MW00387698

Praise for *Treatment of Traumatized Adults and Children*

A major stumbling block to adoption of evidence-based practice in the real world of clinical practice has been the absence of clinician-friendly guides suitable for learning specific empirically supported treatments. Such guides need to be understandable, free of technical research jargon, infused with clinical expertise, and rich with real-life examples. Rubin and Springer have hit a home run with the Clinician's Guide to Evidence-Based Practice series, which has all of these characteristics and more.

Edward J. Mullen
Willma & Albert Musher Chair and Professor, Columbia University

This timely book provides detailed, easy-to-follow procedures for the treatment of traumatized adults and children, based on a solid foundation of empirically based practice. *Treatment of Traumatized Adults and Children*, as well as others in the Clinician's Guide to Evidence-Based Practice series, is a must-read for clinicians who incorporate notions of evidence-based practice in their work.

Tony Tripodi
Professor Emeritus, Ohio State University

In *Treatment of Traumatized Adults and Children*, Rubin and Springer and their contributors boil down more than 20 years of published research and practice to provide the busy practitioner with practical guidance in helping the traumatized. It is an indispensable guide to responsibly bringing relief to those who seek it.

Charles R. Figley,
Tulane University; Editor of *Traumatology*

Rubin and Springer have assembled the practice wisdom of leading practitioners of evidence-based practice interventions, enhancing the likelihood that these practices will be adopted by helping professionals. Each chapter introduces readers to principles that undergird a specific intervention and detailed descriptions of assessment criteria, flow of treatment, and procedural steps. Written in the language of practitioners, this book represents an exemplar for dissemination of evidence-based practice information.

Joanne Yaffe
Associate Professor, University of Utah College of Social Work

Treatment of Traumatized Adults and Children is straightforward and practical, and the step-by-step guides allow even the novice to master the skills needed for effective work with trauma. Marvelous job by the editors and contributors.

Kevin Corcoran
Professor, Portland State University

Clinician's Guide to Evidence-Based Practice Series

Treatment of Traumatized Adults and Children
Allen Rubin and David W. Springer, Editors
Substance Abuse Treatment for Youth and Adults
David W. Springer and Allen Rubin, Editors

ALLEN RUBIN & DAVID W. SPRINGER, Editors

Treatment of Traumatized Adults and Children

Clinician's Guide to Evidence-Based Practice Series

WILEY

John Wiley & Sons, Inc.

Library of Congress Cataloging-in-Publication Data:

Treatment of traumatized adults and children/Edited by Allen Rubin, David W. Springer.

　p. cm.

　　Includes index.

　ISBN 978-0-470-22846-3 (cloth: acid-free paper)

　1. Post-traumatic stress disorder—Treatment.　2. Post-traumatic stress disorder in children—Treatment. 3. Post-traumatic stress disorder—Patients—Rehabilitation.　I. Rubin, Allen.　II. Springer, David W.

RC552.P67T767 2009

　616.85'2100835—dc22

2009004150

Printed in the United States of America

10 9 8 7 6 5 4 3 2 1

Contents

Series Introduction

ONE OF THE most daunting challenges to the evidence-based practice (EBP) movement is the fact that busy clinicians who learn of evidence-based interventions are often unable to implement them because they lack expertise in the intervention and lack the time and resources to obtain the needed expertise. Even if they want to read about the intervention as a way of gaining that expertise, they are likely to encounter materials that are either much too lengthy in light of their time constraints or much too focused on the research support for the intervention, with inadequate guidance to enable them to implement it with at least a minimally acceptable level of proficiency.

This is the first in a series of edited volumes that attempt to alleviate that problem and thus make learning how to provide evidence-based interventions more feasible for such clinicians. Each volume will be a how-to guide for practitioners, not a research focused review. Each will contain in-depth chapters detailing how to provide clinical interventions whose effectiveness is being supported by the best scientific evidence.

The chapters will differ from chapters in other reference volumes on empirically supported interventions in both length and focus. Rather than covering in depth the research support for each intervention and providing brief overviews of the practice aspects of the interventions, our chapters will be lengthier and more detailed practitioner-focused how-to guides for implementing the interventions. Instead of emphasizing the research support in the chapters, that support will be summarized in an appendix. Each chapter will focus on helping practitioners learn how to begin providing an evidence-based intervention that they are being urged by managed care companies (and others) to provide, but with which they may be inexperienced. Each chapter will be extensive and detailed enough to enable clinicians to begin providing the evidence-based intervention without being so lengthy and detailed that reading it would be too time consuming and overwhelming. The chapters will also identify resources for gaining more advanced expertise in the interventions.

We believe that this series will be unique in its focus on the needs of practitioners and in making empirically supported interventions more feasible for them to learn about and provide. We hope that you agree and that you find this volume and this series to be of value in guiding your practice and in maximizing your effectiveness as an evidence-based practitioner.

Allen Rubin, PhD
David W. Springer, PhD

Preface

I F YOU HAVE been treating traumatized clients—or just reading about their treatment, perhaps in anticipation of treating them—you probably have encountered many comments referring to empirically supported trauma-focused interventions that are considered to evidence based. Such interventions include trauma-focused cognitive behavioral therapy (TFCBT), prolonged exposure therapy, and eye movement desensitization and reprocessing (EMDR), which have the best empirical support for treating posttraumatic stress disorder (PTSD). You may also have encountered entire books on each of these interventions and wished you had more time to read them. Perhaps you've seen some research articles reporting outcome studies providing strong empirical support for one or more of these interventions and wished they provided more clinical guidance as to how you could to provide them to your clients. Likewise, you may have read some books that contain chapters on various empirically supported trauma-focused interventions, but have been disappointed with the brevity of specific practice guidelines in those chapters. That is because such books typically just provide very brief thumbnail sketches of the interventions, perhaps accompanied by rather lengthy reviews of the studies that supported each.

If you have had the above experiences and reactions, then this book is for you. Its very detailed, lengthy how-to chapters—with case examples sprinkled throughout—are geared to practitioners who want their practice in treating traumatized clients to be evidence based but who don't have the time to read each book on empirically supported interventions for trauma before feeling that they have enough knowledge to make decisions about which approach to adopt and enough guidance to begin providing the chosen intervention as they learn more about it.

This book is also geared to practitioners who may not have had the time to read research articles about empirically supported interventions for traumatized clients or who may be bewildered by the some of the complex research concepts in those articles or by the diversity of findings from study to study. By reading this book, you will learn what interventions have had the best research support and how to provide them. That's because this book has been written in a user-friendly/practitioner-friendly manner for clinicians who want to learn such things without having to struggle with daunting research and statistical terms. For readers who do not want to accept our conclusions just based on our authority, however, this book provides an appendix that reviews the supporting research.

Another aspect of this book that makes it practitioner friendly and that may enhance its value to practitioners is that every intervention chapter has been authored or co-authored by practitioners who have had extensive experience in the intervention and are clinical experts in it. As you read this book, you may be gratified by the extent to which the chapter authors are communicating more as practitioners and not as ivory tower researchers who don't understand the needs of practitioners. Although the book's editors are housed in academia, we have insisted that our chapters be written in a style that maximizes their utility to practitioners. Moreover, we, too, have had extensive practice experience, and the lead editor has had advanced training in EMDR, has had clinical experience in providing it, and has been teaching a clinical course on the assessment and treatment of traumatized populations.

Although the lengthy how-to detail in this book's chapters will not be as extensive as what you will find in an entire book devoted exclusively to the intervention being described in any particular chapter, it should be enough to get you started in providing the intervention and perhaps helping you decide whether you want to pursue further reading and training in that intervention. Toward the latter end, each chapter will also identify recommended additional reading as well as training options.

As previously mentioned, this book's chapters detail how to provide clinical interventions whose effectiveness with traumatized clients is currently being supported by the best scientific evidence. Thus, the separate chapters cover trauma-focused prolonged exposure therapy, cognitive restructuring, TFCBT, and EMDR. Three chapters describe how to provide such interventions to adults, and two chapters cover providing them to children. In addition to the how-to's of the interventions, each chapter covers their indications and contraindications.

Preceding the five chapters on specific empirically supported interventions is an introduction chapter that identifies commonalities among those interventions. Key among those commonalities is the prerequisite that the interventions be provided in the context of a strong therapeutic alliance. The importance of the therapeutic alliance should not be underestimated—not only in light of the research supporting it as a necessary component of effective treatment with *any* specific intervention approach, but also in light of the widespread misconception that the guidelines for providing empirically supported interventions devalue the importance of the therapeutic alliance and the related misconception that evidence-based practice requires practitioners to function in a mechanistic way following cookbook-like manuals that disregard their practice wisdom and relationship skills. Readers will *not* find such guidelines in *this* volume. Instead, each chapter will reflect our emphasis on the importance of both the need to provide interventions that have had their effectiveness supported by the best research evidence and the need to choose, adapt, and provide those interventions in light of their practice expertise, their knowledge of idiosyncratic client characteristics and circumstances, and their relationship skills.

This book is timely as practitioners are increasingly being urged to provide empirically supported interventions and as those interventions are increasingly being required by third-party payers. Although EBP has become part of the definition of ethical practice, various studies have shown that practitioners rarely engage in the EBP process. Various pragmatic factors have been cited regarding this concern—in particular, real-world time constraints and the difficulty practitioners have in obtaining the needed expertise to begin implementing the interventions with the best empirical support. This book aims to provide that beginning level of expertise in a manner that fits clinician time constraints.

ORGANIZATION

After an introduction chapter (in Part 1), Part 2 of this book provides three chapters on TFCBT. Chapter 2 emphasizes the prolonged exposure therapy component of TFCBT with adults. Chapter 3 emphasizes the cognitive restructuring component of TFCBT with adults. Chapter 4 covers the provision of TFCBT with traumatized children and their caregivers. Part 3 provides two chapters on EMDR, one that focuses on treating adults (Chapter 5) and one that focuses on providing EMDR to children (Chapter 6). The book concludes with a brief afterword, two appendixes, and a glossary. Appendix A reviews the research that provides the empirical support for the interventions covered in this volume. Appendix B describes in detail the evidence-based practice process for readers who would like more detail about that process than is covered in the introduction chapter.

Regardless of which specific approach you use in treating traumatized clients, we hope this book helps you get started in making your treatment of trauma more evidence based. In connection with becoming more evidence based, we hope it also spurs you to pursue further your reading, training, and search for evidence regarding any interventions you decide to adopt or continue using. We would appreciate any feedback you can provide regarding the ways you have found this book to be helpful or any suggestions you may have for improving it. You can e-mail such feedback to arubin@mail.utexas.edu or dwspringer@mail.utexas.edu.

Acknowledgments

S PECIAL THANKS GO to four Wiley staff members who helped make this series possible. In alphabetical order they are: Peggy Alexander, vice president and publisher; Lisa Gebo, senior editor; Sweta Gupta, editorial program coordinator; and Rachel Livsey, senior editor. For this particular volume, we appreciate the fine work of our chapter authors and the helpful feedback they provided to earlier drafts of the complete volume. Thanks also go to the following colleagues who reviewed our submitted manuscript and suggested improvements: Kia Bentley of Virginia Commonwealth University, Lupe Alle-Corliss of California State University at Fullerton, Sherry Cormier of West Virginia University, Waldo Klein of the University of Connecticut, and Albert Roberts of Rutgers University *(deceased)*.

About the Editors

Allen Rubin, PhD, is the Bert Kruger Smith Centennial Professor in the School of Social Work at The University of Texas at Austin, where he has been a faculty member since 1979. While there, he has worked as a therapist in a child guidance center and developed and taught a course on the assessment and treatment of traumatized populations. Earlier in his career he worked in a community mental health program providing services to adolescents and their families. He is internationally known for his many publications pertaining to research and evidence-based practice. In 1997, he was a co-recipient of the Society for Social Work and Research Award for Outstanding Examples of Published Research for a study on the treatment of male batterers and their spouses. His most recent studies have been on the effectiveness of EMDR and on practitioners' views of evidence-based practice. Among his 12 books, his most recent is *Practitioner's Guide to Using Research for Evidence-Based Practice*. He has served as a consulting editor for seven professional journals. He was a founding member of the Society for Social Work and Research and served as its president from 1998 to 2000. In 1993, he received the University of Pittsburgh School of Social Work's Distinguished Alumnus Award. In 2007, he received the Council on Social Work Education's Significant Lifetime Achievement in Social Work Education Award.

David W. Springer, PhD, LCSW, is the Associate Dean for Academic Affairs and a University Distinguished Teaching Professor in the School of Social Work at The University of Texas at Austin, where he is also Investigator of the Inter-American Institute for Youth Justice and holds a joint appointment with the Department of Psychology. Dr. Springer's social work practice experience has included work as a clinical social worker with adolescents and their families in inpatient and outpatient settings and as a school social worker in an alternative learning center with youth recommended for expulsion for serious offenses. He currently serves on the editorial board of several professional journals and on the National Scientific and Policy Advisory Council of the Hogg Foundation for Mental Health. He has co-authored or co-edited several other books, including *Substance Abuse Treatment for Criminal Offenders: An Evidence-Based Guide for Practitioners* and *Handbook of Forensic Mental Health with Victims and Offenders.*

Dr. Springer recently served as Chair of a Blue Ribbon Task Force consisting of national and regional leaders, which was charged with making recommendations for reforming the juvenile justice system in Texas. In recognition of his work with the Blue Ribbon Task Force, the National Association of Social Workers (NASW), Texas Chapter/Austin Branch selected Dr. Springer as the 2008 Social Worker of the Year.

About the Contributors

Robbie Adler-Tapia, PhD is a licensed psychologist who has worked with traumatized children and their families for 23 years. She is certified in EMDR, an EMDRIA Approved Consultant, an EMDR Institute Facilitator, and an EMDR/HAP (Humanitarian Assistance Program) Trainer. With the EMDR HAPKIDS Program, she volunteers to assist with coordinating research, consultation, and training for therapists working with children internationally. She also provided specialty trainings on EMDR with children at the EMDRIA International Conference and at advanced weekend trainings. She co-authored the book *EMDR and the Art of Psychotherapy with Children* and accompanying treatment manual for clinicians.

Joanne L. Davis, PhD is an Associate Professor of Clinical Psychology, Director of Undergraduate Studies in Psychology, and Co-director of the Tulsa Institute of Trauma, Abuse, and Neglect at the University of Tulsa, Oklahoma. She received her doctorate from the University of Arkansas and completed a predoctoral internship at the Medical University of South Carolina and a two-year postdoctoral fellowship at the National Crime Victims Research and Treatment Center in Charleston, South Carolina. Her research interests include the assessment, treatment, and prevention of interpersonal violence and its effects. In recent years, she has focused on the assessment and treatment of chronic nightmares.

Philip W. Dodgson, PhD, is a Consultant Clinical Psychologist in the United Kingdom's National Health Service and in private practice. He holds degrees in psychology from the universities of Oxford, Surrey, and Sussex and is an EMDR Institute and EMDR Europe accredited trainer. Dr. Dodgson's clinical practice is in the treatment of trauma, including working with people who have been victimized by physical, emotional, and sexual abuse and by torture and organized violence. He has worked clinically in the United Kingdom and the Middle East, and taught in the Middle East, Europe, and the United States.

Amy L. Hoch, PsyD, is a licensed psychologist at the Child Abuse Research Education and Service (CARES) Institute at the University of Medicine & Dentistry of New Jersey, School of Osteopathic Medicine, in

Stratford, New Jersey. Dr. Hoch provides individual therapy to children who have experienced abuse and neglect and conducts forensic evaluations concerning allegations of sexual abuse. Dr. Hoch coordinates the Stabilization and Trauma Treatment for Adolescents at-Risk (STTAR) program for teens who have experienced a traumatic event and engage in self-destructive behavior. Dr. Hoch provides workshops on dating violence, sexual assault, and sexual abuse to local high schools and community programs. Dr. Hoch also provides local, national, and international training on trauma-focused cognitive behavioral therapy (TFCBT) and provides supervision, consultation, and training on TFCBT and STTAR.

Elana Newman, PhD, is McFarlin Chair of Psychology, University of Tulsa, Oklahoma; Research Director of the Dart Center for Journalism and Trauma; and a past president of the International Society of Traumatic Stress Studies. Dr. Newman's research in the field of traumatic stress has examined the physical and psychological effects of trauma exposure on adults and children (including meaning of such events), health care costs and trauma, journalism and trauma, occupational health and trauma, research ethics in studying trauma survivors, and substance abuse and trauma. Her recent clinical and supervision work has focused on disseminating best practice for trauma-related disorders, psychological first aid, and trauma-focused interventions for substance users.

Kristi E. Pruiksma received her MA at the University of Tulsa and is currently a PhD student in the Clinical Psychology program. She is research assistant to Dr. Joanne L. Davis and is the lab manager of the Trauma Research: Assessment, Prevention, & Treatment Center (TRAPT) in the Department of Psychology. As a scientist-practitioner, her clinical and research interests include identifying, understanding, and treating difficulties associated with traumatic events; particularly trauma-related nightmares and associated sleep disorders.

Carolyn Settle, MSW, LCSW, is an EMDR Institute Facilitator, an EMDRIA Approved Consultant, and EMDR Humanitarian Assistance Program (HAP) Trainer. Ms. Settle co-authored the book *EMDR and the Art of Psychotherapy with Children* and the associated manual, in addition to co-authoring two journal articles and a chapter in the book *EMDR Scripted Protocols.* She is a co-investigator on a research study focused on the efficacy of using EMDR with children two to ten years of age. Presently, Ms. Settle is an international speaker and provides advanced training workshops. Ms. Settle currently works in private practice in Scottsdale, Arizona.

Gretchen Thomas, MSW is the Director of Sex Offender Treatment in New York City and Long Island, New York, for the Counseling and Psychotherapy Center, Inc. Other experience includes teaching appointments at Columbia and New York Universities; involvement in research projects at Columbia, New York, and Fordham Universities in collaboration with the Centers for Disease Control and Prevention and the New York City Public Schools; and providing consultation and training to the New York City Department of Probation and Criminal Court. She is a doctoral candidate at Columbia University.

PART 1

INTRODUCTION

CHAPTER 1

Introduction: Evidence-Based Practice and Empirically Supported Interventions for Trauma

ALLEN RUBIN

MORE AND MORE clinicians these days want to engage in evidence-based practice (EBP). You may be one of them, and, if so, perhaps that's one reason why you are reading this book. Another likely reason, of course, is your interest in treating people who have been traumatized. Each chapter in this book provides a detailed, practitioner-focused how-to guide for providing a specific intervention approach for trauma survivors—interventions whose effectiveness has been supported by a solid evidence base.

Before describing those chapters, however, this introduction will cover some generic principles about trauma and its treatment. It also will summarize the evidence-based practice process and distinguish the overarching concept of *evidence-based practice* from the provision of specific empirically supported interventions.

GENERAL PRINCIPLES ABOUT TRAUMA AND ITS TREATMENT

DEFINING PSYCHOLOGICAL TRAUMA

Psychological trauma is a subjective and relative phenomenon. Definitions of it vary, depending on whether the focus is on a *Diagnostic and Statistical Manual of Mental Disorders*, 4th edition (DSM-IV) diagnosis of posttraumatic stress disorder (PTSD), adults versus children, and the context of the potentially traumatic event. For a DSM-IV diagnosis of PTSD, to be traumatic the individual must experience, witness, or be confronted by at least one event that causes or threatens death or serious injury, or that threatens the

3

individual's or someone else's physical integrity. The diagnosis also requires that the individual's response involve intense fear, helplessness, or horror. Traumatizing events that are viewed as sufficiently catastrophic to be commonly associated with PTSD include natural disasters, physical and sexual assault, fires, serious automobile accidents and other serious accidents, military combat, torture, and other forms of exposure to violence.

However, people of all ages can be traumatized without a physical threat or a PTSD diagnosis. In Chapter 5 of this book, Dodgson discusses Shapiro's (2001) concept of "large 'T' traumas" and "small 't' traumas." Small t traumas can have a marked impact on a person's life without meeting DSM-IV diagnostic criteria for being considered a traumatic stressor. For example, small t traumas might include adult events such as partnership breakdown or childhood experiences of humiliation.

Consider, for instance, the devoted wife of a successful and admired politician whose secretive and illegal consorting with prostitutes suddenly becomes exposed in the news media. Children, especially, can be traumatized without a physical threat. Consider the teenage daughters of the aforementioned politician. Also, imagine the difference in the degree of psychological trauma between a middle-aged adult learning that his father did not really die in the war but was in an institution for the criminally insane versus an only child aged 12 finding that out for the first time and realizing that his mother has been lying to him.

Regardless of the nature of the trauma and its context, there is agreement that a psychologically traumatic event will demand extraordinary efforts to cope with a sense of helplessness, fear, horror, or disgust. It will shatter basic assumptions and lead to exaggerated appraisals regarding one's vulnerability and self-image and the trustworthiness of other people. It might also be associated with self-blame and notions that life is meaningless.

The meaning and impact of a traumatic event, however, will be affected by its nature and context. A natural disaster—such as a flood, hurricane, or tornado, for example—probably won't induce as much self-blame and lack of trust as would an intentional human act like child abuse, rape, or terrorism. Likewise, the degree to which a traffic accident is psychologically traumatic might depend on whether the survivor was driving and who else was seriously injured or killed. If the traumatic event was an intentional human act, another factor to be considered is the relationship of the perpetrator to the victim. Being sexually abused by a neighbor, albeit horrific, probably will not devastate a child's sense of trust and self-blame as much as being sexually abused by a parent or other close relative.

Also to be considered is whether the client experienced only one isolated traumatic event or multiple such events. Combat veterans with PTSD, for example, often have experienced multiple traumas and consequently are likely to need a much longer treatment regimen than victims of one hurricane. Likewise, children who have been abused multiple times are more likely to have more serious disorders and need more treatment than those who have been abused only once.

Regardless of which evidence-based approach you choose to treat trauma, the foregoing considerations should influence how you intervene. Likewise, before you introduce one of the evidence-based interventions discussed in this volume—interventions aimed at restoring trust and a *realistic* sense of vulnerability—you should first make sure that the client is safe. It would be tragically harmful, for example, to induce an unrealistic sense of trust and safety if the client is still residing in an environment where he or she is vulnerable to ongoing abuse, such as by a parent, sibling, or violent spouse.

ASSESSMENT

Implicit in the preceding considerations is the importance of conducting a thorough assessment before selecting or embarking on one of the evidence-based interventions discussed in this volume. Thus, each intervention chapter in this volume includes attention to assessment processes and issues pertinent to the intervention focus of that chapter. This section, therefore, will focus on generic assessment concepts that apply regardless of the interventions provided to traumatized clients.

Many of the undesirable psychological impacts of trauma on survivors are normal and will not last more than several weeks (if that long). These include such emotions as anger, fear, grief, guilt or shame, numbness, shock, cognitive disorientation, difficulty concentrating, somatic symptoms, problems sleeping or in appetite, being easily startled, interpersonal difficulties, and so on. Most survivors of traumatic events will recover on their own, have their trauma symptoms disappear over time, and not develop PTSD (Friedman, 2006).

DSM-IV Criteria for a PTSD Diagnosis One prime objective of assessment is determining whether the client meets the DSM-IV criteria for a PTSD diagnosis and, if so, its duration and severity. However, that is not the only important assessment objective. As Keane, Weathers, and Foa (2000) point out, a comprehensive assessment would gather information about the client's "family history, life context, symptoms, beliefs, strengths, weaknesses, support system and coping abilities . . . [and] needs to include indices of social and occupational functioning" (p. 32).

As mentioned earlier, the criteria for a DSM-IV diagnosis of PTSD require both of the following: (1) experiencing, witnessing, or being confronted by at least one event that causes or threatens death or serious injury, or that threatens the individual's or someone else's physical integrity; and (2) intense fear, helplessness, or horror in the individual's response. The criteria also include at least one persistent reexperiencing symptom, at least three persistent avoidance or numbing symptoms, at least two persistent hyperarousal symptoms, a duration of the above symptoms of more than 1 month, and clinically significant distress or impairment in important areas of functioning.

Trauma Symptoms Reexperiencing symptoms include intrusive distressing recollections and dreams of the traumatic event. The recollections can include feeling as if the event is actually occurring such as through flashbacks. Flashbacks are not just flashes of memory or intrusive images; instead, they are dissociative episodes. Persons experiencing a flashback will have an altered state of consciousness and be at least partially unaware of their current surroundings. Flashbacks typically last only a few moments, during which time the person has a sense of reliving (not merely recalling) the traumatic event. The flashbacks might involve hallucinations, "such as hearing cries of the dying or seeing images of the dead" (Taylor, 2006, p. 13). Reexperiencing symptoms might also include sensory experiences, "such as seeing unwanted images of the trauma when victims close their eyes, or experiencing smells, tastes, sounds, or emotions experienced at the time of the trauma, such as horror, dread, or helplessness" (Taylor, p. 12). The recollections can include nightmares that might involve waking with nocturnal panic attacks.

Avoidance symptoms involve avoiding stimuli that are associated with the trauma. The symptoms might involve avoiding a particular place where the trauma occurred as well as similar places that are associated with the trauma due to overgeneralization. Abused individuals might avoid people who remind them of the perpetrator of abuse. They might avoid other people in general so as not to be let down by them, and they may feel as if they can't trust anyone anymore. They may have a sense of a foreshortened future in a malevolent world in which they do not expect to have a normal life span or other formerly desired things like a career, a marriage, or children. No longer feeling safe in the world, they might avoid social situations in general. They might avoid feeling optimistic so they won't be disappointed. In turn, they may make no effort to form good relations with others or to further their own self-interest. Avoiding places or people that really are dangerous, however, is not a symptom of PTSD.

Numbing symptoms involve a restricted range of affect, such as being unable to feel love or happiness, the loss of a sense of humor, and a diminished interest in activities that were formerly enjoyable. With severe numbing, the traumatized person might feel dead inside. The numbness might alternate with periods of anger, sadness, anxiety, or other aversive emotions. It might also lead to substance abuse, either to numb the pain and keep the trauma memories away or perhaps as an antidote to the numbness.

Hyperarousal symptoms can come in various forms. Traumatized individuals might be hypervigilant, in a constant state of alert and looking out for danger. They might be easily startled or threatened and misinterpret neutral or ambiguous social cues as threats. For example, not really knowing why peers are laughing, they might misinterpret the laughter as being derisively in reference to them. Hyperarousal might also involve insomnia, although insomnia also could be attributable to reexperiencing or avoidance symptoms, such as repeated awakening from nightmares or staying awake out of a fear of having terrifying nightmares (Taylor, 2006).

Other Trauma Diagnoses   If the client has fewer than the number of symptoms specified for the PTSD diagnosis, there is a "partial PTSD" diagnosis. In addition, the "complex PTSD" or "disorders of extreme stress not otherwise specified (DESNOS)" diagnosis has been proposed for individuals whose traumas have been extremely severe and prolonged—such as early childhood sexual or physical abuse, repeated abuse or battering, being taken hostage, or being incarcerated and tortured—and whose consequent symptoms go well beyond the classic PTSD symptoms (Meichenbaum, 2003). It is beyond the scope of this volume, however, to provide a thorough coverage of all the aspects of making a DSM diagnosis. For that, readers can examine the DSM-IV (American Psychiatric Association, 2000).

If less than 1 month has elapsed since the traumatic event, the individual might be given a diagnosis of acute stress disorder (ASD), the symptoms of which overlap with PTSD symptoms. It has been estimated that 80% of survivors with ASD will develop PTSD 6 months later and that 70% will still have PTSD 2 years after that (Bryant & Harvey, 2000).

Assessing Other Problems   At the end of this introduction are some additional readings on assessing traumatized individuals. Those readings elaborate on the assessment concepts discussed above, as well as some others, such as neurophysical and biochemical symptoms, problems in attention and concentration, trauma-related guilt and shame, cultural considerations, age considerations, and common disorders that co-occur with PTSD, such as depression, substance abuse, anxiety disorders and family dysfunction. I have drawn on those readings in writing this section on assessment, especially those by Foa and Rothbaum (1998), Meichenbaum (2003), and Taylor (2006). One of the readings, by Keane et al. (2000), presents a helpful review of assessment instruments for diagnosing PTSD, including structured diagnostic interviews, self-report questionnaires, and psychophysiological measures. Another, by Turner and Lee (1998), offers a good collection of assessment resources, which can be copied by the clinician. The assessment measures are copyrighted, but the purchaser has permission to photocopy them.

Assessing whether PTSD is accompanied by co-occurring (comorbid) disorders is important. One reason for this importance is the prevalence of comorbidity with PTSD, which has been estimated to be as high as 80% for people in treatment for chronic PTSD (Kessler, Sonnega, Bromet, Hughes, & Nelson, 1995). Over 25% of people with PTSD are estimated to have comorbidity with alcohol or substance abuse (Friedman, 2006).

Assessment of Children As discussed in Chapters 4 and 6 of this book, the assessment protocol for children is different than with adults, and involves the use of special techniques and measures. It is likely to involve observing the child while using play therapy techniques (such as with a sand tray or puppets, or perhaps by drawing pictures). How parents or caretakers interact with the child should be observed. The parent or caretaker also should provide assessment information.

Assessment should also involve evaluating children for behavioral problems, learning disabilities, reading disorders, language disorders, and other developmental disorders. Conducting developmental assessments of children is important not only in treatment planning but also in helping parents understand the child's developmental level and to determine if the child is delayed in any areas. With young children, it also is helpful to assess for sensory integration issues.

Standardized assessment tools may be needed to assess the preceding concerns as well as to assess problems in parents or caretakers, such as their own trauma symptoms, depression, or parenting practices. Table 1.1 lists some useful assessment scales for children. These scales, additional scales, and other special features of assessment with children will be elaborated upon in Chapters 4 and 6. (Assessment tools for adult clients are listed in Chapters 2, 3 and 5.)

Table 1.1
Assessment Scales for Children

Trauma Symptoms

- Children's Impact of Traumatic Events Scale–Revised (CITES-R) by Wolfe, Gentile, Michienzi, and Sas (1991). The CITES-R is a scale used to assess the impact of abuse on children with questions focused on identifying symptoms consistent with post-traumatic stress disorder and can be found online at http://vinst.umdnj.edu/VAID/TestReport.asp?Code=CITESR.
- Children's Reactions to Traumatic Events Scale–Revised (CRTES-R) by Jones (2002) has been used to assess children for symptoms associated with experiencing a traumatic event. The CRTES-R is frequently used in research studies to assess for pre/posttest functioning in children in order to assess for treatment effectiveness.
- Kiddie Schedule for Affective Disorders and Schizophrenia–PTSD section (K-SADS PTSD) semistructured interview for both the child and caregiver regarding the child's exposure to traumatic events and PTSD symptoms (Chambers & Puig-Antich, Hirsch, M. et al. 1985).

- Trauma Symptom Checklist for Children (TSCC) by John Briere et al. (2001) is an assessment tool that identifies symptoms of posttraumatic stress in children aged 8 to 16. The TSCC can be purchased from Psychological Assessment Resources (PAR); www.parinc.com.
- Traumatic Stress Symptom Checklist (TSSC) by Robbie Adler-Tapia (2001) was designed to assess symptoms of traumatic stress in young children aged 0 to 6. This checklist has not been normed or validated, but rather includes symptoms consistent with a diagnosis of PTSD in children, which suggests that the scale has face validity. This scale is available at www.EMDRKIDS.com.
- UCLA PTSD Inventory (Steinberg et al., 1998) is a paper-and-pencil self-report measure that children complete.

Behavior Problems

- Achenbach's questionnaires: The Child Behavior Checklist (CBCL) for younger children ($1\frac{1}{2}$–5) or older children (6–18) (Achenbach, 1991) or the Behavior Assessment Scale (BASC). Each includes caregiver, self, and teacher report forms.

Depression

- Children's Depression Inventory (CDI) (Kovacs, 1985).

Dissociation

- Adolescent Dissociative Experiences Scale–II (A-DES) by Judith Armstrong, Eve Bernstein Carlson, and Frank Putnam is available online at www.caleidoscoop.nl/pdfs/a-des. It consists of 30 items, each followed by a 10-point rating scale from never to always. This scale is helpful for screening for dissociation in adolescents. There is no scoring for this checklist, but, rather, the questions are used to explore the presence of particular symptoms associated with dissociation.
- The Children's Dissociative Checklist–3 (CDC Version 3) by Frank Putnam is available online at www.energyhealing.net/pdf_files/cdc.pdf. This scale is helpful for screening for dissociation in children. There is no scoring for this checklist, but, rather, the questions are used to explore the presence of particular symptoms associated with dissociation.

Parents and Caregivers

- Parent Emotional Reaction Questionnaire (PERQ) by Mannarino and Cohen (1996): assesses abuse-related distress.
- Impact of Events Scale–Revised (Weiss & Marmar, 1997): assesses caregivers' own PTSD symptoms related to their child's trauma.
- Parenting Stress Index (Abidin, 1983): A caregiver self-report questionnaire regarding parenting practices.
- Alabama Parenting Inventory (Frick, 1991): has both child and caregiver report forms.
- A summary of scales is available online in a table entitled "Measures of Child Social–Emotional, Behavioral, and Developmental Well-Being, Exposure to Violence, and Environment Compiled by the Association for the Study and Development of Community," at www.capacitybuilding.net/Measures%20of%20CEV%20and%20outcomes.pdf (downloaded September 26, 2007).

SAFETY AND THERAPEUTIC ALLIANCE

With both adult and child clients, in addition to the preceding considerations, an important part of assessment involves building a therapeutic alliance and assessing safety issues. The next two sections of this chapter will discuss those two areas, starting with the importance of attending to the needs for safety and basic survival resources.

Safety and Resource Provision

Some trauma victims might underestimate or disregard real threats to their safety, such as from an abusive spouse, partner, or parent. They might also underestimate or disregard the risks that their angry outbursts pose to others. Conversely, some clients might be hypervigilant and thus be biased toward overestimating the degree of danger they are in. Zayfert and Becker (2007) recommend assessing safety issues by probing into the recency of the concerned behaviors, the level of threat that they pose, and the conditions under which they tend to increase.

The chapters in this volume describe empirically supported therapeutic treatment approaches for alleviating trauma symptoms that are provided after clients' safety and immediate survival resource needs have been met following the traumatic event(s). A generic principle of trauma treatment is that, if needed, the first priority is to provide crisis intervention or case management to secure a safe environment and basic survival resources for trauma victims. An abuse victim, for example, may need to find a different place to live. Likewise, victims of natural disasters may need temporary housing, clothing, food, financial assistance, and so on. The need to attend to such things first is self-evident and does not require empirical verification, although research could compare the relative effectiveness of alternative case management or crisis intervention approaches to secure such resources. (Here, I am *not* referring to *psychological* forms of crisis intervention. Instead, I am referring to crisis intervention as an approach to provide concrete resources to meet the immediate safety and survival needs of people in crisis.)

The need to provide crisis intervention or case management to help secure a safe environment and basic survival resources is most evident when providing immediate relief to survivors of fires, natural disasters, wars, and terrorist attacks. In that this volume focuses on trauma-focused therapy, we do not provide chapters on crisis intervention or case management. Much has been written about those interventions, however, and readers can examine that literature for detailed guidance on how to provide such immediate relief.

Meichenbaum (2003), for example, lists the following key elements of postdisaster crisis intervention:

- Identifying basic needs of victims (medical, shelter, transportation, etc.)
- Notifying family members

- Connecting victims to needed referrals and resources
- Helping victims negotiate legal, medical, and government services
- Advocating for victims
- Nurturing natural support systems
- Psychiatric referral when indicated
- Helping victims share reactions and experiences

A caveat to keep in mind when examining such literature is that one of the most popular forms of crisis intervention, critical incident stress debriefing (CISD), has not been consistently supported by rigorous outcome studies and in fact has been found to be harmful by some studies. That caveat is most pertinent to the last element in the preceding list (helping victims share reactions and experiences). CISD is a group intervention for survivors of mass traumatic events and is provided in the immediate aftermath of each event. With it, survivors discuss details about their experiences during the traumatic incident, including where they were, what they heard and saw, how they felt, and so on. The survivors also discuss their current emotions and physical symptoms. Service providers let them know that their reactions are normal and give them concrete advice about things to do and not to do to help them deal with their distress (Housley & Beutler, 2007). Although CISD incorporates various generic principles of trauma treatment, it is provided to all survivors, most of whom will recover from the trauma over time without developing PTSD. Various studies have found that CISD actually slows down the natural course of recovery among many of those survivors (Bisson, Jenkins, Alexander, & Bannister, 1993; Carlier, Lamberts, van Uchelen, & Gersons, 1998; Mayou, Ehlers, & Hobbs, 2000; Rose, Bisson, & Wessely, 2001).

In contrast to CISD, critical incident stress management (CISM) excludes the CISD component thought to explain the potentially harmful effects of CISD. Instead of having survivors discuss details about their experiences and feelings, CISM addresses practical issues, debriefs them on what happened, and informs survivors of the availability of treatment resources should they be needed.

CISM, therefore, reflects literature about some general principles for helping trauma victims secure safety and basic survival resources, as discussed by Meichenbaum (2003). With mass traumatic events, for example, intervention must be broadly based and involve multiple agencies. It should target multiple system levels, including the community level, and should include not only the immediate victims, but also their friends, bereaved relatives, and first responding emergency workers. The need to secure social support resources from friends and relatives should not be overlooked. However, the most immediate basic needs (food, water, shelter, etc.) should be addressed first. Special attention should be given to the most vulnerable groups, such as people who are frail or elderly, people who are physically or mentally ill, survivors who are geographically isolated, emergency relief workers, and so on. A case finding effort should be activated so as not to overlook such groups.

Safety concerns pertain not only to harm done by perpetrators of abuse or forces of nature. Some trauma victims are prone to self-harm, such as suicidality, substance abuse, reckless driving, and so on. In addition, some trauma victims may have explosive, angry outbursts that can endanger others. Some such concerns might be addressed as part of the treatment approaches described in this volume. However, some that are evident during assessment may indicate the need to delay the chosen treatment approach until the immediate dangers have been alleviated. For example, clients who physically endanger others with their angry outbursts might be deemed to need an anger management intervention before commencing trauma-focused therapy. Likewise, for some clients who are addicted to drugs or alcohol, detoxification and perhaps other substance abuse treatment may have to precede the trauma-focused therapy. For other clients with less severe substance abuse problems, the clinician might deem resolving the trauma issues as a precondition for alleviating the substance abuse (Zayfert & Becker, 2007).

Volume 2 of this series, *Substance Abuse Treatment for Youth and Adults*, provides a chapter on seeking safety, which is an evidence-based approach for treating co-occurring PTSD and substance abuse. In addition, that volume's appendix reviews the outcome studies that provide the empirical support for the effectiveness of that approach.

For some cases, the efforts to monitor dangerous behaviors and increase safety might occur simultaneously alongside the trauma-focused therapy. Zayfert and Becker (2007), for example, mention one case in which a plan was developed with the client to have him give his guns to a friend so that exposure therapy could commence. In another case, an anorexic client agreed to monitor food intake and body weight during trauma-focused therapy. A third client implemented daily monitoring of suicidal urges during treatment. For more detailed information on handling safety and resource provision concerns when intervening with trauma victims, readers might want to examine the books cited in this chapter by Meichenbaum (2003) and Zayfert and Becker. An older volume that also might be useful is *Handbook of Post-Disaster Interventions* (Allen, 1993).

THERAPEUTIC ALLIANCE

Regardless of the type of client problems clinicians treat—be they trauma related or anything else—one of the most important factors influencing their effectiveness is the quality of the practitioner–client relationship; that is, the therapeutic alliance. Indeed, some research has found that the quality of the therapist's core clinical relationship skills has more influence on treatment outcome than the specific interventions they employ. Although there is some debate as to which set of factors has more influence on treatment outcome, there is little doubt that therapeutic effectiveness is influenced by both the type of intervention employed and relationship factors (Nathan, 2004). A corollary is that no matter how many rigorous studies have empirically supported a particular intervention—and even if that intervention is widely recognized as having by far the best evidence base—whether it will be effective with a particular client will be influenced by the therapist's core relationship skills and the quality of the therapeutic alliance. Readers should bear that corollary in mind as they read about how to provide the interventions to be described in the subsequent chapters of this book.

I'll not delve into the fundamentals of core, generic relationship skills such as empathy, warmth, being nonjudgmental, and so on, that apply regardless of the type of clientele being treated. If you are a practicing therapist or a clinical student taking an advanced course, you should already have those skills. If not, you can read any number of introductory texts that discuss them. For the purposes of this book, however, it's worth examining some guidelines that have been recommended as critical for enhancing your therapeutic alliance with trauma victims per se. In proposing these guidelines, I am drawing on the works of Dworkin (2005), Foa and Rothbaum (1998), Herman (1997), Meichenbaum (2003), Taylor (2006), and Zayfert and Becker (2007).

Of particular importance in working with trauma victims, especially those who are victims of abuse, is restoring their sense of *control* and *empowerment*. During assessment, for example, they should feel that they are in charge of the process of telling their own story. They should feel that they are one step ahead of the therapist in telling that story. For example, the clinician can ask, "Where do you think we should start?" If clients are not yet ready to discuss the traumatic event, they should not be forced to do so. It might take quite a while before they feel sufficiently safe and comfortable in the relationship to reveal the abuse they experienced.

If the client does not bring up the trauma during assessment, but the clinician is aware of it, rather than mention the trauma directly, the clinician could ask whether the client has ever had a very bad experience. If the client had already mentioned the trauma, the clinician could foster a sense of control and empowerment by asking *permission* to discuss the traumatic event. Clients also can be encouraged to share only those aspects of the trauma that they think the therapist needs to know and to keep other things private if they want to. They also can be encouraged to take breaks whenever they want to and stop the discussion whenever they want to. A sense of control and empowerment could also be fostered by encouraging clients to express their goals for treatment and the order in which they would like to work on each.

Also of great importance when working with trauma victims is the need to *validate* the victim's experience. One reason why validation is so important is that many abused victims are disbelieved when they report the abuse to others. Validation implies being somewhat judgmental in becoming the client's ally. When working with victims of abuse or other crimes, for example, Herman (2007, p. 135) asserts:

> The technical neutrality of the therapist is not the same as moral neutrality. Working with victimized people requires a moral stance. The therapist is called upon to bear witness to a crime. She must affirm a position of solidarity with the victim. This does not mean a simplistic notion that the victim can do no wrong; rather, it involves an understanding of the fundamental injustice of the traumatic experience and the need for a resolution that restores some sense of justice.

Another reason for the importance of validation is that the victim might attribute their PTSD symptoms to something that is intrinsically wrong with them and perhaps that they are losing their mind. Thus, it is important for the therapist to communicate to clients that their behaviors and other symptoms are completely understandable in light of the trauma they experienced—that virtually any person would respond similarly.

Moreover, validation is part of empowering trauma victims. Validation and empowerment can also be fostered by commenting on the client's strengths. For example, the therapist could praise clients for entering treatment and having the courage to discuss their painful memories of the trauma(s). They could note how remarkable it is that the client has had the strength to carry on and accomplish things after experiencing the trauma. For example, the therapist could comment on how impressive it is that in spite of what the client went through, she was able to raise her children, keep working, earn her degree, and so on. To further bolster a sense of strength and empowerment, the therapist could ask the client how she managed to accomplish all that after what she went through. At the same time, however, care must be taken not to overdo the focus on strengths. Doing so risks invalidating the client's sense of severe pain and vulnerability. The therapist must balance the comments on client strengths with comments that convey an understanding of that sense of pain and vulnerability.

A caveat to keep in mind about validation is that the clinician should be validating the client's experiences and not the factual truth of what they describe. The clinician has no way of knowing without third-party or other evidence what actually happened in cases where the truth is disputed, such as in court cases.

PSYCHOEDUCATION

In addition to fostering the therapeutic alliance, acknowledging that trauma symptoms are common reactions that people often have to traumatic events is part of the psychoeducation phase of trauma treatment. The term *psychoeducation* means teaching clients about trauma symptoms and their treatment. The importance of the psychoeducation component of effective trauma treatment is reflected in the extensive attention given to that component in each chapter in this book.

Various authors suggest using metaphors as part of psychoeducation to help normalize PTSD symptoms as a natural reaction to trauma and help clients understand that they are not "going crazy." For example, a digestion metaphor compares the thoughts and memories of the trauma to bad food that has been undigested and that keeps coming up and bothering the client until it has been processed. Treatments such as exposure therapy and trauma-focused cognitive behavioral therapy (TFCBT) can be likened to a psychological digestion process that helps clients work through and put the bad thoughts and memories behind them. In EMDR treatment, the digestion metaphor pertains to helping clients integrate (or ingest) into their system and let go of those aspects of the traumatic experience that are no longer needed.

Deblinger, Thakkar-Kolar, and Ryan (2006, p. 407) discuss some of the benefits of normalization during psychoeducation when working with sexually abused children as follows:

> . . . when children learn that child sexual abuse happens to many children, they may feel less alone and stigmatized and possibly reduce their tendency to isolate themselves socially, a common behavioral reaction for children who have been sexually abused. Similarly, when parents learn that the vast majority of child sexual abuse survivors do not disclose their abuse in childhood, they may feel less distressed about the fact that their child did not tell immediately.

Regardless of which empirically supported treatment approach you and the client choose (in a collaborative process), the psychoeducation phase will prepare the client for its use. As part of psychoeducation, it is recommended that you prepare one or more handouts that describe the nature of the client's trauma symptoms (such as PTSD), normalize those symptoms (perhaps using the above psychological digestion metaphor), and describe the nature of the evidence-based treatment options to consider. A handout also could briefly mention that based on the research so far, the intervention(s) appears to have the best chance of helping them.

A handout also should inform clients of any undesirable side effects or discomfort they might experience with the intervention(s). For side effects that are expected to come as a normal part of the treatment process, such as temporary increases in reexperiencing or hyperarousal symptoms during eye movement desensitization and reprocessing (EMDR) or exposure treatment sessions, clients should be informed that a transient increase in those symptoms does not necessarily mean that the treatment is going awry; instead, it may indicate that the treatment is working (Taylor, 2006). Handouts that you can reproduce and give to clients for psychoeducation purposes are provided in the Additional Resources sections of Chapters 2 and 3.

By sharing the foregoing information with clients, they can collaborate with you as to the selection of the treatment approach and provide informed consent for it. By doing so, they might become more committed to the treatment process, which in turn might increase the likelihood of a successful treatment outcome. Informed consent and collaboration are also consistent with the aim of restoring the client's sense of control and empowerment. For guidance on how best to word the digestion metaphor and other parts of the handouts that you might construct, you can examine such sources as Foa and Rothbaum (1998), Greenwald (2005), Taylor (2006), and Zayfert and Becker (2007). The latter source also suggests some additional modalities for conveying psychoeducational information, such as drawing pictures or providing audiotapes for home review.

EVIDENCE-BASED PRACTICE

In its original and most prominent definition, evidence-based practice (EBP) is a five-step *process* in which only one of the steps involves providing an empirically supported intervention (Sackett, Straus, Richardson, Rosenberg, & Haynes, 2000; Thyer, 2004). Thus, the overarching concept of *evidence-based practice* should be distinguished from the provision of specific empirically supported interventions.

The EBP process begins with the formulation of a question seeking evidence about a practice decision. The question could pertain to any level of practice, including questions bearing on administrative or policy decisions. At the clinical level, the most common type of EBP question involves decisions about interventions that have the best evidence supporting their effectiveness. However, alternative questions might pertain to finding the most reliable and valid assessment instrument or learning more about the plight of people suffering from a particular problem.

As alluded to earlier, this volume pertains to EBP questions concerning decisions about interventions that have the best evidence supporting their effectiveness in treating trauma survivors. In formulating such an EBP question, however, more specificity is needed. For example, what *kind* of trauma is involved? What are the client's characteristics? The most effective way to intervene will vary depending on things like the age, gender, and ethnicity of the client; whether the client is a child who has been victimized by multiple incidents of abuse or who has survived a hurricane; whether the client is a rape victim or a combat veteran; whether the client's PTSD diagnosis is or is not comorbid with some other disorder, such as substance abuse; and so on.

After formulating a sufficiently detailed question, the second step of the EBP process involves searching for evidence to answer the question. The most expeditious way to search involves using Internet search engines and electronic literature databases. For example, search terms such as *effective interventions for PTSD* can be entered in Google Scholar, PsycINFO, Medline, or some alternative Internet tool for finding relevant studies. The sources cited in the Additional Readings section at the end of this chapter provide more information on the EBP process, including how to formulate EBP questions and search for evidence. More information on how to do those things will also be provided in Appendix B of this volume.

Once you've found the evidence, the third step of the EBP process involves critically appraising the various studies providing the evidence. Not all studies are equally rigorous. Some works get published despite having flaws that are so egregious that it is difficult to take their conclusions and practice recommendations seriously. At the other extreme are studies that have virtually no serious flaws (although no study is totally devoid of minor flaws). At various points in between those two extremes are studies that have some flaws that seem to be neither trivial nor egregious and that leave the reader unsure of whether or not the studies deserve to guide their practice decisions. A key criterion that tends to distinguish the best studies of intervention effectiveness is whether the study used a randomized experimental design along with unbiased measures of treatment outcome. For more information on appraising research evidence, you might want to examine my book, *Practitioner's Guide to Using Research for Evidence-Based Practice* (Wiley, 2008). Also, Appendix B of this volume summarizes that information.

The final two steps of the EBP process involve selecting and implementing the intervention (in step 4) and then evaluating its outcome (in step 5). You can read Appendix B of this volume or the relevant chapter in my text (mentioned above) to learn more about step 5. Most germane to this volume, however, are some issues in step 4. That's because the intervention you select and implement should not be automatically dictated by your appraisal of the best evidence. According to prominent definitions of the EBP process, EBP is not merely a mechanistic, cookbook approach in which interventions are

Figure 1.1 Integrative Model of EBP

selected and implemented regardless of clinician expertise and knowledge of client attributes and preferences (Gibbs & Gambrill, 2002; Shlonsky & Gibbs, 2004; Thyer, 2004).

Instead, your appraisal of the evidence should be integrated with your clinical expertise and knowledge. The diagram that appears in Figure 1.1 illustrates this integrative EBP process. It shows that clinical decisions should be made by skillfully blending the best research evidence, clinician expertise, and client attributes at the intersection of the circles in the shaded area. Shlonsky and Gibbs (2004) discuss this model as follows:

> None of the three core elements can stand alone; they work in concert by using practitioner skills to develop a client-sensitive case plan that utilizes interventions with a history of effectiveness. In the absence of relevant evidence, the other two elements are weighted more heavily, whereas in the presence of overwhelming evidence the best-evidence component might be weighted more heavily. (p. 138)

Integrating evidence with your clinical expertise might influence not only the selection of the intervention to be implemented, but also *how* it is implemented. Although some developers of empirically supported interventions provide step-by-step manuals to guide the clinical implementation of those interventions, the evidence-based practice process model recognizes that clinicians need not feel compelled to slavishly and mechanically adhere to all the details in how they implement each step. The model recognizes that each individual is unique and that the steps are mainly guiding principles that can be adapted in light of client characteristics and other client problems.

WHY READ THIS BOOK?

Although the integration component enhances the clinician-friendly nature of the evidence-based practice process, engaging in evidence-based practice can nevertheless be quite a challenge for clinicians, regardless of their area of clinical practice. The barriers can be daunting (Mullen, 2004; Rubin & Parrish, 2007).

One common obstacle involves the time and other resources required to search literature databases trying to find evidence supporting the effectiveness of interventions with people and problems that match the clinician's clientele. Added to that is the time it takes to critically appraise the evidence, trying to ascertain which intervention has the *best* evidence from the standpoint of the rigor of the research in the various studies uncovered in the clinician's search. This task can be quite time consuming even if you have been well educated in research methods and still remember what you learned about them.

Moreover, many clinicians either have not had extensive education in research methods or have had that education too long ago to feel confident in trying to appraise the quality of the research evidence in the studies they find relevant to their quest. If you are one of them, then the task of critically appraising the research evidence will be even more time consuming, not to mention your sense that it may be fruitless because you feel you lack the expertise to do it well.

On top of all that, the studies that supply the best evidence often produce a bewildering array of inconsistent findings. Likewise, specific studies almost never give sufficient guidance to clinicians as to how to deliver the intervention that they are empirically supporting. At most, they typically will merely provide a brief overview of the intervention (perhaps less than one page) and cite a lengthy book or manual that clinicians can read to learn more about the intervention from a clinical standpoint. In the area of trauma treatment, for example, one study might cite a volume by Foa and Rothbaum (1998) that focuses on how to provide exposure therapy for rape victims. Another study might cite a volume by Cohen, Mannarino, and Deblinger (2006) that focuses on trauma-focused cognitive behavioral therapy for traumatized children. Still another might cite the Zayfert and Becker (2007) volume that focuses on cognitive behavioral therapy for adults with PTSD or Meichenbaum's (2003) lengthy handbook on that topic. And the EMDR studies are likely to cite Shapiro's (2001) tome on EMDR protocols and procedures. (Each of the foregoing references is listed in the Additional Readings section at the end of this introduction.)

If you have the time and resources to search the literature for evidence on the effectiveness of various alternative interventions for trauma, to critically appraise that evidence in an expert manner from the standpoint of research rigor, and then to read and digest books cited on the various interventions supported by the best evidence, then congratulations; you are truly a renaissance clinician! If so, you may not need to read this book. However, if you don't have enough time or resources for all of that, but still want your practice in treating trauma to be evidence-based, then read on.

The chapters in Parts 2 and 3 of this book provide detailed practitioner-focused how-to guides for those interventions that currently have the best research evidence supporting their effectiveness. The detail in each chapter, naturally, will not be as extensive as what you will find in an entire book devoted exclusively to the intervention being described in any particular chapter. However, it should be enough to get you started in providing the intervention and perhaps helping you decide whether you want to pursue further reading and training in that intervention. Toward the latter end, the chapters will also identify recommended additional reading as well as training options.

At this point, you may be thinking, "Not so fast! Why should I take *your* word for it that the interventions described in this book have the best research evidence supporting their effectiveness?" If so, good for you! A key feature of the EBP process is being a critical thinker, which means in part not just accepting claims based on authority. The fact that I have published extensively in the areas of research methodology and EBP and have taught a graduate course on the assessment and treatment of traumatized populations is no guarantee that I won't mislead you. Consequently, an appendix in this book reviews the research supporting the interventions covered in each chapter. If you have the time and resources to read and appraise that research yourself, by all means go for it! Better yet, don't just rely on the citations that I provide; perhaps you can conduct your own search to try to find better and more recent evidence supporting alternative interventions—things I didn't find in my search. In an ideal world, you would have the time and resources to do all that and not need to rely on my say-so. But this world is far from ideal, and your limited time and resources may require taking some short-cuts; ergo, this book.

CHAPTERS IN THIS VOLUME

The chapters in this book are organized in three parts. Part 1 consists of this introductory chapter only. Parts 2 and 3 then delve into specific interventions that currently have the best research evidence supporting their effectiveness for treating traumatized individuals.

Part 2 contains three chapters on trauma-focused cognitive behavior therapy (TFCBT). In Chapter 2, Gretchen Thomas focuses on a component of TFCBT that has had the most empirical support regarding its efficacy: prolonged exposure (PE). After discussing the theoretical underpinnings of PE, she shows practitioners how to engage clients in imaginal and in vivo exposures, including the use of relaxation techniques to help them remain calm as they confront feared stimuli.

Chapter 3, by Joanne Davis, Elana Newman, and Kristi Pruiksma, extends the coverage of TFCBT by focusing on a major component of that approach that often gets less detailed attention in other readings regarding the how-to's that practitioners need. That component, cognitive restructuring (CR), involves the identification and reworking of maladaptive thoughts. Chapter 3 notes that "most exposure techniques involve small amounts of CR and most CR involves small amounts of exposure." Because CR generally is not provided as a stand-alone therapy, Davis and her colleagues discuss it in the context of a step-by-step approach to TFCBT. They begin by describing the conditions and client attributes for which CR is indicated and contraindicated. Then they cover the following steps:

1. Assessment and case formulation
2. Psychoeducation
3. Eliciting thoughts and assumptions
4. Self-monitoring
5. Reviewing homework
6. Evaluating and challenging thoughts
7. Eliciting alternative thoughts and enhancing cognitive flexibility
8. Practicing skills
9. Maintenance planning

The chapter ends with coverage of additional issues, such as trouble-shooting and supervision.

Chapters 2 and 3, combined, should give readers a firm grasp of the how-to's of TFCBT with adults. They also should provide a good foundation for reading Chapter 4, in which Amy Hoch provides a step-by-step guide for providing TFCBT for traumatized children and their caregivers. For example, the CR material in Chapter 3 will connect to the section of Chapter 4 that deals with cognitive processing with caregivers.

The impact of trauma on children can be particularly devastating, and especially in light of their age and family context, a separate TFCBT protocol is needed for them. Although the TFCBT modalities for adults and children overlap, Hoch shows how TFCBT differs significantly when provided for children. One difference involves the issue of contraindications. For example, the full TFCBT protocol should not be used in cases where abuse is suspected but not yet substantiated. Likewise, it should not be used with clients who have vague memories of the trauma or who do not remember it.

Another important difference involves the need to include parents or alternative caregivers in the assessment and treatment protocol. Indeed, Hoch notes that "engagement with the caregiver is the key to successful treatment." Thus, psychoeducation needs to be provided (separately) to both the child and the caregiver. In the psychoeducation phase as well as later phases, parenting skills get a lot of attention. Another key difference with children involves implementing the exposure aspects of treatment in a manner that fits the child's developmental level. For example, books, games and other props are commonly used to discuss the trauma. An important component of exposure involves writing (with the therapist's help) a developmentally appropriate trauma narrative. Children also need more attention to affect expression and regulation. Likewise, children need a developmentally appropriate approach for dealing with cognitions. Although Hoch emphasizes the need to obtain training and supervision for providing TFCBT for traumatized children and their caregivers, her detailed, step-by-step chapter should give readers an excellent head start.

Part 3 of this book contains two chapters on EMDR. In Chapter 5, Philip Dodgson provides comprehensive coverage of EMDR with traumatized adults. He begins by describing the adaptive information-processing model (upon which EMDR is theoretically based) and linking that model to different intensities of traumatic experiences and symptoms. Dodgson then provides an overview of the eight phases of the standard EMDR protocol, including case examples that illustrate special aspects of EMDR in the case formulation and treatment of PTSD. Next, Dodgson describes in great operational detail (and with case illustrations) the most distinctive features of the EMDR protocol, including the use of bilateral stimulation and related approaches for desensitizing and reprocessing traumatic memories and for replacing negative cognitions about oneself connected to those memories with positive cognitions. After discussing the closure and reevaluation phases of EMDR, Dodgson addresses special aspects of providing EMDR with people who have experienced complex trauma (such as victims of childhood sexual abuse or of torture and organized violence), with people who have recently experienced a traumatizing event, and with people who are in a situation of ongoing conflict. In light of the uniqueness of EMDR, Chapter 5 ends with a relatively extensive section on Additional Resources. That section includes a list of online EMDR resources, sources that provide practice guidelines for using EMDR in the treatment of PTSD, a checklist for assessment and monitoring, and a comprehensive summary of the phases of the EMDR protocol.

In Chapter 6, the final chapter of this book, Robbie Adler-Tapia and Carolyn Settle build on Chapter 5 by describing the special ways in which the EMDR protocol can be adapted when working with children and adolescents. Children who experience trauma are likely to differ from adults who are traumatized in various important ways. Children, for example, are less developed neurologically, and, consequently, trauma can have a greater impact on their neurological development and thus can impede their natural healing process and profoundly impact their future experiences throughout their lives. Children also are less developed cognitively and thus are less able to interpret small t traumas. Consequently, children might interpret such experiences as more traumatic than adults would, and might even experience them as life threatening. Adler-Tapia and Settle discuss a new diagnosis called developmental trauma disorder, in which early life trauma "can cause neurological damage and manifest in learning disabilities, impaired cognitive functioning, as well as mental health and behavioral issues." In light of its importance with children, Adler-Tapia and Settle give considerable attention to how trauma can impact the neurobiology of children and the consequent implications for assessment and treatment.

Adler-Tapia and Settle proceed to discuss the ways in which the EMDR protocol needs to be fine-tuned to meet the developmental needs of children, especially in light of the way in which traumatic memories are stored in their neuronetworks. In addition to the special neurological implications, Adler-Tapia and Settle discuss many other ways in which EMDR for children is unique. To cite just one example, EMDR therapists need to teach children coping skills for dealing with strong emotions and to enhance mastering experiences for stressful situations. Thus, a treatment session might begin by asking the parent and child about something the child did well since the last session. The child's success or accomplishment can then be strengthened and installed as a mastery experience by employing bilateral stimulation.

After covering indications and contraindications for using EMDR with children, Adler-Tapia and Settle discuss each of the eight phases of the EMDR protocol in great detail and with a focus on the unique challenges involved in providing each stage with children. Case examples of five children are employed to illustrate how each phase can be operationalized.

Despite the extensive empirical support for the effectiveness of EMDR, including the consistency among various rigorous meta-analytic research reviews that it is one of the two most effective evidence-based interventions in the treatment of PTSD, its terminology is likely to be new to many clinicians. Recognizing this, the authors of both chapters on EMDR appended a glossary to their chapters. In light of the overlap between the glossaries, and the fact that each included some terms that were not included in the other, I have integrated them into one glossary and put that glossary at the end of this book.

Despite the differences in the treatment approaches described in the five chapters in Parts 2 and 3 of this book, readers can note some commonalities. Each of these approaches requires clients to stop avoiding painful memories of traumatic experiences and instead face them and deal with them in therapy either imaginally or in vivo. Consequently, one key commonality is the recognition that it is vital to establish a strong therapeutic alliance as a prerequisite for providing any of these approaches (as I discussed earlier in this introduction). For example, in Chapter 5, Dodgson notes that key to any psychotherapeutic modality provided to victims of trauma is an attuned therapeutic relationship that enables the client to "feel safe enough to do the work that may entail going into the heart of darkness." Another commonality pertains to the treatment of traumatized children. Both Chapters 4 and 6 stress the importance of involving parents or caregivers in the assessment, treatment planning and psychoeducation phases of either TFCBT or EMDR. In these and various other ways, what you read in each chapter of this book will help you understand and apply material that you read in subsequent chapters.

Time permitting, I hope you can read every chapter in this book. Alternatively, you might be interested only in the chapters on TFCBT or only in the chapters on EMDR. If your practice is limited to working with children and their caregivers, you might opt to read only Chapters 4 and 6, but I would not recommend that because those two chapters build on concepts covered in the adult chapters on their referent treatment approach (Chapters 2 and 3 for Chapter 4, and Chapter 5 for Chapter 6). In addition, if you treat any clients with co-occurring PTSD and substance abuse, then I recommend that you read Chapter 6 of Volume 2 of this series: *Substance Abuse Treatment for Youth and Adults*. As I mentioned earlier, that chapter covers seeking safety, which is an evidence-based approach for treating such clients.

Regardless of which chapters you read, I hope you will find every one of them useful in guiding your practice, perhaps merely by helping you decide which of these interventions you'd like to use and perhaps learn more about. I'll end by reiterating something mentioned in the preface: I would appreciate any feedback you can provide regarding the ways you have found this book to be helpful or any suggestions you may have for improving it. You can e-mail me such feedback at arubin@mail.utexas.edu.

REFERENCES

Achenbach, T. M. (1991). *Manual for Child Behavior Checklist/4-18 and 1991 Profile*. Burlington, VT: University of Vermont, Dept. of Psychiatry.

Adler-Tapia, R. (2001). Traumatic Stress Symptom Checklist (TSSC). Available at www.EMDRKIDS.com.

Abidin, R. R. (1983). *Parenting Stress Index: Manual, Administration Booklet, [and] Research Update*. Charlottesville, VA: Pediatric Psychology Press.

Allen, R. D. (Ed.). (1993). Handbook of post-disaster interventions. *Journal of Social Behavior and Personality (special issue)*, 8, 5.

American Psychiatric Association. (2000). *Diagnostic and statistical manual of mental disorders* (4th ed., text rev.). Washington, DC: Author.

Bisson, J. I., Jenkins, P. L., Alexander, J., & Bannister, C. (1993). Randomised controlled trial of psychological debriefing for victims of acute burn trauma. *British Journal of Psychiatry, 171*, 78–81.

Briere, J., Johnson, K., Bissada, A., Damon, L., Crouch, J., Gil, E., Hanson, R., & Ernst, V. (2001). The Trauma Symptom Checklist for Young Children (TSCYC): Reliability and association with abuse exposure in a multi-site study. *Child Abuse & Neglect, 25, 8*, 1001–1014.

Bryant, R. A., & Harvey, A. G. (2000). *Acute stress disorder: A handbook of theory, assessment, and treatment*. Washington, DC: American Psychological Association.

Carlier, I. V. E., Lamberts, R. D., van Uchelen, A. J., & Gersons, B. P. R. (1998). Disaster-related post-traumatic stress in police officers: A field study of the impact of debriefing. *Stress Medicine, 14*, 143–148.

Chambers, W., Puig-Antich, J., Hirsch, M., et al. (1985). The assessment of affective disorders in children and adolescents by semi-structured interview: Test-retest reliability of the Schedule for Affective Disorders and schizophrenia for School-Age Children. Present Episode Version. *Archives of General Psychiatry, 42*, 696–702.

Cohen, J. A., Mannarino, A. P., & Deblinger, E. (2006). *Treating trauma and traumatic grief in children and adolescents*. New York: Guilford Press.

Deblinger, E., Thakkar-Kolar, R., & Ryan, E. (2006). Trauma in childhood. In V. M. Follette & J. I. Ruzek, (Eds.), *Cognitive–behavioral therapies for trauma* (2nd ed., pp. 405–432). New York: Guilford Press.

Dworkin, M. (2005). *EMDR and the relational imperative: The therapeutic relationship in EMDR treatment*. New York: Routledge.

Foa, E. B., & Rothbaum, B. O. (1998). *Treating the trauma of rape: Cognitive–behavioral therapy for PTSD*. New York: Guilford Press.

Follette, V. M., & Ruzek, J. I. (Eds.). (2006). *Cognitive–behavioral therapies for trauma* (2nd ed.). New York: Guilford Press.

Frick, P. J. (1991). *The Alabama Parenting Questionnaire*. Unpublished instrument. University of Alabama.

Friedman, M. (2006). *Post-traumatic and acute stress disorders: The latest assessment and treatment strategies* (4th ed). Kansas City, MO: Dean Psych Press.

Garratano, L. (2004). *Clinical skills for managing PTSD*. Mascot, Australia: Talomin Books.

Gibbs, L., & Gambrill, E. (2002). Evidence-based practice: Counterarguments to objections. *Research on Social Work Practice, 12*, 452–476.

Greenwald, R. (2005). *Child trauma handbook: A guide for helping trauma-exposed children and adolescents*. Binghamton, NY: Haworth Press.

Herman, J. L. (1997). *Trauma and recovery*. New York: Basic Books.

Housley, J., & Beutler, L. (2007). *Treating victims of mass disaster and terrorism.* Oxford, UK: Hogrefe.

Jones, R. T. (2002). *The child's reaction to traumatic events scale (CRTES): A self-report traumatic stress measure.* Blacksburg: Virginia Polytechnic University.

Keane, T. M., Weathers, F. W., & Foa, E. B. (2000). Diagnosis and assessment. In E. B. Foa, T. M. Keane, & M. J. Friedman (Eds.), *Effective treatments for PTSD* (pp. 18–36). New York: Guilford Press.

Kessler, R. C., Sonnega, A., Bromet, E., Hughes, M., and Nelson, C. B. (1995). Posttraumatic stress disorder in the National Comorbidity Survey. *Archives of General Psychiatry, 52,* 1048–1060.

Kovacs, M. (1985). The Children's Depression Inventory (CDI). *Psychopharmacology Bulletin, 21, 4,* 995–998.

Mannarino, A. P. & Cohen, J. A. (1996). Family related variables and psychological system formation in sexually abused girls. *Journal of Child Sexual Abuse, 5,* 105–119.

Mayou, R. A., Ehlers, A., & Hobbs, M. (2000). Psychological debriefing for road traffic accident victims. *British Journal of Psychiatry, 176,* 589–593.

Meichenbaum, D. (2003). *A clinical handbook/practical therapist manual for assessing and treating adults with PTSD.* Ontario, Canada: Institute Press.

Mullen, E. J. (2004). Facilitating practitioner use of evidence-based practice. In A. R. Roberts & K. R. Yeager (Eds.), *Evidence-based practice manual: Research and outcome measures in health and human services* (pp. 205–210). New York: Oxford University Press.

Nathan, P. E. (2004). The clinical utility of therapy research: Bridging the gap between the present and future. In A. R. Roberts & K. R. Yeager (Eds.), *Evidence-based practice manual: Research and outcome measures in health and human services.* New York: Oxford University Press.

Rose, S., Bisson, J., & Wessely, S. (2001). Psychological debriefing for preventing post traumatic stress disorder (PTSD). *Cochrane Database of Systematic Reviews, 3.*

Rubin, A. (2008). *Practitioner's guide to using research for evidence-based practice.* Hoboken, NJ: Wiley.

Rubin, A., & Parrish, D. (2007). Challenges to the future of evidence-based practice in social work education. *Journal of Social Work Education, 43*(3), 405–428.

Sackett, D. L., Straus, S. E., Richardson, W. S., Rosenberg, W., & Haynes, R. B. (2000). *Evidence-based medicine: How to practice and teach EBM* (2nd ed.). New York: Churchill-Livingstone.

Shapiro, F. (2001). *Eye movement desensitization and reprocessing: Basic principles, protocols and procedures* (2nd ed.). New York: Guilford Press.

Shlonsky, A., & Gibbs, L. (2004). Will the real evidence-based practice please stand up? Teaching the process of evidence-based practice to the helping professions. *Brief Treatment and Crisis Intervention, 4*(2), 137–153.

Steinberg, A. M., Brymer, M. J., Decker, K. B., & Pynos, R. S. (2004). The University of California at Los Angeles post-traumatic stress disorder reaction index. *Current Psychiatry Reports, 6, 2,* 96–100.

Taylor, S. (2006). *Clinician's guide to PTSD: A cognitive behavioral approach.* New York: Guilford Press.

Thyer, B. (2004). What is evidence-based practice? *Brief Treatment and Crisis Intervention, 4,* 167–176.

Weiss, D. S., & Marmar, C. R. (1997). The Impact of Events Scale: Revised. In Wilson, J. P. & Tang, C. S. (Eds.), *Cross-cultural assessment of psychological trauma and PTSD.* New York: Springer, 219–238.

Wolfe, V. V., Gentile, C., Michienzi, T., Sas, L., & Wolfe, D. A. (1991). The Children's Impact of Traumatic Events Scale: A measure of post-sexual abuse PTSD symptoms. *Behavioral Assessment, 13*(4), 359–383.

Zayfert, C., & Becker, C. B. (2007). *Cognitive–behavioral therapy for PTSD: A case formulation approach.* New York: Guilford Press.

ADDITIONAL READINGS

ASSESSMENT

American Psychiatric Association. (2000). *Diagnostic and statistical manual of mental disorders* (4th ed., text rev.). Washington, DC: Author.

Bryant, R. A., & Harvey, A. G. (2000). *Acute stress disorder: A handbook of theory, assessment, and treatment.* Washington, DC: American Psychological Association.

Cohen, J. A., Mannarino, A. P., & Deblinger, E. (2006). *Treating trauma and traumatic grief in children and adolescents.* New York: Guilford Press. (Chapter 2.)

Foa, E. B. & Rothbaum, B. O. (1998). *Treating the trauma of rape: Cognitive–behavioral therapy for PTSD.* New York: Guilford Press. (Chapters 2, 3, & 7.)

Follette, V. M., & Ruzek, J. I. (Eds.). (2006). *Cognitive–behavioral therapies for trauma* (2nd ed.). New York: Guilford Press. (Chapters 2 & 3.)

Friedman, M. (2006). *Post-traumatic and acute stress disorders: The latest assessment and treatment strategies.* (4th ed). Kansas City, MO: Dean Psych Press.

Keane, T. M., Weathers, F. W., & Foa, E. B. (2000). Diagnosis and assessment. In E. B. Foa, T. M. Keane, & M. J. Friedman (Eds.), *Effective treatments for PTSD* (pp. 18–36). New York: Guilford Press.

Meichenbaum, D. (2003) *A clinical handbook/practical therapist manual for assessing and treating adults with PTSD.* Ontario, Canada: Institute Press. (Pages 34–52, 121–142.)

Schnurr, P. P., Friedman, M. J., & Bernardy, N. C. (2002). Research on posttraumatic stress disorder: Epidemiology, pathophysiology, and assessment. *Journal of Clinical Psychology, 58*(8), 877–889.

Shapiro, F. (2001). *Eye movement desensitization and reprocessing: Basic principles, protocols and procedures* (2nd ed.). New York: Guilford Press.

Taylor, S. (2006). *Clinician's guide to PTSD: A cognitive behavioral approach.* New York: Guilford Press. (Chapter 6.)

Turner, S., & Lee, D. (1998). *Measures in post traumatic stress disorder: A practitioner's guide.* Windsor, UK: NFER-Nelson.

Webb, N. B. (2006). *Working with traumatized youth in child welfare.* New York: Guilford Press. (Chapter 4.)

Zayfert, C., & Becker, C. B. (2007). *Cognitive–behavioral therapy for PTSD: A case formulation approach*. New York: Guilford Press. (Chapter 3.)

THE EBP PROCESS

Gibbs, L. E. (2003). *Evidence–based practice for the helping professions*. Pacific Grove, CA: Brooks/Cole.

Rubin, A. (2008). *Practitioner's guide to using research for evidence–based practice*. Hoboken, NJ: Wiley.

PART 2

TRAUMA-FOCUSED COGNITIVE BEHAVIORAL THERAPY

CHAPTER 2

Cognitive Behavioral Treatment of Traumatized Adults: Exposure Therapy

GRETCHEN M. THOMAS

T RAUMA-FOCUSED COGNITIVE BEHAVIORAL therapy (CBT) includes various components. One component, cognitive restructuring, is covered in depth in Chapter 3 of this volume. In this chapter, I'll focus on a component of CBT that is one of the two interventions with the most empirical support regarding its efficacy: prolonged exposure (PE). (The other is eye movement desensitization and reprocessing [EMDR], which is covered in Part 3 of this volume.) I'll also cover anxiety management training (AMT), as an auxiliary component of PE. PE aims to assist the client in confronting feared situations and memories, while AMT teaches clients to decrease their anxiety and use new coping skills.

ASSESSMENT

Prior to administering all CBT treatment programs, it is imperative to conduct a thorough assessment of the client's symptoms. Additionally, it is common to administer repeated assessment measures throughout the treatment course to monitor symptoms and level of functioning. This serves two purposes: (1) to assist the clinician in monitoring the client's process, and (2) to provide the client with evidence of improvement, which can foster a sense of accomplishment, mastery, and confidence. Generic assessment guidelines were discussed in Chapter 1. An extensive coverage of the assessment process that is part of the CBT protocol is provided in this chapter's appendix on assessment.

EXPOSURE: THEORETICAL CONSIDERATIONS

Exposure techniques have been influenced by various theories and principles, including Mowrer's two-factor theory, cognitive theories (e.g., clinical,
personality, and social psychology), Piaget's cognitive development model,
Pavlovian classical conditioning, Skinner's operant conditioning, learning
theory, Beck's cognitive therapy, Lang's theory of fear, and emotional
processing theory. According to Mowrer's two-factor learning theory,
when a client confronts a feared situation or memory without the negative
consequences he or she anticipates will occur, habituation (desensitization)
of the fear is expected to occur (Mowrer, 1960; Foa & Rothbaum, 1998). This
habituation or desensitizing is a goal of treatment.

COGNITIVE THEORY

Another influence, cognitive theory related to posttraumatic stress disorder
(PTSD), is grounded in three disciplines. Clinical psychology explains pathological depression and anxiety disorders, including PTSD, while personality
and social psychology focus on the disruption of cognitive schemas that occur
after a trauma (Foa & Rothbaum, 1998). Schemas are the core beliefs and
assumptions that influence how we interpret information and experiences. In
order to make sense of trauma or to process it, we must change the preexisting
beliefs. This modification of beliefs is based on Piaget's cognitive development model of assimilation and accommodation (Piaget, 1954). Four core
beliefs change after a trauma, namely, beliefs that the world is safe and
meaningful, beliefs of self-worth, as well as beliefs regarding the trustworthiness of others (Epstein, 1991). Traumatic experiences challenge these core
beliefs and require the victim to either assimilate these with old beliefs or alter
his or her beliefs to accommodate the traumatic experience (Janoff-Bulman,
1992). There is often an assumption that all pretrauma schemas or core beliefs
are generally positive in nature (e.g., positive worldview and sense of self).
However, this may not be the case for many people. Their schemas and core
beliefs developed throughout childhood may support negative perceptions of
themselves and the world (Foa & Rothbaum, 1998; Resnick, Kilpatrick,
Dansky, Saunders, & Best, 1993). Traumas will serve to exacerbate and
reinforce these beliefs. Individuals who have been traumatized continually
revise their internal beliefs and perceptions of external events until they are in
agreement with one another (Horowitz, 1986). This process occurs through
reliving the trauma memories.

Another influence on exposure based on cognitive theory is cognitive
therapy developed by Beck to treat depression and later found to be useful
in treating anxiety disorders (Beck, 2005). Beck (2005) suggests that emotional
reactions are based on the meaning we assign to events, not the events

themselves. Different individuals can interpret the same event in different ways, assigning different meanings. Beck further proposes that emotions are associated with specific types of thoughts. For example, if one thinks he is in danger, he tends to feel anxious. Emotional responses that supersede what a given situation is expected to warrant are based on distorted cognitions and interpretations. In cognitive therapy, clients are assisted in recognizing these cognitive distortions, altering them to more healthy and accurate interpretations, which will then evoke emotional responses that fall within a normal and healthy range (Foa & Rothbaum, 1998).

LEARNING THEORY

Exposure is based on the principles of learning theory, including classical and operant conditioning (Foa & Rothbaum, 1998). Behavioral responses are shaped by stimuli that come before (antecedent) and after (consequence) the behavior (Bandura, 1977, 1986). This process can be described as antecedents (A), behavior (B), and consequences (C) (Barkley, Edwards, & Robin, 1999; Feindler & Ecton, 1986). This process can be learned through direct experience or vicariously through observation (Bandura 1977, 1986). Antecedents either directly elicit certain behaviors or they create an opportunity for the behavior to occur. If the behavior is a result of classical conditioning, antecedents are eliciting behavior that is emotionally charged (Friedberg & McClure, 2002). For example, in Case Example 2-1, Naushad was usually molested by his father late at night after he would return home from drinking. The molestation generated aversive physiological, emotional, and cognitive stimuli in Naushad. Suppose Naushad's father slammed the front door when he came home from the bar, which caused anticipatory anxiety and fear in Naushad. Over time, through repeated repetition of the front door slamming paired with chronic sexual abuse that followed, any door slamming shut or a

Case Example 2-1: Naushad

Naushad is a 19-year-old man who was sexually molested by his father until the age of 7, when his father died. He remembers the lights from the bar sign across the street going off and his father coming home drunk. Once home, he would molest Naushad in his bedroom. Naushad remembers the smell of alcohol on his breath and his father's facial hair on his skin. He's having nightmares and flashbacks of his abuse. He does not remember his mother intervening, but he believes she was aware of what was happening. Recently, Naushad was arrested for sexual solicitation in a public park restroom.

similar noise will elicit the same intense anticipatory anxiety in Naushad as the molestation itself. Consequently, Naushad associated being molested with such stimuli as neon bar lights flashing, the smell of alcohol, and feeling the contact of facial hair. In turn, these stimuli continued to provoke anxiety in Naushad later in life.

Classical Conditioning

Similarly, classical conditioning was demonstrated in Pavlov's well-known studies with dogs salivating in response to a ringing bell. The bell (A) was the stimulus, while the act of salivating (B) was the conditioned response. The reward of food (C) was associated with the particular behavior of salivating. Fear is acquired in a similar way through classical conditioning and is maintained through operant conditioning. Skinner further developed these concepts into behavioral engineering and operant conditioning through his experiments with rats. Avoidance behavior is established through operant conditioning. Regarding PTSD, individuals learn that if they avoid a stimulus that triggers fear, they will reduce their anxiety related to the trauma. However, the stimulus they are avoiding may be neutral by nature and threatening only after they assign such a meaning to it. Through avoidance, there is no opportunity for the individual to recognize that the stimulus is not repeatedly followed by trauma so her fear and anxiety is maintained (Foa & Rothbaum, 1998).

Fear

Another theory applied to PTSD and exposure is Lang's (1977) theory of fear. Applied by Foa and Kozak (1986), it suggests that fear is a cognitive structure comprised of fear stimuli, responses, and the meanings assigned to these stimuli. Essential to treatment is the modification of fear structures with pathological aspects. This approach to treatment proposes that in order to form new memories, the feared memories must first be activated (Brom, Kleber, & Defares, 1989), then modified with corrective information that is not compatible with the maladaptive aspects of that memory. This newly created memory should result in a decrease in distressing symptoms.

   A challenge with this approach is first recalling the memory and then organizing different aspects of traumatic memories, which are often disorganized and incomplete. This is followed by correcting the pathological beliefs with corrective information and experience (Foa & Riggs, 1993). The goal of repeating this pattern is habituation and desensitization. Additionally, PTSD treatment aims to correct the client's general belief that he/she is inadequate or ill-equipped to cope with a world that is unsafe. Reducing symptoms brings about confidence in coping skills, while fostering an ability to distinguish safe situations from those that are dangerous (Rothbaum & Foa, 2007).

EMOTIONAL PROCESSING THEORY

To explain why some individuals develop PTSD after a trauma while others do not, Foa and colleagues developed *emotional processing theory*. This is a combination of various theories, including cognitive, learning, and personality theories. Ideally, over time people can recall memories without becoming overwhelmed by the intense emotional experiences of the original event. Emotional processing theory explains fear reduction during exposure and describes emotional reexperiencing as the phenomenon of reliving emotional experiences after the original traumatic event (Foa & Kozak, 1986). There are normal emotional processes involved in the decrease of emotional reexperiencing. Emotional processing theory suggests that successful treatment lies in developing healthy emotional processing that has been impaired for those with PTSD (Foa & Rothbaum, 1998; Rachman, 1980). Exposure corrects the associations between stimulus and response and the inaccurate evaluation of circumstances through deconditioning. First, feared stimuli are introduced by exposure, which activates the fear structure. The pathological elements of this fear structure are then modified by introducing information that is contrary to previous pathological conceptualizations (Foa & Kozak; Foa & Rothbaum).

EXPOSURE TECHNIQUES

The duration and use of exposure techniques vary across studies but commonly consist of 9 to 12 treatment sessions lasting between 60 and 90 minutes (Boudewyns & Hyer, 1990; Boudewyns, Hyer, Woods, Harrison, & McCranie, 1990; Foa & Meadows, 1997; Foa & Rothbaum, 1998; Foa, Rothbaum, Riggs, & Murdock, 1991; Thompson, Charlton, Kerry, Lee, & Turner, 1995). The primary strategies used to alleviate symptoms and develop new ways to cope include exposure through imagination or prolonged *imaginal* exposure, as well as real-life exposures, also called prolonged *in vivo* exposure. Essentially, exposures require clients to repeatedly face their fears by activating and confronting memories. The aim is to improve and correct pathological coping mechanisms (e.g., reexperiencing [Diagnostic and Statistical Manual of Mental Disorders (DSM) B criteria], avoidance/numbing [DSM C criteria], and hyperarousal [DSM D criteria]).

Prolonged *Imaginal* Exposure, or repeatedly activating and reliving the trauma, aims to restructure a client's coping mechanism as applied to trauma memories, while *in vivo* exposure reduces avoidant behaviors related to trauma reminders often found in day-to-day life (e.g., locations, objects, sounds, smells). In vivo exposures allow the client to gradually and incrementally confront avoided situations and understand that they no longer pose a danger to his life or threaten his safety by assigning a new meaning to those situations (Bourne, 2005; Foa & Rothbaum, 1998). Psychoeducation is another component often utilized in the first phase of treatment to explain common reactions to trauma, and mindful breathing is used before and after exposures to assist the client in feeling physically and emotionally relaxed. By facilitating relaxation, mindful breathing creates the exact opposite physiological response the body typically has as a reaction to stress and anxiety (Bourne).

COGNITIVE RESTRUCTURING

Clients with shame, guilt, anger, and rage, in addition to anxiety, may benefit from supplementing other cognitive behavioral techniques with cognitive restructuring (CR). Clients who are most distressed by cognitive distortions that evoke shame and guilt, as well as those clients with anxiety disorders, may benefit from treatment using CR (Foa & Rothbaum, 1998). (For an in-depth discussion on the use of CR, see Chapter 3).

ANXIETY MANAGEMENT TRAINING

Anxiety management training (AMT) uses cognitive restructuring along with relaxation techniques, and has proven to be effective with female assault victims. AMT is based on the notion that anxious reactions are the result of skill deficits. AMT thus provides clients with new skills to manage their anxiety as opposed to fear activation (e.g., exposure) (Foa & Rothbaum, 1998; Meichenbaum, 1974). Efficacy for victims of other forms of trauma is unclear (Foa & Rothbaum).

STRESS INOCULATION TRAINING

Stress inoculation training (SIT) is a form of AMT that provides coping skills to clients through education and training that aim to decrease the client's anxiety in various situations. Examples of these skills include relaxation techniques, breathing exercises, CR, thought stopping, guided self-dialogue, role playing, and covert modeling in an attempt to lower anxiety in various situations. SIT alone, although effective, has not demonstrated greater effectiveness than exposure alone. However, clients who are extremely tense may be hesitant to engage in exposure treatment until their level of tension decreases. In these cases, some suggest that a combination of exposure and SIT is useful (Foa & Rothbaum, 1998).

PROLONGED EXPOSURES

In order to fully grasp how prolonged exposure techniques help clients, and to believe and trust in these techniques, it is important to understand the processes that are being impacted by trauma as well as those that are modified through treatment. Before treatment implementation is presented, a review of the trauma's impact is discussed. For those with PTSD, time does not heal all wounds and there is an inability to integrate and accept trauma experiences as part of the past, so there is a repetitive replaying of trauma memories, including images, psychological states, emotions, and behaviors (Lee, Vaillant, Torrey, & Elder, 1995; van der Kolk & McFarlane, 2007). Traumatic experiences impact the psychological, biological, and social equilibrium of individuals and shade all other experiences, as well as interfere and hinder one's ability to experience and pay attention to current circumstances due to being rigidly fixated on their past (van der Kolk & McFarlane).

Initial therapy should focus on developing a sense of security, safety, control, and predictability for the client. Essentially, we are helping clients to master their stress reactions both physically and biologically, assisting them in coming to terms with their traumatic experience, and creating a secure social support system (van der Kolk, van der Hart, & Marmar, 2007). Effective treatment in one area may have widespread effects on the overall system and secondary implications for problematic symptoms, ultimately affecting the way in which the victim experiences himself, others, and his surroundings (van der Kolk & McFarlane, 2007). However, clients often fear the act of confronting their memories, the memories themselves, and engaging in life in general (van der Kolk & McFarlane). Helping clients to avoid the past will not help them establish a sense of safety or process their trauma. While verbalizing the traumatic experience has been shown to decrease psychosomatic symptoms (Harber & Pennebaker, 1992), simply uncovering and identifying memories is insufficient. Trauma must be activated, modified, and processed. Memory needs to be used to record the past as well as recreate the meaning of past events (van der Kolk & McFarlane, 2007).

Symptom Maintenance and Corrective Experiences

PTSD symptoms are maintained through the client's avoidance. Avoidance behaviors are common to anxiety disorders. Anxiety is formed by creating a connection between a situation (in this case, a traumatic event) and an anxious or fearful emotional response. It creates sensitivity to certain stimuli. This sensitization drives the person to avoid anything related to that feared situation (Bourne, 2005). Prolonged exposures can help the client to confront her fears and process the trauma in a healthier way, by unraveling the connection between negative emotions and the trauma. The client must be in the anxiety-provoking situation but feel relaxed. This will give her a new experience and new feelings of relaxation and calmness to connect to the trauma, which increases her level of functioning while decreasing reexperiencing, avoidant/numbing, and hyperarousal symptoms.

In order to impact the sensitization that has developed, or the connection between the trauma and anxiety, the client must break down the confrontation into small, manageable, and systematic steps using exposures. The idea of using exposures to overcome PTSD symptoms was influenced by several theories and principles (as discussed earlier in this chapter). Essentially, exposure can decondition erroneous associations between stimuli and responses. Correcting these associations between the trauma and fear requires the client to activate the feared situation and respond to it in a relaxed state, which is incompatible with the fear stimuli and situation. Over time, through repeated exposure, the client realizes that memories are not dangerous, memories are different than reality, anxiety does not last forever, and experiencing anxiety and fear does not induce insanity (Foa & Rothbaum, 1998).

Clients may assume that confronting their trauma will increase their anxiety and fear and it may even make them "lose their mind" or "go crazy," never able to return to normal functioning (e.g., "If I allow myself to think about it, that's it, I'll lose it. I'll lose my mind, I can't handle it, I'll have a heart attack. It's like I'm teetering on the edge of complete craziness, and if I do this I'll really cross that line."). Instead, the exposure enhances the client's sense of mastery over the intrusive thoughts, feelings, and memories, allowing him to feel more confident and competent, recognizing those feared situations no longer pose a threat to his life or safety. Clients learn that their negative feelings do increase to a point but can last for only a certain period of time. It is crucial for the client to remain in the situation, tolerate the initial discomfort, and ride it out repeatedly. Retreating will only support those anxious feelings. When clients remain in the feared situation (e.g., reliving of the trauma), they live through an increase and peak of negative emotions. However, on the other side of that peak, they find that their anxiety and fear subside and become less intense. There is no healthy way around these feelings; one must go through them to get to the other side. The exposures provide clients with successful and corrective experiences, giving them personal evidence to counter their worst fears and desensitize themselves or unlearn their anxiety. The more times they do this to retrain themselves, the more quickly their body will learn to react in a relaxed state, allowing their symptoms to dissipate.

The prolonged exposures used to treat PTSD symptoms include imaginal and *in vivo* exposures. Imaginal exposures require the client to relive the trauma, describe it, and feel those same emotions that took place at the time of the trauma. These exposures involve repeated and prolonged exposures to images, scenarios, and flashbacks the client is fearful of (Bourne, 2005). In vivo exposures are practiced for homework to decrease the daily life situations that make people feel anxious or trigger distressing memories related to the trauma, either directly or indirectly. *In vivo* exposures allow the client to confront her fears and avoided situations gradually and incrementally.

Clients can first use imagery and then eventually confront situations and feared stimuli in real life (Bourne, 2005). Before and after exposures, clients can use mindful breathing to help them feel relaxed. Mindful breathing is a technique used to assist the client in being calm during flashbacks or while experiencing negative emotions. It helps create the exact opposite physiological response your body naturally gravitates toward as a reaction to stress and anxiety. It lowers heart rate, respiration rate, and blood pressure, which are all typically altered by stress, anxiety, and fear (Bourne). This technique is also used during the exposure sessions. Tracking clients' practice of mindful breathing can be done in their homework journal. Also for homework, clients are asked to record their avoidance, including the situations, locations, conversations, events, or people they avoid throughout the week. These records are reviewed during treatment sessions.

Trauma Fixation and Information Processing

Unlike other disorders, PTSD symptoms are based in reality, on real trauma experiences, and the meaning individuals assign to these events is as essential as the initial trauma experience (Caruth, 1995; van der Kolk & McFarlane 2007). The trauma memories are not intertwined with previous schemata and are instead independently existing or dissociated (van der Kolk & McFarlane, 2007). The repetitions of the trauma may even play out in the dynamics of interpersonal relationships. With each repetition, distress and sensitization increases, engraving them in the brain (van der Kolk & McFarlane, 2007).

For people with PTSD, the ability to process information is altered in six distinct ways: (1) intrusions; (2) compulsive reexposure to the trauma (harm to others, self-destructiveness, revictimization); (3) avoiding and numbing, inability to modulate arousal; (4) attention distraction and stimulus discrimination; (5) alterations in defense mechanisms; and (6) changes in personal identity. Intrusions do not allow victims to accept the trauma as an event of the past; they keep trauma as a current and ongoing experience. This interferes with healing and often triggers other distressing memories of previous traumas. Instead of tending to other perceptions, clients respond primarily to triggers related to the trauma, creating a biased perception and a limited amount of positive or neutral sensations that are calming or pleasurable.

Regarding compulsive reexposure, some individuals will find themselves in situations that are reminiscent of the trauma, which may help to explain other behavioral and emotional problems, including harm to others through violence, harm to self, and primitive coping behaviors (e.g., suicide, cutting, eating disorders), revictimization (e.g., rape victims, prostitution, drug abuse), and abusive interpersonal relationships (Finkelhor & Browne, 1984; Groth, 1979; Russell, 1986; Seghorn, Boucher, & Prentky, 1987; van der Kolk, 1989; van der Kolk & McFarlane, 2007; van der Kolk, Perry, & Herman, 1991).

Avoiding and numbing are also common symptoms of PTSD that impact one's ability to process information. There is an active avoidance of emotional arousal and a withdrawal from any stimulation, making it increasingly difficult to engage in the present (van der Kolk & McFarlane in van der Kolk, 2007). Clients may avoid reminders, self-medicate through substances, dissociate to keep memories out of their consciousness, socially withdraw, or become generally numb or unresponsive to various emotions.

While individuals may constrict their emotional responses, their bodies continue to respond to stimuli (e.g., exaggerated startle response, hyper-vigilance, restlessness, shutting down, and freezing), and there is an inability to modulate this arousal. They have been conditioned to respond immediately to stimuli without fully understanding why they are even distressed or upset. They may have difficulty articulating their emotional states and continuously anticipate threats to their safety, which takes a toll on their ability to concentrate and process information. Ultimately, it creates distrust in their bodily sensations. Physical sensations and reactions that act as warning signs of threat lose their effectiveness since there is constant mis-firing. This may lead to either exaggerated or inhibited reactions (Reiker & Carmen, 1986; van der Kolk & Fisler, 1994; van der Kolk & McFarlane, 2007).

Processing information is further disrupted by levels of attention, distract-ibility, and stimulus discrimination. People generally need to be able to identify their needs, voice them, and figure how to meet these needs. However, for those with PTSD, there is a loss in ability to identify their needs, an inability to be flexible in responses to external circumstances, a loss of involvement in daily life, difficulty discerning relevant from irrelevant stimuli, and a persistent avoidance of feeling anything by becoming con-stricted (Reiker & Carmen, 1986; van der Kolk & Fisler, 1994; van der Kolk & McFarlane, 2007).

Additionally, there are changes in defense mechanisms and personal identity after trauma. Violence and trauma challenge the views one holds for himself and his capability, as well as others and the world in general. At times there may be a false sense of responsibility for the trauma, which is especially true for those who experience trauma in childhood (see Part 2, this volume). Feelings of shame and humiliation are often dissociated since these emotions are so painful. However, not being in touch with one's own feelings of shame may perpetuate further abuse either through revictimization or perpetration of abuse (Reiker & Carmen, 1986; van der Kolk & Fisler, 1994; van der Kolk & McFarlane, 2007).

PROLONGED EXPOSURE TECHNIQUES

It is possible to consider PE a first-line approach, especially for clients with uncomplicated PTSD mainly consisting of anxiety and avoidance symptoms. It is supported by empirical validation regarding its effectiveness with a variety of trauma populations. PE is the most straightforward program with a simple implementation. This allows for dissemination among clinicians who are not experts in CBT, and it is less intellectually demanding on clients (Foa & Rothbaum, 1998).

As stated previously, the duration and use of exposure techniques commonly consist of 9 to 12 treatment sessions lasting between 60 and 90 minutes (Boudewyns & Hyer, 1990; Boudewyns et al., 1990; Foa et al., 1991; Foa & Meadows, 1997; Foa & Rothbaum, 1998; Thompson et al., 1995). The primary strategies used to alleviate symptoms and develop new ways to cope include exposure through imagination or prolonged *imaginal* exposure to relive the trauma, whereas real-life exposures, also called prolonged *in vivo* exposures, address feared situations. Both of these can vary in duration (Foa & Rothbaum).

Exposure techniques first require the client to activate trauma memories and confront their fears. This activation is followed by repeated modification of the pathological aspects of trauma memories, allowing the client to more fully process the trauma (Foa & Rothbaum, 1998). The ability to process information accurately, as described earlier, is often impaired for clients with PTSD (Foa & Meadows, 1997; Foa, Rothbaum, & Molnar, 1995; Foa, Steketee, & Rothbaum, 1989). Modifying this impairment leads to improvement and correction of pathological coping mechanisms, a decrease in avoidant behaviors and numbing, and diminished hyperarousal. By repeatedly activating and reliving the trauma, PE aims to restructure a client's coping mechanisms as they apply to trauma memories, while *in vivo* exposure reduces avoidant behaviors related to trauma reminders often found in day-to-day life. *In vivo* exposures allow the client to gradually and incrementally confront avoided situations and understand that they no longer pose a danger to his life or threaten his safety by assigning a new meaning to those situations (Bourne, 2005; Foa & Rothbaum, 1998).

Imaginal Exposures: Relive the Trauma in Your Imagination Exposures in imagination require the client to essentially relive the traumatic experience in her imagination. In order for it to become less painful, the client is instructed to close her eyes, place herself in the traumatic experience, and describe the trauma in the present tense out loud as if it were happening now. Initially, the client may be more distressed, but with repeated exposure and processing of the trauma, it will become less painful. This approach may seem counterintuitive to the client, since remembering the trauma is perceived as dangerous, requiring avoidance. Imaginal exposures will aid in modifying this mistaken belief (Foa & Rothbaum, 1998). For imaginal exposures, the more details the clinician knows about the trauma, the easier it will be to prompt the client during imaginal exposures, especially when the client is having difficulty engaging in the exposure (Foa & Rothbaum).

In Vivo Exposures: Facing Your Fears   *In vivo* exposures allow the client to confront avoided situations, locations, objects, sounds, and other trauma reminders that are actually safe in reality. Some avoided situations or locations may in fact be unsafe in general, like an empty parking lot late at night, a deserted street, and so on. For example, in Case Example 2-2, Ieisha should not go to parking garages late at night by herself for *in vivo* exposure since this is the location of her assault and may trigger emotions that are too intense and overwhelming. She may go to the garage with a friend during the day; however, to go by herself at night may be unsafe for Ieisha or for any woman. Clinicians can assist clients in making distinctions between safe and unsafe locations and scenarios. To identify areas of avoidance to target through *in vivo* exposures, clinicians can ask the client to describe ways in which her life has changed since experiencing the trauma. What activities does she no longer participate in? Does she take a different route home so as to avoid the location of her assault? Similar to imaginal exposures, *in vivo* exposures are repeated until the reminders no longer evoke strong negative emotions (Foa & Rothbaum, 1998). Repeated exposure leads to habituation and a decrease in anxiety.

Case Example 2-2: Ieisha

Ieisha is a 29-year-old woman who was carjacked and raped in a parking garage 3 months ago. She states that she is unable to leave her apartment alone without her husband; she cannot drive her car and refuses to go to work or visit with family and friends. She states that she was grabbed from behind, put in a headlock, choked, and pulled backwards, throwing her off balance. She was forced into the backseat of her SUV and was told by her assailant that he had a gun. He began to rape her but could not ejaculate, and he became angry and was screaming at her. Then he put a gun to her head and demanded that she perform oral sex on him.

> She remembers seeing the orange glow of the parking garage lights, feeling the leather seats beneath her body on her bare skin, smelling cigarettes and alcohol on his breath, and hearing classical music.

Initial Treatment Contact: Preparation and Engagement   When planning and preparing for the treatment phase, similar guidelines proposed for the initial assessment contact are again applicable. The clinician must be mindful of practical and logistical aspects of treatment sessions. It may be helpful to have a friend or family member escort the client to the appointment. Following directions, driving, and taking public transportation may be overwhelming while dealing with intense emotions that may arise. Other considerations include the time of the treatment sessions; parking arrangements; the use of staircases, elevators, or restrooms; and the radio or music played in the waiting room lobby, for these may all be reminiscent of the client's trauma scenario. If clients have to drive home or care for children after the treatment sessions (e.g., picking children up from school, watching children at home, etc.) it may be best to reschedule the appointment for a time when another adult can attend to these responsibilities. This allows the client time to acclimate herself to daily responsibilities and tasks after her treatment sessions. In addition to the 90-minute session, allowing for a period of time after the treatment session to act as a buffer is recommended. These sessions are commonly experienced as physically and emotionally exhausting and may compromise alertness and the ability to focus immediately following the session, both of which are necessary to care for children, as well as driving and the like.

When scheduling treatment sessions, one must be mindful of the client's comfort level with the appointment time but also possible interference with other sessions occurring at the same time in neighboring offices. During imaginal exposures used in this treatment and described in more detail below, it is common for clients to become extremely upset. Some clients may cry loudly, scream, or become nauseous, all at a volume that overpowers even white noise machines commonly used by clinicians. Sessions for other clients in the agency may be compromised by their overhearing the imaginal exposure session and your client's distress. It is recommended that session location be carefully planned, either in a space with some distance from other offices or at a 90-minute time period that is uncommon for other clients to have appointments (e.g., early morning, lunch hour, after other appointments have ended for the day, weekends, etc.).

This type of treatment is not appropriate for cubicles or other open office areas. Private space with a door that can be closed is necessary. Other aspects to consider regarding the space in which sessions are to be conducted are the seating arrangements. Clients may find it more comfortable to sit on the floor or have pillows to hold while doing the imaginal exposures. For clients who may become nauseous, having a trash receptacle nearby may be useful. Generally safeguarding the environment is suggested to avoid potential injury. Although clients are asked to sit comfortably, they may move or switch positions during the imaginal exposure part of treatment.

For example, in Case Example 2-3, suppose Lynn is sitting on the floor doing an imaginal exposure of her brother's sexual assault on her as a child. She may be sobbing and throwing her head back in despair or lying down for part of the exposure. This type of reaction cannot be predicted and may not even be something the client is conscious of prior to treatment, but it is possible. Clinicians will learn the physical reactions of each client through initial imaginal exposures. Similar to childproofing a house for infants and toddlers, table or desk corners as well as metal filing cabinets should be located out of range if possible. In this scenario, it may be difficult to tape record the session as described below, but in the best interests of the client it is imperative to make him physically comfortable during imaginal exposures. While we cannot completely safeguard the environment, it is useful to be mindful of these issues while one prepares to meet the client for treatment sessions. All of this preparation and safeguarding sets the stage for treatment sessions to begin.

Case Example 2-3: Lynn

Lynn is a 33-year-old woman who came for treatment after she and her husband separated. She had been promiscuous with both older and younger men throughout her marriage. During her couples counseling sessions, she disclosed that she was sexually molested as a child by her older brother and her cousin. She reports that she engaged in oral, vaginal, and anal sex with her brother, and oral and vaginal sex with her cousin. She states that she believes her mother was aware of the abuse, did not intervene, and instead resented Lynn. The sexual abuse resulted in a pregnancy, and her mother made her have an abortion. She remembers having vaginal infections and bleeding throughout childhood and adolescence, not related to her period but to the sexual abuse and physical aggression. She states that during regular medical appointments, the medical staff did not acknowledge these infections and genital trauma. Lynn reports that she sleeps with the lights on and pillows over her head and that she startles at the slightest noise when trying to sleep. She reports flashbacks and nightmares and avoids family events and gatherings.

This first treatment contact with a client aims to engage the client in the treatment process, develop rapport, and lay the groundwork for a therapeutic relationship. This is especially true if the treatment provider is not the clinician who administered the assessment. The clinician providing treatment should thoroughly review all of the information gathered through the assessment. Ideally, one clinician will administer both the assessment and the treatment program. The relationship between the therapist and client should include genuineness, a positive regard toward the client, warmth, caring, trust, acceptance, encouragement, confidence, and the ability to express empathy and affirmation. As stated previously, given the nature of the presenting problem, clients should be commended for their bravery in taking the first step by asking for help and making changes. Their courage will prove useful throughout this process. Emotional reactions should be normalized and discussed in an empathetic manner. To establish a partnership with the client, it is imperative to remain sensitive to her emotional situation. As described earlier, to enhance engagement it is helpful in this phase to describe the benefits of comprehensive treatment, client strengths and protective factors, treatment objectives, limitations of treatment, and obstacles to treatment success and to identify those support people in the client's life who are aware of the trauma.

Orientation to Treatment and Review of Assessment Findings   The theoretical orientation of PE draws largely from CBT. Used successfully to treat a multitude of disorders and symptoms, especially depression, anxiety disorders, and phobias, CBT is also highly effective in treating people who suffer from PTSD. After the assessment phase, clients are assigned a clinician for treatment. Ideally, the same clinician will work with the client in both the assessment and treatment phases. Clients receive orientation regarding treatment with this model, treatment expectations, session structure, and safety plans. The rationale for treatment using exposures is described to the client and any questions he may have about the model and treatment course are answered. Psychoeducation and literature are provided regarding the symptoms (see Tables 2.1 and 2.5) and treatment model, allowing the client to review this information again at home and with his family or partner. Clients may be so anxious during the initial session that they are not fully focused on the discussion. As mentioned before, clients with PTSD often have difficulty with information processing. Providing the client with handouts regarding the treatment model and common symptoms may help in addressing this issue by offering additional opportunities to review the material.

The findings from the assessment phase are presented in the first treatment session. Mental health diagnoses and subthreshold symptoms that require ongoing monitoring are discussed with the client. Additionally, it is important for the clinician to gather information on current health and mental health services the client is receiving. The client's symptoms and level of functioning both at home and at work are reviewed as well. Clinicians process any reactions to the assessment findings, including the label of a diagnosis and the meaning it has for a client. For some clients there is a sense of relief in knowing that what they have been experiencing is recognized and is common for other individuals exposed to trauma. Consultations with psychiatrists can be scheduled during this initial treatment session for those clients interested in gaining additional information on medication management and how it may work in conjunction with exposure treatment. Other health issues (e.g., high blood pressure, cardiac conditions, trying to conceive, early stages of pregnancy, etc.) should be discussed at this time, since exposure treatment can put stress on the body physiologically. A physical exam may be recommended, as well as consultation with the client's physician to determine physical health contraindications for exposure treatment.

Safeguarding prior to the treatment phase was discussed earlier. Additionally, there are considerations for clinicians throughout the treatment course. Clients again should identify an emergency contact or supportive person in the community, either a family member or loved one who can be contacted by the clinician if the client needs assistance getting home after a session due to distress or exhaustion. This individual will also be someone the client can contact, in addition to the clinician, if suicidal ideation or plans arise in between treatment sessions. As stated previously, clients may have tendencies to engage in self-harming behaviors, including self-mutilation and suicide. Contracts for safety are useful tools at this phase of treatment and present an opportunity to identify supportive people in the client's life as well as community resources and emergency services. Recontracting with clients may be necessary at some point during treatment if suicidal ideation is disclosed during the session. Clients are also instructed to contact the treatment provider or clinician for mental health emergencies. Organizing an on-call schedule among clinicians in your agency who are providing similar treatment may be useful to assist clients in between sessions, if you are unable to be reached. Further instruction may be required to contact emergency medical assistance (e.g., 911, ambulance) or go to the nearest emergency room of a hospital. The likelihood that you will need to implement these plans may not be high; however, it is important to be prepared and design a plan of action with the client and his support system.

TREATMENT STRATEGIES

The treatment course for prolonged exposure consists of 2 assessment sessions and 9 to 12 weekly treatment sessions. Assessment measures are administered both before and after treatment. All sessions are approximately 90 minutes in length (Boudewyns & Hyer, 1990; Boudewyns et al., 1990; Foa et al., 1991; Foa & Meadows, 1997; Foa & Rothbaum, 1998; Thompson et al., 1995). This should allow the client adequate time to review homework from the previous week, complete the imaginal exposure, complete mindful breathing exercises before and after an exposure, and get her homework assignment for the next week. It is essential for clients to leave sessions as calm as possible. Additional sessions may be added, depending on the extent of the trauma and symptoms, as well as the number of trauma memories identified by the client. Regarding staffing, having the same clinician administer the assessment and treatment is advised, as well as the same clinician's meeting with the client throughout the treatment course. Staff changes are disruptive and compromise various aspects of treatment, including the therapeutic relationship and the client's comfort level. The client may feel that treatment has become unpredictable and personally may feel that yet another area of his life is out of his control. Both the client and clinician need to commit to the treatment duration established in order for treatment to be most effective. Regarding treatment modalities, there are two primary strategies used to reduce PTSD symptoms: prolonged imaginal exposures and prolonged *in vivo* exposures (as discussed earlier). Clients who have completed treatment and had their symptoms dissipated may experience events that retrigger PTSD symptoms. These include media coverage of the event (e.g., September 11), memorial services, criminal investigations, and court proceedings (as illustrated in Case Example 2-4). These events and the extent to which they retrigger symptoms may require additional treatment sessions after discharge.

Case Example 2-4: Haley

Haley is a 24-year-old woman who was involved in a car accident with a tractor-trailer when she was a 20-year-old college student. After she had gone home to visit her parents for the weekend, she drove back to college in the evening on a highway frequented by tractor-trailers and other large trucks. There were a total of six lanes, three on each side with a median in between. On that particular day it was rather windy, and when she hit a bump in the highway a gust of wind spun her car to the left, making two rotations, and stopping on the far shoulder of the opposing traffic lanes. Her car was facing oncoming traffic but was across the white line of the shoulder. Technically, she was not in the road. She put her flashing lights on, turned off the ignition, got out of the car, walked up the embankment next to the shoulder, and called her parents. Her father answered the phone and told her to call the police; seconds later, a tractor-trailer hit her car head-on. Her father heard this loud crash and heard Haley scream; then the phone went dead. Her car was totaled, and her father thought she had just been hit by another car. Luckily, Haley had moved to the embankment earlier and was not physically injured, although parts from the car did fall near her. She called her father back, reassured him she was okay, and then called the police. They arrived at the scene of the accident and took photographs as well as statements from both Haley and the truck driver. Later, it was suspected that the truck driver had either fallen asleep or was intoxicated (he had a prior history of driving under the influence). He reported that her car was in the middle of the far lane, not on the shoulder, and that to avoid hitting the car in the lane beside his truck, he drove into Haley's car, totaling it. Legal proceedings have continued for the past 4 years with the driver, his employer, and both insurance companies. More recently, Haley has met with all attorneys involved to answer a series of questions related to the car accident and her life in general. She will need to go to court to testify in 6 weeks and has had an increase in flashbacks and nightmares of the event and difficulty sleeping. She has extreme panic when she attempts to drive—so much so that her roommate has been driving her to work in the morning.

PSYCHOEDUCATION

An important component of PE as well as many other CBT-based programs is psychoeducation (see Part 1 of this volume). Psychoeducation allows the clinician and client to discuss the common reactions to trauma. Additionally, it allows the client to identify and describe the impact the trauma and response symptoms have on the client's life and relationships (see Tables 2.1 and 2.5). Through psychoeducation, the clinician can validate clients' experiences, normalize their reactions, and, for some clients, discuss self-blame and ownership of the trauma. The client's support system of family and friends may not fully understand the impact of trauma and its debilitating effects. Psychoeducation is a useful component of treatment, not just for the client but also for his support system of loved ones. Table 2.1 presents a guide to constructing a psychoeducational handout for clients regarding PE.

THERAPEUTIC RELATIONSHIP

A positive therapeutic relationship requires the therapist to present a non-judgmental and comfortable attitude in general, and specifically when the

Table 2.1

A Guide for Constructing a Psychoeducational Handout for Clients Regarding PE

As suggested by various sources (Foa & Rothbaum, 1998; Giarratano, 2004; Taylor, 2006; Zayfert & Becker, 2007), the following should be addressed in a handout that you can create and give to clients during the psychoeducational phase of treatment to help them understand prolonged exposure.

- **Use simple language and avoid technical terms.** Check with clients to see if they understand what you have written.
- **Use metaphors.** "The way to get over one's fears of swimming or falling off a bike is not by avoiding such things. If you have a toothache, it's better to experience the unpleasantness of dental treatment and put the pain behind you than to avoid it and let the toothache fester. PE is like psychologically digesting undigested bad memories (like undigested bad food) that keep coming up and bothering you."
- **Specify goals.** "The best way to overcome your fears is by facing them gradually, step by step, and in a safe way. Although PE treatment may not enable you to completely rid yourself of all the bad effects the trauma had on you, and it won't mean that the trauma hasn't changed you in some way, scientific studies have found it to be the most effective way to help traumatized people move forward, reduce the unwanted symptoms they are experiencing because of the trauma, and regain control of their lives. In other words, it can help you gain control of your bad memories instead of having those bad memories control you."
- **Specify what is involved in imaginal exposure.** "You will tell me about a bad memory in as much detail as possible, as if it is happening right now. You will tell me about things that you feel, see, hear, smell, taste, or otherwise sense as you think of that memory. You will repeat telling me these things over and over, and as you do so, the memory will become less upsetting to you and you will be better able to put it behind you. We will start with those parts of the memory that you say are easiest for you to talk about and move on to more difficult parts when you are ready to do so."
- **Specify what is involved in *in vivo* exposure.** "When you are ready and willing, you will face situations, locations, objects, sounds, and other things that remind you of your trauma but that are actually safe in reality. You will identify things that are easiest to face in the beginning and will gradually move up—one small step at a time—to other things that, although really safe, are harder to encounter. You and I will work together to make a list of these things in the order in which you feel you can face them."
- **Address issues of pain and control.** "Talking about your bad memories can be scary. Although we will start slowly and at a pace you think will be most comfortable for you, you might feel some emotional pain or discomfort. However, you will be in control at all times and can stop whenever you want to. Like dental treatment, you may feel some discomfort, but we'll try to minimize it."
- **Address possible side effects.** "Talking about your bad memories usually will make your current symptoms a bit worse during the early weeks of treatment. But this typically means that the treatment is really helping you in the long run. We can work together to find ways to reduce any such side effects."
- Let the client know that if he has any questions, you will be happy to discuss them with him.

client discusses the trauma. It is important that the client feels as if she can reveal the intimate details of her trauma without alarming you or making you uncomfortable. It may be the first time the client is sharing these details with another person. This process of disclosure is an honor and a privilege.

Presenting oneself as confident and competent may put the client's mind at ease regarding her decision to receive treatment from you and your treatment program. Normalizing the client's response to trauma as well as assuring her that she is not "going crazy" is essential to treatment. Additionally, recognize how difficult it must be for the client to come forward and ask for help, and commend her on her courage and bravery. It is also important for the therapist to provide support and encouragement. This strengthens the therapeutic alliance, allowing the client to feel comfortable with the therapist and the treatment program (Foa & Rothbaum, 1998).

Mindful Breathing

Mindful breathing is a technique used for decreasing feelings of anxiety and fear, as well as lowering the heart rate, respiration rate, and blood pressure, which are all typically altered by stress, anxiety, and fear. It helps create the exact opposite physiological response your body naturally gravitates toward as a reaction to stress and anxiety (Bourne, 2005). It consists of taking deep breaths through your nose and exhaling through your mouth, all while using your diaphragm or abdomen. It also includes imagery or meditation. These two elements combined, breathing through the diaphragm while practicing calming imagery, is effective in calming the body and decreasing negative feelings such as anxiety and fear. Clients will first learn how to breathe diaphragmatically, then they will learn to use imagery, and finally they will combine the two. It is important to explain the rationale to the client and to move at a slow pace. There is no need to rush through this; remember, it is supposed to be calming, not overwhelming or complicated. Allow them some time to practice each phase of this technique before moving on to the next step. An example of how to present the exercise to the client is provided in the box titled "Therapist Script: Mindful Breathing."

Therapist Script: Mindful Breathing

Today we're going to learn how to breathe in a different way than we're used to, called mindful breathing. Basically, it means to breathe slowly with your abdomen (point to your stomach), which is below the rib cage, while inhaling through your nose and exhaling through your mouth, and at the same time you imagine a peaceful and happy scene. Typically, when we get upset, our breaths become shorter, like we're hyperventilating, which makes our heart race like it's going to pop out of our chest. It can also make us feel anxious and fearful, or like we're going to have a panic attack. Sometimes people feel dizzy, like they're going to faint, or they might feel like they're suffocating. All of these awful sensations are linked to our breathing, so to change those sensations, prevent them from happening, or make them less intense, we need to change our breathing. The amount of tension we're feeling is reflected in our breathing. The style of breathing we'll practice today, called mindful breathing, can help keep you relaxed when you're starting to feel upset or feel those physical sensations I mentioned. I want you to learn this technique before you leave here today because breathing this way can start your body's relaxation response. We're going to tape record our practice session so you can take it home with you and continue to practice for homework. Mindful breathing can be done anywhere, when you have difficulty falling asleep, when you're alone, even if you're around other people or out in the community. We'll use it during our sessions, and I'll have you practice for homework, too. The first few times we do this, it might be difficult to stay focused. This is why we'll need to practice this technique. If at any point it seems too difficult, just let me know and we can take a break. Are you ready to practice with me?

With mindful breathing, instead of your chest, rib cage, and shoulders moving during breathing, they remain as still as possible while your abdomen moves in and out. Clinicians can demonstrate this by taking deep breaths and moving their upper body toward the ceiling and puffing up their chests as they inhale and back down as they exhale (exaggerated, but typical, breathing). The client should be able to observe movement in the shoulders, chest, and rib cage. Clinicians can also simulate hyperventilating by taking quick breaths through a straw. Offering visual demonstrations is helpful for clients who may have difficulty processing information delivered through conversation. Likewise, it is useful for clients to also demonstrate their understanding of these concepts by trying them in front of the clinician. After demonstrating these forms of breathing, the clinician can provide instruction on mindful breathing.

There are several ways to demonstrate mindful breathing to clients. For example, you can tell clients to imagine they have weights on their shoulders, weighing them down, keeping their shoulders and chest still. Instruct them to picture their stomach as a balloon that inflates when they breathe in through their nose, and deflates when they exhale. Again, there should be minimal movement in the shoulders. If the concept is not clear with this explanation, you can instruct clients to lie on the floor with a light object on their stomach (e.g., paper cup, tissue box, small pillow). To understand the idea of breathing with your abdomen, instruct them to puff out their belly and move the object on their stomach toward the ceiling as they inhale through their nose, and back down toward the ground as they exhale through their mouth. Next, clinicians should introduce the element of timing and pace. With mindful breathing, as you inhale through the nose and puff out your diaphragm, you should count slowly to 5. Then, you should slowly count to 5 while exhaling through your mouth. Clinicians can practice this with clients a few times until they can coordinate breathing, the rise and fall of their stomach, and counting.

The next element introduced is imagery. Ask the client to tell you about something that makes them joyful, happy, calm, fulfilled (this can be thinking of their children, their spouse, a favorite vacation, their garden, swimming, etc.). Next, ask them to find a comfortable space (e.g., sitting on the floor, lying down) and close their eyes and imagine the image they identified, pretending they are in that scene in the present tense. For clients who are uncomfortable closing their eyes, they can just sit quietly and look down. Ask them to describe to you what they see in their image, what they hear, what they smell, and what textures they feel in their surroundings. Each question is posed using a quiet and calm voice. Pause in between questions, asking them separately and slowly, allowing plenty of time for the client to answer. If they have difficulty staying with the image in their mind, ask them to go back to the image and describe what they see, keeping them in the present tense. For example, suppose the client imagines a beach scene. An example of how to engage the client in the imagery involving a beach scene is provided in the box titled "Dialogue: Engaging the Client in Imagery." Answering questions related to the five senses, as illustrated in that box, will also be a part of the imaginal exposures.

Dialogue: Engaging the Client in Imagery

THERAPIST (T): You're doing a great job—you seem really calm and comfortable. I want you to imagine that warm sunny beach you told me about. Imagine you're there right now, on this beach (here you can use the description the client gave initially, just use his words and repeat them back to him). Tell me about this beach.

CLIENT (C): It's a sunny day . . . it's warm outside; the sand is warm. It's nice.

T: What do you see on the beach?

C: I see the blue water and the waves crashing and palm trees.

T: Do you hear anything?

C: Well, I can hear the waves. . . . Oh, and I hear seagulls in the background. The wind is rustling the palms and they're moving. I can hear them.

T: That sounds very peaceful. You're doing a great job. (pause) Can you smell anything at the beach?

C: Ummm, I don't know, maybe fish or something fishy . . . but not too bad—not overpowering, just faint, like that beach smell.

T: Tell me more about what you smell.

C: Suntan lotion . . . yeah, I smell suntan lotion. I love that smell.

T: You seem calm and relaxed. (pause) Are you feeling anything or touching anything with your hands or your feet?

C: I feel the sand between my toes. It feels nice. It's warm.

T: You said you can feel the sand between your toes, so now I want you to touch the sand with your hands and fingers. (pause)

C: Okay.

T: What does it feel like? Is it warm? (pause) Is it wet or dry? (pause) Is it heavy or light? (pause)

C: It's dry sand, soft, warm . . . not wet sand. I'm not sitting that close to the water.

T: What else do you see?

> **C:** Little shells.
> **T:** What color are the shells that you see?
> **C:** They're pink. They're really tiny.
> **T:** This all sounds very peaceful. You're doing a great job. Keep going.
> **C:** Well, they're tiny . . . some are smooth . . . some are more rough. They have bumps on them or ridges.

Encourage the client to stay in the image, and once he is fully engaged in the image in the present tense, ask him to try mindful breathing at the same time. Again, he should be still and quiet, focusing on his breathing. Now, instead of describing the image aloud, the client reviews it in his mind silently, staying still, quiet, and focused on his breathing. Allow him to try this for a few minutes. After practicing this skill with the client, it may be helpful to provide him with directions for mindful breathing that he can take home with him. For homework, mindful breathing should be practiced for 5 minutes, three times a day throughout treatment (Foa & Rothbaum, 1998). Clients should also be encouraged to use it when they are feeling anxious, nervous, fearful, or experiencing distressing memories or flashbacks. They can track their use of mindful breathing in their homework journal.

CREATING IMAGINAL AND *IN VIVO* HIERARCHIES

After the clinician has oriented the client to the treatment model, reviewed the assessment findings, and practiced mindful breathing, the client and clinician will create a hierarchy of flashbacks, memories, and nightmares with distress ratings on a scale of 0 to 100, in intervals of 10 (e.g., 10, 20, 30, 40, etc.). As illustrated in Table 2.2, each item will be rated by the client regarding how severe, persistent, or disturbing a particular memory is. This lays the foundation for the imaginal exposures (PE). Treatment will start with the client's choosing a memory from the lower end of the hierarchy.

As illustrated in Table 2.3, a similar hierarchy is created with the client for *in vivo* exposures the client will complete weekly for homework. The client is instructed to list a hierarchy of common things, people, places, and circumstances that trigger anxiety, flashbacks, or reliving experiences, or are reminiscent of their abuser or perpetrator if the trauma is related to assault. This list may include anything that reminds the client of the trauma, for example, a dark room or being alone, certain smells or aromas (e.g., cologne, smoke from a fire, alcohol or smoke on someone's breath), sounds and noises (e.g., gunshot, fireworks, someone walking up a staircase), music (e.g., maybe

Table 2.2
Imaginal Exposure Hierarchy Example: Ieisha's Case (Case Example 2-2)

Distressing Memories	How Distressing Is This? (Scale of 0–100)
1. Getting near my car and feeling uneasy	50
2. Going to the emergency room afterwards	70
3. Talking to the police afterwards	70
4. Realizing he was going to attack me	70
5. Telling my husband afterwards, seeing the look on his face, seeing him cry	80
6. He got on top of me and was yelling and pulling at my pants	80
7. When he stuck his fingers inside me, seeing his face, his reaction	90
8. When he put his penis inside of me, feeling his weight on top of me, smelling his breath (alcohol and smoke)	90
9. He was tracing the outline of my ribs while he said what he planned to do	90
10. He held a gun to my head and told me give him oral sex	100

the attacker listened to a particular style of music; this may be common for adults who were chronically sexually abused), textures (e.g., wool blanket), tastes and flavors, objects (e.g., brand of cigarettes the attacker smoked, weapons, kitchen knives), personal features (e.g., hairstyle, shape of nose, large build, style of dress).

For example, in Nikos's case (for background information on Nikos, see Case Example 2-5), he may list seeing his father questioned by soldiers, hearing the screams of men as he witnessed them being killed, watching the rape of a young girl, and seeing a body burned by napalm. Likewise, for Case Example 2-1, Naushad may list hearing his father come home, come into his bedroom, lock the door, and unzip his pants. He may also include his father pushing him to the ground and telling him to perform oral sex on him. Haley's list (see Case Example 2-4) may include hitting the bump in the highway and having her car spin uncontrollably, finally stopping on the opposite shoulder and facing oncoming traffic, and seeing the tractor-trailer swerve across the road, or the image of her car being totaled and pushed up the embankment. Similar to imaginal exposures, clients will start by choosing an item from the lower end of the hierarchy to complete graduated *in vivo* exposures at home or in the community for homework.

Table 2.3

In Vivo Exposure Hierarchy Example: Ieisha's Case (Case Example 2-2)

Origin of the Triggers	Everyday Triggers	How Distressing Is This? (Scale of 0–100)
1. He was behind me in the parking garage	1. Someone standing behind me	40
2. He had the smell of cigarettes on his breath; he smoked one after he attacked me	2. Smell of cigarettes	40
3. Feeling my skin stick to the leather seat; it was pulling at my skin	3. Leather car seats	40
4. After he raped me, he unwrapped a new pack of cigarettes before he smoked one; it was a cellophane wrapper	4. Sound of cellophane	50
5. Where he attacked me	5. The mall parking lot	60
6. Where he attacked me	6. Any parking lot	60
7. My attacker was male	7. Being near men who are strangers	60
8. I was alone when this happened	8. Driving by myself	70
9. He turned the radio on and played classical music while he raped me	9. Classical music	70
10. I was alone when this happened	10. Being alone in the house	80
11. I'm afraid to fall asleep and have nightmares	11. Sleeping with the lights off	90
12. Lights were on in the parking lot; they had an orange glow. I remember turning my head and looking out the window when he was raping me, trying to go somewhere else in my mind	12. The orange glow of parking lot lights and street lamps	90

Case Example 2-5: Nikos

Nikos is a 43-year-old Greek man who grew up in Cyprus and Greece. He was 9 years old during the Turkish invasion of Cyprus in 1974. His town was bombed and occupied by Turkish and British soldiers. He witnessed civilians being shot and killed, men having their limbs cut off with knives, and other men being taken as prisoners of war (POWs). Nikos has nightmares of people being burned alive with napalm and witnessing women and adolescent girls being raped by soldiers. His family was forced out of their home, never to return, and are still waiting to be compensated for their loss. As a refugee, he and his family lived in a tent community after the invasion. Mostly women, children, and the elderly were in the tents since many men were taken as POWs. Eventually, his family settled in Athens, Greece, and lived with extended family, including his younger cousin, who is getting married and having a traditional wedding in Cyprus. She was born after the war and does not understand why Nikos is "overreacting." Nikos is expected to be a part of this family event but is terrified to go back to Cyprus. He currently lives and works in New York and has started smoking again, is drinking heavily, and is experiencing nightmares and flashbacks related to the war.

Distress Ratings   Distress ratings in the hierarchies for both imaginal and *in vivo* exposures are decided by the client for each individual item on the hierarchy lists. Specific images may be listed. For example, in Case Example 2-6, Joe is holding his comrade as he dies after being shot in Vietnam. Joe will assign a distress rating to that particular image, on a scale from 0 to 100 (e.g., 10, 20, 30, etc.), regarding how severe, persistent, or disturbing a particular memory is, and also in comparison to the other items on the list. For example, Joe may list an image of killing a child who was about to throw a grenade in his direction in Vietnam. Joe considers this second image of killing a child more distressing (score of 90) than the image of holding his friend as he dies (score of 70).

Case Example 2-6: Joe

Joe is a 55-year-old Vietnam veteran and widower. He was trained as a sniper and made dozens of kills in combat. While in Vietnam he used cocaine and shipped packages back to his brother in the United States. Upon returning home, he and his brother sold the cocaine, which led to his involvement in organized crime. He was a hit man and collected money from individuals who owed his superiors. He killed several people or severely injured them after collecting the money they owed, while keeping some for himself. When his boss was brought up on drug charges, they interviewed Joe, and instead of "ratting him out," Joe took the blame for his boss, resulting in a jail sentence of 10 years. While Joe was in jail, his wife passed away without his getting to say good-bye. He's having flashbacks and nightmares of combat, especially memories of kids coming up to his unit with candy, but instead they had grenades. He was ordered to kill several children and women in close-range combat. Additionally, he is having nightmares about his friend who died in his arms after being shot.

In contrast, in Case Example 2-7, Anardo might give a score of 90 to the image of holding his cousin as he died. Although these situations are similar insofar as both men were holding someone as he died, they experience them with different levels of intensity. These ratings are completely decided by the client.

Case Example 2-7: Anardo

Anardo is a 22-year-old man who grew up in the South Bronx of New York City. About a year ago, his cousin was shot in the head and killed during a fight in his neighborhood. Anardo held his cousin in an alley as he died. Since then, he has moved in with his grandmother across town. Anardo is currently suffering from flashbacks and nightmares and avoids family gatherings as well as his old neighborhood and friends. He stays up most of the night and is fearful of falling asleep. Anardo rarely leaves the house and has recently lost his job due to his continued absence.

Distress ratings are used in treatment sessions by the client to report her level of distress during an imaginal exposure. The clinician will ask for her distress rating every 10 minutes. This is an indication, on a scale from 0 to 100, of the distress she is experiencing at that exact moment. As illustrated in Table 2.4, the clinician can chart these ratings and show the chart to the client to demonstrate the rise and fall of anxiety and fear experienced during the

Table 2.4
Distress Ratings Reported During Imaginal Exposure

Distress Level					
100					
90			X		
80					
70					
60		X			
50					
40	X			X	
30					
20					X
10					
Time (minutes)	10	20	30	40	50

exposure. This feedback is helpful to clients and gives a visual representation of their experience in the exposure, and shows the client's progress. Similarly, with *in vivo* exposures, the client will record their distress level before the exposure in their homework journal. After the exposure, the client will record her highest distress level during the *in vivo* exposure and then after its completion.

Imaginal Exposures Imaginal exposures require the client to relive the trauma, describe it, and feel those same emotions that took place at the time of the trauma. By having the client reexperience or relive the traumatic experience repeatedly throughout each treatment session, imaginal exposures increase the client's ability to process memories of the trauma, decreasing symptom severity and frequency. The most effective way to overcome fear and anxiety is to face the situations clients have avoided. Continuing to fear and avoid these situations keeps them alive and maintains their intensity. It is helpful to reassure the client that the body cannot maintain a state of anxiety—it will pass. The body uses adrenaline in under 15 minutes, forcing the mind to refocus on something else. So any fear or anxiety the client experiences will eventually pass if he takes the risk, tolerates the initial discomfort and resistance, and follows through until he completes the exposure (Bourne, 2005). Reassure him that you will be in the room with him and your office is safe. The role of the clinician during the exposures is not the usual dynamic many therapists are familiar with. Throughout the exposure, the clinician's tasks include asking for distress ratings every 10 minutes for the entire 45 to 60 minutes, offering encouragement, and asking sensory questions to keep the client engaged in the image and remaining in the present tense. Helpful comments to encourage the client include, *"Keep going—you're doing a great job," "You can handle this," "These intense feelings will pass if you just stick with it."* Sensory questions that help clients focus on details of the image include, *"Tell me what you see," "Describe what you're hearing right now," "What does it feel like when you touch it?"* In addition to keeping the client in the exposure, there are other challenges the clinician faces (Foa & Rothbaum, 1998).

In Vivo Exposures In vivo exposures are practiced at home or in sessions to decrease the daily life situations that make people feel anxious or trigger distressing memories related to the trauma, either directly or indirectly (see the example of an *in vivo* exposure hierarchy in Table 2.3). As mentioned earlier, *in vivo* exposures allow clients to confront their fears and avoided situations gradually and incrementally. Direct exposure to the stimuli that make someone anxious will assist in decreasing the intensity of symptoms over time. We can make this endeavor manageable if we break it down into small steps and approach the feared situation gradually, systematically, and repetitively. The time it takes to recover is dependent on how regularly the client practices these exercises for homework (Bourne, 2005).

TREATMENT PROGRAM

Let's now examine the foregoing techniques in the context of the overall treatment program, beginning with implementation of imaginal exposure.

IMPLEMENTATION OF IMAGINAL EXPOSURES

At the end of the last assessment session, and prior to treatment, a list or hierarchy of traumatic memories and triggers is created by the client and clinician. Clients are instructed to list flashbacks, images, memories, conversations, nightmares, and reexperiences that are distressing to them. Then each item is given a score by the client—a distress rating—on a scale from 0 to 100, in intervals of 10 (e.g., 10, 20, 30, 40, etc.). Each item is rated by the client regarding how severe, persistent, or disturbing it is for him. This lays the foundation for the imaginal exposures (see Tables 2.2 and 2.4).

Treatment will start with presenting the rationale to the client, giving reassurance, and offering encouragement. The rationale should cover emotional processing, habituation, discrimination between remembering and being traumatized, increased mastery, and differentiation (Foa & Rothbaum, 1998). Clinicians will explain that all imaginal exposures are audiotaped and used by the client for homework assignments. Then the client is asked to choose an item from the lower end of the hierarchy, one that is less moderately distressing since this increases the likelihood of successful completion of the exposure. Additionally, this allows the client to gain a sense of control and accomplishment through the successful and manageable exposure exercises. This success will aid the client in preparing for more distressing items in subsequent sessions.

One imaginal exposure is completed per session, starting at session 2. The clinician should allow between 45 and 60 minutes to complete one imaginal exposure. First the clinician instructs the client to get into a comfortable position (e.g., sitting on the floor, sitting in a chair, holding a pillow). The client is asked to close her eyes and start mindful breathing, staying still and quiet. As mentioned previously, some clients may not feel comfortable closing their eyes; if that is the case, have them look down to minimize distractions from the exercise. This phase of the exercise should last approximately 5 minutes.

After mindful breathing, the client will start the imaginal exposure. The client is instructed to relive the particular scenario from the item they chose from their imaginal exposure hierarchy. The clinician reminds the client that she needs to describe the scenario as if it is happening now. All descriptions are in the present tense. Clients should not imagine themselves watching a movie of the scenario or hovering over the scene, but actually be in the scene as themselves, in their own body, at whatever age or state of mind they were in at the time of the trauma. Starting with a description of the physical qualities of the scene, the client provides details and speaks in the present tense, including the layout of the image and other people present in the image.

Next, the client describes the image as it relates to her senses. The clinician can encourage this thorough description by asking questions such as:

- What's the temperature in the room?
- What do you smell?
- What do you see?
- What do you hear?
- What are you feeling?

Then the client describes what is occurring in the image, what actions are taking place, what is happening. Again, as the client moves through the scene, the clinician poses questions to keep her in the present tense and aware of all of her senses.

Clients often slip back into seeing the image as an outsider or in the past tense. This is common, and the clinician can reengage the client through encouragement, such as, *"You're doing great. Remember to describe what you are experiencing in the present tense, like it's happening to you right now. You can do this; just stick with it."*

When the client has come to the end of the image or memory, she is asked to start again from the beginning, This retelling continues for 45 to 60 minutes. For example: *"That was great. I know it took a lot of courage for you to stay with the image. Take a deep breath and start again from the beginning. Remember to stay in the present tense and tell me what your senses are experiencing."*

Throughout the 45 to 60 minutes, the clinician is asking for distress ratings every 10 minutes and recording them, such as by asking, *"What is your distress rating on a scale of 0 to 100?"* (see Table 2.1). Typically, more details are disclosed each time the client retells or redescribes the scene. Details and significant elements of that particular memory may be brought to consciousness for the first time in years. After the imaginal exposure, the clinician can briefly discuss these newly realized elements. These details may be extremely powerful and meaningful for the client. They might answer questions or offer clarity to the client. These elements may explain things she avoids in her day-to-day life and can influence the structure of *in vivo* exposures. For example, in Case Example 2-3, Lynn was sexually molested as a child by two men in her family, which resulted in a pregnancy. Suppose she relives a memory of when her brother stops molesting her because she starts to menstruate. This gives her clarity regarding who impregnated her—her cousin. This was an aspect of the trauma that haunted her, never knowing if her brother had gotten her pregnant.

Another example is that of Naushad (in Case Example 2-1), who might reveal the details of being molested by his father at night while on a bed with a wool blanket. Throughout his life, he has avoided anything made of wool but didn't understand why. All he knew was that he had a heightened sensitivity to feeling this texture on his skin. Touching wool or sitting in a chair with a wool blanket may be used for his *in vivo* exposures at home. The imaginal exposure provided clarity as to the origin of his sensitivity to wool, as well as a better understanding of why this was something he avoided.

Or suppose Ieisha (in Case Example 2-2), a woman who was attacked and raped in a parking garage late at night, discloses the detail of the attacker unwrapping the cellophane cover of a new pack of cigarettes and smoking next to her after the rape. This detail also offers clarity that can be utilized to facilitate *in vivo* exposures. Ieisha was triggered almost on a daily basis by the sound of cellophane, which is found on numerous household products and is difficult to avoid in daily life (e.g., food wrappers for crackers and dry goods; covers of CDs, DVDs, and boxes of teas; wrapping for household products like sponges, napkins, paper towels, and other packaging). Ieisha was being triggered into flashbacks and intense anxiety when she would hear the sound of cellophane being unwrapped and crushed in someone's hand or thrown in the garbage. With this new information, Ieisha can use this sound in her *in vivo* exposure exercises at home or in a session. Ieisha might also remember the detail of the attacker's turning on classical music in the car before he raped her. If distressing, listening to classical music can be used for *in vivo* exposures at home or in a session. She can sit and listen to classical music, gradually increasing the periods of time or duration, starting with 5 minutes, then 10 minutes, followed by 15 minutes, then 20 minutes, and so on (see Table 2.4 for an example of how Ieisha's distress ratings might be recorded during an imaginal exposure session). Additionally, many of these examples of *in vivo* exposures can be done in the presence of a loved one or support person (e.g., Naushad with the wool blanket, Ieisha with the cellophane and classical music).

After the imaginal exposure is processed for the full 45 to 60 minutes, the client is instructed to return to mindful breathing and her peaceful image for 5 to 10 minutes. Next, the clinician and client discuss the distress ratings recorded throughout the session by the clinician. Usually, there is a steady increase in distress reported, and roughly halfway into the exposure, the distress suddenly decreases and returns to a low level. This graduated increase, peak, and plummet can be demonstrated by a chart (see Table 2.4) and supports what the client was told earlier regarding the body's ability to withstand intense anxiety and fear for only so long. Sharing this with clients will show them they confronted their memories and fears and successfully endured the exercise.

Clinicians are encouraged to remind clients that exposures will allow for symptoms to slowly decrease and become less intense over time. Symptom reduction following exposure occurs when clients realize that remembering the trauma or being in situations that remind them of the trauma does not mean the trauma is being experienced all over again. These memories and situations are not dangerous. It was the meanings clients assigned to them that made them threatening.

What is also demonstrated to clients is the concept of anxiety's not being indefinite. Through these corrective experiences, they learn that anxiety will decrease without having to abandon or avoid the memory or situation. This will challenge their previous thoughts of "going crazy" if they allow themselves to think about the trauma or explore their memories.

Clinicians are encouraged to discuss the client's reactions to the exposure. Are there new revelations? Does she have a different conceptualization of the trauma? These may be questions to discuss with the client. Before the end of the session, the client will choose an *in vivo* exposure to complete from the hierarchy list. For homework, clients will listen to the exposure tape daily before the next session and complete an *in vivo* exposure. Additionally, clinicians should make themselves available via telephone between sessions if the client needs to process emotional reactions from listening to the tape or completing the *in vivo* exposure (Foa & Rothbaum, 1998).

IMPLEMENTATION OF IN VIVO EXPOSURES

At the end of the last assessment session, and prior to treatment, a list or hierarchy is created by the client and clinician of common things, people, places, and circumstances that trigger anxiety, flashbacks, or reliving experiences, or are reminiscent of their abuser or perpetrator if the trauma is related to assault (see Table 2.3). This list will be used for *in vivo* exposures completed at home or in a session and may include anything that reminds the client of the trauma, either directly or indirectly. Then each item is given a score by the client, which is the distress rating, on a scale from 0 to 100, in intervals of 10 (e.g., 10, 20, 30, 40, etc.). Each item is rated by the client regarding how severe, persistent, or disturbing it is for the client. This lays the foundation for the *in vivo* exposures.

In vivo exposures will be introduced by presenting the rationale to the client, giving reassurance, and offering encouragement. The concept of habituation (i.e., decreasing painful reactions to stimuli that remind clients of the trauma through repeated and gradually escalated safe exposures to those stimuli over time) is discussed with the client as well. Similar to imaginal exposures, clients will start by choosing an item from the lower end of the hierarchy to complete graduated *in vivo* exposures for homework at home, in the community, or in a session. Again, by choosing one of the less moderately distressing items, the client is able to achieve success with the exercise from the beginning. This success will aid the client in preparing for more distressing items in subsequent homework assignments.

One *in vivo* exposure is completed per week for homework, starting after session 2. The client should allow between 10 and 30 minutes, depending on the distress rating or intensity, to complete one *in vivo* exposure. If the item is an object, first the client should get into a comfortable position (e.g., sitting on the floor, sitting in a comfortable chair, holding a pillow, being in his favorite room in his home, a place he feels safe and relaxed). The client should close his eyes and start mindful breathing. This should follow with peaceful and happy imaging. Throughout the imagery, the client is mindful of all the details of the scene. Instead of describing them aloud, the client reviews them in his mind silently, staying still and quiet. As mentioned previously, some clients may not feel comfortable closing their eyes; instead, they can look down to minimize distractions from the exercise. This phase of the exercise should last approximately 5 minutes.

After mindful breathing, the client can start by using the item he chose from his *in vivo* exposure hierarchy (see Table 2.3). Through graduated exposure, the client confronts the item he has been avoiding or that is triggering distressing flashbacks and memories. For items that are objects, sounds, textures, sensations, or tastes (e.g., cologne, smoke from a fire, alcohol or smoke on someone's breath, gunshot sound, fireworks sound, particular style of music, wool blanket, weapons, kitchen knives) the client can sit near the object for 5 minutes and look at it, followed by touching the object for 5 minutes, and then holding the object in his lap for 5 minutes.

These graduated exposures of one item can be completed over the course of a week or throughout the day. There should be an increase in intensity by varying the parameters of the exposure. For example, the client may choose to have a support person with her in the exposure (e.g., driving in a car with a friend), vary the length of time with the stimuli (e.g., start off with 5 minute exposure, then 10 minutes, etc.), or choose to be physically close to the object or in the presence of the feared stimuli (e.g., being in the same room with men). Another way to vary the parameters is for the client to complete the exposure at different times of day and night, or be close or far from an exit (e.g., being in the same room with men, but sitting closest to the door) (Bourne, 2005).

This may be more easily explained through a case example. Going back to Case Example 2-2, Ieisha listed on her hierarchy the smell of cigarettes because her rapist smoked a cigarette after he assaulted her. This aroma has made her feel nausea upon encountering it in daily life or in social settings. Ieisha could light a cigarette and allow herself to smell it, increasing the length of time she smells the cigarette over the course of the week. Also, sitting on leather car seats with bare skin was listed on her hierarchy because she remembers the skin on her buttocks and thighs being pulled and pinched on the leather car seats when she was raped. Ieisha could first sit in a car with leather seats with pants on while her husband sits next to her. Next, with her husband, she could sit on the leather seats with shorts on so that she feels the texture of the leather against her skin, and finally she could do this either alone or for a longer period of time.

For items that involve locations or activities (e.g., a dark room or being alone, someone walking up a staircase), it may be helpful to start with a support person accompanying the client. Ieisha lists the parking garage where she was raped as an item on her hierarchy. She could first look at a picture of the parking garage at night with a friend, then drive by it during the day with a friend. These can be followed by driving to the parking garage and parking in it for 5 minutes with a friend, and finally she could stay parked for a longer period of time with a friend or go with her friend in the early evening when the sun has gone down, while there are still plenty of people around on the way home from work. For Ieisha to go to the parking garage by herself at 10 PM when it is fairly empty is not advised and can be dangerous for Ieisha or for any woman.

The client can determine if the graduated exposures should increase by time or independence (e.g., being with someone else or being alone during the exposure). For some trauma locations, the client cannot return to the site. For example, in Case Example 2-5, Nikos, a refugee, may not be able to go home to his town that was invaded by troops. Likewise, in Case Example 2-8, Andre may not be able to return to New York City's Twin Tower site after moving out of state. Also, in Case Example 2-6, Joe is unable to return to the battlefield of Vietnam. In these instances, there can be a focus on photographs of the location, imagery, scenes from movies, or photographs from books, as well as objects and items that elicit reactions from the five senses. Aromas, noises, tastes, and the like can all be used to complete *in vivo* exposures. After the *in vivo* exposure is completed, the client returns to mindful breathing for 5 to 10 minutes. It is important for the client to record in her homework journal the thoughts, feelings, physical sensations, reactions, and distress rating that occurred during the exposure. These can be discussed during the next treatment session.

Case Example 2-8: Andre

Andre is a 38-year-old man who was near the Twin Towers during the September 11th attack on the World Trade Center in New York City. On the street, bodies of people who jumped from the Twin Towers were hitting the ground. As Andre was running to safety, a body almost hit him, but instead landed on the sidewalk next to him. In the aftermath of September 11th, Andre was experiencing too many distressing and overwhelming flashbacks and intrusive memories of dead bodies and body parts, and was avoiding certain locations in Manhattan, which made it difficult for him to do his job within a reasonable amount of time. He recently moved his family out of the city; however, his symptoms continue to impact his ability to stay focused at work and to fall and stay asleep, and are affecting his relationships with his wife and two children.

SESSION STRUCTURE OVERVIEW

Following the assessment sessions, most treatment sessions usually consist of first reviewing homework from the previous session (10 minutes), discussing the agenda for today's session (5 minutes), conducting an imaginal exposure (45 to 60 minutes), and finally assigning an *in vivo* exposure for homework (5 to 10 minutes). Starting from the first appointment, a suggested format to structure your sessions is presented in the box titled "Session Structure." Session materials and content are presented in Table 2.5.

Session Structure

SESSION 1

Session 1 is a designated assessment session in which the assessment clinician gathers information on the trauma itself and the client's response and reactions to the trauma, as well as any stressful life events that occurred prior to the traumatic experience. Additionally, within this first session, the clinician presents the general rationale for PE and introduces mindful breathing (Foa & Rothbaum, 1998).

SESSION 2

Session 2 allows for the client to provide more details related to the trauma, as well as his responses and reactions. The clinician can present the client with a list of common reactions to trauma and spend some time identifying and normalizing the client's responses. After reviewing symptoms, the clinician can present a more detailed rationale for using *in vivo* exposures. With assistance from the clinician, the client then creates a hierarchy of situations he has been avoiding since the trauma. An *in vivo* exposure is identified for the client to complete for homework. It is helpful for the clinician to encourage the client to continue practicing mindful breathing throughout the week, and especially if distressing symptoms arise. It may also be useful to have the client continue to review the common reactions to trauma (Foa & Rothbaum, 1998).

SESSION 3

Session 3 is an opportunity to discuss the assessment findings with the client. Then the rationale for imaginal exposure is presented and the client completes the first imaginal exposure. This exposure will last between 45 and 60 minutes. This will be audiotaped, and the client is instructed to listen to it throughout the week for homework. Additionally, he is asked to complete another *in vivo* exposure for homework (Foa & Rothbaum, 1998).

SESSIONS 4 THROUGH 8

Sessions 4 through 8 consist of imaginal exposures of 45 minutes each. It is also possible for *in vivo* exposures to be completed in the session. During session 8 it is important to reevaluate the client's progress and discuss the possibility of additional sessions to complete the remaining exposures (Foa & Rothbaum, 1998).

Table 2.5
Session Materials and Content

Session 1

Materials

Tape recorder or Dictaphone

Tape player, portable headset, or Walkman

Blank tape

Batteries

Clock or watch

Assessment findings

Psychoeducation handouts for clients (PTSD symptoms, treatment model, mindful breathing)

Hierarchy worksheets

Homework journal

Safety contracts

Content (each component is discussed in further detail below)

Audiotape the session

Orientation to treatment (as described above)

Review of assessment findings (as described above)

Creating imaginal and *in vivo* hierarchies (as described above)

Skill building: Mindful breathing (20 minutes) (as described above)

Assign homework

Homework for Next Session

Practice mindful breathing 3 times per day, and as needed, record in journal

Listen to tape of session 1 two times this week

Record avoidance for this week in journal, daily

Session 2

Materials: Clinician

Tape recorder, Dictaphone

Blank tape

Clock or watch

Hierarchy lists

Hierarchy distress rating sheets

Safety contracts

Materials: Client

Tape from session 1

Homework journal

Content

Audiotape the session

Review homework assignments: Mindful breathing, avoidance, listening to tape of session

Review imaginal exposure hierarchy

Mindful breathing (5 minutes)

Complete imaginal exposure (45–60 minutes)

Mindful breathing (5–10 minutes)

Review *in vivo* exposure hierarchy and choose one for homework

Assign homework and provide the client with audiotape of session

Homework for Next Session

Practice mindful breathing three times per day and as needed; record in journal

Listen to tape of imaginal exposure from session 2 two times this week

Complete *in vivo* exposure three times this week

Record avoidance for this week in journal, daily

Sessions 3–9

Materials: Clinician (treatment sessions 3–9 follow the same format)

Tape recorder, Dictaphone

Blank tape

Clock or watch

Hierarchy lists

(*continued*)

Table 2.5

Continued

Hierarchy distress rating sheets

Safety contracts

Materials: Client

Tape from previous session

Homework journal

Content

Audiotape the session

Review assessment findings and homework assignments: mindful breathing, avoidance, listening to tape of session

Discuss *in vivo* exposure completed for homework

Mindful breathing (5 minutes)

Complete imaginal exposure (45–60 minutes)

Mindful breathing (5–10 minutes)

Choose one *in vivo* exposure for homework

Assign homework and provide the client with audiotape of session

Homework for Next Session:

Practice mindful breathing three times per day and as needed; record in journal

Listen to tape of imaginal exposure from previous session two times this week

Complete *in vivo* exposure three times this week

Record avoidance for this week in journal, daily

DISCHARGE ASSESSMENT

Similar to the assessment that takes places prior to treatment (as discussed in depth in this chapter's appendix on assessment), there is a postassessment at discharge that allows the client and clinician to measure the effectiveness of the treatment program. Accurate assessment both before and after treatment is imperative for all treatment interventions. PTSD may just be one of many issues in a person's life. Clinicians should be well trained in diagnosing and differentiating the full spectrum of psychiatric disorders in adults and be knowledgeable of treatment options in the community.

The postassessment at discharge allows us to measure the client's functioning at the end of treatment, provides us with data we can compare to the intake assessment findings, demonstrates evidence of treatment gains, and identifies areas for continued treatment. The purpose of the postassessment is to: (1) assess current functioning and symptoms at time of discharge, considering the severity and persistence of clinical impairment; (2) determine the client's level of satisfaction with treatment; and (3) review the initial treatment needs and intervention plan and determine if the client has met treatment goals.

The postassessment requires one session of 90 minutes. The assigned treatment clinician can administer the postassessment measures and questionnaires to offer a continuum of care for the client. In addition to the limitations of using self-report measures, there are limitations to having the treatment clinician conduct the discharge assessment. With this type of treatment the therapeutic relationship can be valued immensely by the client, and there may be underreporting of symptoms in an attempt to please the clinician. Clients may have become very fond of their clinician and feel as if they owe them something for the tremendous help they received, and so they may not want to say anything that makes the clinician feel ineffective or incompetent. This may be something to discuss with the client prior to administering measures, as demonstrated in the box titled "Illustrative Script for Introducing Discharge Measures."

Illustrative Script for Introducing Discharge Measures

Before we start the discharge questionnaires, I would like to talk with you about something that's very important to understanding how you are doing now that you and I have completed our sessions. Together, we have had some pretty intense sessions. You should be so proud of yourself for your bravery, first of all, to ask for help, and second, to confront your fears and painful memories. You have come so far and have shown yourself how strong, determined, and courageous you are. I appreciate your thanking me for helping you; however, your success is based on your efforts and your hard work. I am honored to know you and hope that my support has been helpful for you as you went through this process. That is one aspect of my job that I treasure—being able to help others. However, sometimes our work is incomplete and in other ways has just begun. There may be additional services that can assist you in being healthy and successful. Today, we may uncover areas of concern that need to be addressed through additional treatment or support. I want that for you. I want you to get the help you need and deserve to be your best self. So if there are still symptoms that we need to address, I will help you or find someone who can. If you are still having symptoms, that does not invalidate all of the progress you've made here. You've really come a long way, and I'm proud of you. What's most important is that you answer the questions as honestly as possible today. Unfortunately, some clients might not let us know if there's still something that's disruptive to their life. They may feel that they don't want to hurt their therapist's feelings or they think she'll be insulted. Clients may think that if they are honest about the symptoms they still have, it will make the therapist feel like a failure. While caring about someone else's feelings is a wonderful and kind intention, it dishonors you and all of your hard work. We are here to focus on you, not me. The only way we can help you is if you're honest with us. If this seems challenging for you, we can have you meet with another clinician for the discharge assessment. The choice is yours. Whatever makes you feel more comfortable and able to be straightforward is what we'll do today. Okay? Now, are there any questions or concerns that you want to discuss?

Once the postassessment is complete, the clinician should review the findings with the client. Together, they can assess areas of improvement, symptom reduction, and areas for continued treatment. Referrals to the appropriate agencies, clinics, and services should be provided to the client. Additionally, the client is encouraged to contact the clinician if symptoms are retriggered. Clinicians should also discuss that for some clients who have completed treatment, their symptoms have dissipated; however, they may experience events that retrigger PTSD symptoms in the future. These include media coverage of the event, memorial services, criminal investigations, and court proceedings. These events and the extent to which they retrigger symptoms may require additional treatment sessions after discharge.

Content

The primary domains assessed are: (1) types of symptoms experienced at discharge, (2) intensity of symptoms at discharge, (3) frequency and impact of symptoms at discharge, and (4) client satisfaction with treatment program. The postassessment may be difficult to complete due to client factors involved in this process, such as minimization and limited disclosure of symptoms, the intensity of symptoms, and lack of confidence in treatment effectiveness, especially if the clinician involved in this client's treatment is now administering the postassessment, as demonstrated above. Underreporting may occur if the client is concerned with hurting the clinician's feelings or coming across as critical. If you anticipate this issue, it may be in the best interest of the client to have another clinician administer the postassessment to obtain the most accurate information. Having multiple informants may also prove useful in obtaining accurate information regarding symptoms and level of functioning at discharge. The support person the client identified at intake may offer additional insight. When planning, preparing, and administering the postassessment, it is important to consider the individual needs of each client.

Assessment Tools: Structured Interviews and Questionnaires

As mentioned earlier, there are numerous instruments designed to assess exposure to trauma, diagnose PTSD, and assess symptom severity. To compare findings from both the intake assessment and postassessment at discharge most accurately, it is important to use the same measures for both assessments (see Tables 2.7 through 2.9 in this chapter's appendix on assessment). As a reminder, additional instruments have been developed to assess specific types of trauma, such as childhood trauma, domestic violence, war zone trauma, and torture.

CONCLUSION: CHALLENGES FOR CLINICIANS

Working with trauma victims can be a challenging experience. At times it can be particularly draining. For example, watching the client endure an exposure can be painful for the clinician (e.g., she was sobbing uncontrollably, he curled up his body on the floor and was clutching the pillow, she started to make sounds like she was going to vomit, etc.). A clinician's natural inclination is to help others and ease their pain, not exacerbate it. By nature, clinicians want to ease the pain of others, and during the exposures clinicians may think that they are doing more harm than good. It may seem to be most helpful if we stop the exposure and allow the client to retreat; however, this will only reinforce their anxiety and fear and imply that we think they are not capable of facing what haunts them. While these are natural thoughts and feelings for clinicians working with trauma victims, it is imperative to remember that clients need to face their fear in order to desensitize themselves to it. The intensity will pass.

It is important to remind ourselves of the rationale behind this treatment and have supervision with an objective and experienced clinician who is reliable and accessible. It is recommended that supervision sessions be scheduled as soon after the session as possible to allow the clinician to process what they saw, heard, thought, and felt during the session. Audiotapes can be reviewed with supervisors, and if possible videotapes can be monitored for supervision purposes, with the client's consent.

Supervision also can help clinicians deal with feeling guilty for not having the personal experiences their clients have endured. Trauma work may even evoke angry and dismissive feelings in response to the client's helplessness. Although it is difficult to admit these feelings, it is imperative to be aware of your reactions and use them as indicators for when you may need to increase supervision, take a break from trauma-related cases altogether, or seek treatment for yourself. There is a need for support from other trauma clinicians and through supervision with an experienced therapist. It is essential to be aware of your limits and maintain your emotional health in order to provide this type of treatment to your clients. It is important to be praised and to commend yourself as an individual who has accepted the task of helping trauma victims recover from their agony and move forward to lead healthier and fulfilling lives.

VICARIOUS TRAUMA AND SECONDARY TRAUMA SYMPTOMS

Witnessing the impact of trauma on victims makes it difficult to remain objective (McFarlane & van der Kolk, 2007), especially when clients with PTSD tend to recreate their past and become victimized repeatedly in part due to their sense of helplessness. The relationship between a client and therapist is just as susceptible to this dynamic as any other interpersonal relationship. Clinicians sometimes become rescuers, potentially resulting in repetition of the trauma. Clinicians need to be continually aware of their reactions, both positive and negative. Clinicians are not exempt from developing the avoidance and numbing that the general public has toward victims.

When clinicians are exposed to the horrific details of trauma experiences through their clients' accounts, they may become emotionally affected and experience secondary trauma, also called vicarious trauma, which (as discussed by Hoch in Chapter 4 of this volume) can result "from empathic engagement with the client's trauma material" (Saakvitne & Pearlman, 1996). Although not impacted in the same direct ways the victims are, nonetheless these encounters may be difficult to cope with and challenge the clinician's perspective of the world and the capabilities of human beings that have endured such unthinkable atrocities as well as those who have inflicted such severe pain on others for their own gratification. During imaginal exposures, clinicians need to be compassionate and empathetic but maintain a level of professional distance at the same time.

Vicarious trauma can cause the clinician to have symptoms of secondary trauma, including depression and anxiety and other symptoms of PTSD, such as nightmares, avoidant behaviors, rescue fantasies, dissociation, intense guilt, feelings of powerlessness and hopelessness, denial, constricted affect, and minimization (Figley, 1995; Friedman, 2006; Herman, J., 1992; McCann & Pearlman, 1990). Vicarious trauma can compromise a clinician's professional judgment and cause emotional hardship, which can be detrimental to both the client and clinician. And the more symptomatic clinicians become, the less effective they will be.

Secondary trauma symptoms are related to the concept of counter-transference, especially when the clinician is coping with personal issues that are very similar to the client's presenting problem. If so, the clinician may start to have intrusive recollections, avoidant behaviors, and hyper-arousal symptoms in response to their own trauma memories being triggered (Danieli, 1984; Friedman, 2006; Herman, J., 1992; Wilson & Lindy, 1994). Since we know that half of American men and women will be exposed to a traumatic event, it is likely that a number of mental health clinicians have their own personal trauma histories and experiences (Kessler, Sonnega, Bromet, Hughes, & Nelson, 1995).

Clinicians are strongly encouraged to seek their own treatment in addition to supervision support, as needed. In order to help others, it is imperative for clinicians to first care for themselves and evaluate their own capabilities and limitations. In addition to regular supervision, self-care includes having a support system at work, creating and maintaining professional boundaries with clients and with one's caseload (e.g., seeing a variety of clients, not just trauma cases), and engaging in healthy and pro-social activities outside of work, such as exercise, spending time with friends and family, and relaxing (Friedman, 2006).

In the midst of witnessing anguish, dismay, and human suffering when working with trauma victims, there is also the unique opportunity to witness the extraordinary strength, courage, and determination that clients are capable of as they confront their fears. Despite the foregoing challenges, therefore, working with trauma victims can be a fulfilling and rewarding experience. I hope this chapter (as well as the rest of this volume) will help you realize that fulfillment.

APPENDIX: ASSESSMENT IN CBT TREATMENT OF TRAUMATIZED ADULTS

The Assessment Process

Initial Assessment Contact The first contact with a client aims to develop rapport, engage the client in the assessment and treatment process, and provide psychoeducation about common reactions to trauma. Given the nature of the presenting problem, clients should be commended for taking the first step in asking for help. It is not unusual for clients to exhibit uncertainty, despair, self-blame, and shame during this first appointment. These reactions should be normalized and discussed in an empathetic manner. Handout 2-1, which is presented at the end of this chapter, identifies common reactions to trauma and can be reproduced for giving to your clients for the purpose of psychoeducation.

Distress related to trauma symptoms may be compounded by feelings of disconnection and withdrawal from one's family and peer support system. Clients may report that it is difficult to discuss their reactions and symptoms with loved ones because they may not fully understand what the client is experiencing. Many clients report resorting to a life of social isolation and secrecy, which (as mentioned previously) can lead to self-injurious behaviors. It is imperative to assess safety and suicidal/homicidal ideation and plans within this first phase. To enhance engagement, it is helpful to do the following:

- Describe the benefits of comprehensive assessment and treatment.
- Validate the client's reaction.
- Normalize their experiences.
- Identify client strengths and protective factors, as well as identify treatment objectives, benefits, and limitations, as well as obstacles to treatment success (see Table 2.6).

To establish a partnership with the client, it is imperative to remain sensitive to their emotional situation (Friedman, 2006).

Purpose   Accurate assessment is imperative for all treatment interventions. It allows us to measure the client's functioning prior to treatment, assists us in ongoing monitoring throughout the treatment course, and provides us with comparison data for an assessment at discharge, demonstrating evidence of treatment gains as well as identifying areas for continued treatment. In other words, it allows us to measure the effectiveness of our interventions. The purpose of the assessment is to: (1) assess current functioning and symptoms, considering the severity and persistence of clinical impairment; (2) gather details about the trauma and the particular context in which it occurred; (3) determine the client's motivation and commitment to treatment; (4) identify treatment needs and design an intervention plan; and (5) assess goodness of fit between the client and clinician. The assessment may require between one to two sessions of 90 minutes each. It is important to inform clients of the assessment's length so that they are prepared prior to the first appointment. Ideally, the assigned treatment clinician will administer the assessment measures and questionnaires to foster a working alliance with the client immediately. Once the assessment is complete, the client starts treatment within 1 week of the last assessment session. If the assessment is conducted by someone other than the treatment clinician, all information gathered from the initial evaluation should be reviewed thoroughly by the assigned therapist prior to the start of any treatment program (Foa & Rothbaum, 1998).

Content   The primary domains assessed are: (1) the client's history including mental health diagnosis and level of functioning; (2) types of symptoms; (3) intensity of symptoms; (4) frequency and impact of symptoms; (5) amenability to treatment, including motivation to change and compliance with treatment; and (6) prior trauma. The assessment may be difficult to complete due to client factors involved in this process, such as minimization and limited disclosure of symptoms or the extent of the trauma, the intensity of symptoms or reexperiencing the trauma during the assessment sessions, lack of motivation to participate in the assessment, and lack of confidence in treatment effectiveness. When planning, preparing, and administering the assessment, it is important to consider these factors as well as the individual needs of each client.

Assessment Tools: Structured Interviews and Questionnaires   Standardized assessment instruments allow us to assess exposure to trauma, diagnose PTSD, and measure symptom severity; however, a limitation to these tools is that they rely on the client's retrospective self-report. The following tools can be

Table 2.6

Exposure to Trauma Measures

Exposure Measures	Citations
Traumatic Stress Schedule (TSS)	Norris (1992)
Potential Stressor Experiences Inventory (PSEI)	Kilpatrick, Resnick, & Freedy (1991)
Traumatic Events Questionnaire (TEQ)	Vrana & Lauterbach (1994)
Evaluation of Lifetime Stressors (ELS)	Krinsley & Weathers (1995)
Trauma History Questionnaire (THQ)	Green (1996)
Traumatic Life Events Questionnaire (TLEQ)	Kubany et al. (2000)
Stressful Life Events Screening Questionnaire (SLESQ)	Goodman, Corcoran, Turner, Yuan, & Green (1998)
Life Stressor Checklist–Revised (LSC-R)	Wolfe, Kimerling, Brown, Chrestman, & Levin (1996)

used with adult clients to assess exposure to trauma: Traumatic Stress Schedule (TSS) (Norris, 1992), Potential Stressor Experiences Inventory (PSEI) (Kilpatrick et al., 1991), Traumatic Events Questionnaire (TEQ) (Vrana & Lauterbach, 1994), Evaluation of Lifetime Stressors (ELS) (Krinsley & Weathers, 1995), the Trauma History Questionnaire (THQ) (Green, 1996), Traumatic Life Events Questionnaire (TLEQ) (Kubany et al., 2000), Stressful Life Events Screening Questionnaire (SLESQ) (Goodman et al., 1998), and the Life Stressor Checklist–Revised (LSC-R) (Wolfe et al., 1996) (see Table 2.6). Additional instruments have been developed to assess specific types of trauma, such as childhood trauma, domestic violence, war zone trauma, and torture.

A structured clinical interview administered by a clinician is ideal for assessing whether a client meets criteria for a diagnosis. The National Center for PTSD has developed both a diagnostic and symptom severity instrument, the Clinician Administered PTSD Scale (CAPS) (Blake et al., 1995). Additional clinical interviews are listed in Table 2.7. Also, Table 2.8 lists scales that assess symptom severity and level of functioning. As with any instrument, clinicians must be mindful of the reliability and validity of each measure, as well as its applicability to the population or type of trauma being treated. *Reliability* refers to the instrument's ability to produce the same results when it is administered at different times, whereas *validity* refers to the ability of the instrument to actually measure that which it intends to measure (Friedman, 2006).

Process and Procedure   When planning and preparing for the assessment the clinician must be mindful of practical and logistical aspects of the first appointment. For a client to come to the assessment and return home safely,

Table 2.7
Clinical Interviews for Trauma Symptoms

Clinical Interviews	Citations
Clinician Administered PTSD Scale (CAPS)	Blake et al. (1995)
Structured Clinical Interview for DSM-IV (SCID)	First, Spitzer, Williams, & Gibbon (1996)
Composite International Diagnostic Interview (CIDI)	World Health Organization (1997)
Posttraumatic Stress Diagnostic Scale (PDS)	Foa, Casman, Jaycox, & Perry (1997)
Diagnostic Interview Schedule IV (DIS-IV)	Robins, Cottler, & Bucholz (1995)
Davidson Self-Rating PTSD Scale	Davidson et al. (1997)
PTSD–Interview	Watson, Juba, Manifold, Kucal, & Anderson (1991)

it may be helpful to have a friend or family member escort them. Following directions, driving, and taking public transportation may be overwhelming while dealing with the anticipation of intense emotions. Other considerations include the time of the appointment, parking arrangements, the use of staircases, elevators, or restrooms, and the radio or music played in the waiting room lobby, for these may all be reminiscent of the client's trauma

Table 2.8
Symptom Severity and Level-of-Functioning Measures

Symptom Severity and Level of Functioning	Citations
PTSD Checklist (PCL)	Weathers, Litz, Herman, Huska, & Keane (1995)
PTSD Symptom Scale (PSS)	Foa, Riggs, Dancu, & Rothbaum (1993)
PK and PS Scales of the MMPI-2	Lyons & Keane (1992); Schlenger & Kulka (1989)
SCL-PTSD	Saunders, Arata, & Kilpatrick (1990); Ursano, Fullerton, Kao, & Bhartiya (1995)
Impact of Event Scale–Revised (IES-R)	Weiss & Marmar (1997)
Mississippi Scale for Combat-Related PTSD (M-PTSD)	Keane, Gerardi, Lyons, & Wolfe (1988)
Revised Civilian Mississippi Scale	Norris & Perilla (1996)
Penn Inventory	Hammarberg (1992)
Trauma Symptom Checklist–40 (TSC-40)	Briere & Runtz (1989)
Trauma Symptom Inventory (TSI)	Briere (1995)

scenario. For example, recall Case Example 2-2, involving Ieisha, a woman who was attacked and raped while walking to her car at night in an empty parking garage. Ieisha may need a daytime appointment and alternative parking arrangements or an escort to her car because evening appointments after dark may feel too unsafe for her and trigger intense emotional reactions.

Other clients' trauma or assault may have taken place while they are alone in a staircase, elevator, or restroom. A veteran experiencing PTSD, such as Joe (in Case Example 2-3), may be sensitive to overhearing a news program regarding a war abroad while waiting in the lobby. This may trigger flash-backs and an intense emotional reaction, making him feel unsafe where he is trying to seek help. Although we cannot completely safeguard the environment, it is useful to be mindful of the possible triggers the client may encounter before meeting with you for the assessment.

Once in the clinician's office, the assessment begins with an orientation to the program and the expectations for participation if they chose to continue with treatment. Reporting laws for suicidality and homicidality should be discussed along with the completion of administrative forms, such as an authorization to release and obtain information from other providers and informed consent for participation in the program. Copies of these documents are to be provided to clients for their own personal records. Emergency contacts are also identified at this time.

It may be useful to include another informant during the assessment phase (Newman, Kaloupek, & Keane, 2007). For example, a spouse or close friend may be able to provide information to the clinician regarding the client's symptoms and level of functioning. Multiple informants, with the client's consent, may assist in providing a more comprehensive case conceptualization prior to starting the treatment phase. Additionally, referrals to the proper resources can be offered for family members and partners if they are in need of processing the trauma symptoms and reactions of their loved one as well as its impact on their relationship. This may include offering psychiatric consultation and treatment if you choose to also work with members of the client's support system. Psychoeducation about common reactions to trauma is provided, and handouts are given to clients regarding PTSD symptoms and the treatment model, allowing clients to review this information again at home with their family or partner, prior to the first treatment session. This will help to facilitate discussion during the initial treatment contact. In addition to Handout 2-1 (mentioned earlier in this appendix), two other psychoeducational handouts are provided at the end of this appendix, which can be reproduced for giving your clients. Handout 2-2 deals with typically avoided situations; Handout 2-3 is on understanding trauma and its impact.

The assessment clinician administers the diagnostic and clinical interview with the client alone. Throughout assessment, it is important to be mindful of the nature of the trauma and to not take resistance personally. For example, if the client was victimized by another person such as assault, rape, torture, it is common for there to be mistrust and fear, as well as a general pessimistic attitude (Foa & Rothbaum, 1998). Offering the client validation, encouragement, and praise is useful during this phase and may include phrases similar to the following (Foa & Rothbaum, 1998):

- *"It sounds like it was not the right time for you to ask for help until now."*
- *"It takes a lot of courage to come forward and ask for help."*
- *"It sounds like you did the right thing considering the circumstances."*
- *"It's not always best to fight back—sometimes that leads to more violence and aggression."*
- *"Nothing you could have done gave him a right to hurt you this way."*
- *"No one deserves this; I have had other clients tell me they feel similarly."*
- *"That is a very common reaction to traumatic experiences."*

Assessments are conducted at intake and discharge, as well as at follow-up if possible. At discharge, the client will complete the same measures administered during intake. During follow-up, some clinicians may find it useful to administer all prior measures at some point after treatment for follow-up. This may be 3, 6, or 12 months after discharge to determine if the client is able to maintain treatment gains.

A suicide assessment is recommended prior to starting treatment. Suicidality is contraindicated for this treatment protocol. If it is determined that a client has suicidal ideation or plans, it is important to inform them that their depression and suicidality is of primary concern and they will not benefit at this time from exposure therapy. Treatment for depression should be administered first. Referrals to appropriate services are provided if depression treatment is not available on-site. Clients may feel rejected at this point, and their hopelessness may increase. It is important to reassure them and connect them to the appropriate treatment program. Safety contracts may be useful to complete as well as identifying and contacting the client's emergency support person. Clinicians should also adhere to mandated reporting laws regarding suicidality in their jurisdiction (Foa & Rothbaum, 1998; Friedman, 2006; van der Kolk, 2007, from the chapter entitled, "The Complexity of Adaptation to Trauma.")

Upon completion of the assessment, the clinician meets with the client to review the clinician's initial impressions and areas identified as preliminary treatment targets, answer questions the client may have, and discuss motivation and initial plans for treatment. The assessment phase is completed at this point, and a more thorough discussion regarding the results of the assessment is conducted during the first treatment session with the client.

The first treatment session should occur within 1 week of the last assessment session.

SPECIAL CONSIDERATIONS

With each type of trauma, there are different considerations and sensitivities, be it assault, torture, rape, war, military combat, incarceration in a death camp, natural disasters, industrial and automobile accidents, or exposure to violence. During the clinical interview, clinicians must be mindful of the language and labels used, as well as the way these sensitive questions are posed. Many women and men who have experienced sexual assault or been placed in concentration or refugee camps do not identify with the label *victim* or *survivor*. Letting the client take the lead and honoring the language and labels he or she uses will help facilitate the therapeutic alliance.

In addition to being mindful of language used, it is most beneficial to allow the client to assign judgments on severity as they describe the trauma, as opposed to the clinician's assuming one aspect had more of an impact than another. For example, in Case Example 2-4, after being sexually molested by her brother and cousin, Lynn may not identify the sexual assault as the most distressing component, but instead identify her brother pulling away and ending the sexual relationship once she started to menstruate as the most distressing. The feelings of rejection and emotional withdrawal might be more difficult for Lynn to handle than the physical sexual acts.

Regarding pregnancy resulting from abuse, is it worse for a woman to become pregnant by her brother or by an unknown perpetrator? For the client who survived a car accident in which his wife and three children died, is the fact that he lived through this accident something he sees positively or negatively? During the September 11th attacks on the World Trade Center, was it more horrific to have escaped from inside the Twin Towers through smoke and flames or to be outside and nearly hit by the body of someone who jumped from one of the buildings? These questions and experiences of trauma are for the client to assess, clarify, and assign meaning to, not the clinician.

In an effort to be sensitive to the client's willingness to disclose such painful aspects of her life, it is important to allow the client to speak openly about her experiences and their meaning in her life. Sticking to a rigid structure or rushing through measures and cutting off the client in the middle of a story, in order to complete the assessment in its entirety during the first session, is counterproductive. Through discussion, allow the client to provide you with detailed information about the traumatic event in a structure and sequence that is most comfortable for her. Using clinical judgment, we must determine what is most beneficial for the client and therapeutic relationship at any given point in time. It is completely reasonable to conduct the assessment over the course of two sessions if that is more conducive to the client's feeling comfortable.

Comorbidity Exposure to extreme stress impacts the functioning of those exposed to it, including emotional, cognitive, behavioral, physical, and characterological functioning (Cole & Putnam, 1992; Herman, J. L., 1992; Kroll, Habenicht, & McKenzie, 1989; van der Kolk, 1988; van der Kolk, Roth, Pelcovitz, & Mandel, 1993). PTSD is often accompanied by other psychological and substance related conditions that require attention, sensitivity, and ongoing assessment throughout the treatment course. Co-occurring disorders, or those that are present simultaneously with PTSD, are also known as comorbid disorders. People with psychiatric and medical conditions prior to trauma may find that trauma exposure has increased their difficulties. Additionally, many comorbid disorders exacerbate PTSD symptoms and complicate treatment (Foa, Keane, & Friedman, 2000). Prevalence studies indicate that 80% of U.S. patients with chronic PTSD also suffer from other psychiatric disorders, such as depression, phobias, generalized anxiety disorder, other anxiety disorders, conduct disorder, and substance abuse (Kessler et al., 1995). Childhood trauma may create a vulnerability to a variety of psychiatric disorders throughout life including personality disorders, dissociative disorders, eating disorders, substance abuse, and self-mutilation (van der Kolk, 2007, from the chapter entitled "The Phychobiology of PTSD").

For women and men with PTSD, roughly 52% and 28%, respectively, have lifetime prevalence rates of alcohol abuse/dependence. Current prevalence rates for drug abuse/dependence are 35% for women and 27% for men (Foa et al., 2000; Friedman, 2006). Treatment planning should address comorbid symptoms that hinder daily functioning. A comprehensive assessment is a first step in identifying and then treating comorbidities. Clinicians should be well trained in diagnosing and differentiating the full spectrum of psychiatric disorders in adults and should also be knowledgeable of treatment options in the community (see Introduction) (Foa & Rothbaum, 1998; Friedman, 2006).

Adults with Childhood Trauma There may be considerable differences in PTSD symptoms and levels of functioning among individuals who experience trauma in adulthood compared to those who were traumatized as children. The likelihood of multiple traumas may also be greater among adults who were abused as children. Generally, individuals exposed to trauma are often traumatized again, and those who have experienced multiple traumas are more likely to develop PTSD (Burgess & Holmstrom, 1978). Adults who were traumatized as children may have established undesirable patterns of coping, repetitive reliving experiences, and avoidance behaviors that have been reinforced for decades. The considerable length of time between childhood trauma experiences and treatment in adulthood sets the stage for experiencing additional traumas. For adults who were traumatized as children, their long-term adaptations over the life course vary depending on their developmental level at the time of the trauma. Additional factors include temperament, gender, culture, preexisting attachment patterns, and the victim's relationship with those responsible for the trauma (e.g., domestic violence, sexual abuse).

It is imperative to examine where clients have become fixated in their coping and on which specific aspect of the trauma they are focused (Herman, J., 1992; van der Kolk & McFarlane, 2007). The age of the person at the time of the trauma and previous life experiences will also impact the interpretation or the meaning assigned to the trauma. Children tend to blame themselves and assume responsibility for the trauma, resulting in an illusion of control. Burgess & Holstrom (1979) suggest that this distorted sense of control, or keeping the locus of control internal as opposed to external, may prevent helplessness and lend itself to better treatment outcomes, allowing the individual to believe he has the power to make changes.

Exposure to trauma in childhood also has long-term effects that are numerous and complicated, impacting individuals in emotional, somatic, cognitive, behavioral, and characterological ways. Victims of childhood trauma therefore are potentially predisposed to develop a variety of psychiatric disorders, substance abuse, and pathological forms of self-regulation (e.g., eating disorders, self-mutilation) (Cole & Putnam, 1992; Herman, J. 1992; Herman, J. L., 1992; Kroll, Habenicht, & McKenzie, 1989; van der Hart, Steele, Boon, & Brown, 1993; van der Kolk, 1988; van der Kolk, 2007, from the chapter entitled "The Complexity of Adaptation to Trauma").

The biological impact of childhood trauma varies according to developmental level. Most victims of trauma experience hyperarousal and dissociation, as well as problems with attention, self-regulation, and discriminating stimuli. However, for adults with traumatic childhoods, there may be more physiological dysregulation when it comes to stimulus discrimination, especially for those who develop PTSD as a result of child abuse and neglect (van der Kolk, 2007, from the chapter entitled "The Complexity of Adaptation to Trauma"). These individuals tend to go immediately from stimulus to response, without assessing the meaning of the circumstances. Such problems with stimulus discrimination may explain high comorbidity rates between ADHD and PTSD in traumatized children (van der Kolk, 2007, from the chapter entitled "The Complexity of Adaptation to Trauma"). PTSD symptoms in adults, when originated in childhood, may be more severe, persistent, and fixed compared to the symptoms found in adults with more recent trauma. There may be particular differences in regard to variations in attachment patterns, affect regulation, dissociation, absence of self-regulation, and self-destructive behavior.

Secure Attachment as a Protective Factor   Secure attachment bonds buffer children from stressful situations and trauma-induced psychopathology. Additionally, they build capacity both psychologically and biologically, which further assists in regulating arousal. A secure attachment bond fosters the ability to cope with stress by teaching children to take care of themselves, access external support, and rely on others when one's own skills are inadequate (van der Kolk & Fisler, 1994). The single most important determinant of long-term damage or poor prognosis over the life course may lie in the quality of one's attachment to her parent (McFarlane, 1988). This is a factor that is especially meaningful for adults with childhood histories of neglect (van der Kolk & Fisler).

Affect Regulation   One's capacity to deal with external stress, through regulating emotions and behaviors, defines one's sense of self. Adults with problematic childhood self-regulatory processes may have chronic poor self-image, body image, and affect and impulse control, as well as aggression toward self, problems with interpersonal relationships (e.g., isolation, withdrawal, mistrust, suspicion, lack of intimacy), inability to understand cause and effect (e.g., identifying one's own contribution to problems), difficulty functioning in social settings with others (Cole & Putnam, 1992). They may regress to primitive defenses in order to cope with trauma. These problems are often seen in adults with histories of child abuse and neglect. Parenting that is abusive and neglectful may cause chronic hyperarousal, an inability to cope with strong emotions, and problems communicating and understanding emotional signals. This further influences their capacity to deal with future stress and may leave such children vulnerable to psychopathology and trauma throughout the life course (Crittenden, 1994; van der Kolk, 2007, from the chapter entitled "The Complexity of Adaptation to Trauma"). Clients may experience feelings that belong to the trauma as they continuously reveal themselves within interpersonal relationships through the client's own emotions and through the perceived "traumatizing" emotional reactions of others (Litz & Keane, 1989).

Dissociation   Many adults with histories of childhood trauma report that they can leave their body when they are distressed. In a way, they are watching themselves from outside of their own bodies, similar to watching a TV show. There is a detachment from both their body and emotions, and this detachment offers a sense of protection (Gelinas, 1983; Noyes & Kletti, 1977;

van der Hart et al., 1993; van der Kolk, 2007, from the chapter entitled "The Complexity of Adaptation to Trauma"). Adults with dissociation may also have frequent nightmares, flashbacks, and psychosomatic issues, and may engage in self-destructive behavior (e.g., suicide, cutting, substance abuse). Adults with these symptoms often have histories of childhood sexual and physical abuse, domestic violence, and traumatic loss (Bernstein & Putnam, 1986; Saxe et al., 1993; Saxe et al., 1994).

Absence of Self-Regulation and Self-Destructive Behavior Problems with self-regulation may be the most damaging result of trauma for both children and adults. The younger the age of the child at the time of the trauma, the more severe its consequences are regarding regulation of strong emotions (e.g., anger, anxiety) (van der Kolk et al., 1993). Attempts to regain control of themselves, their environments, and their lives may lead clients to utilize a variety of methods such as self-mutilation, eating disorders, and substance abuse. These forms of self-harm may also be indications that the individual in some way holds himself responsible for the trauma or feels shameful or guilty and in turn is inflicting pain inwardly.

Simpson and Porter (1981) suggest self-mutilation may be a primitive reaction to painful experiences, especially with those involving caretakers. Ongoing social isolation and fear may result in self-mutilation (van der Kolk & Fisler, 1994). It is also thought that self-mutilation goes hand in hand with dissociation. Those who harm themselves through cutting or self-mutilation often report the desire to engage in these behaviors to alleviate feeling numb or "dead inside" (Demitrack, Putnam, Brewerton, Brandt, & Gold, 1990; Pattison & Kahan, 1983), or to physically reconnect themselves with their body. Many studies indicate histories of early trauma, including physical and sexual abuse, in those who cut themselves (Bowlby, 1984; van der Kolk, 1987).

The relationship between eating disorders and childhood trauma remains unclear. Studies of populations with eating disorders report childhood trauma histories in roughly 70% while other studies suggest lower rates (Folsom, Krahn, Canum, Gold, & Silk, 1989; Hernandez & DiClemente, 1992; Herzog, Staley, Carmody, Robbins, & van der Kolk, 1993; Pope & Hudson, 1993; van der Kolk et al., 1991).

Additionally, substance abuse populations more often report childhood abuse and neglect histories compared to the general population (Abueg & Fairbank, 1992; Hernandez & DiClemente, 1992; Lisak, 1993). It is thought that particular drugs are chosen for their desired effect, according to the self-medication theory (Khantzian, 1985). Heroin may mute negative emotions (e.g., anger, rage, fear); cocaine may act as an antidepressant; and alcohol may decrease nightmares, difficulty sleeping, and other intrusive memories, thoughts, and feelings (Abueg & Fairbank, 1992; Jellinek & Williams, 1987;

Keane, Gerardi, et al., 1988). These substances may all be considered temporary solutions to safeguard oneself from intense and frequent symptoms of PTSD.

Combat Trauma   Aspects of combat trauma will vary depending on the war. Iraqi war veterans, for example, may be particularly likely to have experienced exhaustion-related problems connected to their multiple extended tours of duty. Vietnam vets, though also vulnerable to exhaustion, may be more likely to suffer from various other aspects of trauma. Let's examine aspects of combat trauma that are experienced somewhat universally by veterans who experience war stressors both as victims and perpetrators of violence (King, King, Foy, Gudanowski, & Vreven, 1995; Breslau & Davis, 1987). These factors include fear, exhaustion, guilt, horror, anger, and inoculation.

Fear   Although seemingly counterintuitive, it is not fear of death and injury that is of primary concern for a soldier. Fear of death and injury in war is experienced by all who are exposed to the trauma of war, and yet we do not see the same high prevalence rates of PTSD in nonmilitary individuals (e.g., medical personnel, civilians), as we do in veterans. What is unique and paramount for a soldier in war or combat circumstances is the fear of not being able to meet the demands and expectations placed on him, including but not limited to killing other human beings or using overt aggressive confrontation. However, being fearful and unable to kill is common. When nonmilitary individuals are faced with threats to their lives (e.g., bombing attacks, shooting) similar to the threat a soldier may experience, while they may develop psychopathology, generally they do so to a lesser extent compared to those expected to kill (e.g., soldiers). Again, for nonmilitary individuals, there is not the *expectation* to kill anyone directly. Those bombed in England and Germany during World War II witnessed death and destruction and experienced fear of being injured or killed, but there was not the same psychological breakdown as seen in WWII soldiers. These two populations experienced similar exhaustion and horror; however, what the civilians did not generally experience was being *expected* to kill another person or looking their potential killers in the face (e.g., civilians being bombed by aircraft, not close-range combat).

Fear should not be underestimated, but it is not the primary factor responsible for causing psychiatric casualties. An exception may be those who survived Nazi concentration camps. Although not expected to kill, on a daily basis they were faced with aggression and death at the hands of sadistic and psychopathic personalities. They had to look these individuals in the face and recognize that another human being hated them to the point that they were slaughtering them like animals, along with their families and their people (Grossman, 1996). This unique expectation to kill should certainly be considered among the etiological factors contributing to psychopathology in veterans.

Exhaustion   Another consideration is the physical and emotional exhaustion in war. This exhaustion consists of the physiological arousal from continual fight-or-flight response and endless surges of adrenaline, lack of sleep, decrease in food intake, and the stress of the physical elements (e.g., weather, temperature, evening darkness). Although these may not cause psychopathology, they may predispose a soldier to seek psychological escape from his circumstances. To cope with these circumstances, soldiers must draw from their internal supplies of fortitude; however, these are limited. The insufficiency of supplies contributes to comrades dying, perceived threat of death or injury, and fear of being overrun by the enemy, and has been shown to directly relate to PTSD (Fontana & Rosenheck, 1999; Grossman, 1996).

Guilt, Horror, and Anger   Guilt is a psychological construct documented as frequent and severe in veterans with chronic PTSD (Beckham, Feldman, Kirby, Hertzberg, & Moore, 1997; Beckham et al., 1996). Exposure to war stressors and atrocities has been found to be significantly related to the severity of PTSD symptoms and longitudinal adjustment (Beckham, Feldman, & Kirby, 1998). Common to war are horrific sounds, smells, feelings, tastes, and sights that will be relived through PTSD symptoms. Soldiers hear the cries of the wounded and smell decaying, burning, and rotting flesh, in addition to blood and feces. Soldiers feel the ground shake and hold their comrades as they struggle to survive or take their last breath before they die. There is the taste of blood and salt from tears. Before their eyes are mutilated bodies, enemies a soldier feels he killed, and fellow soldiers he feels responsible for. An unbearable amount of guilt, horror, and responsibility is experienced. When faced with combat, soldiers are damned if they do and damned if they don't. If they resist killing the enemy, they have guilt for fallen comrades; if they kill the enemy, they have the remorse and shame of killing another human being. To deny the enemy's humanity seems impossible in close-range combat. There is no escaping one's responsibility and culpability in this situation. Many veterans report apologizing to the body after killing someone, as well as vomiting and crying as they are overwhelmed with guilt and shame (Grossman, 1996).

Anger is another construct that has impaired the longitudinal adjustment of veterans with PTSD. Anger reactivity in veterans may lead to impaired relationships with spouses and children, friends, and coworkers (Byrne & Riggs, 1996; Knight, Keane, Fairbank, Caddell, & Zimering, 1984). This further leads to social isolation and emotional control problems (Knight et al., 1984; van der Kolk, Boyd, Krystal, & Greenberg, 1984). Expression of anger has been correlated with frequency of symptoms (Laufer, Yager, Frey-Wouters, & Donnellan, 1981). In combat, anger may serve as a survival skill; however, outside of a war zone, it generally is maladaptive (Novaco & Chemtob, 2002).

Inoculation Seligman's studies of learning in dogs, as it relates to stress inoculation, helps to explain inoculation in military training. In Seligman's studies, dogs were placed in cages and randomly shocked; eventually, dogs gave up trying to escape the shocks by jumping and just resorted to inactivity and helplessness, even when given a way out of the cage. Other dogs were given escape options after only a few shocks, training them to resist apathy and remain hopeful for an eventual escape. In military training, soldiers are exposed to the interpersonal aggression and hostility of their trainers and superiors, with weekend passes as escape. Over time, there is a realization that they can overcome such interpersonal hostility physically and psychologically in training and on the battlefield. Such exposure to intense stress is used to inoculate against psychological trauma (Grossman, 1996).

CROSS-CULTURAL CONSIDERATIONS

PTSD continues to be recognized as a normal response when one is exposed to traumatic events, as is seen in many different countries, cultures, and societies (Foa et al., 2000). Although PTSD cuts across all cultures, races, religions, and ethnicities, we know that cultural influences impact how PTSD is manifested and interpreted (Ahmad & Mohamad, 1996; DiNicola, 1996). It is important to look at the cultural context of trauma and the ways in which the meaning assigned to the trauma is culturally specific. Culture and a sense of community can be considered a protective factor that is both practical and symbolic in nature. It provides individuals with identity and offers cultural defense mechanisms, including a support system of communal values, morals, lifestyles, identities, rituals, a common knowledge base, a security system, and a shared vision for the meaning of life among its people. These supports allow individuals and communities to reorganize themselves in the aftermath of traumatic events.

Bronfenbrenner (1994) suggests that PTSD is grounded in a person's interactions with society and culture. PTSD alters how individuals perceive themselves, their capabilities, others, and the world. The evaluation of oneself and the world is often rooted in one's cultural context. Thus, achieving the treatment goal of modifying pathological views of oneself and the world can be facilitated by considering co-occurring cultural processes that influence healing. One such consideration is the importance of spirituality. In some cultures, the notion of being able to control our own lives and destinies is controversial. Eastern religions typically do not support this idea; however, Hinduism and Islam propose that one must submit to the gods or Allah and in turn fate determines one's life. Currently, it is unclear how religion and spirituality influence how individuals and communities deal with traumatic events (deVries, 2007).

In addition to the implications for individuals, there may also be effects on entire communities, depending on the level and scale of the trauma. Natural disasters and war are examples of large-scale atrocities that attempt to destroy both the individuals' spirit and the basic structure of a community, culture, or nation. Individuals are dependent on their culture for support and healing. This dependence inflicts a deeper sense of loss and an additional trauma, including the loss of structure, predictability, and a sense of safety that was previously offered. The locus of control in individuals who are uprooted and relocated as a result of trauma is altered and increases confusion regarding a sense of belonging and negatively impacts one's view of the future. Cultural processes used for healing and fostering a sense of community, such as rituals and music, may also be distressing reminders of a former life that will never be recovered. For some, engaging in culturally specific activities may continue to reinforce an overwhelming sense of loss and hopelessness. A system (e.g., culture, community, nation) can regress to more primitive forms of being and operating. While this may offer hope in its throwback to simpler times, it may also offer denial and avoidance of pain and suffering (deVries, 2007).

CHALLENGES IN ASSESSMENT

While conducting the assessment sessions, several issues may arise that make this process difficult.

One common problem is noncompliance. Noncompliance is a barrier to both assessment and treatment. It may be an indication of various issues and obstacles and should be explored, with the client being mindful that avoidance is a symptom of PTSD. Discussions of noncompliance and the client's readiness to start treatment should be persistent, encouraging, and sensitive, never condemning or punitive. If clients have difficulty completing assessment sessions, there may be difficulty following through with the treatment program and homework assignments.

Another potential complication seen in assessment sessions is lack of objective criteria regarding symptom frequency and severity. Even with standardized measures, it is easier to count the number of nightmares than it is to objectively quantify feelings of shame and guilt.

For some clients, there may be the concern for secondary gain. For example, veterans receiving treatment through Veterans Affairs may be inclined to report symptoms as more severe and debilitating than they actually are if benefits are dependent on these indicators. As with other disorders and medical conditions, being identified as someone who is "sick" may afford certain benefits, such as limited responsibilities at home and at work, as well as offers of protection and nurturance from family members and friends, all of which reinforce this identity.

Another complication for survivors of sexual assault and other forms of interpersonal violence is that there may be a great deal of shame experienced by the victim. This may hinder their ability to fully report the details of their trauma. It is imperative for the client to feel that the therapist can be trusted and can handle the distress of the client. The clinician can foster this trust by presenting a nonjudgmental attitude, competence, confidence, and sensitivity.

Defining the target behavior for treatment may also be a difficult task when there are multiple severe and persistent symptoms. In order to assess progress in treatment, it is important to identify the symptoms that are most frequent and disturbing. Paying attention to the symptoms the client mentions first or most often, in addition to what is endorsed through the assessment measures, may assist identifying target behaviors to be monitored to assess treatment progress (Foa & Rothbaum, 1998). Once identified, it is essential to repeatedly assess these target symptoms throughout treatment (Foa & Rothbaum).

REFERENCES

Abueg, F. R., & Fairbank, J. A. (1992). Behavioral treatment of posttraumatic stress disorder and co-occurring substance abuse. In P. A. Saigh (Ed.), *Posttraumatic stress disorder: A behavioral approach to assessment and treatment* (pp. 111–146). Boston: Allyn & Bacon.

Ahmad, A., & Mohamad, K. (1996). The socioemotional development of orphans in orphanages and traditional foster care in Iraqi Kurdistan. *Child Abuse and Neglect, 20,* 1161–1173.

Bandura, A. (1977). *Social learning theory.* Englewood Cliffs, NJ: Prentice Hall.

Bandura, A. (1986). *Social foundations of thought and action: A social cognitive theory.* Englewood Cliffs, NJ: Prentice Hall.

Barkley, R. A., Edwards, G. H., & Robin, A. L. (1999). *Defiant teens: A clinician's manual for assessment and family intervention.* New York: Guilford Press.

Beck, A. T. (2005). *Anxiety disorders and phobias: A cognitive perspective.* Cambridge, MA: Basic Books.

Beckham, J. C., Feldman, M. E., & Kirby, A. C. (1998). Atrocities exposure in Vietnam combat veterans with chronic posttraumatic stress disorder: Relationship to combat exposure, symptom severity, guilt, and interpersonal violence. *Journal of Traumatic Stress, 11*(4), 777–785.

Beckham, J. C., Feldman, M. E., Kirby, A. C., Hertzberg, M. A., & Moore, S. D. (1997). Interpersonal violence and its correlates in Vietnam veterans with chronic post-traumatic stress disorder. *Journal of Clinical Psychology, 53*, 7–18.

Beckham, J. C., Roodman, A. A., Barefoot, J. C., Haney, T. L., Helms, M. J., Fairbank, J. A., et al. (1996). Interpersonal and self-reported hostility among combat veterans with and without posttraumatic stress disorder. *Journal of Traumatic Stress, 9*, 335–342.

Bernstein, E. M., & Putnam, F. W. (1986). Development, reliability, and validity of a dissociation scale. *Journal of Nervous Mental Disease, 174*, 727–735.

Blake, D. D., Weathers, F. W., Nagy, L. M., Kaloupek, D. G., Gusman, F. D., Charney, D. S., et al. (1995). The development of a clinician-administered PTSD scale. *Journal of Traumatic Stress, 8*, 75–90.

Boudewyns, P. A., & Hyer, L. (1990). Physiological response to combat memories and preliminary treatment outcome in Vietnam veterans PTSD patients treated with direct therapeutic exposure. *Behavior Therapy, 21*, 63–87.

Boudewyns, P. A., Hyer, L., Woods, M. G., Harrison, W. R., & McCranie, E. (1990). PTSD among Vietnam veterans: An early look at treatment outcome using direct therapeutic exposure. *Journal of Traumatic Stress, 3*, 359–368.

Bourne, E. J. (2005). *The anxiety and phobia workbook.* (4th ed). Oakland, CA: New Harbinger Publications.

Bowlby, J. (1984). Violence in the family as a disorder of the attachment and caregiving systems. *American Journal of Psychoanalysis, 44*, 9–27.

Breslau, N., & Davis, G. C. (1987). Posttraumatic stress disorder: The etiological specificity of wartime stressors. *American Journal of Psychiatry, 144*, 578–583.

Briere, J. (1995). *Trauma Symptom Inventory (TSI): Professional manual.* Odessa, FL: Psychological Assessment Resources.

Briere, J., & Runtz, M. (1989). The Trauma Symptom Checklist (TSC-3): Early data on a new scale. *Journal of Interpersonal Violence, 4*, 151–163.

Brom, D., Kleber, R. J., & Defares, P. B. (1989). Brief psychotherapy for posttraumatic stress disorder. *Journal of Consulting and Clinical Psychology, 57*, 607–612.

Bronfenbrenner, U. (1994). Nature–nurture reconceptualization in developmental perspective: A bioecological model. *Psychological Review, 10*(4), 568–586.

Burgess, A. W., & Holstrom, L. L. (1978). Recovery from rape and prior life stress. *Research in Nursing and Health, 1*, 165–174.

Burgess, A. W., & Holstrom, L. L. (1979). Adaptive strategies in recovery from rape. *American Journal of Psychiatry, 136*, 1278–1282.

Byrne, C. A., & Riggs, D. S. (1996). The cycle of trauma: Relationship aggression in male Vietnam veterans with symptoms of posttraumatic stress disorder. *Violence and Victims, 11*, 213–225.

Caruth, C. (Ed.). (1995). *Trauma and memory.* Baltimore: Johns Hopkins University Press.

Cole, P., & Putnam, F. W. (1992). Effect of incest on self and social functioning: A developmental psychopathology perspective. *Journal of Consulting and Clinical Psychology, 60*, 174–184.

Crittenden, P. M. (1994). Peering into the black box: An exploratory treatise on the development of the self in children. In D. Chichetti & S. L. Troth (Eds.), *Disorders and dysfunction of the self.*

Danieli, Y. (1984). Psychotherapists' participation in the conspiracy of silence about the Holocaust. *Psychoanalytic Psychology, 1*, 23–42.

Davidson, J. R. T., Book, S. W., Colket, J. T., Tupler, L. A., Roth, S., David, D., et al. (1997). Assessment of a new self-rating scale for posttraumatic stress disorder, *Psychological Medicine, 27*, 153–160.

Demitrack, M. A., Putnam, F. W., Brewerton, T. D., Brandt, H. A., & Gold, P. W. (1990). Relation of clinical variables to dissociative phenomena in eating disorders. *American Journal of Psychiatry, 147*, 1184–1188.

deVries, M. W. (2007). Trauma in cultural perspective. In B. A. van der Kolk, A. C. McFarlane, & L. W. Weisaeth (Eds.), *Traumatic stress: The effects of overwhelming experience on mind, body, and society.* New York: Guilford Press.

DiNicola, V. F. (1996). Ethnocentric aspects of PTSD and related disorders among children and adolescents. In A. J. Marsalla, M. J. Friedman, E. T. Gerrity, & R. M. Scurfield (Eds.), *Ethnocultural aspects of PTSD: Issues, research, and clinical applications* (pp. 389–414). Washington, DC: American Psychological Press.

Epstein, S. (1991). Impulse control and self-destructive behavior. In L. P. Lipsitt & L. L. Mitnick (Eds.), *Self-regulartory behavior and risk taking: Causes and consequences* (pp. 273–284). Norwood, NJ: Albex.

Feindler, E. L., & Ecton, R. B. (1986). *Adolescent anger control: Cognitive behavioral techniques.* New York: Pergamon Press.

Figley, C. R. (1995). *Compassion fatigue: Secondary traumatic stress disorders from treating the traumatized.* New York: Brunner/Mazel.

Finkelhor, D., & Browne, A. (1984). The traumatic impact of child sexual abuse: A conceptualization. *American Journal of Orthopsychiatry, 55*, 530–541.

First, M. B, Spitzer, R. L., Williams, J. B. W., & Gibbon, M. (1996). *Structured clinical interview for DSM-IV.* New York: New York State Psychiatric Institute, Biometrics Research.

Foa, E. B., Casman, L., Jaycox, L., & Perry, K. (1997). The validation of a self-report measure of posttraumatic stress disorder. *Psychological Assessment, 9*, 445–451.

Foa, E. B., Keane, T. M., & Friedman, M. J. (2000). Guidelines for treatment of PTSD. *Journal of Traumatic Stress, 13*, 539–555.

Foa, E. B., & Kozak, M. J. (1986). Emotional processing of fear: Exposure to corrective information. *Psychological Bulletin, 99*, 20–35.

Foa, E. B., & Meadows, E. A. (1997). Psychological treatments for post-traumatic stress disorder: A critical review. In J. Spence, J. M. Darley, & D. J. Foss (Eds.), *Annual review of psychology* (vol. *48*, pp. 449–480). Palo Alto, CA: Annual Reviews.

Foa, E. B., & Riggs, D. S. (1993). Post-traumatic stress disorder in rape victims. In J. Oldham, M. B. Riba, & A. Tasman (Eds.), *American Psychiatric Press review of psychiatry* (vol. *12*, pp. 273–303). Washington, DC: American Psychiatric Press.

Foa, E. B., Riggs, D. S., Dancu, C., & Rothbaum, B. (1993). Reliability and validity of a brief instrument for assessing post-traumatic stress disorder. *Journal of Traumatic Stress, 6*, 459–474.

Foa, E. B., & Rothbaum, B. O. (1998). *Treating the trauma of rape: Cognitive behavioral therapy for PTSD.* New York: Guilford Press.

Foa, E. B., & Rothbaum, B. O., & Molnar, C. (1995). Cognitive–behavioral therapy of post-traumatic stress disorder. In M. J. Friedman, D. S. Charney, & A. Y. Deutch (Eds.), *Neurobiological and clinical consequences of stress: From normal adaptation to post-traumatic stress disorder* (pp. 483–494). New York: Lippincott-Raven.

Foa, E. B., Rothbaum, B. O., Riggs, D., & Murdock, T. (1991). Treatment of post-traumatic stress disorder in rape victims: A comparison between cognitive behavioral procedures and counseling. *Journal of Consulting and Clinical Psychology, 59,* 715–723.

Foa, E. B., Steketee, G., & Rothbaum, B. O. (1989). Behavioral/cognitive conceptualization of post-traumatic stress disorder. *Behavior Therapy, 20,* 155–176.

Folsom, V. L., Krahn, D. D., Canum, K. K., Gold, L., & Silk, K. R. (1989). *Sex abuse: Role in eating disorder.* Paper presented at the 142nd Annual Meeting of the American Psychiatric Association, Washington, DC, as cited in van der Kolk, B. A. (2007). The complexity of adaptation to trauma: Self-regulation, stimulus discrimination, and characterological development. In B. A. van der Kolk, A. C. McFarlane, & L. W. Weisaeth (Eds.), *Traumatic stress: The effects of overwhelming experience on mind, body, and society.* New York: Guilford Press.

Fontana, A., & Rosenheck, R. (1999). A model of war zone stressors and post-traumatic stress disorder. *Journal of Traumatic Stress, 12*(1), 111–126.

Friedberg, R. D., & McClure, J. M. (2002). *Clinical practice of cognitive therapy with children and adolescents: The nuts and bolts.* New York: Guilford Press.

Friedman, M. (2006). *Post-traumatic and acute stress disorders: The latest assessment and treatment strategies* (4th ed). Kansas City, MO: Dean Psych Press.

Gelinas, D. J. (1983). The persistent negative effects of incest. *Psychiatry, 46,* 312–332.

Giarratano, L. (2004). *Clinical skills for managing PTSD.* Mascot, Australia: Talominbooks.

Goodman, L., Corcoran, C., Turner, K., Yuan, N., & Green, B. (1998). Assessing traumatic event exposure: General issues and preliminary findings for the Stressful Life Events Screening Questionnaire. *Journal of Traumatic Stress, 11,* 521–542.

Green, B. L. (1996). Trauma history questionnaire. In B. H. Stamm & E. M. Varra (Eds.), *Measurement of stress, trauma, and adaptation* (pp. 366–368). Lutherville, MD: Sidran Press.

Grossman, D. (1996). *On killing.* Cambridge, MA: Little, Brown.

Groth, A. N. (1979). Sexual trauma in the life histories of sex offenders. *Victimology, 4,* 6–10.

Hammarberg, M. (1992). Penn Inventory for Posttraumatic Stress Disorder: Psychometric properties. *Psychological Assessment, 4,* 67–76.

Harber, K. D., & Pennebaker, J. W. (1992). Overcoming traumatic memories. In S. A. Christianson (Ed.), *The handbook of emotion and memory: Research and theory* (pp. 359–386). Hillsdale, NJ: Erlbaum.

Herman, J. (1992). *Trauma and recovery.* New York: Basic Books.

Herman, J. L. (1992). Complex PTSD: A syndrome in survivors of prolonged and repeated trauma. *Journal of Traumatic Stress, 5,* 377–391.

Hernandez, J. T., & DiClemente, R. J. (1992). Emotional and behavioral correlates of sexual abuse among adolescents: Is there a difference according to gender? *Journal of Adolescent Health, 13,* 658–662.

Herzog, D. B, Staley, J. E., Carmody, S., Robbins, W. M., & van der Kolk, B. A. (1993). Childhood sexual abuse in anorexia nervosa: A pilot study. *Journal of the American Academy of Child and Adolescent Psychiatry, 32,* 962–966.

Horowitz, M. J. (1986). *Stress response syndromes* (2nd ed.). Northvale, NJ: Jason Aronson.

Janoff-Bulman, R. (1992). *Shattered assumptions: Towards a new psychology of trauma.* New York: Free Press.

Jellinek, J. M., & Williams, T. (1987). Post-traumatic stress disorder and substance abuse: Treatment problems, strategies, and recommendations. In T. Williams (Ed.), *Post-traumatic stress disorder: A handbook for clinicians* (pp. 103–117). Cincinnati, OH: Disabled American Veterans.

Keane, T. M., Gerardi, R. J., Lyons, J. A., & Wolfe, J. (1988). The interrelationship of substance abuse and posttraumatic stress disorder: Epidemiological and clinical considerations. In M. Galanter (Ed.), *Recent developments in alcoholism* (vol. 6, pp. 27–48). New York: Plenum Press.

Kessler, R. C., Sonnega, A., Bromet, E., Hughes, M., & Nelson, C. B. (1995). Posttraumatic stress disorder in the National Comorbidity Survey. *Archives of General Psychiatry, 52,* 1048–1060.

Khantzian, E. J. (1985). The self-medication hypothesis of addictive disorders: Focus on heroine and cocaine dependence. *American Journal of Psychiatry, 142,* 1259–1264.

Kilpatrick, D., Resnick, H., & Freedy, J. (1991). *The Potential Stressful Events Interview.* Unpublished instrument, Medical University of South Carolina, Charleston, SC.

King, D. W., King, L. A., Foy, D. W., Gudanowski, D. M., & Vreven, D. L. (1995). Alternative representations of war zone stressors: Relationships to posttraumatic stress disorder in male and female Vietnam veterans. *Journal of Abnormal Psychology, 104,* 184–196.

Knight, J. A., Keane, T. M., Fairbank, J. A., Caddel, J. M., & Zimering, R. T. (1984). Empirical validation of DSM-III criteria for posttraumatic stress disorder. Paper presented at the 18th Annual Meeting of the Association for the Advancement of Behavior Therapy, Philadelphia, as cited in Novaco, R. W., & Chemtob, C. M. Anger and combat-related posttraumatic stress disorder. *Journal of Traumatic Stress, 15,* 123–132.

Krinsley, K. E., & Weathers, F. W. (1995). The assessment of trauma in adults. *PTSD Research Quarterly, 6,* 1–6.

Kroll, J., Habenicht, M., & McKenzie, R. (1989). Depression and posttraumatic stress disorder among Southeast Asian refugees. *American Journal of Psychiatry, 146,* 1592–1597.

Kubany, E., Haynes, S., Leisen, M., Owens, J., Kaplan, A., Watson, S., et al. (2000). Development and preliminary validation of a brief broad-spectrum measure of trauma exposure: The Traumatic Life Events Questionnaire. *Psychological Assessment, 12,* 210–224.

Lang, P. J. (1977). Imagery in therapy: An information processing analysis of fear. *Behavior Therapy, 8,* 862–886.

Laufer, K. S., Yager, T., Frey-Wouters, E., & Donnellan, J. (1981). *Legacies of Vietnam: Comparative adjustment of veterans and their peers: vol. 3. Post-war trauma: Social and psychological problems of Vietnam veterans in the aftermath of the Vietnam War.* New York: Center for Policy Research.

Lee, K. A., Vaillant, G. E., Torrey, W. C., & Elder, G. H. (1995). A 50-year prospective study of the psychological sequelae of World War II combat. *American Journal of Psychiatry, 152*(4), 516–522.

Lisak, D. (1993). Men as victims: Challenging cultural myths. *Journal of Traumatic Stress, 6,* 577–580.

Litz, B. T., & Keane, T. M. (1989). Information processing in anxiety disorders: Application to the understanding of posttraumatic stress disorder. *Clinical Psychology Review, 9,* 243–257.

Lyons, J., & Keane, T. (1992). Keane PTSD Scale: MMPI and MMPI-2 update. *Journal of Traumatic Stress, 5,* 111–117.

McCann, L., & Pearlman, A. (1990). Vicarious traumatization: A framework for understanding the psychological effects of working with victims. *Journal of Traumatic Stress, 3,* 131–149.

McFarlane, A. C. (1988). Recent life events and psychiatric disorder in children: The interaction with preceding extreme adversity. *Journal of Clinical Psychiatry, 29*(5), 677–690.

McFarlane, A. C., & van der Kolk, B. A. (2007). Conclusions and future directions. In B. A. van der Kolk, A. C. McFarlane, & L. W. Weisaeth (Eds.), *Traumatic stress: The effects of overwhelming experience on mind, body, and society.* New York: Guilford Press.

Meichenbaum, D. (1974). *Cognitive behavior modification.* Morristown, NJ: General Learning Press.

Mowrer, O. A. (1960). *Learning theory and behavior.* New York: Wiley.

Newman, E., Kaloupek, D. G., & Keane, T. M. (2007). Assessment of posttraumatic stress disorder in clinical and research settings. In B. A. van der Kolk, A. C. McFarlane, & L. W. Weisaeth (Eds.), *Traumatic stress: The effects of overwhelming experience on mind, body, and society.* New York: Guilford Press.

Norris, F. (1992). Epidemiology of trauma: Frequency and impact of different potentially traumatic events on different demographic groups. *Journal of Consulting and Clinical Psychology, 60,* 409–418.

Norris, F., & Perilla, J. (1996). Reliability, validity, and cross-language stability of the Revised Civilian Mississippi Scale for PTSD. *Journal of Traumatic Stress, 9,* 285–298.

Novaco, R. W., & Chemtob, C. M. (2002). Anger and combat-related posttraumatic stress disorder. *Journal of Traumatic Stress, 15*(2), 123–132.

Noyes, R., & Kletti, R. (1977). Depersonalization in response to life threatening danger. *Comprehensive Psychiatry, 18,* 375–384.

Pattison, E. M., & Kahan, J. (1983). The deliberate self-harm syndrome. *American Journal of Psychiatry, 140,* 867–872.

Piaget, J. (1954). *The construction of reality in the child*. New York: Basic Books.

Pope, H. G., Jr., & Hudson, J. I. (1983). Is childhood sexual abuse a risk factor for bulimia nervosa? *American Journal of Psychiatry, 150*(2), 357–358.

Rachman, S. (1980). Emotional processing. *Behavior Research and Therapy, 18*, 51–60.

Reiker, P. P., & Carmen, E. H. (1986). The victim-to-patient process: The disconfirmation and transformation of abuse. *American Journal of Orthopsychiatry, 56*, 360–370.

Resnick, H. S., Kilpatrick, D. G., Dansky, B. S., Saunders, B. E., & Best, C. L. (1993). Prevalence of civilian trauma and posttraumatic stress disorder in representative national sample of women. *Journal of Consulting and Clinical Psychology, 61*(6), 984–991.

Robins, L. M., Cottler, L., & Bucholz, K. (1995). *Diagnostic Interview Schedule for DSM-IV*. St. Louis: Washington University.

Rothbaum, B. O., & Foa, E. B. (2007). Cognitive–behavioral therapy for posttraumatic stress disorder. In B. A. van der Kolk, A. C. McFarlane, & L. W. Weisaeth (Eds.), *Traumatic stress: The effects of overwhelming experience on mind, body, and society*. New York: Guilford Press.

Russell, D. (1986). *The secret trauma*. New York: Basic Books.

Saakvitne, K. W., & Pearlman, L. A. (1996). *Transforming the pain*. New York: Norton.

Saunders, B., Arata, C., & Kilpatrick, D. (1990). Development of a crime-related posttraumatic stress disorder scale for women with the Symptom Checklist–90 Revised. *Journal of Traumatic Stress, 3*, 439–448.

Saxe, G. N., Chinman, G., Berkowitz, R., Hall, K., Lieberg, G., Schwartz, J., et al. (1994). Somatization in patients with dissociative disorders. *American Journal of Psychiatry, 151*, 1329–1335.

Saxe, G. N., van der Kolk, B. A., Hall, K., Schwartz, J., Chinman, G., Hall, M. D., et al. (1993). Dissociative disorders in psychiatric inpatients. *American Journal of Psychiatry, 150*(7), 1037–1042.

Schlenger, W., & Kulka, R. A (1989). *PTSD scale development for the MMPI-2*. Research Triangle Park, NC: Research Triangle Institute.

Seghorn, T. K., Boucher, R. J., & Prentky, R. A. (1987). Childhood sexual abuse in the lives of sexually aggressive offenders. *Journal of the American Academy of Child and Adolescent Psychiatry, 26*, 262–267.

Simpson, C. A., & Porter, G. L. (1981). Self-mutilation in children and adolescents. *Bulletin of the Meninger Clinic, 45*(5), 428–438.

Taylor, S. (2006). *Clinician's guide to PTSD: A cognitive–behavioral approach*. New York: Guilford Press.

Thompson, J. A., Charlton, P. F. C., Kerry, R., Lee, D., & Turner, S. W. (1995). An open trial of exposure therapy based on deconditioning for post-traumatic stress disorder. *British Journal of Clinical Psychology, 34*, 407–416.

Ursano, R., Fullerton, C., Kao, T., & Bhartiya, V. (1995). Longitudinal assessment of posttraumatic stress disorder and depression following exposure to traumatic death. *Journal of Nervous and Mental Disease, 183*, 36–42.

van der Hart, O., Steele, K., Boon, S., & Brown, P. (1993). The treatment of traumatic memories: Synthesis, realization, and integration. *Dissociation, 6*, 162–180.

van der Kolk, B. A. (1987). *Psychological trauma*. Washington, DC: American Psychiatric Press.

van der Kolk, B. A. (1988). The trauma spectrum: The interaction of biological and social events in the genesis of the trauma response. *Journal of Traumatic Stress, 1,* 273–290.

van der Kolk, B. A. (1989). The compulsion to repeat trauma: Revictimization, attachment and masochism. *Psychiatric Clinics of North America, 12,* 389–411.

van der Kolk, B. A. (2007). The complexity of adaptation to trauma: Self-regulation, stimulus discrimination, and characterological development. In B. A. van der Kolk, A. C. McFarlane, & L. W. Weisaeth (Eds.), *Traumatic stress: The effects of overwhelming experience on mind, body, and society*. New York: Guilford Press.

van der Kolk, B. A. (2007). The body keeps the score: Approaches to the psychobiology of posttraumatic stress disorder. In B. A. van der Kolk, A. C. McFarlane, & L. W. Weisaeth (Eds.), *Traumatic stress: The effects of overwhelming experience on mind, body, and society*. New York: Guilford Press.

van der Kolk, B. A., Boyd, H., Krystal, J., & Greenberg, M. (1984). Post-traumatic stress disorder as a biologically based disorder: Implications of the animal model of inescapable shock. In B. A. van der Kolk (Ed.), *Post-traumatic stress disorder: Psychological and biological sequela*. Washington, DC: American Psychiatric Press.

van der Kolk, B. A., & Fisler, R. (1994). Childhood abuse and neglect and loss of self-regulation. *Bulletin of the Menninger Clinic, 58,* 145–168.

van der Kolk, B. A., & McFarlane, A. C. (2007). The black hole of trauma. In B. A. van der Kolk, A. C. McFarlane, & L. W. Weisaeth (Eds.), *Traumatic stress: The effects of overwhelming experience on mind, body, and society*. New York: Guilford Press.

van der Kolk, B. A., McFarlane, A. C., & Weisaeth, L. (2007). *Traumatic stress: The effects of overwhelming experience on mind, body, and society*. New York: Guilford Press.

van der Kolk, B. A., Perry, C., & Herman, J. L. (1991). Childhood origins of self-destructive behavior. *American Journal of Psychiatry, 148,* 1665–1671.

van der Kolk, B. A., Roth, S., Pelcovitz, D., & Mandel, F. (1993). *Complex PTSD: Results of the PTSD field trials for DSM-IV*. Washington, DC: American Psychiatric Press.

van der Kolk, B. A., van der Hart, O., & Marmar, C. R. (2007). Dissociation and information processing in posttraumatic stress disorder. In B. A. van der Kolk, A. C. McFarlane, & L. W. Weisaeth (Eds.), *Traumatic stress: The effects of overwhelming experience on mind, body, and society*. New York: Guilford Press.

Vrana, S., & Lauterbach, D. (1994). Prevalence of traumatic events post-traumatic psychological symptoms in a nonclinical sample of college students. *Journal of Traumatic Stress, 7,* 289–302.

Watson, C., Juba, M., Manifold, V., Kucal, T., & Anderson, P. (1991). The PTSD Interview: Rationale, description, reliability and concurrent validity of a DSM-III based technique. *Journal of Clinical Psychology, 47,* 179–185.

Weathers, F. W., Litz, B. T., Herman, D. S., Huska, J. A., & Keane, T. M. (1995). *PTSD Checklist (PCL)*. Boston: National Center for PTSD.

Weiss, D. S., & Marmar, C. R. (1997). The Impact of Event Scale–Revised. In J. P. Wilson & T. M. Keane (Eds.), *Assessing psychological trauma and PTSD* (pp. 399–411). London: Guilford Press.

Wilson, J., & Lindy, J. (1994). *Countertransference in the treatment of PTSD.* New York: Guilford Press.

Wolfe, J., Kimerling, R., Brown, P. J., Chrestman, K. R., & Levin, K. (1996). Psychometric review of the Life Stressor Checklist-Revised. In B. H. Stamm & E. M. Varra (Eds.), *Measurement of stress, trauma, and adaptation* (pp. 198–201). Lutherville, MD: Sidran Press.

World Health Organization (1997). *Composite International Diagnostic Interview (CIDI),* Version 2.1, Geneva, World Health Organization.

Zayfert, C., & Becker, C. B. (2007). *Cognitive–behavioral therapy for PTSD.* New York: Guilford Press.

ADDITIONAL READINGS

Beck, A. T., Emery, G., & Greenberg, R. (2005). *Anxiety disorders and phobias: A cognitive perspective.* Cambridge, MA: Basic Books.

Beck, J. S. (1995). *Cognitive therapy: Basics and beyond.* New York: Guilford Press.

Bourne, E. J. (2005). *The anxiety and phobia workbook* (4th ed). Oakland, CA: New Harbinger.

Brilliant, A. (2007). Ashleigh Brilliant, POT-SHOTS. www.brilliant-thoughts.com.

Davidson, J. R. T., & Foa, E. B. (1993). *Post traumatic stress disorder: DSM-IV and beyond.* Washington, DC: American Psychiatric Press.

Figley, C. R. (1995). *Compassion fatigue: Secondary traumatic stress disorders from treating the traumatized.* New York: Brunner/Mazel.

Foa, E. B., & Rothbaum, B. O. (1998). *Treating the trauma of rape: Cognitive behavioral therapy for PTSD.* New York: Guilford Press.

Friedman, M. (2006). *Post-traumatic and acute stress disorders: The latest assessment and treatment strategies* (4th ed). Kansas City, MO: Dean Psych Press.

Grossman, D. (1996). *On killing.* Cambridge, MA: Little, Brown.

Herman, J. (1992). *Trauma and recovery.* New York: Basic Books.

Ioannides, P. (1976). *Cyprus dies.* Nicosia, Cyprus: CH. Avdelopoulos, & A. Coutas.

Lew, M. (2004). *Victims no longer.* New York: HarperCollins.

National Center for PTSD web site, www.ncptsd.va.gov.

Schiraldi, G. R. (2000). *The post-traumatic stress disorder sourcebook: A guide to healing, recovery, and growth.* New York: McGraw-Hill.

van der Kolk, B. A. (1987). *Psychological trauma.* Washington, DC: American Psychiatric Press.

van der Kolk, B. A., McFarlane, A. C., and Weisaeth, L. (2007). *Traumatic stress: The effects of overwhelming experience on mind, body, and society.* New York: Guilford Press.

Wilson, J., & Lindy, J. (1994). *Countertransference in the treatment of PTSD.* New York: Guilford Press.

Young, J. E., Klosko, J. S., & Weishaar, M. E. (2003). *Schema therapy: A practitioner's guide.* New York: Guilford Press.

HANDOUTS

The handouts in this section can be reproduced and given to your clients for the purpose of psychoeducation.

Handout 2-1 Common Reactions to Trauma

Emotional Reactions

Fear
Shock
Grief
Outbursts of anger
Irritability
Helplessness
Hopelessness
Guilt
Shame
Resentment
Emotional numbing
Depression
Anxiety
Detachment
Loss of interest

Cognitive Reactions

Repetitive thoughts
Disorientation
Confusion
Difficulty concentrating
Memory loss
Self-blame
Unwanted memories
Indecisiveness
Dissociation
Intrusive recollections of the event
Nightmares
Flashbacks

Physical Reactions

Tension
Headaches

(continued)

Fatigue
Racing pulse
Difficulty falling and staying asleep
Startle easily
Edginess
Change in appetite
Nausea
Panic attacks
Severe agitation
Avoidance behaviors

Reactions Impacting Interpersonal Relationships

Withdrawal
Distrust
Isolation
Change in sex drive
Being judgmental and overcontrolling
Feelings of rejection and abandonment
Avoidance
Intense grief reactions
Estrangement

Handout 2-2 Typically Avoided Situations

Sexual or physical contact, affection with significant others
Standing close to other people
Talking about the trauma
Someone coming up to you from behind
Reading the newspaper, watching television, or listening to the radio
Seeing images or hearing names associated with the traumatic event
Being alone at home
Being alone at night
Walking down the street alone
Going out after dark
Being in a crowd of people
Sleeping with the lights off
Sleeping with the bedroom door unlocked
Sleeping with the windows open or unlocked
Sleeping alone

Getting into a car at night
Walking through a parking lot
Being in a car at a red light or stop sign
Using public transportation
Passing the building or location of the trauma event
Being around men or strangers
Being far from the door or exit of a room

Handout 2-3 Understanding Trauma and Its Impact

INTRODUCTION: WHAT IS TRAUMA?

Traumatizing events include assault, torture, rape, war, military combat, incarceration in a death camp, natural disasters, industrial and automobile accidents, and exposure to violence. Most people will be exposed to catastrophic stress in their lifetime, and most of them will recover on their own from the psychological impact of trauma. However, some will develop posttraumatic stress disorder (PTSD). PTSD is a normal response after exposure to a traumatic event and is seen in many different countries, cultures, and societies. While a natural ability to heal ourselves after trauma may be true for many of us, a significant number of people exposed to a traumatic event develop severe and persistent symptoms that dissipate only when mental health treatment is provided.

COMMON REACTIONS TO TRAUMA

After experiencing a traumatic event, it is normal to experience emotional, cognitive, physical, and interpersonal reactions for several days or weeks. These reactions will vary from person to person. Emotional reactions experienced most often include feelings of fear, shock, grief, anger, irritability, helplessness, hopelessness, guilt, shame, resentment, and numbing. Cognitive reactions may include disorientation, confusion, difficulty concentrating, memory loss, self-blame, unwanted memories, and indecisiveness. Often, these reactions are accompanied by tension, headaches, fatigue, a racing pulse, change in sleeping patterns, startle reactions, edginess, change in appetite, and nausea. For people with PTSD, trauma reminders (such as noises, thoughts, or images) can induce physiological responses and other symptoms.

Interpersonal relationships may be impacted during the immediate aftermath of a traumatic event. For example, it is common to experience

(continued)

withdrawal, distrust, isolation, change in sex drive, and feelings of rejection and abandonment. While these are normal reactions and recovery should be expected, it is often difficult to distinguish between those who will recover on their own and those who will not. In some cases, clinical symptoms of a higher intensity will emerge, including panic attacks, severe agitation, intense grief reactions, depression, anxiety, and the symptoms described below.

Reexperiencing Symptoms

The persistent thoughts, feelings, and behaviors related to the traumatic event may cause psychological distress and abnormal physiological reactions. This unwanted reexperiencing can be so powerful that it does not allow the individual to be fully present in the moment, but rather distracted and distressed by these recollections. It may feel as if the trauma is occurring all over again. Traumatic nightmares and daytime flashbacks can produce feelings of terror, fear, and panic. People with PTSD may be exposed to reminders of the trauma as they go about their daily lives. These trauma-related stimuli may evoke a disconnection with the present. People may feel and think that they have been transported back in time to the traumatic event. This dissociation from the present, paired with a PTSD flashback that simulates the traumatic event, can cause great distress and despair. Some individuals behave as if they are actually experiencing the trauma again, in real time. They may enter a brief psychotic state or acute dissociation, in which they scream in terror, start to panic, and run as if they are once again fighting for their life.

Avoidant and Numbing Symptoms

In an effort to avoid unwanted distress of reexperiencing trauma, PTSD sufferers respond through cognitive, emotional, and behavioral mechanisms, including avoidant and numbing symptoms. Avoidant symptoms, common to anxiety disorders, include attempts to avoid people, places, circumstances, thoughts, and feelings that are reminders of the original trauma. At times, anxiety may seem as if it comes "out of the blue," which offers support for avoidant behaviors. Additionally, it may not be clear what someone is anxious about. Although it may be vague and difficult to specify, it can affect the entire body. On a psychological level, anxiety creates uneasiness and apprehension. Physiologically, it impacts heart rate, muscle tension, sweating, and so on. Behaviorally, it may hinder one's ability to deal with everyday situations. Treating anxiety requires interventions on all three levels—psychological, physiological, and behavioral. Some people with PTSD also experience psychogenic amnesia. For psychological rather than neurological reasons, this is the inability to recall memories related to the trauma. Numbing symptoms are psychological strategies or coping mechanisms used to anesthetize oneself against the distress evoked by reexperiencing symptoms. With numbing, there is a suppression of both positive and negative emotions, leaving the individual devoid of feelings. Psychic numbing is an attempt to block out emotions that are difficult to tolerate and may even seem unbearable.

Hyperarousal Symptoms

Hyperarousal symptoms include difficulty in focusing, irritability, insomnia, and exaggerated startle reactions to unexpected sounds and movements. Hypervigilance, a common feature of hyperarousal, is protective behavior and surveillance paired with a preoccupation for personal safety. Upon entering a room, for example, people experiencing hypervigilance may scan the area in an attempt to quickly identify if this space is safe or not. They may pay particular attention to potentially threatening people, the overall atmosphere of the room, the location of exits, and any signs that suggests this is or is not a safe space. Hypervigilance can hinder one's ability to complete tasks of daily living and get through the day successfully.

CHAPTER 3

Cognitive Restructuring

JOANNE L. DAVIS, ELANA NEWMAN, AND KRISTI E. PRUIKSMA

INTRODUCTION

Cognitive restructuring (CR), the identification and reworking of non-adaptive thoughts, is a major component of cognitive therapy. Cognitive approaches are utilized in the evidence-based treatment of numerous psychological conditions, including posttraumatic stress disorder (PTSD). CR and exposure techniques are considered the key components of cognitive behavioral therapy (CBT) as applied to individuals with trauma-related problems such as PTSD (e.g., Moore, Zoellner, & Bittinger, 2004). Current dismantling studies examining the relative contributions of each component reveal that neither component enhances the other (Moore et al.; Taylor, 2006), although most efficacious evidence-based treatments employ both techniques. Practically speaking, most exposure techniques involve small amounts of CR, and most CR involves small amounts of exposure. However, the optimal integration remains a question for empirical study (Moore et al.; Taylor). Given the documented usefulness of CR and the focus in chapter 2 on exposure techniques, this chapter provides a step-by-step approach to utilizing a CR approach with trauma-exposed individuals.

In general, CR refers to the process of identifying unhelpful or maladaptive thoughts, evaluating such thoughts, and identifying adaptive flexible alternative thoughts. The concept that our beliefs determine our emotional and behavioral consequences above and beyond external experiences has a long history. Indeed, the Greek philosopher Epictetus is often cited as saying, "People are disturbed not by things, but by the views which they take of them." Using this philosophical approach, several theoreticians have promoted similar approaches to cognitive therapy in general and CR in particular. Although many aspects of the approaches are similar, there are some distinctions among the various theorists. A comprehensive review of the different approaches is beyond the scope of this chapter; instead, we describe two major theoreticians who developed CR and the key differences in their approaches. Then, using a general approach to cognitive therapy, borrowing from these theorists' ideas and others, we provide a general step-by-step approach to CR that has been developed specific to trauma populations. Throughout the chapter, we integrate theory, evidence, and practical advice and provide case examples.

The major theorists typically associated with the CR technique are Albert Ellis and Aaron Beck. Initially, CR emerged from Ellis's Rational Emotive Behavior Therapy, in which he focused on 12 irrational beliefs that individuals commonly held that clients needed to learn to confront and dispute (Ellis & Dryden, 1997). In the Ellis version of CR, the overall goal of intervention was to directly confront and alter those core beliefs that are hypothesized to be responsible for maintenance of disorders. Aaron Beck, focusing at first on depression (Beck, Rush, Shaw, & Emery, 1979), theorized that systematic distortions caused and maintained depression. Beck's technique was similar to Ellis's, although his process focused on leading clients to restructure their own thoughts rather than directly confront clients' thoughts. These initial cognitive conceptualizations did not specifically address PTSD or other posttrauma reactions. Several authors have since expanded cognitive theory to explain responses to traumatic events.

COGNITIVE THEORY AND COGNITIVE RESTRUCTURING AS APPLIED TO PTSD

Within cognitive behavioral theories of PTSD, trauma-related thoughts are often conceptualized as a form of a conditioned response. The basic behavioral models of PTSD propose that salient stimuli or cues present during and after the traumatic event are associated with fear-inducing trauma stimuli through classical conditioning, which then may generalize to other stimuli over time (e.g., Becker, Skinner, Abel, Axelrod, & Cichon, 1984; Foa & Kozak, 1986; Litz & Keane, 1989; Mowrer, 1960). For example, the song playing in the car at the time of an automobile crash becomes associated with the fear and arousal experienced at that time. Over time, all music of that genre becomes conditioned with fear. Then, operant conditioning maintains the fear and anxiety response during which avoidance behaviors, emotional numbing, and other behaviors are reinforced. In the example of a motor vehicle accident, avoidance of driving and music reduce anxiety and are then reinforced. Cognitive theorists augmented behavioral models of PTSD by including an emphasis on the ways in which thoughts and cognitive appraisals of the situation could be learned and then reinforce other maladaptive reactions to trauma. For example, thoughts can be conditioned. In the case example of the car accident, the driver was listening to the music and thinking about how happy he was about a current intimate partner at the time of the accident. Now every time the driver thinks about relationship happiness, he becomes uneasy. Cognitive behavioral therapists would theorize that the thought itself has become associated with the fear and arousal; then operant conditioning could lead to avoidance of thoughts related to relationships or interpersonal avoidance. Similarly, cognitive appraisals of the accident could lead to problems. Perhaps the driver blames himself for being distracted by the music as the reason for the accident so that self-blame creates or amplifies problems. In fact, all thoughts about responsibility might become generalized to elicit fear and arousal.

Several theorists have elaborated upon the role of trauma-related thoughts within this framework. Foa and colleagues (Foa & Kozak, 1986; Foa & Rothbaum, 1998; Foa, Steketee, & Rothbaum, 1989) applied Lang's (1979) bioinformational theory of emotion to trauma responses. Lang conceptualized fear as a "cognitive structure that serves as a program for escaping danger" (Foa & Rothbaum, p. 74). This fear structure is conceived as a network of associations in the brain that includes information about the feared event (and stimuli associated with it), the person's responses to the event (including behavioral, verbal, and physiological), and the meaning of the event and responses to the event. After trauma exposure, the network links trauma memory in new patterns of associations that may or may not accurately represent fear and danger. Nonpathological fear structures would link true dangerous elements to fear. For example, a victim of child physical abuse may associate her parents with danger, particularly when her parents have been drinking. This individual will respond to her parents with fear, but will not respond similarly to other adults. Pathological fear structures develop when nonthreatening stimuli become associated with fear and interpretations of danger. For example, risk of injury may be associated with fauna present in a conflict zone for a soldier, danger may be linked to a non-dangerous smell (e.g., cologne of a perpetrator), or feelings of incompetency may be linked to the color of surroundings where a person was assaulted. Given the extensive network of associations, many false alarms may result in response to various emotional, behavioral, physiological, and cognitive stimuli. Foa and colleagues posit that cognitive therapy needs to modify the fear structure so that the connections between elements are reduced and corrective information is learned, thus reducing or changing the problematic rigid content.

Ehlers and Clark's (2000) cognitive model of PTSD emphasizes slightly different components. Although they also rely on learning theory and network theory, they accentuate the linkage among memories and thoughts. Ehlers and Clark believe that it is the original and ongoing problematic appraisals of the trauma and the immediate and long-term effects of trauma as currently threatening that initiate and maintain PTSD. For example, it is not the intrusive symptoms of PTSD, but the labeling of such intrusive symptoms early on as life-threatening, which maintains the condition we know as PTSD. Ehlers and Clark also believe that the links between the trauma memory and autobiographical memory create problems of biased recall, overestimation of threat, and/or a nonadaptive autobiographical sense of oneself. These appraisals, in turn, are associated with dysfunctional behaviors and strategies.

Finally, Brewin, Dalgleish, and Joseph's (1996) cognitive model of PTSD elaborates on Foa and colleagues' ideas about fear networks by suggesting that there are two types of memories: (1) verbally accessible memories (VAMs) that can readily be retrieved and modified where meaningful narrative information is stored; and (2) situationally accessible memories (SAMs), where fragmented sensory information is stored. They argue that SAMs need to be integrated into VAMs by first using prolonged exposure and then CR.

While the mechanisms emphasized in each of these theories differ, all theories highlight that individuals with PTSD experience new associations among trauma- and non-trauma-related emotions, behaviors, physiological reactions, and cognitions. Trauma-related problems in cognitive appraisals and overaccessibility of negative emotions emerge from the new pattern of misaligned associations. Theorists generally agree that realistic flexible cognitions need to be created by strengthening or weakening different connections between beliefs, feelings, and memories.

With respect to the content of trauma-related cognitions, theorists basically agree about the content of problematic thoughts, although they differ in how they organize these types of thoughts. For example, Resick and Schnicke (1993) focus on five of the seven themes that McCann and Pearlman (1990) identified as problematic for trauma survivors: safety, trust, power, esteem and intimacy. Other cognitive therapists emphasize the three beliefs that Janoff-Bulman and Frieze (1983) noted were affected by experiencing a traumatic event: "1) the belief in personal invulnerability; 2) the perception of the world as meaningful and comprehensible; 3) the view of ourselves in a positive light" (p. 3). Epstein (1991) identified four core beliefs thought to be affected by trauma: the world is benign, the world is meaningful, the self is worthy, and people are trustworthy. Roth and colleagues (Roth & Lebowitz, 1988; Roth & Newman, 1991) divide the beliefs into emotional and cognitive themes that incorporate these ideas but include concerns about loss, legitimacy, influence of culture, alienation, and shame. Despite these conceptual differences regarding the categorization of thoughts, there is relatively common agreement about the phenomenology of these trauma-related nonadaptive thoughts.

In summary, CR is a core component of evidence-based, trauma-focused, cognitive and cognitive behavioral treatments. However, the relative emphasis, particular techniques employed, and degree of structure vary across interventions. In fact, much debate and research is now assessing to what degree CR is the essential ingredient as opposed to exposure for trauma-focused cognitive behavioral treatment with varying results by sample, acuteness of symptoms, and sample type (e.g., Resick et al., 2008; Bryant et al., 2008).

INDICATIONS AND CONTRAINDICATIONS

As with any therapeutic approach, CR is not likely to work the same for all clients. Increasingly, research has focused on identifying which clients with what particular problems may do well with various approaches to treating trauma-related problems. The following section reviews the relevant issues and empirical findings regarding indications and contraindications for a CR approach.

Traumatic events can affect individuals in a variety of ways. Although the majority of individuals who experience a traumatic event do not suffer from long-term problems (Bonnano, 2005), a minority may suffer any combination of problems including, but not limited to, acute stress disorder, PTSD, anxiety, depression, dissociative reactions, interpersonal problems, and sleep disorders (Foa & Rothbaum, 1998; Zayfert & Becker, 2007). Therefore, a thorough assessment to determine the nature and severity of primary problems and co-morbid issues is indicated (Foa & Rothbaum; Resick & Schnicke, 1993).

CONTRAINDICATIONS

For any therapeutic treatment, safety is of primary concern. For individuals presenting with trauma-related problems, the following specific issues should be assessed: suicidal, parasuicidal, and homicidal thoughts and behaviors; comorbid substance abuse and dependence (Foa & Rothbaum, 1998; Resick & Schnicke, 1996; Taylor, 2006); and continued risk for assault, such as in the case of a victim living in a domestic violence situation (Taylor). If these problems are of sufficient severity that the client needs to focus all of his/her resources on them, cognitive restructuring for trauma-related problems should not be initially implemented. Instead, these problems may require immediate intervention first. For others, these issues may not exclude the use of CR; rather, these issues may need to be addressed prior to, or in conjunction with, trauma treatment.

Matthews and Litwack (1995) suggest that CR may not be appropriate for clients demonstrating psychosis or mental deficits (e.g., autism, mental retardation), or who are in extreme emotional states (e.g., manic). They also argue that CR requires a degree of cognitive ability to think about one's thoughts and engage in logical problem solving. They state that CR "is more appropriate with clients who are grounded in reality, are verbal, possess an adequate memory, and are intellectually competent" (p. 42). CR requires insight into thoughts, feelings, behaviors, and interactions with others. Also, clients need to be open to taking personal responsibility. Clients most likely to benefit from CR also exhibit a degree of motivation, commitment, and self-discipline to engage in therapy, complete homework assignments, and experiment with the cognitive techniques learned in therapy. Therefore, clients who are unable to demonstrate these abilities may not benefit from CR.

Although these suggestions are reasonable, there is evidence suggesting that CR may be appropriate with a broader range of psychological problems than originally thought. For example, there is evidence that broader treatments that emphasize CR—embedded within an overall treatment package of psychoeducation, breathing retraining, and coordination of community treatment—can be successfully employed with clients suffering from PTSD and comorbid severe mental illness in both individual (Mueser et al., 2008; Rosenberg, Mueser, & Jankowski, 2004) and group formats (Mueser et al., 2007). Studies investigating these treatments generally find improvements in PTSD symptoms, perceived health, negative trauma-related beliefs, knowledge about PTSD, and case manager working alliance.

INDICATIONS

CR has been effectively used for a wide variety of psychological conditions. Specific to trauma-exposed samples, cognitive approaches have been compared to other evidence-based approaches, including prolonged exposure, to determine if one approach is better than another or if the combination of approaches results in better treatment outcomes. At this point, it is difficult to recommend one approach over the other. Thus far, it appears that exposure and CR generally result in similar outcomes and their combination does not have an additive effect on outcome (Foa et al., 2005; Marks, Lovell, Noshirvani, Livanou, & Thrasher, 1998; see Foa, Rothbaum, & Furr, 2003, and Moore et al., 2004, for a review of the literature). Specifically, when the standard prolonged exposure protocol is used, which includes both imaginal and *in vivo* exposure, CR does not appear to enhance PTSD treatment (e.g., Foa & Rauch, 2004). However, when only imaginal exposure is used, the addition of CR results in greater reductions of PTSD symptoms, depression symptoms, and maladaptive cognitive styles than imaginal exposure alone (e.g., Bryant, Moulds, Guthrie, Dang, & Nixon, 2003).

Foa and Kozak (1986) propose that trauma-related anxiety and fear are represented in a fear network, and modification of the structure requires emotional engagement with feared stimuli and incorporation of new information. Certain emotions, such as anger, shame, and guilt are thought to interfere with emotional engagement/processing of traumatic events during natural recovery or during exposure therapy (Brewin et al., 1996; Hembree, Marshall, Fitzgibbons, & Foa, 2001; Joseph, Williams, & Yule, 1997; Lee, Scragg, & Turner, 2001; Riggs, Dancu, Gershuny, Greenberg, & Foa, 1992). Therefore, exposure treatments, which aim to engage the individual with feared stimuli in order to modify the fear network, may be less effective for individuals who do not engage emotionally with the stimuli. Given this hypothesis, CR and other cognitive techniques have been suggested to be especially beneficial for addressing intense emotions other than fear, such as anger, shame, self-blame, and guilt (Brewin et al., 1996; Foa & McNally, 1996; Foa & Rothbaum, 1998; Pitman et al., 1991; Resick & Calhoun, 2001; Resick, Nishith, Weaver, Astin, & Feuer, 2002).

The research literature, to date, reveals a slightly more complex set of findings. In one study, anger and guilt improved similarly across conditions of CR alone, exposure alone, and CR and exposure (Marks et al., 1998), whereas in another study a treatment that combines written exposure and CR (Cognitive Processing Therapy) had more of an effect on two of four subscales on a measure of guilt than did PE (including imaginal and in vivo exposure) (Resick et al., 2002). Drawing firm conclusions is difficult, however, as each of these studies used different measures of anger and guilt.

Thus, at this point in time, it appears that exposure and CR generally result in similar outcomes and their combination does not have an additive effect on outcome. Further, areas thought to be specifically targeted by CR (i.e., negative cognitions) appear amenable by exposure alone. However, it remains possible that some individuals may be more likely to respond to one treatment or another. Moore et al. (2004) note that our ability to detect these pretreatment variables that may influence outcome is limited due to: (1) the high response rates to CBT treatments and (2) the lack of power to adequately evaluate the relation of individual differences to specific treatments. Clearly, more research is needed to specifically determine which individuals, with what presenting complaints, will do better with one form of treatment versus another.

SUMMARY

Overall, it appears that few conditions are contraindicated for CR. Much of the research, however, has evaluated CR as part of a broader treatment. Thus, it is unclear how the results might generalize to CR alone. When CR is evaluated as an addition to another component, it does not appear to have an additive effect compared to prolonged exposure alone, although it may have advantages over imaginal exposure alone. Finally, there is limited evidence at this point that CR may result in better treatment outcome than prolonged exposure for indices of guilt.

STEP-BY-STEP

The information covered below is drawn from a large number of sources including Zayfert and Becker (2007), Foa and Rothbaum (1998), Beck et al. (1979), Najavits (2002), Ellis and Dryden (1997), and Resick and Schnike (1993). Whereas we generally think of treatment approaches according to session-by-session guidelines, we chose to structure the information in this chapter in a different way. As CR is not generally conducted as a stand-alone approach, but rather incorporated into broader cognitive and cognitive behavioral approaches, we determined to present the approach as a series of steps, not sessions. This format allows for providing important information about the order of therapy that we believe to be most logical, but is flexible enough to be used as part of another approach. The specific steps include assessment and case formulation, psychoeducation, eliciting thoughts/assumptions, self-monitoring, reviewing homework and identifying unhealthy thoughts, evaluating and challenging thoughts, eliciting alternative thoughts/enhancing cognitive flexibility, practicing skills, and maintenance planning.

Our approach assumes the use of the general cognitive therapy approach to treatment, including: (1) a collaborative working relationship and strong alliance between the therapist and client; (2) a present-centered, time-limited, and goal-oriented approach; (3) the importance of homework; (4) a focus on changing thoughts, behaviors, and emotions; and (5) an educative approach designed to teach clients to be their own therapists. Although the approach is present centered, we also incorporate a focus on patterns or themes of unhealthy cognitions that may be related to the traumatic event, similar to several trauma-specific cognitive approaches. Three cases are utilized to illustrate various points throughout the chapter. While these cases are drawn from our clinical practice, they represent amalgamations of various clients. The names have been changed, and any resemblance to an individual person is unintended.

STEP 1: ASSESSMENT AND CASE FORMULATION

Assessment   Assessment is a key component of the cognitive approach throughout the treatment process. A comprehensive assessment will include, but is not limited to, the evaluation of diagnostic considerations, physical difficulties, substance use, strengths and weaknesses of the client, trauma history, and social support. Ideally, a multimodal assessment will include, at minimum, both structured interviews and self-report measures (for additional information on conducting assessments prior to PTSD treatment, readers are referred to Foa & Rothbaum, 1998, and Zayfert & Becker, 2007). For purposes of this chapter, we focus only on the assessment of unhealthy beliefs. To conduct CR, the therapist must identify what beliefs may be creating and maintaining dysfunctional behaviors and symptoms; therefore, assessment of these beliefs is clearly warranted. Also, ongoing self-report measures of beliefs can be useful if during treatment clients are having difficulties identifying problematic beliefs. The measures listed below may assist with identifying potential problematic themes and targets for treatment.

Trauma-Specific Cognitive Measures   One trauma-specific measure is the *Personal Beliefs and Reactions Scale* (PBRS; Resick, Schnicke, & Markway, 1991). The PBRS is a 55-item self-report scale that assesses cognitions thought to be affected by sexual assault, including those related to safety, trust, control, esteem, intimacy, negative rape beliefs, self-blame, and undoing. Although the scale was designed for use with victims of sexual assault, it can be modified to assess cognitions related to other types of trauma (e.g., Kaysen, Lostutter & Goines, 2005). Another trauma-specific measure is the *Posttraumatic Cognitions Inventory* (PTCI; Foa, Ehlers, Clark, Tolin, & Orsillo, 1999). The PTCI is a 36-item measure with three subscales: Negative Cognitions about the Self, Negative Cognitions about the World, and Self-Blame. The World Assumptions Scale (Janoff-Bulman, 1989) is a 32-item measure assessing posttrauma beliefs. Three scales assess beliefs about the benevolence of the world, meaningfulness of the world, and self-worth. There are eight subscales that address assumptions about the benevolence of the world, benevolence of people, luck, justice, randomness, control, self-worth, and self-control. The *Trauma Attachment Belief Scale* (TABS; Pearlman, 2003 is an 84-item measure assessing disruptive beliefs about self and others. In particular, the measure focuses on beliefs about safety, trust, power, esteem, intimacy, and control.

General Cognitive Measures   Several measures are available to assess cognitions not specific to trauma. For example, the Schema Questionnaire (Young, 1994) was developed to assess 16 early maladaptive schemas. The questionnaire is available in two forms. The long form consists of 205 items, and the short form consists of 75 items. The Cognitive Style Questionnaire (Alloy et al., 2000) is an extended version of the Attributional Style Questionnaire (Peterson et al., 1982) and was developed to assess attributions, consequences, and self-characteristics following 12 negative and 12 positive events. The Dysfunctional Attitude Scale (Beck, Brown, Steer, & Weissman, 1991) consists of 40 items designed to assess adherence to implicit rules and conditions for self and others thought to be related to depression. The Leahy Emotional Schema Scale (Leahy, 2002) consists of 50 items comprising 14 dimensions "along which emotional schemas may be understood" (p. 180).

These scales can be useful in identifying global schemas and/or attributions to address in treatment.

Ongoing Assessment Ongoing assessment is an important aspect of the cognitive approach, and we highly recommend using two forms of ongoing assessment in your work with trauma victims. The first is weekly completion of measures. These are typically conducted at the beginning of the session or while the client is waiting for the session to begin and should take no longer than 5 to 10 minutes to complete. Weekly assessments allow for a quick determination of the client's status and change over the previous week and throughout the course of treatment. This allows the clinician to gauge if the client is changing at a rapid pace. If the client shows rapid deterioration, the therapist can conduct a more in-depth assessment to determine the cause and, if necessary, temporarily refocus treatment to attend to the crisis or stressor. Weekly assessments also provide the therapist information about the point at which changes begin to occur. This may be important when considering mechanisms of change generally, as well as specific aspects of the treatment that work well for a particular client. The specific measures utilized each week will depend in part on the case formulation (e.g., if the individual is suffering from insomnia, you may want to assess sleep quality and quantity each week). As this treatment is designed for trauma-related difficulties, giving brief self-report measures of PTSD, depression, and anxiety is recommended. Another method of assessment is self-monitoring of symptoms, behaviors, and thoughts between sessions. Daily monitoring is important, as it often provides a clearer perspective of patterns and relationships among situations, thoughts, feelings, and behaviors.

Case Conceptualization Prior to beginning treatment, a thorough assessment identifies presenting problems, history, functional and dysfunctional beliefs, triggers, coping strategies, level of impairment, learning history, symptoms and diagnosis, cultural issues, anticipated treatment obstacles, and treatment plan (see Taylor, 2006). Although assessment is often considered distinct from treatment, assessment is the first phase of clinical intervention (Newman, Kaloupek, & Keane, 1996). Using assessment tools, a clear understanding of the person's experiences and a clear case conceptualization is generated, which provides a road map for intervention. The case formulation allows for increased consistency throughout the treatment process. It places the client's difficulties within the context of the theoretical approach and provides an anchor for the treatment plan, a common language between the therapist and client, and a means of checking progress. A case formulation is not something that is completed at the beginning of the therapeutic process and never examined again; rather, it is shaped during initial sessions but regularly revised as part of a fluid and flexible approach to therapy. Typically, a therapist starts with a set of hypotheses about a client, checks their veracity with the client, and continues to adjust and reconsider the hypotheses as necessary. Important aspects of case formulation are responsive to initial and ongoing assessments.

STEP 2: PSYCHOEDUCATION

Upon completion of the initial assessment and case formulation, the next step is to help the client understand the therapeutic approach. During psycho-education, information about the client's symptoms and struggles, as well as the theory and evidence about the approach, is typically provided. While there is little evidence for psychoeducation as a stand-alone intervention, it is an important component of the therapeutic process. As stated by Judith Beck:

> Most patients feel more comfortable when they know what to expect from therapy, when they clearly understand their responsibilities and the responsi-bilities of their therapist, and when they have a clear expectation of how therapy will proceed both within a single session and across sessions over the course of treatment. The therapist maximizes the patient's understanding by explaining the structure of sessions and then adhering to that structure. (p. 25)

It is well-known that a client's positive expectations of treatment success significantly predict favorable treatment outcome (e.g., Lambert & Barley, 2001). Perhaps explaining the rationale helps the client form positive expec-tations and a sense of hopefulness. Similarly, understanding the approach may facilitate a client's ability to consistently and fully engage in the therapy process, ask questions about the structure and process, discuss fears and concerns, and clarify the roles and tasks of therapist and client. This process of clarification may bring to light clients' erroneous notions about their expe-riences or diagnoses that can be useful to address early in treatment. Finally, the clear expectations of each party's roles and responsibilities communicated during psychoeducation may foster collaboration and enhance the therapeu-tic alliance.

Overview of Cognitive Restructuring Psychoeducation initially focuses on providing an overview of the therapeutic approach. This synopsis includes information about the basics of the cognitive approach as described earlier (e.g., strong alliance, the importance of homework, learning to be one's own therapist) as well as how the approach conceptualizes and addresses the clients' particular problems. Then we detail the principles of the cognitive model, emphasizing that cognitive biases and cognitive shortcuts are essential for human beings to adaptively function. We explain how core beliefs and schemas (systems of core beliefs) are developed and how they can pose problems in functioning. Finally, we stress how therapy will focus on transforming problematic interpretations of life experiences to self-enhancing but accurate accounts of these experiences. A typical psychoeducational script is provided in Handout 3-1, "A Psychoeducational Script." This handout, which appears in the Handouts section at the end of this chapter, may be copied and provided to clients. The explanation provided to the client, as illustrated in that script, can be substantially simplified. Case Example 3-1 illustrates how to teach clients about the cognitive model. Handout 3-2, "Event/Thoughts/Consequences Worksheet," can be reproduced and disseminated to clients to help them understand the relationship of events, thoughts and feelings, and behaviors. It can also assist them with their own monitoring. That handout appears in the Handouts section at the end of this chapter.

Case Example 3-1: Teaching Clients about the Cognitive Model

THERAPIST: I would like to tell you a bit about the treatment and what you can expect while we are working together. First I will tell you about the ideas behind the treatment. Then I will explain some of things we will do. I am going to draw a picture of three things that are connected:

The basic idea of the treatment is that your emotions and behaviors are connected to the way that you think about things. Typically, every behavior that we do (other than breathing) has a feeling and thought that comes before it. Then the behavior can cause another thought and feeling that causes another behavior. We have done this thinking–feeling–behavior pattern so many times, it becomes so automatic we don't even know it—it's a habit. Although we often think that we respond emotionally and behaviorally to situations, we actually are responding to how we think about situations. How does that sound so far?

CLIENT: Well, I don't know—I've never thought about it like that.

T: It is a kind of different way of thinking about ourselves. Much of the time we tend to believe that our emotional and behavioral responses stem directly from some experience; for example, if I am sitting in a meeting for work and raise my hand to talk about an idea and my boss doesn't acknowledge me, I might be annoyed at her and ignore her for the rest of the day. I would attribute my irritability to my boss's behavior. However, if we break it down, we can see that it is not really the situation that led to my response, but my interpretation of the situation. So, if my interpretation of her behavior is that she is angry with me about something and does not want me to share my ideas in meetings, I would be annoyed or angry and respond accordingly. Let's say the same thing happened to you—how would you feel if you were in a meeting and your boss did not call on you?

C: Well, I guess maybe she figures I don't have anything good to say.

T: You are not important enough to bother listening to?

C: Yeah, like, why does she have her hand up? She never has ideas.

T: Okay, so if you thought you were not important enough to be listened to, how would you feel?

C: Small.

T: Can you tell me more about that?

C: Well, I guess I would be embarrassed that I had wanted to say something and would just want to hide, like, melt into the wall.

T: So if you thought that you were not important enough for her to call on you, you would feel embarrassed for having put your hand up, for wanting to contribute.

C: Probably. I'd guess I'd also feel sad that I'm not important, that it is okay to ignore me.

T: Embarrassed and sad. That's pretty different from my response of feeling angry. What is different in those two examples?

C: How we end up feeling about what the person did to us.

T: But if the person did the same thing in both examples, why would we feel differently?

C: Well, I guess we're thinking that she meant something different both times.

T: But she did not act any different, did she?

C: I guess not. She didn't change.

T: So what changed?

C: I thought she meant something different than you did.

T: Right—the only thing that changed was how we thought about, or interpreted, her behavior. What if you thought that she must be really stressed out and really busy and wasn't paying attention?

C: I guess I might be worried about her. Maybe I would offer to help her out with something.

T: So it sounds like you're saying that your feelings would be different—you would feel concerned about your boss instead of angry or sad.

C: That's right.

T: You also said that your behaviour would be different—instead of ignoring her or melting into the wall, you might approach her and see if there was anything you could do to help her out. So the same event can have different meanings for different people or the same person at different times.

C: How can it be different for the same person at different times?

T: Well, can you think of a time that you might be more likely to think that your boss believes you are unimportant?

C: Ummm, all the time? [small laugh] I guess if I'm already feeling down, it would make sense to me that she would think that.

T: That's right—sometimes we seem to interpret lots of things in a negative way—no matter what the situation. This may happen more when we're feeling down or really distressed—it's like we have these basic negative beliefs about ourselves that tend to come up when we're not feeling well and we are more likely to interpret situations in a negative way. If we were sad and not feeling very good about ourselves, we might believe that the other person thinks we are unimportant. Or we would be more likely to assume that the boss was angry with us because we probably screwed up in some way . . . just more evidence that we are worthless. This would increase the chance that we would feel depressed and hopeless about the situation. It is not hard to imagine that these basic beliefs may affect how we feel. Does this make sense?

C: Yeah.

T: Okay—now, our job together is to identify the thoughts and feelings that come after an event and help you rework the thoughts and feelings so you have a different outcome that is healthier for you.

Trauma Reactions   Once the client appears to understand the general cognitive model, the next step is demonstrating how this model explains reactions to trauma. As reported earlier, several information processing and cognitive behavioral theories exist that lend themselves to the understanding of the negative effects of trauma, particularly the development of PTSD. While the underlying principles are generally the same, it will be important to connect the explanation with the therapist's specific treatment approach. Opinions differ as to whether the introduction of common reactions to trauma should explicitly incorporate the direct experiences of the client. Zayfert and Becker (2007) suggest that clinicians may choose to begin with a hypothetical distant example, as some clients may not be ready to fully engage in a discussion of their trauma experience at this early stage of treatment. Further, they propose that distress related to the client's own experiences may limit certain clients' abilities to fully attend to the information. Others (e.g., Foa & Rothbaum, 1998) utilize the client's own material while presenting the common reactions as standard practice. Resick and Schnicke (1993) believe that for certain clients who feel a need to share their story, using an interactive dialogue to incorporate the client's experiences during this introduction can enhance the client's understanding and engagement in treatment At this point, whether one approach is more appropriate than another is an empirical question. Each clinician will need to consider what may be in the best interest of the client. The clinician has to weigh the client's ability to tolerate the information with the strength of the client's avoidance strategies, all while not assuming the client is overly vulnerable. If the client can tolerate this level of discussion of his or her trauma at the beginning of individual therapy, then it may be best to directly incorporate the client's experience since it communicates understanding of the client's experience, facilitates some exposure to trauma-related material, and helps demonstrate the specific applicability of cognitive restructuring to the client's worldview. In groups, some therapists suggest that in-depth discussions of traumatic history be avoided so as to not trigger distress in other members (e.g., Najavits, 2002), although this depends on the purpose and composition of the group. In certain groups, it may be helpful to use examples that are both specific and general to facilitate learning. Handout 3-3, "Cognitive Theory of Trauma Responses," provides general information that can be reproduced and provided to clients as the basis for explaining trauma responses to them (see also Foa & Rothbaum, 1998); Resick & Schnicke, 1993); and Zayfert & Becker, 2007). It appears in the Handouts section at the end of this chapter.

Concerns about Change   Clients may be hesitant to approach changing thoughts and reactions to events, particularly if they have histories of early or ongoing abuse. Despite the degree of pain they are experiencing, some clients may perceive that changing behaviors and thoughts will put them at greater risk for danger or abuse. It is essential that the therapist understand that concerns about change are legitimate and address these concerns, if applicable. An illustration of how to do so is presented in the dialogue in Case Example 3-2.

Case Example 3-2: Addressing Client Concerns About Change

THERAPIST: Let me give you an example. Suppose a child was badly hurt by someone who was supposed to protect him. He might grow up thinking that all people are not trustworthy. It is the lens he sees the world with, like a pair of tinted glasses that colors all he sees. So when anyone approaches him—a teacher, a child care worker, another child—he has the thought, "This person will hurt me. I have to protect myself and not trust them." The child would probably be quite anxious and fearful, or might develop a shell against other people.

CLIENT: That would be a good thing—then others won't have the chance to hurt him.

T: Over time, this may protect him in certain ways, but it also does not allow him to learn in school, have friends, or have loving relationships. Then the child may develop thoughts like "I am unlovable" and "I am alone," since people will leave the child alone. Over time, the child will have more troubles. What do you think about this?

C: Being alone still might be better than being hurt again.

T: That may be. But what if that child could change that thought to "some people are trustworthy and some are not, and I have to figure out who to trust."

C: Then he might be safe but still have people close to him.

T: Right—the child would still be able to protect himself, but also allow some people to help him. The child might be cautious but still able to trust some people. That is what we will do together—figure out what thoughts are affecting your symptoms and experiences and help you change those thoughts in ways that still protect you, but help you handle things in ways that are helpful to you. I think of it like a road—if you see a sign that says the road is curvy and under construction and you slow down, the road is less stressful for you and you may prevent an accident. If you don't see the sign, you have to work harder when you are on that road to stay calm and safe. We want you and your body to work less hard and be safe on your travels through life. Like driving, you have control of this process and can slow it down or speed it up based on the weather conditions, how you feel that day, how much traffic is around you, and so on. You need to learn how to correctly identify and anticipate the road conditions.

C: Being in control—I like that. Deciding to slow down or speed up depending on what's around me.

T: That's right. Now this may sound easy, but you have been engaged in this thinking pattern for so long and so automatically, you are going to have to retrain yourself. Some of the thoughts are so tangled up with other thoughts, we are going to have to figure out which are the most important to address. Some clients like to think about this work as training for a marathon; others have told me it is like being a detective searching for clues. In any case, you are going to have to do a lot of

> work. Working together, we will try different ways to help you identify and change thoughts in ways that will make you feel safer, stronger, and healthier. Also, the people who have the most success in this treatment practice between sessions, so you will need to do a little work each day. Like an athlete, you need to train to learn these skills. Are you ready? Any questions?

Summary Psychoeducation provides the groundwork for treatment, but psychoeducation should not be conceived of as a "one-shot intervention." Even clients who attended to the information well are likely to not have fully understood and integrated all the information. Therapists can increase their clients' understanding of the information by following the guidelines in Table 3.1. We now turn to the next step in this approach: eliciting automatic thoughts.

STEP 3: ELICITING THOUGHTS/ASSUMPTIONS

Changing negative thoughts requires first identifying what those thoughts are. As these thoughts are automatic, just recognizing them may be challenging. We typically begin by asking a client to describe a situation in the previous week that elicited a negative emotional response. When teaching this step for the first time, it may be helpful to start with a non–trauma-related situation, as minimizing trauma-related affect may heighten the client's

Table 3.1
Psychoeducation Guidelines for Enhancing Client Understanding

- Provide handouts that the clients can review on their own (such as those in the Handout section at the end of this chapter). We recommend that the client be assigned to read over the handouts and formulate questions to ask at the beginning of the next therapy session.
- Review the information. It is a good idea to find out what the clients took away from the psychoeducation by asking them at the next session to explain to you the cognitive model and common trauma reactions. Hearing them explain their understanding can be very valuable in correcting any miscommunications or misperceptions.
- Repeat the information throughout the therapy. This can be done through using different examples and specific material that the client brings up during sessions. The rationale can be reiterated and reinforced at various times during the treatment to further aid the client's understanding and acceptance of the approach.

understanding. Of course, as depicted in Case Example 3-3, a seemingly non–trauma-related situation may ultimately end up being about the trauma. This example illustrates that rarely do emotionally charged situations bring up a single thought and a single emotion. Further, it shows that the first thought and emotion that the client identifies may not be the primary ones responsible for most of the distress. While Diane was angry with her sister when she called, it seems that the anger was less related to not having time to hear about the wedding plans and more related to both: (1) her incapacity to share in her sister's joy; and (2) thoughts about her sister's and parent's denial of her rape. Further, underlying her anger was guilt regarding her own response to her sister.

Case Example 3-3: Eliciting Responses—Reactions from Diane, Beginning with a Non–Trauma-Related Situation

Diane is a 22-year-old recent college graduate. She was raped by an acquaintance during her sophomore year. Although she reported the rape to campus officials, they did not find the man at fault. Diane also disclosed her experience to her family, who reacted to her with disbelief, particularly after the official ruling of the college.

[Diane and the therapist have finished psychoeducation and are about to begin identifying automatic thoughts].

THERAPIST: Let's start to practice with a situation that happened this past week. It does not have to be a situation related to the rape. Did something happen last week that you had a strong negative emotional response to?

DIANE: Yes—my sister is getting married in the spring and she is always calling me about this detail or that detail. I get really annoyed after a while—I've got so much going on. I mean, I'm happy for her, but I just don't have it in me right now.

T: Okay, the situation is that your sister called about the wedding again. What was your emotional response?

D: Anger—I was nice to her on the phone, but got off as soon as I could.

T: And what were you thinking?

D: I don't have time to hear all about every little detail. I wish she would stop calling me.

T: You are too busy with work to hear about her plans.

D: Yes. Well, I mean I am busy, but also, I don't think I want to hear them. She and my parents all act like nothing ever happened to me and life goes on as usual. My life doesn't go on as usual—I have to deal with what happened.

T: When you have those thoughts—that you are the one who has to deal with this and they don't acknowledge what happened—what emotions do you feel?

D: I'm angry—very angry. Why would I lie about such a thing? Why don't they believe me?

T: So you think "they don't believe me" and you feel anger. Is there another emotion you are feeling?

D: Yeah, I also feel guilty for feeling angry—does this therapy cover that? [*Diane smiles*] I feel badly for not being able to be happy for her—she deserves to have a wonderful wedding. What happened to me really shouldn't interfere with that.

T: Okay, now you're thinking "I can't be happy for my sister" and you feel guilty.

D: Right; but then I get angry again because the rape is interfering—is not allowing me to be normal.

T: Let's go ahead and write down the situation, the thoughts, and the feelings that go with them.

Other challenges may emerge when engaging in thought identification, including difficulty identifying emotions or thoughts and/or confusing thoughts and facts. Each of these problems is described below.

Difficulty Identifying and Focusing on Feelings   Some clients will have more difficulty identifying feelings than others. Indeed, one of our authors (E.N.) recognized a significant difficulty in helping female substance abusers, especially those within the first year of sobriety, be aware of or distinguish between their thoughts and feelings. It is unclear if this is due to residual effects of substances (e.g., Gonzalez et al., 2004) or increased anxiety sensitivity (Stewart & Conrad, 2003) or represents a long-standing pattern of self-medicating in response to unpleasant feelings and thoughts (Stewart & Conrad). Regardless of the reason, considerable emphasis needs to be placed on identification and articulation of feelings and thoughts among this group and possibly others. For non–mental health professionals, distinguishing types of inner experiences and cataloguing these experiences may simply be unfamiliar and require developing a new vocabulary and habits. Case Example 3-4 illustrates how to help a client identify feelings.

Case Example 3-4: Helping Sally Identify Feelings

Sally is a 26-year-old woman who is 3 months pregnant and has a 4-year-old child. She is in residential treatment for methamphetamine abuse. She tested positive for methamphetamine abuse during a routine prenatal exam and was brought to the attention of social services. She was offered the opportunity for treatment to retain parental rights over her 4-year-old child and baby. Although methamphetamine was her primary drug of choice, she abused other substances as well, starting at age 10. When assessed at intake, she reported an extensive trauma history, including physical and sexual abuse throughout childhood, adult physical and sexual assault related to obtaining and manufacturing substances, multiple car accidents, and exposure to multiple natural disasters. She met criteria for chronic PTSD, so auxiliary treatment of her PTSD symptoms was recommended. Sally had never had more than a few days of not abusing a psychoactive substance, and the treatment team was concerned that she lacked the coping skills to tolerate direct therapeutic exposure. Further, it was hypothesized that cognitive therapy to help her alter her trauma-related thoughts and behavior might be more successful than exposure as it could be readily integrated into her cognitive behavioral substance-abuse treatment. During the assessment, staff determined that Sally had difficulty identifying her feelings, so the therapist opted to help Sally self-monitor her feelings before focusing on her thoughts.

THERAPIST: How are you feeling today, Sally?

SALLY: Fine.

T: Fine is not a feeling. Take a deep breath and take a moment and notice what emotions you may be experiencing.

S: I have no idea how I am feeling. Bad. Good.

T: That's a great start. You are feeling both bad and good. I really want to understand your experience and since bad and good have so many different meanings to different people, let's see if we can understand more about what feeling bad and good means to you. What feels bad?

S: I had an argument with my boyfriend this morning. I got up late.

T: Let me interrupt you here, you are describing things that happened to you and I want to focus on *feelings*. So, what did you feel when you argued with your boyfriend?

S: Mad. Annoyed.

T: Those are great descriptions of feelings, though I am sorry you felt that way. Your sense of mad may be very different from my experience of mad. I'd like to understand more about what that feeling is like for you. When you felt mad this morning, what sensations in your body did you notice?

S: My face got flushed. I felt tense all over.

T: Where was most of the tension?

S: My shoulders and arms.

T: Did you heart beat faster?

S: A little bit.

T: How about when you got up late . . . how did you feel?

S: Grumpy.

T: Any sensations in your body?

S: No, not that I remember.

T: Those words and your bodily reactions are helping me understand exactly how you are feeling. Thanks. The more I understand your feelings, the more I can help you. Here is a list of feelings that people sometimes have. Let's go over all these feelings. Are there any feelings that you have never experienced or don't know what they mean? *[The client was provided a feeling list to help her identify her own feelings. For adults with severe deficits, it may be useful to review in this fashion any restrictions in emotional experiencing that are common among those with PTSD or substance abuse. Often, for children, a book of feelings is constructed.]* How about if you practice identifying feelings this week? This is very important, as it is the first step in helping you learn how to cope with your feelings and thoughts. We can't figure out how to teach you skills for responding to pain, until we understand the type of pain and what conditions cause or magnify the pain. So this week I'd like you to carry around this feeling list with you. Whenever you sit down to begin a group or individual counseling session, I'd like you to review the list and write down the feelings you are having.

The therapist chose to pick a regularly scheduled activity that could help cue the client to conduct this self-assessment. In addition, the therapist thought this exercise might enhance the client's experience of other therapies, and allow other therapists to address this skill. For other clients, this exercise might be scheduled through the use of an alarm clock, each time a client exits transportation, or any other marker. In this case, feelings were explored each week and the therapist used the opportunity to meet the following goals: (1) help client monitor internal states, (2) communicate an ability to understand the client's internal states thus strengthening the working alliance, and (3) help the client experience success and optimism about her ability to change.

Difficulty Identifying and Focusing on Thoughts   While Sally (in Case Example 3-4) had difficulty identifying her emotions, other clients have more difficulty identifying thoughts. For example, in Case Example 3-5, Allan, a 67-year-old veteran, was very engaged with his feelings but initially had difficulty determining the thoughts preceding his feelings. Allan is currently single, although he divorced twice. He has 5 children, three from his first marriage and two from his second. In addition to losing numerous friends and comrades in Vietnam, he was wounded in the right leg—an injury severe enough to send him home. Allan described his suffering from PTSD since coming home, although there were times when the symptoms seemed to subside substantially. When asked, Allan recognized that his better periods occurred when he was busy and content with his work quality and productivity, and his relationships were going well. Allan's symptoms increased significantly following the U.S. invasion and occupation of Iraq. He reported that he felt it was another Vietnam—a pointless war that would destroy the lives of many. Allan reported overwhelming feelings of guilt related to making it back from Vietnam while so many did not, and then hearing and watching ongoing news of the war, knowing his comrades were still there fighting and dying. He described intolerable flashbacks to the disturbing images and feelings from the past that materialized if he saw news coverage of the ongoing war in Iraq—flashbacks that stopped him in his tracks. Subsequently, he tried to avoid seeing or hearing any war-related news coverage or having war-related conversations. In addition to guilt, Allan reported substantial feelings of anger and sadness. When asked to consider the thoughts underlying his feelings, he had great difficulty.

Case Example 3-5: Helping Allan Identify Thoughts Underlying His Feelings

THERAPIST: You said you became angry with your cousin over the weekend?

ALLAN: Yeah, I was able to walk away from him, but I fumed all weekend.

T: What were you thinking that made you angry?

A: He just kept pushing my buttons—I started to argue with him, but I could feel myself starting to lose control. My fists were clenched and my heart was pounding.

T: It sounds like you were really upset and you were able to notice some clear physiological signs of that. I wonder, though, what were you thinking about?

A: That he didn't know what the hell he was talking about—all about how we have to support the troops and I should know that. Yeah, I should know—I was there; he was not. You don't support them by continuing to send them over there, not allowing them to come home when they are supposed to. You don't know what that does to a person.

T: Can you tell me more about what you mean by "you don't know what that does to a person"?

A: I mean it's hell, absolute hell. And sometimes all you have to hang on to is knowing that you're going home—you count the days down. That's about the only thing that makes it bearable. Then to find out that you have to stay another 3 months—well, that just messes with a person, you know?

T: So it is accurate to say that you are angry because you believe the soldiers are not being treated well?

A: Yeah, and everyone is talking about it like they know. They don't.

T: What thoughts are running through your mind when you hear people talking "like they know"?

A: That if they had a clue about what it's like, they would never have even gone over there. They pretend to be all concerned, buying their yellow stickers.

T: But you think they don't care?

A: That's right. I think that I was there, and no one—not the government, not society—no one cared about me or my men.

T: You think no one cares, and that makes you angry.

A: Yes, very angry.

At this point, the therapist might have Allan complete an event, thought, emotion, and behavior form (see Appendix A) to illustrate the cognitive model. If Allan continues to have difficulties identifying thoughts, the therapist may consider providing him with options, similar to using a feeling checklist. The therapist will need to take care, however, to not lead him to endorsing a specific thought or belief.

For those clients who still struggle with identifying thoughts, therapists can try using imagery or role playing (Beck, 1995). Some clients report thinking in images as opposed to words, so engaging with the client using imagery may be especially helpful. For example, the therapist can ask clients to visualize a recent situation that made them upset. At various points in the imagery, the therapist can query, "What is going through your mind right now?" Therapists can also role play distressing situations and use the same query when the client appears to become upset. Beck also recommends being aware of automatic thoughts in addition to those that the client identifies initially. For example, if a client is afraid of going to a store by herself and identifies thoughts while she is at the store, the therapist may want to query about automatic thoughts she may have prior to and after going to the store. Further, it may be helpful to determine which thought was most salient or distressing for a given situation.

Thoughts versus Facts　Often, clients will confuse thoughts with facts. For example, many people who have experienced a violent assault believe that they are unable to do the things they used to do because they are always in danger. This belief of constant danger is, for those individuals, a fact—not a guess, not an interpretation, not a question. The therapist might help the client understand that thoughts are our best guesses given the information we have at hand. These thoughts could be right or wrong. The previously described exercise in which a client identified other reasons why a boss might not acknowledge a worker can be adapted to help clients distinguish between thoughts and facts. The therapist can pose the question to the client, "If all these thoughts are possible following the same event, how can they be facts?"

Additionally, it may be important to normalize reactions by emphasizing that it is natural and reasonable to behave based on beliefs and emotions. The therapist can then explain that if those beliefs are incorrect and emotions unwarranted, acting on them may lead to some uncomfortable situations. This can be illustrated to the client also, using the previous example: "In the example with the boss, if I believe that the individual is angry with me, and I respond by acting rudely, my boss may very well end up being angry with me." The client can then be asked about possible consequences related to other thoughts and feelings in that situation. For trauma-related problems, survivors often believe that it is better to be in a relationship with someone than to be alone. This thought may propel the person to stay in unhealthy or abusive relationships. Instead, if clients believe it is better to be alone than in a destructive relationship, they may make choices that allow them to find better, more life-affirming relationships. Similarly, if trauma victims believe they are failures, they may seek out experiences or interpret events to illustrate a shortcoming. If, however, a trauma victim believes that he made mistakes but is not a failure, then he can use events and feedback to learn and become healthier.

Note: For some individuals, distinguishing between thoughts and feelings or thoughts and facts may be challenging to understand. In such cases, clinicians need to not spend too much time and energy distinguishing the two, especially if the clients are becoming frustrated and unable to under-stand the key points. In our experience, it is sometimes helpful to start simpler and help the client understand that outer experiences [events] can affect inner experiences [thoughts and feelings] which can subsequently affect other outer experiences [behaviors].

STEP 4: HOMEWORK AND SELF-MONITORING

In order to facilitate the ability to change thinking habits, clients need to practice these skills daily. Through daily practice, clients will have opportunities to observe their successes and failures in skill delivery and outcome. Then they can address their unique concerns with the therapist. Furthermore, such daily practice and appraisal will help the client develop the ability to self-assess how well he is implementing the skills, so he can learn to self-correct and change patterns as needed. Homework, especially self-monitoring assignments, typically is implemented to achieve these goals. Homework can help cement ideas learned in session through practice and monitoring outside of the therapist's office. Homework can also assist in bringing to light challenges and areas to focus on in therapy not previously discovered.

Tailoring the nature of the self-monitoring homework to the particular struggles of the client will maximize effectiveness. Assigning homework that is too difficult or confusing for the client may result in feelings of frustration, hopelessness, and/or despair. At the beginning of cognitive restructuring, as clients are learning the basics underlying the therapy, they may need to work on identifying what their thoughts and feelings are, before identifying how events, thoughts, feelings, and behaviors are connected. For example, Sally's therapist asked her to work initially on identifying her feelings. This may be done using a feeling checklist or a monitoring form in which the client identifies particular events and subsequent feelings. Handout 3-4 provides a form that you can duplicate and use with clients and is presented in the Handouts section at the end of this chapter.

As described earlier, some clients may not have had any experience monitoring thoughts; for these clients, considerable emphasis may need to be placed first on helping individuals identify their thoughts before connecting those to feelings and behaviors. A sample script from a group session addressing the challenges of monitoring thoughts is presented in Handout 3-5, "A Script to Help Clients Identify Their Thoughts," in the Handouts section at the end of this chapter. You can reproduce that handout and provide it to clients to help them identify their thoughts.

Clients can be assigned to just identify the situation and thoughts initially before continuing on, using Handout 3-6, "Thought Identification Form," which you can duplicate and give to clients. If the client does not have difficulty identifying feelings or thoughts, you can assign Handout 3-2, "Events, Thoughts, Feelings, and Behaviors Worksheet." If you are concerned about the client's ability to tolerate thoughts of the traumatic event, you can ask the client to complete the worksheets for non-trauma-related situations and thoughts initially.

Increasing Adherence   A key component of trauma response (with or without PTSD) is a tendency to avoid thinking about the traumatic event. This avoidance may include avoiding homework assignments and, perhaps, avoiding treatment all together. For some clients, not completing homework assignments may be a defense against strong negative emotions related to memories of the trauma. For others, it may be a lack of understanding of the nature of the particular assignment. Others may not fully trust the clinician and may not be prepared to reveal certain information about themselves. While it will be important for the clinician to determine the underlying reason for the clients' avoidance, it may be helpful to acknowledge the tendency to avoid trauma stimuli, including homework. The therapist and client can then actively problem solve strategies to increase compliance, as illustrated in Case Example 3-6.

Setting homework at the appropriate skill level, anticipating problems with adherence, and helping the client to problem solve potential obstacles to completing homework are important steps in maximizing the chance that clients will be successful. Next we turn to reviewing the homework once it is completed.

Case Example 3-6: Problem Solving Homework With Allan

THERAPIST: For the next week I'd like for you to monitor your thoughts and feelings a couple of times a day. I have these sheets for you to fill out. As we discussed in the beginning of the session, what you do outside of therapy is very important. The work we do in session will provide you with information and guide you along, but it is what you do between sessions that will determine how quickly you start to see an improvement in your symptoms.

ALLAN: Okay.

T: What do you think about doing this assignment over the next week?

A: [grins] Well, I was actually a bit irritated at first—it felt like being back in school. But I get your point. I'm doing this for me, and I'm in charge of getting better.

T: That's right. Let's use that as an example to fill in the first sheet right now. The event was that I assigned you some homework. What was your thought?

A: This is like being back at school—I haven't had someone tell me what to do in a long time.

T: Good—what were you feeling?

A: Irritated.

T: Excellent—what was your behavior?

A: Well, I probably wouldn't have done it.

T: But that is different now?

A: Yeah. Now I'm thinking that this is my life and I'm in control. It's up to me to do the work. This is about me, not someone telling me what to do.

T: Okay, so what are you feeling now?

A: Charged up. Ready to do this.

T: And your behavior?

A: I will fill these out by next session.

T: Okay, great. Do you have any concerns about doing the homework?

A: Well, I guess if this is going to make me think about 'Nam and all that, I would worry about going off on someone or getting really upset.

T: That's a good point, and something that might be helpful to think about now. Can you tell me what usually happens when you are faced with a cue about the war and feel yourself becoming upset?

A: I usually try to get out of the situation fast—I'm worried that I'll hurt someone.

T: That sounds like a good strategy for a lot of situations—getting away before you act on your anger. I'm wondering if there are situations that are more difficult to escape from—what do you do in those situations?

A: If I'm in the middle of a job or something and can't walk away, I'll try to tune out in my head.

T: Can you tell me more about that?

A: Sometimes I'll start singing a song in my head—something I used to listen to in 'Nam. Or I'll keep telling myself that it is not their fault that they don't understand. How could they? No one could unless they were there.

T: Okay. Another thing you could try is what you did in session—if you start to get upset, tell yourself why you are doing the homework, that you are working to get better and feel better. Even if it is hard at first, it will get easier with time.

A: Yeah, I could do that.

> T: So it seems that you have a number of strategies to use if you start becoming upset while doing the homework. Other than not wanting to think about the trauma and worrying about how you'll react, is there anything else that might get in your way of completing the homework?
>
> A: Not really. Time, I guess; I get really busy during the week and I might forget.
>
> T: Okay, let's see if we can figure this out. Is there any time of the day that you are less busy?
>
> A: Usually, I take my time over breakfast, reading the paper. Then right after work I sit and go through the mail before going for a run.
>
> T: Do you think that you would be able to fill out a form once in the morning and once right after work?
>
> A: Yeah, I can do that.

STEP 5: REVIEW HOMEWORK AND IDENTIFICATION OF UNHEALTHY THOUGHTS

The first thing that should occur in the following session is a review of the homework. Starting the session reviewing the homework and devoting significant time to it in the session will help the client understand how important it is. Any difficulties completing the homework should be addressed and problem solved. It may be that the homework was too difficult for the client, the client continued to avoid in fear of eliciting memories and emotions related to the trauma, or other unanticipated obstacles got in the way. Barriers to homework completion should be fully addressed, as it is a central component of the cognitive approach.

Initially, the homework review will consist of identifying unhealthy cognitions. Later, it will involve helping the client to evaluate and challenge those cognitions and evaluate the results of behavioral tests of the cognitions. For trauma-exposed clients, the therapist may decide to start with general unhealthy cognitions, and later focus on trauma-specific cognitions.

What Is the Problem With Problem Thinking?   We all engage in some distorted thinking at times. This may happen more frequently when we are under stress and may cause us some difficulties, although those difficulties are usually temporary. Greater problems likely come when the distorted thoughts are frequent, extreme, and immutable. An important point to help the client understand is that there is nothing inherently wrong with negative feelings and to help them distinguish between healthy negative feelings and unhealthy negative feelings, as illustrated in Case Example 3-7.

Case Example 3-7: Helping Diane Identify and Discuss Unhelpful Cognitions

Diane brought in her homework sheets (see Handout 3-2) in the third session. She chose one to focus on in session. The therapist then helps her identify and discuss the unhelpful cognitions.

THERAPIST: You have three thoughts listed for the time when you were in the parking lot and a man was behind you. Why don't we take them one at a time?

DIANE: Okay. Well, my first thought was "he is going to rape me."

T: What do you think about that thought?

D: At that moment, I thought it was true.

T: And now?

D: I still think it's true—probably the only reason he didn't was that I ran away.

T: So you're pretty sure that if you hadn't run away, he would have raped you.

D: Yes.

T: Okay—this thought may be one of those unhealthy types of thoughts we've been talking about. In a minute, we'll look at a list and see if we can identify which one it might be.

D: But wouldn't you feel the same if you were in the parking lot and someone was walking close behind you?

T: I might; I don't know. But it is important as we go along to distinguish between healthy negative thoughts and unhealthy ones.

D: What do you mean?

T: Well, everyone has negative thoughts, and the point of therapy is not to make you think positively all the time.

D: I think I'm getting confused; I thought my problem was that I had negative thoughts and they made me feel bad.

T: Well, while everyone has negative thoughts, people who have PTSD or other forms of anxiety/depression tend to engage in these thoughts more frequently and adhere to them more strongly. For example, it is healthy and not uncommon to feel sad and think that it will be hard to go on when someone close to you dies. Similarly, it is normal to think that you might still be in danger and feel scared after going through a violent assault. However, thinking that your life is over and you are incapable of coping with anything without your loved one is not rational—it is an extreme way of thinking. Thinking that everyone is dangerous and you can no longer trust anyone is an extreme way of thinking. Extreme thoughts may lead to intense emotions that last for a long time and have a real negative impact on one's functioning.

Diane's Thought Diary from Handout 3-2

Day	Activating Event	Thoughts/Beliefs	Emotional Consequence	Behavioral Consequence
5/20	Man walking out to parking lot behind me	He is going to rape me I am vulnerable I can't protect myself	I feel scared and angry	I run to my car and drive away quickly, crying

Types of Distorted Thoughts   Three common types of distortions are as follows:

1. Labeling, which means making sweeping generalizations about ourselves or others
2. Overgeneralizing beliefs based on a few incidents
3. Catastrophizing, or believing the absolute worst about a situation and emotional reasoning

Providing explanations about the different types of distorted thoughts can help clients gain distance from the content of their painful thoughts and engage in analyzing their thinking processes with new perspective.

There are many sources available that provide various categorizations of unhealthy thought patterns. We provide a list of the more common ones in Handout 3-7, "Types of Unhealthy Thoughts." That handout can be used during the session while helping clients identify their particular thought patterns and reproduced and given to clients to utilize while doing the homework identifying their own distorted thoughts.

Tracking Symptoms   We recommend tracking clients' symptoms over time. A powerful way of helping clients understand their progress is by graphically plotting symptoms. The client's particular case formulation will guide which symptoms should be tracked, although it typically makes sense to track weekly symptoms of PTSD, depression, and anxiety in trauma-exposed individuals. Providing a visual representation of progress in therapy can help clients understand changes they've made. Sometimes identifying particular times of improvement or worsening can help clients identify what changes may have been occurring during those times that can be applied to other targets of change.

Present- Versus Past-Focused Approaches While classic cognitive approaches are present-focused and evaluate current thoughts, some trauma-focused cognitive approaches are past-focused and evaluate thoughts related to their traumas and the meaning of the trauma in clients' lives. The approaches do not need to be mutually exclusive, however. Distorted cognitions that continue to emerge for clients may be related to or a reflection of underlying beliefs. Resick and Schnicke (1993) refer to these as "stuck points"—areas that represent unprocessed or unresolved aspects of trauma. These areas include power/control, safety, intimacy, esteem, and trust. If these areas appear relevant, it may be important to assign homework specifically addressing these areas. It may not be possible to fully address the automatic thoughts until these underlying beliefs or stuck points are addressed. This is discussed further in Step 6.

STEP 6: EVALUATING AND CHALLENGING THOUGHTS

Once clients can identify underlying thoughts, the next step is to help them evaluate and challenge the accuracy of their thoughts and the impact of holding those beliefs. Given the numerous techniques available to help clients achieve this goal, this section will not be a comprehensive review of every technique available. Instead, we will focus on general guidelines and considerations, then review some common techniques.

Choosing the Thought Once clients are able to identify their thoughts and feelings and have begun to identify patterns or categories of unhelpful thinking, the therapy moves toward evaluating specific thoughts. The first challenge for the therapist is determining which thought to evaluate. Typically, the therapist chooses a thought that: (1) is posing difficulty for the client and (2) can be successfully challenged so the client can experience mastery. There is debate in the field whether to start with a highly distressing thought or less distressing thought. It may be helpful initially to begin with a less distressing thought in order to teach the process of CR and give the client a fairly easy sense of mastery and enhance motivation to target the more difficult thoughts. Alternatively, targeting a difficult thought could result in greater distress relief initially (Zayfert & Becker, 2007). Another consideration is whether to focus on automatic thoughts or underlying beliefs. Although it is not always necessary to distinguish between thoughts and beliefs, the therapist may realize that a client's automatic thoughts indicate a pattern representative of broader beliefs. For many clients, it may be more effective and efficient to target the underlying beliefs directly (Foa & Rothbaum, 1998; Zayfert & Becker). For example, for many trauma survivors, automatic thoughts are related to feeling unsafe. If therapists identify an underlying belief of vulnerability, a more efficient approach may be to target this belief for restructuring.

Finding the Evidence The next step in evaluating thoughts is to gather evidence for and against the thought. Numerous metaphors have been used to describe this process, including acting as a scientist, a detective, or an explorer. The main idea is to help clients try to broaden their perspective and to not assume that beliefs are facts, set in stone. Any technique that can challenge a client to question evidence, perspective, and/or interpretations can assist in this goal; techniques can range from formal exploration (as illustrated in Case Example 3-8) to the appropriate use of humor.

Case Example 3-8: Helping Allan Evaluate His Thoughts

THERAPIST: Now that you are comfortable identifying the relationship between thoughts and feelings and you are able to see patterns in your thinking, it's time to start digging down and evaluating the thoughts. The first step in doing this is to act almost like a detective, looking for clues or evidence that support your thought and clues or evidence that do not support your thought.

ALLAN: Okay, sounds interesting.

T: What is one of your more common thoughts that you would like to start with? *[At this point the therapist is unsure of the relative distress related to Allan's various thoughts and decides to start with a frequent thought].*

A: I guess the one that really gets me going is that no one cares about me.

T: Okay—yes, you tend to have that thought frequently. And that also is a thought that seems to lead to significant anger.

A: Definitely.

T: I'd like you to rate how much you believe that thought, "no one cares about me," from 0 to 100; 0 would mean you did not believe it at all, 50 would mean that you believe it's about half true, and 100 would mean it's absolutely true, no doubt about it.

A: I guess it would be about a 90.

T: How do you feel when you think "no one cares about me"?

A: Angry and sad.

T: Okay. So, detective, let's make a list of what we uncover to support and not support the belief that no one cares for you.

A: Well, of course, there was the way we were treated when we got back.

T: How did people respond?

A: They'd pick fights with me at bars, calling me names.

T: Who did this?

A: A lot of people—seemed like stuff would happen everywhere I went.

T: Were there people who were happy that you came home?

A: Yeah, most of my family and some of my old friends.

T: How did you know they were happy?

A: Well, I don't know. I guess they told me they were. And they were there for me—left me alone when I needed it, but always tried to include me in things.

T: It seems like although some people were cruel, others were happy to have you back and were supportive of you.

A: Right.

[The therapist and Allan continued to gather evidence for and against. Following is an evidence list they ended up with.]

THOUGHT: NO ONE CARES ABOUT ME

Evidence For

People were mean and picked fights with me.

People don't understand what happened over there and believe things that aren't true about me.

I can't keep a relationship with a woman.

Evidence Against

My family was happy I came home.

My family supported me emotionally and financially until I got work.

I got to know some great guys through groups at the VA.

There were a lot of times when my marriages seemed to be going well.

I have a good relationship with my kids.

T: What do you think when you look at this list?

A: Seems to be more stuff against my thought than for it.

T: I agree.

A: But that doesn't mean that my thought isn't true.

T: Correct. It doesn't. However, it seems that we can't assume that it is necessarily true either, can we?

A: No, I guess not.

T: So if you rated that thought again, how much would you say you believe it's true, from 0 to 100.

A: I guess I'd have to say about 50.

T: The belief in your thought, "no one cares about me," just went from a 90 to a 50. Of course, the situation didn't change in the past 5 minutes that we have been talking about it. What happened?

A: Well, I looked at things that matched up with what I was thinking and what didn't—it seemed there was more stuff against what I was thinking.

T: Okay—you were able to evaluate what evidence there was for and against your thought. Now that you think it is about half true, how do you feel? [Therapist brings this positive experience back around to the treatment rationale.]

A: It's weird. I don't feel as angry or sad. Maybe a bit confused right now.

T: So by changing your thought, your feelings also changed. It's normal to feel confused at first. You are evaluating thoughts that you believed to be true—maybe even facts—for a long time. It may take some time to consider this more before you feel comfortable thinking about things in a different way. [It is important for the therapist to acknowledge the discomfort with this new way of thinking. The therapist will want to follow up with this at the next session to see how the client is feeling about his new perspectives.]

As you initiate the process of evaluating thoughts, it is important that therapists not shy away from finding evidence to support the thought that is being evaluated. When the therapist attends to the evidence for the belief, it gives her more credence and does not seem like the she is "stacking the deck" to make a point. It is important that clients are taught to evaluate all aspects of their thoughts to determine what is rational.

Extreme Thinking One aspect of the thought to evaluate is whether clients' wording suggests extremes in their thinking. For example, do they consistently use words such as *always, never, should, forever, need, must,* or *can't?* If so, this suggests rigidity in thinking that may be particularly challenging to evaluate. It is helpful to have clients identify these extreme words when they do their homework to indicate potential stuck points or indications of unhealthy underlying beliefs.

Overgeneralization Overgeneralizing from a single incident is a common type of thought distortion. A good way to help clients recognize overgeneralization and evaluate the impact of such overgeneralization is to help them think through probabilities of such incidents occurring. For example, Diane felt unsafe most of the time and, as illustrated in her thought record above, she believed that the man following her in the parking lot was planning to rape her. After enduring an awful rape by one man, she extended her belief to assume that nearly all men were dangerous and wanted to hurt her. The consequence of these global beliefs about men included increased isolation, failure to pursue intimate relationships since the rape, and great distress when alone with a man or in a situation (walking across a parking lot) in which she felt vulnerable with a man. The therapist worked with Diane to consider the likelihood that that she would be raped by the man in the parking lot or the next man that she was alone with in the library. Questions the therapist asked (and Diane considered) included:

- How many men do you know?
- How many of them have hurt you?
- Are there any men that you trust?
- How many times have you been alone with a man?
- How many times have you been raped?

The aim here is not to quash a client's experience, but to enable a client to consider realistically the probability of something terrible happening again. The therapist should not try to convince the client that the probability is 0%—this is disingenuous and untrue, and chances are the client will not believe it, and rightfully so. It also reinforces dualistic thinking. Underestimating risk also potentially puts a client at greater risk. The goal of this exercise is to help the client understand that the probability is less than 100%, and to use evidence to determine the actual degree of risk.

Am I Disregarding Important Aspects of the Situation? When negative schemas are activated, an individual's perspective narrows. People begin to pay attention to information that fits with their schema and to ignore information that does not. Thus, one of the important questions for a client to consider is whether there is important information about the situation that is disregarded. As illustrated in Case Example 3-9, Sally's distortions tend to revolve around her history of choosing to use drugs and its impact on her parenting. When Sally was not using drugs, she demonstrated positive parenting skills; however, she also accurately perceived that her drug use negatively affected her parenting. This latter realization led to significant feelings of guilt that were almost unbearable for Sally, increasing her risk for using; she also felt hopeless about her potential to be a good mother. A struggle in therapy was helping her to attend to the positive aspects of her parenting.

Case Example 3-9: Helping Sally Recognize Positive Aspects of Her Parenting

THERAPIST: From your homework, it looks like there were several situations in which you had the thought, "I'm a terrible parent."

SALLY: Yes, I feel that all the time.

T: Is it okay if we examine that thought today?

S: Well, that one is not going to change.

T: Sounds tough. Are you willing to give it a try?

S: I guess.

T: Tell me about what happened the last time you had that thought. [*Sally describes the only time she used in the past week. It was after her daughter had gone to school. Sally had been quite out of it when it was time to pick her daughter up and had asked her mother to get her daughter*].

S: So, obviously, I don't deserve to be a mom.

T: Well, before we make a decision about that, let's think about this. You said you used around 9 AM, after you dropped Jamie off at school. What did you do before Jamie went to school?

S: The usual, I guess.

T: What is that?

S: You know, I got her up, made her breakfast, got her dressed, dressed myself, and then I drove her to school.

T: Sounds like a busy morning.

S: Not really; well, not unusual anyway.

T: So, before you used, you got up, took care of your daughter, got her ready, then drove her to school.

S: Well, yeah. But I'm not winning any mother of the year award for that—that's just normal stuff.

T: That's quite a comparison to make—either you are mother of the year or you are a horrible parent. [*Therapist notes the black-and-white thinking.*]

S: I guess that's a bit much . . . but still, getting my child up and ready for school doesn't make me a great parent.

T: Would you say that it was an important thing to do?

S: Sure. She's got to be dressed and ready for school, and I'm a big believer in having breakfast.

T: It sounds like that is a good parenting thing to do—getting your child up and ready for school and making sure she has breakfast. Do you agree?

S: Yeah, but that doesn't make up for what I did after I dropped her off.

T: But if you're going to think about how you are as a parent, doesn't it make sense to consider the good things as well as the not so good things?

> **S:** I guess. But I think the bad things outweigh the good things.
>
> **T:** That may be; we'll continue to look at it. But right now, if you take the good things into consideration, can you say that you are a horrible mom?
>
> **S:** That seems a bit harsh now.
>
> **T:** What seems more accurate?
>
> **S:** I don't know. Maybe that I'm not a very good mom, but I have done some good things for Jamie.
>
> **T:** How would you feel if you thought that?
>
> **S:** I think I'd still feel unhappy and angry at myself, but, I don't know— the weight doesn't seem as heavy now.
>
> **T:** Okay, so by considering *all* aspects of your parenting, the good *and* the not so good, you feel somewhat less depressed and angry.
>
> Now that Sally and the therapist have gone through an example of looking at different aspects of Sally's parenting, the therapist asks Sally to continue doing this over the next week for homework.

Basing Thoughts on Feelings Rather Than Facts   Often, clients find that thoughts associated with intense emotions are more deeply entrenched and more difficult to evaluate dispassionately. Emotional reasoning, a type of common cognitive distortion, refers to assuming that the situation is true because that is how it feels to the client. As illustrated in Case Example 3-10, Diane believed that she truly was in danger most of the time because she felt so afraid. Further, she believed that she was unable to protect herself in part because of how afraid she felt. Her overpowering sense of fear led her to believe she was unsafe. For situations where emotional reasoning is used, it can be helpful to introduce the idea of treating these beliefs as hypotheses instead of facts; so for Diane's thought, "he is going to rape me," the therapist might help Diane focus on the facts of the situation, not feelings.

> **Case Example 3-10: Helping Diane Focus on Facts, Not Feelings**
>
> **THERAPIST:** Sometimes when we have thoughts that are related to strong feelings, such as fear, it's hard to imagine that they may not be true. It seems they must be true because of how we feel.
>
> **DIANE:** Right. I wouldn't be so afraid if there were nothing to be afraid of.
>
> **T:** Let's think about that. Our bodies do have ways of helping us to sense danger. What does your body do when you begin to feel afraid?

D: Well, it feels like my hair is standing on end, my heart starts to pound, and I feel like I can't breathe.

T: Okay, that is your body getting ready to run, fight, or freeze—whatever would help most in the situation. Has there ever been a time that your body reacted like that and there wasn't anything to be afraid of?

D: The other night I was getting ready for bed and heard something. I got really scared and my heart started pounding.

T: What were you thinking at the time?

D: That someone was breaking in and I was in trouble.

T: What happened next?

D: Turns out it was my cat messing with an empty box I had put in the dining room.

T: It sounds like even though your body responded with fear and you were afraid, your thought of "someone is trying to break in and I'm in trouble" was not accurate.

D: Yeah, but I didn't know that at the time.

T: Okay. You had to get the evidence to figure it out—evidence that the noise was your cat playing with a box, not someone breaking in. What did you think when you realized it was your cat?

D: Thank God!

T: And how did you feel?

D: Relieved.

T: Okay, so even though you were really scared, your thought turned out to be inaccurate, right?

D: Yeah, I guess.

T: And the way you figured that out was that you looked for and found evidence that it was your cat and not someone breaking in. That is what we are going to focus on next—how even if you feel something very strongly, it does not always mean that it is necessary to feel that way. Just as with finding the cat, we're going to look for evidence for other thoughts and figure out how to determine whether they are accurate.

Guilt   A struggle that many trauma survivors have is dealing with feelings of guilt related to aspects of the traumatic event or how they responded to the traumatic event. As previously noted, feelings of guilt, shame, and anger may respond better to CR than to other approaches. Case Example 3-11 illustrates addressing Sally's guilt about mothering, which also seems to relate to her values about mothering and femininity.

Case Example 3-11: Addressing Sally's Guilt about Mothering

Throughout therapy, Sally continued to deal with how painful it was to acknowledge feelings of guilt about being an inadequate parent. Although Sally had typically conceptualized her feelings as depression and anger at herself, it became increasingly clear that she was experiencing tremendous guilt. This then became the focus of therapy.

THERAPIST: You said you felt guilty for what you did to your daughter and that feeling was intolerable to you. It was so bad that you almost left the facility. First, I want to ask, what helped you stay? *[This is done to shore up coping skills.]*

SALLY: I thought about what would happen to my child if I left.

T: That's great. You thought about the consequences. What else?

S: That my family would say I told you so—you can't do anything right.

T: Okay, when you were feeling guilty, what were you saying to yourself?

S: I don't know. *[At this phase in treatment, Sally was still not able to monitor thoughts while she was experiencing strong emotions, although she was able to do this when calm.]*

T: Well, let me take a couple of guesses, but you have to tell me which, if any, are right.

I messed up that day.
I am a total f— up as a parent.
I can't do anything right. I will never be a good parent. I might as well use.
I am a failure as a woman and a mom.

S: All of them. I don't think I ever told myself it was "that day," just that I messed up in general. I was all about what a f—k up I am.

T: So let's talk about the difference of saying different things to yourself. You said you really screwed up in general. What if you told yourself, "I really screwed up that day choosing drugs over my child." How would that make you feel?

S: Bad, but not as bad as I felt.

T: How about, "I am a horrible parent and don't deserve to be with my kid."

S: That would make me use.

T: So that's another example of how your thoughts may affect your behavior. Remember how we talked about thinking errors. This is an example of overgeneralization, all-or-nothing thinking, and emotional reasoning. Do you recognize them? *[Therapist tries to get Sally to identify her own distorted thoughts.]*

S: Not really. *[Sally looks frustrated.]*

T: You were frowning when you said that. What were you thinking just then?

S: That we've been through this before and I should know it by now.

T: Remember when you were telling me about learning the new computer system at work?

S: Yeah.

T: It took a few weeks to really understand it, right? How did that feel?

S: Very frustrating.

T: And now?

S: Well, now I know it really well. They've even asked me to start training other people.

T: So it was frustrating and took a while to learn a new system, but now you are the local expert.

S: *[smiles]* Well, sort of.

T: Learning to think differently about things going on in your life is similar. It seems weird and frustrating for a while, but pretty soon it will start to come pretty naturally.

S: Okay.

T: Okay, let's take overgeneralization. Remember, this means that you assume things to be true for many situations based on only a few examples of behaviors.

S: So I'm assuming that I am a terrible parent because I chose to use drugs a few times and wasn't there for Jamie *[her daughter].*

T: Right. Were there times that you chose not to take drugs and were there for Jamie?

S: Yeah.

T: Okay, so it seems like we're talking about the difference between saying "I made some big mistakes with my child" versus "I made mistakes with my child all the time."

S: Well, that does seem different, but it doesn't erase the bad things I did.

T: You're right, it doesn't. Remember, this therapy is not about painting a rosy picture of the world, but of having a realistic perspective. *[Therapist reiterates the rationale and emphasizes the goal of rational thinking.]* Okay, let's try the next one—can you see how your thoughts about parenting are an example of all-or-nothing thinking?

S: All or nothing . . . well, I guess that would be that I think I can be either a good mom or a bad mom—there is no in between.

T: Right. How about emotional reasoning?

S: I'm not sure about that one.

T: Emotional reasoning means that you think something is true because of the way that you feel.

S: Oh, so I feel guilty because of what I've done, which makes me a horrible parent. *[Sally starts to cry.]*

T: Exactly—and like we've talked about before, feeling a certain way is not proof that your thoughts are accurate. Last time we met, we talked about looking at all aspects of the situation, and you did that for homework this week. What did you find?

S: I found that when I really thought about how I am with Jamie, there are a lot of things I am pretty good at, although my mistakes are big ones.

T: Previously, you said that you were a total failure as a parent and you felt guilty, angry, and sad. What can you conclude about your parenting now?

S: I've made a lot of mistakes that have been hurtful to her, but I have also loved her and supported her. I'm still not winning any awards, but overall I'm not a horrible parent.

T: How do you feel when you say that?

S: I still feel bad, but not as bad as before.

T: Has the guilt changed?

S: Yes, I feel a lot less guilty.

T: How about the anger?

S: Yes, that seems a bit less.

T: And the sadness?

S: I still feel quite sad. But I also feel like there are some good things I've done that I can keep doing and even get better at. That makes me feel a bit hopeful.

There were a lot of different feelings that Sally was struggling with. Although the primary feeling was guilt, if that were the only feeling that the therapist had focused on, Sally might still be confused about her progress. By evaluating each feeling separately, Sally was able to identify some significant reduction in guilt, giving her a greater sense of control, even though she still felt a lot of anger and sadness. This also allows the therapist to better target future interventions at Sally's feelings of anger and sadness.

T: Okay, our goal now is to increase the number of healthy thoughts you have and decrease the number of unhealthy thoughts.

Functionality of Thoughts Finally, one needs to examine the functionality of particular thoughts, even thoughts that are typically dangerous and need attention. Several Vietnam veterans with whom we have worked found the possibility of committing suicide a comforting option if the pain got too extreme. The option gave them an illusory sense of control and willingness to engage in emotionally difficult psychotherapy. The thoughts were infrequent and, there was no history of acting upon them. The clients believed in the honor of their word and set up contracts with the therapists about what they were and were not willing to do should the thoughts get intense. Therefore, as unusual as it sounds, it was decided that focusing on the occasional suicidal thought was not an appropriate target of intervention, as they seemed to be facilitating treatment, not interfering!

Evaluating thoughts involves many different questions and ways of examining them. There are a number of worksheets available for assisting clients in monitoring and evaluating their beliefs and emotional responses. One worksheet that is particularly comprehensive is from Multiple Channel Exposure Therapy (Falsetti & Resnick, 1997). This worksheet can be broken into several different steps as the client progresses. The full worksheet is presented in the Handouts section as Handout 3-8, "Events–Thoughts–Feelings Worksheet."

An important note about validation: One of the trickiest aspects of implementing CR with trauma survivors is doing so without invalidating the person's experience. It takes skill and effort to help clients understand that their fears, while based in reality in that something horrific did happen to them, still may be exaggerated or distorted in some way. Many survivors, especially of interpersonal abuse and/or chronic/repetitive trauma, feel that their experience has been denied, ignored, and invalidated. In many cases, the experience of changing and challenging thoughts can be experienced by the client as the therapist not believing the client, minimizing the client's experiences or suffering, and/or not understanding the client's perspective (Linehan, 1993). Thus, challenging trauma-related thoughts requires very careful application. First, it is especially helpful to use terms like *unhelpful, nonadaptive,* or *unhealthy* thoughts rather than terms like *irrational, crazy,* and the like. Second, special care needs to be given to identify the reason for the development of the schemas themselves, however maladaptive or adaptive they are, before changing them. In her treatment of borderline clients, Marsha Linehan (1993) uses the phrase "finding the kernel of truth" (pp. 241–242) in the client's interpretation. If the therapist can identify the feeling or belief that the client is experiencing, then it is easier to work toward challenging the client's thoughts. In addition, reminding the client of the rationale of cognitive restructuring and focusing and continuously strengthening the interpersonal alliance can also help the client feel supported. It may also help to directly address the possible sense of invalidation (Leahy, 2003), as illustrated in Case Example 3-12.

Case Example 3-12: Addressing Diane's Possible Sense of Invalidation

Diane and the therapist are reviewing her thought record from the previous week.

THERAPIST: The thoughts you identified in this situation suggest a sense of powerlessness in that situation. Is that accurate?

DIANE: Yes. I just knew that he was going to try to hurt me, and like last time, what was I going to do? I couldn't fight off a man that size.

T: That sounds very scary. *[validating Diane's feelings]* Given what you've gone through, it would be natural to be very scared if someone were about to hurt you again. *[further validation]* Let's look at your thoughts: "He is going to rape me; I am vulnerable; I can't protect myself." Can you identify any of these thoughts as being similar to the unhealthy thoughts we discussed last week?

[Therapist hands her the list of types of unhealthy thoughts.]

D: I don't know. Can they be unhealthy if they are true?

T: Great question. At this point, we still don't know if they were true or not, right? We are going to talk about how to evaluate that in a minute.

D: Wait a minute. You are saying that I'm lying—that I'm getting freaked out over nothing. My mom says that, too.

T: I don't think you're lying at all. Do you often have the sense that people don't believe what you are saying?

D: Well, they certainly did not believe me about being raped—the police, my mom, everyone. They thought that I just got in over my head, I guess.

T: That must have been difficult—to go through such a terrifying experience and then to have people not believe you. *[validation]*

D: Yeah. I even started questioning it myself.

T: It is going to be important as we continue through therapy to let me know if what we do in here makes it seem like I don't believe you. *[Here, the therapist recognizes that questioning may serve as a cue to the client to interpret the therapist's as unbelieving, so she is highlighting this issue to help in the future].* What we're doing right now is trying to see if there is a pattern of thinking that you use that is related to your feeling scared all the time. *[explaining rationale]* The thoughts may be accurate or inaccurate, we don't know yet. But either way, it doesn't mean that you are lying. *[Therapist reiterates the rationale.]* As we discussed before, when we go through traumatic events, it is not uncommon for your perceptions to change—how you perceive yourself, others, and the future are likely to be affected. What I'd like to do is to help you figure out what your thoughts are now and if there is any pattern to your thinking.

D: Okay, I don't know if there is a pattern, but the way I see it, everything certainly has changed since the rape.

T: So, let's start with the first thought: "He is going to rape me."

The therapist is now able to continue helping Diane identify the type of thoughts she is having.

Step 7: Eliciting Alternative Thoughts/Enhancing Cognitive Flexibility

When clients are able to engage in good detective work and evaluate evidence for and against their thoughts, determine their belief in the thought, and determine whether it is an overgeneralization or based in feelings instead of facts, the client is ready to start generating alternative thoughts/beliefs. Modifying beliefs involves three distinct processes: (1) generating alternative thoughts; (2) evaluating if the alternative belief is helpful and reflects reality; and (3) applying that alternative thought in various situations. In the beginning, the therapist may have to help out with developing alternative thoughts, but it is important to have the client generate alternatives. This will allow more opportunities for skill development. Furthermore, it is believed that clients are more likely to "own" the thoughts if they come up with them.

When beginning the process of generating alternative thoughts in collaboration with a client, the therapist should have a working hypotheses about more functional beliefs for the client based on the case formulation, although that might not be shared with the client. This belief should be realistic, flexible, and culturally appropriate and should help the client achieve goals or better functioning. For example, in Case Example 3-12, the therapist believed that Diane's thought, "He is going to rape me," might be replaced with "although the possibility exists that men can rape, there is little evidence that this particular man is going to rape me now." The therapist was concerned that "he is not going to rape me" would not be the ideal adaptive thought for Diane, as it was unclear if Diane was indeed able to monitor safety cues. The therapist conjectured that a flexible thought that allowed Diane to focus on monitoring the situation might be most useful. A working hypothesis, although it may be modified, will allow the therapist to ask better questions about the situation and decide how much to probe.

Typical maladaptive and adaptive trauma related beliefs tend to focus on issues of danger and safety, controllability, meaning of life, hopelessness, self-esteem, expectation of others as dangerous or rejecting, fear of symptoms and self-blame. While some beliefs are idiosyncratic and unique to individuals, it

Table 3.2
Common Trauma-Related Thoughts and More Adaptive Beliefs

Type of Belief	Maladaptive Beliefs	Adaptive Beliefs
Legitimacy	Everyone thinks I am overreacting and I should be able to put it behind me.	It is going to take me and others time to work through this.
	My trauma reactions mean I am crazy.	Although unpleasant, my trauma-related reactions do not mean I am crazy.
World benevolence/ justice	The world is dangerous.	Some aspects of the world are unsafe and others are safe and predictable.
	The world is malevolent.	There is both good and bad; some aspects of life are rewarding.
Trust	I will be exploited always if I am not careful.	Some people may try to take advantage of me, but most will not.
	It is unsafe to get close to people; people are untrustworthy.	Some people are untrustworthy, but many can be trusted.
Esteem	I am incompetent.	There are many things that I do quite well.
	I fail at everything I try.	
	The numbness I feel makes me a horrible wife and parent. I will never recover.	I will continue to try and do my best and learn from my mistakes.
		The numbness is part of my PTSD condition, which I am working on. It does not mean I am a bad family member.
Hope	I'll never be the same again.	I will always remember what happened, but it doesn't have to define me. I can overcome its effects.
Power/ Choice	I'm a powerless little girl again.	I did the best that I could, and I am able to control many things in my life.
	I could have stopped it.	I did what I could, but I could not stop it.
	It was my fault.	It was not my fault. I did not cause this to happen.

is useful for therapists to anticipate common problematic thoughts associated with trauma and common alternative thoughts. Table 3.2 lists several common trauma-related thoughts and more adaptive beliefs.

Generating and Evaluating Alternatives   The first goal is to help the client consider alternative interpretations of the same situation. There are several useful questions to ask that can start this process. For example:

- Is there another way of looking at this?
- What are other possible outcomes?

- What evidence do I have to support these other explanations? What evidence do I need?
- How else could I have interpreted their behavior/the situation?
- Is there a more adaptive way to look at the situation?
- Are you judging people or yourself with labels that are healthy or unhealthy?

In Case Example 3-13, Sally discusses her feelings of helplessness in an interpersonal relationship.

Case Example 3-13: Helping Sally Consider Alternative Interpretations

SALLY: I feel trapped by him.

THERAPIST: What thought is associated with that?

S: I can't control the situation.

T: Okay, how much do you believe that thought?

S: 100%.

T: Okay, let's look at that thought: "I can't control the situation." Let's do what we did before and review the evidence for and against this thought. *[They review the evidence for and against; the therapist then asks Sally to conclude what she learned.]*

S: I can't control the person—that is true. Everyone makes their own choices. But I can influence how he sees me.

T: Great job. Okay, when you are saying to yourself "I can't control the situation," that makes you feel trapped and helpless, correct? Those feelings of powerlessness are probably similar to what you felt when you were abused as child. *[Here, the therapist is using interpretation to help the client understand the feelings with the hope that it will help the client generalize new thoughts when she feels helpless. It is also used to convey that the therapist understands the depths of the client's pain].* What other thought can you replace that with?

S: I can control the situation?

T: Well, that's a possible alternative thought—based on the evidence for and against that thought that we just talked about, can you say that you *can* control the situation? *[The therapist is introducing the idea of evaluation of the thoughts. For some clients it may be useful to separate these steps, but the therapist chose to combine these steps for this client.]*

S: No.

T: So you're probably not going to want to replace a thought with something that is not true. While you wish you could control the other person and that would be a positive thought for you, we don't want to replace it with happy untrue thoughts. I've found that at first as clients are practicing this skill, the first alternative thought is typically a happy thought that is not accurate. That will change as you practice. Let's go back and look at the evidence against the thought to help you generate an alternative. What evidence do you have against "I can't control the situation"?

S: Well, I don't control the situation, but sometimes he listens to what I say, if I have the nerve to say it.

T: Excellent, you caught yourself generalizing from one experience and focusing on the negative. That's a great observation. So sometimes he listens to what you say—knowing that, maybe, we can generate a different thought. What ideas do you have about how to turn that into an alternative thought?

S: Well, sometimes what I say makes a difference.

T: Right, so how about something like "I can't control the outcome of the situation, but I can control what I say and do"?

S: Well, that is true.

T: How would you feel if you were able to say this to yourself—"I can't control the outcome here, but I can control my contributions to this interaction"?

S: I think I would feel a bit safer and less afraid. I might be able to speak up a bit more.

T: Great, that might be a thought to tell yourself when you hear yourself say "I can't control the situation." Can you practice this during the next week when you feel trapped or find yourself saying "I can't control this situation"?

S: Yes, I can do that.

T: In addition to practicing this, our goal is to keep asking yourself, "What else could I say to myself instead of the initial thought or belief that would be more helpful to me?" So this week I really want you to focus your homework on identifying alternative thoughts, evaluating them, deciding which will help you the most, and practicing saying them to yourself.

   Although not necessary, the therapist could also use this opportunity to review previous skills, and begin to help the client consolidate skills as they evaluate what would be most useful for them.

T: While we're at it, can I use this example to go over some skills we were working on last week and tie them to skills this week? Would this be all right with you?

S: Sure.

T: We talked a bit about using words indicating extremes. What part of the thought "I can't control the situation" sounds extreme?

S: The "can't" part.

T: Right. So when you hear "I can't" in your thoughts, let's talk about what things you might want to replace it with.

S: I could say, "I feel like I can't."

T: Right. Or "I choose not to try," "I feel unable to," "I'm afraid to"— you get the idea?

S: Yes.

T: Now what else is extreme about the statement "I can't control the situation"?

S: I guess now that we're talking about it, the whole idea of control is a bit extreme. Except when it comes to someone hurting someone else, most of the time we don't have control over situations.

T: Excellent. You are really doing well at analyzing and generating new thoughts! Now let's talk more about the thought " I can't control what will happen here." When you tell yourself that, are your thoughts stemming from feelings rather than facts?

S: A little bit . . . I feel so helpless, so that might be part of it.

T: Exactly, so you are using emotional reasoning?

S: Yes—thinking that I'm helpless because I feel helpless.

T: How about asking yourself if you are "overgeneralizing from a single incident"?

S: That I'm not so sure about. Maybe my sense of helplessness comes from the abuse and addiction, but I have plenty of examples of times I could not influence him.

T: Okay. That's a good point, so you are not overgeneralizing since you have examples in both directions. How about disregarding important parts of the situation?

S: That's what I think I did, when I gave up all together. I knew I couldn't control him, and thought that meant I couldn't control any part of the situation.

It is not uncommon for clients to struggle to imagine what they would feel, as they are likely to have a low degree of belief of this alternate thought at this point. Clients may feel some discouragement or concern about whether this approach will work—they may be able to recognize that the evidence does not all point to the veracity of their thought, but they probably do not believe the alternative thought or feel any different at this point. It will be important to address this and let them know that they are just at the beginning of this process. The more practice they have at looking at all sides of a thought/belief, the degree to which they believe it will change and subsequently their feelings will change. For example, Allan sometimes felt great shame for seeking psychotherapy services. He identified his thought as "I am less of a man for not handling this all on my own." Case Example 3-14 illustrates how the therapist works constructively with Allan to address his lack of belief in the alternative thoughts.

Case Example 3-14: Helping Allan Address His Lack of Belief in Alternative Thoughts

THERAPIST: What would be an alternative thought?

ALLAN: I am more of a man for not handling it on my own.

T: That's a possibility, but I am concerned about you just stating the opposite—more than, less than. Can you think of another?

A: Well, sort of. Umm, it takes guts to come here, ask for help, and work on this stuff. I have to swallow my pride and get help. I think it's not just an opposite. One could say I am more of a man for seeking the help I need.

T: How much do you believe that?

A: Just a little, about 5%.

T: Okay, so you really don't believe it, but if you did, how would that make you feel?

A: I think it would make me feel good about myself if I really thought that.

T: How much do you believe "I am less than a man for coming here"?

A: 95%.

T: How does that make you feel?

A: Really shitty. I don't want to do the work then. But honestly, that is how I feel.

T: I am glad you are being honest. You are just starting out, and the goal will be to get you to look at all the sides of the thought and eventually the degree to which you are able to test out and believe alternative thoughts, the easier it will get. You are off to a great start in being willing and able to generate healthier thoughts.

Difficulty Generating Alternatives Sometimes when clients experience trouble generating alternatives, it may be helpful to have them utilize techniques that provide them with some distance from their habitual patterns of interpretation or affect. For example, if clients are unable to generate alternatives, and evaluate them fully, it may be useful to have the clients pretend they are evaluating the situation of a friend. So in the case of Allan in Case Example 3-14, it might be useful to ask him to evaluate if he thinks the men who served with him that go to the VA for mental health services are weak. He might consider engaging in a behavioral experiment in which he asks several people what they think of a person who seeks help for mental health services despite his pride. Alternatively, the client can pretend that the person with the thought is a character on television, in a book, or a movie. It may even be useful to have him imagine that he is looking back at the thought 10 years into the future. When a thought seems especially resistant to alternatives, it may be useful to evaluate what is maintaining that particular belief. For example, family or friends might be reinforcing that belief.

When the Thought Is True   Some clinicians may hesitate to evaluate an automatic thought for fear that the thought is true. Then what? It is important for therapists to remember that not all of the client's thoughts are likely to be distorted, and if this particular thought is true, it is not cause for panic. If it appears that the client's thought is not distorted, but is an accurate representation of the situation, then the therapist is faced with several options. First, the therapist can question the client about what it means that the thought is accurate. Often, this will reveal some erroneous conclusions. For example, in Case Example 3-13, several of Sally's automatic thoughts revolved around making some bad decisions about using substances. As Sally and the therapist evaluated that thought, they concluded that it was true—she had indeed made some bad decisions. However, the conclusion that Sally drew, "I'm a failure as a parent," was not accurate. The therapist and Sally then switched to evaluating that thought.

Second, the client's automatic thoughts may reveal an actual problem or skill deficit that could be addressed in session. For example, in Case Example 3-14, Allan had often talked about the great difficulty he had when people brought up politics. His typical response was to get angry if the person did not agree with his position and walk away or become violent. In evaluating his thoughts, he and the therapist discovered that while some of his anger stemmed from the belief that no one understood or cared about him, it also stemmed from feelings of inadequacies about being able to control his emotions. If the client is accurately describing a deficit in behavior, an excess in behavior, or inappropriate behaviors that are creating problems, then there are a number of activities that the therapist can assign/help with to correct the problem. For Allan, the therapist suggested that some time be spent working on affect regulation. Additional strategies include skill training, problem solving, role playing, and assertiveness training—to name a few.

Additional Cognitive Techniques   The breadth of cognitive techniques available is beyond the scope of this chapter. Other works that include detailed descriptions of various cognitive techniques include Foa and Rothbaum (1998), Zayfert and Becker (2007), Leahy (2003), and Beck (1995). While not all works are trauma focused, most techniques can be used with trauma-related problems.

Behavioral Techniques   In addition to evaluating thoughts through various cognitive techniques, behavioral techniques are frequently used in evaluating thoughts and in determining alternative thoughts. Typically, behavioral techniques are implemented to test out particular thoughts. Essentially, a client is asked to test out a specific belief with an action. For example, in Case Example 3-3, Diane was struggling with relating to her sister, who was planning her wedding. Diane thought that her sister did not believe that she was raped. The therapist and Diane agreed that the thought may or may not be true, which decreased her anger somewhat. Diane also agreed that the only way to know for sure would be to ask her sister directly. The therapist and Diane discussed various ways of asking her sister, possible reactions her sister might have to being asked this question, and how Diane would handle them. Diane agreed to ask her sister the following week. When she returned to the next session, there was a notable difference in her affect. She appeared calmer and happier than the therapist had ever seen her. Diane reported that she and her sister had a long talk. Her sister reported not talking to her about the rape because she was afraid of upsetting her sister, not because she did not believe her. This helped Diane feel validated. They were also able to discuss their parents' reactions. Her sister agreed that it was hard to understand why her parents responded as they did and thought that their response was more related to not wanting to believe it happened instead of not believing it happened.

There are several important considerations when using behavioral strategies. First, when setting up behavioral experiments, the therapist should maximize the chance that the client will be successful. While this is never guaranteed, there should be a strong probability of success. In fact, similar to beginning evaluating thoughts, the therapist may want to assign a simple experiment and is very likely to succeed. Similarly, it is important to be sure that the test does not place the client in greater danger. If one is testing out how safe a client might be walking to a parking lot, the therapist might want to ensure that this is conducted for the first time in a relatively safe neighborhood in the middle of the day where there are lots of people. Second, as there is really no way to guarantee success, the therapist should prepare the client for many possible outcomes. In our experience, even if experiments are not successful, the clients seem to handle the outcomes well if the therapists prepared them in advance. As with all aspects of this type of therapy, the behavioral strategies should be determined collaboratively with the client. Further, as noted by Dobson and Hamilton (2003), it is important to be very clear about the specific behavior to be engaged in—at the beginning when the assignment is set, and afterwards in reviewing what was done. Often, even if the behavior was conducted as specified, the conclusions that the client draws from the assignment may be inaccurate.

Additional Behavioral Techniques   Again, a full review of available behavioral techniques is beyond the scope of this chapter. Other works that include detailed descriptions of various behavioral techniques include Foa and Rothbaum (1998), Zayfert and Becker (2007), and Beck (1995).

STEP 8: PRACTICING SKILLS

Once a client can generate alternatives, evaluate a realistic/fair interpretation, and select an alternative, he can benefit from repeated opportunities to practice implementing the alternative thought. It will also be important for the client to continue practicing his skills in many different situations in order to generalize what he learned. Therapy can also focus on anticipating new and different situations in which negative cognitions may emerge. Clients can practice their skills in session to handle these potential situations. Role playing various situations may be especially helpful here.

STEP 9: MAINTENANCE PLANNING

As the client continues to improve, it is important to begin planning for termination. Generally, this includes maintenance planning and relapse prevention. Many clients will become anxious as termination approaches. Often, this relates to concerns about relapsing once they are no longer in treatment and sliding back into old habits, and subsequently the reemergence of symptoms. Some practical strategies include spreading sessions out as the time for termination approaches, scheduling a booster session for 1 to 3 months after treatment, and discussing how the client can maintain treatment gains after therapy ends.

Often, clients do not realize how far they have progressed in treatment. As previously discussed, it might be helpful to make a graph of their progress, using the periodic assessments implemented throughout treatment, to illustrate the decline in symptoms and improvement in other areas. A visual representation can be quite powerful "evidence" for how much clients have improved. Having clients identify areas of their lives that have improved beyond their particular symptoms or presenting problems can also illustrate how far they have come, as illustrated in Case Example 3-15.

Case Example 3-15: Helping Diane Realize Her Progress

THERAPIST: I would like for you to think about anything that may have changed over the past 3 months. How are you compared to when you started?

DIANE: I can't believe we're almost done—it has gone by so quickly.

T: Yes, you've certainly done a lot of work over the past few months.

D: I definitely feel different—I was such a mess when I started. Now I don't feel afraid all the time and actually feel even happy sometimes.

T: As you know, I have been keeping track of your progress over time. This is the graph that I showed you of your weekly PTSD symptoms when we were about halfway through. At that point you were really starting to make progress, and you've continued to improve since then.

D: Wow! I really have. I didn't realize my symptoms had gone down that much.

T: Are there other ways that things are different for you now?

D: Absolutely. I'm sleeping much better, which has made a huge difference. I am much more focused and able to concentrate at work.

T: How about relationships—has anything changed in that area?

D: Well, I still don't think I'm ready to date anyone, but I am spending more time with my girlfriends. They are very supportive, and I think that is what I need right now.

T: Has the way you think about the rape changed?

D: Yes. It was definitely a life-altering experience, but I don't have to let it define who I am. I can never erase what happened, but I think I've put it into perspective. I don't know that I'll ever forgive him [the rapist], but I don't think that's what I need to be focused on right now.

T: Okay—like we talked about last week—that may be something that you can address in the future, but you don't need to worry about that now.

D: Right, now the focus is me.

Helping the client become her own therapist is an important tenet of the cognitive therapy approach. To facilitate maintenance of treatment gains, therapists can encourage clients to continue using the skills they learned in therapy and apply them in new and different circumstances. For example, an important part of Diane's therapy was learning that it was okay to feel and express anger toward her mother for not believing her about the rape. Diane identified that she had difficulty expressing her true feelings in other situations as well. Part of the last two sessions were spent identifying specific situations in which she felt discomfort expressing herself and role playing different ways of handling the situation.

It is also important to anticipate that there may be times when circumstances get tough and clients may begin experiencing symptoms again. The therapist and client can outline what those situations might be (e.g., times of high stress, experiencing another trauma). Clients can be encouraged to use their new skills during those times. They should also know that the expectation should not be to handle all situations perfectly, but to use difficult times as an opportunity to hone newly acquired skills.

Sometimes, however, that may not be enough, so we think it is important to talk to clients about seeking additional help in the future. This may include a booster session to focus on trauma-related issues, or they may choose to work on other problems. It can be helpful to outline signs or symptoms, based on the case conceptualization, of when seeking help might be appropriate. For some clients, seeking additional treatment may be viewed as a sign of failure. The therapist may need to apply some final cognitive restructuring to help clients perceive additional treatment as an opportunity to further process important events in their lives and further increase their quality of life. We have found it useful to describe booster sessions similarly to a booster dose of vaccine to extend the effectiveness of the intervention. It is not a sign of failure but a need to enhance the effectiveness of the "first dose" of treatment.

Troubleshooting

Dealing with Reluctance/Resistance   Most clinicians are well aware of the benefits of using well-designed homework assignments for the progress of therapy. Sometimes clients may have difficulty completing assignments. Beck (1995) identified a number of ways to increase compliance with homework assignments. One way to increase the potential for compliance and success is to match the assignments to the relative abilities of clients. Some clients will need more time with the basics, while others will catch on rather quickly. Beck suggests erring on the side of assignments that are too easy, rather than too difficult, to help promote a sense of mastery in clients. Clinicians should also explain clearly the rationale for each assignment. The more clients understand the purpose and likely benefit for them, the more likely they are to engage.

Further, it is important to follow one of the basic tenets of cognitive therapy and approach homework as a team. If clients are a part of determining how best to monitor symptoms or challenge particular thoughts, they may be more invested in carrying out the homework. Clinicians can also take an "all is grist for the mill" approach to homework by using either completed homework or helping clients to identify thoughts that got in the way of completing homework in session. Both are likely to be helpful in more fully under-standing clients and helping them to improve. Clinicians may also want to ask clients to start the assignment in session so that any problems in under-standing the assignment can be addressed.

A number of problem-solving techniques can be employed if the client has difficulty remembering to do the assignments, including using a day planner to write out assignments and plan for time to complete them. Many clients may find that carrying the assignment in a notebook or a reminder on their car dashboard, refrigerator, or bathroom can be useful. Problem-solving tech-niques can also be helpful to anticipate obstacles the clients may face when trying to complete assignments. Finally, while clinicians should try to set up assignments that clients will likely succeed at, it is important to consider and plan for negative outcomes. Establishing from the beginning that many out-comes are possible may help increase clients' cognitive flexibility as well as ready them to handle multiple scenarios.

Comorbidity   Clients presenting with multiple difficulties are often thought to be inappropriate for a PTSD-specific therapeutic approach. The research does not support this assumption, however. Empirical evidence suggests that increasing complexity of presenting complaints does not necessitate increas-ing complexity of treatment approaches (e.g., Feeny, Zoellner, & Foa, 2002; Foa et al., 2005). Further, many studies find that therapies that target PTSD have a generalized impact. Often, when the PTSD symptoms start to abate, improvement occurs in other areas as well. At times, however, it may be necessary to refocus treatment in the case of an immediate crisis, significant increase in depressive symptoms, or thoughts of suicidality. Indeed, for some clients, it may be necessary to implement other treatments first or in conjunc-tion with CBT for PTSD.

Fortunately, treatments developed specifically to address PTSD have also been shown to alleviate comorbid problems such as depression (Bryant, Moulds, Guthrie, Dang, & Nixon, 2003; Foa, Dancu, Hembree, Jaycox, Meadows, & Street, 1999; Foa, et al., 2005; Foa, Rothbaum, Riggs, & Murdock, 1991; Paunovic & Ost, 2001; Resick et al., 2002) and general anxiety (Foa et al., 1999; Foa et al., 1991; Paunovic & Ost). Additionally, treatment packages with empirical support have been developed to specifically address PTSD with comorbid problems. Specifically, *Multiple Channel Exposure Therapy* (MCET; Falsetti & Resnick, 1997; Falsetti, Resnick, & Davis, 2005) targets PTSD and comorbid panic attacks, and *Seeking Safety* (Najavits, 2002) addresses PTSD and comorbid substance use. It remains unclear, however, whether combi-nation treatments are always necessary. For example, Hien, Cohen, Miele, Litt, and Capstick (2004) compared a cognitive behavioral treatment that targets PTSD and substance use with a cognitive behavioral therapy that only targets substance use and community care. They found that both cognitive behavioral therapies resulted in significant improvements, while the community care group worsened. Further, the treatments did not differ from each other.

Sleep Disturbance and Nightmares   A growing literature suggests that sleep disturbances, including nightmares, may be resistant to psychological treatments that broadly target PTSD symptoms (e.g., Davis, DeArellano, Falsetti, & Resnick, 2003; Forbes, Creamer, & Biddle, 2001; Keane et al., 1989; Schreuder, van Egmond, Kleijn, & Visser, 1998; Scurfield, Kenderdine, & Pollard, 1990; Zayfert & DeViva, 2004) as well as pharmacological agents (e.g., cyproheptadine; Clark et al., 1999; Jacobs-Rebhun et al., 2000; sertraline; Davidson, Landerman, Farfel, & Clary, 2002). If ongoing assessment reveals that clients continue to struggle with insomnia or nightmares, clinicians should consider implementing treatments specific to these sleep difficulties (see Davis, 2008; Krakow et al., 2001; Morin, 1993) and/or a referral to a sleep medicine specialist.

Dissociation and Numbing   Dissociation and numbing are not uncommon responses to overwhelming trauma—at the time of the trauma and subsequently in response to reminders of the trauma. These responses may increase with the initiation of treatment focused on working through the impact of traumatic events as clients struggle to find ways of coping with increased distress (Jaycox & Foa, 1996). Cognitive techniques may be particularly helpful, depending on the issues underlying the dissociative/numbing response. Clinicians will want to determine what these issues are and target restructuring in those areas, teach coping strategies including grounding techniques and relaxation, and consider modifying their approach to slow down and use a more gradual approach that will enable clients to experience some increased confidence in their abilities to tackle these difficult issues (Jaycox & Foa).

Agitation   While some increase in distress and anxiety is not unexpected in trauma treatments, at some point clients' agitation may interfere with their progression in treatment. Again, we recommend a graduated approach, such as dealing with less troublesome thoughts or thoughts that are less directly related to the traumatic event. We would also recommend skills training in affect regulation for individuals who have difficulty tolerating intense affect (see Cloitre, Koenen, Cohen, & Han, 2002).

Making Cognitive Restructuring Your Own   Implementing trauma-related CR relies heavily on the technical skills and creativity of the therapist. Many therapists erroneously believe that CR is simply reading aloud a particular manual with a client without the use of clinical judgment, creativity, and tailoring to specific clients. This is false. Effective implementation of CR requires building and maintaining a strong therapeutic relationship; conceptualizing the client's symptoms, thoughts, and goals accurately; choosing which thoughts to target, providing examples and suggestions that work for a particular client in a particular setting and culture; selection and creation of behavioral experiments; and careful timing of interventions. Furthermore, a therapist's understanding of a particular client's strengths and weaknesses becomes critical in applying CR interventions in a manner that is most effective.

Timing Interventions   Therapists are encouraged to allocate time as they see fit for each client on each therapeutic goal; it may take some clients several weeks to master a particular skill, or some clients may work very quickly. Pacing is dependent on the client's abilities and life circumstances as well as the clinician's ability to pace and effectively communicate with the client. For example, in working with individuals who have recently experienced mild head injury or recently ceased psychoactive substance abuse, it may take longer to master certain skills. Some therapists may want to regularly review or revisit previous topics to crystallize learning.

Creativity   Therapists are encouraged to use images, examples, metaphors, and terminology that fit their therapeutic style and are appropriate to the client's education, culture, region, work history, ethnicity, and background. Some therapists may be more skilled at using metaphors, whereas others excel in visual imagery. Finding innovative and compelling ways to describe reactions and helping clients foster openness to flexible adaptive thinking is one of the artistic technical aspects of conducting CR.

Self-Disclosure   Therapists may vary in the degree to which self-disclosure is used in session. For example, in helping clients rethink and cope with trauma-related irritability, we divulge how when a car abruptly moves in front of ours, we think to ourselves, "Oh, that person is in a terrible rush. I hope they are able to safely deal with the problems they are trying to solve." We discuss with clients how interpreting the situation that way soothes us and makes us calmer than alternative situations. Furthermore, when appropriate, we describe how we practice such behavior by sending good wishes, blessings, or prayers when we encounter fire trucks, policemen, or ambulances with flashing lights on the road. Using self-disclosure that is appropriate to clients' goals and needs is one way in which each therapist, consistent with his or her style, can implement CR creatively. However, caution should always be used when using any form of self-disclosure; therapists must be vigilant that the benefits to the client outweigh any potential harm and that such disclosure is always in the service of the client. We typically recommend that neophyte therapists avoid the use of self-disclosure.

Using the Relationship   While CR requires a solid therapeutic alliance (Beck, 1995), the therapeutic interactions between the therapist and client may not typically be an explicit area of focus for CR. For clients who can tolerate it, addressing trust schemas affected by trauma within the relationship may be useful. Often, midway in treatment, when trust with others may become a target for intervention and it is clear that the client trusts the therapist, we have found it useful to ask clients to consider how they would respond to treatment if they carried a particular thought with them about the therapist. Similarly, we might discuss how the client began trusting the therapist. Explicitly addressing trust within the therapeutic relationship needs to be considered carefully as it could, in some cases, undermine the working alliance rather than help the client address faulty assumptions about trust. For example, for a client with a long history of betrayal by people in power who believes that it is just a matter of time before the therapist abuses his power, specifically using the relationship to discuss trust may backfire. Instead of changing maladaptive schemas about trust, it may in fact have the client feel less trust in the therapist.

SUPERVISION AND HOW TO OBTAIN TRAINING

SUPERVISION AND COGNITIVE THERAPY IN GENERAL

Although there is little evidence confirming the efficacy of clinical supervision, it is believed that novice and experienced therapists may benefit from supervision or consultation (Liese & Beck, 1997). Supervision of CBT therapists typically utilizes the same basic therapeutic tenets of CBT to achieve supervisory goals (Rosenbaum & Ronen, 1998). Rosenbaum and Ronen suggest several tenets of CBT to be applied to supervision. Similar to therapy sessions, supervision should be systematic, goal-directed, and collaborative. Supervisors may choose to utilize practice and experiential techniques, such as additional readings or behavioral experiments. Beck (1995) suggests that supervision might focus on modifying the supervisee's professional maladaptive cognitions, such as "I can't structure the session," my client "won't like the structure," "she won't do homework," or "she'll feel denigrated if I evaluate her thinking" (p. 74). The supervision experience should also be person focused, with goals and objectives shaped to the specific educational needs and desires of the supervisee.

Some issues that are likely to be a focus of supervision include honing case conceptualization skills, selecting appropriate thoughts and beliefs to modify, and maximizing the use of homework assignments. We have also noticed that learning to balance flexibility and creativity with technical skill adherence tends to be an area that needs attention in supervision. Beck (1995) presents a list of questions to consider when a problem in therapy arises. These questions are intended to help therapists and supervisors identify the nature of the problem and determine a course of action. Specifically, questions are presented to determine in which of several broad categories the problem is arising, and in which specific elements of that category. The broad categories include diagnosis, conceptualization, treatment planning, therapeutic alliance, structure or pace of the session or both, socialization of the client to the cognitive model, dealing with automatic thoughts, accomplishing goals in and across sessions, or the client's processing of session content. This may be a useful tool for supervisors and therapists to review in addressing potential problems.

As emphasized elsewhere in this chapter, therapists may need assistance in validating and empathizing with clients without validating their dysfunctional beliefs and restructuring beliefs that are held very strongly by the client and are unyielding and resistant to change (Taylor, 2006). Therapists may rush to challenge thoughts prior to satisfactorily communicating understanding of the client's perspective. Helping therapists appropriately pace validating and challenging comments may be a target of supervision. For novice therapists, in particular, help in selecting which thought to focus on can be useful. Safran, Vallis, Segal, and Shaw (1986) suggest targeting thoughts and beliefs that are more central to the client's problems and the relative strength of that belief. Strong beliefs that are closely associated with problems should be targeted first and foremost. Modifying beliefs with more leverage is likely to be a time-efficient and effective method.

Often, spiritual and cultural issues related to maladaptive trauma-related beliefs need attention. Specifically, restructuring alternative healthy beliefs that are consistent with faith traditions can be challenging in unfamiliar faith traditions. One of our clients who was brutally abused in childhood and then kidnapped and sadistically tortured was convinced this was punishment for a past life. Therapeutically, this sense of blame and control was problematic, but it was consistent with her faith tradition. In supervision, consultation with appropriate clergy and review of religious practice helped the therapist determine alternative beliefs that were culturally consistent. It was suggested that beliefs about valuing one's current worth and implementing good deeds that could change the future could be implemented successfully. Another Catholic client who believed her sexual abuse was a sin was encouraged to talk to her priest about sin as a behavioral experiment. Rather than talk, this client decided to confess her abuse as a sin; the priest refused to absolve her of her sins, since he declared she had not sinned at all. Instead, he asked her to step out of the confessional area and join him in the sanctuary to pray for the soul of her perpetrator.

SUPERVISION AND TRAUMA COGNITIONS RELATED TO VICARIOUS TRAUMATIZATION

Although the client's reactions, behaviors, needs, and goals are the primary focus of the therapeutic relationship, the therapist's reactions and beliefs may be challenged and changed during the process of collaborating with clients in trauma-focused work (McCann & Pearlman, 1990). When serving as a witness to traumatic events, therapists' worldviews may also be changed in ways that are maladaptive. McCann and Pearlman believe therapists may be likely to experience changes in cognition in the areas of safety, trust, power, and evil in the world. In order to help clients create new meanings that are adaptive, therapists' ability to create personal adaptive meanings must be proficient. Therefore, supervision and consultation that focus on regular assessment of these areas and healthy self-care may be critical for enhancing the therapist's ability to implement CR effectively.

PROFESSIONAL ORGANIZATIONS: COGNITIVE/COGNITIVE BEHAVIORAL THERAPY

The American Institute for Cognitive Therapy
www.cognitivetherapynyc.com
136 E. 57th Street, Suite 1101
New York, NY 10022
Phone: 212-308-2440
Email: intake@cognitivetherapynyc.com

Association for Behavioral and Cognitive Therapies (ABCT)
www.aabt.org
305 7th Avenue, 16th Fl.
New York, NY 10001
Phone: 212-647-1890
Fax: 212-647-1865

Beck Institute for Cognitive Therapy and Research
www.academyofct.org
One Belmont Avenue, Suite 700
Bala Cynwyd, Pa 19004-1610
Phone: 610-664-3020
Fax: 610-664-4437
Email: beckinst@gim.net

International Association for Cognitive Therapy
www.the-iacp.com

PROFESSIONAL ORGANIZATIONS: TRAUMA

American Professional Society on the Abuse of Children (APSAC)
www.apsac.org
350 Poplar Avenue
Elmhurst, IL 60126
Phone: 630-941-1235
Toll Free: 1-877-402-7722
Fax: 630-359-4274
E-mail: apsac@apsac.org

American Psychological Association Division 56: Trauma Psychology
www.apatraumadivision.org

Anxiety Disorders Association of America (ADAA)
www.adaa.org
8730 Georgia Ave., Suite 600
Silver Spring, MD 20910
Phone: 240-485-1001
Fax: 240-485-1035
Email: information@adaa.org

Institute on Violence, Abuse and Trauma (IVAT)
www.ivatcenters.org
10065 Old Grove Road
San Diego, CA 92131
Phone: 858-527-1860 x. 4160 (Main Line)
Fax: 858-527-1743
Email: IVAT@alliant.edu

The International Society for Traumatic Stress Studies (ISTSS)
www.istss.org
60 Revere Drive, Suite 500
Northbrook, IL 60062
Phone: 847-480-9028
Fax: 847-480-9282
E-mail: istss@istss.org

The International Society for the Study of Trauma and Dissociation (ISSTD)
www.isst-d.org
8201 Greensboro Drive, Suite 300
McLean, VA 22102
Phone: 703-610-9037
Fax: 703-610-9005
E-mail: info@isst-d.org

REFERENCES

Alloy, L. B., Abramson, L. Y., Hogan, M. E., Whitehouse, W. G., Rose, D. T., Robinson, M. S., et al. (2000). The Temple–Wisconsin Cognitive Vulnerability to Depression Project: Lifetime history of Axis I psychopathology in individuals at high and low cognitive risk for depression. *Journal of Abnormal Psychology, 109,* 403–418.

Beck, A. T., Brown, G., Steer, R., & Weissman, A. N. (1991). Factor analysis of the Dysfunctional Attitude Scale in a clinical population. *Psychological Assessment: A Journal of Consulting and Clinical Psychology, 3,* 478–483.

Beck, A. T., Rush, A. J., Shaw, B. F., & Emery, G. (1979). *Cognitive therapy of depression.* New York: Guilford Press.

Beck, J. S. (1995). *Cognitive therapy: Basics and beyond.* New York: Guilford Press.

Becker, J. V., Skinner, L. J., Abel, G. G., Axelrod, A., & Cichon, J. (1984). Sexual problems of sexual assault survivors. *Women and Health, 4,* 5–20.

Bonanno, G. A. (2005). Resilience in the face of potential trauma. *Current Directions in Psychological Science, 14,* 135–138.

Brewin, C. R., Dalgleish, T., & Joseph, S. (1996). A dual representation theory of posttraumatic stress disorder. *Psychological Review, 103,* 670–686.

Bryant, R. A., Mastrodomenico, J., Felmingham, K. L., Hopwood, S., Kenny, L., Kandris, E., et al. (2008). Treatment of acute stress disorder: A randomized controlled trial. *Archives of General Psychiatry, 65,* 659–667.

Bryant, R. A., Moulds, M. L., Guthrie, R. M., Dang, S. T., & Nixon, R. D. (2003). Imaginal exposure alone and imaginal exposure with cognitive restructuring in treatment of posttraumatic stress disorder. *Journal of Consulting and Clinical Psychology, 71,* 706–712.

Clark, R. D., Canive, J. M., Calais, L. A., Qualls, C., Brugger, R. D., & Vosburgh, T. B. (1999). Cyproheptadine treatment of nightmares associated with posttraumatic stress disorder. *Journal of Clinical Psychopharmacology, 19,* 486–487.

Cloitre, M., Koenen, K. C., Cohen, L. R., & Han, H. (2002). Skills training in affective and interpersonal regulation followed by exposure: A phase-based treatment for PTSD related to child abuse. *Journal of Consulting and Clinical Psychology, 70,* 1067–1074.

Davidson, J. R., Landerman, L. R., Farfel, G. M., & Clary, C. M. (2002). Characterizing the effects of sertraline in post-traumatic stress disorder. *Psychological Medicine, 32,* 661–670.

Davis, J. L. (2008). *Treating post-trauma nightmares: A cognitive behavioral approach.* New York: Springer.

Davis, J. L., DeArellano, M., Falsetti, S. A., & Resnick, H. S. (2003). Treatment of nightmares related to post-traumatic stress disorder in an adolescent rape victim. *Clinical Case Studies, 2,* 283–294.

Dobson, K. S., & Hamilton, K. E. (2003). Cognitive restructuring: Behavioral tests of negative cognitions. In W. T. O'Donohue, J. E. Fisher, & S. C. Hayes (Eds.), *Cognitive behavior therapy: Applying empirically supported techniques in your practice* (pp. 84–88). Hoboken, NJ: Wiley.

Ehlers, A., & Clark, D. M. (2000). A cognitive model of posttraumatic stress disorder. *Behavior Research and Therapy, 38,* 319–345.

Ellis, A., & Dryden, W. (1997). *The practice of rational emotive behavior therapy* (2nd ed.). New York: Springer.

Epstein, S. (1991). Impulse control and self-destructive behavior. In L. P. Lipsitt & L. L. Mitnick (Eds.), *Self-regulatory behavior and risk: Cause and consequences* (pp. 273–284). Norwood, NJ: Ablex.

Falsetti, S. A., & Resnick, H. S. (1997). *Multiple Channel Exposure Therapy: Therapist manual*. Charleston: Medical University of South Carolina.

Falsetti, S. A., Resnick, H. S., & Davis, J. L. (2005). Multiple Channel Exposure Therapy: Combining cognitive behavioral therapies for the treatment of posttraumatic stress disorder with panic attacks. *Behavior Modification, 29*, 70–94.

Feeny, N. C., Zoellner, L. A., & Foa, E. B. (2002). Treatment outcome for chronic PTSD among female assault victims with borderline personality characteristics: A preliminary examination. *Journal of Personality Disorders, 16*, 30–40.

Foa, E. B., Dancu, C. V., Hembree, E. A., Jaycox, L. H., Meadows, E. A., & Street, G. P. (1999). A comparison of exposure therapy, stress inoculation training, and their combination for reducing posttraumatic stress disorder in female assault victims. *Journal of Consulting and Clinical Psychology, 67*, 194–200.

Foa, E. B., Ehlers, A., Clark, D. M., Tolin, D. F., & Orsillo, S. M. (1999). The Posttraumatic Cognitions Inventory (PTCI): Development and validation. *Psychological Assessment, 11*, 303–314.

Foa, E. B., Hembree, E. A., Cahill, S. P., Rauch, S. A., Riggs, D. S., Feeny, N. C., et al. (2005). Randomized trial of prolonged exposure for posttraumatic stress disorder with and without cognitive restructuring: Outcome at academic and community clinics. *Journal of Consulting and Clinical Psychology, 73*, 953–964.

Foa, E. B., & Kozak, M. J. (1986). Emotional processing of fear: Exposure to corrective information. *Psychological Bulletin, 99*, 20–35.

Foa, E. B., & McNally, R. J. (1996). Mechanisms of change in exposure therapy. In R. M. Rapee (Ed.), *Current controversies in the anxiety disorders* (pp. 329–343). New York: Guilford Press.

Foa, E. B., & Rauch, S. A. (2004). Cognitive changes during prolonged exposure versus prolonged exposure plus cognitive restructuring in female assault survivors with posttraumatic stress disorder. *Journal of Consulting and Clinical Psychology, 72*, 879–884.

Foa, E. B., & Rothbaum, B. O. (1998). *Treating the trauma of rape: Cognitive-behavioral therapy for PTSD*. New York: Guilford Press.

Foa, E. B., Rothbaum, B. O., & Furr, J. M. (2003). Augmenting exposure therapy with other CBT procedures. *Psychiatric Annals, 33*, 47–53.

Foa, E. B., Rothbaum, B. O., Riggs, D. S., & Murdock, T. B. (1991). Treatment of posttraumatic stress disorder in rape victims: A comparison between cognitive-behavioral procedures and counseling. *Journal of Consulting and Clinical Psychology, 59*, 715–723.

Foa, E. B., Steketee, G. R., & Rothbaum, B. O. (1989). Behavioral/cognitive conceptualizations of post-traumatic stress disorder. *Behavior Therapy, 20*, 155–176.

Forbes, D., Creamer, M., & Biddle, D. (2001). The validity of the PTSD checklist as a measure of symptomatic change in combat-related PTSD. *Behaviour Research and Therapy, 39*, 977–986.

Gonzalez, R., Rippeth, J., Carey, C., Heaton, R., Moore, D., Schweinsburg, B., et al. (2004). Neurocognitive performance of methamphetamine users discordant for history of marijuana exposure. *Drug and Alcohol Dependence, 76*(2), 181–190.

Hembree, E. A., Marshall, R., Fitzgibbons, L., & Foa, E. B. (2001). The difficult to treat patient with posttraumatic stress disorder. In M. J. Dewan & R. W. Pies (Eds.), *The difficult to treat psychiatric patient* (pp. 149–178). Washington, DC: American Psychiatric Press.

Hien, D. A., Cohen, L. R., Miele, G. M., Litt, L. C., & Capstick, C. (2004). Promising treatments for women with comorbid PTSD and substance use disorders. *American Journal of Psychiatry, 161,* 1426–1432.

Jacobs-Rebhun, S., Schnurr, P. P., Friedman, M. J., Peck, R., Brophy, M., & Fuller, D. (2000). Posttraumatic stress disorder and sleep difficulty. *American Journal of Psychiatry, 157,* 1525–1526.

Janoff-Bulman, R. (1989). *World Assumptions Scale.* Unpublished measure, University of Massachusetts at Amherst.

Janoff-Bulman, R., & Frieze, I. H. (1983). A theoretical perspective for understanding reactions to victimization. *Journal of Social Issues, 39,* 1–17.

Jaycox, L. H., & Foa, E. B. (1996). Obstacles in implementing exposure therapy for PTSD: Case discussions and practical solutions. *Clinical Psychology and Psychotherapy, 3,* 176–184.

Joseph, S., Williams, R., & Yule, W. (1997). *Understanding post-traumatic stress: A psychosocial perspective on PTSD and treatment.* Chichester, UK: Wiley.

Kaysen, D., Lostutter, T. W., & Goines, M. A. (2005). Cognitive processing therapy for acute stress disorder resulting from an anti-gay assault. *Cognitive and Behavioral Practice, 12,* 278–289.

Keane, T., Fairbank, J., Caddell, J., Zimering, R., Taylor, K., & Mora, C. (1989). Clinical evaluation of a measure to assess combat exposure. *Psychological Assessment, 1,* 53–55.

Krakow, B., Hollifield, M., Johnston, L., Koss, M., Schrader, R., Warner, T. D., et al. (2001). Imagery rehearsal therapy for chronic nightmares in sexual assault survivors with post-traumatic stress disorder: A randomized controlled trial. *Journal of the American Medical Association, 286,* 537–545.

Lambert, M. J., & Barley, D. E. (2001). Research summary on the therapeutic relationship and sychotherapy outcome. *Psychotherapy: Theory/Research/Practice/Training, 38,* 357–361.

Lang, P. J. (1979). A bio-informational theory of emotional imagery. *Psychophysiology, 16,* 495–511.

Leahy, R. L. (2002). A model of emotional schemas. *Cognitive and Behavioral Practice, 9,* 177–190.

Leahy, R. L. (2003). *Cognitive therapy techniques: A practitioner's guide.* New York: Guilford Press.

Lee, D. A., Scragg, P., & Turner, S. (2001). The role of shame and guilt in traumatic events: A clinical model of shame-based and guilt-based PTSD. *British Journal of Medical Psychology, 74,* 451–466.

Liese, B. S., & Beck, J. S. (1997). Cognitive therapy supervision. In C. E. Watkins (Ed.), *Handbook of psychotherapy supervision* (pp. 114–133). New York: Wiley.

Linehan, M. M. (1993). *Cognitive behavioral therapy of borderline personality disorder.* New York: Guilford Press.

Litz, B. T., & Keane, T. M. (1989). Information processing in anxiety disorders: Application to understanding of post-traumatic stress disorder. *Clinical Psychology Review, 9,* 243–257.

Marks, I., Lovell, K., Noshirvani, H., Livanou, M., & Thrasher, S. (1998). Treatment of posttraumatic stress disorder by exposure and/or cognitive restructuring. *Archives of General Psychiatry, 55,* 317–325.

Matthews, L., & Litwack, L. (1995). Cognitive restructuring. In M. Ballou (Ed.), *Psychological interventions: A guide to strategies.* Westport, CT: Praeger.

McCann, I. L., & Pearlman, L. A. (1990). *Psychological trauma and the adult survivor: Theory, therapy, and transformation.* New York: Psychology Press.

Moore, S. A., Zoellner, L. A., & Bittinger, J. N. (2004). Combining cognitive restructuring and exposure therapy: Toward an optimal integration. In S. Taylor (Ed.), *Advances in the treatment of posttraumatic stress disorder* (pp. 129–149). New York: Springer.

Morin, C. M. (1993). *Insomnia: Psychological assessment and management.* New York: Guilford Press.

Mowrer, O. H. (1960). *Learning theory and behavior.* New York: Wiley.

Mueser, K. T., Bolton, E. E., Carty, P. C., Bradley, M. J., Ahlgren, K. F., DiStaso, D. R., et al. (2007). The trauma recovery group: A cognitive-behavioral program for posttraumatic stress disorder in persons with severe mental illness. *Community Mental Health Journal, 43,* 281–303.

Mueser, K. T., Rosenberg, S. D., Xie, H., Jankowski, M. K., Bolton, E. E., Lu, W., et al. (2008). A randomized controlled trial of cognitive-behavioral treatment for posttraumatic stress disorder in severe mental illness. *Journal of Consulting and Clinical Psychology, 76,* 259–271.

Najavits, L. M. (2002). *Seeking safety: A treatment manual for PTSD and substance abuse.* New York: Guilford Press.

Newman, E., Kaloupek, D. G., & Keane, T. M. (1996). Assessment of posttraumatic stress disorder in clinical and research settings. In B. A. van der Kolk, A. C. McFarlane, & L. Weisaeth (Eds.), *Traumatic stress: The effects of overwhelming experience on mind, body, and society* (pp. 242–273). New York: Guilford Press.

Paunovic, N., & Ost, L. (2001). Cognitive-behavior therapy vs exposure therapy in the treatment of PTSD in refugees. *Behavior Research and Therapy, 39,* 1183–1197.

Pearlman, L. A. (2003). *Trauma and attachment belief scale.* Los Angeles: Western Psychological Services.

Peterson, C., Semmel, A., von Baeyer, C., Abramson, L. Y., Metalsky, G. I., & Seligman, M. E. (1982). The Attributional Style Questionnaire. *Cognitive Therapy and Research, 6,* 287–300.

Pitman, R. K., Altman, B., Greenwald, E., Longpre, R. E., Macklin, M. L., Poiré, R. E., et al. (1991). Psychiatric complications during flooding therapy for posttraumatic stress disorder. *Journal of Clinical Psychiatry, 52,* 17–20.

Resick, P. A., & Calhoun, K. S. (2001). Posttraumatic stress disorder. In D. H. Barlow (Ed.), *Clinical handbook of psychological disorders: A step-by-step treatment manual* (3rd ed., pp. 60–113). New York: Guilford Press.

Resick, P. A, Galovski, T. E., O'Brien Uhlmansiek, M., Scher, C. D., Clum, G. A., & Young-Xu, Y. (2008). A randomized clinical trial to dismantle components of cognitive processing therapy for posttraumatic stress disorder in female victims of interpersonal violence. *Journal of Consulting and Clinical Psychology, 76*, 243–258.

Resick, P. A., Nishith, P., Weaver, T. L., Astin, M. C., & Feuer, C. A. (2002). A comparison of cognitive-processing therapy with prolonged exposure and a waiting condition for the treatment of chronic posttraumatic stress disorder in female rape victims. *Journal of Consulting and Clinical Psychology, 70*, 867–879.

Resick, P. A., & Schnicke, M. K. (1993). *Cognitive processing therapy for rape victims: A treatment manual.* Newbury Park, CA: Sage.

Resick, P. A., Schnicke, M. K., & Markway, B. G. (1991). *Cognitive content and post-traumatic stress disorder.* Presented at the International Society of Traumatic Stress Studies conference. Washington, D.C.

Riggs, D. S., Dancu, C. V., Gershuny, B. S., Greenberg, D., & Foa, E. B. (1992). Anger and post-traumatic stress disorder in female crime victims. *Journal of Traumatic Stress, 5*, 613–625.

Rosenbaum, M., & Ronen, T. (1998). Clinical supervision from the standpoint of cognitive-behavior therapy. *Psychotherapy, 35*, 220–230.

Rosenberg, S. D., Mueser, K. T., & Jankowski, M. K. (2004). Cognitive-behavioral treatment of PTSD in severe mental illness: Results of a pilot study. *American Journal of Psychiatric Rehabilitation, 7*, 171–186.

Roth, S., & Lebowitz, L. (1988). The experience of sexual trauma. *Journal of Traumatic Stress, 1*, 79–107.

Roth, S., & Newman, E. (1991). The process of coping with sexual trauma. *Journal of Traumatic Stress, 4*, 279–297.

Safran, J. D., Vallis, T. M., Segal, Z. V., & Shaw, B. F. (1986). Assessment of core cognitive processes in cognitive therapy. *Cognitive Therapy and Research, 10*, 509–526.

Schreuder, B. J. N., van Egmond, M., Kleijn, W. C., & Visser, A. T. (1998). Daily reports of posttraumatic nighmares and anxiety dreams in Dutch war victims. *Journal of Anxiety Disorders, 12*, 511–524.

Scurfield, R. M., Kenderdine, S. K., & Pollard, R. J. (1990). Inpatient treatment for war-related post-traumatic stress disorder: Initial findings on a longer-term outcome study. *Journal of Traumatic Stress, 3*, 185–201.

Stewart, S. H., & Conrad, P. J. (2003). Psychosocial models of functional associations between posttraumatic stress disorder and substance use disorder. In P. C. Ouimette, & P. J. Brown (Eds.), *Trauma and substance abuse: causes, consequences, and treatment of comorbid disorders* (pp. 29–55). Washington, DC: American Psychological Association.

Taylor, S. (2006). *Clinician's guide to PTSD: A cognitive-behavioral approach.* New York: Guilford Press.

Young, J. D. (1994). *Cognitive therapy for personality disorders: A schema-focused approach* (rev. ed.). Sarasota, FL: Professional Resource Press/Professional Resource Exchange.

Zayfert, C., & Becker, C. C. (2007). *Cognitive-behavioral therapy for PTSD*. New York: Guilford Press.

Zayfert, C., & DeViva, J. C. (2004). Residual insomnia following cognitive behavioral therapy for PTSD. *Journal of Traumatic Stress, 17*, 69–73.

ADDITIONAL COGNITIVE/COGNITIVE BEHAVIORAL READINGS FOR THERAPISTS

Beck, J. (1995). *Cognitive therapy: Basics and beyond*. New York: Guilford Press. (A list of additional readings is included.)

Beck, J. S. (1995). *Cognitive therapy for challenging problems: What to do when the basics don't work*. New York: Guilford Press.

Leahy, R. L. (2003). *Cognitive therapy techniques: A practitioner's guide*. New York: Guilford Press.

Lyddon, W. J., & Jones, J. V. (2001). *Empirically supported cognitive therapies: Current and future applications*. New York: Springer.

ADDITIONAL RESOURCES FOR CLIENTS

Burns, D. (1999). *The feeling good handbook*. New York: Penguin Group.

Burns, D. (1999). *Feeling good: The new mood therapy*. New York: Avon Books.

Greenberger, D., & Padesky, C. (1995). *Mind over mood: Change how you feel by changing the way you think*. New York: Guilford Press.

Hickling, E. J., & Blanchard, E. B. (2006). *Overcoming the trauma of your motor vehicle accident: A cognitive-behavioral treatment program workbook*. New York: Oxford University Press.

McKay, M., Davis, M., & Fanning, P. (2007). *Thoughts and feelings: Taking control of your moods and your life* (3rd ed.). Oakland, CA: New Harbinger.

Najavits, L. M. (2002). *A woman's addiction workbook: Your guide to in-depth healing*. Oakland, CA: New Harbinger.

ADDITIONAL TRAUMA RESOURCES

Briere, J. (1996). *Therapy for adults molested as children: Beyond survival* (2nd ed.). New York: Springer.

Briere, J. (1992). *Child abuse trauma: Theory and treatment of the last effects*. Newbury Park, CA: Sage.

Davis, J. L. (2008). *Treating post-trauma nightmares: A cognitive behavioral approach*. New York: Springer.

Falsetti, S. A., & Resnick, H. S. (1997). *Multiple Channel Exposure Therapy: Therapist manual*. Charleston: Medical University of South Carolina.

Falsetti, S. A., Resnick, H. S., & Davis, J. L. (2005). Multiple Channel Exposure Therapy: Combining cognitive behavioral therapies for the treatment of post-traumatic stress disorder with panic attacks. *Behavior Modification, 29*, 70–94.

Foa, E. B., Keane, T. M., & Friedman, M. J. (Eds.). (2000). *Effective treatments for PTSD: Practice guidelines from the International Society for Traumatic Stress Studies*. New York: Guilford Press.

Foa, E. B., Keane, T. M., & Friedman, M. J. (2005). Guidelines for treatment of PTSD. *Journal of Traumatic Stress, 13,* 539–588.

Foa, E. B., & Rothbaum, B. O. (1998). *Treating the trauma of rape: Cognitive-behavioral therapy for PTSD*. New York: Guilford Press.

Hickling, E. J. & Blanchard, E. B. (2006). *Overcoming the trauma of your motor vehicle accident: A cognitive-behavioral treatment program therapist guide*. New York: Oxford University Press.

Linehan, M. M. (1993). *Cognitive behavioral therapy of borderline personality disorder*. New York: Guilford Press.

Linehan, M. M. (1993). *Skills training manual for treating borderline personality disorder*. New York: Guilford Press.

Najavits, L. M. (2002). *Seeking safety: A treatment manual for PTSD and substance abuse*. New York: Guilford Press.

Pearlman, L. A., & Saakvitne, K. W. (1995). *Trauma and the therapist: Counter-transference and vicarious traumatization in psychotherapy with incest survivors*. New York: Norton.

Resick, P. A. (2001). *Cognitive processing therapy: Generic version*. St. Louis, MO: University of Missouri–St. Louis.

Resick, P. A. (2001). Cognitive therapy for posttraumatic stress disorder. *Journal of Cognitive Psychotherapy: An International Quarterly, 15,* 321–329.

Resick, P. A., Monson, C. M., & Chard, K. M. (2007). *Cognitive processing therapy: Veteran/military version*. Washington, DC: Department of Veterans' Affairs.

Resick, P. A., & Schnicke, M. K. (1993). *Cognitive processing therapy for rape victims: A treatment manual*. Newbury Park, CA: Sage.

Saakvitne, K. W., & Pearlman, L. A. (1996). *Transforming the pain: A workbook on vicarious traumatization*. New York: Norton.

Zayfert, C., & Becker, C. B. (2006). *Cognitive-behavioral therapy for PTSD: A case formulation approach*. New York: Guilford Press.

HANDOUTS

The handouts in this section can be reproduced and given to your clients.

Handout 3-1 A Psychoeducational Script*

The cognitive model suggests that problems with negative feelings, such as depression and anxiety, develop through biases in thinking. Everyone has biases, or filters, that help us to sort out what to pay attention to in our everyday lives and what things to ignore. This ability to sort information is very important, as there is so much going on around us all the time—we couldn't possibly pay attention to it all! And we might be worse off if we tried to! We need these filters to function. The ability to figure out quickly what information we should pay attention to and what we should ignore is very important, as we have constant streams of information around us every day.

So if we all have filters, where is the problem? The problem comes from overuse of particular filters that are not helpful to use. If the filters allow us to focus only on information that leads to negative thoughts and problematic feelings, we are in big trouble. As we are growing up, we all develop core beliefs—those basic ideas we hold about ourselves, others, and the world. They are so basic to us that we do not even question whether they are true or not. For example, tall people know they are tall, and that causes them to duck automatically when they approach a low ceiling.

Our core beliefs can have a great influence on how and what we think. They help us to filter information that is not considered important or relevant. They can also help us make connections between new information and old information. Some of these core beliefs are negative (I am worthless) and may be activated during times of stress. We call this activation a "trigger" sometimes. When triggered, these beliefs filter out positive information and allow in only negative information that supports our core beliefs. So if you have the core belief that you are a failure, you will see everything through that filter. You will pay attention to information that seems to support the idea that you are a failure and ignore information that does not support that belief. When core beliefs are activated, unhealthy assumptions, rules, and attitudes are also activated. These serve to further direct attention toward information that will support our beliefs. For example, if the core belief of "I am worthless" is activated, we may assume that because we are so incompetent, we have to work extra hard in order to just keep up with our coworkers. Of course, working hard is not necessarily a problem. These assumptions, attitudes, and rules become problematic if they are not flexible or if they generalize too broadly across situations. For example, if a mother has a core belief of "I am unlovable," one of her "rules of living" may

---

*You may want to simplify this handout, which explains the cognitive model.

be that she must be loving and nurturing at all times or she is a bad mother and her children will not love her. While there is nothing wrong with being loving and nurturing, if this rule is inflexible, it does not leave room for the mother to take time for herself or become irritated at her children.

If we see everything through a filter, we are likely to make some mistakes about how things really are—these are called *thinking errors*. For example, if a threatening core belief (the world is a dangerous place) is triggered, this will narrow your perspective and color how you perceive everything going on around you. You will look for and pay more attention to potentially threatening information and danger cues. If a hopeless core belief (I am worthless) were activated, you would pay attention to any information that might suggest you had failed in some way and ignore all successes. Feelings or emotions are associated with different types of thoughts. For example, feelings of anxiety are associated with perceptions of danger, while feelings of anger are related to thinking that something is unfair or that someone treated you badly.

Finally, negative assumptions, rules, and attitudes lead to negative automatic thoughts. These are thoughts that just pop into our heads (e.g., I always screw things up). Often, we don't even realize it is happening. For example, consider a worker who has the belief that he is incompetent. The employee works really hard on a project and his boss stops by to tell him how pleased he is with the result. The employee thinks, "He wouldn't be so impressed if he knew it took me twice as long as it would someone else." So, in spite of evidence to the contrary (boss's praise), the employee's first thought is consistent with his core belief—that he is incompetent. The fact that the thoughts are automatic does not mean they are true. The problem is that we have them, and generally believe them, without considering whether they are true or false; having them and believing them increases the chance that we will feel depressed and hopeless about the situation. It is not hard to imagine that the activation of these negative thoughts may affect how we feel.

Handout 3-2 Event–Thoughts–Consequences Worksheet[*]

Activating Event	Thoughts/Beliefs	Emotional Consequence	Behavioral Consequence
Raise hand in meeting and boss does not acknowledge me	She is mad at me. I must have screwed something up.	Worried, anxious	Hide in office and fret
Raise hand in meeting and boss does not acknowledge me	I am unimportant to my boss.	Depressed, rejected	Go home early and go to bed

| Raise hand in meeting and boss does not acknowledge me | She must be in a bad mood. Why is she taking it out on me? | Angry | Fume around the office; respond angrily to others |
| Raise hand in meeting and boss does not acknowledge me | She must be really stressed out and distracted. | Concerned | Check on boss later that day and return to work |

*Handout 3-2 can be used to help clients understand the relationship of events, thoughts, and feelings and behaviors. It can also assist them with their own monitoring.

Handout 3-3 Cognitive Theory of Trauma Responses[*]

If the way you think about everyday situations has an impact on your mood, it would not be surprising that the way you think about a traumatic event would also impact your mood. This can happen in a number of ways. First, if the trauma did not fit your beliefs about yourself, other people, or the world, your mind would not know what to do with that information, although it may still trigger those basic negative beliefs. If your mind is unable to process the trauma, it may keep replaying the information until you can somehow make sense of it. This may be why you have intrusive thoughts and nightmares about the trauma. Of course, most people do not like thinking about the trauma, so they try to avoid anything that reminds them of the trauma, including people, places, and situations. If the avoidance continues for a while, your mind is not able to process the information, which actually makes the impact of the trauma last longer. Not being able to process the information may also explain hyperarousal—if you are unable to make sense of the trauma, chances are that you may still feel that you are in danger and your body stays aroused, waiting to respond to the danger. Second, if you have negative core beliefs already, the trauma might provide support for them. So a trauma may reinforce and strengthen prior beliefs, perhaps making them more extreme and maintaining symptoms over time.

If the information about the trauma does not fit with your underlying beliefs, there are three ways that your mind can handle it. First, you can alter the information to fit the beliefs (assimilate) or alter the beliefs to fit the information (accommodate). For example, suppose you believe that the world is basically a safe place and that you will avoid accidents if you drive carefully and follow the rules. If you are then hit by another driver who was speeding,

*This handout provides general information that can be reproduced and provided to clients as the basis for explaining trauma responses to them (see also Zayfert & Becker (2007), Foa & Rothbaum (1998), and Resick & Schnicke (1993)).

you may assimilate, or alter, the information by convincing yourself that you are to blame for the accident, that you must not have been paying attention. If you were to accommodate the information, you might change your beliefs to suggest that sometimes, even if we are really careful, other people's carelessness can endanger us. A third possible response is overaccommodation. This process involves an extreme distortion of the belief system. For example, instead of changing the belief to suggest that sometimes other people's carelessness can result in harm to us, you may believe that the world is a very dangerous place; all drivers are reckless and can never be trusted. Overaccommodation may result in very rigid thinking, making it very difficult for you to consider other alternatives (Resick & Schnicke, 1993).

Whether you assimilate, accommodate, or overaccommodate information about the trauma, experiencing traumatic events like combat, rape, or a severe car accident may activate your core beliefs.

Handout 3-4 Feeling Identification Form

Day	Event	Feeling

Handout 3-5 A Script to Help Clients Identify Their Thoughts

Lots of people may not even be aware they are having thoughts, since this is not something they are used to noticing. The type of thoughts we want you to monitor over the next week are called "automatic" because they just seem to pop up out of nowhere; also, they may come and go so quickly that we are not aware of them. In fact, we may be much more aware of the emotions that come after the thoughts than the thoughts themselves. The good news is that you can train yourself to notice thoughts. People whose thoughts come and go so quickly may need to catch their thoughts, like catching a butterfly or lightning bug. One way to do this is to stop at various times of the day and ask yourself, "What am I thinking right now?," and keep track of it. You could decide to do this at the beginning of each group session you have or at the start of your meals, or program your clock to go off and ask yourself this question. Learning how to do this may seem awkward at first, but just like a sport, you need to practice to get good at it. Eventually you will be able to identify your thoughts fairly easily.

Handout 3-6 Thought Identification Form

Day	Event	Thought

Handout 3-7 Types of Unhealthy Thoughts

All or nothing	Perception that situations are absolutes, are one way or another, without allowing for gray areas or flexibility	I am powerless versus I am in control You are a buddy or an enemy
Overgeneralization	Assuming from one situation	I was victimized, so I will always be a victim
Personalization	Taking responsibility for some negative outcome unrelated to your actions	He died that day because I was not there to save him
Mind reading	Assuming you know what another is thinking	He thinks I'm worthless
Magnification	Focusing on the negative aspects of yourself or a situation	I'm a failure because I failed the test
Minimization	Not focusing on the positive aspects of yourself or a situation	It wasn't really a rape
Predicting the future	Assuming you know what will happen in a given situation	I know he'll leave me eventually
Emotional reasoning	Defining situations by how you feel about them	I am in danger because I am afraid
Catastrophizing	Focusing on the worst possible outcome	A flashback means I am losing my mind
Superstitious thinking	Believing that there is a link between events when no link exists	I was wearing shorts when I was raped; if I wear shorts again I'll be in danger

Handout 3-8 Events–Thoughts–Feelings Worksheet[*]

A. Event (something happens):

_____

_____

_____

_____

_____

B. Thoughts/Beliefs (what you say to yourself about what happened):

_____

_____

_____

_____

_____

C. Feelings/Behaviors (what you feel—sad, mad, glad, scared—and what you do when you say the above (B) to yourself?)

_____

_____

_____

_____

_____

Complete the following about your thoughts in B.

1. What is the evidence for this thought?

_____

_____

_____

2. What is the evidence against this thought?

_____

_____

_____

3. Rate the probability that this thought is true on a scale from 0 (not at all true) to 100 (completely true):

_____

4. Am I using words indicating extremes in my thinking, for example: always, never, should, forever, need, must, can't, every time?

_____

5. Are my thoughts based on feelings rather than facts?

_____

6. Am I overgeneralizing from a single incident?

_____

7. Am I disregarding important aspects of the situation?

_____

8. What else could I say to myself instead of the initial thought or belief?

_____

_____

_____

_____

_____

9. If I were able to say this how would I feel?

_____

_____

_____

*Reprinted, with permission, from Falsetti, S. A., & Resnick H. S. (1997). *Multiple Channel Exposure Therapy: Patient manual*. Charleston: Medical University of South Carolina.

CHAPTER 4

Trauma-Focused Cognitive Behavioral Therapy for Children

AMY L. HOCH

TRAUMA

Exposure to trauma can yield significant and potentially lifelong problems for children, their families, and society. Children and adolescents with trauma histories routinely exhibit symptoms of posttraumatic stress disorder (PTSD), which often goes undiagnosed and untreated. This may result in the continuation and escalation of destructive and disruptive behaviors, such as violence, suicidal ideation, sleeplessness, attention problems, running away, and substance abuse. Consequently, there is a need for mental health professionals proficient in trauma-informed care to provide the needed treatment for these children and serve as the expert voice in understanding and responding to the needs of these youth.

The most damaging types of trauma include early physical and sexual abuse, neglect, emotional/psychological abuse, exposure to domestic violence, and other forms of child maltreatment. The Child Maltreatment Annual Report (U.S. Department of Human Services, 2006) states that there were over 905,000 substantiated victims of child maltreatment in fiscal year 2006, as reported to child protective services across the nation. Of those 905,000 victims, 64.1% were neglected, 16% were physically abused, 8.8% sexually abused, 6.6% were emotionally/psychologically abused, and 15.1% were maltreated in other ways, including abandonment, threat of harm, and in utero exposure to drugs. Furthermore, an estimated 3.3 million children and 10 million adolescents witness violence in their homes each year, and these youth are at higher risk for child maltreatment (Carlson, 1998; Straus & Gelles, 1996).

Of course, these statistics are likely an underestimate of the prevalence of abuse since they speak only to those reports of child maltreatment that get reported to child protective services and that are substantiated. It is also unclear how many of these children were exposed to more than one kind of trauma. Epidemiological research suggests a higher incidence of children's exposure to complex trauma. The National Child Traumatic Stress Network's (NCTSN) Complex Trauma Task Force defines complex trauma as "children's experiences of multiple traumatic events that occur within the caregiving system, that are chronic, and begin early in childhood" (Cook, Blaustein, Spinazzola, & van der Kolk, 2003). The Third National Incidence Study of Child Abuse and Neglect utilized a nationally representative sample of 5,600 professionals across 842 agencies in 42 countries (Sedlak & Broadhurst, 1996) to look at the incidence of abuse and neglect. The data were examined using the Harm Standard, including only youth who have experienced harm from the abuse or neglect. An estimated 1,553,800 children were abused or neglected in 1993, including 217,700 sexually abused children, 338,900 physically neglected children, 212,800 emotionally neglected children, and 381,700 physically abused children. When the Endangerment Standard, defined as children who experience abuse or neglect that puts them at risk or harm, was used, the estimated incidence of child abuse and neglect nearly doubled (2,815,600).

The NCTSN Complex Trauma Taskforce (Cook et al., 2003) identified seven domains of impairment observed in children exposed to complex trauma. The domains include:

1. Attachment
2. Biology
3. Affect regulation
4. Dissociation
5. Behavioral regulation
6. Cognition
7. Self-concept

An understanding of these domains becomes important when creating a treatment plan for traumatized youth. Treatment providers must have an understanding of the differences between more acute trauma, a single-event traumatic experience, and complex trauma so that best practices are followed and youth are not retraumatized.

In over 80% of maltreated children, insecure attachment patterns have been observed. Children who grow up being exposed to chaos, violence, and repeated abandonment fail to develop appropriate developmental abilities, including language, verbal processing, and the ability to make organized decisions (Siegel, 1999). Maunder and Hunter (2001) reported that early disrupted attachment in humans can lead to further problems in adulthood, including increased risk of poor physiological and psychosocial functioning. Specifically, three pathways are affected: (1) increased sensitivity to stress; (2) difficulty modulating emotions without outside support; and (3) problematic support-seeking behavior including dependency or withdrawal.

Recent research documents the effects trauma has on the biological system. The NCTSN Complex Trauma Taskforce's White Paper on Complex Trauma edited by Cook and colleagues (2003) states that in early childhood, trauma creates biological vulnerability by increasing risk for disorders in reality orientation (e.g. autism), learning (e.g. dyslexia), or cognitive and behavioral self-management (e.g., attention deficit hyperactivity disorder [ADHD]). In middle childhood and adolescence, the brain is developing the ability to make decisions necessary for functioning in the world and with others. In the absence of supportive relationships, traumatic events may lead to problems in self-regulation (e.g., eating disorders), relationships (e.g., conduct disorders), thought problems, or a combination of these areas, resulting in borderline personality disorder and/or chronic addiction.

Children exposed to chronic trauma are vulnerable to emotional and behavioral dysregulation disorders, including major depression (Putnam, 2003) and oppositional defiant disorder (Ford et al., 2000). Trauma is associated with deficits in executive functioning (Beers & DeBellis, 2002), which in turn result in an increase in impulse control disorders. Frequently, youth displaying these behaviors are thought to be purposefully manipulative. In reality, risky behaviors, including self-injury, sexualized behavior, and aggression, may be reenactments of aspects of the trauma or maladaptive means of trying to regulate their experiences. Overall, a history of childhood trauma increases the risk of poor outcomes, including substance use and abuse, suicidality and self-injury, teen pregnancy and paternity, criminal activity, and revictimization (Anda, 2002).

Dissociation falls along a continuum of experience, from getting engrossed in a movie to loss of time during a traumatic event. Putnam (1997, p. 7) defines dissociation as the "the failure to integrate or associate information and experience in a normally expectable fashion." During a traumatic event, dissociation can have a protective effect by allowing the child to cut off from or compartmentalize his or her feelings, thoughts, and/or behaviors so they are more manageable. Unfortunately, dissociative responses may become habitual so that even under minor stress, dissociation is triggered and youth zone out important information (e.g., lessons in school, potential perpetrator's behavior) or shut off beneficial feelings (e.g., love, excitement).

Significant effects on cognition have been documented in abused and neglected children. These children show lower IQs and are more likely to be found in the developmentally delayed spectrum of cognitive functioning

(Sandgrund, Gaines, & Green, 1974). Across a variety of trauma exposures, maltreated children are more frequently referred for special education services (Shronk & Cicchetti, 2001), have lower grades and poorer scores on standardized tests, and have higher rates of grade retention and dropout (Cahill, Kaminer, & Johnson, 1999; Kurtz, Gaudin, Wodarski, & Howing, 1993; Leiter & Johnson, 1994; Trickett, McBride-Chang, & Putnam, 1994).

It is well documented that childhood trauma has an adverse impact on psychosocial functioning in both childhood and adult years. Youth who experience childhood trauma are at increased risk for experiencing posttraumatic stress disorder (PTSD), depression, substance abuse, academic difficulties, delinquency, and teenage pregnancy, as well as revictimization (Finkelhor, 1995; Kelley, Thornberry, & Smith, 1997). More recent research suggests that the developing brain is also adversely affected by chronic PTSD in childhood (DeBellis et al., 1999). Felitti and colleagues (1998) link childhood abuse and household dysfunction with the leading causes of death in adulthood, including heart disease, cancer, chronic lung disease, fractures, and liver disease.

When the Harm Standard incidence numbers are used, the total annual cost of child abuse and neglect is estimated at $94 billion (Fromm, 2001). Hospitalization, chronic health problems, mental health, child welfare, law enforcement, and judicial system costs are the direct costs ($24.4 billion) associated with child abuse and neglect. Indirect costs ($69.7 billion) include special education, juvenile delinquency, adult mental health and health care, lost productivity to society, and adult criminal behavior.

The developers of trauma-focused cognitive behavioral therapy (TFCBT), Judy Cohen, MD, Esther Deblinger, PhD, and Anthony Manarino, PhD, have been clinicians and researchers in the field of trauma for over 20 years. TFCBT has evolved from original studies (Cohen & Mannarino, 1996; Deblinger, Lippmann, & Steer, 1996; Deblinger, McLeer & Henry, 1990; Deblinger, Stauffer, & Steer, 2001), manuals (Cohen, Deblinger, Mannarino, & Steer, 2001), and books (Cohen, Mannarino, & Deblinger, 2006; Deblinger & Heflin, 1996) by the developers and more recently a National Institute of Mental Health (NIMH) multisite study (Cohen, Deblinger, Mannarino, & Steer, 2004) that compared TFCBT to a more nondirective supportive mode of treatment with sexually abused youth and their nonoffending caregivers.

The randomized, controlled multisite study occurred over a 5-year period at both the University of Medicine & Dentistry of New Jersey–School of Osteopathic Medicine's CARES Institute and the Center for Traumatic Stress in Children and Adolescents at Allegheny General Hospital in Pittsburgh. Two hundred twenty-nine children between the ages of 8 and 14 were assigned to either TFCBT or nondirective supportive treatment. All the children had substantiated sexual abuse, but most of them had experienced other traumatic events as well. Significant improvement occurred across both treatment models; however, children randomly assigned to trauma-focused CBT, as opposed to children assigned to client-centered therapy, showed greater improvement with respect to PTSD, depression, behavior problems, shame, and feelings of perceived credibility and interpersonal trust (Cohen et al., 2004). Participating parents demonstrated similar superior benefits in response to trauma-focused CBT in terms of general levels of depression, abuse-specific distress, parental support, and skills in responding their children's behavioral and emotional needs. Although there have been some outcome investigations examining other abuse-specific treatments, several recent critical reviews of the empirical literature have clearly established this trauma-focused CBT model as the treatment of choice at this time for children who have suffered sexual abuse and their families (Saunders, Berliner, & Hanson, 2003; Substance Abuse and Mental Health Services Administration, 2004).

It is noteworthy that some of the basic elements found in the trauma-focused CBT interventions are incorporated in many of the treatment approaches described in the clinical literature. Authors from a variety of theoretical orientations report that some type of trauma-focused process is important to effective treatment with victims of trauma (Benedek, 1985; Friedrich, 1991; Pynoos & Nader, 1988; Terr, 1991). The National Child Traumatic Stress Network (NCTSN) identified the following list of core components for effective trauma treatment:

- Risk screening and triage
- Systematic assessment, case conceptualization, and treatment planning
- Psychoeducation
- Addressing stress reactions
- Trauma narration and organization
- Emotion regulation and anxiety management
- Facilitating adaptive coping
- Parenting skills and behavior management
- Promoting adaptive developmental progression
- Addressing grief and loss
- Promoting safety skills
- Relapse prevention
- Evaluation of treatment response
- Engagement/addressing barriers to treatment

Many of these core components of trauma treatment are directly included in the TFCBT model. The other components are also included but perhaps less directly addressed in writings on the model.

THE FOUNDATION OF TFCBT

The primary values of the TFCBT model are conveyed by the acronym CRAFTS (Cohen et al., 2006):

- **C**omponents based
- **R**espectful of cultural values
- **A**daptable and flexible
- **F**amily focused
- **T**herapeutic relationship is central
- **S**elf-efficacy is emphasized

TFCBT is a components-based approach to treatment. The skills taught in TFCBT are matched to the individual needs of the client and presented in a manner that builds on previously learned skills.

An inherent value of TFCBT is its respect for cultural, religious, familial, and personal values. Through each phase of TFCBT, the therapist attempts to understand and validate the family's values so that treatment can be supported by the larger systems impacting on the family.

Adaptability and flexibility are necessary for the success of TFCBT. Rather than a rigid treatment protocol to which the client must conform, TFCBT seeks to adapt to the needs of the family while effectively addressing PTSD, depression, shame, and behavior problems.

Family involvement is a key component of TFCBT. When a child is traumatized, it affects the entire family. Therefore, the involvement of caregivers, as well as siblings and extended supports if appropriate, helps to heal the whole system. If the family participates in treatment, skills are more likely to generalize beyond the therapy room.

The therapeutic relationship is the foundation of TFCBT. Providing a trusting, validating environment for the child and family allows deeper work to be done. A supportive relationship counteracts feelings of shame and distrust and provides the necessary safety net to confront avoidance related to the trauma.

Self-efficacy for caregivers and children is the long-term goal of TFCBT. It is hoped that by providing them with coping skills and safety skills with which a feeling of mastery is created, children and families will improve their overall functioning.

A frequent concern and misconception about TFCBT is that it is rigid and has little respect for the therapeutic alliance. Good TFCBT is neither rigid nor disrespectful of the therapeutic relationship. Just the opposite! The most effective TFCBT balances a strong therapeutic relationship with purposeful technique, creativity, and validation. The experience and clinical skill you bring to TFCBT will only make the treatment model more effective for your individual client.

The mental health field is now emphasizing the need for evidence-based treatment. Like the medical field, mental health is being held accountable for treatment outcomes. With the push to learn and use evidence-based treatments, some clinicians feel that their clinical judgment and creativity are being questioned. TFCBT allows one to strike a balance between a well-studied treatment model, the needs of the client, and the strengths of the clinician. Its effectiveness lies with specific issues: PTSD, depression, shame, and behavior problems related to sexual abuse. Adaptations with physical abuse and domestic violence have been made and are being researched. The model has been studied using a linear approach to the components; however, agencies and individuals have adapted the model by using only certain components. These adaptations, while necessary for the model's ongoing evolution, should not be confused with the model. Fidelity is important for treatment outcome. As a clinician learning this model, it is important to first practice it with fidelity so the therapist can understand its strengths and weaknesses and one's own process within it. Thus, in the following pages, the model will be outlined as a linear progression as seen in Figure 4.1.

The remainder of this chapter should be thought of as a detailed summary of TFCBT that outlines a more comprehensive explanation of the model in the co-developers' book, *Treating Trauma and Traumatic Grief in Children and Adolescents* (Cohen et al, 2006). The structure, rationale and creative ideas for implementation are their ideas unless cited otherwise.

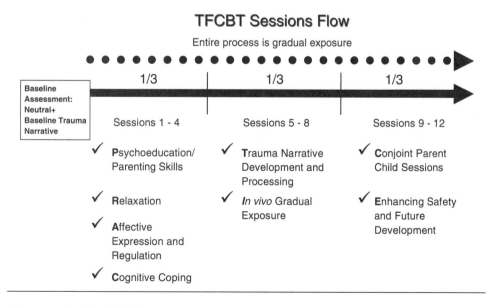

Figure 4.1   The TFCBT Model

THERAPIST TRAINING

Since this chapter outlines how to apply TFCBT in clinical practice, it is important to talk about clinical skill and training. Trauma work is both challenging and rewarding. Regardless of previous training and preferred treatment modality, specific training in working with traumatized clients is needed. This chapter is not a substitute for the necessary reading, training, and supervision required to utilize TFCBT effectively and safely with clients. There are various resources available for such training in TFCBT. A good starting place would be the two books outlining the TFCBT model: *Treating Sexually Abused Children and Their Nonoffending Parents* (Deblinger & Heflin, 1996) and *Treating Trauma and Traumatic Grief in Children and Adolescents* (Cohen et al., 2006).

Through a grant from Substance Abuse and Mental Health Services Administration (SAMHSA), researchers and psychologists from the Medical University of South Carolina (MUSC), in collaboration with the TFCBT developers, were able to create a web-training program on TFCBT that is available to any clinician (www.musc.edu/tfcbt). The web training provides information on each component of the model, provides information sheets and scripts for use by clinicians, and offers video clips of therapists demonstrating various aspects of the model. Free continuing education credits are offered for completion of the training. A separate web training is available on TFCBT for traumatic grief (www.musc.edu/ctg).

While books and web-based training provide didactic learning opportunities, face-to-face training opportunities are critical for learning how to apply TFCBT to real cases. Basic and advanced TFCBT trainings are offered both nationally and internationally. These 1- to 3-day training opportunities provide opportunities for discussion and practice on the TFCBT components as well applications to special populations.

Finally, to practice TFCBT with safety, effectiveness and fidelity, supervision and consultation are encouraged. There is no better way to learn TFCBT than to have weekly or monthly consultation on cases, perhaps including feedback on audio- or videotaped sessions. Experts in TFCBT provide consultation to professionals and agencies around the world.

IS TFCBT RIGHT FOR MY CLIENTS?

TFCBT is appropriate for substantiated cases of child maltreatment (e.g., physical abuse, sexual abuse, domestic violence) and other documented traumatic events (e.g., homicide/suicide of a loved one; natural disaster). In the case of child maltreatment, the substantiation could come from child protective services (CPS), a medical professional, the prosecutor's office, or another mental health evaluator. Substantiation is important in cases of child maltreatment because of the possible involvement of CPS and other legal entities. Therapy should be kept separate from an investigation so that the therapist is not serving a dual role as evaluator and therapist.

Given that TFCBT is a structured model of treatment, it is important to have some acknowledgment by a professional that the abuse has happened so that the therapist can directly acknowledge the trauma within the first session. In cases where abuse is suspected or the child is displaying sexualized behavior without a known history of sexual abuse, TFCBT should not be used. Instead, in the case of suspected abuse, the child should be referred for an abuse evaluation with a trained professional, who can better determine what has or has not happened to the child. That evaluator can then go to court if needed and make recommendations for treatment. In this way, the evaluator is part of the investigation and can speak to the allegations in court if necessary, and the therapist–client relationship remains protected. If abuse is not substantiated, a more nondirective approach to treatment may be more appropriate. If a disclosure occurs in the context of more nondirective treatment, abuse-specific treatment can then begin. However, even with less structured treatment, components of TFCBT can be used to provide education and safety skill training. In the case of sexualized behavior without any disclosure of abuse, various components of the TFCBT model may be used to address the behavioral issues: parenting skills to help caregivers manage the sexualized behavior; relaxation, affective expression and regulation, and cognitive coping to help both caregivers and children understand the function of the sexualized behavior and how to redirect themselves; psychoeducation about sexual abuse and sexual behavior; and enhancing safety and future development to provide prevention education and safety skills. The trauma narrative and cognitive processing components of the model would not be used since there was no reported traumatic event. If, during the course of treatment using some of the TFCBT components, abuse is disclosed, a report to CPS should be made. Following the investigation by CPS, direct discussion about the child's abuse can then take place.

Clients who have vague memories or don't remember the trauma are not appropriate candidates for TFCBT, because there is not a clear memory to process. TFCBT is built on the model of gradual exposure, a process of incremental exposure to anxiety-provoking memories and material over the course of treatment. The goal of gradual exposure is to reduce anxiety and avoidance associated with the trauma. By facing one's fear in a manageable manner, the trauma becomes manageable as well. This process will be elaborated on later in the chapter. Without a clear memory of the trauma, narrative and cognitive processing work would be impossible and/or risky. TFCBT is not about pulling for traumatic memories; it is about processing the ones that are distressing to the client. The therapist does not want to be in the position of possibly creating, changing, or influencing memories, especially if the case is involved in litigation.

It is important to remember that TFCBT does not solve *all* problems. Triaging cases for appropriate services is necessary. Children, adolescents, and caregivers whose behavior is extremely risky or unsafe (e.g., active suicidal ideation and attempts, active psychosis, active substance abuse) may need more intensive services or, at the very least, adjunctive services in addition to TFCBT. For example, if a caregiver is actively using drugs or alcohol and his ability to get to sessions or manage his behavior in sessions is affected, it may be necessary to suspend TFCBT until after the caregiver has obtained substance abuse treatment. However, even though risky behaviors are present, the TFCBT model may still be used. For many adolescents, suicidal ideation and other risky behavior (e.g., cutting, risky sexual behavior) are a means of managing the strong emotions they are having related to the abuse. Relaxation, affective regulation, and cognitive coping skills can sometimes very quickly get those behaviors under control within the 12 sessions. Some adolescents may need an extended stabilization period during which coping skills are taught and psychoeducation about trauma and trauma triggers is provided. In either case, TFCBT can still be utilized. The therapist's assessment of the client and family will dictate how quickly they can proceed with more direct trauma work as stabilization improves.

TFCBT is predicated on social learning theory with an emphasis on skill building as well as exposure and processing. Exposure is a well-validated treatment for anxiety and PTSD that "exposes" clients to reminders of the trauma that they eventually habituate to so that they no longer create anxiety. Foa, Molnar, & Cashman (1995) successfully used a prolonged exposure technique with rape victims. Deblinger et al. (1996) then adapted the model for children and adolescents by providing gradual increments of exposure to trauma beginning with general information about the trauma and eventually talking directly about the client's traumatic experience(s). TFCBT incorporates other important components that positively impact on children's and parents overall functioning in the aftermath of trauma.

WHAT DOES TFCBT LOOK LIKE?

TFCBT is made up of 12 weekly 90-minute sessions. An example of one such midtreatment session is provided in Table 4.1. Forty-five minutes are spent with a nonoffending caregiver, and 45 minutes are spent with the child or adolescent. If unable to provide 90-minute sessions, 16 to 20 60-minute sessions are equivalent. With 60-minute sessions, 30 minutes are spent with the child and 30 minutes with the caregiver. In early sessions, children and caregivers are seen separately by the therapist. As sessions progress, joint sessions occur to enhance communication between child and caregiver(s). Depending on the child's/caregiver's situation, other adaptations may need to be made. For example, if a caregiver has a difficult work schedule, the therapist might meet with the caregiver one week and the child the next.

Table 4.1
Example of One 90-Minute Session from Midtreatment

	Goals	Activities	Time
Child–Individual Session	Review rationale for gradual exposure	Review child's gradual exposure work from prior sessions	30–40 minutes
	Reduce distress associated with the abusive experience	Continue to add additional "chapters" to child's book by providing choices of topics to focus on	
	Elicit abuse-related thoughts and feelings	Reinforce education about child sexual abuse when disputing dysfunctional beliefs	
	Process and dispute dysfunctional thoughts	Prepare for joint session with caregiver. Role play sharing the "chapter" from the child's book as well as praise for the caregiver	
Caregiver–Individual Session	Reduce distress associated with the child's abusive experience	Share the child's gradual exposure work	30–40 minutes
	Elicit abuse-related thoughts and feelings	Assist in applying cognitive coping skills to combat dysfunctional beliefs	
	Process and dispute dysfunctional thoughts	Prepare for joint session with child. Role play caregiver's comments to the selected "chapter" of the child's book as well as praise.	
	Assist caregiver in managing child's behavior at home		
Joint Session	Promote open communication about the child's experience of abuse	Child shares a "chapter" from gradual exposure book	10–20 minutes
	Provide an opportunity for the caregiver to model comfort when discussing the abuse	Mutual exchange of praise	
	Strengthen caregiver–child relationship		

Sometimes children are placed in foster care after child maltreatment is reported. If the plan is for reunification, it may be helpful to include both the foster parent and the caregiver in treatment. This can be done in several ways. Separate sessions with each party are best in the beginning so that the therapist can get to know everyone and there are no conflicts regarding contact. Usually, the foster parent brings the child since they are living together. They move through the model as described throughout this chapter. Since the foster parent has a direct effect on the child with regard to daily contact and behavior management, these issues should be addressed. At a different time, the caregiver comes to session with the therapist and follows a parallel process. Work with the caregiver usually focuses more on the trauma, including pyschoeducation and the caregiver's thoughts and feelings about the trauma. Parenting skills also should be addressed so that the transition home is successful. Joint sessions can be done separately with both the foster parent and the caregiver, although the child may want to talk directly about the trauma with only the caregiver. That decision is the child's to make. The overall goal is to work directly with the foster parent on current issues so as to stabilize behavior problems and provide support and work on transition/long-term issues with the caregiver so that reunification is successful. The therapist may continue working with the family for a period of time after reunification takes place so as to solidify the gains made in therapy.

If the nonoffending parent is unable to participate in therapy, another support person can be included. Foster parents, residential staff, child protection workers, mentors, older siblings, and grandparents are all possible support people who can participate in the therapeutic process. If a caregiver cannot participate, the therapist can use the model with children and adolescents alone, as the model can still be effective in addressing depression, shame, and PTSD. However, if the child or adolescent is having significant behavior problems, it is important to motivate the caregiver to participate in sessions. Without caregiver involvement, behavior problems are likely to continue and/or escalate.

The entire treatment process is considered gradual exposure. Gradual exposure refers to the gradual process of encouraging the child to confront and discuss trauma-related thoughts and other reminders. At the point of intake or assessment, children and caregivers are asked questions about the trauma. Discussion related to the trauma becomes more specific and detailed as the sessions progress. At termination, ideally, the child and caregiver are able to talk more openly and with less discomfort about the trauma.

ENGAGEMENT

Since the caregiver's functioning after a traumatic event impacts the child's functioning, engagement with the caregiver is the key to successful treatment. Practically speaking, the caregiver is usually the one transporting the child/

adolescent to sessions, so if the caregiver and child do not come to sessions, treatment can't happen. Transportation, child care, work schedules, and other issues may present obstacles to a caregiver's participation in therapy. It is important to address these obstacles at the point of referral so a plan can be implemented to manage them. These practical issues can significantly impact the caregiver's motivation to participate in treatment. Clinicians and agencies may need to brainstorm about what they can offer clients who have difficulty accessing treatment: volunteers who provide child care and snacks/meals for families who have sessions over meal times, transportation vouchers, and so on. If the clinician or agency cannot offer such incentives, they should brainstorm with the caregiver how they can access their own resources to help them get to sessions.

Beyond the practical issues previously mentioned, other factors may impact a caregiver's motivation to participate in the child's/adolescent's treatment. Some caregivers are avoidant of the trauma themselves. Others don't understand their role in the process, so they think only the child should be meeting with the therapist. Some foster parents don't understand why they should be included in therapy when the trauma did not happen in their care. Regardless of the reason, it is the therapist's job to motivate the caregiver to participate fully in treatment. In Dialogue 4-1, the therapist is speaking to a parent who wants to just drop off her son for therapy and pick him up after the session is over. In this scenario, the therapist's goal is to validate the caregiver's feelings and worries and then help her see that her participation would benefit the child. After a traumatic event, caregivers often feel helpless and ineffective. They may feel scared to participate because they fear being judged by the therapist. It is the therapist's job to offer praise and hope and orient their role in the process of helping their child.

Dialogue 4-1: Motivating Caregiver Participation

THERAPIST: I understand that your schedule is very busy, so it would just be easier to drop off Jamal and pick him up at the end of the session. As a single mom, you are working really hard to fit everything in, so I admire your commitment to get him here to therapy. I know it may seem like an extra burden to wait here with him and meet with me as well. In the short run, it may feel like that, but in the long run, I think you'll see that with your participation, therapy will go faster and better. Even though I can help your son by talking to him about the sexual abuse, you are the most important person in his life, and you, more than I ever could, can help him get through this. Do you realize how important you are to him and how he will deal with the sexual abuse?

> **Mom:** No, I guess I just thought that since he didn't tell me about the abuse, he didn't feel comfortable talking to me about it. I keep thinking I should have known what was happening, and maybe if I had been a better mother, Jamal would have come to me sooner. I just get upset when I start talking about this, so maybe it's better that I not come. I don't think I can help him.
>
> **Therapist:** It's understandable that you get upset talking about the abuse. Even though Jamal was the one sexually abused, you've been affected by this as well. That's another reason why I meet with all the parents of the kids I see in therapy. Parents have questions and worries about their child and what happened. Just like you, many parents wonder why their children didn't tell them sooner and then wonder what to say to their children about the abuse. That's where I can help. In our sessions together, we can talk about and practice how to talk to Jamal about the abuse so you feel comfortable. In the end, you two will feel more comfortable talking about the abuse. Even though kids can talk to me about what happened, their parents are really the people they want and need the support from. You are already giving Jamal a lot of support by bringing him here. My job is to give you the support you need so you can keep giving it to Jamal.

ASSESSMENT

Prior to treatment, a comprehensive assessment should be done as a means of informing treatment and evaluating progress over time. Each agency and/or clinician may have an individualized intake assessment they currently use; however, it is important to assess the child's functioning across the following domains, again conveyed by the acronym CRAFTS (Cohen et al., 2006):

- *Cognitive problems:* Dysfunctional thinking and negative thoughts about self, learning problems, attention and concentration issues
- *Relationship problems:* Chaotic, risky, and/or volatile relationships; peer and family conflicts, withdrawal and social anxiety related to social situations
- *Affective problems:* Strong feelings that can trigger impulsive behavior, difficulty self-soothing, dysregulated affective states
- *Family problems:* Attachment issues, parent–child conflicts, parenting and behavior management problems
- *Traumatic behavior problems:* Risky behavior that is used as a means of coping with strong feelings; oppositional and/or sexualized behavior

- *Somatic problems:* Headaches, stomachaches, sleep problems, anxiety or tension, hyperarousal

To help provide a rationale for using the model, the assessment should include measures for PTSD, depression, shame, and behavior problems in children and adolescents. For PTSD, there are several measures that provide clinical information to the therapist. The Kiddie Schedule for Affective Disorders and Schizophrenia—PTSD section (K-SADS PTSD) semistructured interview elicits information from both the child and caregiver on the child's exposure to traumatic events and PTSD symptoms (Kaufman et al., 1997). The UCLA PTSD Inventory (Pynoos & Nader, 1998) is a paper-and-pencil self-report measure that children complete. The Trauma Symptom Checklist for Children (TSCC) (Briere, 1996) is a self-report measure on a variety of trauma-related symptoms, including PTSD, anger, dissociation, depression, and sexual problems. There are versions for school-aged children and young children.

Depression can be assessed using the Children's Depression Inventory (CDI) (Kovacs, 1983) for children or the Beck Depression Inventory, 2nd edition (BDI-II) (Beck, Steer, & Brown, 1996) for adolescents and caregivers. Shame can be measured by a self-report shame questionnaire developed by Feiering and Taska (1998).

Behavior problems as well as adaptive behavior can be evaluated using Achenbach's questionnaires: the Child Behavior Checklist (CBCL) for younger children (1–5) or older children (6–18) (Achenbach & Rescorla 2001) or the Behavior Assessment Scale (BASC), each of which have caregiver, self, and teacher report forms.

Caregivers should also be assessed using measures that evaluate their own depression, abuse-related distress, and parenting practices. Besides the BDI-II, the Parent Emotional Reaction Questionnaire (PERQ) by Cohen & Mannarino (1996) is a valuable indicator of abuse-related distress. The Impact of Events Scale–Revised (Weiss & Marmar, 1996) can also be used with caregivers to evaluate their own PTSD symptoms related to the child's trauma.

Given that TFCBT is effective at decreasing child and caregiver depression and abuse-related distress, as well as behavior problems and shame in children, a clinician needs to be able to provide pretreatment data on these issues to families so as to provide a rationale for using TFCBT.

The pretreatment assessment should be considered part of the gradual exposure process. During the assessment, children and caregivers are asked questions about the traumatic event(s). They are asked to think about the event and sit with thoughts, feelings, sensations, and reminders about the abuse. While formal treatment has not yet begun, it is important to consider the total therapeutic experience as gradual exposure. Assessment is part of that therapeutic process. Feedback from the assessment to both caregivers and children is an important part of engaging families and orienting them to the TFCBT model.

TFCBT COMPONENTS

Let's consider the following PRACTICE acronym as a means of remembering the components used in TFCBT (Cohen, et al., 2006). Each will be discussed below:

- **P**sychoeducation and **P**arenting skills
- **R**elaxation
- **A**ffective expression and regulation
- **C**ognitive coping
- **T**rauma narrative development and processing
- **I**n vivo gradual exposure
- **C**onjoint parent child sessions
- **E**nhancing safety and future development

As stated previously, the TFCBT model has been researched using these components in a relatively linear fashion across treatment sessions as shown in Figure 4.1. While each component is discussed separately, it is important to also consider the bigger picture and understand how the components are integrated.

Psychoeducation

The First Session with Caregivers Psychoeducation begins in the first treatment session and continues throughout each additional session in various ways. In the first session, psychoeducation refers to providing feedback on the assessment, orienting the client to the TFCBT model, and providing general information about such things as trauma, PTSD, and other mental health issues related to trauma.

Obviously, in the first session with both caregivers and children/adolescents, rapport building is imperative. Rapport building does not mean you have to wait to start doing TFCBT. Rapport building is about building connection and trust with the caregiver. Treating them with respect and orienting them to treatment is part of both psychoeducation and rapport building. This occurs at the same time. In a directive treatment like TFCBT, you can structure the rapport building to maximize the efficiency of the session. Directing the session to the assessment is a good starting place because it allows the therapist to immediately become trauma focused, validate his or her thoughts and feelings about the assessment process, and begin providing a rationale for the use of TFCBT. Dialogue 4-2 represents how a therapist might provide feedback about the assessment and transition to orienting caregivers to trauma-focused therapy.

Dialogue 4-2: Providing Feedback about Assessment and Orienting Caregivers to TF-CBT

THERAPIST: Thank you for coming today, Ms. Smith. I know the last time you were here you completed a variety of questionnaires about your daughter's thoughts, feelings, and behavior. I wanted to go over the results of that assessment and talk about the kind of treatment I think would be best for Janelle. One of the questionnaires you and Janelle completed was about posttraumatic stress disorder, or PTSD for short. Have you ever heard of that?

MOM: It sounds familiar.

THERAPIST: PTSD is a reaction to a traumatic event, like the domestic violence your daughter witnessed. When children or adults live in an environment where violence or abuse happens, they are affected by it in a variety of different ways. Each person reacts differently, but Janelle and you reported that Janelle has nightmares and trouble sleeping. When things remind her of the fighting she witnessed, she gets upset and she tries not to think about the fighting she saw. She also reported that she has more difficulty concentrating; she gets angry a lot and she feels on edge or overly watchful much of the time. Those are all PTSD reactions. Given that you were a victim of domestic violence, you may notice that you have some of those same reactions.

Another questionnaire you completed had to do with depression. Both you and your daughter report having some depression symptoms. That is common when you are dealing with trauma. On another questionnaire you completed that asked about Janelle's behavior, you reported that she is having some behavior problems, including aggression, defiance, and lying, and she's reporting a lot of physical problems like headaches and stomachaches. Kids who have been exposed to fighting in their home are at risk for having problems with their behavior. When kids don't know how to deal with their feelings, they act it out. The good news is that PTSD, depression, and behavior problems are very treatable. In fact, the kind of treatment we do here has been shown to be very effective in decreasing PTSD, depression, and behavior problems.

You have already done two of the most important things for Janelle in helping her deal with the domestic violence. You believe and support her by bringing her here to therapy. Second, you are coming here with her. Research shows that parents who participate in therapy with their kids have better results. The goal is not for you to be in therapy forever. The goal is for you and Janelle to be able to think about and talk about the domestic violence with me first and then eventually together. When therapy ends in 12 sessions or so, you will know how to keep talking about it if and when it comes up.

It is easier to provide a rationale for TFCBT if caregivers and children report symptoms of PTSD, depression, shame, and/or behavior problems. It is important to validate caregivers' concerns, worries, and fears related to their child's symptoms and provide accurate information about trauma to help provide perspective. Many caregivers have concerns about abuse-specific treatment, including talking directly about the abuse. In the first session, the therapist continues to assess caregivers' worries and concerns about treatment, so this is important information to have. The therapist then has an opportunity to talk about what exposure is and the benefits it can yield. Sometimes providing caregivers' with a metaphor is helpful. A common metaphor that can be used is likening the therapy process to cleaning a wound (Cohen et al., 2006). Dialogue 4-3 illustrates this and other metaphors. These metaphors can be used with children and adolescents as well. The goal is to convey that talking about the abuse is helpful and it will be done in a way that is manageable.

Dialogue 4-3: Metaphors That Can Be Used in the Rationale for TFCBT

THERAPIST: Therapy is a little bit like cleaning out a wound. When you first get injured, you may want to ignore the cut because of your worry that it will hurt to clean it out and take care of it. You may be able to ignore it for a while, but eventually it will become infected if you don't take care of it. Just like therapy, as you start to clean out the wound after it is infected, it may sting a little bit and hurt, but after you clean it, it won't hurt as much and you will be able to let it heal. There may still be a scar that you can look at and remember the injury. You can look at that scar with pride and know that you got through something difficult.

> The therapist can emphasize that the process of talking about the abuse is a gradual one by using another metaphor:
>
> THERAPIST: Have you ever gotten into a swimming pool when the water is really cold? Well, talking about the sexual abuse is a lot like that. You may not want to get in at first, but if you go slowly it isn't so bad. First, you put your foot in, and your foot gets used to the water. Then, you put your legs in, and they get used to it. Eventually, you get your whole body in, and then the water doesn't seem so cold.

Another goal of the first session with a caregiver is to obtain a commitment from her as to her participation. Engagement with the caregiver is often the key to success with TFCBT. Practically speaking, caregivers are often the ones who get their children to the sessions. Their presence in treatment allows you to address the abuse. Of course, it is important to emphasize to caregivers that with their support and presence in the therapy process, their child will do better in treatment. Helping caregivers understand their role in therapy and their influence over their child's recovery gives them a sense of purpose and control. For many caregivers, this can counteract feelings of guilt, shame, and helplessness around the abuse.

It is important to clarify for caregivers that they are participating in their child's treatment. Many caregivers have their own history of trauma, for which they may not have received treatment. Emphasize to caregivers that TFCBT may trigger thoughts and feelings about their own trauma history, but the treatment is for their child. Caregivers will learn skills and information that may indirectly impact how they manage their own trauma experience, but the therapist is not working with them on their own trauma. If needed, the therapist should make a referral to the caregiver for his or her own treatment.

The first session is a time to partner with the caregiver and enlist their knowledge and support. Spending time understanding their previous history with mental health providers; cultural, religious, and familial values; family strengths; and worries about the sexual abuse will allow for open discussion about why it may be difficult to participate in abuse-focused treatment at times. Many caregivers have strong beliefs about the value of therapy, especially abuse-focused therapy:

- *"Why do we have to make her talk about it?"*
- *"Won't she just forget it?"*
- *"If you make her talk about it, she will just be more upset."*
- *"We don't talk about such private things with outsiders."*
- *"Therapy is only for crazy people."*

Clients may not initiate discussion about some of these issues, so it is the therapist's job to listen for these concerns and/or directly ask about these issues so one can remove any obstacles to participation in treatment. Of course, practical obstacles may also exist, such as transportation problems, child care issues, and scheduling. It is important to problem solve these issues in the beginning so treatment is not delayed or terminated in the middle of trauma work.

An important goal of the first session with caregivers is to instill hope and confidence. Caregivers may be dealing with their own PTSD and depression symptoms related to their child's abuse. They may be struggling with thoughts such as:

- *"My child's life is ruined."*
- *"I am a horrible parent for not protecting my child."*
- *"Life will never be the same."*

With accurate information about abuse and confidence in effective treatment strategies, it is the therapist's job to help the caregiver see what he or she has already done to make the situation better. For example, telling a caregiver that she has already done the most important thing for her child—believing her—is a way to praise the caregiver and show her that there are protective responses in which she has engaged. Conveying to caregivers that PTSD and depression are treatable conditions and that most children who have been sexually abused lead productive, happy lives is also important psychoeducation that instills hope. Caregivers often walk into the first session feeling helpless, hopeless, and scared. The therapist must balance validation of these feelings with active questioning and problem solving as to how one can look at the situation in a different way. An example of such a balanced dialogue is presented in Dialogue 4-4.

Dialogue 4-4: A Balanced Dialogue

FATHER: I'm not sure what to do. Ever since my wife killed herself, my son has been withdrawn and depressed. I don't know what to say to him. I'm having enough trouble as it is.

THERAPIST: You and your son are both struggling with your feelings since your wife's suicide. You don't know how to talk to him. It's understandable that you don't know how to act or what to say around him, but I wonder, what would you say to him if you could?

Without the validation, clients may feel that the therapist is just trying to throw psychoeducation at them and change their thoughts. Balancing validation with education and problem solving allows clients to take information and move forward with an action plan.

Lastly, especially if there are behavior problems with the child or adolescent, an introduction to behavior management skills is beneficial in the first session. Starting with the concept of praise, one can continue building on the theme of hopefulness. Caregivers often come to a first session with a list of problems and things that are going wrong at home, at school, and at work. Asking them to identify things that are going well is one way of helping them to shift their focus to more positive events. Introducing the concept of praise as a behavior management tool and as a way to counteract some of their negative or depressing thoughts can be a way to end the first session on a positive note.

Provide some initial guidelines for praise:

- Praise should be given in a purely positive manner with no negative tags attached.
- Praise should be given consistently.
- Praise is most useful when given immediately after the positive behavior.
- Specific praise is more effective than global praise. The more specific you can be about what you like, the more the person will learn from it.

After providing some psychoeducation on praise, have the parent identify specific behaviors for which they would like to praise their child. Have the caregiver practice giving the praise following the previous guidelines and coach him if he has difficulty. In the individual session with the child, the therapist can also provide psychoeducation on praise and practice identifying and saying something positive to the caregiver. If both parties do well with the practice, a brief joint session to exchange praise may be a positive ending to a first session. Dialogue 4-5 illustrates such a joint session, consisting of a mother, her daughter, Sarah, and the therapist.

Dialogue 4-5: A Joint Session to Exchange Praise

THERAPIST: As a way to end our first session together, I thought it might be nice to share some praise with each other. Over the next 12 weeks we will talk a lot about praise, and one of the things we will be practicing here and at home is praising each other as much as possible. When we catch people doing things we like, it's important to tell them so they keep doing them and so everyone feels good with each other. Who wants to go first?

> **DAUGHTER:** I will. Mom, thank you for playing Monopoly with me last night. I know it's not your favorite game, so I'm glad you played it with me anyway.
>
> **MOM:** I had fun. Sarah, I really like it when you play nicely with your brother and share your toys with him. I love to see the two of you smiling and laughing together.
>
> **THERAPIST:** You both gave great praise! You were very specific about what you liked from the other person. Over the week, when you do something fun together or like something the other person has done for you, tell her right away. Great session!

PARENTING SKILLS

Parenting skills are also discussed and taught throughout the entire model, both as a means of supporting the strengths in the family and as a means of actively addressing behavior problems. Behavior problems can be triggered and/or exacerbated by a traumatic event. If, during the assessment, the caregiver reports that the child/adolescent has specific behavior problems, psychoeducation on behavior management should be offered and practice should be reinforced.

Caregivers' behavior management skills are often influenced by cultural and family values, so it is important to elicit from the caregivers information about discipline and reward practices in their family. It will be important to tailor the information and practice to the family's individual needs. Regardless of individual values, it is important to convey to caregivers that behavior problems are not uncommon in children/adolescents who experience a traumatic event. The therapist should convey a sense of hope and confidence about that the behavior can be managed.

As stated previously, a good place to start is with praise because it focuses on catching the child being good/appropriate, which in turn helps everyone in the family shift their focus to what is going well. So often, in families affected by trauma, life becomes sad, chaotic, or scary. Guiding caregivers to notice what is going well helps them to see there is life beyond trauma.

Praise should also be used to actively increase a behavior that the caregiver wants to see more of. In one of the early sessions, the caregiver and therapist should identify such a behavior and discuss what to say and do when the caregiver notices the child engaging in that behavior. For example, if a caregiver wants to see less fighting between the child and his brother, the therapist must first help the caregiver define the positive behavior to look for. In the midst of stress, caregivers can easily resort to labeling behaviors only in negative terms. With guidance and prompting, the caregiver can be helped to identify the desired behavior as "the child playing cooperatively with his brother." When the caregiver identifies specific behaviors to notice, she is more likely to catch the child engaging in those behaviors.

The next step is to teach the caregiver how to praise. Guidelines for giving praise were previously provided. After discussing how to praise, the therapist must create opportunities for the caregiver to practice using praise in the office and at home. Facilitating brief joint sessions to share praise or giving homework assignments during which caregiver and child must share one praiseful statement each day are means of engaging caregivers in practicing the skills.

Additional behavior management skills should be taught to decrease negative behaviors. These skills include active ignoring, time-out, appropriate consequences, and work chores. Active ignoring is the skill of not reacting to minor, annoying behavior from a child/adolescent. Some caregivers report constant yelling, lecturing, and punishment going on in the home after a trauma event. Everyone is so stressed that they become reactive to everything around them. The caregiver eventually feels like all she does is yell and reprimand the child. In this situation, the therapist and caregiver(s) just prioritize the behavior problems. Obviously, behaviors that present safety concerns, such as aggression or running away, should not be ignored. Other behaviors like whining, rolling eyes, and sighing are behaviors that can be ignored. Picking only certain battles to wage will help the caregiver and the child. The battling can then be replaced with praise and pleasant activities.

Many caregivers have strong feelings about corporal punishment. Exploring and processing the caregivers' beliefs about spanking and other physical discipline is important. It is important to share that using physical discipline with children who have been physically violated in some way can be confusing to those children and leave them with the message that it is okay to hit or hurt someone. An alternative to physical discipline is the use of time-out. If done correctly, time-out can be very effective at reducing and/or eliminating problematic behavior. The child is offered an opportunity to calm down and regain control by being put into a quiet, nonstimulating environment. The caregiver should explain to the child why she is being placed in time-out and how long the time-out will last. A rule of thumb is that the duration in minutes should not exceed the child's age (e.g., a 6-year-old should be in time-out for 6 minutes). The child is told that the timer will begin once her screaming/yelling stops. During the time-out, the caregiver should remain calm and refrain from making eye contact with the child and/or talking to the child.

Many caregivers need help identifying appropriate consequences for children. Caregivers may fall into the trap of removing all privileges for months at a time and then becoming frustrated when there is nothing to take away. The therapist can provide guidelines for appropriate consequences, including giving an older child a work chore as a consequence. Rather than removing a privilege, assigning a work chore to the child requires that he must give back to the family in repair for his actions. Most importantly, therapists can emphasize the need for consistency and reinforce this concept in sessions with the caregiver when reviewing homework on behavior management.

It is the therapist's job to model the very behavior management skills being taught to the caregiver. When caregivers are given homework to praise their child, the therapist must consistently follow through with asking about the homework at the beginning of each session, thereby stressing its importance. In addition, when the caregiver reports efforts at change, the therapist must praise the caregiver. If caregivers do not follow through on homework, the therapist provides a consequence such as having the caregiver do the homework in the waiting room while his child is seen by the therapist.

Since many children experience behavior problems after a traumatic event, it is important for the therapist to assess the severity of such problems and have a good understanding of how to help caregivers manage the behaviors. The therapist's role here can be thought of as a coach. With behaviors that pose a safety risk, such as sexualized behavior, more immediate action is advised.

Sexualized Behavior It is not uncommon for sexually abused children to engage in inappropriate sexual behavior with other children because of what has been done to them. In addition, children may engage in other sexualized behaviors such as compulsive masturbation, making sexual sounds, imitating sexual activity in play, and talking in a sexualized manner. These behaviors, more than other behaviors, can create strong reactions in both caregivers and therapists. Although difficult, it is important to remember that treatment for sexual behavior problems is similar to treatment for other, more general behavior problems.

First, the clinician must assess whether the behaviors are common or uncommon in children of that age. Caregivers sometimes assume that any sexual behavior is problematic and/or a possible sign that the child will become a perpetrator. The clinician need will need to not only provide psychoeducation on developmentally appropriate and inappropriate behavior but also help caregivers manage their own emotional reactions to such behavior.

Friedrich (1991) identified the following behaviors as uncommon in children who have not been sexually abused:

- Putting his/her mouth on another person's private areas
- Making sexual sounds
- Asking others to engage in sexual acts

- Imitating intercourse
- Inserting objects in the vagina/anus
- Masturbating with an object

These behaviors are of concern and should be addressed in a treatment plan, whereas the following behaviors are commonly observed in children:

- Being shy with strange people
- Walking around in underwear
- Scratching crotch
- Touching private areas at home
- Walking around nude
- Undressing in front of others

Providing caregivers with psychoeducation about sexual behavior in children can help them gain perspective, know when and how to respond, and manage their feelings about such behavior.

If the sexual behavior is problematic, safety should be assessed. Are there other children in the home? What kind of supervision is provided? What is the layout of the house? Do the children share bedrooms? If the child is touching other children in and/or out of the home, arrangements may need to be made for increased supervision, private bedrooms, and informing teachers and other parents about the need for monitoring.

Although joint sessions are usually saved for later in treatment, sexualized behavior that presents a safety concern may need to be addressed in a first session with both the children and caregivers. Acknowledgment that the behavior has occurred and discussion about safety should follow. The therapist can address the issue in a joint session with the caregivers and child in the manner illustrated in Dialogue 4-6.

Dialogue 4-6: Addressing Safety in a Joint Session

THERAPIST: Before you leave today, we want to talk about house rules so that everyone feels safe. I'm going to give everyone a chance to come up with some rules, but one rule should be about touching private parts. It's not okay to touch anyone else's private parts or have them touch yours. Sometimes when kids have been sexually abused, they think about touching other people's private parts because that is what happened to them. I know that you, Jose, have touched other kids and that's one of the reasons you are here to talk to me so you can learn not

> to do that anymore. Because we want everyone to feel good about being together at home and safe, I thought we should practice what to do, Jose, if you have the urge to touch someone's private parts. If you think about touching someone else on their private parts, you can go and tell your mom or dad *before* you do it. If you go and tell them *before* you do it, they will help you do something else instead. They will not be mad at you and you won't get in trouble. They want to help you learn how to be safe. Let's practice how that might go.

Ideally, the therapist should meet individually with the caregivers to prepare them for such a session. The therapist should coach them on what to say if their child comes to them with such an urge and how to handle any emotional reaction they have. Caregivers should be encouraged to respond in a positive, supportive manner by thanking the child for coming to tell them, asking the child to share any feelings he or she has, and redirecting the child to another activity.

It is also important to discuss with caregivers the need for appropriate touch and physical affection. Because caregivers and other adults have emotional reactions to sexualized behavior, they may respond by withdrawing from the child and feeling fearful of any direct physical contact. Of course, those emotional reactions should be validated and discussed so appropriate physical contact can continue. All people need physical contact to thrive. When children's needs are not met, they try to meet them in less adaptive ways, sexualized behavior being one of them. To prevent that from happening, the therapist must educate the caregivers on the child's needs and discuss ways they can continue to provide love, affection, and physical contact in ways that make them feel comfortable. If caregivers do not feel comfortable hugging or kissing their child, other touches can be substituted: holding hands, sitting closely, high fives, brushing hair, and so on.

After role playing the interaction with the child and caregivers, other house rules should be identified, and consequences for breaking the house rules should be clarified. It is important to predict for caregivers that, like any other behavior one is trying to change with a new response, the behavior is likely to increase before decreasing. If the sexualized behavior becomes more forceful, coercive, or dangerous, more restrictive interventions may need to be made and/or child protective services may need to be involved.

The First Session with Children/Adolescents   Psychoeducation in the first session with children and adolescents is not dissimilar from that of their caregivers. Orienting youth to treatment and providing feedback about the assessment will differ depending on the developmental level of the youth. Therapists may introduce younger children to treatment by introducing themselves as a "talking doctor who talks to kids about their feelings about touching." Assessment feedback should be given in simple terms such as "all those questionnaires you filled out tell me that you are feeling really sad right now and have a hard time thinking about the touching that happened to you." Older children can be given more in-depth explanations about treatment and the results of their assessment. The therapist is providing gradual exposure by talking directly about the reason for treatment and the way the trauma is affecting the child/adolescent. Similarly to caregivers, providing this orientation and feedback allows the therapist to then easily convey a rationale for talking about the trauma directly. The "wound" and "swimming pool" metaphors work nicely here.

Engagement and rapport building with the child/adolescent is extremely important. The relationship between therapist and client will greatly impact on their ability to confront and process the traumatic event. Spending time getting to know each other is important to understanding the whole child, not just the abuse victim. Obtaining information about strengths, talents, activities, and goals provides information that can be used in later sessions to move through avoidance, fear, and sadness. The manner in which the therapist obtains this information is also important.

The Sternberg et al. research (1997) indicates that children provide more spontaneous, detailed information when individuals ask open-ended questions. Asking questions in such a way and allowing children the time and space to answer with as much information as possible teaches children to provide a more comprehensive narrative. If therapists are able to teach the child how to talk in more detail from the very first session, that skill can translate to more comprehensive trauma narratives later on in treatment. Examples of such rapport-building methods include, "Tell me about school," "What is your family like?," "I'd really like to hear everything about your best friend."

If the child responds with only minimal answers, encouraging her to "tell me more about that" may elicit more information. The key is to reinforce the child for giving as much information as possible, including thoughts, feelings, and sensations. The therapist maximizes time spent in the initial session with rapport building by also teaching a skill that can be later applied to the trauma narrative. This skill can also be applied to another task for the first session: the baseline assessment.

Baseline Assessment The baseline assessment is the combined process of eliciting a neutral narrative and a baseline trauma narrative from the child in the first session (Deblinger, Behl, & Glickman, 2005). The goal is to assess how much spontaneous information a child delivers in response to an open-ended question, first about a benign event and then about the traumatic event. The comparison between the amount and kind of information presented by the child allows the therapist to know how quickly information about the trauma can be presented to the child. If a child is able to talk easily about the trauma, the therapist may be more direct about the trauma as well and move more quickly through the components. However, if the child is avoidant about the trauma, the therapist knows more gradual steps may need to be taken to talk about the trauma and more coping skills may need to be taught. The other goal of a baseline assessment is to introduce direct discussion about the trauma so the child knows that the therapist is comfortable talking about it.

A neutral narrative is a narrative about a recent event or day elicited by the therapist from the client. The child is asked to provide a detailed description, including thoughts, feelings, and body sensations about the event. The goal of the neutral narrative is to see how much information a child can provide given an open-ended question. The baseline trauma narrative is elicited by the therapist immediately after the neutral narrative. The child is asked to tell about the traumatic event in as much detail as she provided in the neutral narrative. The goal of the baseline trauma narrative is not to process the abuse by but to see how comfortable the child is talking about the abuse. The therapist assesses comfort level, spontaneous details, and vocabulary by comparing the neutral narrative to the baseline trauma narrative. This process further facilitates teaching the child how to communicate about events with as much detail as possible since the therapist is asking the child to give information in a certain manner. Both the neutral narrative and baseline trauma narrative, in combination, are used for evaluative purposes, not processing the abuse.

After some initial rapport building, using open-ended questions, the child is told to tell the therapist about an event that happened in the recent past. The therapist may know of a specific event to ask about because the caregiver may have reported on a recent birthday, holiday event, or outing. These contained events provide good neutral narratives. If the therapist is not aware of any recent events that the child could describe in detail, tell the child to describe her day, from the time she woke up until she came to see the therapist. Dialogue 4-7 presents an example of what the therapist might say.

Dialogue 4-7: Asking a Child to Describe Her Day

THERAPIST: Now that I know a little bit about you, I'd like you to tell me about your day so I can get an idea of what a regular day is like for you. I want you to tell me as much detail as possible about your day from the time you woke up this morning until you came to see me. I want to know what you did, your thoughts, your feelings, and even how your body felt. Don't leave anything out.

The neutral narrative, like other rapport-building questions, allows the child to provide as much spontaneous information as possible. Younger children may require more prompts to provide details. Prompts like "Then what happened?" and "How did you feel?" are appropriate; however, the goal of the neutral narrative is to assess the child's level of spontaneous narrative, speech patterns, and comfort level, so too many prompts are not advised. Frequent interruptions should not occur. Children can usually provide some level of detail to their narrative but don't include thoughts, feelings, and body sensations. The therapist should then prompt for at least one of these details so children know that the therapist wants to hear that information as well. If children consistently don't include feelings or thoughts in their narrative, the absence of those details gives the therapist valuable information about how the child communicates.

When the child finishes her neutral narrative, the therapist should provide her with praise for how much information she provided. Then the therapist elicits a baseline trauma narrative. The therapist tells the child to describe, in as much detail as she did the neutral narrative, about the referral incident, as illustrated in Dialogue 4-8.

Dialogue 4-8: Eliciting a Baseline Trauma Narrative

THERAPIST: Wow! You gave me a lot of details about your day. I feel like I have a good idea what your day is like. Thank you. Now what I'd like you to do is tell me, in as much detail as you told me about your day, about your cousin touching you on your private parts. Just like before, I want to know about what happened, your thoughts, your feelings, and even how your body felt.

The transition between the neutral narrative and the baseline trauma narrative should be smooth so the therapist can compare the two narratives and assess for any differences in speech patterns, body language, feeling vocabulary, details, and so on. Again, the goal of obtaining a baseline trauma narrative is *not* to process the trauma. The therapist should sit back and allow the child to spontaneously provide as many details as possible. Only when the child stops talking or needs helping starting should a question be asked. A rule of thumb is that the number of questions between the neutral narrative and the baseline trauma narrative should be about the same. The therapist does not want to inadvertently convey that she is more interested in the trauma details. The therapist should remain as neutral as possible. Dialogue 4-9 provides an example of a baseline assessment with a 6-year-old male child who was sexually abused by his grandfather.

Dialogue 4-9: Example of a Baseline Assessment with a 6-Year-Old Male Child Who Was Sexually Abused by His Grandfather

THERAPIST: So Joseph, your mom told me that you had a picnic yesterday for the Fourth of July. I want to hear all about it, starting with what happened before the picnic and everything that happened during the picnic, even how you felt, what you were thinking, and even how your body felt inside.

JOSEPH: The picnic was fun! I got to help my mom make cupcakes for the picnic. I ate two of them. They were good.

THERAPIST: Then what happened?

JOSEPH: My cousin Blake came to the picnic and we played soccer. I can kick the ball really far. He has a sister and she always wants to play with us, but we don't want her to play.

THERAPIST: What else happened at the picnic?

JOSEPH: We had hot dogs and hamburgers and we got to watch the fireworks.

THERAPIST: How did you feel at the picnic?

JOSEPH: I was happy. We had fun.

THERAPIST: That sounds like a great picnic! You had fun with your cousin and you got to eat lots of good food and see the fireworks.

JOSEPH: Yeah, it was fun.

THERAPIST: Thanks for telling me all about it. Now I want you to tell me all about your grandfather touching you in a not okay way, just like you did with the picnic—your feelings, your thoughts, and everything that happened.

JOSEPH: [looking down] My grandpop touched my pee-pee. It was nasty.

THERAPIST: How did that make you feel?

JOSEPH: Mad.

THERAPIST: How did your body feel when he touched your pee-pee?

JOSEPH: It felt yucky.

THERAPIST: So you feel mad that your grandpop touched your pee-pee. It was nasty and it made your body feel yucky. You were very brave to tell me about your grandpop touching your pee-pee, especially since you just met me today. Over the next 12 weeks we're going to learn about okay and not okay touching and talk more about what your grandpop did. Right now, we're going to talk about feelings.

From the baseline assessment, the therapist learns how willing and comfortable the child is talking about the trauma. That information allows the therapist to plan the treatment more effectively. If a child talks easily and openly about the trauma, the therapist knows they can perhaps move more quickly through the components. However, if a child responds to the baseline trauma narrative directive by looking down and shrugging his shoulders and refuses to respond to prompts, the therapist knows the child might be more reluctant to talk. The therapist knows she will then have to be more creative about motivating the child and creating opportunities to talk about the trauma in a nonthreatening manner.

It is important to remember that the baseline assessment is evaluative in nature. It is the combination of the neutral and baseline trauma narratives that provides information to the therapist about the child's ability to talk about the trauma in comparison to a neutral event. Differences in vocabulary, body language, tone of voice, and detail should be noted and considered when talking about the trauma throughout treatment.

Many therapists have a strong reaction to asking about the traumatic event in the first session. They worry it will retraumatize the child and think more time for rapport building is needed. If a pretreatment assessment was done with the child prior to his first session, the child has already been asked about the traumatic event. If not, the baseline assessment serves part of that purpose. Children and adolescents arrive for a first session knowing that they are there to talk about the trauma. Since most children do not initiate discussion about the trauma, they look to the therapist to make the first move. Why? Sometimes the disclosure process has been difficult and triggered strong emotions in those around the child. The child may then think that he shouldn't talk about the trauma because people get upset and/or bad consequences follow. Therapists need to show youth that they can handle hearing about the trauma.

Initiating discussion about the trauma may be a relief to many children. They are waiting for the therapist to be clear about the reason for the session and to break the ice by first saying the words "sexual abuse" or "not okay touching." Initiation of this topic also conveys to the child that the therapist views them as strong and brave. Of course, it is important for therapists to consider their own thoughts and feelings about the child and directive trauma treatment. Those thoughts and feelings will impact on a therapist's ability to talk openly and comfortably about the trauma. If a therapist is new to trauma treatment or to cognitive behavioral therapy, initiating discussion about these topics can feel awkward, in which case the therapist's discomfort may cause her to remain silent about the trauma and prolong other parts of therapy, sometimes to the child's detriment. Therefore, it is essential for therapists to be aware of their own part in this process.

Whether a child provides a detailed baseline trauma narrative or cannot respond verbally to the directive, the process provides a transition step to orienting the child to treatment. Dialogue 4-10 provides an example, after facilitation of the baseline assessment, of what the therapist might say. If time allows, the session can then transition to the next set of components that address coping skills:

- **R**elaxation
- **A**ffect expression and regulation
- **C**ognitive coping

The focus of these components is teaching the child or adolescent a variety of coping skills that he or she can utilize to reduce any emotional or behavior dysregulation that has occurred. The components do not have to be taught in the order presented. Likewise, the amount of time spent on these components and the number of skills taught will depend on the individual needs of the child or adolescent.

Dialogue 4-10: Transitioning to Treatment

THERAPIST: It's okay if you can't tell me about your cousin touching you. I'm someone you are just meeting today and we are still getting to know each other. But that's one of the reasons you are here. Over the next 12 weeks or so we are going to talk about the touching and learn about okay and not okay touching and other things. The more we talk about touching, the easier it gets to talk about it.

Caregivers should also be taught these skills in their sessions for the same reasons they are taught to children and adolescents. Caregivers often have their own distress related to the abuse. Relaxation, affect tolerance, and cognitive coping skills can be helpful for caregivers to learn to manage their own symptoms. In addition, it is important for caregivers to know and learn the skills for their child's sake so that caregivers can eventually take on a therapeutic role with the child and coach him or her on using the skills.

With these components, as with all of them, therapists are encouraged to use their creativity and clinical judgment. Coping skills should be taught with developmental level in mind. The therapist is providing the client (caregiver and child) with a toolbox of various tools, some of which they will use often and some of which they won't use at all. Their toolbox should include skills that impact many dimensions, including their feelings, their thoughts, and their body, since trauma impacts on all of these areas.

Relaxation

Progressive Muscle Relaxation   There are a variety of relaxation exercises that can be taught to children, adolescents, and families. Progressive muscle relaxation (PMR) is a method of tightening and releasing areas of the body in order to relax the muscles and calm the body. There are numerous scripts for PMR that can be found in anxiety and stress reduction books as well as downloaded from the Internet. With young children, using visual cues is helpful, including acting first like a "tin soldier" while tensing their whole body and then like a "rag doll," making their body limp. One can also show children the difference between cooked and uncooked spaghetti to make the point that the tense body is hard and stiff while the relaxed body is loose and floppy.

This is a skill that should be first practiced in the office with the client so that coaching can occur. With dissociative clients, relaxation is often difficult and can trigger a dissociated state. It would be important to talk about the possibility of "zoning out" during an exercise such as this and plan for what to do if that should happen. Pairing the PMR with some grounding techniques such as keeping the eyes open and maintaining awareness of the chair underneath one's body can be helpful.

Breathing   Focused breathing exercises are an excellent way of relaxing. Breathing is the body's natural relaxation mechanism. Just telling oneself to "relax" doesn't necessarily have a relaxing effect on the body. Breathing can create relaxation within the body. With children, "belly breathing" can be a way to direct their breathing to relax. Belly breathing can be demonstrated by sitting in a chair or lying on the floor. Direct the child to breathe in deeply through his nose until the belly sticks out, and then blow out through the mouth until all the air is gone. Using props like a balloon or bubbles can make it even more fun.

Visualization   Visualization can be a powerful tool used with or without other relaxation techniques. Clients can be directed to create their own safe or calming image they can access in times of anxiety. In session, they can be directed to draw the image and put it at home or in school as a reminder to stay calm. Visualization can also be used as a means of confronting one's fears. For example, after being sexually abused, a child may be fearful of walking outside alone because she is worried the perpetrator may attack her. In response, the therapist can guide the client through a series of visualizations that move her closer to the desired outcome. In this case, the therapist might ask the client to visualize herself walking outside the house and standing on the porch. The next step might be to see herself walking to the end of the driveway. Eventually, the child visualizes walking around the corner to a friend's house. The visualization should be paired with breathing or other relaxation techniques to pair the anxiety-provoking image with calm. For more general purposes, there are a variety of published guided visualizations for children of all ages, including the books *Starbright* and *Moonbeam*, both by Maureen Garth.

Affect Expression and Regulation

It is important to assess the child's ability to identify feelings, to express them, and to tolerate strong, painful emotions. This process can start in the first session with the baseline assessment and continue in the same or subsequent sessions by having children and adolescents identify a range of general feelings. The therapist can make a list on the board, use a feelings chart, or play charades. No matter how one does it, the first goal is to assess the child's feeling vocabulary and build it if it is limited, so that the child has the words to express both general events and those related to the traumatic experiences. After the child creates a list of general feelings and talks about them, he or she can be directed to identify the trauma-related feelings.

This exercise serves multiple purposes: It allows continued rapport development by sharing various experiences that trigger different emotions; it provides the clinician with information about a child's emotional vocabulary and comprehension; and it initiates discussion about the traumatic event in a relatively nonthreatening manner. Obviously, younger children will identify fewer feelings (e.g., mad, sad, happy, and scared), while older adolescents may create an extensive list of emotions. For all children, the goal is to create a list of feelings that offers a range of feelings that can be used to express how they feel about the trauma. If not identified by the child, the therapist will want to include on such a list the following feelings: mad, sad, scared, embarrassed/ashamed, guilty, and confused. It is important to include such "positive" feelings as brave, proud, and love. Some children will express feelings of pride at being able to tell someone about the abuse; brave for being able to tell the perpetrator "no"; and love for still loving the perpetrator despite what he or she did. After the child expresses his feelings about the trauma, the therapist should explain that many children have mixed feelings about the trauma and, in fact, there are no right or wrong feelings to have.

Affect regulation skills will also vary depending on the child's developmental level and need. For children with anger/aggression problems, anger management skills will be important to teach. One way to begin teaching anger management is to ask children to identify where in their body they feel anger. If a child is able to use a physical sensation as a cue to recognizing anger, he can then be directed to handle the anger in a healthy way. Several options should be taught. First, children can learn to express their anger with words using "I" statements. Next, children can be taught to redirect their anger into a physical activity, including running or playing basketball. Children can also be taught to calm themselves down with relaxation, yoga, reading, or listening to music. Therapeutic board games can also be used to teach and reinforce healthy expression of anger. Angry Animals by Kidsrights and Peace Path are two such examples. It is important that a variety of techniques be taught, given that different techniques work in different situations.

For children who have experienced a traumatic loss, techniques to manage their sadness and grief should be addressed. Children can be taught to express their feelings in a letter to the loved one who died. Creating a scrapbook with pictures and memories of the loved one is another way to help them address their feelings. As with any strong emotion, children can be encouraged to identify and sit with their feelings of sadness using relaxation and/or breathing. The website on using TFCBT with traumatic grief (www.musc.edu/ctg) is an excellent resource for learning specific coping strategies and processing techniques for use with children and families who have suffered a traumatic loss.

Reexperiencing and arousal symptoms can lead to such problems as flashbacks, sleep problems, and attention problems, all of which can be addressed with different coping skills. Many children with complex trauma issues resort to using risky behaviors as a way of controlling their pain. Affect tolerance skills should be taught to reduce or sit with the painful emotions so that behavior can be better managed as well.

Marsha Linehan (1997) speaks at length about the damaging effects of emotion dysregulation, an inability to manage strong feelings. She created a model of treatment specifically designed to help adults learn how to modulate their feelings. Her model has since been adapted for adolescents by Alec Miller (2007). A core skill both speak about is mindfulness. Mindfulness is the ability to notice and identify one thing at a time. It is the ability to be in the moment, tolerating one's feelings, thoughts, and body sensations without judgment. Children can be taught mindfulness by observing everyday objects, including coins, rocks, and shells. The other senses can be included in mindfulness activities, including listening to a piece of music, chewing a piece of gum, feeling a feather, or smelling a scented candle. Children can be encouraged to focus on one sense at a time to observe the experience and report on it. As children get better at attending to an experience, they can be asked to focus on the experience for longer periods of time. The complete participation and involvement in each sensory activity can distract a child from overwhelming emotion. *Peaceful Piggy Meditation* (MacLean, 2004) is a wonderful book that teaches children how to be mindful. Mindfulness is a core skill that enhances other affect regulation skills. The more aware children become, the more they can identify their feelings, tolerate them, and act in thoughtful ways rather than with impulsivity.

Mindful awareness of feelings is the first step in regulating them. Older children can be helped to identify triggers for their flashbacks, sleep disturbances, and urges to engage in risky behaviors. With increased awareness of triggers comes an increased ability to intervene. Mindfulness alone can be taught to help children and adolescents sit with strong emotions and ride the ebb and flow of their intensity without reacting. This skill is especially important for children with posttraumatic stress symptoms who often try to forget or avoid memories and feelings about the trauma. The skill of mindfulness teaches tolerance for sitting with those thoughts and feelings rather than pushing them away.

Grounding skills can be added to contain flashbacks, intrusive thoughts, and nightmares. In response to flashbacks, children and teens can be instructed to focus on the here-and-now by identifying objects in their immediate environment. In addition, engaging in a physical activity like jump rope, pushups, or basketball can ground a child in his/her body. Mental grounding can be taught by teaching the child to play a "concentration" game in their head or with someone else. For example, a child may be coached to subtract backwards from 100 by 3s or choose a category, such as animals, and identify an animal beginning with each letter of the alphabet (e.g., armadillo, bear, crow, etc. . . .). A therapist might practice such mindfulness/affect tolerance skills at the beginning and end of each session to anchor the trauma work done in the middle of the session. Not only does the practice provide additional reinforcement of the skill but it provides a structure to the session that allows containment of thoughts and feelings related to the trauma.

Affect tolerance skills can be categorized into two domains: those that are used to manage strong, immediate reactions and those that are practiced on a daily basis to buffer stress and build positive experiences. After a traumatic event, children's lives may become chaotic. Routines may be disrupted and more emphasis may be placed on the negative impact of the trauma. It is important to provide education to children and caregivers about the buffering effects of balanced nutrition, exercise, sleep, and play. Children can be encouraged to engage in at least one positive and productive activity each day. Positive, productive activities reinforce optimism, self-worth, mastery, and laughter, all of which improve affect tolerance. See Linehan (1997) and Miller (2007) for additional resources on emotion regulation and mindfulness.

Cognitive Coping

One of the premises of CBT is that thoughts impact feelings. Cognitive coping is the skill of identifying the relationship between a person's thoughts, feelings, and actions and talking to oneself differently so as to change feelings (i.e., self-talk). To teach cognitive coping, the cognitive triangle is used, as

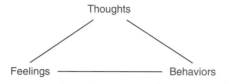

Figure 4.2 Cognitive Coping Triangle

illustrated in Figure 4.2. The therapist describes the connection between thoughts, feelings, and actions as he or she draws the cognitive triangle on the board, as illustrated in Dialogue 4-11.

Dialogue 4-11: Describing Connections between Thoughts, Feelings, and Actions

THERAPIST: Thoughts, feelings, and actions are all connected. We often think feelings just happen all of a sudden out of nowhere. In fact, feelings have a lot to do with the way we think, what we say to ourselves, or even images that pop into our head. If you were about to take a test and you said to yourself, "I'm so stupid. I'm never going to pass this test," how would you feel?

CHILD: Sad. Nervous.

THERAPIST: Right, so what would you do as you sit there telling yourself you're stupid and feeling sad and nervous?

CHILD: I'd just write down the answers as quickly as possible and get done with it.

THERAPIST: So, first you tell yourself you're stupid and you'll never pass the test. Then you start to feel sad and nervous and that leads you to get through the test as fast as possible. See the connection?

In the first third of treatment, cognitive coping is taught as a coping skill to both caregiver and child. Depending on the strengths and problems presented within treatment, children and adolescents can use cognitive coping to reinforce or improve self-esteem, relaxation, safety, and hopefulness. Practicing on more benign issues first allows the child or caregiver an opportunity to learn the skill, in a gradual manner, on issues that are not directly related to the abuse. Later in treatment, after the narrative is written, cognitive processing can be done to change cognitive distortions or inaccuracies associated with the trauma. Cognitive processing is a more in-depth process of talking through the trauma, gaining new perspective, and making meaning of it. Cognitive processing may involve some cognitive coping techniques like identifying and changing distorted thoughts to more accurate or helpful ones. Cognitive processing can also involve role plays, experiments, and dialogue between the therapist and client that allows the client to see the trauma in a new way. Think of cognitive coping as a precursor to cognitive processing.

It is important not to begin direct cognitive processing of the abuse until after the child's narrative has been written. More will be written about this later, but the danger of processing abuse material too early, before one has heard the child's "story," is that the child may experience the processing as invalidating. In essence, when you process information, you are telling the child he needs to think differently about the event. Until the therapist fully hears the child's story and bears witness to it, he or she should not seek to change it. Research shows that if the therapist does not validate the client first, before working on cognitive restructuring, the client becomes anxious and may not be able to take in the new information being provided (Miller, Rathus, & Linehan, 2007). Therefore, it is important to fully validate the client's experience before exploring it for change.

After children identify their feelings associated with the trauma, the therapist can easily transition to talking about how thoughts and feelings are related. The cognitive triangle can be drawn to show the connection between thoughts, feelings, and actions. For older children, a cognitive diamond can be drawn to show the relationship between thoughts, feelings, body sensations, and actions.

Younger children may need to be educated on the difference between feelings, thoughts, and actions. A fun way to teach children these concepts, while also engaging their bodies, is to outline the cognitive triangle in tape on the floor. Indicate which points of the triangle represent thoughts, feelings, and actions. On notecards, write examples of each category (e.g., I want to go outside; sad; running). As the therapist reads each example, the child must jump to that point on the triangle. Providing information in a fun, engaging manner helps the child tolerate the information and stay focused. For younger children, reading the book *The Little Engine That Could* shows an example of positive self-talk. Older children may more easily understand that people talk to themselves all day long. Drawing a person with a thought bubble over the head is a way of helping the child visualize this concept. A good book for school-aged children that highlights the concept of cognitive coping is *The Hyena Who Lost Her Laugh*.

Once the child understands the difference between thoughts, feelings, and actions, the therapist can begin to talk to the child about how self-talk directly impacts how one feels. Explain to the child that two people can have the same thing happen to them but have different feelings about it. For example, the therapist might describe the scenario in Dialogue 4-12.

Dialogue 4-12: Explaining How Self-Talk Impacts Feelings

THERAPIST: Let's say two people go to a party. The first person walks in and everyone turns to stare at her. She thinks to herself that no one will want to talk to her, that she is not dressed right and that she doesn't fit in. How does she feel then? And what does she end up doing? The second person walks in and has the same thing happen, everyone turns to stare at her, but this person says to herself that she can't wait to meet everyone and that she is going to have a great time at the party. How does she feel? And then what does she do?

The therapist then wants to highlight that the different thoughts in each scenario led to different outcomes and that thoughts have a powerful impact on how we feel and then how we act. Children can then be instructed to notice and observe some of their own thoughts. The therapist can also refer back to the list of trauma-related feelings that the child identified earlier and ask about thoughts associated with those feelings. Those thoughts can be documented for future use. Since this is still early in treatment, the therapist should be assessing the child's thoughts, not necessarily processing them. The therapist might say, *"Thank you for sharing those thoughts with me. Now I understand better what goes through your mind when you think about your sister touching you on your private area. We are going to learn about sexual abuse and how to handle thoughts about sexual abuse that are bothering you."* The therapist can then provide a rationale for teaching the skill of cognitive coping, which the child can first use to address more benign issues such as sleep problems, separation or test anxiety, or other worries.

Cognitive coping with caregivers should follow the same trajectory, although their thoughts and feelings about the abuse are often processed earlier, as they talk about their own experience. A thought log, such as the one in Table 4.2, can be used with caregivers to identify distressing feelings related to the abuse and thoughts associated with those feelings.

After eliciting a variety of feelings and thoughts and validating them, the therapist can then help the caregiver identify more accurate or helpful thoughts. In the beginning of treatment, cognitive coping can help caregivers with related issues such as behavior management. For example, a caregiver may be overindulgent with a child after surviving a hurricane. With exploration, the caregiver identifies feelings of guilt when the child misbehaves and the caregiver has to decide what to do about discipline. With the thought log, the caregiver identifies that when she feels guilty, she says to herself, *"My daughter has been through so much. She deserves a break."*

Table 4.2
Example of a Caregiver Thought Log

Feeling	Thought	Accurate/helpful thought	New feeling
Anger	He is just like his father!	My son is a child. Just because he's angry doesn't mean he will be like his father.	Less angry
Guilt	It's my fault my son is so angry.	Even though I stayed in an abusive relationship, I did the best I could at the time. I need to set limits to help my son now.	Hopeful

The therapist can then help the caregiver identify the thoughts that keep him from effectively disciplining the child and work with the caregiver on using self-talk that reinforces responding to misbehavior with consistent, firm consequences. As the child's narrative is developed and shared with the caregiver, further processing of the abuse can occur for the caregiver.

Trauma Narrative Development and Cognitive Processing

Preparation for Writing a Narrative   As the client moves into the second third of treatment, more focused work is done on the traumatic event(s). This phase of treatment should also follow a process of gradual exposure, usually beginning with psychoeducation about trauma and abuse. Depending on the child's history of trauma, the therapist can provide both the child and caregiver with general information about that type of trauma (e.g., sexual abuse, physical abuse, domestic violence, suicide, natural disaster, car accident). It is often easier for people to learn about and talk about these issues in general before answering questions about their own personal experiences.

With children, the psychoeducation can be done in a fun, engaging manner by playing a game with questions and answers. For example, questions such as the following help the child talk about the subject within a more neutral yet structured framework:

- *"Why don't most kids tell about sexual abuse?"*
- *"Why don't most kids tell about domestic violence in their house?"*
- *"What are some feelings kids have who have been through a flood?"*

They can talk about themselves without saying they are talking about their experience and they can take in new information that may help them to begin thinking about the trauma in a different way. Deblinger, Neubauer, Runyon, & Baker (2006) developed the game What Do You Know?, which has question cards, in both English and Spanish, about such topics as domestic violence, sexual abuse, physical abuse, and personal safety. The cards can be used individually with children and caregivers or in a game format with children and caregivers competing against each other. There are a variety of good information books on trauma that can be used during the psychoeducation component, such as those listed in Table 4.6, which appears under Additional Resources at the end of this chapter.

Caregivers should also be provided information about the traumatic event(s) via fact sheets, articles, or books that can be further discussed and processed. Fact sheets in English and Spanish can be found in the TFCBT web training at www.musc.edu/tfcbt under the psychoeducation component. In addition, information on various traumas can be found on the NCTSN web site at www.nctsn.org. For both children and caregivers, the information can be later used to further process distorted or unhelpful thoughts related to the trauma.

After children are provided psychoeducation on the traumatic event(s), books, games, and other means can be used to discuss the trauma in a more personalized way. For young children, books about a child's experience with sexual or other traumatic events can provide a model for discussion about the child's own experience. Two such books are *Please Tell!* (Jessie, 1991) for younger children and *Strong at the Heart* (Lehman, 2005) for adolescents. Games with questions and scenarios about the traumatic event can present further education while also eliciting some personal details about the child's experience. KidsRights created two such games. Survivor's Journey is a board game about sexual abuse, and Breakaway is a game about various kinds of interpersonal violence: sexual abuse, physical abuse, and verbal abuse. In keeping with the gradual exposure model, the therapist is introducing structured, engaging, fun materials that help the child talk about both general and personal information related to the traumatic event.

Books, games, and other props also can pair a different affective experience with the trauma. Other props that might be used are poems, music, and magazine articles. Often, children enter treatment having talked about the trauma under strong emotional circumstances. Both child and caregiver may feel mad, sad, upset, worried, scared, or embarrassed when they talk about the abuse. Within the context of a game or a book, both children and caregivers can infuse hope, pride, laughter, and relaxation with talking about the trauma. Obviously, therapists can be creative with this component by introducing ways that their individual client will engage with the material. The therapist's knowledge and attunement to their client will help decide how best to engage the client around this material.

If the child read a book about another child's trauma experience, it is very easy at this point to introduce the concept of writing his or her own book about what happened. Many children feel excited and empowered to write about their own experience. The idea that what they have to say is important and helpful to others is healing. Of course, the therapist's presentation of this idea is also important. As with all gradual exposure activities, the therapist must be willing to hear the child's story and bear witness to his or her experience. If the therapist is unsure, worried, scared, or overwhelmed, he may inadvertently encourage further avoidance by not initiating this next step or initiating it an ambivalent manner. Notice the difference in the following two introductions to writing a narrative:

1. "Now that you've read a book about another child's experience, I think it would be a great idea to write your own book about the sexual abuse that happened to you."
2. "I know it may be hard and maybe you're not ready, but would you like to write your own book?"

The first introduction sounds more confident and sends the message that the child is ready for this next step. Of course, the child may have anxiety about beginning to talk in a detailed way about his trauma, but that is why the process remains *gradual* and safe in that the therapist will be coaching the child to use the coping skills he learned earlier in treatment. Practicing the coping skills, while writing the narrative, is good *in vivo* experience. (As will be discussed later, *in vivo* exposure refers to the gradual and repeated contact with a feared object or activity in real life.)

A first step in writing a narrative with a child is to create a hierarchy of "chapters" for the book. The therapist should have at least a general idea of the events surrounding the trauma and propose what chapters to include in the book if the child falters. With very young children, the therapist will make a list of chapters and give the child choices to write about. With older children, the therapist should work collaboratively with them to arrive at a chapter list that is comprehensive. In both situations, the therapist allows the child to have as much control as possible, thereby counteracting feelings of helplessness.

With an adolescent who was sexually abused over a period of years by her stepfather, a list of chapters might include:

- How people found out about the abuse
- The first incident of sexual abuse
- The last incident of sexual abuse
- The incident of abuse that is hardest to think about
- The relationship with the stepfather before the abuse started

- The medical exam
- Interview with child protective services or police
- Counseling
- Going to court

After writing these chapters, a final chapter that focuses on "advice to other kids," "how I feel now about the abuse," or "what strengths I've gained from this experience" can be written as a way to help the child put the experience in perspective.

With a young child who witnessed the homicide of her mother by her father, the chapter list might read:

- The time my dad hurt my mom
- Another time my dad hurt my mom
- A time my mom had to go to the hospital
- A time the police came to the house
- When my dad stabbed my mom
- Talking to the police
- Going into foster care

Writing the Narrative   After creating a list of "chapters" for the narrative, have the child choose where he wants to begin. Giving the child the choice allows him control and provides the therapist with an understanding of what facet of the traumatic event is easiest to begin talking about. It is important for the therapist not to assume what might be the hardest for the child to talk about.

Ideally, the therapist writes the narrative as the child dictates the details of what happened. In this way, young children and/or children who have difficulty reading or writing can create a book. As the therapist writes, he can control the pace of the child's narrative and prompt for details. Each chapter should be as contained as possible so the child can be instructed to start at the beginning and describe what happened, including thoughts, feelings, and body sensations in as much detail as possible. After completing the chapter, the therapist and/or child can reread the finished product out loud. Dialogue 4-13 illustrates how a therapist may begin the process of writing a trauma narrative.

Once the therapist introduces the idea of creating a book, the therapist and client identify a list of chapters to write. As stated previously, with young children, the therapist can create a list of chapters and just give the child choices. Once the chapters have been identified, ask the child which one they want to start with and begin, as illustrated in the second part of Dialogue 4-13.

Dialogue 4-13: Beginning the Process of Writing a Trauma Dialogue

THERAPIST: Now that we read the book about terrible things happening, I think it would be a great idea to write your own book about what happened to you. The book would be just for you to take home.

CHILD: I don't think I can write a book.

THERAPIST: I know it sounds hard, but I'm sure you can do it. I will be your secretary so you don't have to do any writing at all. Since you are the author, all you have to do is tell me what to write down and I will. After we are done, I can type it on the computer for you and you can even add pictures if you want. I think it will be great!

CHILD: Okay!

Once the chapters have been identified, ask the child which one he wants to start with and begin.

THERAPIST: Okay, so you want to start with the chapter on the first time you saw your dad hurt your mom. I want you to think back to that day and tell me in as much detail as possible what happened—starting with how the fight started; where you were; your thoughts, feelings, and body sensations; and everything that happened. Start when you're ready and I'm going to write down everything you say. I might have to ask you to talk slowly if I can't keep up. I want to make sure I get every word.

CHILD: Well, I was playing upstairs in my room and I heard my dad start to yell. I didn't know what was going on, so I went downstairs to see. I saw my mom on the floor and my dad was standing over her yelling at her. Then he hit her on the head. I didn't like that. I started to cry. Then my dad heard me and he slammed the door shut so I couldn't see, but I could still hear him yelling.

THERAPIST: How did you feel when you saw your dad hit your mom?

CHILD: I felt sad and scared. I was afraid he was going to hit me.

THERAPIST: How did your body feel inside?

CHILD: Like there were butterflies in my tummy.

THERAPIST: Great job! Let me read back to you what I wrote down so you can make sure I got it right.

If a child talks easily, the therapist should not interrupt the flow of thoughts. One goal of writing a trauma narrative is to allow time for the child to sit with and tolerate his feelings and thoughts about the trauma. Interrupting to ask for details hinders that process. Of course, many children have difficulty talking about the abuse and/or avoid certain words or parts of their experience. If a child has difficulty starting to talk or becomes silent in the middle of talking about an incident, the therapist can use open-ended questions to facilitate further details (e.g., *"Can you tell me, from the beginning, where you were and what you were doing before he touched you or what happened next?"*). If a child talks easily but leaves out certain parts, the therapist can ask further questions when it is reread, rather than interrupting the flow of the narrative while it is being told. While rereading the chapter, the therapist can ask open-ended questions like:

- "I'm wondering what you were thinking here."
- "What were you feeling after he left the room?"
- "You said he came into the room and touched you and then you ran out of the room. I wasn't there so I'd like to know everything that happened."
- "After he came into the room, what happened next?"
- "Then what happened?"

Rereading the chapter and eliciting further details provides another layer of exposure to the experience. Time permitting, more than one chapter can be written in a session. If there are concerns about the child's becoming upset, allow time at the end of session to practice coping skills. Coping skills can be coached as chapters are being written as well. At the end of each session, the therapist should check in with the client to assess how he is feeling. Praise and encouragement should be provided.

Depending on the length of each chapter and the necessity, chapters can be reread at the beginning of each new session so as to provide further exposure to the material. Once all chapters are written, the client can organize them and choose a title. Artwork can be included as well, depending on what engages the child in the activity and helps him to process his experience.

With that in mind, a trauma narrative does not necessarily mean one has to write a book. The more important goal is that the child process his experience in a way that is engaging so he will complete the process. For many children, writing is a difficult or boring task, even when the therapist is doing the writing. Other means of creating a narrative include drawing, poetry, songwriting, puppet shows, and structured play. Matching a client's interests to the experience of telling his story often is the deciding factor in whether a child creates a narrative. If a child is avoidant, it is the therapist's job to find a way to motivate him to process the trauma and make it a meaningful experience.

As the narrative is being written, the therapist's job is to validate the child's experience by hearing it and accepting it as it is told. Structured cognitive processing is better left until the narrative is done. If a therapist is too quick to jump in and change thoughts or feelings, the child may feel reticent to share additional details. After the identified chapters are written, the final chapter of the narrative can serve as a means of solidifying what needs to be processed. In the last chapter, the child can discuss what he has learned since coming to counseling; how he views the trauma differently now; and/or what strengths he has gained and how they will be used in the future. This chapter should capture the new perspective the child has on the traumatic event. Sometimes the process of creating a narrative is all that is needed for a child to make meaning of his experience, and so a final chapter can be written rather quickly. For others, more intense cognitive processing of distorted or inaccurate thoughts may need to be done before a final chapter can be written. Examples of two completed narratives can be found in Tables 4.3 and 4.4.

Table 4.3
Trauma Narrative Written by a 10-Year-Old boy Who Witnessed Domestic Violence

Chapter 1: Introduction

Hello! I'm Joe. I'm 10 years old and I'm in the fifth grade. I like to listen to music and play video games. I also like to go to the movies with my mom. I'm writing this book to tell people about me. It was sad for me when my parents weren't there for me, so I want other kids to know how it feels to be sad about things that happen to them and that it can turn out fine!

Leaving Our Home

I was sad when child services took us out of our house. First they called us at night and said they were coming the next day. My mom said they weren't going to take us. I was crying bad. The next morning a DYFS lady came and said, "I'm taking all your kids." My mom said, "No you ain't!" Then they had to call a big lady in to hold my mom back. I didn't like that. I felt so mad that I wanted to punch her. I said, "You're not taking us, dummy." Then they just took us in a van and I never saw my mom after that. I was panicky. I said, "I want my mom!" But then I got the feeling that we weren't living right. My brother told me that. He said we'd all go into foster homes and it would be all right. He told me not to fight it. There was nothing to fight about. I felt better.

Life with Mom

I was in the house watching TV and my mom came home. My mom was watching TV with me. My stepdad came in the door and saw my mom's phone book. He got mad and slapped her across the face. I felt mad. I thought that better not be me. He made me scared sometimes because he had a gun. After that, I told my mom we should leave. We told him a lie that we were going somewhere else and got a motel room. I was playing video games and my mom was reading a book. I heard a loud noise and I got scared bad. I jumped up onto the bed. When we looked up we saw John's face in front of the window. He yelled, "Open up the door!" and after that, he took out the air conditioner from the window and got in the room. He tried to hit my mom and then me and my brother called the cops. I don't like that when someone hits my mom. I got mad. The cops came and took him to jail, but a friend bailed him out. After that, me and my mom went to live with my grandma and we never saw him again. He used to sell puppies for drugs. He used to come home drunk and run into the refrigerator. We'd try to take care of him and give him an ice pack but then he'd get up and hit my mom. He'd call my mom a slut. Me and my brothers would jump on him and hit him. One time I hit him with a lamp. The glass flew everywhere and he bled. He wasn't a stepdad. I felt mad at my mom for staying with him. He'd tell her he'd help her buy a house but he never gave her a penny. One time he hit us hard with a metal stick. Me and my brothers told him to stay away from my mom. He left the house and then came back and hit us with a metal stick on the leg. He threatened to kill my mom. My grandma was nice. She gave my mom money and we never saw him again.

Fighting

Me and my brother were coming home. We came in the motel room and sat down when we heard screaming. My mom was in Room 101 and we were in a friend's room, Room 102, chillin'. We heard screaming, and my mom called our name. We ran into the room and saw my stepdad smacking my mom, punching her and kicking her inside the hotel. I felt mad. I thought I should hit him with something. I called the cops and he threatened my mom. My stepdad said that when he got out of jail he'd hurt my mom. I felt mad because he said that. The cops came and he tried to run away and hide in the building but they found him and put him in jail. After that we went to the park so he couldn't find us.

I was 8 years old when my mom first got married. We were all living at my grandma's house. No one was home but me, mom, my brothers and my sister. He started stuff and then she called him a bitch. I was happy because that was the first time she ever cussed at him. He was starting stuff with her and she cussed at him. He went to the kitchen and got a butcher knife out of the drawer and put it to her neck. He said, "You're so lucky because I could kill you right now." She said, "Do it!" and picked up a chair. She tore off the chair leg and said, "Bring it on." She threw it at his head but he ducked. She stayed because he was bad. He kills people. She was afraid to say no to him. I was afraid something bad was going to happen to her and then he'd do something to us.

My Foster Home Now

I got sent to foster care because of my stepdad doing mean things like hitting my mom and hitting us. Someone called child services on my mom because of the hitting and because she was drinking a lot. They came to my grandma's house when we were there and I felt sad and mad. They took me and my siblings to different foster homes. The first time I ever went there my brother had to spend the night because I was sad and scared about everything. My foster mom was the only one there and my foster dad was at work. When he came home I felt scared because I didn't know how he'd be. After a while, I got used to it. I like the way they treat us. They don't treat me like my stepdad did. They treat me like how I should be treated. My sister and brothers all wanted to come live with me because they don't like their foster homes. In the beginning I used to visit with my brothers and sister but now I don't really anymore. I feel sad and mad about that. I'd like to go see them.

Counseling

My foster parents told me that it would be nice to come to counseling. My caseworker came to pick me up. She was nice to bring me to counseling. We were late getting there the first time. I could only meet with Dr. Amy for 10 minutes. In counseling, we talk and we draw and we write about good things and bad things. Sometimes I feel mad and sad and upset. I like counseling because I can get my anger out and it helps me to stop thinking about a lot of stuff like what my mom and dad did. It helps me just go on.

(Continued)

Table 4.3

(Continued)

Advice to Kids

Do not be mad when you get put in a foster home. Don't fight it because it's not going to get you anywhere. You can be mad but don't take it out on people by hitting them. You can be sad and mad. It helps me to talk to people. You can talk to your mom and dad or a psychologist. When I was little my mom was drinking a lot of beer. It made me mad because she couldn't take care of me and we had to go into foster care. I didn't like when my mom drank. If your parents are drinking, you should call the cops. The cops can find them a place where they can stop drinking.

Domestic violence is when a mom and a dad hit each other and fight. It's not OK. If your parents are fighting, don't jump in the middle. Go call 911. Sometimes people can get killed. When kids see their parents fight, they may want to fight too because they don't know how to handle their anger. But fighting doesn't get you anywhere. If you are a woman with a guy who is doing drugs or hitting you, you should leave. It will be good for the kids because they will feel safe.

Table 4.4

Trauma Narrative by a 6-Year-Old Boy Who Was Sexually Abused by His Brother

You Are Not My Friend

Introduction

Hi! My name is Daryl. I like to play basketball. I am in kindergarten. I live with my mom and dad and my brother, Tyrone. Tyrone sexually abused me. I'm writing this book to help stop sexual abuse from happening to other kids.

Chapter One

I was in bed sleeping and Tyrone walked over to my bed, pulled my pants down, and put his finger in my butt. I felt sad and mad. I was thinking he is not my friend. My butt hurt. He went back to bed and layed down. I pulled my pants up. I felt mad.

Chapter Two

Another time Tyrone touched me was when I was downstairs on the couch sleeping. He was right there next to me. He pulled my pants down and then he bit my butt cheek. I felt sad and mad. Then he went back upstairs back to sleep. Everyone else was asleep. I couldn't tell my mom because she was asleep and I couldn't tell my dad because he was asleep. He didn't say sorry.

When I Told

I was outside. My mom asked me what was wrong and has Tyrone bothered me. I said yes. She said, "What did he do?" I said he put his finger in my butt. She said, "We're going to find out." I felt sad. After I told my mom, the police came. They kicked down the door. I felt mad. Some guy with glasses took us to the police station. He took us upstairs to this room. We talked to the man about Tyrone. I felt happy that Tyrone got in big trouble but sad because he had to live somewhere else.

Coming to the Doctor

Someone drove me and my mom and my sister to the doctor. It was really bad. My mom came in the room with me. I took off my pants and my shirt. First, he checked me on my private parts and then he checked in my butt. That felt bad. Then he brought a TV and a camera that showed by butt on TV. I felt bad, but he told me everything was OK. He gave me stickers because I was good.

Coming to Counseling

The first day I came to see Dr. Amy, my dad and mom brought me. I felt good and sad. I felt happy about coming to counseling. We play and we learn the names for private parts: breasts, butt, vagina, and penis. I learned that sexual abuse is when someone touches you in your private parts. Kids feel mad when they get sexually abused. Sexual abuse happens to a lot of kids. You should tell if it happens to you.

In the Future

In the future, I want to be a painter. I'm doing good in school and I like to play putt-putt golf. I'm proud of myself for doing great work and writing this book. I feel better now that I came to counseling. I know it's not my fault. I love my brother but I don't like what he did.

Cognitive Processing   For caregivers, cognitive processing happens at various levels throughout the therapy process. Caregivers frequently present for treatment with common thoughts:

- *"This has ruined my child's life."*
- *"I should have known he was a child molester."*
- *"I can't ever trust anyone again."*
- *"Why didn't he tell me?"*

These thoughts often involve underlying concerns about trust, parenting ability, and the child's well-being. Although caregivers do not write their own trauma narrative in TFCBT, they tell the therapist their own story of how they learned about the abuse. Thought logs, such as the one in Table 4.2, are utilized in session and for homework to encourage caregivers to notice their thoughts and feelings about the abuse. Validation is used to acknowledge the caregivers' thoughts and feelings. As psychoeducation about trauma is presented and the child's narrative is read, more problematic thoughts may be voiced. Sometimes, psychoeducation and reading a child's narrative may help a caregiver process the abuse on her own. Other times, they need more focused cognitive processing that involves helping them utilize the cognitive coping skills already taught. Some caregivers need even more processing that involves evidence gathering, Socratic questioning, and/or role plays. These techniques can also be used with children and adolescents.

For children and adolescents, cognitive processing occurs after the bulk of the narrative has been written and the child has expressed her feelings, thoughts, and body sensations in the narrative. It is at this juncture that the therapist reviews the narrative and identifies feelings, cognitions, and body sensations that were problematic. With older children and adolescents, this process can be done collaboratively. With younger children, only the therapist will identify the issues to address. With all children and adolescents, the therapist then checks in with the client about where he or she is at with an identified feeling, thought, or body sensation. For example, in the body of the narrative, a child wrote, *"After he touched me on my vagina, I felt scared and dirty."* The therapist wants to know if the child *now* feels scared and dirty. As stated previously, sometimes the psychoeducation and discussion about the abuse processes that feeling and thought without specifically focusing on them. If the child said, "No, I don't feel scared anymore because I was able to tell and he can't hurt me anymore," then further processing may not need to be done. The child's response suggests there has already been processing going on in treatment. To capture and reinforce this new perspective, the therapist can have the child create a last chapter to the book that incorporates the new way of thinking. A final chapter might be titled, "What I Learned in Therapy" or "What I Think about the Abuse Now."

If, however, the child continues to feel "scared" and/or "dirty," more direct cognitive processing should be done using the previous techniques mentioned: evidence gathering, Socratic questioning, and/or role playing. The goal of each of these techniques is to help the child see her situation in a new, more helpful way, in contrast to the distorted, inaccurate, or unhelpful way she is viewing the abuse. Psychoeducation can help some children understand their situation better and therefore see it in a different way. Other children may be able to identify the correct or helpful way to view the situation in their head but not in their heart.

Evidence gathering is devising an experiment to show children how their thinking is altered. For example, after being sexually abused, a child may believe that *all* men sexually abuse kids. To show the child the inaccuracy of her thinking, the therapist might ask the child to identify all the men/boys that she knows. After identifying and writing down the names of all the men/boys the child knows, the therapist can have the child circle all of the men/boys that sexually abused her. The child can then see that most men/boys do not sexually abuse children. Having the child collect her own evidence about a distorted or inaccurate belief helps her to gain a new perspective and believe in it more strongly.

Socratic questioning is the process of asking the child or caregiver questions to help them see the abuse from a new perspective. A child who was sexually abused may continue to believe that "sex is dirty" even after receiving psychoeducation on sexual abuse and talking about his/her own sexual abuse experience. To help the child gain a new perspective, the therapist might ask a series of questions that helps shake the foundation of the child's belief. The exchange in Dialogue 4-14 is an example of Socratic questioning.

Dialogue 4-14: An Example of Socratic Questioning

CHILD: I never want to have sex with anyone. It's so dirty!
THERAPIST: What makes sex so dirty?
CHILD: Well, that's what my uncle did to me and that was gross.
THERAPIST: Was what happened to you sex or sexual abuse?
CHILD: Sexual abuse I guess.
THERAPIST: Well, what's the difference between sex and sexual abuse?
CHILD: Sex is when two people who love each other decide to have sex together. Sexual abuse is when an adult forces a child to touch them on their private parts.
THERAPIST: So, is sex dirty or is sexual abuse dirty?
CHILD: Sexual abuse.
THERAPIST: Why is it important to think about the difference?
CHILD: Because someday when I love someone I can decide to have sex with them.
THERAPIST: How will that experience be different?
CHILD: I will be older and the person won't force me to do anything I don't want to. We will love each other.
THERAPIST: Does that sound dirty?
CHILD: No.

Having the child role play someone else, like her best friend or therapist, can have a therapeutic effect as well. These techniques are both ways to provide children with those "aha" moments. With a role play, the child must convince the therapist (playing her) that her thoughts are distorted or inaccurate. The very act of trying to convince the therapist and stating accurate/helpful information out loud helps the child solidify those statements in her own mind. Dialogue 4-15 illustrates a role play between the therapist and an 8-year-old boy who was in the car when his mother was killed in a car accident. He is struggling with guilt and the thought that he should have died, too.

Dialogue 4-15: Illustration of a Role Play

THERAPIST: One of the things that you write in your narrative is that you feel guilty about not being able to save your mother from dying in the car accident. Do you still feel that way?

CHILD: Yes. Even though we've talked about it and I know accidents happen to people and it's not my fault. I still think that maybe if I had done something more, she might have lived.

THERAPIST: Okay, let's do a role play. I want you to play your best friend, Josh, and I'm going to be you. I'm going to come and talk to you about how I feel and I want you to be a good best friend, Okay?

CHILD: Okay.

THERAPIST: Hi, Josh! Can I talk to you?

CHILD: Sure.

THERAPIST: I've been thinking a lot about my mom and how she died. I feel really bad about it. I'm afraid to tell you what I did.

CHILD: You can tell me.

THERAPIST: I think you'll be mad at me. Maybe you won't even be my friend anymore.

CHILD: Listen, you can tell me and I won't be mad.

THERAPIST: Okay . . . I think it's my fault that my mom died in that car accident.

CHILD: No way. Why?

THERAPIST: After we hit the truck and the car flipped over, I should have done something to help her get out of the car before it blew up.

CHILD: What could you have done?

THERAPIST: I don't know. Maybe undone her seat belt and pulled her out.

CHILD: How could you do that when you were caught in the car, too?

THERAPIST: I don't know.

CHILD: Well if you were stuck yourself, how could you get her out? Plus, how much did your mom weigh? Would you have been able to pull her out?

THERAPIST: I don't know. She was a lot bigger than me.

CHILD: What about the police people that came to the accident. They got you out. Why didn't they get your mom out?

THERAPIST: They tried, but before they could get her out the car blew up. They took me first. I should have told them to get her out first.

CHILD: They made the decision, not you. Would they have listened to you?

THERAPIST: I don't know, but do you think it's my fault?

CHILD: No. You were trapped inside the car, too, and even if you got out of your seat belt, your mom was too heavy to pull out. The police were in charge, and they made the decision to pull you out, so it's not your fault.

THERAPIST: Are you sure?

CHILD: I'm sure. You were only 7 years old then. You weren't strong enough and you didn't make the decisions.

IN VIVO GRADUAL EXPOSURE

The process of gradual exposure across sessions may include a specific focus on a problematic area about which a child is avoidant. With a narrative, exposure is covert, meaning the child is asked to remember, think about, and talk about events that have happened in the past. *In vivo* exposure refers to the gradual and repeated contact with a feared object or activity in real life. Some traumatized children develop fears that affect their overall functioning. Some fears may be directly associated with traumatic events (e.g., fear of sleeping in a bedroom where sexual abuse occurred, fear of getting in a car after a car accident) and others may not (e.g., fears of leaving the house or separating from a parent). The child may avoid people, places, or things that appear benign but are somehow associated with the trauma in the child's mind (e.g., smells, people who like like the perpetrator, tone of voice, thunderstorms, water). These are sometimes referred to as *traumatic reminders* or *triggers*.

Traumatic reminders can trigger a variety of symptoms: avoidance or withdrawal, strong emotion, flashbacks, dissociation, and impulsivity. The child can appear to have severe mood swings when, in reality, a reminder of the trauma is causing an automatic response. The trigger, which was originally paired with the trauma, has now become a reminder of the abuse. The reaction is experienced on many levels: cognitive, emotional, physiological, and behavioral. For example, a child who survived a school shooting incident finds herself on the floor, shaking when she hears the sound of a car backfiring. Her body automatically responds to the perceived threat by falling to the ground and shaking. She feels intense fear at that moment as if she is back in school on the day of the shooting.

In addition, specific and global fears can develop after a traumatic event. For example, after disclosing that his uncle had been sexually abusing him in his bed over a period of months, Adam did not want to sleep alone. Instead, he wanted to sleep with his parents in their bed. After the disclosure, Adam's parents felt sad and upset for their son. They wanted to protect him and keep him safe, so they let Adam sleep with them for several months. Over those months, Adam became even more avoidant of his bedroom and complained of not wanting to enter his bedroom at all.

Through a process of *in vivo* gradual exposure, Adam was gradually reintroduced to his bedroom. First, Adam's parents were directed to spend time with Adam in his bedroom playing with him, beginning with short intervals (5–15 minutes) and moving up to longer intervals (45 minutes to 1 hour). As Adam became more comfortable and was given praise for his efforts, he was required to start sleeping in his bed. At first, Adam's mother or father slept with Adam in his own bed until he fell asleep. Adam's parent would then leave the room and return to their room. If Adam woke up in the middle of the night and came to his parents' bedroom, he was directed back to his bed by one of his parents, who again would lie down with him until he fell asleep. As time went on, Adam's parents put him to bed without staying with him. If he came in their room in the middle of the night, they again directed him to his own bed. Over time, they no longer had to stay with Adam in his room. He went to bed on his own and stayed in his bed the whole night.

This process of in vivo behavioral exposure helps to reduce or eliminate children's stress reactions so that they can function more effectively. A desensitization plan should be developed with the caregiver(s) or other support people (e.g., teachers, coaches) to resolve the avoidance.

The therapist first creates a hierarchy of situations that create anxiety. The child is introduced to each situation, beginning with the least anxiety provoking. The following list is an example of such a hierarchy that might be used with the previous example:

- Playing in bedroom with parents for 5 minutes
- Playing in bedroom with parents for 15 minutes
- Playing in bedroom for 45 minutes
- Sleeping in own bed with one parent until asleep
- Sleeping in own bed

The therapist should create a list of people, places, or things that the child can gradually be exposed to in real life. For the plan to be effective, the exposure must occur in the context of a safe and supportive environment, including the therapist's office or other safe locations. The therapist would not want to do *in vivo* exposure in the bedroom where the sexual abuse happened or at the site of the car accident. These locations may elicit so much fear and anxiety that the traumatic association is strengthened. During the exposure process, the child is coached to use coping skills to manage any anxiety. In this way, the traumatic reminder is being paired with a state of calm. As the child practices visualizing or engaging in the feared situation while also practicing coping skills to manage the anxiety, a new association will develop. Over time, the child learns to manage her fear and anxiety and cope with the situation.

Conjoint Parent–Child Sessions

The sessions up until this part of treatment have been used to assess how well the caregiver is able to handle hearing about the child's trauma. *Is the caregiver able to hear about the child's trauma without triggering significant stress reactions in the caregiver? Is the caregiver able to use coping skills to manage his own stress if it occurs? Is the caregiver able to be present and validate the child regarding his trauma?* If the therapist assesses that the caregiver can hear the trauma narrative and provide validation and praise, joint sessions can be facilitated by the therapist. However, if the caregiver is not emotionally ready to hear the child's narrative, more preparation may need to be done. If not, individual sessions with the caregiver may continue beyond the child's sessions or a referral for individual therapy can be made to the caregiver with the hope that at a later time, he could return to participate in that phase of treatment.

Caregivers may need more preparation for several reasons: (1) their own trauma history is interfering with the ability to tolerate their child's trauma; (2) they may have distorted or inaccurate thoughts about the trauma might create difficulties in a joint session; and/or (3) they are extremely emotional or become dysregulated when talking about their child's trauma. These situations may require further psychoeducation about trauma, coping skills training to manage feelings and reactions, and/or additional cognitive processing.

Following a gradual exposure model, at least three conjoint sessions should occur. The first session is often centered around general information about the specific trauma (e.g., sexual abuse, physical abuse, natural disaster, etc.). The therapist can facilitate a "game show" during which caregiver(s) and child compete over answering questions about the specific trauma the child experienced. A therapeutic game may be played to review and impart information about the trauma. Two games mentioned earlier are appropriate for the joint session: Breakaway and Survivor's Journey, both by KidsRights. Another game is called Let's Talk About Touching (Cavanagh-Johnson, 1992). The therapist can be creative and adapt traditional games to include trauma information. For example, one can play checkers or Jenga and attach questions to each piece that the child or caregiver has to answer when they move. The therapist can also make "word find" games on the computer that include words related to the trauma that the child and caregiver have to define. Since this is the first conjoint session focused on trauma-related material, the goal is to create a comfortable, affective experience that contrasts any strong emotions so far associated with the trauma. In other words, the therapist wants to create an experience in which the caregiver and child are having fun, feeling happy, and laughing so that these emotions, rather than ones previously associated with the trauma (e.g., sadness, shame, etc.), become paired with talking about and thinking about the trauma.

As part of the therapist's individual time with both child and caregiver, preparation for the joint session should occur. With the child, the therapist might review the information to be discussed in the joint session. With the caregiver, preparation should include orienting the caregiver to the goals of this first joint session: (1) create a comfortable, fun atmosphere for the child that counteracts feelings of sadness, shame, and fear associated with the abuse, in other words, have fun playing the game; (2) create a space for open communication about the trauma; and (3) show the child that the parent is comfortable talking about and hearing about trauma. Knowing the goals of the joint sessions helps a caregiver focus on specific outcomes and also manage her anxiety about beginning to talk about the trauma.

In keeping with what caregiver(s) have learned about parenting skills, it is also important to prepare the caregiver to provide the child with praise. Joint sessions should be facilitated to allow many opportunities for praise and positive feelings. Review with the caregiver(s) what praise is and how to do it, focusing specifically on how they might introduce it in each of the joint sessions. The caregiver can also review any coping skills she may need to use in the joint session to manage strong feelings.

A second joint session might focus on sex education and safety skills. Again, the therapist might introduce sex education by way of a quiz or structured conversation. Please see Table 4.5 for several sex education resources that offer quizzes and activities that can be used in a joint session.

Both child and caregiver may need to discuss rules for communication around these subjects, since they may evoke strong feelings and beliefs. For children who experience physical abuse or domestic violence, sex education may be broadened to include information about healthy relationships and conflict resolution.

Safety skills can be role played with both child and caregiver. Depending on the type of trauma experienced, safety skills may include how to respond to a notice of evacuation, safety planning for domestic violence situations, or boundary setting with a bully. More discussion on these topics appears in the next section.

The final joint session, separate from the last session which should be celebratory in nature, should focus on the child's reading the trauma narrative to their caregiver(s). At this point, the child and caregiver(s) have come together at least twice to discuss the abuse in a more general way. A comfortable, supportive atmosphere has been facilitated to now talk specifically about the trauma.

Table 4.5

Sex Education Resources for Joint Session Activities

My Body, My Self for Girls, workbook
Author: Lynda Madaras and Area Madaras
Publisher: Newmarket Press
ISBN#: 1-55704-441-4

My Body, My Self for Boys, workbook
Author: Lynda Madaras and Area Madaras
Publisher: Newmarket Press
ISBN#: 1-55704-230-6

Sexuality Curriculum for Abused Children and Young Adolescents and Their Parents
Author: Toni Cavanagh-Johnson

The Teen Relationship Workbook
Author: Kerry Moles, CSW
Publisher: Wellness Reproductions and Publishing, Inc.
1-800-669-9208

Preparation with the child should focus on re-reading the narrative a final time or parts that are more difficult. The therapist should discuss what worries or fears the child has and how to cope with them in the joint session. Behavioral rehearsal of those coping skills can be done as well. Have the child practice using coping skills learned earlier in treatment so that he is more likely to use them if he needs to during the joint session.

With the caregiver, the therapist should also review any worries or fears the caregiver has and discuss how to manage any anxiety the session may create. Caregivers should be instructed to use any of the coping skills they learned earlier in treatment to manage any strong feelings that are triggered in the joint session. Review how the caregiver will respond to the narrative with praise, comments, or questions. The final joint session should be a time during which the caregiver provides praise and positive comments about the child's narrative, so questions that might be heard as blaming or critical by the child should not be made in the joint session. For example, if a caregiver wants to ask the child why he didn't yell, scream, or fight back when the sexual assault occurred, the therapist should talk to the caregiver about why that question may be experienced as blaming to the child and provide more psychoeducation to the caregiver to help him understand why most kids don't fight back.

The more practice one does with a caregiver, the better. However, even with good preparation, caregiver(s) sometimes freeze or ask a question that may be interpreted by the child as critical or blaming. Try to problem solve any challenges before the session, but if necessary, jump in during the joint session to redirect or mediate any conflicts. If, despite the therapist's best efforts to prepare caregivers for the joint session, the caregiver does ask a question that the child may perceive as negative, the therapist may jump in and do some damage control. Dialogue 4-16 is an example of such an exchange. Sometimes caregivers react to their own worries or fears and then respond in an impulsive or reactive way. It is the therapist's job to get them back on track. Remember that the goal of this session is to facilitate open, positive communication about the traumatic event.

Dialogue 4-16: Doing Damage Control in a Conjoint Parent–Child Session

THERAPIST: After hearing your daughter's book that she wrote, what would you like to say to her?

DAD: I'm really proud of how well you are able to talk about the sexual assault. You did a wonderful job writing a lot of details about the assault, talking to the police, and having a medical exam done. You are so brave! It's just so hard for me to understand why you couldn't scream for help or run away when the assault was happening.

THERAPIST: I think what you mean to say is that it's really hard to understand how people just get scared and freeze when they are being attacked. It feels scary to know that can happen to anybody. You're not saying it's your daughter's fault, right?

DAD: No, no, not at all.

THERAPIST: In fact, what have we learned about why people do freeze during a stressful event, Katie?

KATIE: Your body gets so scared it goes into shock and it can't move.

THERAPIST: Exactly! I'm very impressed you remembered that, Katie. Dad, what did Katie do after she got unfrozen that was very brave?

DAD: She told her teacher what happened and her teacher called me.

THERAPIST: Right! What do you want to say to Katie about how brave she was for telling?

DAD: I'm really proud of you for being able to tell. I know that must have been hard.

There may be issues that require further cognitive processing in the joint session. For example, if, at the time of an abuse disclosure, a caregiver becomes angry and yells at the child, "Why didn't you tell me sooner?" it might be necessary to address this issue in the joint session. Through individual sessions with the child, the therapist will have some sense of how that kind of reaction might have affected the child. It is the therapist's job to facilitate a discussion about the caregiver's reaction in the joint session. Ideally, the therapist would prepare the caregiver to apologize for his response and articulate that the caregiver was mad at the perpetrator, not the child. In addition, the therapist would want the caregiver to reinforce how proud he is that the child told at all. Dialogue 4-17 illustrates how a therapist might prep a parent to address the issue of why the child didn't tell sooner in a joint session. This interaction takes place with the individual session with the parent, in this case a mother.

It is important to practice how the exchange might go in case the therapist needs to edit the caregiver's statements. Some caregivers may need more than one prep session, so plan accordingly. After the prep session with the caregiver, the joint session can be facilitated.

At the end of the joint sessions, the child and caregiver(s) should feel more comfortable talking directly with each other about the traumatic event(s). These sessions set a foundation for ongoing, future discussion about the trauma as well as related topics such as sex education, safety, and relationships.

Dialogue 4-17: Preparing a Parent to Address the Issue of Why the Child Didn't Tell Sooner in a Joint Session

THERAPIST: Now that I've read you your daughter's book about the sexual abuse, I want to talk to you about one issue she talks about in her book. In her book, she mentions that one of your reactions to her disclosure was to ask her why she didn't tell sooner. Of course, that question is totally understandable given that you were shocked to hear that your daughter had been sexually abused. You felt horrified that you hadn't known sooner. From your daughter's perspective, though, how might she hear that question?

MOM: She might think I'm mad at her for not coming to me sooner.

THERAPIST: Yes, in fact, she said in her book that she felt bad after you asked her that. Even though you have done a wonderful job telling her how proud you are of her for telling and coming to counseling, we want to make sure she isn't left with any bad feelings about not being able to tell right away. In order to do that, I want you to address the issue with her in the joint session after she reads you her book. How might you do that?

MOM: Well, I guess I can reassure her that I did not think it was her fault and she did the right thing by telling.

> **Therapist:** Wonderful! I think it would also be important for you to add that you were not and are not mad at her for not telling you. You may need to explain to her that your reaction was out of shock and anger at the perpetrator, not her. Let's practice! After your daughter finishes reading her book, you can praise her for what a wonderful job she did. Then you can initiate a discussion about this issue. Pretend I just finished reading my book and now it's your turn to talk.
>
> **Mom:** Marisol, that was an incredible book! I'm so proud of you for being able to talk and write about the abuse. I'm glad you can talk to me about it. There's one part of your book I want to talk about because I wonder if you think I'm mad at you for not telling me sooner about the abuse. I'm sorry I reacted so strongly by asking you why you didn't tell me sooner. I was shocked and sad and mad, not at you but at your uncle for touching you. I realize now that you were too scared to tell me. I'm just glad you told your grandma so the abuse could stop. Please don't think I'm mad at you. I couldn't be more proud!
>
> **Therapist:** That was terrific! You apologized and explained what you were feeling at the time. You reassured her you were not mad at her and you praised her for telling someone, even if it wasn't you. This is really important because we want her to feel like she can tell anybody if something happens again.

Enhancing Safety and Future Development

The last phase of treatment should be focused on learning skills that will maintain and further the gains already made in treatment. These skills include open communication between child and caregiver(s), age-appropriate sex/relationship education, and safety skill training. Individual and joint session time is spent on these skills so that the therapist can provide specific information to both child and caregiver and then bring them together to discuss and practice the skills.

Sex/Relationship Education   Age-appropriate sex education is important for all youth, but especially for children and adolescents who have been sexually abused. Children who have been sexually abused have experienced an inappropriate "sexual" activity. They are at risk for inaccurate and/or distorted thoughts related to their bodies, sex, and relationships. To set the stage for healthy sexuality, it is important that children who have been sexually abused understand the difference between sex and sexual abuse.

For those children who have experienced other kinds of interpersonal trauma, sex education should include education about healthy relationships, boundary setting, and conflict resolution. In addition, peer relationships, bullying, and teasing should be discussed.

Of course, this topic can trigger much anxiety for many caregivers and therapists. All caregivers come to treatment with their own history of trauma, parenting, and sex education. Before talking to the child about sex education, it is important for the therapist to first discuss the topic with the caregiver so as to understand her cultural and family values and comfort level with the topic. Families have different beliefs about masturbation, gender roles, sex before marriage, abortion, and birth control. Before discussing any of these topics with the child/adolescent, it is important to understand the caregivers' beliefs. It is not in the child's best interest for the therapist to be saying something in contrast to the caregiver. For example, a therapist may want to normalize masturbation with a child; however, if the parent believes that masturbation is sinful based on the family's religious beliefs, the caregiver may feel upset that the therapist is providing information on masturbation to the child that is in direct contrast to the family's religious values. Ground rules must be established regarding the family's religious and cultural values with regard to these topics. Once ground rules have been set, the therapist can move forward providing information to children. The information will, of course, be dependent on the child's age, maturity, and developmental level.

Therapists also have experiences, attitudes, and feelings that impact their ability to educate clients about sex and sexuality. If a therapist is uncomfortable or judgmental about these topics, it can create discomfort for clients and possibly avoidance related to sex education and further trauma work. The therapist's ability to be self-aware and recognize any discomfort related to these topics will help the therapist separate his own needs from the client's.

For very young children, sex education should include teaching the correct names for their private parts and helping them learn to distinguish between okay, not okay, and confusing touches. As children get older, puberty should be discussed, including an understanding of menstruation and wet dreams. Girls are starting to menstruate as early as 7 and 8 years old. It is important they hear correct information from their caregivers to ease any anxiety they might have about their bodies. Adolescents may need information on sexuality, birth control, sexually transmitted infections, and healthy relationships. Adolescents exposed to domestic violence can benefit from psychoeducation on healthy versus unhealthy relationships, the cycle of abuse, and how to deal appropriately with conflicts in relationships. The *Teen Relationships Workbook* (Moles, 2001) is a wonderful resource for handouts and activities on these issues.

Depending on the needs of the child/adolescent, the therapist may spend more or less time on this topic, with the ultimate goal of opening the topic for discussion between caregiver and child so that after treatment ends, the conversation will continue.

Safety Skill Training   Children and adolescents may feel disempowered and fearful after a traumatic event. The goal of safety skill training is to improve the child's sense of empowerment and decrease anxiety related to future social situations. Given the risk for revictimization after exposure to interpersonal violence, safety skill training should promote awareness, problem-solving skills, and assertive communication. Safety skill training, like other skills, must be taught according to the child's developmental level and with the caregiver's involvement so that skills will be maintained after termination.

With very young children, concrete rules like "don't talk to strangers" are taught to help keep them safe. Developmentally, very young children need specific safety rules to follow; however, it is also important to start teaching them awareness skills. Awareness refers to both internal and external awareness. Children can be taught to pay attention to what is going on inside their bodies—body signals—that tell them how they are feeling. If a child is uncomfortable, she can be encouraged to leave the situation, go somewhere safe, and tell someone. External awareness involves teaching children to be good observers of their environment. *What are the safe places/people I can go to if I feel uncomfortable?* Teaching children what confident body language is and having them practice it is helpful with integrating the concepts of internal and external awareness.

Many traumatized children have fears and anxieties related to the abuse happening again. These children may have hundreds of "what if" questions related to safety, many of them directly related to the perpetrator coming back or making contact with them. The skill of problem solving helps children/adolescents think through these scenarios on their own, rather than being given black-and-white rules to follow. It teaches children that their brain is a tool and that thinking through various scenarios helps them to be able to trust their feelings and body signals. The reality is that there are no hard-and-fast rules for safety. The rule "Don't talk to strangers" is a perfect example of this. While adults teach children this rule, they break it almost every day talking to the cashier at the checkout or asking directions from a pedestrian. The skills of awareness and problem solving help children listen to their own feelings and strategize. Dialogue 4-18 illustrates how a therapist might introduce problem solving to an 11-year-old boy, Brian, who was bullied at school.

Dialogue 4-18: How a Therapist Might Introduce Problem Solving to an 11-Year-Old Boy Who Was Bullied at School

THERAPIST: Okay, Brian, you said before that you're still afraid of going to school because you worry that other boys will tease you and punch you. Let's think through what you can do if that happens. Describe a situation you are worried about.

BRIAN: What if some boys follow me home after school and try to jump me?

THERAPIST: Okay . . . what's a tool you have that might let you know you're about to get jumped?

BRIAN: Maybe I see them following me?

THERAPIST: Yes, you might see them following you or hear them following you. We call that skill *awareness*. When you're walking home, the more aware you are, the safer you are. You may be used to walking home thinking about all the things that happened at school or all the homework you have to do when you get home. You may even walk and talk on your cell phone. How do those things affect your awareness?

BRIAN: I may not be paying as much attention.

THERAPIST: Exactly! So let's say you notice the boys following you. What can you do then?

BRIAN: I can walk faster.

THERAPIST: Yes, you can walk faster. What else can you do?

BRIAN: I can go to someone's house and call my mom.

THERAPIST: Good idea! What else?

BRIAN: I don't know.

THERAPIST: What if you notice there are other people on the opposite side of the street?

BRIAN: I could walk across the street and stay near them.

THERAPIST: Yes, bullies want an easy, available target, so if you make yourself less available by being aware and/or being near other people, you make yourself safer. Let's say, though, that you don't notice the bullies until they start talking to you and teasing you. What can you do then?

BRIAN: I can tell them to leave me alone.

THERAPIST: Yes, but how would you do that?

BRIAN: I don't know.

THERAPIST: How can you tell them to leave you alone with confidence and assertive communication? Talk to me like I'm one of them.

BRIAN: I want you to leave me alone.

> **Therapist:** I really liked that you told me what you wanted me to do; you looked me in the eye and you had a strong voice. Those things make you look more confident. Great job! Is there anything else you can do to stay safe if some boys follow you and start to jump you?
>
> **Brian:** I can yell for help.
>
> **Therapist:** Yes, you can yell for help, but how can you be really specific about what you need when you yell for help?
>
> **Brian:** I can yell that I need help because someone is bothering me.
>
> **Therapist:** Great job, Brian!

Assertive communication is another important piece of safety skill training and involves identification of boundaries, learning how to say "no" and communicating congruently between one's nonverbal and verbal language. For all safety skills, behavioral rehearsal, or practice, is absolutely necessary for learning. Creating challenging role plays for children and their caregivers also makes the sessions fun and engaging. Children/adolescents can identify real-life situations they experience that can be used for practice (e.g., being teased on the bus; having a teacher grab you by the arm and yell at you; someone shoving you; parents fighting). Practicing using "I" statements while using confident body language can be done first with uncomfortable touch scenarios that do not involve physical or sexual abuse and then graduate to more difficult scenarios that do involve inappropriate touch. To practice using "I" statements, the child can be given a scenario to which she has to respond with an "I" statement, followed by what the child wants the person to do. For example, the therapist tells the child that her friend comes up behind her and snaps her bra. The therapist then asks the child to respond with assertive communication, using confident words and body language. The child responds by saying, "I feel uncomfortable when you snap my bra. Don't touch me again!" After the child thinks through what she might say, the therapist role plays the scenario with the child to provide further practice. The therapist can coach the child on using direct eye contact, a strong voice, a serious face, and confident body posture.

Obviously, the issue of touching a client in a role play scenario should be carefully thought through by each individual therapist. Each therapist has her own boundaries, and no role play should involve touch of an inappropriate nature. For example, when practicing uncomfortable, nonabusive scenarios, the therapist may discuss with the child putting his hand on the child's shoulder as such a behavior. The child is asked to assume that makes her uncomfortable. For abuse scenarios, the child can designate a certain body part, such as the elbow, as a "private area" so that in the role play, when the therapist touches the child on the elbow, the child must practice using assertive language. For clarity and safety, it is often best to practice these skills with both the child and caregiver in the room so no miscommunication arises and caregivers can continue to practice the skills with their child after sessions end.

NONSUPPORTIVE OR AMBIVALENT CAREGIVERS

Although TFCBT was researched with supportive, nonoffending caregivers, the treatment model has been used with nonsupportive and ambivalent caregivers in clinical practice. In many instances, TFCBT can be utilized successfully with these families. Sometimes, however, families may participate in treatment longer than twelve 90-minute sessions. The course of treatment may differ as well.

Even more than other caregivers, nonsupportive caregivers require incredible validation from the therapist. Validation can be difficult for therapists to give because of the nonsupportive stance of the caregiver. In addition, referral agencies may share their own judgments about the caregiver, which may impact the therapist's viewpoint about the caregiver prior to any direct contact with him or her. Therefore, it is extremely important that therapists remain attuned to their own thoughts and feelings about the caregiver so that they do not react impulsively or with negativity toward the caregiver or become overprotective of the child/adolescent, thereby creating an unhealthy split.

With nonsupportive caregivers, rather than jumping into psychoeducation about trauma and/or labeling the abuse, the therapist should allow the caregiver to tell her story about what happened and then use the caregiver's words to reflect back what has been offered. For example, in the case of a child who was whipped by his stepfather with a belt buckle, the mother denies that her son was physically abused. Instead, she describes what her husband did as "chastising" the child. Early in treatment, in the service of developing rapport and trust with this mother, the therapist should refer to what happened as "chastising." If the therapist is too quick to label the referral incident, there is a risk that the caregiver will drop out of treatment.

As the caregiver's perspective is validated, psychoeducation can be gradually introduced as a means of helping the caregiver broaden her perspective. If the caregiver's perspective shifts and she becomes more supportive of the child, TFCBT can proceed as described. If not, more individual work may need to be done with the caregiver with the hope that she will eventually believe and support the child.

Unfortunately, some caregivers remain unsupportive of their children, usually because of the caregiver's own issues, including substance abuse, trauma, and domestic violence. If the therapist assesses that the caregiver cannot be supportive of the child, joint sessions should not be conducted. The child can be seen individually and proceed with TFCBT without sharing the information with the caregiver. Obviously, the caregiver's nonsupport becomes an issue to process with the child so that he can gain an understanding of why the caregiver is reacting that way. The processing may involve psychoeducation about the parent's stance; work on acceptance of the parent's position; and/or Socratic dialogue about the situation. If possible, it may be helpful to identify other people in the child's life who can provide support.

TERMINATION

So the question is, "How do you know when to end?" One way of approaching this question is to return to the pretreatment assessment and evaluate goals for treatment. When reevaluating a client at the end of treatment, it is important to remember that TFCBT was not intended to solve all of the client's problems. The strength of TFCBT is in reducing PTSD, depression, shame, and behavior problems, so one way of determining termination is to reassess these issues. A posttreatment assessment completed prior to an anticipated end to therapy can be helpful for several reasons: (1) more objective data is are obtained in making a decision about termination; (2) if any problems still remain, the assessment provides a focus for continuing treatment; and (3) it provides feedback to clients and therapist about the outcome of treatment.

Many therapists have their own assumptions about when clients are ready to end therapy. With trauma clients, even more assumptions may be present. Such beliefs, like the following three, are not uncommon among caregivers and therapists:

- *"Sexually abused children need to be in therapy forever."*
- *"If the child does not stay in therapy, he will become a perpetrator."*
- *"These kids need more support even after talking about the abuse."*

The therapist's subjective evaluation of the client's progress may impact the decision to end treatment. Therefore, it is important to balance objective data with subjective clinical judgment when making decisions about termination. In addition, both clients and therapists work better when they are working toward a goal—in this case, termination. If clients and therapists know they are working toward a defined ending, motivation may remain high and more focused work may be done. Rather than thinking that all the work must be done in the initial sessions, consider a phase approach to treatment in which clients return to treatment after an initial phase of TFCBT. For some clients, a phase approach helps them weather different developmental periods or trauma reminders (e.g., court). In this way, clients can feel successful completing each phase, perhaps making it more likely they will return if necessary.

Obviously, termination will depend on the context in which therapy began. For clients who were referred for treatment because of an abusive or traumatic event, TFCBT may be more focused and contained. For other clients who are living in a residential facility, TFCBT may be one part of the larger treatment paradigm. After the trauma work is done, additional cognitive behavioral work or supportive treatment related to other issues may begin.

For all clients, however, termination should be a time of celebration. Some therapists refer to termination as *graduation,* a milestone the client has reached for which they should be proud. Termination becomes a time for review of all the information learned and a reflection on a new perspective regarding the trauma. In the final sessions, obstacles and challenges should be addressed so that caregivers do not think it necessary to just return to therapy when the first problem arises. If the therapist has done his job, the caregiver and child should now feel excited (and also nervous perhaps) about flying solo. The caregiver can always call the therapist for support and problem solving, but caregivers are expected to take over as coach.

There are various issues to consider when making the decision to end treatment. First, are the child's and caregiver's PTSD and depression symptoms sufficiently reduced. The posttreatment assessment should provide one piece of information related to this question. It is also important to consider how comfortable the clients are talking about the abuse in session and with each other. Avoidance, arousal, and reexperiencing symptoms should be evaluated, such as by considering the following concerns:

- Are the clients having flashbacks or nightmares?
- When clients are reminded of the sexual abuse, do they withdraw or refuse to talk about it?
- How comfortable were the clients reading and talking about the trauma narrative?
- Are the clients reporting more positive moods and experiences?
- How are their sleeping and eating habits?

Another issue to consider is behavior. For example, the following should be considered:

- If there were significant behavior problems reported at the onset of treatment, have those decreased or been eliminated?
- Is the caregiver using appropriate and consistent behavior management strategies? How often is praise being used?

- Even if behavior remains problematic in some areas, are coping skills being used at all?

Shame is a feeling frequently reported by victims of sexual abuse. Shame can be counteracted in treatment through education, talking about and processing the abuse experience, and learning safety skills that create confidence and empowerment. Shame can be assessed both verbally and nonverbally at the end of treatment. The following two questions should be considered:

1. Do clients have any lingering distorted thoughts related to shame (e.g., I feel dirty inside)?
2. How do clients use their voice and hold their body in general and when they talk about the abuse?

Another area to consider when determining the right time for termination is relationships. Because interpersonal violence can impact an individual's worldview regarding trust, intimacy, and relationships, interpersonal conflict, withdrawal, and social problems can be consequences of abuse. If functioning with peers, family, and friends remains problematic, termination may be delayed.

Given the many ways abuse can impact a child's overall functioning, therapists may be reluctant to end treatment at all. It is important to balance the goals of trauma-focused therapy with the family's need for accomplishment. When children and caregivers' work toward an outcome that is realistic and provides a sense of success, they feel good about coming to therapy and view it as a positive experience. These families may be more likely to return if and when therapy is needed. In this way, phases of treatment may occur that coincide with developmental milestones or environmental shifts. Each time a new phase of treatment is completed, the family feels a sense of accomplishment and self-efficacy, which further counteracts feelings of depression and shame.

VICARIOUS TRAUMATIZATION

It is important to consider the impact of trauma on the therapist given that TFCBT is a treatment model that requires direct discussion about the traumatic event. Vicarious traumatization is "a transformation of the helper's inner experience resulting from empathic engagement with the client's trauma material" (Saakvitne & Pearlman, 1996). It is the act of connecting with one's clients and taking the risk of bearing witness to their stories that changes the therapist.

Just as clients are changed by their traumatic experience, so are therapists. Therapists can develop symptoms of PTSD, depression, and anxiety related to the stories they take in day in and day out. Their behavior may change as well as their beliefs about the world, themselves, and others. There are several contributing factors to vicarious traumatization, including the nature of the therapist's work, organizational support, and cumulative exposure to traumatic material.

A therapist working in an agency where the only clients are victims of trauma is more at risk for developing vicarious trauma. Such a therapist is hearing details about people's traumatic experiences on a daily basis. In contrast, a clinician employed at a community mental health center is working with a variety of clients with diverse issues. Cumulative exposure to traumatic material and a lack of diverse job responsibilities increases the risk of vicarious traumatization.

Another contributing factor is the level of organizational support. Therapists reduce their risk of vicarious trauma if their job description provides variety (e.g., direct client contact, case management, supervision, consultation to other professionals, etc.). If client contact expectations are too high without enough support and supervision, therapists may be more affected. Supervision is one way of providing support to therapists and directly addressing vicarious trauma on a regular basis.

Similarly to clients, therapists can be impacted across a variety of domains: cognitive, emotional, behavior, interpersonal, physical and spiritual. The impact can affect the therapist on a personal and professional level. Personally, the therapist can have problems with concentration, irritability, impatience, intimacy, somatic complaints, loss of purpose, cynicism, and high absenteeism.

Because vicarious traumatization can have such far-reaching consequences, part of any trauma-focused work must include support for the clinician. Saakvitne and Pearlman (1996) recommend the following:

- *Awareness.* Clinicians, supervisors, and administrators must be attuned to the risk of vicarious traumatization and actively incorporate supports into the work environment, including realistic client expectations, diverse job responsibilities, regular breaks, additional training, and supervision/consultation.
- *Balance.* Clinicians must work to create a balance between work, play, and recovery. In mental health, the needs of clients can seem overwhelming. With traumatized clients, especially children, therapists may feel more responsible for their safety and well-being, thereby working more hours with fewer breaks and less support.

- *Connection.* Maintaining connections to family, friends, and other professionals provides support and a more balanced perspective. It allows one to see that there is life other than and beyond trauma. Regardless of one's religious beliefs, connecting to a higher power or higher purpose in life allows one to make meaning of what they take in each day.

Vicarious trauma should not be confused with burnout, which is also a risk in the trauma field. Burnout is more a function of stress triggered by long hours, little or no vacation, anxiety-provoking job duties, and few breaks in the day. Vicarious trauma creates stress, but the distinguishing factor is that vicarious trauma changes individuals—who they are, how they relate to others, and how they see the world. That is why it is important to involve oneself in other experiences that create a balanced perspective.

CONCLUSIONS

There are three overarching premises to this treatment approach. First, several studies have demonstrated (Cohen et al., 2004) that children are not likely to initiate discussions about their abuse or focus on abuse-related difficulties without the structure and guidance of the therapist. Therefore, this approach requires the therapist to take a collaborative role with the caregiver and child to provide abuse-related information and focus on the family's traumatic experience. Part of this structure necessitates modeling comfort and open communication about difficult topics such as sexual abuse and sexuality.

Second, the involvement of a nonoffending caregiver has been routinely demonstrated to positively impact outcome for children (Deblinger et al., 1996). The relationship the child has with his caregivers greatly outweighs the therapeutic relationship. Therefore, it is the role of the therapist to work collaboratively with caregivers and empower them to act as a therapeutic and supportive resource for the child even after therapy is terminated.

Finally, this model is most successful when good technique is combined with a strong therapeutic relationship and creativity. The components of the model can be used as a guide. Each client may have a different journey as they navigate the components because the therapist will use metaphors, props, and examples that motivate that individual client.

It is recognized that the field is still very much in its infancy in terms of our understanding of how to best respond to the psychosocial needs of children and their families in the aftermath of trauma. Thus, continued research is needed to further clarify the critical ingredients of treatment and to increase the availability and accessibility of evidence based models such as the one described above.

REFERENCES

Achenbach, T. M., & Rescorla, L. A. (2001). *Manual for the ASEBA School-Age Forms & Profiles*. Burlington, VT: University of Vermont, Research Center for Children, Youth and Families.

Anda, R. (2002, November). The wide ranging health effects of adverse childhood experiences. Paper presented at the 18th Annual Meeting of the International Society for Traumatic Stress Studies, Baltimore, MD.

Beck, A. T., Steer, R. A., & Brown, G. K. (1996). *Manual for the Beck Depression Inventory–II*. San Antonio, TX: Psychological Corp.

Beers, S. R., & DeBellis, M. D. (2002). Neuropsychological function in children with maltreatment-related posttraumatic stress disorder. *Journal of Psychiatry, 159*, 483–486.

Benedek, E. (1985). Children and psychic trauma: A brief review of contemporary thinking. In S. Eth & R. S. Pynoos (Eds.), *Post traumatic stress disorder in children*. Washington DC: American Psychiatric Press.

Briere, J. (1996). *Trauma Symptom Checklist for Children (TSCC) professional manual*. Odessa, FL: Psychological Assessment Resources.

Cahill, L. T., Kaminer, R. K., & Johnson, P. G. (1999). Developmental, cognitive, and behavioral sequelae of child abuse. *Child & Adolescent Psychiatric Clinics of North America, 8*, 827–843.

Carlson, B. E. (1998). Children's observations of interparental violence. In A. R. Roberts (Ed.), *Battered women and their families*. New York: Springer.

Cavanagh-Johnson, T. (1992). *Let's talk about touching: A therapeutic game*. Toni Cavanagh-Johnson, Ph.D., Pasadena, CA.

Cohen, J., Deblinger, E., Mannarino, A. P., & Steer, R. (2001). The importance of culture in treating abused and neglected children: An empirical review. *Child Maltreatment, 6*(2), 148–157.

Cohen, J., Deblinger, E., Mannarino, A. P., & Steer, R. (2004). A multisite, randomized controlled trial for children with sexual abuse-related PTSD symptoms. *Journal of the American Academy of Child and Adolescent Psychiatry, 43*, 393–402.

Cohen, J. A., & Mannarino, A. P. (1996). A treatment outcome study for sexually: Abused preschooler children: Initial findings. *Journal of American Academy of Child and Adolescent Psychiatry, 35*(1), 42–50.

Cohen, J. A., Mannarino, A. P., & Deblinger, E. (2006). *Treating trauma and traumatic grief in children and adolescents*. New York: Guilford Press.

Cook, A., Blaustein, M., Spinazzola, J., & van der Kolk, B. (Eds.). (2003). Complex trauma in children and adolescents. White paper from the National Child Traumatic Stress Network.

DeBellis, M. D., Baum, A., Birmaher, B., Keshavan, M. S., Eccard, C.H., Boring, A. M., et al. (1999). Developmental traumatology part I: Biological stress systems. *Biological Psychiatry, 45*, 1259–1270.

Deblinger, E., Behl, L., & Glickman, A. (2005). Treating children who have experienced sexual abuse. In P. Kendall (Ed.), *Child and adolescent therapy*, third edition. New York: Guilford Publications.

Deblinger, E., & Heflin, A. H. (1996). *Treating sexually abused children and their non-offending parents: A cognitive behavioral approach.* Thousand Oaks, CA: Sage.

Deblinger, E., Lippmann, J., & Steer, R. (1996). Sexually abused children suffering posttraumatic stress symptoms: Initial treatment outcome findings. *Child Maltreatment, 1*(4), 310–321.

Deblinger, E., McLeer, S. & Henry, D. (1990). Cognitive behavioral treatment for sexually abused children suffering post-traumatic stress: Preliminary findings. *Journal of the American Academy of Child & Adolescent Psychiatry, 29*(5), 747–752.

Deblinger, E., Neubauer, F., Runyon, M.K., & Baker, D. (2006). *What Do You Know? A therapeutic game about child sexual, physical abuse and domestic violence.* CARES Institute and the National Child Traumatic Stress Network.

Deblinger, E., Stauffer, L. B., & Steer, R. (2001). Comparative effects of supportive and cognitive-behavioral group therapies for young children who have been sexually abused and their non-offending mothers. *Child Maltreatment, 6,* 332–343.

Feiring, C., Taska, L., & Lewis, M. (1998). The role of shame and attributional style in children's and adolescents' adaptation to sexual abuse. *Child Maltreatment, 3,* 129–142.

Felitti, V. J., Anda, R. F., Nordenberg, D., Williamson, D. F., Spitz, A. M., Edwards, V., et al. (1998). Relationship of childhood abuse and household dysfunction to many of the leading causes of death in adults: The adverse childhood experiences (ACS) study. *American Journal of Preventive Medicine, 14,* 245–258.

Finkelhor, D. (1995). The victimization of children: A developmental perspective. *American Journal of Orthopsychiatry, 65*(2), 177–193.

Foa, E. B., Molnar, C., & Cashman, I. (1995). Change in rape narratives during exposure therapy for PTSD. *Journal of Traumatic Stress, 8,* 675–690.

Ford, J. D., Racusin, R., Ellis, C., Davis, W. B., Reiser, J., Fleischer, A., & Thomas, J. (2000). Child maltreatment, other trauma exposure, and posttraumatic symptomatology among children with oppositional defiant and attention deficit hyperactivity disorders. *Child Maltreatment, 5,* 205–217.

Friedrich, W. N. (Ed.). (1991). *Casebook of sexually abused children and their families.* New York: Norton.

Fromm, S. (2001). *Total estimated cost of child abuse and neglect in the United States.* Prevent Child Abuse America.

Garth, M. (1993). *Moonbeam: Meditations for children.* New York: HarperOne.

Garth, M. (1991). *Starbright: Meditations for children.* New York: HarperOne.

Jessie. (1991). *Please Tell!* Center City, MN: Hazelden Foundation.

Kaufman, J., Birmaher, B., Brent, D., Rao, U., Flyyn, C., Moreci, P., Williamson, D., & Ryan, N. (1997). Schedule for Affective Disorders and Schizophrenia for School-Age Children- Present and Lifetime Version (K-SADS-PL): Initial reliability and validity data. *Journal of American Academy of Child & Adolescent Psychiatry, 36*(7), 980–988.

Kelly, B. T., Thornberry, T. P. & Smith, C. A. (1997). *In the wake of childhood maltreatment.* Washington, DC: U.S. Department of Justice.

Kovacs, M. (1983). The Children's Depression Inventory: A self-rated depression scale for school-aged youngsters. Unpublished manuscript, University of Pittsburgh School of Medicine.

Kurtz, P. D., Gaudin, J. M., Wodarski, J. S., & Howing, P. T. (1993). Maltreatment and the school-aged child: School performance consequences. *Child Abuse & Neglect, 17,* 581–589.

Lehman, C. (2005). *Strong at the heart: How it feels to heal from sexual abuse.* New York: Melanie Kroupa Books.

Leiter, J., & Johnson, M. C. (1994). Child maltreatment and school performance. *American Journal of Education, 102,* 154–189.

Linehan, M. (1997). *Cognitive-behavioral treatment of borderline personality disorder.* New York: Guilford Press.

MacLean, K. L. (2004). *Peaceful piggy meditation.* Morton Grove, IL: Albert Whitman & Company.

Maunder, R. G., & Hunter, J. J. (2001). Attachment and psychosomatic medicine: Developmental contributions to stress and disease. *Psychosomatic Medicine, 63,* 556–567.

Miller, A., Rathus, J., & Linehan, M. (2007). *Dialectical behavior therapy with suicidal Adolescents.* New York: Guilford Press.

Moles, K. (2001). *The teen relationship workbook.* Plainview, NY: Wellness Reproductions and Publishing.

Putnam, F. (1997). *Dissocation in children and adolescents: A developmental perspective.* New York: Guilford Press.

Putnam, F. (2003). Ten-year research update review: Child sexual abuse. *Journal of the American Academy of Child and Adolescent Psychiatry, 43,* 269–278.

Pynoos, R. S., & Nader, K. (1988) Psychological first aid and treatment approach to children exposed to community violence: Research implications. *Journal of Traumatic Stress, 1,* 445–473.

Saakvitne, K. W., & Pearlman, L. A. (1996). *Transforming the pain.* New York: Norton.

Sandgrund, H., Gaines, R. & Green, A. (1974). Child abuse and mental retardation: A problem of cause and effect. *American Journal of Mental Deficiency, 79,* 327–330.

Saunders, B. E., Berliner, L., & Hanson, R. F. (Eds.). (2003). *Child physical and sexual abuse: Guidelines for treatment* (Revised Report: April 26, 2004). Charleston, SC: National Crime Victims Research and Treatment Center. Available at www.musc.edu/cvc/

Sedlak, A., & Broadhurst, D. (1996). Executive summary of the third national incidence study of child abuse and neglect (NIS-3). *National Clearinghouse on Child Abuse and Neglect Information.* Washington, DC: U.S. Department of Health and Human Services.

Shronk, S. M., & Cicchetti, D. (2001). Maltreatment, competency deficits, and risk for academic and behavioral maladjustment. *Developmental Psychology, 37,* 3–17.

Siegel, D. J. (1999). *The developing mind: Toward a neurobiology of interpersonal experience.* New York: Guilford Press.

Sternberg, K. J., Lamb, M. E., Hershkowitz, I., Yudilevitch, I., Orbach, Y., Esplin, P. W., et al. (1997). Effects of introductory style on children's abilities to describe experiences of sexual abuse. *Child Abuse and Neglect*, *21*, 1133–1146.

Straus, M. A., & Gelles, R. J. (1996). *Physical violence in American families*. New Brunswick, NJ: Transaction.

Substance Abuse and Mental Health Services Administration (SAMHSA). Model Programs web site. Available at http://modelprograms.samhsa.gov. Accessed 2004.

Terr, L. C. (1991). Childhood traumas: An outline and overview. *American Journal of Psychiatry*, *148*(1), 10–20.

Trickett, P., McBride-Chang, C., Putnam, F. (1994). The classroom performance and behavior of sexually abused females. *Development & Psychopathology*, *6*, 183–194.

U. S. Department of Human Services, Administration on Children, Youth, and Families. (2000). *Child maltreatment, 1998: Reports from the states to the National Child Abuse and Neglect Data System*. Washington DC: Government Printing Office.

Weiss, D. S. & Marmar, C. S. (1996). *Impact of Events Scale-Revised*. National Center for PTSD.

ADDITIONAL RESOURCES

Table 4.6
Psychoeducation/Trauma Narrative Resources

Domestic Violence

A Place for Starr
Author: Howard Schor
Publisher: KidsRights
To order, call: 1-800-892-5437

A Safe Place to Live
Author: Michelle A. Harrison
Publisher: KidsRights
ISBN#: 1-55864-090-8 (Also available in Spanish)

Living with My Family: A Workbook
Author: Wendy Deaton & Kendall Johnson
1-800-266-5592

Sexual Abuse

Please Tell!
Author: Jessie Otten Weller
Publisher: Hazelden Foundation

Strong at the Heart
Author: Carolyn Lehman
Publisher: Melanie Kroupa Books

A Guide for Teen Survivors: The Me Nobody Knows
Author: Barbara Bean and Shari Bennett
Publisher: Jossey-Bass Publishers

Back on Track: Boys Dealing with Sexual Abuse
(boys 10 and up)
Author: Leslie Bailey Wright and Mindy B. Loiselle

I Can't Talk About It: A Child's Book About Sexual Abuse
Author: Doris Sanford
Publisher: Gold'n Honey Books
ISBN#: 0-88070-149-8

How Long Does It Hurt?
(teens)
Author: Cynthia L. Mather (1994)

Shining Through: Pulling It Together After Sexual Abuse, 2nd edition (CSA)
(for girls 10 and up)
Author: Mindy B. Loiselle and Leslie Bailey Wright

When I Was Little Like You
Author: Jane Porett
Publisher: Child Welfare League of America
ISBN#: 0-89486-776-8
202-638-2952

In Their Own Words: A Sexual Abuse Workbook for Teenage Girls
Author: Lulie Munson and Karen Riskin

General Trauma/Traumatic Grief

Brave Bart: A Story for Traumatized and Grieving Children
Author: Caroline Sheppard
Publisher: The Institute for Trauma and Loss in Children

A Terrible Thing Happened
Author: Margaret M. Holmes
Publisher: Magination Press

When Dinosaurs Die: A Guide to Understanding Death
Author: Laurie Krasny Brown and Marc Brown
Publisher: Little, Brown, & Company
ISBN#: 0-316-10917-7

PART 3

EMDR

CHAPTER 5

EMDR and PTSD

PHILIP W. DODGSON

THE PERSON IN my office reaches for his leg which is in pain, and then his neck, and comments that he has not been sleeping well. His sleep is disturbed by nightmares, night terrors, and sometimes he wakes, screaming. He has problems with relationships and feels unable to get involved with others. He feels alone and isolated, and as though his life will not last for very long. Rami has posttraumatic stress disorder (PTSD), which he relates to his experience of imprisonment, torture, and violence in his country of origin.

Jane also has PTSD. She was involved in a motor vehicle accident in which her life and the lives of her children were threatened. She had surgery on her legs and finds it difficult to walk without using a wheelchair, which is embarrassing and clumsy. An effective businesswoman, Jane is frustrated by her inability to do the things she was able to do before the incident and by her dependence on others. She is jumpy and irritable, withdrawn socially, and avoids situations that remind her of the incident, including driving and being driven.

These symptoms of intrusion, avoidance and arousal in relation to a specific traumatic event or events characterize PTSD. Rami and Jane were helped by eye movement desensitization and reprocessing (EMDR).

EMDR was developed by Francine Shapiro from an observation in 1987 that eye movements had an impact on emotional arousal (Shapiro, 1989a, 1989b, 1991, 1995). It is a complex, integrative psychotherapy approach (Lipke, 2000; Shapiro, 2002a) that focuses on a specific experience or experiences, and the images, thoughts, feelings and bodily sensations associated with them: the information stored in the brain and nervous system. EMDR enables a person to reprocess maladaptively stored information to an adaptive resolution.

Of course, a person does not come to therapy because she wants to "reprocess maladaptively stored information"! People usually come into therapy because they are experiencing current disturbance or distress, and it is this that becomes the initial focus of a consultation. However, present disturbance is usually rooted in previous experience. The past experiences give a charge to the present, and both past and present can affect (and give affect to) future thoughts, feelings and behaviors. A comprehensive approach to therapy will, therefore, address the past, the present, and the future.

EMDR does this, and in this chapter the EMDR approach to psychotherapy will be outlined. It will give the practitioner a background into the theory and practice of EMDR, with practical clinical illustrations, and it will look at the ways in which EMDR approaches the past, present, and future in relation to posttraumatic stress.

Rose was in her 50s when she began therapy to help her with hearing intrusive voices and with her sense of shame. The "voices" were of two people who had hurt her deeply and the shame was associated with their deeds and accusations.

Jason had been a police officer and previously was in the military in a war zone when he and his colleagues came under fire, and another unit was destroyed. He came into therapy because he was having nightmares and bad dreams. He had pains in his body and mind, and he was agitated, felt worthless, and was unable to sleep.

Paul was a young man who was able to form casual relationships but would damage relationships when they became meaningful and intimate. He was sociable but isolated and avoided situations in which he might become closely involved with someone, and in which he might love and be loved. He had been sexually abused in childhood and had symptoms of PTSD.

This chapter is about these people and others affected by the psychological sequelae of trauma, including PTSD. These people and their events are real, though details and identities have been changed to preserve confidentiality.

PTSD, ADAPTIVE INFORMATION PROCESSING, AND EMDR

Posttraumatic Stress

People present with a range of symptoms and associated events, some of which meet the criteria of the two major systems of classification for mental disorders, the *International Classification of Diseases* (ICD-10; World Health Organization [WHO], 1993) and the *Diagnostic and Statistical Manual of Mental Disorders* (DSM-IV-TR; American Psychological Association [APA], 2000). These have similar but slightly different criteria for the diagnosis of PTSD, but both are limited in not taking into account what has been termed *complex trauma* (Herman, 1992), and they do not include the range of life events that can result in symptoms of posttraumatic stress (Gold, Marx, Soler-Baillo, & Sloan, 2004).

Symptoms of complex PTSD include alterations in affect regulation, consciousness, and self-perception, changes in the perception of the perpetrator, and in relationships with others, and changes in systems of meaning (Herman, 1992) and somatization (Pelcovitz et al., 1997). These are cognitive, affective, and sensory changes, and they are related to long-term trauma, including "totalitarian control," such as in situations of torture and organized violence; childhood emotional, physical, and sexual abuse and exploitation; and domestic violence (Herman, p. 121).

Paul, who was unable to form emotionally intimate and reciprocal relationships, tried to block off feelings about his earlier experiences of child sexual abuse and the ways in which that had been dealt with when he reported it to his parents. His self-perception was one of shame and stupidity. He blamed himself for what had happened, and in a subsequent incident in which he was raped at the age of 16, his beliefs about himself were negative—that he was guilty, dirty, and worthless because he should have known better. He identified with the abuser and with the person who raped him.

For Paul, these changes in self-perception included a sense of stigma and a pejorative sense of being different from other people. As with Paul, such changes following long-term trauma can include becoming preoccupied with the perpetrator of the abuse, and changes in the ways in which a person relates to others, including distrust and isolation, or a search for and fear of someone by whom to be cared about, loved, or rescued.

The symptoms of complex posttraumatic stress may also include changes in a person's system of meaning in relation to faith, belief, belief in self, and feelings of hopelessness and despair. These are often associated with the core existential question of "Who am I?" It could be argued that such a question is at the heart of all psychological dysfunction and therapy.

A comprehensive approach to the treatment of posttraumatic stress will, therefore, need to address symptoms of intrusion, avoidance, and arousal, but also address negative beliefs about the self and others; trust and mistrust; attachment and loss; faith and hopelessness; and, in some part, the question of "Who am I?"

Shapiro (2001) has also extended the concept of trauma to include not only what she described as "large T" traumas, such as those outlined above, but also "small t" traumas, which are experiences that have had a marked impact on a person and evoke somatic responses and negative beliefs about the self (p. 4). These include life events such as partnership breakdown, but also other experiences such as instances of humiliation or embarrassment in childhood, often in school, which had a significant impact on the individual, without meeting any of the current diagnostic criteria for a traumatizing stressor.

Some life events have been found to be significant in the development of PTSD symptoms. For example, Mol et al. (2005) found that people who had experienced life events such as marital discord or unemployment in the past 30 years had more symptoms of PTSD than did people who had experienced a "traumatic" event such as an accident or disaster in the same time period. Other small t traumas are familiar to many people. As we reflect back on our childhood, many of us will find such moments, incidents, or experiences that come to mind. As we do so, we are likely to experience something of the bodily sensations—the smells, tastes, sounds, and feelings—that went with that original incident. We might also notice negative thoughts about our self that, to some degree, have become embedded in our sense of self, though often not clearly articulated. And we may see an image of the incident. This is a recall of sensory, rather than narrative, information and is a link into a memory network.

Sensory experiences are often powerful links with the past—smell, taste, bodily sensations. The pain in Rami's leg, and now in his groin, becomes much more marked when he is feeling vulnerable and when he thinks about the time when he was kicked and beaten by the guards. And the reprocessing of these memories is most readily accessed through these bodily sensations.

Given these extensions of the concept of trauma, in complexity and ubiquity, to include ongoing experiences of abuse, imprisonment and torture, and awareness of apparently minor incidents that evoke disturbing sensory responses, the clinician exploring the history with a client will be sensitive to repeat traumatic experiences, to apparently smaller traumas that nevertheless have had an impact on a person's sense of well-being or sense of self, and to traumas such as the loss of a loved one (through death, separation, or divorce) or the breakdown of a relationship. The clinician will also be aware of negative beliefs about the self expressed by the client, often as a throw-away line, and the bodily sensations that the client experiences and reports— or the unspoken sensations expressed in body language and other nonverbal communications.

When Jane is reprocessing her memory of the motor vehicle accident in which she was hit by a vehicle head on, as she speaks she touches her neck, then her leg, and her facial expression says that she feels in pain. The pain is similar to the pain she experienced in her neck and her leg at the time of the crash.

As Paul talks about the rape, and feels the physical sensations associated with it, he quietly comments, "It was disgusting," and, later, "I'm a bad person."

Given these extensions of the concept of trauma, a theoretical model of present disturbance and past experience needs to take into account both the large T and the small t sources of disturbance or pathology and the cumulative impact of physical, emotional, or psychological captivity, as well as the events identified by the DSM-IV and ICD-10 as sources of PTSD. Shapiro's model of adaptive information processing (Shapiro, 1995, 1999, 2001, 2006, 2007) does this.

ADAPTIVE INFORMATION PROCESSING

The notion that past experiences affect the present was at the basis of Freud's theory of the mind (Freud, 1949). It is also central to a learning theory account of thoughts, feelings, and behavior (Wachtel, 1977). Drawing on current models of the mind and neurobiology, Shapiro (1995, 1999, 2001; Stickgold, 2002; van der Kolk, 1996) developed the concept of an adaptive information processing system that was descriptive in the sense that it could account for the clinical experiences described by clients and clinicians, and predictive in that it could be used to inform the therapeutic approach of EMDR and predict what might be expected to occur in new situations or with new applications.

The Adaptive Information Processing (AIP) model (Shapiro, 2001) is an account of the ways in which the brain is thought to process experiences (information), usually to an adaptive resolution that contributes to a sense of worth, well-being and effectiveness. It has at its center the view that the body's natural tendency is toward a state of health and, as a physical wound needs cleaning, and may need physical interventions to facilitate its healing, so the mind has a natural tendency toward health or well-being, "a dynamic drive towards mental health" (Shapiro, p. 64), and the role of therapy is to facilitate that process.

This model proposes that new learning, behavior and experiences must be assimilated into the system and accommodated into existing memory networks. This is consistent with Piaget's (1952) account of learning, in terms of assimilation of new material and accommodation of new information into existing knowledge, memories, or neural pathways.

In the AIP model, memory networks are the basis of thoughts, feelings and behavior, and the default position is for the brain to process information, new experiences, from disturbance to an adaptive resolution. Information in memory networks contains related images, thoughts, emotions, and physical sensations, including olfactory and auditory information or memories. The model also suggests that memory networks are organized around or built upon the earliest related event. Present behavior and experiences are influenced by past behavior and experiences (information), and in cases where an adaptive resolution has not been reached, present pathology is rooted in, and charged by, dysfunctionally stored memories (information).

In the case of trauma, this processing can naturally occur. However, in the case of PTSD, this processing has not occurred (or not occurred fully) and, typically, people talk of the present experience of the past event as being associated with emotions, sensations, and negative beliefs, rather than as an integrated experience which is accessible to thought and reflection and is part of a story. This can lead to a sense of re-living the experience as though it were happening now.

When Jane feels the pain in her neck, or Paul the sensation of blood on his legs, these feel like present experiences, not past events. When Rose feels sick at the smell of a man's after-shave that reminds her of her former husband and the rape that he perpetrated on her with another man, the sickness and sense of shame feel like present experiences, not like past events. When Jason cowers in the corner of the room at the sound of noise outside, this is a present experience, not a narrative account of a past event.

A key feature of the AIP model is that early experiences can "get locked in the nervous system" (Shapiro, 2001, p. 123) and give cognitive, emotional, and somatic charge to a current situation, especially when, to use the phrase from DSM-IV, the present situation "symbolizes or resembles" (DSM-IV; APA, p. 468) an aspect of the earlier event. However, the symbolization or resemblance may not be direct or appear to be logical, and it may not be accessible to traditional forms of interpretation or cognitive restructuring. When Martin, a firefighter, freezes on seeing a black bag in my office, he is not at that point able to tell me it is like a charred body part. He feels fear, smells smoke, and senses death. The previous experience is not recalled as a cognitive, reflective act. The past experience is repeated as an involuntarily distressing or disturbing state, not as a story to be told, and retold, and developed on reflection, but as an experience now.

These memories (or information) are thought to be stored in the non-declarative, or sensory system, which is not readily accessible through verbal mediation (Lipke, 1992; Shapiro, 2002b; van der Kolk, 1994). We feel, fear, and act with such memories, rather than reason them. They are not well integrated with the declarative, verbal, and adaptable memory networks that can be accessed through conscious channels, usually at will (Brewin, Dalgleish, & Joseph, 1996; Squire, 1994), and they are less responsive to cognitive or interpretative interventions. A treatment approach, therefore, will need to access these memories in the modalities in which they are stored: sensory, somatic, and emotional, and sometimes as irrational beliefs. And the client is likely to come to therapy saying, "I have a pain in my leg (or side)," "I feel bad when my boss challenges me," "I can't succeed at college, or in a sports team," "I cannot get close to other people," "I wake screaming and have bad dreams," "Can you help me?"

Given this, it is important in addressing present difficulties to explore, access, and reprocess earlier, "touchstone" memories because it is these that give charge to the present difficulties, and it is these that feel as though they are here in the present.

This model of processing and reprocessing is central to EMDR, and is reflected in working with the past, and the present, and the future. The purpose of EMDR is to help the client reprocess the information stored from past experiences and, in doing so, address and reprocess recent incidents that are charged by those past experiences. Then, the EMDR approach looks to process ways in which future occurrences or triggers of disturbing material may be adaptive and effective rather than dysfunctional—time present, time past, and time future.

In the following section, EMDR is described in detail, but first there is a description of the development of EMDR and the formulation, reprocessing and evaluation stages of the EMDR approach.

EMDR

Although Shapiro initially called the process that she had discovered *eye movement desensitization* (EMD; Shapiro, 1989a), she later became aware, from research and clinical practice, that the changes experienced by people as part of the EMDR process were more fundamental than the state changes of reduced anxiety, and reduced anxiety in relation to a specific event. People described substantial and enduring trait changes in their sense of self and in their interactions with others. In response to this, Shapiro introduced the term *reprocessing* because she realized that the "desensitization and cognitive restructuring of memories" and "the elicitation of spontaneous insights and an increase in self-efficacy" appeared to be by-products of the approach (Shapiro, 2001, p. 13), at the heart of which was the adaptive reprocessing of disturbing memories or experiences. EMD became EMDR (Shapiro, 1991, 1995, 2001).

In retrospect, it seems as though the therapeutic approach was addressing some of the issues outlined by Herman (1992), such as alterations in the sense of self, alterations in consciousness, alterations in the perception of others, including perpetrators, and alterations in systems of meaning—in addition to alterations in affect and arousal.

EMDR became a comprehensive psychotherapy approach, with a specific methodology that included the elements of images, beliefs about the self, emotions, and bodily sensations. The approach included a methodology around case conceptualization and treatment, and a range of protocols was developed, derived from the standard protocol that is the basic framework on which all interventions are developed. Shapiro's (2001) text describes these interventions in detail.

What Does EMDR Look Like?   In a sense, developing skills as an EMDR clinician is like learning a language, where it is important to know the vocabulary but also the syntax or grammar.

The standard protocol is like the basic syntax of the EMDR. It gives a structure in which to work. Like a language, without an understanding of the structure and becoming familiar with its use, there is no fluency and there can be a loss of meaning. When the syntax and vocabulary become an integral part of a person's way of thinking, then it is possible to make meaningful adaptations, to interweave clauses and subclauses, to incorporate new words and test out new structures. But the starting point is the basic structure.

In this section, the basic structure is outlined. In the following section, it is described in detail. But first, a warning.

A Warning   EMDR is a powerful psychotherapy approach that is both effective and efficient in the treatment of PTSD, and there is increasing evidence of its effectiveness with other disorders (for reviews, see Dodgson, 2007a; Maxfield, 2007; and Spector, 2007). There is also evidence that fidelity to the model and treatment procedures and protocols positively correlates with successful outcome (Maxfield & Hyer, 2002; Shapiro, 1999).

While this chapter gives an introduction to EMDR, it is not a replacement for training and personal experience of the approach, nor is it a substitute for reading Shapiro's detailed text (Shapiro, 2001). Practitioners need formal training and consultation from accredited trainers and consultants in order to work effectively, safely, and, therefore, ethically with EMDR in both simple and complex cases, and Shapiro (2001) is required reading. Details of training and consultation resources are given in the EMDR web sites listed in the Additional Resources section at the end of this chapter.

An Integrative Psychotherapy Approach   Practitioners from different schools of psychological therapy will recognize in EMDR elements of their own theory and practice. EMDR draws on the received wisdom of other modalities, but does so in a way that forms a new and distinctive psychotherapy approach.

The therapist with a psychoanalytic background will recognize free association, and a dual representational model of the mind, conceptualized in psychodynamic therapy as conscious and unconscious. The cognitive behavioral psychotherapist will recognize cognitive structures and schemata, while the psychoanalytic therapist will recognize the significance of the influence of past learning on present behavior. The client-centered therapist will understand the importance of the client's being at the center of the process, and the gestalt therapist will recognize the value of imagery. Therapists with backgrounds in the body therapies will value the role of sensory awareness, and those with a background in hypnosis will recognize some components such as the affect scan, which has similarities with the affect bridge of Watkins (1971) and Watkins and Watkins (1997).

EMDR, however, is not simply a sum of these parts. EMDR differs from other therapies in its focus on memory networks and specific targets from the recent and distant past. It differs in the way in which it focuses on past, present and future; and it differs in the way in which it facilitates reprocessing and places the clinician in the role of facilitator.

What Is New About EMDR?   A number of elements of EMDR will be new to the clinician trained in other approaches. One will be the focus on "targets" for reprocessing. Targets, to borrow from a neurobiological model, are nodes in the memory networks: significant points that link channels of association and may represent unprocessed experiences that are stored in such a way that they charge present experiences and behavior. The nodes, or targets, are the primary focus of EMDR reprocessing, and identifying these, listing, grouping, and ranking them, is part of the history taking process of EMDR (Shapiro, 2001).

Four other aspects of EMDR are likely to be unfamiliar to the clinician. First, because it is the client—or the client's brain or nervous system—that is doing the reprocessing, the role of the clinician is that of a facilitator, enabling the client to do the work and intruding on that process as little as possible. Thus, in the reprocessing phases of the therapy, clinicians are minimal in their interventions, and there to enable the client to trust the process and that reprocessing will lead to an adaptive resolution. When asked about the most difficult thing in beginning to work in the EMDR approach, a clinician said to me, "The thing I found most difficult about EMDR was keeping out of the way."

I have sometimes thought of the clinician as a catalyst; but a catalyst remains unchanged in the course of a chemical reaction, and this is not so with the EMDR clinician. While not intrusive, the presence of the clinician is an engaging presence and one in which the clinician will not remain unchanged. The clinician will be touched by the process and attuned to the client.

Second, because of its name, *eye movement desensitization and reprocessing,* the clinician new to EMDR is likely to focus on eye movements as the principal difference between EMDR and other therapy approaches. However, as we have seen, eye movements are only one form of bilateral stimulation, and bilateral stimulation is only one part of the approach. Nevertheless, the use of bilateral stimulation (visual, auditory, or tactile) will be new and can feel different for the clinician who is used to a distance between clinician and client and to less direct intervention than there is when using eye movements that track the clinician's hand, or taps or sounds.

Third, because of the importance of past events and experiences on current experiences and the effect of both past and present on future modes of being, the clinician and client need to consider the past, the present, and the future; a full treatment plan includes working with material from the recent and distant past, and the present, and the future.

The fourth element of EMDR that may be new to the clinician is the structure of the approach. EMDR is an eight-phase psychotherapy approach. It is built on a framework that includes a standard protocol and developments of that protocol for different problems or diagnoses, and interweaves within the core protocol to deal with situations such as blocked responses or incomplete reprocessing.

The Standard Protocol EMDR is not a psychotherapy approach for the untrained or inexperienced practitioner. It builds on the skills that a clinician already has. These include listening, being attuned with the client, enabling the client to feel safe and secure enough to talk about difficult things, and formulating with the client an understanding of the difficulties and of the ways in which these can be addressed. The framework of the eight phases of the standard protocol can be reassuring to both client and clinician, and give each a sense of security and being understood. Like the syntax of a language, it can be used effectively and creatively in order to enable clinician and client to articulate the various dimensions of the material with which the client presents. To use the terminology of Ryle (1975), it is a frame, not a cage.

The standard protocol is the basic syntax of EMDR. It gives a structure within which to work and within which the client can process information. As with language, without an understanding of the structure and familiarity with its use, there can be a loss of meaning and the form of words may make no sense. When the syntax and vocabulary become an integral part of a person's way of thinking, and of their repertoire, then it is possible to communicate with a common understanding, and it is possible to make meaningful adaptations, to interweave clauses and subclauses, and to incorporate, or even create, new words. But the starting point is the basic structure. The basic structure of EMDR is the eight phases of the standard protocol, which are described below.

The Approach: Eight Phases of EMDR The eight phases of EMDR are: Client history; Preparation; Assessment; Desensitization; Installation; Body scan; Closure; Reevaluation. What follows is a brief introduction to the eight phases and then a detailed account of the implementation of those phases in the EMDR psychotherapy approach.

While the eight phases of EMDR are sequential, they are not fixed. During the Reevaluation phase, for example, more material may be accessed that needs a further, more detailed, history taking, preparation, and assessment before focusing on further desensitization and reprocessing.

Client History EMDR begins with listening to the client as he tells his story, and bringing together a history that includes significant incidents and experiences (large T and small t traumas), and the thoughts, images, emotions, and sensations that are associated with those experiences. The story will include present triggers that reevoke feelings from the past, and will identify future goals and the hopes and apprehension that may go with them. The phase is not a single, one-off phase. During the course of therapy, new aspects of a person's background may emerge and the history phase will be revisited.

Preparation The purpose of the Preparation phase is to introduce a person to the EMDR methodology and to the reprocessing phases of Desensitization, Installation, and Body scan. Preparation also includes the introduction of bilateral stimulation, usually eye movements but also tactile taps or auditory tones.

During the Preparation phase, the client is introduced to some coping strategies. These include affect management techniques, such as relaxation and using affirming imagery as resources to strengthen the sense of self and safety. The client is also asked to establish an image of a safe or special place to which he may go in his mind if he needs to lower the level of disturbance. This is an important part of the approach because it leaves with the client the ability to control the sessions, and, importantly, it leaves the client with choices.

Assessment In the Assessment phase, the client is asked to call to mind the traumatic memory or incident and a picture representing that incident. With the image in mind, she is asked to identify a negative belief about herself, associated with the incident but having an impact on the present sense of self, and emotions associated with the memory and the negative belief. The client is asked to rate the degree to which she feels disturbed by the incident, using the 0–10 Subjective Units of Disturbance (SUD) scale, where 0 represents "no disturbance or neutral," and 10 represents "the highest disturbance you can imagine" (Wolpe, 1969), and to note where she feels the disturbance in her body.

Because EMDR addresses the past, the present, and the future, the client is also asked to bring to mind a positive belief that he would prefer to have about himself and to give a rating of the present validity of that belief (while holding in mind the traumatic incident) using the Validity of Cognition (VoC) scale, in which 1 represents "completely false" and 7 represents "completely true." Typically, before the reprocessing phases, the SUD will be 5 or above. The VoC will be 4 or less.

The Assessment phase acts as a bridge between the history, preparation, and reprocessing parts of the therapy. It draws together the material identified in the earlier phases and brings them more sharply into focus for reprocessing.

Desensitization   The Desensitization phase is the first of the three reprocessing phases. It is in this phase that the client is asked to focus on the image, which is internal, while following another stimulus, the bilateral stimulation of eye movements, taps, or tones, which are external. This dual attention to the past and the present, to internal and external stimuli, is thought to be one of the components of EMDR that facilitates change (Lee, Taylor, & Drummond, 2006).

One of the key elements of the Desensitization phase is the brief exposure to traumatic memories, accompanied by the dual attention stimulus of the bilateral eye movements, tones, or taps. Following a set of bilateral stimulation, the client will be asked to take a breath and report on what is happening now and what he is noticing now. In this, there is free association and the process follows the lead of the client. The clinician does not interpret or comment. The clinician simply remains present and, in response to the client's response, says, "Go with that," before beginning another set of bilateral stimulation.

These two features, brief exposure to the traumatic memory and free association, are different from the procedures used in cognitive behavioral and exposure approaches where prolonged exposure and maintaining a focus on the traumatic memory are key to the process. Indeed, brief "doses" of exposure and freedom to associate, which may include distancing from the memory, are counterintuitive to the exposure-based approaches of cognitive behavioral therapy (CBT; Boudewyns & Hyer, 1996).

In the course of the Desensitization phase, reprocessing will sometimes become stuck, and the clinician will help the client to "jump-start" the natural process by briefly intervening with a cognitive interweave, such as a brief Socratic questioning in which a short series of questions is asked of the client to help her loosen stuck beliefs, or by inviting the client to notice the thoughts, feelings, or bodily sensations that she is experiencing. The client might also be asked to return to the target memory and the negative cognition, and again notice what she is feeling in her body.

Other than in such brief interweaves, the clinician remains present but not intrusive in the Desensitization phase, anticipating that the client will move to adaptive processing of the information, given the space and environment in which to do so.

Desensitization to a specific experience is considered complete when no new material or sensations are experienced and when the SUD score, ideally, is 0 and Validity of the Positive Cognition score, ideally, is 7.

Installation *Installation* is perhaps too mechanical a word for this part of the methodology, which is designed to link the positive beliefs a person has about himself (the positive cognition) with the memory of the original incident that has been reprocessed. In her early studies and clinical practice, Shapiro (1999) noticed that the negative beliefs that people had about themselves in relation to traumatic incidents were often spontaneously changed into positive beliefs, and this was incorporated into the protocol. In the reprocessing phases of EMDR, a client is likely to move from distress to smiling, from negative to positive emotions, and from negative to positive beliefs. The installation phase harnesses this naturally occurring change by coupling the positive cognition with the traumatic memory, and accompanying this with bilateral stimulation. It also prepares the client for the next stages of therapy, dealing with the present and the future.

One other aspect of the Installation phase is that, because it brings together a positive cognition and the original incident and bilateral stimulation, any residual unprocessed negative information associated with the incident or with holding a positive belief about the self is likely to emerge and be accessible for reprocessing.

Body Scan One of the strengths of EMDR is the attention to nonverbal information, including imagery, smells, tastes and sounds, but also including other bodily sensations, such as tension or discomfort.

At the point in the therapy when the reprocessing appears to be complete in relation to a specific target, the client is asked to close her eyes, keep in mind the positive Cognition, and bring her attention to the different parts of her body, starting with her head and working downward, noticing any tension, tightness, or unusual sensation. If such sensation is experienced, it is processed with bilateral stimulation. If there is none, then the positive sensation is processed with bilateral stimulation and the client has reached the Closure phase.

Closure In the Closure phase, the client is advised that processing may continue between sessions and that it is helpful to make a note of any disturbance or disturbing thoughts or dreams so that these can be addressed at a subsequent consultation. The client is also reminded of the self-care techniques such as relaxation. There is no specific "homework" other than to keep the "log": brief bullet-point notes of experiences to bring to the next consultation.

Complete reprocessing of a single aspect of the trauma may not happen within a single session, and closure is then the closure of an incomplete session. Here, in addition to the advice about ongoing processing, and keeping a note of significant experiences, the client is reintroduced to the affect management procedures such as relaxation, using visual imagery and a safe or special place, and other resources. The purpose is to ensure that the client leaves the consultation with a sense of safety and well-being.

Reevaluation   An important phase in the EMDR psychotherapy approach is the Reevaluation phase. This happens (after the first consultation) at the beginning of each session and is a time for reevaluation of the processing of the material of the previous session, bringing to mind the target memory or incident and asking for an SUD and VoC rating. Where these indicate that there is residual material to be reprocessed in relation to the original target (the SUD score is more than 0 or 1 and/or the VoC score is less than 7 or 6), the clinician and client return to the target and continue with the reprocessing.

Where the previous material has been processed effectively (SUD ideally at 0, VoC ideally at 7), the client and clinician will discuss the material and may reflect on the client's experience of the reprocessing and the material that emerged in the previous session, in other sessions, or between sessions. The client and clinician will also discuss the next "target" of reprocessing. This is a less structured part of the protocol, and it links with the ongoing process of taking a history, and assessment of specific targets.

Past, Present, and Future   When the reprocessing of a past event has been completed, the client will process material associated with present triggers, and also address the ways of responding to future possibilities—future templates.

The present triggers will become a focus of the assessment and reprocessing protocol in order to process any dysfunctional or residual material associated with the triggers themselves.

Work on the future templates or possibilities also uses the framework of the standard protocol, this time with the future possibility as the focus of processing. This is a form of mental rehearsal in which the client brings to mind a future situation that would have been disturbing prior to reprocessing, but plays it through, as though on a video, in the light of their new experience, with the positive cognition and with a positive outcome. This is accompanied by bilateral stimulation and may reveal further material to be reprocessed or may simply complete the three-pronged approach of EMDR, working with the past, the present, and the future.

EMDR IN CASE FORMULATION AND THE TREATMENT OF PSTD

When Rami came into my office, he had been referred by his general physician for help because he was not sleeping, he had been waking at night shaking and shouting out, and during the day he had been experiencing considerable pain. He felt afraid to go out and would stay in his room with the blinds closed, protecting himself from the world outside. He wanted help with these difficulties, and he felt like an outsider. English was not his first language, and we arranged for an interpreter.

Jane was referred by her lawyers. She was unable to let her children cross the road without her, and she was frightened about driving or being in a car. She felt angry with herself and other people and was irritable with her children. Jane was in some pain, especially when walking, which she did with a stick. Most of the time, she used a wheelchair.

In the first meeting with each of these people, they talked about why they had come for help and about the things that they were experiencing. Rami said that he was an asylum seeker. Jane said that she had been working until the time of the road traffic crash and was embarrassed at being unable to work, and about her dependency on other people.

With Rami, it was not possible, or necessary, at this stage to go into detail about what had happened to him. The focus was on his present difficulties and how he felt about being here in a consultation with an interpreter and someone whom he saw as being in authority. He found it difficult to talk, not knowing whether to trust the interpreter or me, but he was able to give an outline of how he needed help. The initial focus was one of trust, and safety.

Jane was able to give a more detailed account of what she was experiencing now, and of the road traffic crash that had changed her life. She was able to engage quickly, and there was a sense of rapport or attunement: therapeutic relatedness (Dworkin, 2005). Jane also spoke about her marriage and children, and a little bit about her background and childhood. She had divorced 5 years ago but was happy with her life and felt that she had had a good childhood, although her parents might have wanted her to be more conventional. Toward the end of the initial consultation we spoke briefly about EMDR, and I gave her an information sheet that included web site addresses where she could gain more information.

For Rami and Jane, the primary diagnosis was of PTSD, but the presentations were completely different, and the case formulation and treatment plans were also different. But, in both cases, EMDR had begun as they came into the room, with the need to establish a therapeutic relationship, and to begin to identify issues that would later be significant in establishing and sequencing the therapeutic work and in addressing issues from the past, the present, and into the future.

Past, present, and future are the temporal dimensions within which EMDR is framed. The AIP model gives a framework for understanding the issues from the past and their relation to the present and the future, and EMDR case formulation works from that model, identifying present difficulties and past experiences associated with them, and how the client could plan things to be in the future.

The image of a mind map can be a helpful metaphor here. In creating a mind map, free association, or "brainstorming," leads to a picture of different thoughts, images, ideas, beliefs, sensations, and hopes, often grouped in clusters and connected firmly or loosely to one another, looking like a network of neurons and dendrites. In EMDR, it is the information networks that form the map of thoughts, feelings, and actions, and within these networks there are focal points, or nodes, that represent significant experiences (small t or large T traumas) that may become the targets of reprocessing.

For Rami, there were large T traumas from his time in his country of origin, and also trauma associated with being an asylum seeker and an outsider. Some of these would be small t traumas, not meeting criterion A of the DSM-IV diagnostic criteria for PTSD (APA, 2000, p. 467). For Jane, the large T traumas included the motor vehicle accident, but also her experience of hospitalization. Other, small t traumas were likely to include issues around her divorce, and may include, as with most of us, experiences from childhood.

CASE FORMULATION

Case formulation in EMDR begins as a process with the referral of a client, and draws on information from verbal and nonverbal interactions with the client and with the referrer. Among the questions being addressed in case formulation are whether a client at this point in his life is able to use EMDR and whether the clinician, at this point in her training and her experience of the EMDR psychotherapy approach, has the necessary skills, experience, time, and supervision to help this particular client at this particular time.

From the referrer and client, the clinician will be wanting to know about the presenting issues and will be making an assessment of the client's current stability and availability, both in practical and in psychological terms. Key to the assessment will be whether there are focal issues that can be addressed through the EMDR approach, including problems in the present, experiences in the past, and anticipated hopes for the future. The AIP model gives a lens through which to see the client's presentation and the client's history in the ways that were described above.

Essential in case formulation and the decision to go ahead with EMDR psychotherapy is informed consent, based on accurate information and given without constraint. For the clinician and client, there will be questions about presentation, diagnosis, and ego strength or coping skills. There will be an exploration of attachment, dissociation, personal and social support, and inquiries about medical conditions and medication. Above all, there is a need to be aware of a sense of safety and trust.

From the clinician, the client and referrer will want information about EMDR, the background to EMDR, and whether it is an appropriate approach for them. They may be helped by an information leaflet, web site addresses, and published material on EMDR, such as the international guidelines that recommend EMDR in the treatment of PTSD (see Additional Resources at the end of this chapter), and research including more than 20 randomized controlled trials of the efficacy of EMDR, that indicate that EMDR is both an effective and efficient psychotherapy for PTSD (Maxfield, 2007; Spector, 2007). They should be informed of the clinician's training and experience in EMDR and the outcome data for the clinician's practice. Other sources that some clients might find helpful, and listed in the Additional Resources section, are the EMDR Network web site (which includes guidance on choosing a clinician), several research review papers, and the *Handbook for EMDR Clients* (Luber, 2005).

As with all therapies, the client should seek answers to questions about the clinician's qualifications and registrations, training and accreditation in EMDR, and supervision or consultation. She should ask about the clinician's experience in working with material similar to that with which the client wants to work, and she will also need to know about the clinician's availability and, where relevant, the costs. The initial consultations should lead to a formulation of the issues to be addressed. There should also be an indication of the ways in which these will be approached in therapy, how long the treatment is likely to take, and the anticipated outcomes.

Case formulation, then, draws on the traditional elements of history taking and preparation but with specific differences relating to EMDR. Because of this, even in situations where a history has been taken by another clinician, the EMDR clinician will need to take a history from the AIP perspective. Even for an apparently single-incident trauma experienced by a person with a robust personality, with good ego strength and appropriate support, it is important to work with the client on a full history. This will help build the therapeutic relationship and will enable the clinician and client to make choices about how to structure the therapy and target the reprocessing. It should also mean that the clinician and client will be working with fewer surprises. It is good to have a picture of the background within which a person is working, and where there may be potential difficulties.

In a single-incident presentation, the clinician will focus on that incident and look for present triggers. Bringing the event to mind, the clinician will also work with the client to see whether the present difficulties relate to previous experiences, including the recent and distant past. This will be done through asking the client about his past, developmental and attachment history, and any small t or large T experiences.

Sanya did not have PTSD but did experience work-related traumatic stress. She was anxious about confronting her boss, a director of the organization in which she worked. She described a collusive relationship between her boss and another director, whom she felt was being turned against her. Sanya found it difficult to work with her boss and talk with her about the issues. She felt "like a kid" when she went in to work, although she was head of a successful department and was well qualified and well experienced. Asked about earlier times in her life when she had felt like this, Sanya spoke about school, where she had been bullied, and about home where, at times, she had felt overlooked and in the way.

The presenting target in her story was confrontation with her boss, and one particular incident seemed to capture the essence of this. There was a picture of her boss looking angry and confronting her, and feelings associated with the picture were of humiliation and worthlessness. Reflecting back on her life, other "nodes" were identified: a specific time at school when she had been bullied and called names, and a time at home when her parents had sent her to school without support.

Sometimes, however, direct questioning does not readily link with past experiences, and the floatback technique, developed by Brownrigg and Zangwill (Young, Zangwill, & Behary, 2002), or the affect scan, developed by Shapiro (1995, 2001), is more helpful. These focus on emotions and bodily sensations, and, in the case of the floatback technique, negative cognitions.

In the affect scan, the client is asked to bring to mind an image of the incident, notice what emotions she is experiencing and where she feels this in her body, and to let herself go back to an earlier time in her life when she had similar feelings or sensations.

In the floatback technique, the client is asked to bring to mind an image of the incident together with the negative cognition or belief about the self associated with the incident, to notice what emotions he is experiencing and where he is feeling them in his body. The client is then asked to let his mind "float back" to an earlier time in his life to when he first had similar thoughts (of the negative cognition) and feelings (of the identified emotion) in his body. The client is encouraged not to force anything—just to let his mind float back (Zangwill, 2005). When the floatback reaches an incident, that incident is likely to be a touchstone event, though sometimes a further floatback from that event will take the client to an earlier event that is the touchstone.

The affect scan and floatback are powerful but gentle approaches and integrate well with the History phase and the Preparation, Assessment, and Reevaluation phases of EMDR. I often use a combination of both approaches, asking the client to bring to mind the experience she is having and notice what she is feeling in her body, notice any negative words or beliefs about herself that go with that experience, and what emotions she is feeling, and then let herself float back, not push it, just float back, to an earlier time in her life when she has experienced similar thoughts, feelings, or sensations. If the client does not relate to one of the dimensions (does not have a negative belief or cannot articulate the emotions), then the third element—in this case, bodily sensation—will be what is attended to by the client as the place from which to float back.

Sanya brought to mind the picture of her boss looking angry and confronting her. Her negative belief was that she was a kid and worthless. Her feelings were of shame and anger, and she felt tense in her stomach and chest. Asked to bring these to mind—"just notice" them—Sanya was then asked to let herself float back to an earlier time in her life when she had had similar thoughts, feelings, or sensations. She arrived at a particular time at a bus stop when she had felt alone and despairing as she waited for the school bus, which did not come. It was this that fueled her emotions, beliefs, and bodily sensations when confronted with her boss. It was this that was the touchstone event, and it was this that became the first target of reprocessing.

In a complex presentation, the process of taking a history is the same, but more complex. Instead of one "index" incident, there may be several. Instead of one touchstone event, there may be several, although the clinician and client will look for the earliest or most poignant that seems to be the primary source of the present pathology and a suitable starting point for reprocessing. Elements like personal and interpersonal resources may need more time to work on (Luxenberg et al., 2001), and the client may need new affect management skills to help deal with intense levels of emotion. In complex trauma, attachment and trust may be particularly significant and may take time to address and time to build. At the beginning of therapy, positive beliefs about the self and a sense of personal integrity may be difficult to identify, and during therapy, dissociation may mean that different approaches need to be taken in preparation for the reprocessing phases of treatment. The clinician beginning with EMDR will want to build experience with simpler cases before addressing complex trauma.

Sometimes a client will ask for treatment without a clear presenting problem, but with a sense that "something has happened" to him, or with a physical sensation, such as a pain in the neck or of something stuck in his throat. The issues here are more complex. EMDR can be very effective in enabling a person to reprocess material that is not verbally accessible. The "image" needed as a target for the reprocessing phases may be a picture, but it may also be a somatic sensation, a taste, smell, sound, or bodily sensation. Such an image may be the access point for a memory network.

However, EMDR is not a metal detector, and the EMDR approach cannot be used with a view to locating or identifying memories that a person feels may be there and feels may relate to incidents or experiences that she thinks could have occurred but cannot remember. The EMDR approach can be used to enable a client to process current difficulties, and this may lead to material from the past that needs to be reprocessed, but this is not evidence of an event having occurred, and it is inappropriate to use EMDR or any psychotherapy approach as a means of uncovering suspected issues, rather like an archaeological dig.

This is important in considering a referral with a potential forensic involvement in criminal or civil law, such as an alleged abuse or rape case, or in personal injury litigation. It is important not to use any therapeutic approach as a way of trying to uncover memories, and it is equally important to be aware that material disclosed in EMDR may or may not be an accurate representation of a factual occurrence in time.

EMDR enables the client to access stored information. *Information* and *memory* are sometimes used as interchangeable terms, but memory is often seen as relating to a specific event in the external world, one that would be recognized as a consensus reality. However, memory is not fixed or static and does not usually play as a video in a temporal sequence. Memory changes, and we do not know whether the information that is accessed in EMDR relates to an event in the external world. Other evidence would be needed to corroborate that. However, we also do not know that the information does not relate to an event or events in the external world. Information that emerges during EMDR is neither a true nor a false memory in itself; it is simply information. In considering a referral, it can be important to make this clear to the referrer and to the client.

It can also be important to make the client and referrer aware that a person's recall of an incident may change during EMDR. The memory may become less clear, and details that were recalled before EMDR may not be readily available after reprocessing. Similarly (and unpredictably), new information and new details may emerge, as illustrated in Case Example 5-1.

Case Example 5-1: Jane Recalls Helpful Details during Desensitization

When Jane came for EMDR psychotherapy, she came with vivid, intrusive memories of the road traffic crash that included images, emotions, and bodily sensations. Her thought about herself when she thought of the crash was, "I am to blame," even though the other driver was prosecuted for driving without due care. Jane felt responsible because her son was in his seat in the back of the car and she felt to blame, and that she was a "bad person," because she thought that she had put him at risk.

During the Desensitization phase of EMDR, Jane recalled that she had insisted that her son wear his seat belt. Without that, he would have been thrown through the car windshield and would almost certainly have been severely injured or killed. As it was, because of what she remembered as her insistence that he wear the seat belt, Jane realized that she was not to blame and that, as she now recalled, she had probably saved her son's life.

The added detail helped Jane considerably. She recalled telling her son that he must use his seat belt, but the clinician has no way of knowing whether this actually occurred. In this case, the clinician is not being asked to make that judgment. However, were a case of neglect to have come to court, the clinician may have been called to give evidence, since Jane's testimony before EMDR would have been different from her testimony after reprocessing. The evidence that the clinician could have given would have been based on factual evidence of what occurred in therapy, not factual evidence of the incident with the seat belt.

Another element that needs to be addressed in forensic cases is that during reprocessing, images may fade. When Jane had reprocessed the memory of the oncoming vehicle just before the point of impact in the motor vehicle accident, she said that detail of the memory had faded.

Rami, who had intrusive memories and nightmares of a number of incidents from his time in prison, said in an evaluation phase that when he had been reprocessing memories it was as though they became dimmer and more distant. In one case, he said it was as though the vivid image was erased. He still had a memory of the event. He still recognized it as a disturbing event. But it was no longer haunting him, it was no longer "in my face," and he no longer felt that he was to blame. His emotional responses to the incident were of sadness but not of personal violation or responsibility.

Were Rami to have given evidence at an immigration tribunal hearing, or Jane given evidence in a court case, each may have been concerned at the distancing of the memory and the lack of detail and current emotional impact. And, for example, in a rape case, a lawyer or client might want to ensure that in giving evidence or a witness impact statement, the power of the emotion was still present. Again, before beginning therapy, these are matters that may influence informed consent, and they are matters about which the client might want to consult a lawyer.

These two accounts also point to the importance of taking a detailed history, especially in cases where there may be a forensic involvement. A detailed history will include a client's narrative account of what happened, often as a part of a semistructured interview, and may include questionnaires and checklists such as the Clinician Administered PTSD Scale checklist (Blake et al., 1995), the Impact of Event Scale (Horowitz, Wilner, & Alvarez, 1979), and the Dissociative Experiences Scale (Bernstein & Putnam, 1986), details of which are given below. The narrative account, questionnaire material, and semistructured interview based on DSM-IV diagnostic criteria (APA, 2001) will help in giving a picture of the client before treatment and, therefore, before any changes during the course of treatment. In some cases, best practice would be to recommend an external assessment by a third-party clinician.

WORKING WITH DIFFERENT PRESENTATIONS OR DIAGNOSES

An implication of the AIP model is that EMDR could be successful with nonorganic disorders where there is a significant event or experience that gives charge to the present disorder, but less so with organically based disorders, although the diagnosis of an organic disorder may itself be traumatic and a focus of reprocessing. In line with this, research is developing, for example, in fields such as EMDR with depression, anxiety, and the psychological impact of cancer. There are also developments in the fields of pain management, including the management of phantom limb pain (Schneider, Hofmann, Rost, & Shapiro, 2007), chemical dependency (Popky, 2005), specific phobias (de Jongh & Broeke, 2007), and treatment of sexual offenders (Ricci, Clayton, & Shapiro, 2006). For more information about these applications and others, see the EMDR Institute web site, listed in the Additional Resources section. It is important, however, that the clinician only uses EMDR where there is research evidence for its effectiveness, or significant clinical evidence to suggest that it is an appropriate approach. In this case, the client needs to know the basis on which EMDR is being suggested, and any possible risks, as illustrated in Case Example 5-2.

Case Example 5-2: Rose Gives Informed Consent

Rose was tormented by hearing voices. The voices were of two people, the most prominent of which was her former husband, who had raped her. At the time of this referral, there was little evidence of the use of the EMDR approach with people who heard voices, but it seemed clear from the history taking that the voice was an intrusive experience that was likely to be a symptom of PTSD. The EMDR approach has enabled Rose to address traumatic memories from the recent and distant past but has also helped her to deal with the voices (Dodgson, 2007b). The voices have been targets for reprocessing, and this has given Rose a sense of greater control and distancing from the voices that she now sees as aspects of her own mind rather than individuals in her own head. Rose chose to engage in EMDR and to work with the experience of voices, knowing that it was a new approach and that there was as yet no research evidence of EMDR being used in this way. She gave informed consent.

INFORMED REFERRAL

Because of national and international guidelines that recommend EMDR in the treatment of PTSD (see the Additional Resources section), and because of clinical success, clinicians practicing EMDR are likely to have an increase in referrals, some of which may be based on unrealistic expectations.

Although research suggests that EMDR is an efficient psychotherapy approach, not requiring extensive homework (Davidson & Parker, 2001; Jaberghaderi, Greenwald, Rubin, Dolatabadim, & Zand, 2004; Van Etten & Taylor, 1998), and needing fewer sessions (Van Etten & Taylor), it is not a "quick fix" and it is not a "cookie cutter" or "one size fits all." EMDR is a comprehensive psychotherapy approach and as such, while it has clear structures, it is responsive to the individual client and will vary, for example, in the number, length, and frequency of sessions needed. The needs of Jane and those of Rami are considerably different.

While the reprocessing of information from a single trauma may take three to six sessions (Marcus, Marquis, & Sakai, 1997; Rothbaum, 1997; Scheck, Schaeffer, & Gillette, 1998; Wilson, Becker, & Tinker, 1995), these will be set in a context of having established a therapeutic relationship, taken a history, engaged in preparation and assessment work with the client, and checked that the client has ego strength and personal resources to deal with the work which can entail reprocessing painful memories and experiences, some of which may not be apparent at the initial consultation. Treatment of a single trauma may take three to six sessions. Treatment of complex trauma will take considerably longer.

This can lead to some difficulties with referrals. As the EMDR practitioner becomes known, he is likely to be referred a wide range of cases, and there is a temptation to become a "hero innovator" (Georgiades & Phillimore, 1975). So caution needs to be taken with regard to idealized referrals that assume a rapid and successful outcome—assumed by the referrer, the client, or a third-party funder. The client and referrer need to be informed of the clinical approach and the length of time that treatment might take.

INFORMED CONSENT

It can be argued that no form of psychological therapy should be undertaken without the explicit informed consent of the client. Given that working with PTSD will include the client revisiting some of the stressful incidents that feed the present pathology or difficulties, it is wise to ask for written consent, after the client has had the opportunity to read the client information sheet, scan the Internet and ask any questions of others or the clinician about what therapy entails. The interaction between past and present is important. Even in an apparently straightforward case such as a motor vehicle accident, there may be hidden touchstone memories that emerge during therapy and the client may feel vulnerable and exposed. In making an informed decision about consent, the client needs to know that this can happen. He will also need to know that processing may continue between sessions and there may be increased levels of intense emotion.

In practice, I give an information sheet and consent form to a client after the first consultation and ask for the completed form after answering any questions, usually at the beginning of the Preparation phase. The consent form used should be adapted to meet the requirements of national or state legislation and the requirements of the professional indemnity insurers covering the clinician.

As with other aspects of therapy, giving informed consent may be an ongoing process, as illustrated in Case Example 5-3. In particular, when a client is giving consent to reprocessing early material—for example, involving child molestation—the clinician may need to be aware both of the adult, informed client, and of those aspects of the client that may be childlike or compliant, linked with the past, and perhaps acquiescing to a process, while simultaneously resisting it. Similarly, with victims of rape, torture, or organized violence, there are likely to be dissociated memory networks, and compliance should not be assumed to be consent.

Case Example 5-3: Informed Consent as an Ongoing Process

Arleen was an adult in her early 40s and was working in a full-time job. She was able to conduct her life effectively, but was troubled by a difficult sexual relationship in which intimacy was avoided, and caresses triggered times from childhood in which she had been sexually abused. Wanting to deal with this, Arleen sought EMDR psychotherapy from an experienced practitioner and gave consent to treatment. However, when it came to reprocessing some very difficult material from childhood, Arleen was resistant at one level, though giving what appeared to be informed consent at another. The reality was that when Arleen had been abused, she had been forced to acquiesce to the abuse and feel that she was to blame because of this. In therapy, the child parts of her information system, the memory networks associated with the times of abuse in childhood, were acquiescing to treatment, while the parts of her mind associated with adult decisions were concerned that the time was not yet right to do this. First, it was important to address the fears that remained from childhood and charged the present responses. In this case, the therapy itself was acting as a trigger. Having recognized this, the clinician was able to address this with Arleen, and to work with issues to do with dissociation.

Timing Considerations

Timing considerations are about whether this is the right time for the client and the clinician to engage in assessment or therapy. This has three aspects: (1) the timing of the initial consultation; (2) the timing of the reprocessing phases; and (3) the frequency and length of sessions.

Ideally, the initial consultation needs to be planned so that client and clinician can arrange a further consultation within, say, a week, because material is likely to emerge that will be difficult for the client and emotionally charged. There may be an element of shame, anxiety, or fear.

Georgie had never spoken with anyone about the abuse that she had experienced as a child. Her father had told her that if she ever told anyone, her mother and sister would be punished. As she began to speak about what had happened, the fear that she had experienced in childhood reemerged, and Georgie felt treacherous and ashamed. She also wondered what the clinician would think of her and wondered herself about what she had said.

If Georgie had not met again with the clinician, those thoughts, fears, and bodily sensations are likely to have remained locked, and in some respects Georgie's experience of the consultation would have been like a repeat of the abuse that she had experienced as a child and the injunction of silence and secrecy that went with it.

In talking about an issue that has been kept secret, the client will often "realize" what has happened—in the sense that the articulation brings the material into the outside world and, in a sense, declares to the client the external reality of his present, internal, experience. Revisiting that experience in the following session affirms both the internal and the external experience of the client and the sense that the clinician has seen what the client means. Like Vladimir in *Waiting for Godot,* implicit in the client's presence is the request,

"You're sure you saw me, you won't come and tell me tomorrow that you never saw me!"[1] If problems with identity are part of the issues with which a client is struggling as a consequence of earlier complex trauma, then this sense of being known, and held in mind, is vital.

Further considerations about timing include whether the client has current or imminent life events that will stretch her emotional resources to a degree that working on traumatic material may not be viable at this stage. These might include, for example, pregnancy and childbirth, hospitalization, taking an examination, and giving a major presentation or appearing in court. These might not be good times to begin therapy; however, the potential benefits of effective treatment may outweigh any possible risks. And in some cases of litigation, a person's claim for ongoing psychological injury may be challenged if the claimant has not sought appropriate psychological treatment.

The second aspect is the timing of the reprocessing phases so that there is safety and stability for the client and clinician. It is important that sufficient time be given for the client to be able to reprocess material from the recent and distant past, process present triggers, and practice in imagination future templates or ways of dealing with situations or people that he associates with the traumatic event or events. It takes time to tell the story. As noted above, while a single trauma may need three to six sessions to reprocess, more complex presentations will need longer (Edmond, Rubin, & Wambach, 1999; Maxfield & Hyer, 2002; National Institute for Clinical Excellence [NICE], 2005; van der Kolk, 2007).

There is a caveat here in that sometimes a clinician or client will prevaricate—deferring the start of a reprocessing session as a form of avoidance. EMDR can be very effective very quickly. While it might be dealing with information stored from experiences many years before, the reprocessing is of memory networks presently stored in the nervous system, and the reprocessing can be very rapid.

The third aspect of timing includes the length of sessions and their frequency. The notional length of a psychotherapy session varies, though it is typically 45 or 50 minutes. For the initial history taking and the reprocessing consultations, it is helpful to schedule a double session of, say, 90 minutes because the material with which the client is working may take longer to speak about and longer to reprocess fully than the usual 45 to 50 minutes (NICE, 2005, p. 16). While the length of some sessions may be double at the beginning of treatment and in the reprocessing phases, as treatment progresses (and as the clinician becomes more experienced in the

---

1. This excerpt from *Waiting for Godot* by Samuel Beckett (1956) is reprinted with permission of Faber & Faber and Grove Atlantic.

EMDR approach), the client and clinician may find that the standard 45 or 50-minute hour (Lindner, 1954) is sufficient.

The frequency of sessions may vary. Usually, at the beginning of therapy, these will be scheduled weekly. Occasionally, more frequent sessions will be helpful at the beginning or during the Desensitization phase to help with stabilization, but usually weekly sessions usually are enough, and the space between them allows time for further spontaneous processing and for consolidation. As therapy progresses, the space between sessions may be increased to two weeks, then a month, and then at, say, 3- or 6-month follow-up.

For some clients, it will be important to schedule appointments at specific times of day, for example, after work or at the end of the week, as reprocessing (and processing after session) can itself be demanding, and it is good to have space to reflect after a session. For other people, it may be helpful to schedule at the beginning of the day. Rose finds it difficult to leave the house. Anxiety in the anticipation of leaving the house later in the day builds to a point where sometimes she is unable to do so. For Rose, early sessions are more helpful.

A final note on timing and availability: Many EMDR clinicians ensure that the client knows that he can access the clinician's office by phone between sessions, should he need to do so. Experience shows that this is reassuring to the client, as a kind of insurance, but it is seldom used.

CLIENT–CLINICIAN RELATIONSHIP

The container for effective psychotherapy is an attuned therapeutic relationship (Dworkin, 2005; Hopenwasser, 2008; van der Kolk, 1987) in which the client feels good enough and safe enough to do the work that may entail going into the heart of darkness (Silver & Rogers, 2002). This is no different in EMDR. There needs to be a sense of trust. The client needs to feel safe in working with potentially difficult or painful material, and the clinician needs to feel able to work with the client in reprocessing this material. Such a relationship may take a long time to develop, especially where there are significant issues of attachment and betrayal, as is often the case in complex PTSD. However, the sense of attunement may also be fairly rapid, with the clinician and client able to engage in the process from the first consultation, as illustrated in Case Example 5-4.

By contrast, Rami took time to develop a relationship in which he felt safe and could trust the clinician, and other clients have wanted to know something about the clinician's experience, checking out the clinic's web site, and other Internet links, and wanting to know about the research evidence for EMDR. Time is spent on the clinician's and client's understanding the issues and testing out the sense of safety before going further with the eight phases of EMDR.

Case Example 5-4: A Rapid Attunement in EMDR Training

I recall working with a man participating in a 1-day workshop on the assessment and treatment of PTSD, which included an introduction to EMDR. As the day evolved, it seemed appropriate to offer a live EMDR consultation, and he volunteered to do this. He successfully processed a disturbing experience that had troubled him on a day-to-day basis for many years, but not sufficiently for him to have sought therapeutic help. At the beginning of the consultation, he had found the initial experience of focusing on the issue and addressing the problem moderately disturbing. After 20 minutes of reprocessing, his level of disturbance had reduced from 6 to 0 and his sense of himself in relation to the experience was positive. There was a trait as well as a state change.

Noticing that there was little intervention from the clinician, some people from the rest of the class observing the process wondered if the "client" had experienced this as "cold." The client responded that it had been a warm experience and there had been a marked sense of intimacy, even though the clinician had not intruded on the client's space. There was a sense of attunement, without there having been a long period of getting to know one another.

THE EIGHT PHASES OF EMDR

Phase 1: History

The purpose of the History phase is to assess the suitability of the client for EMDR psychotherapy, and to identify material for reprocessing, including small t and large T traumas. These potential targets will comprise experiences from the present and the recent past, but may also relate to experiences from the distant past that are earlier than those with which the client initially presented.

It is during the History phase that information that will be used in the reprocessing phases (Desensitization, Installation, and Body scan) begins to be more clearly identified and a provisional structure and targeting sequence takes shape. The History phase addresses: client selection, evaluating affect tolerance and dissociation, noting negative and positive cognitions, identifying and clustering targets, and, where appropriate, the touchstone event, and developing a targeting sequence and treatment plan. Occasionally, it will include teaching affect management skills.

The reprocessing phases are detailed below but outlined here because in the History phase the clinician will be keeping in mind the elements of the reprocessing phases and the relevant material that the client may describe when speaking about her history. The reprocessing phases include (1) an initial focus on an incident, memory, or experience, and identifying (2) an image that represents that experience, or the worst part of it. They also include identifying (3) a negative cognition associated with the target incident or experience, and (4) a positive cognition that represents what the client would like to believe about herself now. The client is then asked to rate (5) the validity of that cognition, using a 1-to-7 scale, which is described below. With the original incident or image brought to mind, the client is asked, (6) "What emotions do you feel now?" and (7) to rate on a scale of 0 to 10 how disturbing the incident feels to her now. Finally, the reprocessing phases include attention to (8) bodily sensations and the use of bilateral stimulation such as eye movements, tones, or taps. Because these elements are a core part of the reprocessing, in the history, preparation, and assessment phases the clinician and client will be working toward bringing these elements to mind.

The History phase, then, is a time for the client to speak freely about his experience and explore this with the clinician who, among other things, will listen for elements that will be part of the later reprocessing. Careful history taking, in which a client is able to unfold his story, or fragments of his story, and be aware of the thoughts and feelings associated with it, is a reflective and often moving experience and one in which the relationship of trust between client and clinician is fostered. It is an important part of the therapeutic process and, in some cases, will take many sessions; in others, it may be completed in an initial consultation. It is also a time of bearing witness—in simply hearing what the client has to say, and seeing what the client means.

Although the History phase is less structured than the reprocessing phases, a framework is important. The consultation(s) may be guided by published semistructured interviews, such as the Structured Clinical Interview for DSM Disorders (SCID-CV; First, Spitzer, Gibbon, & Williams, 1997), or be more loosely based on a classification system such as the DSM-IV (APA, 2001). The consultations may be more open-ended but have that sort of framework in mind, and always the clinician will be aware of an experience or experiences that may form an initial focus of reprocessing, together with the image, thoughts, emotions, and sensations that are linked with that experience. The clinician may ask direct questions of the client, for example, about an image or a negative cognition, a thought, an emotion, or sensation. Sometimes the clinician may ask the client to complete questionnaires to help in this process and to establish baseline measures of the difficulties the client is experiencing, their frequency and their severity. Baseline measures are helpful to them both, in planning therapy and monitoring progress, and to referrers in identifying the outcome of therapy. They are also helpful, together with outcome measures, in contributing to research on the effectiveness of treatment approaches. Always, the clinician will work with the client so that it is the client who is selecting the targets for the work.

Client Suitability for EMDR Psychotherapy   Before or during the initial consultation, the clinician will discuss with the client her expectations of therapy and what she would hope for as an outcome. General physical and mental health needs to be considered, and whether intense levels of emotion could exacerbate any medical conditions. In particular, the clinician and client will want to consult the client's medical practitioner about any neurological history, including seizures, and about other conditions, including pregnancy, which might be affected by increased levels of emotion. There is no research evidence of contraindications for EMDR on medical grounds, but it is always wise to consult. With epileptiform seizures, the use of eye movements is not advised, and this is also the case with eye pain. There are, however, other choices of tactile or auditory stimulation.

The clinician will also want to consult the client's medical practitioner or psychiatrist if there is evidence of a major mental disorder, and work in partnership in providing treatment. If there is a risk to the client or others, an inpatient admission might be considered during the reprocessing phases. There is no research evidence of contraindications for EMDR with psychotropic medications, though clinical practice suggests that a client needs to have a sufficient level of arousal for reprocessing to occur, and use of benzodiazepines may limit this. Discussion with the client's medical practitioner may include assessing the viability of reducing or withdrawing from benzodiazepines during therapy. Reprocessing while taking psychotropic medication may be affected by state-dependent learning, and may need further work if the medication is discontinued. Usually, a short series of assessment and reprocessing sessions will help to consolidate the reprocessing work that was done when the medication was being taken.

Self-medication also needs to be taken into account, especially alcohol and substance misuse. Where a client has been alcohol or substance dependent, the reprocessing of experiences from the past may elicit a desire to respond as in the past, and therefore increase the risk of alcohol or substance misuse. This is not always so. Sometimes the reprocessing effects a change in the experience of wanting to self-medicate as the emotional charge of the past experiences reduces. Again, this is something that should be discussed with the client and with his medical team. There is a specific *EMDR Chemical Dependency Treatment Manual* (Vogelmann-Sine, Sine, Smyth, & Popky, 2004) and literature on impulse control available from the EMDR Humanitarian Assistance Program (HAP) web site (see Appendix B) and Popky (2005).

Affect Management and Dissociation Specific approaches to affect management will be outlined in the Preparation phase, detailed below. In the History
phase, it is important to identify whether a person has access to feelings and
emotions, and whether these are appropriate and managed effectively by the
client—neither overwhelmed by them nor overdefended from them, for
example, by dissociation.

Assessment of a client's readiness for working with the EMDR approach
will therefore include assessing the client's ability to manage intense emotion
and also the degree to which she is likely to dissociate. The Dissociative
Experiences Scale II (DES II; Carlson & Putnam, 1993) can be helpful in
this because it gives a qualitative sense of what a person is experiencing as
well as a quantitative indicator of severity. The DES II is a 28-item self-report
questionnaire that measures the frequency of a person's reported dissociative
experiences, including experiences of a clinical and nonclinical nature. The
items are scored on an 11-point Likert scale (from 0 to 100 in 10-point
increments), and the total scale score is calculated by summing the scores
on each of the 28 items and dividing the sum by 28. Total scale (mean) scores
of 20 and above indicate the need for further exploration by the clinician
(Carlson & Putnam, 1993).

Clinical indicators of dissociation and dissociative disorders are also
important. Summarizing the clinical signs of dissociative disorders, Puk
(1999) notes that these include years of unsuccessful psychotherapy with
little progress (Kluft, 1985; Putnam, Guroff, Silberman, Barban, & Post, 1986),
depersonalization and derealization (Putnam et al.), memory lapses (Putnam
et al.), flashbacks and intrusive thoughts, somatic symptoms (Putnam, 1989),
sleep disturbance (Lowenstein, 1991) and the Schneiderian symptoms of
hearing audible voices, experiencing 'made' feelings that feel as though
they are from outside the person, or having 'made' thoughts and behavior
(Kluft, 1987; Puk; Ross et al., 1990) that feel controlled from outside. Where
these are present, dissociation should be considered, and a fuller assessment
for a dissociative disorder needs to be made. This is especially so with DES II
scores above 30.

A clinician working with clients with dissociative disorders should have
taken formal training in treating people with dissociative disorders and have
considerable experience of working in the EMDR approach. It is beyond the
scope of this chapter to provide such training and the necessary supervision
to equip the clinician to work with EMDR and clients with dissociative
disorders. Again, the reader is advised to consult the Shapiro (2001) text.
For the more advanced clinician, *Healing the Heart of Trauma and Dissociation
With EMDR* (Forgash & Copeley, 2007) is an excellent review of the integration of EMDR and ego state techniques (Watkins & Watkins, 1997) in working
with trauma and dissociation. The DVD, *Deepening EMDR Treatment Effects*

Across the Diagnostic Spectrum: Integrating EMDR and Ego State Work (Forgash, 2005) is also recommended.

Negative Cognitions   The history is part of the narrative that a person creates to help bring meaning, and in some cases a sense of identity, in relation to life events. As with any story, the language in which it is spoken or written, the omissions and inclusions, and the ways in which it is told and experienced, are all part of the story and of the person's own sense of meaning. As he hears the story, the clinician is listening for potential foci or targets for reprocessing, and for negative and positive beliefs—cognitions—about the self that may go with them. As these begin to emerge, sometimes as throw-away comments, it is helpful to record them in the clinical notes. A simple indicator such, as >t or >nc, in the margin of the notes can draw attention, in this case to a potential target (>t) or negative cognition (>nc).

A negative cognition is a presently held self-referencing belief (an "I" statement) about the self that is negative, irrational, and generalizable from the specific incident to which it relates to other situations in which a person finds herself and has concern. The negative cognition will relate to the client's presenting issues and resonate with her associated affect. When a negative cognition has been accurately identified, a client will often respond with a lump in her throat or other emotional response because the negative cognition has touched on an irrational, negative, core belief about self. It can be like a lightning conductor going to earth.

Sarah was concerned about relationships and a sense that people thought that she was selfish. She described a background in which she had been well supported, financially and emotionally, in her family but had been bullied and humiliated at school. During floatback, she recalled a specific time when a friend had rejected her and an earlier time when she had been trapped by a group of school students and humiliated.

Sarah chose to work with the memory of rejection by her friend and brought an image of this incident to mind. Asked what words went best with that memory, that described a negative belief about herself, Sarah reflected on a number of words: *selfish, unwanted, bad.* It was quite easy for her to identify this negative cognition as "I'm a bad person" because it was a thought that she frequently had about herself.

John did not find it easy to bring to mind a negative cognition when thinking about being humiliated at school because of wetting the bed. It took him time to reflect on what he thought or feared that this said about him: "I'm dirty," "unacceptable," and in exploring this further, he touched on "I'm not a man."

Shapiro (2001) suggests that negative cognitions fall into three domains: responsibility, safety, and choice. She further delineates responsibility into cognitions relating to self-worth, such as "I am unlovable," "I'm worthless," "I'm bad," and those relating to action, and a sense of guilt. These include cognitions such as "It's my fault" and "I should have ... [done something]." Further exploration of these cognitions, however, is likely to lead to more fundamental self-statements, and beliefs that are associated with self-worth and shame. Exploring negative cognitions can include asking questions such as, "What do you fear that this says about you?," "What do you think other people think this says about you?," and "What in your worst moments do you think this says about you?" The negative cognition is negative, self-referencing, and irrational. It is not a question of what a person rationally knows about himself, but one of what he fears in his guts.

The other two domains, safety and choices, may also have deeper referents. Negative cognitions relating to safety would include "I'm vulnerable," "I'm unsafe," or "I'm going to die," but these are presently held beliefs, not statements of the past. "I was vulnerable when the rapist attacked me" is a statement of fact. "I am vulnerable [when I bring this incident to mind]" is a presently held, irrational, self-referencing belief—a negative cognition. Similarly, the negative cognitions associated with choices, or control, such as "I'm out of control" or "I'm powerless," will be presently held beliefs as the person brings the traumatic incident to mind. They are not statements of a past reality, such as "I was out of control [when being assaulted]."

Negative cognitions relating to safety and choices may also have underlying beliefs associated with them that can be explored by asking similar questions, such as "What do you fear this says about you?," and can lead to cognitions such as "I'm not a man," "I'm unlovable," or "I'm bad." Interestingly, these are often associated with attachment and/or shame.

Positive Cognitions   In the same domains of responsibility, safety, and choice, a person is likely to have positive beliefs or hopes. These also are self-referencing, "I" statements, but they describe the person's hoped-for direction of change or growth, and they take the person from the past and present into the future. Sometimes, especially with complex trauma, a person will find it very difficult to express a positive belief about herself, and the positive cognition will need to wait until later in the protocol, in the Installation phase, when the client and clinician return to the positive cognition and explore whether it still fits or another is more fitting.

The positive cognition has a number of characteristics. It is 180 degrees from the negative cognition, but is not simply a negation of the negative statement, such as "I'm not bad." The positive cognition is, at least, a possibility. It is not an absolute that would be unattainable, such as "I am not going to die" or "I will always succeed," but is a statement tempered by reality: "I am safe enough now," "I can succeed." Sometimes, as in complex trauma, a person will arrive at a positive cognition in stages, such as "I could be lovable," "I can be lovable," "I am lovable," developing over the course of therapy. Case Example 5-5 illustrates arriving at a positive cognition in stages. A positive cognition is also not a wish that things had been different, as illustrated in Case Example 5-6.

Case Example 5-5: Sarah's Positive Cognition Changes

Sarah's positive cognition was "I'm a good friend," but in the Reevaluation phase, after an incomplete reprocessing session in which the target experience was the rejection by her friend, it became clear that this positive cognition, "I'm a good friend," did not resonate well with her feelings about herself. Her negative cognition had been "I'm a bad person," and, on reflection, the positive cognition, "I'm a good friend," was clearly not in the same domain as "I'm a bad person," and not 180° from it. The positive cognition would be "I'm a good person."

Was this apparently slight difference important? And did it affect reprocessing? It was important because it reflected Sarah's way of dealing with her belief about herself that she was a bad person. She dealt with this by trying to be friends with others through doing what they wanted instead of appropriately expressing her own views and needs. In the Reevaluation phase, Sarah realized that the positive cognition, "I'm a good friend," reflected this. The positive cognition was a way of saying, "I'm a bad person but if I try to be a good friend, people will like me," whereas "I'm okay as I am" was an affirmation of herself. "I'm okay as I am" was 180° from the negative cognition, "I'm a bad person," and it was a desired future state that represented a fundamental trait change. "I'm okay as I am" became the positive cognition, later used during the installation phase. Interestingly, between sessions, Sarah had deepened a relationship with a friend and said that, for the first time with a partner, she had felt able to be herself.

Case Example 5-6: Sam's Positive Cognition Cannot Turn Back the Clock

Sam was raped by her father and felt abandoned by him. As each episode of molestation ended, her father would call her names and tell her she was disgusting. Sam wanted her father to tell her that he loved her. Her negative cognition was "I'm unlovable." She wanted her positive cognition to be "My father loved me"—a wish to turn back the clock and for things to be different. Together with the negative cognition, there was a sense of being alone and unacceptable, and, in exploring the negative beliefs that Sam had about herself, a great deal of therapeutic work was done that later contributed to the reprocessing. The work was not a reframing or restructuring of the negative belief; it was an exploration of it and a journey further into some of the depths of a sense of isolation and darkness: "Don't tell me you never saw me." The work on the positive cognition was similar in that it explored the meaning to Sam of her father's physical, sexual, and emotional abuse and denial of her, and the partial destruction or disintegration of her sense of self. Arriving at the positive cognition "I'm lovable as I am" was a huge step forward that became integrated in the reprocessing phases. And it was generalizable from the specific incident to Sam's life as a whole.

Forms and Questionnaires   Although asking a person to complete forms and questionnaires can seem impersonal, it can also be an integral part of the therapeutic work and one that the client will value. I routinely use three questionnaires in a standard posttraumatic stress (PTS) evaluation, together with a semistructured interview that follows the DSM-IV criteria for a diagnosis of PTSD, as does the Clinician Administered PTSD Scale (CAPS; Blake et al., 1995). The three questionnaires are: the CAPS Life Events Checklist, the Impact of Event Scale (IES; Horowitz, Wilner, & Alvarez, 1979), and the Trauma Symptom Inventory (TSI; Briere, 1995). The Dissociative Experiences Scale (DES; Bernstein & Putnam, 1986), described above, is also used where the TSI shows an elevated Dissociation score. Many EMDR clinicians do not use the TSI, but routinely use the DES with all clients. Where there is need for further structured information, additional questionnaires may be used.

Being with the client or available to him as he completes the questionnaires can be helpful for clarification. A client with reading difficulties will complete the questionnaires together with the clinician, though the clinician needs to be careful not to influence the client's responses. Where English is not the client's first language, it is important to work with the client, or the client and an interpreter, though the validity of the questionnaire will not have been established and the results need to be treated with caution. In some cases, the differences in language make the use of questionnaires unhelpful. Some questionnaires are available from the publishers and some service providers in a range of languages, together with normative data (see, for example, the United Kingdom's Medical Foundation for the care of victims of torture (www.torturecare.org.uk), and the EMDR HAP Program (www.emdrhap.org). I do not often use questionnaires with refugees and asylum seekers because it can evoke memories of formal immigration procedures.

The Clinician Administered PTSD Scale (CAPS) Life Events Checklist
This is a very helpful checklist that enables clients to respond without being asked direct detailed questions by the clinician, as illustrated in Case Example 5-7. In my experience, it is best given to the client after meeting with her, or even during the first consultation, when a client–clinician relationship has begun to be established and the client knows the person, the clinician to whom the information is being given.

The checklist comprises a list of 17 "difficult or stressful things that sometimes happen to people" (CAPS checklist; Blake et al., 1995). The list includes natural disasters; transportation accidents; assault; sexual assault or unwanted or uncomfortable sexual experience; and exposure to a war zone, toxic substances, and severe human suffering. It also includes illness; sudden, violent death; death or harm the respondent caused to others; and other stressful events or experiences. The last item on the checklist is "any other stressful event or experience," but I have found it helpful to add three further items: self-harm (for example, attempted suicide, cutting, other . . .); *any* major or minor surgery or hospitalizations; and termination of pregnancy, miscarriage, or difficult birth. The extended checklist is shown in Table 5.1.

The respondent is asked to think of his entire lifetime and check a box that indicates which of these have happened to him; which he has directly witnessed with his own eyes or other senses; and which he has learned about happening to someone close to him, someone he loves. A person may check one or more of the columns or may check the last two alternatives: "not sure" or "doesn't apply." This is a tick-box exercise, but one that can be very reflective and thought provoking, and clinically very helpful. The advantage of using the checklist rather than covering each of the items in interview is that the client is prompted by the items on the checklist and can respond by ticking a box, rather than saying yes or no. Some people find ticking the box much easier.

Having completed the checklist, the clinician goes through it with the client, asking her to tell them more about what she has experienced. This begins to give a map of a person's large T and small t history, and, while explaining what the various items refer to, a person will often make throw-away comments that are essentially negative, and sometimes positive, cognitions.

Table 5.1

Extended CAPS Checklist

In this questionnaire you are being asked to think about events *in your entire lifetime.*

Name: _____ Date: _____ ID: _____

Interviewer: _____

Listed below are a number of difficult or stressful things that sometimes happen to people.

For each event, check one or more of the boxes to the right to indicate that: (a) it *happened to you* personally, (b) *you witnessed* it happening to someone else, (c) *you learned about* it happening to someone close to you, (d) *you're not sure* if it fits, or (e) it *doesn't apply* to you. Be sure to consider your *entire life* (growing up as well as adulthood) as you go through the list of events.

Event	Happened to Me	Witnessed It	Learned About It	Not Sure	Doesn't Apply
1. Natural disaster (for example, flood, hurricane, tornado, earthquake)					
2. Fire or explosion					
3. Transportation accident (for example, car accident, boat accident, train wreck, plane crash)					
4. Serious accident at work, home, or during recreational activity					
5. Exposure to toxic substance (for example, dangerous chemicals, radiation)					
6. Physical assault (for example, being attacked, hit, slapped, kicked, beaten up)					
7. Assault with a weapon (for example, being shot, stabbed, threatened with a knife, gun bomb)					
8. Sexual assault (rape, attempted rape, made to perform any type of sexual act through force or threat of harm)					
9. Other unwanted or uncomfortable sexual experience					

(continued)

Table 5.1 (Continued)

Event	Happened to Me	Witnessed It	Learned About It	Not Sure	Doesn't Apply
10. Combat or exposure to a war zone (in the military or as a civilian)					
11. Captivity (for example, being kidnapped, abducted, held hostage, prisoner of war)					
12. Life-threatening illness or injury					
13. Severe human suffering					
14. Sudden, violent death (for example, homicide, suicide)					
15. Sudden, unexpected death of someone close to you					
16. Serious injury, harm or death you caused to someone else.					
17. Any other very stressful event or experience					
Added by Dodgson, P.W.:					
18. Self-harm (for example, attempted suicide, cutting, other)					
19. Any major or minor surgery or hospitalizations					
20. Miscarriage or termination of pregnancy					

Reprinted, with permission, from Blake, D. D., Weathers, F. W., Nagy, L. M., Kaloupk, D. G., Gusman, F. D., Charney, D. S., et al. (1995). *The Clinician-Administered PTSD Scale* (*CAPS*). New York: Wiley.

Case Example 5-7: Completing the CAPS Checklist Helps Mary Identify a Trauma

Mary is a police officer who was working in a specialist unit and had been working on a particularly difficult case. She had spoken with her occupational health department about this and had been referred for a psychological assessment and, if appropriate, therapy. Mary had been troubled by the material in the case but had not expressed why. In completing the CAPS Checklist, she came to items 8 and 9: "Sexual assault" and "Other unwanted or uncomfortable sexual experience," for which she checked "Happened to me." On going through the items later, she said that she would not have spoken about this, though she knew that she needed to, but it had been much easier simply to tick the box. The earlier "touchstone" event of being abused by a family member was the initial focus of desensitization.

Clustering The checklist, together with the open interview, enables the client and clinician to begin to draw together the things that have happened. Some of these will form clusters around the people involved, the type of trauma, or the location. If so, then one incident is likely to be the most significant in the cluster and the most representative of it. Here, the SUD scale (Wolpe, 1969) and the IES (Horowitz et al., 1979) can help. The SUD scale is a semantic differential scale in which 0 represents "no disturbance or neutral" and 10 represents "the highest disturbance you can imagine." It was used by Shapiro in her initial study of EMD (Shapiro, 1989a) and is used in the Assessment and Reprocessing phases of EMDR.

In the History phase, the SUD scale can be used to assess the degree of disturbance experienced as the client brings to mind specific incidents identified in the history or in the completion of the CAPS checklist. Where incidents are clustered, the SUD scale is used in relation to the event that is representative of that cluster or of the worst incident or experience in the cluster. When used in this way, it is possible to create a hierarchy of disturbing events that can help the client and clinician identify what might be the most appropriate incidents or experiences to target first. In this way, a draft plan of a targeting sequence can be established. While "clustering" and "establishing a targeting sequence" can sound overstructured and controlled, in clinical experience the structure can give a sense of reassurance to the client—that the clinician understands what he is doing and that there is form and order in what often feels to the client like a kaleidoscope of chaos or pain. The sense of order can be supportive and containing.

Use of the SUD scale can also be helpful in forensic cases, where the court is likely to want to know what degree of disturbance was experienced by the client before the client received treatment. And it can be helpful for referrers, health insurance providers, and researchers because it gives a numerical tag to subjective experience before and after treatment.

The Impact of Event Scale The IES (Horowitz et al., 1979) can be used in a similar way. It was the first published questionnaire to focus on the intrusion and avoidance symptoms of posttraumatic stress, and it is very widely used. The original version, which predates the inclusion of PTSD in the *Diagnostic and Statistical Manual of Mental Disorders, 3rd edition* (DSM-III; APA, 1980), is a 15-item questionnaire that yields scores on two dimensions of posttraumatic stress: intrusion and avoidance. The more recent Impact of Event Scale–Revised (IES-R; Weiss & Marmar, 1997) was extended to include a measure of hyperarousal.

The IES and IES-R scales refer to one event (not events) and may therefore be used for several aspects of the process of a traumatic experience, such as the index event of a road traffic crash, the experience of being hospitalized, and the experience of being interviewed by the police. The scales may also be used for different events. So, for example, because the questions refer to the 7 days prior to (and including) the day on which the IES is completed, the present psychological impact of a recent motor vehicle accident can be compared with the present psychological impact of a motor vehicle accident 10 years earlier, as measured by the scale.

The disadvantage of the IES and IES-R (and other metrics, including the SUD) in forensic cases is that they are self-report measures. However, if the idea of triangulation—the synthesis of data from different sources—is accepted, the self-report measure represents one source, one angle, from which to view the impact of an event. In this case, self-report measures, together with data from other sources, such as the clinical interview and third-party information, can be examined for congruence and, therefore, be considered in weighing the evidence.

In the standard EMDR protocol, the IES may be used in the History phase to measure the impact of selected events and in the Reevaluation phase or at treatment closure and follow-up as indicators of outcome.

Brent was a 19-year-old who was suffering from posttraumatic stress following a rape. He told the story of an earlier incident, when he was a child, in which he had been raped by two men in a public washroom. Sore and bleeding, he walked home, where his parents reprimanded him for being late and his father beat him for telling untruths. An IES was used in relation to each of these experiences—the recent rape, the historic rape, and the return home to his parents. Scores on the IES indicated that the memory of the encounter with his parents was more intrusive than the memories of the rapes. The memory of the encounter with his parents became the first focus of reprocessing.

The Trauma Symptom Inventory The Trauma Symptom Inventory (TSI; Briere, 1995) is a 100-item questionnaire that yields scores on 10 clinical scales associated with posttraumatic stress, and 3 validity scales. It is one of a family of questionnaires that includes the Detailed Assessment of Posttraumatic Stress (DAPS; Briere, 2001) and the Trauma Symptom Checklist for Children

(TSCC; Briere, 1996). Scores are transcribed onto a clinical profile, together with the standardized T scores. Because the profile is visually presented on a graph, the standardized T scores can be seen clearly by the respondent and can be plotted before, during, and after treatment, so the client (and the referrer) can see developments. The clinical scales are Anxious Arousal; Depression; Anger/Irritability; Intrusive Experiences; Defensive Avoidance; Dissociation; Sexual Concerns; Dysfunctional Sexual Behavior; Impaired Self-Reference; and Tension Reduction Behavior. High scores correlate with high severity.

Going through the profile with the client can be helpful in that, for example, where there is a high defensive avoidance or dissociation score and a low intrusive experiences score, it can be explained to the client that, as treatment progresses, the defensive avoidance and/or dissociation scores are likely to improve, and the intrusive experiences may get worse before they get better. Clients usually find this reassuring and often complete the sentence, ". . . worse before it gets better." This can certainly be a help when it comes to the reprocessing phases of EMDR and the client has been informed that it can be difficult for a time.

The TSI profile can also help the clinician in forming a clinical picture and identifying what needs to be done first. For example, if there is a high Depression score but lower Intrusive Experiences and Dissociation scores, does the reprocessing need to be the first target or should the depression be treated first, or are they interrelated such that as the traumatic material is reprocessed, the symptoms of depression are likely to lift?

When the client has completed the questionnaire and the profile has been plotted, I give feedback by showing the profile to the client and discussing with him what the profile shows and how it is likely to change.

The client's story and treatment plan In telling her story, the client will have identified presenting issues and traced the sensory, emotional, or cognitive elements of these that are charged by earlier, dysfunctionally stored experiences. The clinician will have been listening for material that will inform the later part of the EMDR protocol. These include:

- Incident(s) or experience(s)—small t and large T traumas
- Images—pictures, sounds, smells, touch, taste
- Cognitions—negative beliefs about the self in relation to the identified incidents
- Emotions—associated with the identified incidents
- Sensations—associated with the identified incidents and present triggers
- Beliefs—overall beliefs about the self, the incidents, and life

The History phase is an important element of EMDR. It draws together the information that is needed for reprocessing, and it prepares the client for the rest of the therapeutic work. It is not a phase that closes. At various times, more history is likely to emerge, and the approaches used in the History phase, such as the floatback technique or affect scan to identify a touchstone event, will be used again.

The initial outcome of the History phase will be the development of a treatment plan and targeting sequence. Although this may change and be modified in the light of further information that emerges during the course of therapy, the form of the plan will be similar, reflecting the past, present, and future dimensions of the work. The plan will identify affect management skills and list the present problems. It will note the events from the recent and distant past that are difficult in themselves or that fuel the present problems, and it will provide a draft targeting sequence plan that will give the client and clinician a preliminary map for the journey of reprocessing.

The usual approach to reprocessing is first to target the touchstone event, then to reprocess material chronologically. The advantage of this is that the earlier experiences are likely to act as feeder memories for later experiences, and in reprocessing the earlier experiences, some of the channels of association are cleared. Having reprocessed past events, the treatment plan is to process present triggers and finally to work with future templates or ways of dealing with similar situations or experiences in the future.

The treatment plan developed from the History phase is likely to include background information comprising a psychosocial history; forensic and social issues; clinical presentation including dissociation, stabilization, and medical issues; and attention to the clinician–client relationship and timing. The plan will identify specific presenting problems, including traumatic experiences, incidents, and memories representing the presenting problems, and earlier experiences and touchstone events associated with the presenting difficulties. Where possible, there will be identified negative and positive cognitions and an awareness of emotions and bodily sensations. The experiences will be included in a targeting sequence that will usually begin with the earliest experience and then proceed chronologically. Sometimes the most traumatic event will be at the top of the sequence, and sometimes it will be the most recent, but in these cases the reprocessing is likely to reach into earlier events or experiences. The treatment plan will also identify present triggers that evoke the responses from these experiences in the recent and distant past. And it will identify hopes for the future. All these elements will be important in the reprocessing phases, and the work done in the History phase will create a culture in which the reprocessing work can be done.

PHASE 2: PREPARATION

The Preparation and History phases interrelate. Both include elements of establishing a sound client–clinician relationship, working with the client about what can be expected and what needs to be addressed. Both include informing the client about adaptive information processing and EMDR.

The Preparation phase also includes an introduction to the logistics of the reprocessing phases of EMDR, and the development of a portfolio of affect management strategies, such as relaxation, a safe place exercise, and the use of imagery in developing resources. The purpose of the Preparation phase is twofold: (1) to help a client prepare for reprocessing material that may be distressing and to give informed consent, and (2) to prepare a client for the logistics of the reprocessing phases by introducing him to the mechanics of bilateral stimulation and to the seating arrangements needed to accomplish that.

Education and Expectations Many aspects of education and expectations about PTSD and EMDR will have been covered in the History phase. In the Preparation phase, there is the opportunity to answer any questions and to remind the client of the AIP model and the way in which it relates to EMDR. The description can also give the client assurance that she will be in control. The client is at the center of the process. The following is a suggested summary explanation of the process:

> When a disturbing event occurs, it can get locked in the nervous system with the original picture, sounds, thoughts, feelings, and body sensations. EMDR seems to stimulate the information and allows the brain to reprocess the experience. That may be what is happening in rapid eye movement (REM) sleep. The eye movements (tones, tactile) may help to process the unconscious material. It is your own brain that will be doing the healing, and you are the one in control. (Adapted from Shapiro, 2001, p. 431; 2008, p. 26[2])

Informed Consent Given the background information provided to the client in the History phase, in the Preparation phase, any questions that the client may have about EMDR can be addressed by the clinician, and it is usually at this stage that the client would complete and sign the consent form.

Logistics The sitting position adopted in the reprocessing phases of Desensitization, Installation, Body scan, and Closure has been described as

---

2. Excerpts from Shapiro (2001) *Eye Movement, Desensitization and Reprocessing: Basic Principles, Protocols and Procedures* are reprinted with permission of Francine Shapiro and Guilford Press.

"ships that pass in the night." The clinician sits alongside the client, each facing in the opposite direction. Where eye movements are used as the bilateral stimulation, guided by the clinician's hand, the clinician will need to sit with the client to the right, if right handed, or left, if the clinician will use her left hand to guide the eye movements, and close enough for the client to see the clinician's hand clearly, but in soft focus, usually about 12 to 18 inches, or 30 to 45 centimeters.

Distance between the clinician and client needs to be controlled by the client because a sense of safety, well-being, and control is essential in developing and maintaining a good therapeutic relationship and in enabling the client to feel safe enough to work with difficult, and sometimes unexpected, material. The clinician needs to sit close enough for the client to be able comfortably to track the clinician's fingers. Usually, this will mean parallel to but facing the client with, say, 2 or 3 inches' (about 10 centimeters) distance between the chairs, side to side. It is helpful if the clinician's chair is on wheels. I use a gas-elevated desk chair on wheels, which I can lower to be at the same level as the chair on which the client is sitting. Where this is not possible, the client and clinician use similar chairs—though in some circumstances, such as when working in the field, in a person's home, or in a shelter, for example, it is necessary to improvise and adapt.

The seating arrangement of "ships that pass in the night" is partly determined by the use of bilateral stimulation and partly by the clinician's role in the therapy. The clinician is there to facilitate the reprocessing and not to get in the way of it. So he needs not to get in the way of the client's field of vision and movement. It is best if the client is facing a space with a blank wall so her field of vision is not affected by "noise." This is true not only when eye movements are the modality that the client chooses for the bilateral stimulation, but also when auditory or tactile stimulation is used, and when eye movements track an electronic light bar rather than the clinician's hand. The client needs a neutral background, or "wallpaper," and the space in which to get up and move around, should she need to. Care also needs to be taken to avoid the client's looking into a light source, such as a window, which can give a strobe effect if using eye movements tracking the clinician's hand.

Bilateral Stimulus There are several kinds of bilateral stimulation that may be used in EMDR. While in the early stages of the development of EMDR, eye movements (as the name implies) were thought to be central to the process (Shapiro, 1989a, 1989b), clinical practice and research (Bauman & Melnyk, 1994; Foley & Spates, 1995; Shapiro, 1991, 1994, 1995, 1999, 2001, 2002b) showed that other forms of bilateral stimulation were also effective. These include tactile and auditory stimulation, such as hand taps or tones. It was also found that these could be facilitated by the clinician directly or through electronic equipment that includes lights moving across the field of vision, taps administered through small vibrating pulsars (they look like small pebbles or rods), or tones or other sounds played through earphones. I use handheld grips that deliver a variable vibration or can be connected to head phones, for sound. They also have a light on each grip and can be used for bilateral stimulation of eye movements by placing one grip on each side of the client's field of vision. The speed and intensity of the tactile and auditory stimuli can be varied as can the speed of the bilaterally flashing lights. Details of suppliers are given in the Additional Resources section.

Sometimes clinicians ask whether tones or other sounds, such as music or the sound of sea lapping on the beach, make a difference. Given that the bilateral stimulation is there to facilitate processing, tones, which are more neutral than music or natural sounds, are likely to be better. However, sometimes bilateral stimulation will be used during resource installation, for example, during relaxation, when music or natural sounds can be soothing.

Another question often asked is whether the client should keep his eyes open or closed. The bilateral stimulation is thought to serve a number of functions. One of these is the dual attention to internal and external stimuli. In bringing to mind a memory or experience, the client is attending to internal information. In attending to an external focus such as the movement of a clinician's hand, the sound of tones or the sensation of taps or vibrations, he is drawn to external information, and there is a demand for dual attention to the two stimuli—internal and external. For this reason, the bilateral stimulation (BLS) is sometimes referred to as the dual-attention stimulus (DAS).

Research has shown that a distancing from the traumatic material is associated with learning and reprocessing (van der Kolk, 1996, 1997). In closing the eyes, the client tends to focus on internal stimuli, and this can be particularly helpful when accessing early memories or experiences. The lack of external distraction, other than tones or taps, can allow the client to remain with the internal information and for connections to be made within the information network. However, this can also mean that the client dissociates—puts a screen between herself and the information she is processing, or distances herself from the present moment and gets lost in the internal material. While in some situations this can be helpful, enabling the client to titrate the emotional loading, or charge, of the experience, it can also inhibit processing because the experience, image, cognition, and emotion are not brought together. And if the client is dissociating, there is a sense in which she is not fully in the room. Most of the time during reprocessing, it will be helpful for the client to maintain open eyes during the bilateral stimulation and certainly during the feedback of "what is there" for her *now,* after each set.

What is important is that the client and clinician have choices. For the client, this extends not only to the type of bilateral stimulation but also to its speed, distance or intensity, and proximity or volume. The client may also tell the clinician whether the number of bilateral sweeps (center to right to left and back again to center) is sufficient, too much, or not enough. The speed of eye movements, or other bilateral stimuli, is related to function. Rapid, saccadic eye movements have been found to enhance reprocessing, and the emergence of previously dormant information (Christman, Garvey, Propper, & Phaneuf, 2003). Slow eye movements have been associated with reduced levels of arousal, and are used in the safe place exercise and preliminary resource development and installation (Smyth, Rogers, & Maxfield, 2004). In the preparation phase, slow eye movements are used, and in short sets of, say, four to six sweeps.

Stability   Bilateral stimulation when attending to a memory is a new experience for most people, and many clients have a fear about visiting traumatic memories and reexperiencing them, because of the emotional charge that often goes with them. A metaphor can help in this, such as the metaphor of traveling on a train or bus:

> Sometimes people think of this [reprocessing] as a train or bus journey where they "just notice" the experience, like watching the scenery go by—the images, thoughts, and so on are just like watching the scenery go by. (Adapted from Shapiro, 2001, p. 130)

The metaphor can be helpful for a number of reasons. It can be referred to during reprocessing in order to give a sense of reassurance if the material becomes very intense. It can enhance the sense of going on a journey toward adaptive resolution and the feeling that unneeded material gets off, and new, adaptive, material gets on. Clearly, if the person has been in a train or bus crash, another metaphor, such as watching the material on a screen, can be helpful. And in places where there are no trains, the bus is preferred!

Affect Management   Relaxation and affect management techniques can also be important in giving a client a sense of safety and stability. Although sometimes taught and used in the History phase, for example, with particularly vulnerable clients, these techniques are usually introduced in the Preparation phase. One such approach, usually introduced in the Preparation phase, is the "safe place" exercise.

The safe place exercise has a number of functions. Because it parallels the process of the EMDR standard protocol, it gives the client an introduction to the process without addressing difficult material. It also gives the clinician an indication of the ways in which a client is likely to respond to bilateral stimulation, including his sense of stability, and it is often a good indicator of the client's suitability and readiness for the reprocessing phases. If the client is not able to access a safe place, there will be more work to be done in history taking and in the development of personal resources.

In the safe place exercise, sometimes called the special place because some clients do not have a sense of safety, the client is asked to think of a place—in reality or in her imagination—in which she feels safe, or calm, or special. It is best if this does not include other people because people can change and what may seem safe at one point may feel unsafe at another. I recall a client saying that her safe place was with her partner—until he left her 4 weeks later. Sometimes a person will find this safe or special place difficult to locate and may need to look for somewhere in which she can feel strong or can have courage. Occasionally, this will be clinician's office.

Having identified a safe place, the client is asked to bring it to mind and notice what emotions and sensations are associated with it: bringing to mind a picture of the place and noticing what he sees, what he feels, and perhaps what he smells. The clinician helps him enhance this imagery by quietly drawing attention to positive thoughts, feelings, and sensations. As the image and sensations come clearly to mind, the clinician adds a short, slow set of about four to six eye movements, tones, or taps (BLS), and if the client is experiencing a positive response, this is repeated several times. The client is then asked to think of a word that can act as a key to the safe or special place, and the clinician uses the key (or cue) word together with the imagery of the safe place, and adds in a short set of BLS.

The safe place can be used during the reprocessing phases but can also be used away from the clinical sessions. So the client needs to be able to cue herself to use the key word to access the safe or special place. To practice this, the client is asked to bring up the cue word and the image of the special place and notice the emotions and sensations that go with it. She is then asked to think of something mildly disturbing—a recent event, such as rushing to get to the consultation—and to notice the feelings and sensations that go with this mild disturbance, and then use the key word to go back to the safe place. The client may need help in first going through this process of moving from disturbance to the safe place and "toggling" between the two—going from the one to the other—but it is a skill that can bring a sense of control and well-being, and safety. Having been guided in this by the clinician, the client is supported in doing this herself. Instead of eye movements, the client might use taps, by gently tapping her thighs, alternating from one to the other slowly, about six times.

Sometimes the safe place exercise will trigger traumatic material. When this is so, the clinician will stop the exercise and talk with the client about this.

Together, they will identify the material and targets that need to be reprocessed and, usually, make a note for these to be included in the targeting sequence plan. Very occasionally, it will be possible to begin to reprocess this material at this stage, but this is dependent on a sense of safety and stability and a sound sense of attunement between client and clinician.

Other forms of affect management include relaxation techniques that use a degree of distancing but also maintain an awareness of the present moment. Dual attention to the inner and outer world, the past experience and the present moment is a significant part of the EMDR paradigm. EMDR is not a form of prolonged exposure (Boudewyns & Hyer, 1996; Rogers et al., 1999; Rogers & Silver, 2002), but it does include times of focusing on elements of the traumatic memory and reprocessing them in the present. During reprocessing, the levels of affect are likely to change and may at times become more intense. At other times, they may become less intense. It is important, therefore, that the client is able to tolerate this range of affect or to use approaches to titrate the affective material so that it can be reprocessed effectively.

The purpose of reprocessing is not to precipitate or generate an abreaction, but to enable a person effectively to process maladaptively stored experiences to an adaptive resolution. Similarly, the purpose of reprocessing is not simply to ameliorate present difficulties by reducing the level of affect or disturbance, which would be desensitization (EMD) without the reprocessing (EMDR) and would help to bring about a state change rather than the trait change that is associated with the adaptive resolution of disturbing material. Reprocessing occurs best when the client's level of arousal is within what has been called the *window of tolerance* (Siegel, 1999, p. 253) in which there is a sufficient level of arousal for the client to be aware of the image, beliefs, emotions, and sensations, but within a framework of tolerance that allows dual attention to the material and to the present moment to occur.

One example of a relaxation technique is the light stream (Shapiro, 2001), in which the client is asked to focus on a disturbing body sensation(s) and consider its shape, size, color, temperature, texture, and sound. He is then asked to bring to mind a color that he associates with healing and imagine that a light of this color is coming in through the top of his head and encompassing the shape in his body. The light is limitless: The more that is used, the more there is available. As the light focuses on the shape, the client is asked to notice what happens to the shape and its size and its color. Gradually, the shape is likely to dissolve, together with the sense of disturbance, and the light is able to radiate throughout the whole of the person's body. The process is closed by inviting the person to notice his present surroundings, gradually to become aware of the sounds, sensations, and light around them, and, in his own time, to open his eyes (based on Shapiro, 2001, pp. 244–246).

The light stream and other relaxation techniques are available in audio form from the EMDR HAP web site, as listed in the Additional Resources section.

Resource Development Some clients feel as though they have few personal resources on which to draw, especially people with a history of complex trauma and difficulties in early attachment. For some people, this will mean building on the developing sense of attachment with the therapist. For others, it will include developing imaginary resources such as a strong person, an image, or a figure that gives them a sense of well-being. The kinds of imaginary figures can include fictional or cartoon characters such as Aslan (Lewis, 1950), the Lion King (Allers & Minkoff, 1994), Mario (Miyamoto, 1981), and Wonderwoman (Moulton Marston, 1942). For some, it will include accessing the stronger or supportive parts of their self: a supportive ego state (Forgash, 2005). A more detailed account of resource development and installation (Korn & Leeds, 2002; Leeds, 1998; Leeds & Shapiro, 2000) can be found in Shapiro (2001).

PHASE 3: ASSESSMENT

The Assessment phase refers not to a global assessment or evaluation of the client's presentation, but to the specific assessment of a memory or experience and its associated image(s), cognitions, emotions, and bodily sensations. This is a structured assessment and the introduction to the reprocessing stage of the therapy. It includes a numerical evaluation of the degree of disturbance associated with the target incident (the SUD scale) and a numerical indication of the validity of a positive cognition (the VoC) in relation to the incident when both are held together in the present moment—now. While the History and Preparation phases have flexibility in the interaction with the client, fidelity to the protocol is important in the Assessment and Reprocessing phases.

In the Assessment phase, the client is asked to call to mind (1) the traumatic memory or incident, (2) a picture representing that incident, (3) a negative cognition associated with the incident but having an impact on the present sense of self. The client will also be asked to bring to mind (4) a positive belief that she would prefer to have about herself, and to give (5) a rating of the present validity of that belief (while holding in mind the traumatic incident) using the VoC scale described earlier. Returning to incident and the words of the negative cognition, the client is asked what (6) emotions are experienced with the memory and the negative beliefs in mind, and then (7) to rate the degree to which she feels disturbed by the incident, using the 0 to 10 SUD scale described earlier and to note (8) where she feels the disturbance in her body. Typically, before the reprocessing, the SUD will be 5 or above, and the VoC will be 4 or less.

If the EMDR procedure is like using a language, in which it is important to learn the syntax, or structure, and the vocabulary, it is in the structure and vocabulary of the Assessment phase that the clinician will find it particularly helpful to be fluent. Rather like learning a language and using a phrase book at the beginning, some clinicians will find it helpful to use a worksheet similar to the one included in the Additional Resources section. This can be a prompt and will become the clinical notes. Other clinicians will find it helpful to learn the protocol by rote so that it becomes easy, and seamless, to move into it from the rest of the consultation.

The structure of the protocol in the Assessment phase is:

1. Incident
2. Image
3. Negative cognition
4. Positive cognition
5. VoC
6. Emotion
7. SUD
8. Bodily sensation

The Standard Protocol What follows is the EMDR standard protocol for reprocessing a single incident or experience, following the History and Preparation phases. A summary is included in the Additional Resources section. With special situations or presentations, this protocol is adapted, as shown in the next section on working with recent events and complex PTSD. However, the standard protocol is the root framework—the syntax—on which all other protocols are built. I found it helpful to learn this protocol verbatim.

Unlike the History and Preparation phases, it is important to follow through the detail of the protocol as it is written, although with experience there may be some variations depending on the client's level of under-standing, and on clinical need. The structure and words within the structure have been developed to enable the client to bring to mind a target incident or experience, together with the images, beliefs, emotions, and bodily sensations associated with that incident, and the protocol builds up, like a crescendo, to a point where the different dimensions of the target are brought into sharp focus with maximum charge. Shapiro (2001) likens this to bringing into play the laser beams of image, beliefs, emotions, and sensations to focus on the incident or experience to facilitate reprocessing.

Instructions Important in the Desensitization phase is the feedback from the client. What the clinician needs to know is that things have changed—change indicates processing. The clinician does not need to know the detail of the change, nor does he need to discuss the change with the client. Indicators of change can be seen in the client's facial expressions and body language and the information that he gives. In anticipation of this, during the assessment phase, the clinician will let the client know:

> What we will be doing often is a simple check on what you are experiencing. I need to know from you exactly what is going on, with feedback that is as clear as possible. Sometimes things will change and sometimes they won't. I'll ask you how you feel from 0 to 10; sometimes it will change and sometimes it won't. I may ask if something else comes up; sometimes it will and sometimes it won't. There are no "supposed to's" in this process. So just give feedback as accurately as you can as to what is happening, without judging whether it should be happening or not. Let whatever happens happen. We'll do the eye movements for a while, and then we'll talk about it. (Shapiro, 2001, p. 431)

The stop signal Client control and safety are important elements of EMDR. In the History and Preparation phases, the clinician will have worked with the client on the development of personal resources, and on affect management skills such as the light stream and the safe place to help in feelings of safety and well-being. Here, in the assessment phase, the client is reminded of the safe place and introduced to the stop signal, which gives the client control over the session. When a client uses the stop signal, usually by raising her hand, the clinician will immediately stop bilateral stimulation and will usually remind the client of the safe place, helping her to bring it to mind by using the key word as a cue and describing sensations that the she has associated with it. The reason that this is an agreed signal rather than a verbal response—"Stop!"—is that when a person is reprocessing, he may shout "Stop!" or other words to the perpetrator of the assault, or the oncoming motor vehicle, as part of the journey through reprocessing, rather than as an instruction to the clinician.

In the standard protocol with single-incident PTSD, the stop signal and safe place are seldom used. However, it is important that the client is able to have control over the process and also that he is able to remain within the window of tolerance with arousal levels that are neither too high nor too low, and which will be optimal for reprocessing. In introducing the stop signal or reminding the client of it, the clinician may say: *"If at any time you feel you have to stop, raise your hand"* (Shapiro, 2001, p. 431).

Mechanics During the Reprocessing phases, the clinician will usually sit closer to the client and alongside her, as described earlier. The clinician first needs to check with the client that this is acceptable: *"I'm going to come and sit* *closer to you. Is that okay?''* If using eye movements, the clinician will ask: *"Is this a comfortable distance and speed?''* (Shapiro, 2001, p. 431).

Where tactile stimulation is being used, the clinician will check this out, as in the Preparation phase, usually placing a book or cushion on the client's lap, with the client's hands palm down on the cushion and the clinician alternately tapping the back of the client's hands. I use the middle two fingers of my own hands to do this lightly but firmly. When the clinician is using electronic equipment, such as a light bar, pulsars, or tones through earphones, the distance between the client and clinician may be greater and will depend on the client's comfort and the length of the cable. The clinician still needs to keep out of the line of vision of the client.

The starting point in the Desensitization phase is the past memory, incident, or experience—the target issue.

1. **Target issue:** The target has been identified in the History and Preparation phases. In a single incident, with no significant history, usually this will be the index event—the incident itself—and the following question may be redundant: *"What incident (or experience) would you like to work on today?''* (Shapiro, 2001, p. 431). With more complex presentations, the target incidents, memories, or experiences will have been identified in the targeting sequence plan and the sequence agreed to by the client. However, if the previous session was an incomplete session, or if on review of the previous target during reevaluation the SUD is greater than 1, the target will be the memory or experience that was the target of the previous session. If new material has emerged between sessions or during a previous session, then this will be included in the targeting sequence and may have priority because of the immediacy of the memory or experience (e.g., a dream) and its present emotional charge. The target incident or experience addresses the past dimension of reprocessing.

2. **Image:** Having brought a target incident or experience to mind, the client is asked: *"What picture represents the worst part of that incident (or experience)?''* (Shapiro, 2001, p. 431). Sometimes the client will not have a picture but may have some other image, sensation, or representation of the incident, such as a sound, taste, tactile sensation, or smell. In that case, the sound, taste, sensation, or smell is taken as the image or sensation that represents the worst part of the incident. Sometimes the client will find it difficult to identify the worst part of an incident or experience, in which case the clinician may ask for the image or sensation that represents it or is associated with it. The image or sensation brings the past (stored information) into the present moment.

3. **Negative cognition (NC):** The client is now asked: *"What words go best with that picture (sensation) and express a negative belief about yourself now?''*

(Shapiro, 2001, p. 431). Here, the client and clinician may draw on material from the previous phases of history and preparation in which negative beliefs about the self will have been noted. These will often be "throw-away" lines or phrases used by the client, as described earlier in the History phase. The NC is a presently held, negative, self-referencing belief—an "I" statement in the present tense. It links the present and the past by tapping into presently held, irrational beliefs about the self, associated with the target experience from the past.

4. **Positive cognition (PC):** The next stage of the assessment is for the client to bring to mind a positive cognition: *"When you bring up that picture (or sensation)/incident (or experience), what would you like to believe about yourself now?"* (Shapiro, 2001, p. 431). The PC is a presently desired, positive, self-referencing belief—an "I" statement in the present tense. It is not simply a negation of the negative cognition. Examples of PCs are given in the History phase above. Occasionally, client may be unable to identify a PC (such as "I can be strong") and may need to begin by using a conditional, such as "I could be strong." In some cases, particularly in complex PTSD, a client may be unable to access a PC at this stage and will do so in the Installation phase. The PC begins to address the future dimension of EMDR.

5. **Validity of Cognition (VoC):** The client is then asked about how valid that Positive Cognition feels when he brings to mind the target incident: *"When you think of that picture (sensation)/incident (experience), how true does that [positive cognition] feel to you now on a scale of 1 to 7, where 1 feels completely is totally false and 7 feels completely is totally true?"* (Shapiro, 2001, p. 431). Because this brings together the past, present and future in a setting in which the client's primary focus is on the past (stored information) and the present, the client may initially find the use of the VoC scale difficult and it may need some further, brief explanation. Usually slowly repeating the statement above, or slightly rephrasing it, will be enough. The VoC links the future goal with the present reality.

6. **Emotions:** The focus on emotions returns the client to the dual attention between present and past—outer and inner—present moment and stored information. The client is asked: *"When you bring up that incident and those words [negative cognition], what emotion(s) do you feel now?"* (Shapiro, 2001, p. 431). This is one of the laser beams that focus on the target experience and the associations with it. Sometimes clients will give descriptions of thoughts, rather than emotions or feelings, and there may be some cultural differences in this. The clinician needs to be sensitive to cultural issues but to be aware that this laser is one of emotion and feeling, rather than thought. It may be seen in a bodily

reaction, and articulating that feeling or emotion helps to bring it into the awareness of the present moment and its links with the past.

7. **Subjective Units of Distress (SUD) scale:** The SUD scale may have been used earlier in the History phase. The client is asked: *"On a scale of 0 to 10, where 0 is no disturbance or neutral and 10 is the highest disturbance you can imagine, how disturbing does it feel to you now?"* (adapted from Shapiro, 2001, p. 431). The value of the SUD here is in giving an indication of the subjective sense of disturbance in relation to the target incident and being able to compare this before and after desensitization. It may also be used from time to time during the reprocessing phases to give an indication of movement, and where the client is in relation to the material being reprocessed.

8. **Location of body sensation:** The final stage of the Assessment phase, which immediately precedes the desensitization phase, focuses on bodily sensation. The client is asked: *"Where do you feel it* [the disturbance] *in your body?"* (Shapiro, 2001, p. 431). There is no need for the clinician to describe the disturbance, even by using the client's own words. This can take the client into a cognitive or verbalized conceptualization of the disturbance that is unlikely to represent the whole of the experience. Sometimes the clinician will use the SUD score given by the client. If the SUD score was, say, 8, the clinician may say, "Where do you feel that 8 in your body?" This leaves the client with the sensation without explaining it or explaining it away.

The client is now on the threshold of the Desensitization phase of reprocessing. The image, beliefs, emotions, and sensations associated with the target incident or experience have been brought into focus and the Desensitization phase is ready to begin.

Sometimes, however, because of time constraints, the Assessment phase will not be followed immediately by the Desensitization phase. There may be a gap, for example, between sessions. When this is so, immediately before the Desensitization phase, the client will again need to bring into focus the target incident, and the image (or sensation) that goes with that incident. The clinician will ask the client to bring these to mind, together with the negative words that go with the image of the incident. The client will be asked to notice her emotions and, "on a scale of 0 to 10, where 0 is no disturbance or neutral and 10 is the highest disturbance you can imagine, how disturbing is the incident to you now?," notice where she is feeling it in her body, and follow the clinician's fingers or other bilateral stimulation. This is so that the various dimensions of the experience are held together, and the laser beams of image, cognitions, emotions, and sensations are brought into focus on the target at the start of the reprocessing.

PHASE 4: DESENSITIZATION

The Desensitization phase is the engine of EMDR. Like an engine, it can go at different speeds and operate in different gears. And sometimes it will stall, needing a jump-start or a push-start to get back into motion. Like an engine, it will drive other mechanisms, such as the reprocessing systems, and will draw on the fuel of the client's images, cognitions, emotions, and sensations associated with the target experiences—and it may take the client down other routes, or channels of association. To extend the analogy further, the client may be thought of as the driver and the clinician as the navigator.

It is in this desensitization phase that the client brings to mind the target experience for reprocessing and the images, cognitions, emotions, and sensations associated with it, and during a series of bilateral stimulation, allows the material to reprocess, by letting "whatever happens, happen." At the end of each set, the clinician will ask the client to take a breath, let go, and respond to the clinician's question, "What's there for you now?" It is in this phase that the client is most likely to discover new associations, sometimes surprising to him and to the clinician, who needs to attend the client, be attuned and bear witness to the process, but to keep out of the way of the reprocessing or, more accurately, not to impede it.

In the course of desensitization, processing will sometimes become stuck, and the clinician will help the client to jump-start the natural process by briefly intervening with a cognitive interweave, as described below, or by inviting the client to notice the thoughts, feelings, or bodily sensations that she is experiencing. Sometimes, to reengage the reprocessing, the clinician will ask the client to return to the target experience and the negative cognition, notice what she feels in her body, and say, "Go with that," followed by a set of bilateral stimulation. Other than in such brief interjections, the clinician remains present but not intrusive, anticipating that the client will move to adaptive processing of the information, given the space and environment in which to do so.

The desensitization phase is considered complete when no new material or sensations are experienced and when the SUD, ideally, is 0 and the VoC, ideally, is 7.

Changes Indicating Processing   How can you tell when someone is processing information? Bearing in mind the dimensions of image, cognitions, emotions, and sensations associated with the target experience, the processing is going to bring into play changes in one or more of these dimensions at any one time. Sometimes the changes will be clearly visible in facial expressions, bodily movement, and sensations; changes in feeling expressed in words or in tears, smiles, or laughter; and changes in cognitions. Sometimes the changes will be slight—a fleeting facial expression; sometimes they will be dramatic—an abreaction; and sometimes they will be a simple statement, "It is different." And while the clinician might want to satisfy his curiosity about what is happening, that is all he needs to know: It is different. One of the most difficult things for the experienced clinician who is new to the EMDR approach is simply to say, "Go with that," in response to the client's response after a set of bilateral stimulation, a breath, and the question, "What's there for you now?" At the beginning, this takes trust in the process. Later, the confidence is built on experience.

There are other indications of processing. The memory may become less distinct; sometimes it will be sharper and more detail will be added. Sometimes the image will fade or lose its color or impact; sometimes it will become more clear and have more color or more light and shade. Sometimes the image will change completely, opening up a new channel of association.

At times, the cognitions will change, becoming more positive, or expressed in terms of relationship with other people in the target incident, such as telling the perpetrator what the client really thinks about her, and who was responsible for the perpetration of abuse. Sometimes emotions may change; for example, the client will be more sad, or angry, or more compassionate toward himself.

As illustrated in Case Example 5-8, during reprocessing, the client may experience changes in bodily sensations—sounds, tastes, smells, feelings, touch—that are linked with the target incident or associated with it, and changes in bodily sensations, for example, in their color, shape, intensity, or location. At times, there may be a sense of numbness, or "nothing": when something happened prior to it, "nothing" can be an indicator of change!

Case Example 5-8: Rami Experiences Neck Pain and Then Relief During Reprocessing

The pain that Rami experiences in his neck when reprocessing the memory of being hooded, with a rope around his neck, and escorted to an execution yard, becomes acute. He touches his neck and stares blankly into space. He continues with the reprocessing and bilateral stimulation. The emotions become more intense as he hears the gunshot that kills his friend beside him. He continues reprocessing. The pain becomes more severe and is then followed by relief. He continues reprocessing, and the memory becomes less immediate, and the sense of guilt that he survived transmutes to sadness at the loss of his friend. He continues reprocessing: "Nothing." There is further reprocessing with bilateral stimulation, and he comments, "I can be okay as I am."

The client who is new to EMDR can be surprised at the changes, and some clients become concerned that they cannot hold onto the original memory or image and do the eye movements or other bilateral stimulation at the same time. Reassurance that this is okay, and that no one can do that, will often help the person to move with the process and "let whatever happens, happen."

Occasionally, the clinician and client will be surprised at extreme shifts that others might think of as defensive avoidance or a "flight into health." Polar changes in cognition are an example of this (Shapiro, 2001, p. 85), such as changing from a sense of personal guilt to "It's not my fault" in a few sets of bilateral stimulation. How does the clinician know that this is not a defensive flight into health? Ask the client to go back to the original target, bring to mind the image, notice what she experiences in her body, and say, "Go with that," followed by bilateral stimulation. If there is more material, it will emerge. If the client is deliberately blocking, it is likely that the clinician will be able to see that. If the channels of association are clear and the target experience has been reprocessed, this will be seen in the bodily sensations, emotions, cognitions, and feedback following the bilateral stimulation.

Returning to target, asking the client to bring to mind the original experience being worked on in this session, is important at the end of each channel of association, and also when the person seems to be stuck, or "in his head," not allowing the reprocessing to move freely. The client's returning to target and noticing what he feels and where that is in his body often moves him back into reprocessing at the emotional and sensory levels, as well as cognitively. It is a good regrounding of the process, linking into what is there of the original material or information, and it is helpful not only when the client seems stuck, but also when the clinician feels stuck or unsure.

Memories, or information, are not stored in isolation. They are linked into an information network that has channels of association linked to the target memory. In the desensitization phase, coming to the end of such a channel is usually indicated when the client gives the same neutral or positive response, such as "It's okay now," after two or three consecutive sets of bilateral stimulation. However, the networks are complex, and, during reprocessing, associations within and between networks are likely to be made. Sometimes these can be surprising, jumping to material of which the client and clinician were unaware. The changes may be to networks associated by links with a participant in the experiences, such as being bullied by father, to a time of being beaten by father, to seeing father beat mother. They may be associated by stimuli such as the sound of police sirens, car horns, brakes screeching, moving from the common sensation of sound in one experience to the sound in another. Sometimes they are linked by bodily sensation.

Becky was in the mountains when she had a serious cycle accident and was taken into the hospital where she was agitated and unable to communicate in the local language. Because of her agitation, the nursing staff held her down and eventually raised a cot side to the bed and strapped her in. When reprocessing this memory, the material moved from the hospital to a memory in childhood when she had been held down and had felt vulnerable and in danger. The networks were linked by the common sensation of being restrained.

Managing Affect As noted earlier, there is a window of tolerance within which reprocessing is optimal, with the arousal levels of the client being neither too high nor too low. This will vary for each person, but sometimes the client will need help in maintaining an optimal level of arousal and in titrating the emotional material to accomplish this. At the extreme, the stop signal will be used by the client to control the levels of emotion, and affect management techniques will be introduced to bring down the level of arousal.

The stop signal interrupts the reprocessing rather than facilitates it, although often after a brief break, the client will want to return to the process. To facilitate the ongoing processing, the levels of arousal, or the impact of traumatic images, cognitions, emotions, and sensations, can be managed in other ways. The first is to support the client as she goes through the emotional material. Sometimes the analogy of a dream can help: When the nightmare reaches the most critical or disturbing point, the sleeper wakes up and the processing that can occur in dreams is not completed. It is interrupted and the person is left with disturbing feelings. In EMDR, it is possible to continue through that most disturbing part of the experience and come to a resolution, but to do so the person needs to keep going or to return to the reprocessing later. Another analogy is that of driving a vehicle through a tunnel and keeping the foot on the accelerator. Continuing to drive can get one through the tunnel more quickly.

The second approach to managing the impact of images, cognitions, emotions, and sensations is to titrate the impact. Many clients are able to gain control over the image by seeing it as though on a video screen and turning down the intensity, the focus, or the color. Black-and-white pictures are less vivid than images in color: gray blood is less intense than red blood. Turning down the color can help some clients view the scene (or scenery, to use the train metaphor) at a level of intensity at which they can begin to process the material. Similarly, taking the action out of the scene so that, for example, the perpetrator is seen in still pictures, rather than in motion, or putting the scene at a distance, can help in bringing the process back into the frame of the window of tolerance. Conversely, where processing has become blocked because of underarousal, adding color or action, or increasing proximity can bring the client's levels of arousal up to the sill of the tolerance window and within it.

Reassuring the client that she is doing okay, reminding her to "just notice," and that this is "old stuff," "it's in the past," "it's over," can be helpful. Some clients find it reduces levels of arousal to put a barrier between themselves and the material they are reprocessing, for example, like a glass screen through which they can safely see what is happening. And as the sense of safety increases, the screen can gradually be removed.

If changing the perception of the image of the incident can effect changes in processing, so can attention to cognitions, emotions and sensations. Focusing on one rather than all of these can reduce arousal; extending the focus from one to all of these can increase it. The development of personal resources that give confidence can be also helpful, including the resource that is the presence of the clinician, as illustrated in Case Example 5-9.

Case Example 5-9: The Clinician Accompanies Martin to the Morgue (Imaginally)

Martin was present at a major fire in which colleagues had lost their lives. He had to visit the mortuary to identify bodies, and he had a haunting memory of one of them. He was frightened by the image that he saw, and of the basement mortuary. He had to go through a door to get into it and terrified himself with the thoughts of what was inside. Processing became stuck: Martin wanted to go into the morgue but wanted to be accompanied. He asked the clinician to go with him in his mind and at one point reached out to hold the clinician's arm to give him a sense of safety and that he was not alone. He was able to continue to reprocess the memory, and subsequently to think about his colleagues who had died. These were sad thoughts, but not haunting and intrusive, and when, in the future, he needed to think about death or the incident itself, he was able to imagine being accompanied by the clinician, and to gain a sense of strength from that. He had developed a resource and internalized (installed) it.

Unblocking Processing When It Is Stuck   What happens when processing becomes stuck? To draw on the metaphor of a bus or car journey, when the vehicle gets stuck, it needs a push. If it cannot be restarted, it may need a push-start or jump leads; but when it does so, it needs this only briefly. The people push it to start; they don't continue pushing it for the rest of the journey. The vehicle continues under its own power: The engine is reengaged. So it is with processing. Sometimes the processing will become stuck and the client needs help to get it restarted, to reengage the gears.

Changing the direction of the eye movements might do this, or the speed, volume, or pressure of the bilateral stimulation. Occasionally, changing the modality of the bilateral stimulation (having first told the client) will help to push-start the reprocessing, and at times the client who has closed her eyes during bilateral stimulation might find that opening them helps her to continue processing. Sometimes, as described above, the client needs help to bring the target information back into focus for a moment, by returning to the image, emotions, and sensations associated with it, adding bilateral stimulation and going from there. There are, however, *no "supposed to's" in this process,* and the clinician needs to be supportive and affirming in enabling the client to *let whatever happens, happen.*

Cognitive Interweave A very effective way of facilitating processing when it becomes stuck, for example, when the client is "looping"—repeatedly returning to the same material or the same negative belief—is to use a cognitive interweave. A fuller account of this is given in Shapiro's (2001) book. As the name suggests, this is a brief statement, question, or short sequence of questions that is interwoven into the therapeutic process by the clinician and helps the client to link different information networks, as illustrated in Case Example 5-10.

> **Case Example 5-10: Jason's Cognitive Interweave**
>
> Jason had an enduring sense of guilt about a time when his ship was coming under attack and he had not reached out to a colleague who was crying for help: "It was a real, real, real cry for help." Jason felt that he should have done something, and that he was a failure, worthless. He described the setting:
>
> JASON: You had to hear him cry. It wasn't just . . . wasn't just . . . wasn't just a small thing. It was a cry for help. It was a real, real, real cry for help.
>
> THERAPIST: Go with that. [bilateral stimulation] Let go. Take a breath. What's there for you now?
>
> JASON: You had to be there—action stations. A real, real human cry. I should have responded; should have offered my arm. I can't believe I didn't do it.
>
> THERAPIST: Go with that. [bilateral stimulation] Let go. Take a breath. What's there for you now?
>
> JASON: It was bad enough [not offering my arm]. It was barbaric.

THERAPIST: Go with that. [bilateral stimulation] What's there for you now?

JASON: It still frightens me now, being there [at action stations].

Later in the reprocessing, Jason began looping, feeling frustrated that he had not comforted his colleague by putting his arm round him or saying to him that things would be okay. Several sets of bilateral stimulation were followed by a response that he felt frustrated that he had not done something. The cognitive interweave was giving new information about fear:

THERAPIST: So what would have happened if you had put his arm around him?

JASON: It would have been all right if it hadn't been for the chief. I think the chief was scared. You could smell the fear.

THERAPIST: What happens when people are scared?

JASON: They [defecate].

THERAPIST: Anything else?

JASON: They [urinate].

THERAPIST: Do you know what else they often do?

JASON: No.

THERAPIST: They freeze. [bilateral stimulation] Take a breath. Let go. What's there for you now?

JASON: It was very frightening.

THERAPIST: Go with that. [bilateral stimulation] Let go. Take a breath. What's there for you now?

JASON: It was a big attack, one of the biggest we'd been in. Nevertheless, I still wish I could. . . .

THERAPIST: Go with that. [bilateral stimulation] Take a breath. Let go. What's there for you now?

JASON: I feel that's a positive. That's quite nice.

THERAPIST: Go with that. [bilateral stimulation] What's there for you now

JASON: Yeah. I was scared.

THERAPIST: Go with that. [bilateral stimulation] What's there for you now?

JASON: I know I always wanted my mom when it was happening.

THERAPIST: Go with that. [bilateral stimulation] What do you notice now?

JASON: I feel a bit more positive.

In further reprocessing, Jason said that he felt quite relaxed. "I feel like I've done something. I feel that I've achieved something. A bit of a sense of achievement." He said that he had a sense of purpose and that he felt better about himself. Later, he said, "I can be worthwhile."

The cognitive interweave may trigger new information, as it did with Jason, and there may be new insights. It may help the client challenge an existing dysfunctional belief. It may add a different perspective to a memory or experience, for example, in helping the client to view an incident from the present situation as an adult, rather than the past experience as a child. As a child, the victim may have been told that he was to blame and carried with him that sense of guilt, often through to adulthood. In adulthood, then, he has the child's perspective of "I'm to blame," rather than the adult's perspective that the child was vulnerable, dependent, and manipulated by the perpetrator. Reasoning with the client is unlikely to help him change, but the cognitive interweave may help him make connections that link memory networks in such a way that the adult perspective, which the client already has in other memory networks, can be accessed in relation to this memory.

The purpose of the cognitive interweave is to parallel spontaneous processing by linking into existing networks. The interweave might be educational, introducing new information, such as information about involuntary physiological responses of arousal when a person is sexually stimulated, even against their will. It might use the approach "I'm confused . . . " to bring in a gentle challenge to the logic of what has been said in the looping. It may use the Socratic method in which a brief series of questions is asked by the clinician and responded to by the client, and results in a gentle challenge to the client's premise, or negative belief, that is at the root of the looping or the block. As illustrated in Case Example 5-11, a typical example that draws from the perspectives of an adult and a child is when a client has been attacked by an assailant or perpetrator who is bigger, stronger, and/or older than the client was at the time of the assault, but the client is stuck with a sense of guilt, that it was his fault, and that he is to blame.

Case Example 5-11: Using Socratic Questioning in Tammy's Cognitive Interweave

Tammy thought that it was her fault when her father used to beat her and plunge her into a bath of very hot water. "I must have done something wrong." During the reprocessing, she arrived at a sense that she should have done something about it, and she looped on this concept, repeating, "It's my fault. I should have done something." The cognitive interweave used "I'm confused" and the Socratic method:

THERAPIST: I'm confused. . . . [Tammy waits.] You were how old?
TAMMY: Between 6 and 10 or 11.
THERAPIST: And your father was how old?

TAMMY: I don't know. About 40.

THERAPIST: Who was in control?

TAMMY: He was.

THERAPIST: Go with that. [bilateral stimulation]

   Other forms of a cognitive interweave could have been, from the adult perspective:

THERAPIST: If you saw your niece (daughter, son, a child) who is 6 put into a very hot bath by their father, whose fault would you think it was?

TAMMY: His.

THERAPIST: Go with that. [bilateral stimulation]

Finally, reprocessing can also be blocked because the root of the block lies in earlier material that has not yet been processed: a feeder memory that is "contributing to the current dysfunction, and blocking processing of it" (Shapiro, 2001, p. 189) or a blocking belief (Shapiro, 2001, p. 192). These may be accessed using the floatback or affect scan described earlier, asking the client to bring to mind the blocked response, notice what negative words go with it, and what he feels in his body, and float back to an earlier time in his life when he had similar thoughts or feelings. When such an experience is identified, it becomes a focus of reprocessing.

Whenever the reprocessing is interrupted, through a cognitive interweave, reprocessing a the source of a blocking belief, or through other intervention, it is important to return to original target of that session, to bring to mind the incident, the negative cognition and the bodily sensations that go with it, and to continue the desensitization and reprocessing. This may not be immediately after the interjection, but it will usually be in the course of that session. The desensitization phase is considered complete when, on returning to the target experience, the SUD is 0 and the VoC is 7. Occasionally, the SUDs will be 1 or the VoC 6, if there are ecological reasons why a person feels that he cannot go to 0 or 7.

PHASE 5: INSTALLATION

Installation is perhaps too mechanical a word for this part of the methodology, which is designed to link the positive beliefs a person has about herself with the original incident. First, the client is asked whether the positive cognition that was identified during the assessment phase is still appropriate or whether another cognition fits better. If a new positive cognition is selected, then it is used; if not, the original positive cognition is used. In either case, the client is asked to think of the target incident and the words of the positive cognition and rate on the VoC scale how true the words feel to her *now*. This is followed by a set of bilateral stimulation, a breath, *"Let go,"* and a rating again of the VoC, on the 1-to-7 scale. This process is continued as long as the VoC is becoming stronger, either numerically or in what the client is saying. Occasionally, further material for reprocessing will emerge during the installation phase. When this happens, the process returns to the desensitization phase in order to process the new information. Usually, however, the VoC remains at 7, and when it has stayed there for two or three sets of bilateral stimulation, the clinician moves with the client on to the body scan.

Phase 6: Body Scan

A key part of the EMDR process is the focus on bodily sensation. Indeed, a bodily sensation may itself be used as a target (Shapiro, 2001) even when the sensation is "phantom" (Schneider et al., 2007; Wilensky, 2006). The purpose of the body scan is to check out this dimension of the processing, so that any unresolved sensations that may link to unprocessed aspects of a memory or experience may be "just noticed" and, with further bilateral stimulation, processed to an adaptive resolution.

In the body scan, the client is asked to close his eyes and keep in mind the original memory and the positive cognition while bringing his attention to the different parts of his body from head to toes and noticing where there is any tension, tightness, or unusual sensation (Shapiro, 2001, p. 74). If any sensation is reported, it is followed by bilateral stimulation and usually fades after two or three sets. Where, rarely, new material emerges, then the process returns to the desensitization phase to reprocess the new material. More usually, where processing is complete and the body scan reveals no areas of discomfort or unusual sensation, then there is often a sense of well-being. This completes the reprocessing phases, when the SUD score is 0, the VoC is 7, and there is a clear body scan. It is time to move to closure.

Phase 7: Closure

The purpose of the closure phase is to ensure the safety of the client at the close of a session, and to prepare the client for possible ongoing processing between sessions. While "homework" is not a part of the EMDR approach, the client may need to be reminded of resources she might use between sessions, such as affect regulation, guided self-imagery, and relaxation. It is also helpful to ask the client to make a note of anything that comes up for her between the closure and the next consultation, which will begin with the reevaluation phase, during which there will be a time to review what has happened in the reprocessing session.

At closure, the client is advised that processing may continue between sessions and that it is helpful to make a note of any disturbance or disturbing thoughts or dreams so that this can be addressed at a subsequent consultation. The client is also reminded of the self-care techniques such as relaxation. There is no specific homework other than to keep a log of any significant experiences, what triggered them, and the images, cognitions, emotions, and sensations that went with them. For ease of recording, this can be put into a table, a so-called TICES grid (Shapiro, 2001) in which rows refer to (1) triggers, (2) images, (3) cognitions, (4) emotions, and (5) sensations, and columns refer to days of the week.

Complete reprocessing of a single aspect of the trauma may not happen within a single session, and closure is then the closure of an incomplete session. Here, in addition to the advice about ongoing processing and keeping a note of significant experiences, the client is reintroduced to the affect management procedures such as relaxation, using visual imagery and a safe or special place, and other techniques. The purpose is to ensure that the client leaves the consultation with a sense of safety and well-being.

PHASE 8: REEVALUATION

For the clinician, the reevaluation phase begins at the end of a session, when the client has gone and the clinician is taking time for personal reflection on the consultation and the reprocessing. During the consultation, the clinician will have noted areas that may need to be addressed further. Sometimes this will be noted during the reprocessing phases, but then is not the time for clinician to explore, interpret, or comment because to intervene then, other than with a brief interweave, would be to intrude into the reprocessing.

For the client, the reevaluation phase opens each session after the first. It is a time for revisiting the targets of the previous reprocessing, and reevaluating on the 0-to-10 SUD scale, the degree of disturbance experienced now by the client. It is also a time for reflection on the previous session and the intervening time between that session and the present one. Once again, this is a less tightly structured phase, like the history and preparation phases, and it may lead to further exploration of the client's history and of issues that may have been missed or not known earlier. The clinician will ask the client if he has any notes from his experiences between sessions and in particular will ask about any dreams or intrusive thoughts; any times of discomfort or disquiet; and any new reflections, insights, or memories.

In reevaluating the work done in the previous session, a client will be asked to bring to mind the incident with which she had worked. She will be asked what image is in mind, what thoughts come up with that image, and what emotions and sensations she is experiencing. And she will be asked to rate on the SUD scale how disturbing is the incident to her now. If there is any disturbance, this is reprocessed until there is an SUD of 0, a VoC of 7, and a clear body scan. Where this does not happen, the reevaluation phase may lead into reformulation of a part or parts of the treatment plan. It may indicate new targets that need to be addressed and new insights, emotions, and beliefs that need to be addressed, incorporated, or processed.

Where the previous material has been processed effectively, the client and clinician will discuss the material and may reflect on its meaning, and then move to identify the next target of desensitization.

When processing of a past event has been completed, the client will process present triggers and also future possibilities or templates. Present triggers are those experiences that take the client back to the traumatic memory and evoke feelings from the past, experienced in the present. Having reprocessed the traumatic memory and its associations, the targets for the reprocessing are now the recent or present triggers, together with the image, beliefs, emotions, and sensations associated with them. Sometimes this will reveal further material to be reprocessed, in which case the full protocol is followed for reprocessing. More usually, the reprocessing will be complete, with an SUD of 0 and a VoC of 7, and it is time to move on to the next stage: processing the future templates.

Future templates are sketches of how a person wants to be in response to situations or experiences that previously would have likely triggered traumatic memories from the past. The processing is a form of mental rehearsal in which the client brings to mind a future situation that would have been disturbing, but plays it through, as though on a video, in the light of his new experience, with the positive cognition and with a positive outcome. This is accompanied by bilateral stimulation and may reveal further material to be reprocessed or may simply complete the three-pronged approach of EMDR, working with the past, the present, and the future.

In the final session of a completed series of therapy, the reevaluation will look back over the whole experience of the therapy, the issues that have been addressed, and the targets that have been reprocessed. It will also be a time for completing again any of the measures used at the beginning of therapy and feeding back the results of this evaluation to the client.

For a lengthy illustration of the assessment, reprocessing, and closure phases of EMDR, you can read Case Example 5-12, which involves Jane, the subject of this chapter's first case example. In addition, the Additional Resources section at the end of this chapter provides a thorough summary of the assessment, desensitization, installation, body scan, and closure phases of EMDR.

Case Example 5-12: The Assessment, Reprocessing, and Closure Phases of EMDR

When Jane came for EMDR psychotherapy, she came with vivid, intrusive memories of the road traffic crash that included images, emotions, and bodily sensations. Her thought about herself when she focused on the crash was "I'm to blame." Jane described a history in which she had experienced a breakdown in her marriage but a childhood that seemed well grounded and supportive and one in which she felt loved and felt good about herself. Reflecting on her history, the sense of being to blame was associated with the breakdown of her relationship, but for Jane the focus was on the road traffic crash itself and its sequelae.

In the history and preparation phases, we developed a treatment plan that addressed past, present, and future, and a target sequence to do with the incident itself, hospitalization, and issues to do with her marriage. Jane was concerned about the crash and felt guilty about her young son, who was a passenger in the car she was driving, having just picked him up from school. What follows is an account of the assessment, reprocessing (desensitization, installation, and body scan), and closure phases, which is based on Jane's work and similar cases. I am indebted to Dr. Francine Shapiro for permission to reprint the EMDR protocol here and to include client data. In the following dialogue, instead of prefacing the remarks by who said them, the therapist's comments will be in italics, and Jane's will be indented and in roman font.

Assessment

Hello Jane, today we have planned to begin the reprocessing. Is that OK with you?

Yes.

What we will be doing is a simple check on what you are experiencing, I need to know from you what is going on, with feedback that is as clear as possible. Sometimes things will change and sometimes they won't. [Jane nods.] I'll ask you how you feel from 1 to 10; sometimes it will change and sometimes it won't. I may ask if something else comes up; sometimes it will and sometimes it won't. There are no "supposed to's" in this process. So just give as accurate a feedback as you can as to what is happening, without judging whether it should be happening or not. Let whatever happens happen. We'll do the eye movements (taps or tones) for a while, and then we'll talk about it.

That's okay. I understand.

Do you remember, we talked about a safe place, a place where you feel safe, or special. It was . . . ?

It was at home in my garden when I was a child. I can remember the smell of the flowers. . . .

That sounds good! Remember, if at any time you feel you have to stop, raise your hand and I will stop, and begin to talk about your safe place.

Yes, that's okay.

What will you do if you want to stop?

[Jane raises her hand.]

And can I just check the eye movements? Is it okay if I move closer to you?

Yes, that's fine. That's okay.

I'm going to put my hand in front of your face and then move it away. Is that okay?

Sure.

[With clinician's hand in position at the center line of the Jane's vision and moving away from the Jane's face] *Is this a comfortable distance?*

Yes, just a bit further—that's fine.

[Starting bilateral stimulation slowly, then increasing the speed, watching the client's eyes for movement and any sign of discomfort, and having checked about spectacles or contact lenses. Use about 6 to 8 continuous sweeps from center line to right or left, then to left or right, and back to center.] *And is this a comfortable speed?*

Yes.

1. Incident

We have agreed that the focus today will be on the road traffic crash; can you just describe that to me briefly?

The car was coming toward me. James was in the back [of my car]. I had just picked him up from school.

2. Image

What picture represents the worst part of the incident?

The car coming toward me—and the screech. . . . And my son was in the back of the car. . . . The car coming toward me. [Tearful]. I thought it was the end.

3. Negative Cognition

What words go best with that picture that express a negative belief about yourself now?

I'm frightened. It wasn't my fault; there was nothing I could do. I feel I'm to blame because my son was there. I shouldn't have put him at risk.

What do you feel that says about you?

I'm a bad person.

Are the negative words that go with that picture, "I'm a bad person"?
Yes.

4. Positive Cognition

When you bring up that picture, what would you like to believe about yourself now?
I'd like to think I could have done something. It could have been different. I'm a good mother, really.
Is that, "I'm a good mother" or "I'm a good person" that you would like to believe about yourself now when you bring up that picture?
Both. I'm a good mother; I'm a good person. I'm a good person.
"I'm a good person"?
Yes. Yes—I'm a good person.

5. Validity of Cognition (VoC)

When you think of that picture (incident or experience), how true do those words, "I'm a good person," feel to you now on a scale of 1 to 7, where 1 feels completely false and 7 feels completely true?
Well, I know I'm a good person.
When you think of the road traffic crash and that picture of the car. . . .
I should have done something [begins to cry] . . . 3

6. Emotion

When you bring up that picture, and those words, "I'm a bad person," what emotion(s) do you feel now?
Sad. Guilty. . . . I'm ashamed.

7. Subjective Units of Disturbance (SUD)

On a scale of 0 to 10, where 0 is no disturbance or neutral and 10 is the highest disturbance you can imagine, how disturbing does it feel to you now?
8, 9? . . . 9

8. Bodily Sensation

Where do you feel it in your body?
Here [stomach] . . . and here [chest] . . . and in my head.

DESENSITIZATION

I'd like you to bring up that image, those negative words, "I'm a bad person," notice where you are feeling it in your body, and follow my fingers.

[Bilateral stimulation (BLS)—eye movements. No need to count them; watch for facial and bodily expressions. As a guide begin with, say, 24 to 30 sweeps.]

[Client follows clinician's hand with her eyes. Tearful.]

That's it. . . . You're doing fine. . . .

[Ends BLS after about 24 to 30 sweeps, taking the cue to stop from watching the client's face that seems to have come to an emotional plateau.]

Take a deep breath. . . . Let go. . . . What's there for you now?

I can just see the car—it's red. And the screech of brakes. . . .

Go with that. [BLS] *Take a deep breath. . . . Let go. . . . What's there for you now?*

It's funny. I can't see the car so clearly but I can feel . . . I've got a pain in my stomach.

Go with that. [BLS] *Take a breath. . . . Let go. . . . What do you notice now?*

I can feel my legs. I can't move. I'm scared.

Go with that. [BLS] [Client takes a breath.] *Let go. . . . What's there for you now?*

It's strange. I can't see the car anymore. I feel calm.

Go with that. [BLS] [Client takes a breath.] *Let go. . . . What's there for you now?*

Nothing. It's the same.

Go with that. [BLS] *Take a breath. . . . Let go. . . . What's there for you now?*

The same.

When you go back to that original experience [waits for the client to bring the original target to mind], *what do you get now?*

[Cries]

Go with that. [BLS]

[Jane is distressed and crying as she processes material. Her facial expressions indicate that there are changes occurring.]

You're doing fine. This is old stuff.

It's my son. He could have gone through the windshield. He could have been killed. [Cries]

Go with that. [BLS] *Take a deep breath. Let go. What's there for you now?*

He's wearing a seat belt. I remember telling him to put it on before we started. He didn't want to but I told him he had to. . . .

Go with that. [BLS] *Take a breath. Let go. What do you notice now?*

If he hadn't had a seat belt, he'd have been killed. [Cries.] I think I saved his life.

Go with that. [BLS] [Client takes a breath.] *Let go. What's there for you now?*

I think I saved his life. If I hadn't told him to put his belt on. . . .

Go with that. [BLS] *Take a deep breath. Let go. What do you notice now?*

I'm okay. I did the right thing. It was a [dreadful] crash, but I did the right thing. It was okay.

Go with that. [BLS] [Client takes a breath.] *Let go. What's there for you now?*

Nothing. I did the right thing.

And if you go back to the original experience, what do you get now?

Nothing. It was a dreadful crash and we're safe now.

Go with that. [BLS] *Take a breath. Let go. What's there for you now?*

I'm okay. We're safe now. I did the right thing.

So when you bring up that experience—the crash—on a scale of 0 to 10, where 0 is no disturbance or neutral and 10 is the highest disturbance you can imagine, how disturbing does it feel to you now?

Not really disturbing; 2.

Go with that. [BLS] *Take a breath. Let go. What's there for you now?*

No. Nothing. It's okay now. It's still horrible. But it's okay. It's a memory.

Go with that. [BLS] *What's there for you now?*

I'm just glad we're both safe. We're alive.

Go with that. [BLS] *What's there for you now?*

Nothing. I'm okay.

Go with that. [BLS] *Take a breath. Let go. What's there for you now?*

Nothing. I'm okay.

And when you bring up the experience, on a 0-to-10 scale, where 0 is no disturbance or neutral and 10 is the highest disturbance you can imagine, how disturbing does it feel to you now?

It's not disturbing. It's horrible—a memory—but it's okay.

[Smiles] *Zero is no disturbance and 10 is the highest?*

Now? Zero.

INSTALLATION

You've done well. I'd like to go back to the words "I'm a good person." Do those words still fit, or is there another positive statement that you feel would be more suitable?

No, they still fit. I *am* a good person. I'm okay.

Think about the original incident and those words, "I'm a good person." From 1, completely false, to 7, completely true, how true do they feel?

Six, 7. [Decides] Seven.

Hold them together. [BLS] Take a breath. . . . Let go. . . . On a scale of 1 to 7, how true do those words, "I'm a good person," feel to you now when you think of the original incident?

Seven. I *am* a good person. Seven.

You sound sure.

I am. I did what was right. I'm okay. I'm a good person as I am.

Body Scan

Close your eyes and keep in mind the original memory and the words, "I'm a good person." Then bring your attention to the different parts of your body, starting with your head and working downward. Any place you find any tension, tightness, or unusual sensation, tell me.

I feel okay. Just something in my stomach.

Just notice that. [BLS] Take a breath. . . . Let go. . . . What's there now?

Nothing. I'm okay.

[BLS] *What's there now?*

Nothing. It's gone.

[BLS] *What's there now?*

I'm fine. It's gone. [Smiles]

Closure

You have done really well. You've done some good work today. How are you feeling?

I'm feeling okay. I can't really believe it. I always thought it was my fault—I was guilty because of my son. I feel okay about that now.

It sounds as though you have experienced new positive thoughts and insights?

I have. I had forgotten about the safety belt. It's okay.

The processing we have done today may continue after the session. You may or may not notice new insights, thoughts, memories, or dreams. If you do, just notice what you are experiencing. Take a snapshot of it—what you are seeing, feeling, thinking, and the trigger. Keep a log, using the TICES grid we spoke about. I think you have a copy: Triggers, Images, Cognitions, Emotions, and Sensations. And remember to use the relaxation technique daily! We can work on this new material next time. If you feel it necessary, call my office.

In the following consultation, the work in this session was reviewed. Jane said that she still felt that she had done the right thing and that she remembered insisting that her son use the safety belt. Asked to bring the original incident to mind, of the car coming toward her, and the screech, and her son in the back of the car, and the words, "I'm a bad person,"

Jane said that "on the 0-to-10 scale, where 0 is no disturbance or neutral and 10 the highest disturbance you can imagine," the score was 0.

In this session, Jane spoke more about her experience in the crash and also about her time in the hospital after the incident. Again, a target memory became the initial focus of reprocessing, this time of being on a gurney in the hospital and being told she needed surgery. The safe place was the same, but the negative and positive cognitions were, "I'm weak," and "I can be strong." Reprocessing continued until the SUD was 0 and the VoC 7.

In a subsequent session, there was discussion about her marriage, but the sense of "I'm a good person" and "I can be strong" had generalized from the earlier reprocessing, and Jane felt much more positive about her present situation and did not feel that she needed to reprocess issues to do with her marriage. When she brought to mind the image of her ex-husband, her SUDs rating was 1.

Having reprocessed the material to do with the crash and the hospitalization, Jane focused on present triggers. These were the sound of traffic, especially the screeching of brakes, and taking her son to school. In processing these present triggers, Jane was asked (1) to bring to mind the sound of brakes screeching, and (2) an image that represented that; she was asked for words that went with that image, that described (3) a negative belief about herself now. It was difficult to find words, but "I'm vulnerable" seemed to fit. The (4) positive cognition was, "I can be safe." The (5) VoC was initially 3 and moved to 6. The (6) emotion was "anxious" and (7) the SUD initially 4. The (8) bodily sensation was in Jane's stomach. After reprocessing, the SUD was 9 and the VoC was 1. Jane said that she thought that these were realistic because accidents do happen, but she was more comfortable in the street with traffic, and she was beginning to let her son go to school with others rather than only with her.

The future template was to do with road traffic, but also to do with driving. In the future template, the incident becomes the imagined future situation in which things go okay. There can be variations in this, with some things going okay and some things being difficult. The future template enables a person to run a video of how it could be and also a video of how to deal with things when they go wrong. For Jane, the future template had to do with driving again. At the time of the consultations, this was not possible because of her leg injuries, but it was something that she wanted to be able to do. Her positive cognition, "I can be strong," helped her in this and was linked to images of driving.

As noted above, this part of the EMDR approach is similar to mental rehearsal practiced by athletes and others, and it has been used in performance enhancement in a number of settings (Lendl & Foster, 2003). I have used the EMDR approach with members of a football team, a tennis player, and executives.

Here, Jane used the approach successfully to build confidence, and when her leg injuries recovered sufficiently, she was able to buy a well-constructed vehicle with an automatic transmission in which she felt safe enough, and which she could drive.

EMDR WITH OTHER TYPES OF TRAUMA AND SITUATIONS

EMDR WITH COMPLEX TRAUMA

So far, this chapter has mainly focused on aspects of a single traumatic incident. In this section, the more complex issues of Rami, Paul, and Rose will be outlined, and approaches to working with complex trauma will be noted.

Fundamental to working with people who have experienced complex trauma is the development of safety and trust. Often, there are issues to do with early attachment, and the internal sense of self may well have been violated. The relationship with the clinician may, therefore, take time to develop, and rapport and attunement may be gradual. Similarly, because of the importance of trust, the early phases of EMDR—history, preparation, and assessment—are also likely to take much longer.

Rose, Paul, and Rami had complex presentations. For Rose and Paul, there was a sense of rapport and trust early in therapy, but the deeper level of safety and trust would take time to develop in a way that would enable them to share the more difficult aspects of their experiences. In the case of Rose, it took several years, not of regular weekly therapy, but of periods of therapy and then breaks. Initially, the sessions were weekly, but later there were times when they were every two weeks, or three, moderated by availability but also by the degree to which Rose was able to deal with the intensity of the material and the affect that the material evoked. Rose was helped in this by having the support of a mental health worker from the mental health team and one from the day center of which she was a member. Without the framework of a safe environment, and access to mental health workers on a day-by-day basis, it would have been very difficult for Rose to have done the therapeutic work. The importance of a supportive network, social network, or family is key.

Paul was able to engage in therapy over the period of about a year, without the support of a multidisciplinary team. He had good ego strength and regular employment, and a small network of good friends. However, it was some time before he was able to address, in therapy, issues cloaked with shame and with the sense that he did not deserve to get better.

One of the ways in which Paul and Rose were able to reprocess their feelings of shame was to bring to mind the sense of shame and the time in their life about which they felt most ashamed. In an adaptation of the standard protocol (Dodgson, 2007b), the image of themselves at that time became the target for reprocessing, together with the negative belief about the self at that time, that gave charge to the feelings of shame. This is similar to, but not the same as, the standard negative cognition, such as "I don't deserve to get better." It differs in that it is a negative belief about the self in the past, a belief such as "You are disgusting," as the person holds in mind an image of the self from the past, the self of whom they are ashamed.

It was not possible, at the beginning of working with the sense of shame, for either Paul or Rose to find anything positive to say about themselves and, in the case of Rose, to begin to attempt to have positive thoughts about herself precipitated an onslaught of abuse from the voices that she experienced in her head. The positive cognition, therefore, was not elicited at this stage. Without the positive cognition and the VoC rating, the assessment and desensitization phases followed the adapted protocol; the image of "the self that was shameful" was the target of the reprocessing, together with the negative belief about the self at that time, and the emotions, SUD, and bodily sensations associated with it.

For Paul, this reprocessing was completed over two sessions. For Rose, it took many sessions spread many months apart, with other work done in between, and gradually returning to the issue of shame when it was appropriate to do so, building on the work that had been done in the reprocessing the last time the issue had been addressed. By contrast, with the initial rejection of her shamed self, in a recent consultation Rose said that she felt proud of the little girl Rose who had gone through so much and had survived. And she thought that she could use some of that strength, or resilience, to help deal with present difficulties. The self of whom she had been ashamed had become a resource, though there were other aspects of herself of which she was still ashamed and that would be addressed at another time.

Rami developed a sense of rapport quite quickly and strengthened this as his experience of EMDR therapy became deeper. At the beginning, there were difficulties because of the presence of an interpreter, but gradually, Rami had enough confidence in himself to start to use the English that he knew, and to express himself, verbally and nonverbally. After a short time, an interpreter was not needed. Without the interpreter, and as the clinical work developed, Rami was able to reprocess material associated with shame and fear, and with the sense of guilt that he carried with him. In order to enhance the sense of immediacy of the material, during the reprocessing phases, I asked Rami to use his language of origin, and only later to describe in English, if he wanted to, the material with which he had been working. As a clinician, it is possible to see how a person is reprocessing, without needing to know the detail.

For Jason, the question of trust was a different one, but one that is often an issue with military personnel and with members of the emergency services. Sometimes it is associated with shame, sometimes with a wish not to contaminate others with the knowledge, images, and sensations that a person has experienced in the field of war or in the course of policing, or working as a paramedic or firefighter. Occasionally, this anxiety is expressed in terms of the confidentiality or official secrecy of the material. Sometimes it remains unspoken. I often think that the client can sense the degree to which the therapist can bear to hear what the client needs to tell. And the more familiar the therapist becomes with disturbing material, the more disturbing the material that the therapist will encounter.

So an important point in working with complex trauma is for the therapist to care for himself, for example, by regulating his caseload and attempting to maintain a balance in which there are some more simple cases as well as the potentially disturbing ones. It is also important for the clinician to access EMDR for himself when needed, and have adequate support and supervision.

There are also two other areas of work that I would like to mention. One is working with people who have recently experienced a traumatizing event. The other is working in a situation of ongoing conflict. Again, in both domestic and other ongoing conflict, safety is a significant issue, and the usual focus on responsibility, safety, and choice changes first to a focus on safety, including practicalities of safety in an otherwise unsafe situation. In domestic violence, this may mean involving other agencies. In situations of war or other ongoing conflict, this may mean being as safe as can be in an unsafe setting.

WORKING WITH PEOPLE WHO HAVE RECENTLY EXPERIENCED A TRAUMATIZING EVENT

In working with people who had recently experienced traumatic events, Shapiro (2001) noticed that the client was often able to give a sequential account of the events but that the information associated with various aspects of the memory was not fully integrated, and the processing of one aspect of a trauma did not generalize to others. In order to address this, Shapiro described an adaptation of the standard protocol that included obtaining a narrative account of the event, targeting and processing the most disturbing aspect of the memory, and then targeting and processing the rest of the narrative in chronological order. To do this, the client is asked to visualize the whole sequence of the event, with his eyes closed, and reprocess it as disturbance arises (Shapiro, 2001, p. 225). This is repeated until the client can visualize the sequence without disturbance, and then visualize the sequence with eyes open, coupled with the positive cognition. The process concludes with a body scan and moves on, as in the standard protocol, to processing any present triggers, and the future templates.

Working in a Situation of Ongoing Conflict

Adaptations of this protocol have been used in situations of ongoing conflict with adults and with children (Shapiro, & Laub, 2008; Silver & Rogers, 2002; Wesson & Gould, 2008; Zaghrout-Hodali, Alissa, & Dodgson, 2008), and there is an EMDR protocol for work in military and disaster areas (Shapiro, 2004). There may be difficulty in working with people affected by recent incidents in a present situation of conflict. It may, for example, be difficult for a person to access a positive cognition and, because of the sense of justice or injustice, it may sometimes also be difficult for the person to access a negative cognition. In a setting of ongoing conflict, a person is likely to need to be guarded and strong.

People confronted with trauma respond in different ways. One way may be through dissociation. There are specific ways of addressing the spectrum of dissociation. These include techniques for bringing a person's focus "back into the room," such as those described by Knipe (2008) to enhance present orientation, through to working with people with dissociative identity disorder, such as the approaches described by Forgash & Knipe (2008), Paterson (2008), and Paulsen (2008), which integrate ego state work (Watkins & Watkins, 1979, 1997) with EMDR. It is beyond the scope of this introductory chapter to describe these approaches in detail or to introduce to the clinician sufficient skills to work with complex cases. Forgash and Copely (2008) give a detailed account of such approaches and, as has been done here, they strongly advise appropriate training and clinical supervision.

CONCLUSION

In this chapter, I have tried to describe the EMDR psychotherapy approach and introduce you to some of the issues involved. A number of times, I have noted that this chapter is not a substitute for Shapiro's comprehensive text, nor is it a substitute for training and supervision. EMDR is an integrative psychotherapy approach that will draw on the existing skills and experience of the clinician. As the clinician becomes familiar with the approach, there will be a fluidity, as there can be with language, and the clinician will find ways of working with her experience and with the protocols to help people who have encountered trauma reprocess the stored information associated with that trauma, and reprocess their sense of self. As one client said:

I look back, and EMDR transformed me. I had an initial fear but the treatment itself was quite relaxing and very interesting. It was a treatment I had no knowledge of but after the first session, I was sold on it. It's been brilliant. Quite relaxing, a comforting way of dealing with the issues that I had. The anxiety was put by as soon as the treatment started. I can't sing its praises enough. It's been fantastic for me—and with someone [clinician] in a comfortable situation and seeing the light at the end of the tunnel and putting bits and pieces together, I feel more positive, more me, and able to go back to work and deal with a similar situation. I can talk to people about what happened.

And another client wrote:

I had never heard of EMDR treatment before. Although the process was fully explained, I was naturally apprehensive and in some ways sceptical [sic.] about its success. However, once the treatment started, I couldn't believe its effectiveness. With my eyes following my consultant's movements, I quickly found myself back at the incident that caused me to receive treatment in the first place. This helped as I was able to process disturbing thoughts in my time, allowing my mind to literally wander where it wanted to. I found taking a deep breath after each [set of eye] movements in EMDR helped enormously, allowing me to focus my mind.

With each session of the treatment, I started to experience the feeling of distance from the incident, almost like I was walking away from it. At one time, I can remember it was like looking at the scene from above. The incident no longer felt real. The constant churning of the stomach that I had suffered many times had gone.

These feelings were in stark contrast to when I first saw my consultant for treatment: negative thoughts, flashbacks, nightmares, and the feeling that something terrible was about to happen to those closest to me was an everyday occurrence. I was in a state of heightened anxiety and felt terrible.

After completing various questionnaires, my consultant diagnosed post-traumatic stress disorder. I remember feeling very worried about my situation and how I would ever get out of it.

EMDR [the reprocessing phases] was then used in a number of subsequent sessions and I responded well. I credit the treatment as a big influence in my recovery. However, why it has worked so well for me is not just down to EMDR itself. Being comfortable with my consultant was a huge overriding factor. With EMDR, I found at times you just didn't know where your mind would take you. Having someone there who you are fully comfortable with and can trust allows you the safety net to process those thoughts further.

Paul said that EMDR had enabled him to have a sense of himself as a man. For Rami, EMDR brought a sense of safety and well-being, and hope for the future. Rose said, "Without EMDR, I don't think I would be here now." But that is another story, for another time.

APPENDIX

Summary of Assessment, Desensitization, Installation, Body Scan, and Closure

ASSESSMENT

1. Incident

The clinician agrees with the client in deciding what will be the focus of the work in this session.

> What we will be doing is a simple check on what you are experiencing, I need to know from you what is going on, with feedback that is as clear as possible. Sometimes things will change and sometimes they won't. I'll ask you how you feel from 0 to 10; sometimes it will change and sometimes it won't. I may ask if something else comes up; sometimes it will and sometimes it won't. There are no "supposed to's" in this process. So just give as accurate a feedback as you can as to what is happening, without judging whether it should be happening or not. Let whatever happens happen. We'll do the eye movements (taps, or tones) for a while, and then we'll talk about it.

The client is then reminded of the stop signal and the safe or special place.

> If at any time you feel you have to stop, raise your hand.

The clinician also checks with the client the speed and distance or intensity of the bilateral stimulation.

> Is this a comfortable distance (volume, pressure) and speed?

2. Image

This is a still "snapshot" of the worst part of the incident. Sometimes it will be a sensory experience.

> What picture represents the worst part of the incident (memory or experience)?

3. Negative Cognition

This is a negative "I" statement, in the present tense—a presently held, negative, self-referencing belief.

What words go best with that picture that express a negative belief about yourself *now?*

4. Positive Cognition

This is an "I" statement, in the present tense, in the same domain as the negative cognition but 180° away from it. It is a positive statement and does not contain negatives, such as "I'm not a bad person."

When you bring up that picture, (incident, experience), what would you like to believe about yourself *now?*

5. Validity of Cognition (VoC)

The VoC scale is an indicator of the degree to which a person believes in the validity of a positive cognition *now.*

When you think of that picture (incident or experience), how true do those words (repeat the Positive Cognition—in the first person, present tense) *feel* to you *now* on a scale of 1 to 7, where 1 feels completely false and 7 feels completely true?
1 2 3 4 5 6 7

6. Emotion

The client is asked about the emotions he or she is feeling now.

When you bring up that picture (incident or experience), and those words (repeat the negative cognition—in the first person, present tense), what emotion(s) do you feel *now?*

7. Subjective Units of Disturbance (SUDs)

The SUD scale is an indicator of the degree to which a person feels disturbed *now,* in this case in relation to the target experience, the image and the negative cognition.

On a scale of 0 to 10, where 0 is no disturbance or neutral and 10 is the highest disturbance you can imagine, how disturbing does it *feel* to you *now?*
0 1 2 3 4 5 6 7 8 9 10

8. Bodily sensation

This question is self-explanatory.

Where do you feel it (the disturbance) in your body?

DESENSITIZATION

The Desensitization phase begins with focusing on the image, negative cognition, emotions, and body sensations:

I'd like you to bring up that image, those negative words (repeat the negative cognition—first person, present tense), notice where you are feeling the disturbance in your body, and follow my fingers (or tones, or taps).

The bilateral stimulation begins slowly but increases to a speed that is as fast as the client can comfortably tolerate. The clinician will occasionally make quiet affirming comments, such as:

That's it. . . . Good. . . .

As the client is processing, especially with intense emotion, it can be helpful to make the occasional quiet comment such as:

You're doing fine. . . . It's old stuff. . . . Just notice. . . .

It can also be helpful to use the train or bus metaphor:

It's like the scenery going past.

After a set of bilateral stimulation, the client is invited to:

Take a breath. Let go.

And is then asked:

What's there for you *now?* or What do you notice *now?*

If the client reports movement or change, the clinician continues with another set of bilateral stimulation, starting with the words:

Go with that. . . .

This process continues until the client's report is positive or neutral or until the client repeats the same response for two or three consecutive sets of bilateral stimulation. In both cases, return to the original target and ask the client:

When you go back to the original memory or experience (name the target), what do you get *now?*

When the client reports something, say:

Go with that.

and do another set of bilateral stimulation. Continue with the process as above. When the client reports no change, ask the client:

When you bring up that experience, on a scale of 0 to 10, where 0 is no disturbance or neutral and 10 is the highest disturbance you can imagine, how disturbing does it *feel* to you *now?*
0 1 2 3 4 5 6 7 8 9 10

If the SUD is 0, move on to the Installation phase. If the SUD is 1 or greater, continue the processing and repeat the above processes.

Sometimes the SUD will stay at 1. If this is so, ask:

Where do you feel that "1" in your body?

and follow the response with a set of bilateral stimulation.

It can be tempting to accept an SUD of 1 and think that it is "good enough." However, often the "1" will represent some residual material and two or three sets of bilateral stimulation will enable the client to reprocess this. Occasionally, the client will have reasons for the SUD's staying at 1, such as out of respect that someone died. Shapiro described this as being "ecologically sound" (Shapiro, 2008, p. 126). If this is so, move to the Installation phase.

INSTALLATION

The Installation phase links the positive cognition with the target experience and uses bilateral stimulation to help strengthen the association. It also links the past and present into the future. Sometimes during the bilateral stimulation, the client will access more material, in which case the Desensitization phase continues before returning to the Installation phase. The Installation phase is introduced by the client's bringing to mind the original memory, experience, or picture, and the clinician's asking:

Do the words (repeat the positive cognition—an "I" statement in the present tense) still fit, or is there another positive statement you feel would be more suitable?

The client responds. If the positive cognition still fits, the clinician continues with that. If another positive cognition has a better fit for the client, then that replaces the original PC. Where, in some cases, there has not been a positive cognition identified in the Assessment phase, the clinician will ask for one now.

When you bring that picture to mind, what would you like to believe about yourself *now*?

With the original positive cognition confirmed, or a new positive cognition identified, the clinician asks for a VoC:

Think about the original incident and those words (repeat the selected positive cognition), from 1, completely false, to 7, completely true; how true do they feel?
1   2   3   4   5   6   7
Hold them together.

The clinician leads the client in a set of bilateral stimulation, and then asks:

On a scale of 1 to 7, how true do those words (repeat the positive cognition) *feel* to you *now* when you think of the original incident?

The clinician continues repeating this process as long as the VoC continues to increase or the positive material strengthens. When the VoC reaches 7, repeat the process until the material no longer strengthens (often two or three sets), and then move to the body scan.

If the client continues to report a VoC of 6 or less, check the appropriateness of the positive cognition, or whether there is a blocking belief that prevents it from becoming a "7." If there is a blocking belief, then this will be reprocessed by returning to the Desensitization phase, using the blocking belief as a staring point. Sometimes, as with the SUD at 1, there may be ecologically sound reasons why a VoC does not reach 7, in which case the clinician will move to the body scan.

BODY SCAN

The Body Scan is the third of the reprocessing phases and checks out whether there is residual disturbance that the client is experiencing in her body sensations. The clinician asks:

> Close your eyes and keep in mind the original memory and the words, (repeat the selected positive cognition). Then bring your attention to the different parts of your body, staring with your head and working downwards. Any place you find any tension, tightness, or unusual sensation, tell me.

If any sensation is reported, do a set of bilateral stimulation. If the sensation is positive, the bilateral stimulation will help to strengthen it. If the sensation is one of discomfort, the clinician continues to reprocess it using the bilateral stimulation until the discomfort subsides.

CLOSURE

Reprocessing sessions may be complete or incomplete. A complete session will end with an SUD of 0 and a VoC of 7 and have a clear body scan. An incomplete session is one in which the material has not yet reprocessed to an adaptive resolution. The SUD will be above 0 and the VoC below 7, and the client will still feel some disturbance. The body scan may not have been completed or if there has been a body scan, there is still unprocessed disturbance.

In closing a completed reprocessing session, the clinician will have told the client that it is time to close the session and will have encouraged the client in what he has done:

> You have done some good work today. How are you feeling?

The clinician will help the client debrief the experience, for example, by asking:

> What new positive thoughts or insights have you experienced?

> or

> What do you feel you have gained from today?

The clinician may also share briefly with the client his own observations of what has happened during the session. This is not a time for lengthy discussion about the session, partly because processing is likely to continue after the session, and the clinician will still want to avoid impeding that. There will be more time for reflection at the beginning of the next session, during the reevaluation phase. In closing the session, the clinician may say:

> The processing we have done today may continue after the session. You may or may not notice new insights, thoughts, memories, or dreams. If you do, just notice

what you are experiencing. Take a snapshot of it (what you are seeing feeling, thinking, and the trigger), and keep a log (on the TICES grid). Remember to use the relaxation technique daily. We can work on this new material next time. If you feel it necessary, call me (my office).

In an incomplete Desensitization session, the clinician will not go through the Installation phase or the body scan because these can lead to new material that needs to be processed. The clinician will be helping the client to feel safe and to draw from the experience of the session and leave with a sense of well-being. The clinician will tell the client it is time to close the session:

We are almost out of time, and we will need to stop soon.

The clinician will give encouragement and support, such as:

You have done some very good work and I appreciate the effort that you have made. How are you feeling?

The clinician will also check to see whether it is necessary to use a containment exercise, such as the light stream, safe place, or other resource. If so, the clinician will go through this with the client.
In closing the session, the clinician might review with the client:

What do you feel you have learned today?

And follow with the debriefing paragraph on "The processing we have done today. . . . "
The closure phase closes the session. Afterward, the clinician may spend some time reflecting on the session and planning the next one, looking through the targeting sequence and the treatment plan. In a sense, this is the beginning of the reevaluation phase that will open the following consultation.
In the closing session of EMDR psychotherapy, the clinician and client will review the issues that have been addressed through the course of therapy, including targets that have been reprocessed, and will complete any Assessment and outcome measures.

ACKNOWLEDGMENTS

Appreciation is expressed to the following for their support in the preparation of this chapter: Clare Dodgson; Clio Berry; Sussex Partnership NHS Foundation Trust; the clients who have taught me much of what I have written here; and the EMDR Clinical Governance Group, including Brenda Roberts, Maeve Crowley, Teresa McIntyre, and Shawn Katz.
This chapter draws extensively on the work of Dr. Francine Shapiro and colleagues at the EMDR Institute. A detailed account of the EMDR approach to psychotherapy is included in Dr. Shapiro's seminal book: *Eye Movement Desensitization and Reprocessing: Basic Principles, Protocols, and Procedures* (Shapiro, 2001). This chapter is in no sense a substitute for the more detailed and

extensive work in Shapiro's book. No reading, however, can take the place of clinical training and supervised practice. Readers of the present chapter are strongly advised to take up the accredited basic training in EMDR and to work with an accredited EMDR consultant in supervising their practice.

REFERENCES

Allers, R., & Minkoff, R. (1994). *The lion king.* Burbank, CA: Walt Disney Feature Animation.

American Psychiatric Association. (1980). *Diagnostic and statistical manual of mental disorders* (3rd ed.). Washington, DC: American Psychiatric Press.

American Psychiatric Association. (2000). *Diagnostic and statistical manual of mental disorders* (4th ed., rev.). Washington, DC: American Psychiatric Press.

Bauman, W., & Melnyk, W. T. (1994, March). A comparison of eye movements and finger tapping in the treatment of test anxiety. *Journal of Behaviour Therapy and Experimental Psychiatry, 25*(1), 29–33. Abstract retrieved May 21, 2008, from www.ncbi.nlm.nih.gov/pubmed/7962578.

Bernstein, E. M., & Putnam, F. W. (1986). Development, reliability, and validity of a dissociation scale. *Journal of Nervous and Mental Disease, 174,* 727–735.

Blake, D. D., Weathers, F. W., Nagy, L. M., Kaloupek, D. G., Gusman, F. D., Charney, D. S., et al. (1995). The development of a clinician-administered PTSD scale. *Journal of Traumatic Stress, 8,* 75–90.

Boudewyns, P. A., & Hyer, L. A. (1996). Eye movement desensitization and reprocessing (EMDR) as treatment for posttraumatic stress disorder (PTSD). *Clinical Psychology and Psychotherapy, 3,* 185–195.

Brewin, C. R., Dalgleish, T., & Joseph, S. (1996). A dual representational theory of post-traumatic stress disorder. *Psychological Review, 103,* 670–686.

Briere, J. (1995). *Trauma Symptom Inventory.* Odessa, FL: Psychological Assessment Resources.

Briere, J. (1996). *Trauma Symptom Inventory for Children.* Odessa, FL: Psychological Assessment Resources.

Briere, J. (2001). *Detailed Assessment of Posttraumatic Stress (DAPS).* Odessa, FL: Psychological Assessment Resources.

Carlson, E. B., & Putnam, F. W. (1993). An update on the Dissociative Experiences Scale. *Dissociation, 6*(1), 16–27.

Christman, S. D., Garvey, K. J., Propper, R. E., & Phaneuf, K. A. (2003). Bilateral eye movements enhance the retrieval of episodic memories. *Neuropsychology, 17*(2), 229–231.

Davidson, P. R., & Parker, K. C. H. (2001, April). Eye movement desensitization and reprocessing (EMDR): A meta-analysis. *Journal of Consulting and Clinical Psychology, 69*(2), 305–316.

de Jongh, A., & Broeke, E. (2007). Treatment of specific phobias with EMDR: Conceptualization and strategies for the selection of appropriate memories. *Journal of EMDR Practice and Research, 1*(1), 56–66.

Dodgson, P. W. (2007a). EMDR: An integrative psychotherapy approach. *Impuls: tidsskrift for psykologi*, 61, 3, 42–55.

Dodgson, P. W. (2007b, June 16). *Shame: The adaptive information processing model and introduction of the "protocol interweave" in EMDR with victims of torture, rape and organised violence.* Paper presented at the 8th EMDR European Conference of EMDR Europe, Paris.

Dworkin, M. (2005). *EMDR and the relational imperative: The therapeutic relationship in EMDR treatment.* New York: Routledge.

Edmond, T., Rubin, A., & Wambach, K. G. (1999). The effectiveness of EMDR with adult female survivors of childhood sexual abuse. *Social Work Research*, 23(2), 103–116.

First, M. B., Spitzer, R. L, Gibbon, M., & Williams, J. B. W. (1997). *Structured Clinical Interview for DSM-IV Axis I Disorders, Clinician Version (SCID-CV).* Washington, DC: American Psychiatric Press.

Foley, T., & Spates, C. R. (1995, December). Eye movement desensitization of public-speaking anxiety: A partial dismantling. [Electronic version]. *Journal of Behaviour Therapy and Experimental Psychiatry*, 26(4), 321–329.

Forgash, C. (2005, May). Deepening EMDR treatment effects across the diagnostic spectrum: Integrating EMDR and ego state work. Two-day workshop presentation. New York: Advanced Educational Productions.

Forgash, C., & Copeley, M. (2007). *Healing the heart of trauma and dissociation with EMDR.* New York: Springer.

Forgash, C., & Knipe, J. (2008). Integrating EMDR and ego state treatment for clients with trauma disorders. In C. Forgash & M. Copeley (Eds.), *Healing the heart of trauma and dissociation with EMDR* (pp. 1–59). New York: Springer.

Freud, S. (1949). *The Ego and the id.* (J. Rivere, Trans.). London: Hogarth Press.

Georgiades, N. J., & Phillimore, L. (1975). The myth of the hero innovator and alternative strategies for organisational change. In C. C. Kiernan & W. F. P. Woodford (Eds.), *Behaviour modification with the severely retarded* (pp. 313–319). Amsterdam: Associated Scientific Publishers.

Gold, S. D., Marx, B. P., Soler-Baillo, J. M., & Sloan, D. M. (2004). Is life stress more stressful than traumatic stress? *Journal of Anxiety Disorders*, 19(6), 687–698.

Herman, J. (1992). Complex PTSD: A syndrome in survivors of prolonged and repeated trauma. *Journal of Traumatic Stress*, 5(3), 377–391.

Hopenwasser, K. (2008). Being in rhythm: Dissociative attunement in therapeutic process. *Journal of Trauma and Dissociation*, 9(3), 349–367.

Horowitz, M., Wilner, M., & Alvarez, W. (1979). Impact of Event scale: A measure of subjective stress. *Psychosomatic Medicine*, 41, 209–218.

Jaberghaderi, N., Greenwald, R., Rubin, A., Dolatabadim, S., & Zand, S. O. (2004). A comparison of CBT and EMDR for sexually abused Iranian girls. [Electronic version]. *Clinical Psychology and Psychotherapy*, 11(5), 358–368.

Kluft, R. P. (1985). The natural history of multiple personality disorder. In R. P. Kluft (Ed.), *The childhood antecedents of multiple personality* (pp. 198–238). Washington, DC: American Psychiatric Press.

Kluft, R. P. (1987). First-rank symptoms as a diagnostic clue to multiple personality disorder. *American Journal of Psychiatry, 144*, 293–298.

Knipe, J. (2008). Loving eyes: Procedures to therapeutically reverse dissociative processes while preserving emotional safety. In C. Forgash & M. Copeley (Eds.), *Healing the heart of trauma and dissociation with EMDR* (pp. 181–225). New York: Springer.

Korn, D. L., & Leeds, A. M. (2002). Preliminary evidence of efficacy for EMDR resource development and installation in the stabilization phase of treatment of complex posttraumatic stress disorder. *Journal of Clinical Psychology, 58*(2), 1465–1487.

Lee, C. W., Taylor, G., & Drummond, P. D. (2006). The active ingredient of EMDR: Is it traditional exposure or dual attention? *Clinical Psychology and Psychotherapy, 13*(2), 97–107.

Leeds, A. M. (1998). Lifting the burden of shame: Using EMDR resource installation to resolve a therapeutic impasse. In P. Manfield (Ed.), *Extending EMDR: A casebook of innovative applications* (pp. 256–281). New York: Norton.

Leeds, A. M., & Shapiro, F. (2000). EMDR and resource installation: Principles and procedures for enhancing current functioning and resolving traumatic experiences. In J. Carlson & L. Sperry (Eds.), *Brief therapy strategies with individuals and couples* (pp. 469–534). Phoenix, AZ: Zeig, Tucker, Theison.

Lendl, J., & Foster, S. (2003). *EMDR "Performance Enhancement" for the workplace: A practitioners' manual* (2nd ed.). San Jose, CA: Performance Enhancement Unlimited.

Lewis, C. S. (1950). *The lion, the witch and the wardrobe*. New York: Macmillan.

Lindner, R. (1954). *The fifty-minute hour*. New York: Bantam Books.

Lipke, H., (2000). *EMDR and psychotherapy integration: Theoretical and clinical suggestions with focus on traumatic stress*. Boca Raton, FL: CRC Press.

Lowenstein, R. J. (1991). An office mental status examination for complex chronic dissociative symptoms and multiple personality disorder. *Psychiatric Clinics of North America, 14*(3), 567–604.

Luber, M. (2005). *Handbook for EMDR clients*. Hamden, CT: EMDR HAP.

Luxenberg, T., Spinazzola, J., Hidalgo, J., Hunt, C., & van der Kolk, B. (2001). Complex trauma and disorders of extreme stress (DESNOS) diagnosis, part two: Treatment. *Directions in Psychiatry, 21*(26), 395–415.

Marcus, S., Marquis, P., & Sakai, C. (1997). Controlled study of treatment of PTSD using EMDR in an HMO setting. *Psychotherapy, 34*, 307–315.

Maxfield, L. (2007). Current status and future directions for EMDR research. [Electronic version]. *Journal of EMDR Practice and Research, 1*(1), 6–14.

Maxfield, L., & Hyer, L. A. (2002). The relationship between efficacy and methodology in studies investigating EMDR treatment of PTSD. *Journal of Clinical Psychology, 58*, 23–41.

Miyamoto, S. (1981). *Donkey kong*. Kyoto, Japan: Nintendo.

Mol, S. S. L., Arntz, A., Metsemakers, J. F. M., Dinant, G.-J., Vilters-van Montfort, P. A. P., & Knottnerus, J. A. (2005). Symptoms of post-traumatic stress disorder after non-traumatic events: Evidence from an open population study. *British Journal of Psychology, 18*, 464–499.

Moulton Marston, W. (1941, December). *All star comics*, 1(8). New York: DC Comics (All-American Publications).

National Institute for Clinical Excellence. (2005). *Post-traumatic stress disorder: The management of PTSD in adults and children in primary and secondary care*. London and Leicester, UK: Royal College of Psychiatrists and British Psychological Society.

Paterson, M. C. (2008). Changing cognitive schemas through EMDR and ego state therapy. In C. Forgash & M. Copeley (Eds.), *Healing the heart of trauma and dissociation with EMDR* (pp. 121–139). New York: Springer.

Paulsen, S. (2008). Treating dissociative identity disorder with EMDR, ego state therapy, and adjunct approaches. In C. Forgash & M. Copeley (Eds.), *Healing the heart of trauma and dissociation with EMDR* (pp. 141–179). New York: Springer.

Pelcovitz, D., van der Kolk, B. A., Roth, S., Mandel, F., Kaplan, S., & Resick, P. (1997, January). Development of a criteria set and a structured interview for disorders of extreme stress (SIDES). [Electronic version]. *Journal of Traumatic Stress* 10(1), 3–16.

Piaget, J. (1952). *The origins of intelligence in children*. (M. Cook, Trans.). New York: International Universities Press. (Original work published 1936.).

Popky, A. J. (2005). DeTUR, an urge reduction protocol for addictions and dysfunctional behaviours. In R. Shapiro (Ed.), *EMDR solutions: Pathways to healing* (pp. 167–188). New York: Norton.

Puk, G. (1999). Clinical signs of dissociative disorders. In F. Shapiro (Ed.), *EMDR Institute manual*. Pacific Grove, CA: EMDR Institute.

Putnam, F. W. (1989). *Diagnosis and treatment of multiple personality disorder*. New York: Guilford Press.

Putnam, F. W., Guroff, J. J., Silberman, E. K., Barban, L., & Post, R. M. (1986). The clinical phenomenology of multiple personality disorder. *Journal of Clinical Psychiatry*, 47, 285–293.

Ricci, R. J., Clayton, C. A., & Shapiro, F. (2006). Some effects of EMDR treatment with previously abused child molesters: Theoretical reviews and preliminary findings. [Electronic version]. *Journal of Forensic Psychiatry and Psychology*, 17(4), 538–562.

Rogers, S., Silver, S. M., Goss, J., Obenchain, J., Willis, A., & Whitney, R. L. (1999). A single session, group study of exposure and eye movement desensitization and reprocessing in treating posttraumatic stress disorder among Vietnam war veterans: Preliminary data. *Journal of Anxiety Disorders*, 13(1-2), 119–130.

Rogers, S., & Silver, S. M. (2002). Is EMDR an exposure therapy? A review of trauma protocols. *Journal of Clinical Psychology*, 58(1), 43–59.

Ross, C. A., Miller, S. D., Reagor, P., Bjornson, L., Fraser, G. A., & Anderson, G. (1990). Schneiderian symptoms in multiple personality disorder and schizophrenia. *Comprehensive Psychiatry*, 31, 111–118.

Rothbaum, B. O. (1997). A controlled study of eye movement desensitization and reprocessing in the treatment of posttraumatic stress disordered sexual assault victims. [Electronic version]. *Bulletin of the Menninger Clinic*, 61(3), 317–334.

Ryle, A. (1975). *Frames and cages: The repertory grid approach to human understanding*. Brighton, UK: Sussex University Press.

Scheck, M. M., Schaeffer, J. A., & Gillette, C. (1998). Brief psychological intervention with traumatized young women: The efficacy of eye movement desensitization and reprocessing. *Journal of Traumatic Stress, 11*(1), 25–44.

Schneider, J., Hofmann, A., Rost, C., & Shapiro, F. (2007). EMDR and phantom limb pain: Theoretical implications, case study, and treatment guidelines. *Journal of EMDR Practice and Research, 1*(1), 31–45.

Shapiro, E., & Laub, B. (2008). Early EMDR intervention (EEI): A summary, a theoretical model, and the recent traumatic episode protocol (R-TEP). *Journal of EMDR Practice and Research, 2*(2), 79–96.

Shapiro, F. (1989a). Efficacy of the eye movement desensitization procedure in the treatment of traumatic memories. *Journal of Traumatic Stress Studies, 2,* 199–233.

Shapiro, F. (1989b). Eye movement desensitization: a new treatment for post traumatic stress disorder. *Journal of Behaviour Therapy and Experimental Psychiatry, 3,* 211–217.

Shapiro, F. (1991). Eye movement desensitization and reprocessing procedure. From EMD to EMDR: A new treatment model for anxiety and related traumata. *Behaviour Therapist, 14,* 133–135.

Shapiro, F. (1994). Alternative stimuli in the use of EMD(R). *Journal of Behavior Therapy and Experimental Psychiatry, 25*(1), 89–91.

Shapiro, F. (1995). *Eye movement desensitization and reprocessing: Basic principles, protocols and procedures* (1st ed.). New York: Guilford Press.

Shapiro, F. (1999). Eye movement desensitization and reprocessing (EMDR) and the anxiety disorders: Clinical and research implications of an integrated psychotherapy treatment. *Journal of Anxiety Disorders, 13,* 35–67.

Shapiro, F. (2001). *Eye movement desensitization and reprocessing: Basic principles, protocols and procedures* (2nd ed.). New York: Guilford Press.

Shapiro, F. (Ed.). (2002a). *EMDR as an integrative psychotherapy approach: Experts of divers orientations explore the paradigm prism.* Washington, DC: American Psychological Press.

Shapiro, F. (2002b). EMDR 12 years after its introduction: Past and future research. *Journal of Clinical Psychology, 58*(1), 1–22.

Shapiro, F. (2004). *Military and post-disaster field manual.* Hamden, CT: EMDR Humanitarian Assistance Program.

Shapiro, F. (2006). *New notes on adaptive information processing with case formulation principles, forms, scripts, and worksheets.* Hamden, CT: EMDR Humanitarian Assistance Programs.

Shapiro, F. (2007). EMDR, adaptive information processing, and case conceptualization. *Journal of EMDR Practice and Research, 1*(2), 68–87.

Siegel, D. J. (1999). *The developing mind: Toward a neurobiology of interpersonal experience.* New York: Guilford Press.

Silver, S. M., & Rogers, S. (2002). *Light in the heart of darkness: EMDR and the treatment of war and terrorism survivors.* New York: Norton.

Smyth, N. J., Rogers, S., & Maxfield, L. (2004, September 10–12). *What about eye movements? A research update for EMDR practitioners.* Paper presented at the EMDR International Conference, Montreal, Canada.

Spector, J. (2007). Eye movement desensitisation and reprocessing (EMDR). In C. Freeman & M. Power (Eds.), *Handbook of evidence-based psychotherapies: A guide for research and practice*. London: Wiley.

Squire, L. R. (1994). Declarative and nondeclarative memory: Multiple brain systems supporting learning and memory. In D. L. Schachter & E. Tulving (Eds.), *Memory systems* (pp. 203–232). Cambridge, MA: MIT Press.

Stickgold, R. (2002). EMDR: A putative neurobiological mechanism of action. *Journal of Clinical Psychology, 58*(1), 61–76.

Van der Kolk, B. A. (1987). *Psychological trauma*. Washington, DC: American Psychiatric Press.

van der Kolk, B. A. (1996). Trauma and memory. In B. A. van der Kolk, A. C. McFarlane, & L. Weisaeth (Eds.), *Traumatic stress: The effects of overwhelming experience on mind, body and society* (pp. 279–302). New York: Guilford Press.

van der Kolk, B. A. (1997). The psychobiology of posttraumatic stress disorder. In J. Panksepp (Ed.), *Textbook of Biological Psychiatry* (pp. 319–344). Hoboken, NJ: Wiley-Liss, Inc.

van der Kolk, B. A., Spinazzola, J., Blaustein, M. E., Hopper, J. W., Hopper, E. K., Korn, D. L., et al. (2007). A randomized clinical trial of eye movement desensitization and reprocessing (EMDR), fluoxetine, and pill placebo in the treatment of posttraumatic stress disorder: Treatment effects and long-term maintenance. *Journal of Clinical Psychiatry, 68*(1), 37–46.

Van Etten, M. L., & Taylor, S. (1998). Comparative efficacy of treatments for posttraumatic stress disorder: A meta-analysis. *Clinical Psychology & Psychotherapy, 5* (3), 126–144.

Vogelmann-Sine, V., Sine, F., Smyth, N. J., & Popky, A. J. (2004). *EMDR chemical dependency treatment manual*. Hamden, CT: EMDR HAP.

Wachtel, P. L. (1977). *Psychoanalysis and behavior therapy*. New York: Basic Books.

Watkins, J. G. (1971). The affect bridge: A hypnoanalytic technique. *International Journal of Clinical and Experimental Hypnosis, 19*(1), 21–27.

Watkins, J. G, & Watkins, H. H. (1979). The theory and practice of ego state therapy. In H. Grayson (Ed.), *Short-term approaches to psychotherapy* (pp. 176–220). New York: Human Sciences Press.

Watkins, J. G, & Watkins, H. H. (1997). *Ego states: Theory and therapy*. New York: Norton.

Weiss, D., & Marmar, C. R. (1997). The Impact of Event Scale-Revised. In J. Wilson & T. Keane (Eds.), *Assessing psychological trauma and PTSD*. New York: Guilford Press.

Wesson, M., & Gould, M. (2008). *Intervening early with EMDR on military operations*. Manuscript submitted for publication.

Wilensky, M. (2006). Eye movement desensitization and reprocessing (EMDR) as a treatment for phantom limb pain. *Journal of Brief Therapy, 5*(1), 31–44.

Wilson, S. A., Becker, L. A., & Tinker, R. H. (1995, December). Eye movement desensitization and reprocessing (EMDR) treatment for psychologically traumatized individuals. *Journal of Consulting and Clinical Psychology, 63*(6), 928–937.

Wolpe, J. (1969). *The practice of behavior therapy* (1st ed.) New York: Pergamon Press.

World Health Organization. (1993). *International classification of diseases and related health problems* (10th ed.). Geneva: Author.

Young, J. E., Zangwill, W. M., & Behary, W. E. (2002). Combining EMDR and schema-focused therapy: The whole may be greater than the sum of the parts. In F. Shapiro (Ed.), *EMDR as an integrative psychotherapy approach: Experts of diverse orientations explore the paradigm prism* (pp. 181–209). Washington, DC: American Psychological Press.

Zaghrout-Hodali, M., Alissa, F., & Dodgson, P. W. (2008). Building resilience and dismantling fear: EMDR group protocol with children in an area of ongoing trauma. *Journal of EMDR Practice and Research*, 2(2), 106–113.

Zangwill, W. M. (2005). *Floatback technique*. Retrieved June 8, 2008, from www.emdrandtraining.com/FloatBack.doc.

ADDITIONAL RESOURCES

EMDR WEB SITES

EMDR Association United Kingdom and Ireland: www.emdrassociation.org.uk
EMDR Europe: www.emdr-europe.org
EMDR Humanitarian Assistance Program (HAP): www.emdrhap.org
EMDR Institute: www.emdr.com
EMDR International Association: www.emdria.org
EMDR Network: www.emdrnetwork.org/index.html
EMDR and Training: http://emdrandtraining.com
Neurotek Corporation: http://neurotekcorp.com/index.htm
PTSD: www.ncptsd.va.gov

SOURCES WHOSE GUIDELINES RECOMMEND EMDR AS EFFICACIOUS IN THE TREATMENT OF PTSD

American Psychiatric Association. (2004). *Practice guideline for the treatment of patients with acute stress disorder and posttraumatic stress disorder*. Arlington, VA: American Psychiatric Association Practice Guidelines.

American Psychological Association: Clinical Division Taskforce. Chambless, D. L., Baker, M. J., Baucom, D. H., Beutler, L. E., Calhoun, K. S., Crits-Christoph, P., et al. (1998). Update on empirically validated therapies. *Clinical Psychologist*, 51, 3–16.

Australian Centre for Posttraumatic Mental Health. (2007). *Australian guidelines for the treatment of adults with posttraumatic stress disorder: ASD and PTSD treatment guidelines*. Melbourne, Victoria: ACPHM.

Bleich, A., Kotler, M., Kutz, I. & Shalev, A. (2002). *Guidelines for the assessment and professional intervention with terror victims in the hospital and in the community*. Jerusalem: A position paper of the (Israeli) National Council for Mental Health.

Chemtob, C. M., Tolin, D. F., van der Kolk, B. A., & Pitman, R. K. (2000). *Eye movement desensitization and reprocessing*. In E. B. Foa, T. M. Keane, & M. J. Friedman (Eds.), *Effective treatment for PTSD: Practice guidelines form the International Society for Traumatic Stress Studies* (pp. 139–155, 333–335). New York: Guilford Press.

CREST. (2003). *The management of post-traumatic stress disorder in adults*. Belfast: Clinical Resource Efficiency and Support Team, Department of Health, Social Services and Public Safety.

Department of Veterans Affairs and Department of Defense. (2004). *Clinical practice guideline for the management of post-traumatic stress*. Washington, DC: VA/DD.

Dutch National Steering Committee Guidelines Mental Health Care. (2003). *Multi-disciplinary guideline anxiety disorders*. Utrecht, Netherlands: Quality Institute Health Care CBO/Trimbos Institute.

INSERM. (2004). *Psychotherapy: An evaluation of three approaches*. Paris: French National Institute of Health and Medical Research.

National Institute for Clinical Excellence. (2005). *Post-traumatic stress disorder: The management of PTSD in adults and children in primary and secondary care*. London and Leicester: Royal College of Psychiatrists and British Psychological Society.

Sjöblom, P. O., Andréewitch, S., Bejerot, S., Mörtberg, E., Brinck, U., Ruck, C., & Körlin, D. (2003). *Regional treatment recommendation for anxiety disorders*. Stockholm: Medical Program Committee/Stockholm City Council.

CHAPTER 6

Healing the Origins of Trauma: An Introduction to EMDR in Psychotherapy with Children and Adolescents

ROBBIE ADLER-TAPIA AND CAROLYN SETTLE

INTRODUCTION

What if the brain had a similar mechanism for healing psychological injuries as the body does, just like a finger can heal a cut? Imagine tapping into that healing process in the brain and helping a child who witnessed her brother accidentally killed by a school bus, who then developed a school phobia, be able to return to school and eliminate her depression. What if you could help a foster child with a history of severe and chronic abuse, reduce his disruptive symptoms within a 9-month period so that he could stabilize and be adopted? Eye movement desensitization and reprocessing (EMDR) can be used in psychotherapy to help children heal from stressful experiences of both traumatic and developmental origins. And, while EMDR is not a magic wand, it is remarkable in its efficiency in reducing or eliminating significant mental health symptoms and healing the origins of trauma.

This chapter is written for clinicians who have had little or no exposure to the EMDR treatment methodology or for those who may have wondered what it is and how it works. The goal of this chapter is to summarize the use of EMDR with children with case presentations woven through the steps of the EMDR protocol. As a potential paradigm shift for child and adolescent therapists who have been trained in child development and play therapy, this chapter will not only explain why EMDR with children and adolescents makes sense, but why EMDR is the treatment of choice for many children presenting with symptoms of trauma. The experienced child therapist will also learn how child development, play therapy, and other child-focused therapies can be integrated to overall case conceptualization with the eight phases of the EMDR protocol.

Initially, this chapter provides a brief description of EMDR. While Chapter 5 covered EMDR with adult clients, this chapter will focus on translating the EMDR protocol into child language from a developmentally grounded perspective for use with child clients. Given that focus, this chapter will minimize coverage of generic EMDR content that was already covered in Chapter 5. However, some overlap is inescapable. For example, like Chapter 5, this chapter will address the Adaptive Information Processing (AIP) theory that underlies the eight phases of the EMDR treatment protocol. This chapter also includes a brief theoretical overview of trauma and the impact on neurodevelopment as it guides psychotherapy. With a detailed explanation of the description, purpose, and concepts of each phase of the EMDR protocol, this chapter describes the clinical implications and procedural considerations for effectively using EMDR with children through each phase of the protocol. The chapter concludes with information for clinicians to learn how to get basic training in EMDR and advanced training in using EMDR with children. Integrated throughout this chapter are practical applications for successfully using EMDR in psychotherapy with children in order to heal the origins of trauma.

With this introduction to EMDR, the reader should note that throughout this chapter, the terms *client* and *child* are often interchanged, and any reference to a child includes children and adolescents unless otherwise noted. Finally, the terms *parent* and *caregiver* refer to the child's primary caregiver.

WHAT IS EMDR?

Eye movement desensitization and reprocessing is a psychotherapy treatment methodology created by Francine Shapiro (1989a, 1989b). EMDR is a comprehensive psychotherapy treatment approach based on an eight-phase model that was originally focused on treating trauma in adult clients (Shapiro, 1995, 2001). The EMDR treatment methodology is based on the Adaptive Information Processing Theory proposed by Shapiro as an explanation for why EMDR is an efficacious treatment (Shapiro, 1995, 1997, 2001, 2007). Since Shapiro created EMDR, the protocol has been expanded for use with child and adolescent clients (Adler-Tapia & Settle, 2008; Greenwald, 1999; Lovett, 1999; Tinker & Wilson, 1999).

ADAPTIVE INFORMATION PROCESSING THEORY

Francine Shapiro (2001) developed the Adaptive Information Processing (AIP) model to explain the mechanisms by which EMDR assists clients in moving disturbance to adaptive resolution. EMDR is a comprehensive treatment methodology, while AIP is the comprehensive theoretical approach to psychotherapy. In the AIP model, Shapiro theorized that the human organism is hard-wired to assimilate new information and to move to adaptive resolution when presented with experiences causing high arousal. In the event that the level of arousal is overwhelming and traumatic to the individual, the adaptive information processing progression is thwarted and healthy processing does not continue. Instead, the event is stored with all the emotions, sensations, and perceptions that the individual experienced at the time of the event. When the traumatic event is stored in its original form because the information processing system was not able to process the overwhelming event, that event does not continue processing through to adaptive resolution.

The AIP model (Shapiro, 2001) concludes that emotional, behavioral, and mental health symptoms originate from the maladaptive storage of previous life events. These events are stored in memory networks that link to the present though channels of association that can be triggered at any time manifesting in the client's current symptoms. Memory networks are stored information from the client's life experiences that connected through common links (channels of association) such as the same smell, sound, body sensation, or other sensory relationship where the individual's brain made the association between experiences. In the future, as those stored memory networks are activated, the client experiences disturbances and dysfunction in their current lives. Maladaptively stored memory networks cannot link with up with current resources to be reprocessed through to adaptive resolution, thus causing symptom manifestation. By using EMDR, the therapist assists the client in reprocessing those maladaptively stored events by linking those with positive experiences allowing the client to come to adaptive resolution of the maladaptively stored information and resolution of symptoms.

GETTING STARTED WITH EMDR

Why Would I Want to Be Trained in EMDR?

Many research studies have supported EMDR's effectiveness and efficiency (see this book's Appendix A). New research suggests that EMDR also helps children improve their resiliency (Zaghrout-Hodali, Alissa, & Dodgson, 2008). For a review of the research on EMDR with children, the reader is referred to *EMDR and the Art of Psychotherapy with Children* (Adler-Tapia & Settle, 2008).

In addition, when therapists are frustrated in the lack of progress that they are seeing with child clients, EMDR provides a clinical road map for working with early childhood trauma, including traumas related to attachment that are not always amenable to traditional talk therapy or play therapy. The template of the eight phases of EMDR offer a design for integrating the best practices in child psychotherapy into a comprehensive treatment approach that incorporates the most efficacious interventions of play therapy, art therapy, attachment therapy, and affective and sensory-based treatment techniques. This chapter will offer opportunities for the EMDR-trained therapist to integrate the most efficacious techniques of other treatment protocols into the EMDR eight-phase model. In order to pursue training, the therapist must begin with basic training in EMDR.

WHAT CONSTITUTES BASIC TRAINING IN EMDR?

Individuals interested in basic and advanced trainings in EMDR can explore details at the EMDR International Association (EMDRIA) web site at www.emdria.org. There are trainings provided by commercial trainers, universities, and by the EMDR Institute (www.emdr.org) in the United States, while training is available in more than 80 countries worldwide. The Basic Training in EMDR in the United States has recently been changed to meet the EMDRIA standards. In the United States, EMDRIA requirements for basic training consists of 10 hours of lecture, 10 hours of practicum, and 10 hours of consultation in order to complete basic training. For information on training in EMDR in countries throughout the world, links are available at the EMDRIA web site.

ADVANCED TRAINING IN EMDR WITH CHILDREN

After completing basic training, therapists can participate in advanced trainings in many areas, including specialty trainings in using EMDR with children. Advanced trainings that have EMDRIA approval can be used as continuing education units for certification in EMDR and for other state and national licensing requirements in the United States. It is important to note that specific requirements are unique to each country. This information can also be accessed at the EMDRIA web site.

INTEGRATING EMDR INTO PRACTICE AFTER BASIC TRAINING

In basic training in EMDR, therapists participate in practicum experiences aimed at providing practice for the therapist to return to their offices to begin using EMDR. Integrating EMDR into practice after basic training is best tackled when therapists jump into the application of EMDR in clinical practice soon after training while the information is still fresh. As with any new information or clinical intervention, there is a learning curve and period of time that therapists need to practice before becoming comfortable with the protocol. Using the protocols provided in basic training and explaining to the client that the therapist is using a script for the protocols may be uncomfortable for the therapist, but clients are typically accepting, especially as the therapist demonstrates the benefits of using EMDR.

Because basic training is presented primarily for adult clients, it may be initially challenging to start using EMDR with children. With previous training in treating children, therapists need to begin bridging the language and clinical skills necessary to apply the EMDR protocol to the treatment of children and adolescents. Therapists need to take the mind-set that how you will receive and interpret information within the AIP theory during interactions with children requires attunement to the unique way that each child expresses their individual struggles. This attunement then guides the therapists' maneuvering through the eight phases of the EMDR protocol. In order to bridge the basic training paradigm to the practice of EMDR with children and adolescents, at the end of this chapter there are recommendations for getting started in using EMDR with children, including resources for therapists.

TRAUMA

As discussed in Chapter 5, Shapiro (1989a, 1989b) devised a therapeutic process she called EMDR in which the therapist guides the client through a series of procedural steps in order to access the maladaptively stored information. By accessing those memory networks, the EMDR protocol focuses on reprocessing the accessed information so that the client can proceed with the healing process. Since Shapiro's work initially focused on using EMDR for treating trauma in adults, this chapter includes theoretical foundations on trauma and trauma in children in order to provide the reader with a basis for exploring the EMDR protocol applied to the treatment of children and adolescents.

DEFINING TRAUMA

For the purposes of this chapter, trauma is defined as anything that negatively impacts the psyche. When a traumatic event occurs in early life, the child continues through life with dysfunctionally stored material manifesting in current symptomatology. What experiences the child engages in or avoids is impacted by those previous life experiences. With children, this traumatic event can also impact neurological development and all future experiences in the child's life. This etiological event thus prevents the individual's natural healing process from functioning at full potential.

A medical analogy can help illustrate how to explain what happens with EMDR to children and parents. For example, the therapist tells of a 10-year-old girl who was riding a go-cart and fell off, causing a severe injury to her left knee. After her parents and the child cleaned out the injury and applied medication, the wound was treated in order to allow the healing process to take place; however, the wound did not heal. The wound became infected, and the child and her parents were not able to care for the wound; therefore, the parents took the child to the medical doctor for assistance. The medical doctor used professional techniques to clean the wound and applied a prescription antibiotic to the wound and asked the parents to continue to apply the antibiotic for 10 days in order for the wound to heal. Even though the child and her parents did the best they could to treat the injury, the injury was such that the child required professional assistance to clean the wound in order that the natural healing process could take place.

The therapist can explain that, as in the foregoing medical analogy, when something emotionally traumatic happens in a child's life, parents and friends try to help, but they don't always have the skills to help the child and therefore require professional assistance. This is when the services of a psychotherapist are needed.

ACUTE TRAUMA

Children may have experienced stressful life situations or events from which clinical symptoms arise. These include adjustment disorders, acute stress disorder, and—at the extreme end of the continuum—posttraumatic stress disorder (PTSD) and dissociation. When this occurs, children can initially present with clinical indicators of an adjustment disorder where the child is struggling to adjust to specific life situations or events. Children with acute stress disorder are responding to an extreme stressor with symptoms that are of an acute nature and have occurred within 4 weeks of the traumatic event. If those symptoms continue more than an additional 4 weeks, the child could eventually meet the criteria for a diagnosis of PTSD. Even though the diagnostic criteria for acute stress disorder and PTSD require a traumatic event, children may have extreme responses to a traumatic event—including severe symptoms—that are less severe than described in the *Diagnostic and Statistical Manual of Mental Disorders, 4th edition, Text Revision* (DSM-IV-TR) (American Psychiatric Association, 2000). This is a common occurrence when children experience medical procedures. Children may respond with symptoms that would meet the criteria for PTSD after having surgery to have tubes put in their ears. It is important to not place so much emphasis on the situation or event, but rather note that there is an event and the child is responding with symptoms subsequent to the event. In some cases, symptoms suggest that the child has experienced a traumatic event, but neither the parent nor the child is able to identify the event. When this happens, psychotherapy can be helpful to prevent the child from experiencing long-term consequences from being exposed to trauma. Children may react to developmental milestones with distress that can contribute to symptoms suggestive of trauma.

DEVELOPMENTAL TRAUMAS

In addition to traumas that meet the criteria defined in the DSM-IV-TR, children can experience developmental traumas or "small t" traumas that are events that might not be experienced or interpreted as traumatic to an adult. These developmental traumas are events that cause distress for the child because the child is not cognitively able to interpret the event, but instead experiences the event as disturbing or life threatening. Developmental traumas can arise adjacent to regulatory tasks such as sleeping, potty training, school, separation from parents, and medical interventions as examples. Case Example 6-1 illustrates a developmental trauma.

Case Example 6-1: A Developmental Trauma

Two-year-old Andrew was a calm little boy who had been successfully sleeping through the night in his own crib. After visiting the pediatrician, Andrew's parents learned that Andrew needed surgery to correct a minor genetic issue. So the parents scheduled Andrew's surgery and took Andrew to the doctor without explaining anything to Andrew. Andrew went to the doctor, was sedated, and went to sleep, and when he awakened he was in pain from his surgery. After Andrew returned from the doctor's office, Andrew had difficulty sleeping, wanted to sleep with his parents, and often woke up screaming. Following his surgery, Andrew associated sleeping with waking up in pain. By using the EMDR protocol, the therapist had Andrew's parents tell a story of a little boy that incorporated all the details of Andrew's experiences with a bad thought (negative cognition) of "When I go to sleep I wake up in pain" and a good thought (positive cognition) of "I can sleep and wake up without an owie." The therapist reprocessed this traumatic event with Andrew and his family until Andrew adaptively reprocessed the traumatic memory to an adaptive resolution, allowing Andrew to no longer associate sleeping with pain. With AIP theory this medical event that Andrew was unable to understand most likely was the etiology of his trauma symptoms.

> These developmental traumas can leave an impact that impacts functioning as the child grows and can contribute to adult symptomatology if not reprocessed.

ATTACHMENT, TRAUMA, AND DISSOCIATION

If the child experiences trauma in his earliest relationship, and that relationship is less than secure, and the child then experiences additional traumas, the child is then at risk to develop symptoms of dissociation. Children who have experienced abuse and neglect often present with a particularly difficult symptom presentation that can be challenging for even the seasoned child therapist. EMDR provides an efficacious treatment protocol that allows the therapist to work with developing resources in the child with attachment trauma while also reprocessing traumatic events that can lead to chronic and severe mental health and physical symptoms. Within the EMDR protocol there is the opportunity to provide reparative work even without a healthy attachment figure and to provide the child with a clinical intervention to address current symptoms while also creating a positive template for the future. Therapists who have encountered frustration and lack of direction for treating children with such severe and chronic trauma have a guide for case conceptualization that can lead to more successful outcomes in psychotherapy. Case studies and clinical interventions for children with severe and chronic trauma—including attachment trauma—are included throughout this chapter.

INDICATIONS OF TRAUMA SYMPTOMS WITH CHILDREN AND ADOLESCENTS

Parents and therapists may not recognize symptoms of trauma in children and thus do not assess for trauma when working with children in psychotherapy. Each child brought to a therapist's office for treatment needs to be assessed for trauma. Events that may not be assessed as traumatic for adults can be experienced as traumatic for children. With a definition of trauma as anything that negatively affects the psyche, therapists need to recognize that with children this can entail anything that impacts the course of normal development. Assessment tools have been included for evaluating trauma in children and adolescents in the Client History and Treatment Planning section of this chapter, with references for therapists to further consider the indications of trauma with child and adolescent clients.

Why is it imperative for therapists to assess for trauma in children and adolescents? As discussed in the next section of this chapter, several authors have concluded that trauma can impact neurodevelopment and manifest in learning disabilities and other disorders with children and adolescents.

TRAUMA AND THE IMPACT ON NEURODEVELOPMENT: IMPLICATIONS FOR PSYCHOTHERAPY WITH CHILDREN AND ADOLESCENTS

Recently, Bessel van der Kolk, Bruce Perry, and Dan Siegel have written about the impact of trauma on the developing mind and suggested that trauma changes the actual neurobiology and neurodevelopment of the brain (Perry, 2006; Siegel, 2007; van der Kolk, 2005). When using EMDR with children, the therapist is in a unique role of having the opportunity to intervene at a time when neurodevelopment is most rapid and malleable and treatment can have its greatest impact.

DEVELOPMENTAL TRAUMA DISORDER

Understanding how trauma affects development is imperative for all therapists. Van der Kolk suggested a new diagnosis—"developmental trauma disorder" (2005). With developmental trauma disorder, van der Kolk has written that early life trauma experiences can cause neurological damage and manifest in learning disabilities, impaired cognitive functioning, as well as mental health and behavioral issues. Van der Kolk concluded that "The diagnosis of PTSD is not developmentally sensitive and does not adequately describe the effect of exposure to childhood trauma on the developing child . . . they tend to display very complex disturbances with a variety of different, often fluctuating, presentations" (p. 404). It behooves the treating therapist to understand that treating traumatized children is a complicated process as the child's ongoing developmental processes and fluctuating responses that are ever influenced by the environment change each time the child enters the therapist's office. Even the experience of participating in therapy affects the child's development as the therapist can provide opportunities to learn, make connections, and process life experiences. It is vital that the treating therapist approach case conceptualization with children especially from the understanding of developmental processes with awareness that developmental tasks may have been missed, altered, or yet to be attempted.

Van der Kolk (2005) has included various tasks to be included in treatment approaches with children, including "establishing safety and competence, dealing with traumatic reenactments, and integration and mastery experiences." In the EMDR protocol as explicated in this book, therapists will understand how these tasks are all integrated and can be successfully maneuvered when the therapist understands the theoretical underpinnings along with the goals and objectives of using EMDR in psychotherapy with children.

Neurosequential Development

Perry (2006) has proposed a neurosequential treatment protocol that includes EMDR. Perry has studied the clinical needs of maltreated and traumatized children and integrated theories of neurobiology and neurodevelopment to explain how children respond to trauma. Perry's studies and theories have created recommendations for the treatment needs of traumatized children. Perry has provided a framework for understanding children's responses to traumatic events based on theoretical models of neurodevelopment. Perry has proposed "Key Principles of Neurodevelopment and Neurobiology" that provide a way of organizing and interpreting children's responses to trauma. Perry suggests that children are responding from brain stem–based behaviors when threatened as the brain's alarm system interprets any stress as a threat to the individual. Perry suggests that chronically traumatized children respond with an increased baseline where the brain is more reactive to stress and that this increased baseline causes more reactive and emotional dysregulation in children who are chronically responding from a position of trauma and distress. These children are often diagnosed with mental health disorders and are difficult to parent. Perry also theorizes that children who have experienced a chronic trauma history develop a neurological system that is in a persistent state of fear. Because these children are in this chronic state of alarm, their physical and mental health are impacted, which leads to maladaptively stored states and experiences.

AIP theory postulates that current symptoms are driven by maladaptively stored experiences that contain all of the memories, emotions, and body sensations the individual experienced at the time of the traumatic events. By using an EMDR treatment protocol, the therapist taps these maladaptively stored memory networks in order to bring them to adaptive resolution. Perry's writings hypothesize that the way to change children and their neurological systems is through repetition. By tapping those maladaptively stored memories, reprocessing the memories to adaptive resolution, and then installing mastery and positive templates with EMDR, the therapist offers the child replacement experiences with which to change the neuropathways and future development.

Perry's theory also surmises that brain development is sequential and occurs most rapidly earlier in life. By understanding all the theories of human development and how trauma can divert the normal developmental process, therapists can return to those events to reprocess those events with

EMDR. Perry concluded that "All the best cognitive-behavioral, insight-oriented or even affect-based interventions will fail if the brainstem is poorly regulated" (pp. 39). That individual who experiences a constant state of arousal cannot talk away or think away or act away that physiological experience. With EMDR, the therapist taps the physiological state with which the client presents, explores the origins of the state and then reprocesses the experience in order to improve the client's ongoing state and modulate arousal. The client's ability to regulate their state can be treated with EMDR. We have hypothesized that EMDR is effective because it can short-circuit the chain of traumatic memory that follows a specific traumatic event by tapping into a much more powerful brain stem–diencephalic memory—the association created in utero (Perry, 2006, p. 39).

Finally, Perry proposes that some neurological systems are easier to change than others and that the human brain has evolved from a different world. Because of this, Perry recommends that psychotherapy must be organized in a manner to best treat the neurobiology that already exists. The plasticity of the brain varies, depending on the area of the brain impacted and the specific stage of development. Within the EMDR framework, therapists may need to focus time on helping children develop emotional literacy and self-nurturing and mastery experiences. Providing this internal scaffolding for children can create a base with which the child can learn to reprocess previous traumatic events and become more resilient to current and future stressors.

This chapter cannot begin to capture the significance of Perry's research and theories; however, it is important for the reader to note that these models of development and treatment integrate with the AIP theory and using EMDR in the treatment of children. Understanding how experiences in the world impact neurodevelopment and neurobiology is important for therapists to create reparative experiences in psychotherapy and to create interventions that impact the parenting and environment in which the child lives.

NEUROBIOLOGY, MIRROR NEURONS, ATTACHMENT, AND RELATIONSHIPS

Siegel began integrating attachment theory, neurobiology, and the implications of how the brain interprets and processes relationships both in the environment and in psychotherapy. In his book *Parenting from the Inside Out* (Siegel & Hartzell, 2003), Siegel discussed how parenting impacts neurodevelopment. In his most recent book, *The Mindful Brain* (2007), Siegel explores how integrally related neurobiology is with psychotherapy.

Of special interest is the exploration of mirror neurons in the brain and how these mirror neurons theoretically connect two people in a state of resonance and potentially form the basis for the healing that occurs within a therapeutic relationship. Understanding how our therapist relationships develop with our child clients and their families is critical to understanding the elements of successful models of psychotherapy with children.

With AIP theory and newly formulated theories of neurobiology, physiology, and the impacts of trauma on the development of the neurosystem, theories of child development provide a comprehensive theoretical framework to approach clinical work with children.

The theoretical foundations provided by the theories included in this chapter provide a framework for the therapist to assess the child's development and explore areas of thwarted development where varying degrees of traumatic events have changed the course of healthy development of the child. These traumas, once identified, can be reprocessed with EMDR in order to restore the process of healthy human development for the child.

PSYCHOTHERAPY WITH CHILDREN AND ADOLESCENTS

What happens when children and adolescents are not resilient and struggle to recuperate from exposure to traumatic events? At a minimum, children may demonstrate distress that manifests in somatic, emotional, and behavioral problems. More severely traumatized children may manifest symptoms consistent with significant psychiatric disorders. Psychotherapy to treat these symptoms can prevent the long-term sequelae of exposure to trauma, especially when the symptoms are addressed early. Research has not only found that childhood distress and trauma contribute to increased adult mental health and medical issues, but also impact neurodevelopment. Given the significance of these findings, early interventions with children exposed to trauma have the potential to change the trajectory of children's futures by addressing the adverse impact of childhood experiences.

In one study, Felitti et al. (1998) assessed the impact of childhood stressors on adult medical issues. By surveying more than 9,000 individuals who had been treated at a local health clinic with the Adverse Effects of Childhood Scale (AECS), the authors concluded that "The findings suggest that the impact of these adverse childhood experiences on adult health status is strong and cumulative" (p. 251). The authors suggested that mental health interventions are necessary to change the future of individuals who have experienced childhood abuse and dysfunction in the home and who are therefore at increased risk for not only mental health issues, but also medical problems. With this trajectory, there is even more compelling reason supporting the necessity of early intervention with children and adolescents.

AIP AND THE EMDR MODEL AS A TEMPLATE FOR A COMPREHENSIVE APPROACH TO CHILD PSYCHOTHERAPY

AIP WITH CHILDREN

AIP theory postulates that memories are a combination of sensory input, thoughts, emotions, physical sensations, and a belief system but may actually have metacognitions. Accessing and processing of neuronetworks is different for children because children have not fully developed a belief system with which to understand and process an event or experience. In spite of the fact that children have not developed the same cognitive processes nor have as extensive language skills as adults, the AIP model still explains personality development as well as the development of dysfunction and pathology in children. AIP theory proposes that the information must be accessed, stimulated, and then moved toward adaptive resolution (Shapiro, 2007). The child client must be able to access and communicate this information. For this reason, therapists must assess development in the client prior to proceeding with the EMDR protocol because children present at varying stages of development. The therapist then needs to fine-tune the EMDR protocol to meet the developmental needs of the client. If, according to AIP, the assimilation of events into the associative memory network and accommodations of the client's previous identity to encompass it can be considered the basis of personality development (Shapiro, 2007), the earlier the intervention the more positive the impact on the personality and the individual's overall health. AIP suggests that for children with extensive abuse and neglect histories, this learning and adaptive resolution cannot take place because they have insufficient internal resources and positive experiences to transform the initial dysfunction. When working with children in psychotherapy, the therapist also has a unique opportunity to provide opportunities for developing internal resources and positive experiences through resource development and mastery skills as part of the EMDR treatment protocol.

Children often store memories in sensory/motor format; therefore, children may not have a coherent narrative to describe to the therapists. However, children can report sensations that arise when neuronetworks are probed. This is when the use of play therapy and art therapy techniques are indicated to facilitate the treatment process within the eight phases of the EMDR protocol.

THE EIGHT PHASES OF EMDR

The next section of this chapter is organized by using the eight phases of the EMDR protocol as headings. As discussed in Chapter 5, the eight phases of EMDR include client history and treatment planning, preparation, assessment, desensitization, installation, body scan, closure, and reevaluation (Shapiro, 1995). Each phase of EMDR includes treatment goals and interventions to be accomplished before proceeding; however, this organization in no way suggests that the protocol is linear and sequential. On the contrary, the psychotherapy process with actual clients is often circular, with the therapist needing to return to earlier phases of the protocol as more information arises during each phase of treatment. This is true of almost any treatment methodology in that as the therapist works with the client, the therapist learns more about the client's history, becomes attuned to the client, and gains new insights into the uniqueness of the client, which impacts the treatment goals in an ever-changing and dynamic process.

With child clients, the therapist is also noticing how the child's development impacts treatment from session to session. Theories and concepts of child development are integrated into the EMDR protocol with child clients. In addition, it is important to assimilate other techniques used in child psychotherapy along with the foundations and techniques from attachment therapy into case conceptualization throughout the eight phases of the EMDR protocol. Therapists need to use all their clinical skills and tools to create a therapist's toolbox that can be integrated into the EMDR eight-phase treatment protocol. This is not to suggest that all other clinical skills or training be abandoned, but instead that therapists consider how organizing treatment and case conceptualization is a comprehensive process with the eight phases of EMDR. While reading the explanations of each phase of the EMDR protocol, the astute therapist will recognize clinical skills from attachment therapy, play therapy, and cognitive behavioral therapies, to name a few.

THREE-PRONGED APPROACH

EMDR is a three-pronged approach that conceptualizes treatment based on past–present–future goals for treatment. Therapy begins with the identification of symptoms that are the manifestations of maladaptively stored information. As therapy progresses, maladaptively stored events from the past are reprocessed through to adaptive resolution and then treatment focuses on present triggers that need to be targeted. Once past events and present triggers are cleared, the therapist guides the client to the future, where the client processes a positive future template until the future event is anticipated absent of distress. Any distress for the future is conceptualized as anticipatory anxiety and/or missing skills that the client is taught. Anticipatory anxiety is reprocessed to adaptive resolution while missing skills are taught and practiced. This three-pronged approach guides the eight phases of the EMDR protocol.

INDICATIONS AND CONTRAINDICATIONS FOR USING EMDR WITH CHILDREN

EMDR is a psychotherapy treatment model in which the therapist approaches case conceptualization from the AIP theoretical model. The first two phases of EMDR include client history and treatment planning and preparation, which will both be described in detail later in the chapter.

In general, the initial phase of EMDR, client history and treatment planning, parallels similar practices in other treatment models. The second phase of EMDR is the preparation phase, in which the therapist assesses the client's stability and resources to continue with the next phases of the EMDR protocol. It is during the first two phases of the EMDR protocol that the therapist may need to pace how long the treatment episode remains in the preparation phase, focused on stabilization and skill building. Depending on the client's needs for stabilization, support, and resource development, the clinical venue may remain in the preparation phase for some time without proceeding to the trauma-processing phases of the EMDR protocol. It is in the trauma-processing phases of EMDR where contraindications arise. In general, contraindications to EMDR are based on the stability of the client and the organicity of the symptom presentation.

EMDR can be used to process traumatic events and the secondary traumatic experiences that can arise from psychiatric diagnoses that are typically considered to have organic etiology such as attention deficit hyperactivity disorder (ADHD) and bipolar disorder. This is not to suggest that EMDR alleviates the symptoms of organically based psychiatric disorders, but instead EMDR can be used to treat the secondary symptoms the client might experience from having to cope with a disorder. For example, many clients have struggled with being successful in school and been called "lazy" before being diagnosed with ADHD. It is the client's memory of being called lazy and the impact of that event that can be reprocessed with EMDR.

In case conceptualization, the therapist needs to assess how and when to proceed with each phase of the EMDR treatment. One consideration is the mental health and physical stability of the client. Using the trauma-processing phases of EMDR would not be indicated with clients who are not medically or psychiatrically stable, but instead the therapist would refer for additional evaluation and pace the course of treatment focused on stabilization as indicated. Therapists may also consider providing supportive therapy if the client's environment is unstable.

When working with children, the therapist needs to consider the child's environment and family stability. If parent or family stability is of concern, best practice would suggest that the therapist consider interventions to help the child cope with the environment and refer the parent for treatment as indicated. This is true of most clinical work with children and not unique to EMDR. Finally, it is important for the therapist to pace the therapeutic interventions. Therapists would consider extraneous variables that may impinge on the therapeutic process such as the client's impending medical care or the therapist's upcoming vacation. The competent therapist would not consider beginning trauma processing the session before the therapist is leaving on a 2-week vacation or the day before the client is due for surgery.

Finally, EMDR trauma processing would not be indicated if the client's symptoms are based on a lack of information or specific skill. For example, a child may be afraid of giving a speech because the child has never given a speech and needs assistance in writing the speech and with presentation skills. Part of case conceptualization with EMDR is considering what skills the client has and what the client needs. In this case, the therapist may choose to refer the child for a class in public speaking, and once the child has acquired the needed skills, the therapist will reassess the need for any treatment of any remaining anticipatory anxiety.

WHAT MAKES EMDR WITH CHILDREN DIFFERENT THAN EMDR WITH ADULTS?

The EMDR psychotherapy model is a comprehensive template for case conceptualization in psychotherapy for adults as well as adolescents and children. The entire EMDR protocol can be used with young clients when therapists learn how to translate the protocol into both the verbal and nonverbal language of children. Because EMDR was created for use with adult clients, as is described in Chapter 5, therapists may need to partake in additional training to gain expertise in using EMDR with children. There are books and training programs that the therapist can access following basic training in EMDR. Information on advanced trainings in using EMDR with children and adolescents is included at the end of this chapter.

As with any psychotherapy model, therapists who work with children need to adjust the intervention to match the developmental level of the individual child. With EMDR, the course of treatment may also be shorter because the child has not developed the expansive neuronetworks that an adult who has lived longer and had more life experiences may have developed. Because of this, as the therapist implements the EMDR protocol, children often move through the protocol faster and more efficiently than adults.

Also, children interpret the world by creating their own narrative of the event that is filtered through the lens of their brief life experiences. With younger children, many events are stored in sensory–motor memories; therefore, the therapist needs to use techniques that allow the child to express himself through nonverbal means, such as play therapy and art therapy techniques.

Finally, because of their abbreviated life experiences, children are less likely to have fully developed their personality. This provides an opportunity for interventions that can return the child to his own course of normal development.

This is a general overview of how EMDR is different with children than with adults, and the above points will be expanded through the eight phases of the protocol with children. The remainder of this chapter is organized to discuss each of the eight phases of EMDR, with a focus on the unique challenges to accomplishing the phase with young clients. With each phase of the protocol, included are the purpose and description of the specific phase along with clinical considerations and procedural implications to guide the practitioner working with child clients. In order to explicate the specific protocol, case studies that demonstrate how a therapist uses the EMDR protocol with children through all eight phases are woven throughout this chapter.

This chapter will use case illustrations of EMDR with children through the phases of EMDR to help explicate the EMDR protocol. The cases of five children (Julia, Steven, Andrew, Max, and James) are included. We'll start with Case Example 6-2, which follows Julia's case through the treatment protocol. Later, we'll examine other illustrations.

Case Example 6-2: Julia and the Bus Accident

Seven-year-old Julia was referred to psychotherapy after she watched her 10-year-old brother's death in a school bus accident the previous year. Even though Julia's entire family had received grief counseling, Julia became increasingly more anxious about going to the school she had attended for several years. Julia knew her teacher and classmates very well, and they were all very supportive; however, Julia began to have stomachaches in class and frequently went to the school nurse. Then Julia's stomachaches started taking place before school, contributing to frequent absences. Julia's parents tried many things to get her to go to school, including driving Julia to school because they thought the bus would be traumatizing. But Julia would scream and cry in the car as her parents sat in the school parking lot trying to calm her, to no avail. By the time Julia was brought in for EMDR, she had constant stomachaches, was moody and irritable, and appeared depressed and was no longer attending school. Julia's course of EMDR therapy will be woven through the eight phases of the protocol.

THE EIGHT PHASES OF THE EMDR PROTOCOL
IN PSYCHOTHERAPY WITH CHILDREN

CLIENT HISTORY AND TREATMENT PLANNING PHASE

Client history and treatment planning is the first phase of the EMDR protocol, which parallels most other types of treatment. Therapists in most treatment modalities are trained to collect a client history and identify treatment issues in order to aid in the treatment planning process.

Description and Purpose   The purpose of Phase 1 of EMDR, client history and treatment planning, is to gather information about the client's history and symptoms that spurred the client to seek treatment and to create a treatment plan to guide the psychotherapeutic process. Most therapies begin with some type of intake that includes collecting the client's history that provides the basis for treatment planning. During client history and treatment planning, the therapist is also establishing a relationship with the client and developing rapport. Because EMDR is a client-centered treatment that focuses on the identification and resolution of symptoms, the therapist is focused on developing a clinical alliance with the client, within which the healing process occurs.

With EMDR, the unique addition to the client history-taking process is that the therapist listens for the client's negative self-perceptions, beliefs, and cognitions, as well as emotions and unique body sensations, as the client describes his or her presenting issues. The therapist notes aspects of the client's presentation in each of these areas to be further explored in later phases of the EMDR process. The themes with which clients present—including negative self-perceptions, beliefs, and cognitions—would be considered in any psychotherapy intake process by clients and included in treatment planning; however, the significance of these issues is at the root of symptom manifestation from an AIP theoretical perspective.

With children, the therapist is listening to what the child says along with what the therapist observes from the child and between the child and his caregivers. Not only is the therapist gathering data; she is also observing the child's development, play, interactions with caregivers, and the meta-communications demonstrated in the therapist's office. Along with the therapist's previous intake protocol, she is listening for what life events are possibly contributing to the child's symptom presentation. The therapist begins case conceptualization by considering the child's mastery of developmental tasks based on the child's chronological age and achievement of psychosocial, emotional, behavioral, cognitive, and developmental tasks of childhood and adolescence. As the therapist assesses the child's treatment goals, she then needs to explain EMDR to the child and caregivers.

Explaining EMDR to Both Parents and Children   It is important to explain EMDR to both parents and children in terms that all family members can understand. Client understanding of the EMDR methodology is imperative in engaging the child and family in the therapeutic process. Once the child and family have consented to the treatment process, the therapist then gathers information to aid in case conceptualization. The explanation of EMDR needs to be provided in a language that meets the child and care-givers at their developmental level and level of psychological savvy. There are books (Adler-Tapia & Tapia, 2008; Gomez, 2007) that can be used to explain EMDR to children and then guide children through the phases of EMDR. (These books will be described near the end of this chapter.) By reading Gomez's book to tell the story of EMDR and then using the work-book by Adler-Tapia & Tapia, the therapist can begin helping clients to understand the efficacy of EMDR while collecting data for use in the EMDR protocol. Therapists can incorporate play therapy techniques and drawing with children of all ages to develop rapport, engage the client, and assess the child's comprehension and expressive skills. Therapists have used creative and innovative techniques to explain EMDR to children and guide children through the stages of the EMDR protocol. The procedural steps of the protocol need to be adjusted to the unique presentation of the individual child based on an accurate assessment of the child's development and the therapist's attunement to the child.

Case Conceptualization in EMDR with Children   Therapist case conceptualiza-tion in treating children with EMDR includes integrating both the parent input and child input in the process of collecting a client history and writing a treatment plan for psychotherapy. Clinical practice suggests that what par-ents identify as issues and what children identify may be very different. From a case conceptualization perspective, the therapist is attempting to listen for how the trauma is stored for the child. A child's experience of a traumatic event is frequently stored in unusual and surprising ways. Children may identify a traumatic event in an imaginative manner such as a spider that is a metaphorical representation of the child's fear. A child may explain that she cannot go to the bathroom because there is a spider in the bathroom that might jump on her. What the therapist knows from the parent is that the child has had difficulty using the restroom since a family pet was hit by a car. This is the beginning of the process of examining how the child experiences the world and manages the distressing and traumatic events that have brought her to therapy.

Symptom presentation may also be discrepant between children and parents. Symptoms that are of concern to parents may not seem as important to the child. Parents will often identify external symptoms, while children will often report internal symptoms. For example, the parent may bring the child for misbehaving in school, while the child is reporting stomachaches from having to go to a different classroom for resource class because the child is struggling with reading. The parent is focused on treating the behaviors, while the child is focused on the internal distress that is theoretically driving the behaviors.

The difference between what children present and what parents present is also important in treatment planning. It is important to ask parents how they will evaluate the child's progress in therapy. Ask the parents how they hope the child will be acting, behaving, and feeling when therapy is completed. What are the parents' goals for their child's therapy? It is critical to also ask the child how she wants to think, feel, and behave or what she wants to be able to do instead of what she's doing now.

It is important for the therapist to explore both parent input and child input throughout the EMDR treatment process in order to capture a comprehensive treatment course for the child. Once the therapist has conducted the intake and written an initial treatment plan, therapy then proceeds with the preparation phase of EMDR.

Clinical Considerations   During the first phase of EMDR, the therapist needs to consider the use of standardized assessment tools for evaluating child development, trauma, and dissociation. Since children and adolescents are in a constant state of growth, assessing the client's current stage of development is important to making adjustments to the languaging of the EMDR protocol. The therapist's goal is to become attuned to the child in order to assess how to talk to the child. For this reason, it is important for the therapist to gather information about the child's developmental milestones and current functioning as the treatment process begins and throughout the course of psychotherapy.

Evaluating Children in Psychotherapy   In order to most effectively treat children, it is important to assess their current level of functioning and to note any developmental issues that may impact the course of EMDR therapy. Therapists must consider the benefit of cognitive/intellectual assessment, academic/achievement assessment, and developmental assessment based on the use of standardized assessment tools. Therapists can request previous testing from schools that include both intellectual and achievement assessment or refer families for cognitive assessments of children if there is a concern regarding intellectual functioning or learning disabilities. Conducting developmental assessments of children is important not only in treatment planning, but also in helping parents to understand the child's developmental level and to determine if the child is delayed in any areas of development.

In addition to developmental scales, it is helpful to assess for sensory integration issues, especially with young children. Even though sensory integration is a symptom of other mental health issues, including autism and Asperger's disorder, sensory integration dysfunction (SID) is most often diagnosed by occupational therapists.

Most mental health professionals in a treatment role with children will use academic, cognitive, and developmental assessments conducted by other professionals; however, mental health professionals in treatment roles will often conduct emotional and behavioral health assessments of children as part of a comprehensive treatment plan.

In addition to intellectual, achievement, developmental, and behavioral issues, it is important for therapists to assess children for symptoms of trauma and dissociation (Adler-Tapia & Settle, 2008). It is important for therapists to be aware of the document *Guidelines for the Evaluation and Treatment of Dissociative Symptoms in Children and Adolescents* (ISST-D, 2004). Therapists can access documents for assessing trauma in children, including the Child's Reaction to Traumatic Events Scale (CRTES; Jones, 2002) and assessment tools for assessing dissociation in children—the *Child Dissociative Checklist, Version 3* (CDC) (Putnam, 1997) and for adolescents—the *Adolescent-Dissociative Experiences Scale* (Armstrong, Carlson, & Putnam, 1997).

Assessing Children's Readiness for Therapy/Selection Criteria   The most significant issue in the successful treatment of children is engaging the child in the therapeutic process. To successfully engage the child in therapy, the therapist needs to first assess the child's readiness for treatment and willingness to engage in the therapeutic process. This is vital because the child rarely is the one who initiates therapy. The therapist can initially play with the child and ask him, "What did your mommy or daddy tell you about why you came to see me?" The therapist needs to ask some type of question that explores what the child has been told by the caregiver and the child's expectations for being at the therapy session. This initial discussion then leads the therapist to the opportunity to discuss therapy, the therapist's role, and the purpose for therapy. The therapist can also use this opportunity to explain mental health and psychotherapy in developmentally appropriate terms.

During this interaction, the therapist is continuing to become attuned to the child and is assessing the child's level of comfort and safety in the office. Will the child engage in a play activity with the therapist? What is the child's level of comfort in separating from the parent? What is the child's level of activity, and how does the child explore the office? A child with a secure attachment should gradually take greater interest in exploring the office, while either physically or visually checking in with the parent. This checking-in process should decrease as the child establishes a comfort level with the therapist and the office setting.

While developing the therapeutic relationship with the child, the therapist may have an opportunity to install mastery. If the therapist feels a level of attunement with the child, the therapist may determine that installing a mastery experience will benefit the child and engage the child in the therapeutic process. Additional information for installing a mastery experience will be discussed later in this chapter.

Monitoring Children's Symptoms EMDR is a symptom-focused treatment protocol in that therapists begin by asking children and caregivers what brought them into therapy, what are the child's specific symptoms and what are they hoping to accomplish in treatment. How will the child be behaving, feeling, and thinking if and when therapy is successful? With EMDR, these symptoms are evidence of maladaptively stored information that is driving the symptoms. Symptoms may originate directly from the traumatic event, from intrusive images, nightmares, triggers in the current environment (including the avoidance of places, smells, or events), issues of personal responsibility, safety, mortality, regulatory issues, or unresolved fears.

Throughout the course of treatment it is important to monitor positive and negative symptoms. The therapist is ever aware of how the original symptoms may have changed, new symptoms may have arisen, or previous symptoms may have abated during and between sessions. It is important to monitor progress in the child's life. This is significant especially with parents who may believe that the therapist will want them to report only negative behaviors and symptoms. Ask the parents for the child's strengths and accomplishments in addition to the child's challenges in order to help parents focus on the child's progress. Parents may report additional symptoms at the beginning of treatment as they become more observant of their children and begin to realize what constitutes a symptom with a child. By educating parents about children's responses to trauma and how children experience life events in different ways than adults, parents often become more perceptive and insightful into children's experiences. This is also an opportunity for therapists to point out the child's progress in treatment. The goal is for the parent to become a more active and astute member of the child's treatment team.

Therapists need to encourage parents to use a written monitoring form to note symptoms and progress. Specific symptoms therapists should consider when working with children and adolescents are changes in sleep, eating, concentration, bowel and bladder control, headaches, stomachaches, other somatic complaints, changes in relationships, behavioral issues, and school challenges. These symptoms should be assessed at the origination of treatment and throughout the course of treatment.

Providing Psychoeducational Information   In addition to monitoring the child's behavior between sessions, therapists need to teach parents about children's reactions to distressing and traumatic experiences. It is important for therapists to explain the etiology of children's symptoms and behavioral issues. This can enhance parents' insights and understanding of their children and can facilitate engaging parents in the therapeutic process. It is also beneficial to provide written psychoeducational materials about trauma, abuse, and other children's issues for parents and children to read between sessions. There are many books and web sites (which will be identified near the end of this chapter) to which one can refer children and parents for more information.

Providing psychoeducational information and materials to children and parents is necessary to help families understand how children deal with distress and to aid in gaining skills in relaxation, stress management, emotional literacy, and parenting. Also necessary is allowing families to ask questions in sessions and to practice new skills in sessions, with the therapist's guidance.

Additional competencies in effectively using EMDR include the therapist's role in EMDR and case conceptualization. Therapist's use of self and skills at building relationships and modeling interaction skills for parents and emotional literacy are part of successful interventions. Therapists who work with children need to be active and flexible in their work with children and families and to be creative at juggling the child's needs, the parents' needs, and the needs of the family while weaving therapeutic interventions into the session of psychotherapy. At each step of the EMDR protocol, the therapist also should contemplate the procedural considerations and clinical implications in case conceptualization in treating children. This includes the assessment of attachment and level of trauma that can realistically be tackled during this episode of care. The issue of attainable goals is an on-going consideration when treating children. For example, therapists working with children with attachment trauma can consider when it may be beneficial for the parent–child relationship for the parent to hold the child in their lap as the child reprocesses a memory. Assessment of the child's needs, the parents' needs, and therapeutic goals is an ongoing and fluid process.

Creating a Targeting Sequence Plan   The final step of the client history and treatment planning phase of EMDR is to create a targeting sequence plan. The targeting sequence plan is a list of events or targets that are interpreted by the child as potentially traumatic. A target is an issue, incident, experience, memory, or dream from the client's life. The targeting sequence plan consists of clustering the client's maladaptively stored events related to a specific negative cognition in order to organize the focus of reprocessing. With the EMDR protocol, the therapist guides the client through the process of developing the negative cognition, which is the negative belief that the client has about herself and the exploring how the client learned this belief. (Negative and positive cognitions will be discussed in greater detail during the assessment phase of EMDR later in this chapter). Initially, the therapist asks the client, "How did you learn or when do you first remember thinking 'I'm not good enough?'" Clients will often recall events that the client believes contributed to this negative belief. What the client recounts as the first time the client remembers thinking "I'm not good enough" is considered the touchstone event, or the first time a traumatic event that contributed to the client's belief negative believe about herself. As illustrated in Case Example 6-3, the therapist explores with the client past events when the client also thought "I'm not good enough" and then explores present triggers that also reinforce the client's belief that "I'm not good enough." Once the therapist organizes this sequence from past events and present triggers, the therapist then explores with the client future concerns that the client has when the client anticipates thinking "I'm not good enough" in the future.

Case Example 6-3: Steven's Touchstone Event

Sixteen-year-old Steven reported struggling with completing his research paper for his history class because he never felt that the paper was good enough. With this symptom, the therapist then asked Steven, "If you believe this is true, that your paper is not good enough, what does that say about you?" With probing, Steven concluded that his negative belief about himself was "I'm not good enough." The therapist then asked Steven to recall an earlier time when Steven first thought "I'm not good enough." Steven recalled several events, including an incident in first grade in which he failed a spelling test in school. This event was identified as the touchstone event or the event that most likely began Steven's belief that "I'm not good enough." The therapist then guided Steven through the process of identifying previous events when Steven also had this same thought of "I'm not good enough." After listing the past events and identifying current triggers for this same thought, the therapist then asked Steven to identify future concerns when he anticipated not believing that he is good enough, and Steven identified his fear of presenting his paper to his 10th-grade class. This series of events, triggers, and anticipatory anxiety became the targeting sequence plan for Steven's EMDR treatment.

With younger children, who often have shorter sequences of events contributing to the child's current symptoms, and because children are often present focused, the targeting sequence plan may be short or consist of the original symptom or trigger that brought the child into therapy, the maladaptively stored event that is driving the current symptoms, and the concern that the symptom will carry into the future.

As in Julia's case, her school avoidance became school phobia that eventually caused Julia's parents to seek treatment for Julia. The targeting sequence plan for Julia consisted of the bus accident in which Julia's brother was killed, Julia seeing her brother's picture at school, her fear of the school buses, her current school phobia, and her future that predicted ongoing distress and avoidance of school. This was Julia's targeting sequence plan for continuing through the remaining steps of the EMDR treatment protocol.

It is important to remember that if the child is too overwhelmed by the process of defining the targeting sequence plan, the therapist may need to move to the preparation phase. It is in the preparation phase of EMDR where the goals are to teach self-soothing and calming, emotional regulation skills and resource development and installation (RDI) that may be necessary before being able to identify a targeting sequence with many children because of the developmental overlay and distress that arises from interviewing children about past traumatic events. RDI is an advanced EMDR protocol (Leeds, 1998) taught in basic training in EMDR to advance the client's skills is self-soothing and calming. RDI will be discussed in depth later in the chapter.

From Client History and Treatment Planning to the Preparation Phase of EMDR   At the end of the client history and treatment planning phase, when the therapist has gathered all relevant information and created a working treatment plan, developed a working relationship with the child and caregivers, and considered case conceptualization for this unique client, the therapist can explain the next step in the psychotherapy process to transition into the preparation phase of EMDR. The goal of the preparation phase is to assess the child's resources and teach needed resources for treating the child's specific symptoms. Case Example 6-4 illustrates transitioning to the preparation phase with Julia.

Case Example 6-4: Client History and Treatment Planning with Julia

After the therapist completed a comprehensive history and developed a treatment plan with Julia, he noted that one of the things that bothered Julia the most was the last time she saw her 10-year-old brother. In addition, the school had placed a plaque with her brother's picture by it as a memorial and it hung in the corridor, where Julia was reminded of her brother's death every day at school. Julia's parents contacted the school, and even though the school removed the plaque, Julia still refused to go to school.

The therapist decided to proceed with the EMDR protocol and explained EMDR to Julia and her parents by saying that sometimes bad things happen and the brain doesn't always fully "digest" the bad things, so when this happens, EMDR can help the brain digest things and help people feel better. The therapist ended this session with Julia's agreement to start with the preparation phase of EMDR at her next session.

PREPARATION PHASE

Description and Purpose During the second phase of EMDR, the therapist's primary goal is to prepare the client for reprocessing during the remaining phases of EMDR. Most therapies assess the client's resources and then facilitate the client's learning needed skills in order to improve his functioning. Assessing for affect management, affect tolerance, emotional regulation skills, self-soothing skills, and other needed skills is important to any type of therapy and is the focus of the preparation phase of EMDR. The final goal of the preparation phase is to teach clients the mechanics of EMDR, which are described in detail in this section of the chapter.

The initial goal of the preparation phase is to teach children the ability to titrate the impact of intense emotions. The more the child feels capable of managing intense affect and self-soothing, the smoother and more effective the therapeutic process. Children especially need to feel powerful and competent in therapy in order to actively participate in the healing process. When children are feeling overwhelmed by their intense emotions, they are much more likely to be reluctant to participate in therapy.

EMDR in Multimodal Treatment with Children During the preparation phase, any previous skill-building activities that the therapist has typically used in psychotherapy can be implemented and taught to the client. Guided imagery, systematic desensitization, assertiveness training, dialectical behavior therapy (DBT), trauma-focused cognitive behavioral therapy (TFCBT), or any other interventions the therapist has found to be beneficial in working with children are equally important to consider teaching a child during the preparation phase or at any other time she assesses that the child needs particular skills to be successful in therapy. For example, children often benefit from learning how to take deep breaths for self-soothing and pro-gressive muscle relaxation exercises. With EMDR, it is helpful to teach children resource skills and install mastery experiences in order to provide the scaffolding from which children can build healthy experiences and reprocess traumatic events.

Emotional Resources, Coping, and Mastery Skills for Children   The goal for teaching children resourcing, coping skills, and enhancing mastery experi-ences is to assist the child in creating his own toolbox of skills to be used both in therapy and in his daily life for more advanced coping. This toolbox includes an EMDR skill entitled safe/calm place. The safe/calm place is a protocol taught during the preparation phase when the therapist explains the mechanics of EMDR. This safe/calm place protocol is discussed later in the discussion of the preparation phase of EMDR. With child clients, the therapist reviews the child's resources in each session and reminds the child to use those resources at home and school. Ultimately, the effectiveness of the therapeutic process is for the child to be able to take the skills learned in the therapist's office and apply those skills in his life outside the office.

Teaching Children Skills for Dealing with Strong Emotions   Children benefit tremendously from learning techniques for dealing with strong emotions and coping with the memories that arise during the course of psychotherapy and from experiences in their lives. Creating and enhancing new skills, while enhancing mastery experiences the child has recalled, help create a positive foundation for children to deal with reprocessing traumatic events in therapy. Mastery experiences are those identified by the child as times when the child felt successful or masterful in a situation that might have been difficult. The therapist can ask the child to report one event since the last session when the child attempted something stressful or difficult and he felt that his efforts had been successful. Identifying situations and events when the child was successful are important resources for children.

Exploring mastery experiences and coping skills are especially important for children who are reluctant to address symptoms and traumatic memo-ries in therapy. In case conceptualization, the therapist must regularly note the skills the child currently possesses, as well as the additional skills she will need in order to cope with therapeutic and life challenges. One recommendation is that therapists need to be aware of children's genre including games, books, movies, television shows, sports, and other current child activities. It is helpful to ask children about what they like and how they spend their free time when they have a choice as possible clues to resources and mastery experiences for the child. The therapist can also use this information to create mastery experiences in the office.

Resourcing, coping, and mastery skills also provide empowerment, mentalizing, positive foundation, emotional regulation, and boundaries and limits for children to learn, improve, and practice in their lives. Each of these competencies assists children in dealing with life stressors and processing whatever maladaptively stored information needs to be reprocessed during EMDR. The following definitions can assist the reader in understanding how these terms are used in this chapter. With children, *empowerment* is defined as the ability to feel competent to make choices and to be able to advocate on one's own behalf. *Mentalizing* is the ability to understand one's own intentions and the impact one has on others and the ability to hypothesize the intentions of others and recognize how others' intentions impact the child. A *positive foundation* is defined for the purpose of resourcing and mastery as creating a positive foundation with which children can tackle daily situations in order to set them up to meet the challenge of reprocessing trauma. *Emotional regulation* is the child's ability to regulate his own intense emotions. By teaching the child an array of skills, psychotherapy is both beneficial and fun for the child. Children even enjoy teaching their newly acquired skills to parents, siblings, and friends.

It is also helpful to children when therapists teach relaxation skills, breathing, mindfulness, guided imagery, progressive muscle relaxation, and other calming and self-soothing skills and techniques.

Breathing Techniques   Breathing is one of the simplest and most important techniques to teach children. Children can be taught to lie on the floor and put a book on their stomach so they learn to breathe from the bottom of their stomach. This works for older children, but with younger children, the therapist can have the child exaggerate blowing up a balloon and learning to take really deep breaths and exhaling. With older children, it is also possible to teach them to learn to take longer and deeper breaths by simply counting and increasing the count to take longer and deeper breaths.

Guided Imagery   With guided imagery, the child can choose a comfy place to sit in the office and then the therapist can ask the child to select a real or imaginary favorite place where the child feels most comfortable. Next the child can then be instructed to take a guided tour of his favorite place as the therapist asks him questions that elicit all the senses about the place: "When you see your favorite place, what do you smell? What do you hear? How does your body feel?" The therapist can then enhance the child's responses by using short (2–4 saccades), slow sets of bilateral stimulation. "Bilateral Stimulation (BLS) is any external movement that produces alternating stimulation of the two sides of the client's body to get alternating activation of the two sides of the brain" (Adler-Tapia & Settle, 2008, p. 26). A saccade is one full pass of BLS from side to side.

The therapist can also ask the child to identify something that feels really relaxing to him and then have him draw a picture of whatever he identifies. One child identified floating in the pool as very relaxing, while another child identified walking through an imaginary castle. These images and sensations can also be enhanced with the use of short, slow sets of BLS.

Relaxation Skills In addition to breathing techniques and guided imagery, children can be taught relaxation skills. Teaching children relaxations skills is extremely beneficial no matter what the presenting symptoms. Relaxation skills can incorporate breathing, guided imagery, and the "butterfly hug," which was created by Lucinda Artigas in 1997 during her work with survivors of Hurricane Paulina in Acapulco, Mexico. The butterfly hug is a type of BLS and can be used as a self-soothing technique (Jarero, 2001). The therapist can demonstrate how the child can cross her arms and with alternating slow taps on her own arms help herself to self-soothe and calm as the child notices what is happening to her by using mindfulness. As the child continues with the alternating taps, she can then pretend that what she is observing is just like clouds passing by as she takes deep breaths. The butterfly hug is also part of the EMDR group protocol or butterfly hug protocol described later in this chapter.

Containers Containers are any type of tangible object that can be used to store intense emotional affect from which the child needs a break or for resources and skills the child needs for self-soothing and emotional regulation. A container can be a box, a jar, or any object that holds something else. Containers are a fun and creative activity for children. Food storage containers can be used both in the office and for the child to take with her in order to deposit anything she feels she needs to contain both in therapy and in her daily life. For example, a child can use containers at school when she experiences intense emotion, but the opportunity is not available to express the emotion and it needs to be contained until later. Containers can also be used in a positive light to include all the resources and skills the child needs to be able to cope in her life. The child can create a container to put in all her resources in order to have those available as needed. Sometimes this means writing all the resources on a piece of paper to put in the container or toolbox that the child always has available. Children can be encouraged to draw pictures or create figures or symbols to represent their safe place, or resources, or people who help them to be calm and self-soothe.

Some children choose to leave their containers in a safe place in the office and then make deposits and withdrawals to their containers each time they return for a session. A child makes a deposit in an actual container when he needs to contain something he is not ready to process and then later makes withdrawals from the container for processing in the therapy session. It is especially important to explain to children that whatever is deposited (i.e., a dream, an emotion, a monster, a fear, a memory) must later be withdrawn for later reprocessing; otherwise, the container will overflow and interfere with their lives. Containers serve as very powerful resources and mastery experiences for children in the psychotherapy process and for titrating the impact of intense emotions.

Techniques for Discharging Intense Emotions   Various techniques in the office teach children to more effectively discharge intense emotions and the body energy children typically experience with intense emotion. This includes things like drawing an angry picture, noticing their disturbing feelings and kicking their legs or stomping their feet in time with the BLS, identifying the top 10 things for letting the air out of the balloon, jumping jacks, running laps, swimming, and other appropriate physical activities for releasing energy in order to self-calm. This is an opportunity for therapists to incorporate play therapy and art therapy techniques that the therapist has previously used in treating children.

Calming and Soothing Skills and Techniques   In addition to breathing, guided imagery, and progressive muscle relaxation, therapists can teach children other ways to help calm themselves. Calming techniques such as the use of transitional objects, dream catchers, singing, dancing, drumming, positive affirmations, and other play therapy and art therapy techniques can be used to help children improve coping and self-soothing.

Mastery Skills for Children   Children are most likely to be scheduled for psychotherapy because of emotional or behavioral concerns identified by their parents. Parents are quick to identify issues or symptoms with children, but are much less likely to identify the child's strengths or accomplishments. A strengths-based model, where the treatment focuses on enhancing the child's and family's strengths, can model and teach a strengths-based approach to children and families. This is integrated into each session starting at the beginning of each session where the therapist asks the child and parent about something the child did well since the last session. The child's successes and accomplishments can then be strengthened and installed as mastery experiences for children by adding BLS to strengthen the memory.

You can install resources, as discussed earlier in this chapter, or have the child identify something that makes him feel good about himself or something he has accomplished, which is called a *mastery skill.* A mastery skill is something that is installed that is a memory or experience that makes child the feel competent. This can be about a time when the child learned to ride a bike, his first day of school, a good grade on a test, or even a positive experience with sports. One goal of mastery is to identify an experience that is already stored in a positive memory network and strengthen the memory with BLS. This serves several purposes, including creating a positive foundation and feeling for the child, and it helps to get the child to associate positive affect with BLS. Focusing on mastery will help the child become more confident in himself and in the therapeutic process before trying to process traumas. If necessary, the therapist can remind the child that he can use his mastery experience to assist in making him feel more confident. Installing a mastery experience is quite helpful when a child is reluctant to work on a target or explore his current symptoms. The therapist can also teach children mastery skills to be used as resources.

The therapist can also have a child participate in more extensive RDI protocols that include identifying mastery experiences.

Sometimes children may need mastery skills in order to cope with upcoming stressful events, such as going to court and testifying. In this type of situation, it is helpful to ask the child to identify a time in his life when he was initially scared to do something, but in spite of his anxiety or fear he did it anyhow and was proud of what he accomplished. The therapist can say to a child, *"Tell me about a time when you were really scared to do something, but you did it anyway and were very glad that you did it."* The child's answer can then be installed as a mastery experience.

Procedural Considerations for Mastery Skills   If the child becomes overwhelmed by affect, he is most likely to attribute the discomfort to EMDR and the therapeutic process. Like adults, children need time to integrate what is occurring in therapy without becoming overwhelmed. Teaching containers, affect management, resourcing, and mastery skills are all critical parts of the process; however, the therapist's hesitancy to target the most severe trauma can delay the process when the child may not need as much skill building as the therapist implements. Therapists often express angst about targeting the most horrendous traumas with their child clients. Therapists need to consider whether the child is prepared to reprocess the target memory, but it is the therapist who is not prepared to handle the child's trauma, which stalls the therapeutic process. Therapists may experience vicarious trauma from the severity of the child's experiences; therefore, it is important for therapists to always be aware of their own countertransference issues with children and to participate in ongoing self-care.

Resource Development and Installation (RDI) Skills for Children   Andrew Leeds first published his protocol for RDI skills for adults in 1998 in order to provide a template for clients to develop skills for accessing maladaptively stored memory networks while being able to cope with the sometimes intense affect associated with the memories. Since then, Dr. Deborah Korn and Dr. Leeds (2002) have tested the efficacy of the RDI protocol for use during the preparation phase of EMDR to enhance stabilization of adults with complex PTSD. RDI has been taught in the basic EMDR trainings. The goal of RDI is to enhance the ability of the client for emotional regulation and improve the capacity for coping with intense affect during EMDR reprocessing.

Once the child has successfully identified as many resources as necessary to participate in targeting a memory for reprocessing, the therapist can return to the assessment phase to begin with a memory. Sometimes the child may have been able to process a memory, but other memories may be overwhelming, indicating that the child may be in need of additional resources.

It is important for the therapist to remind the child during each session to use her resources and mastery skills both during the session and at home. If the child has drawn any pictures of resources or created any symbols of other resources, the therapist can have her look at the picture or hold the symbol to help anchor the resource. In addition to developing children's resources, children benefit from learning how to label and express their emotions.

Emotional Literacy   Emotional literacy is the ability of a child to label and describe emotions. The child's unique neurological development impacts her verbal ability and awareness of emotions. If children struggle with identifying, labeling, and describing emotions, the therapist will need to teach emotional literacy and weave skill building into the EMDR protocol. As children are able to more successfully express how they feel, children often experience a greater mastery of their intense emotions and behaviors.

It is helpful to offer opportunities for children to enhance their emotional literacy skills while also encouraging parents to teach and encourage the appropriate expression of emotions at home. This is an opportunity for therapists to model skills for children and parents during sessions of psychotherapy.

Mindfulness and Body Awareness   Children also benefit from learning to be mindful of their own unique responses both internally and externally, as well as learning to read their own bodies. In learning mindfulness, children learn to be aware of their own thoughts (metacognitions), emotions, actions, and motivations. This is an unfolding process that is impacted by development. Because children are very present oriented and limbic driven, developing mindfulness is a basic unfolding skill. As children become aware of themselves, their own emotions, choices for actions, and motivations, they are better able to understand themselves and others. Mindfulness and body awareness can be interwoven into therapy. One art therapy technique to teach children aspects of mindfulness and body awareness is to have the child lie on a large piece of paper and have the parent trace the child's outline on the paper. The therapist can teach the child about how sometimes we can see on the outside when we are hurt, like when we have a cut or bruise; however, sometimes it's hard to tell what's hurting on the inside. This technique proceeds with either having the child identify on the drawing where he might feel hurt on the inside such as in his head, heart, stomach, or other body parts, or by having the child place bandages on the picture. This intervention serves as a projective technique and an opportunity to teach the child about body awareness. Once the child can identify a symptom such as chronic stomachaches, therapists can use this to teach mindfulness. The therapist can explain that sometimes stomachaches come from eating something that bothers our stomach or tummy, while other time our stomachs hurt because we are worried or afraid. Teaching mindfulness and body awareness can also help the therapist to identify where the child holds his distress or memories of a traumatic experience. There are many resources for therapists to learn mindfulness and body awareness and to teach children these skills. Body awareness will become even more important in the EMDR protocol as the therapist moves to the remaining phases of the protocol where children are asked to identify body sensations.

Techniques for Distancing and Titrating Intense Affect   In addition to teaching children skills for self-soothing and calming, the therapist needs to remind children and parents that these skills can be practiced outside the therapist's office, especially if the child needs to distance from intense affect. Children are very likely to avoid intense affect by becoming sleepy, increasing activity level, changing the subject, or using various avoidance skills. It is crucial to any therapy to teach children how to distance themselves from intense affect before it becomes overwhelming or to titrate the affect in order that it is manageable. There are many skills for distancing and titrating affect, including having the child imagine changing the color of the affect, changing the volume, or imaging the uncomfortable or distressing image or experience on a screen.

One effective technique is to teach children to imagine that they have a remote control for a television while identifying which channels hold comfortable feelings, images, people, or resources, while other channels hold the distressing feelings, emotions, memories, or situations. The child then is given the power to change the channel as necessary to distance or titrate intense affect. Children may want to draw a picture of a remote that labels resources for them to use. In addition to learning to distance and titrate intense emotions, children may need to learn techniques for appropriately discharging intense emotions.

Techniques for Discharging Intense Emotions   Children may be enrolled in psychotherapy for inappropriately expressing intense emotions that manifest in behavioral issues. In addition to exploring what emotions underlie children's behavioral symptoms, therapists need to help children learn to express their intense emotions more appropriately in order to reduce behavioral problems. Therapists can teach children new words to express themselves or appropriate skills for expressing intense affect, such as using jumping jacks to discharge the energy behind frustration or anger. These skills can be used at home and school in order for children to express themselves and feel understood without getting in trouble for behavioral problems. Therapists can weave techniques into sessions in order to improve children's skills. Depending on the amount of distress in the child's life, some children many need more advanced skills. Techniques for discharging intense emotions can include skills for self-soothing and calming.

Calming and Soothing Skills and Techniques   As previously discussed, children can be taught relaxation, imagery, and mindfulness and these skills can be used on a regular basis to self-soothe. In addition, it is helpful to explore what the child has used thus far for calming themselves. These successes can be installed as mastery experiences, so the therapist can ask the child, *"Tell me about a time when you were really angry and you didn't get in trouble."* Therapists can also use children's hobbies as techniques for self-soothing. If a child plays basketball, she can be encouraged to safely play basketball when feeling frustrated in order to calm herself and discharge negative energy. Some children read, draw, or use physical activities to help themselves to relax. There are many skills and techniques that can be used with children that help them feel more powerful and successful.

Skills for between Sessions   Children need to be instructed and reminded to use all of their resources, calming and soothing skills, safe/calm place, and containers between sessions for improving coping. It is helpful to predict that the issues addressed in therapy may continue to process outside of sessions and the child has skills to empower him to cope more effectively with symptoms and stressors. Parents also can be asked to demonstrate skills and cue children to use newly acquired skills.

Teaching the Mechanics of EMDR   It is during the preparation phase that clients are also taught the mechanics of EMDR. These include the train metaphor, stop signal, safe/calm place, and BLS, in addition to skills for affect management, emotional literacy, and stabilization. These mechanics are part of the basic training (Shapiro, 2008) that therapists learn with adjustments to help children and adolescents understand EMDR. This begins by explaining the mechanics of EMDR in simple terms.

Train Metaphor   The train metaphor is used in EMDR to teach the child to manage the information and intense affect that can potentially be activated during reprocessing. The child is taught to imagine being on a train looking out the window noticing their issues as just scenery going by. Old memories, body sensations, emotions, and symptoms are considered scenery that is just passing by as the individual participates in EMDR to reprocess the maladaptively stored information to adaptive resolution. Since many children have not had the experience of a train, it is important to identify a metaphor that the child can understand.

Stop Signal   The stop signal is used for the client to signal the therapist that the client needs to stop reprocessing and take a break because the client is feeling overwhelmed. The client and therapist have identified a specific signal that the therapist understands is about the client asking the therapist to stop reprocessing and have the client move to the client's safe/calm/comfortable place. Stop signals with children are important and can be elicited from even very young children with adjustments to the directions the therapist uses. With children, teaching the stop signal can be as simple as having the child hold up their hand to signal that the therapist should stop.

Bilateral Stimulation (BLS)   One of the nuances of using EMDR is learning how to implement the different types of bilateral stimulation. Bilateral stimulation includes eye movements, tactile and auditory stimulation. In EMDR training, therapists are encouraged to use only eye movements because the research on EMDR is almost entirely based on eye movements as bilateral stimulation.

Eye movements can be elicited by the therapist by moving your fingers as taught in EMDR training. For children, the therapist can put stickers or draw figures on the therapist's fingers to assist the child to track. Therapists can also use penlights on the floor or wall for the client to follow or purchase specialized equipment for eliciting eye movements. Children will track with their eyes and enjoy the use of puppets or finger puppets, stuffed animals, or other toys selected by the child to increase the child's focus on the eye movements.

In addition to assessing the client's ability to track the type of bilateral stimulation, the number of saccades also impact the client's ability to track the stimulus.

It is important to determine the number of saccades that are necessary when working with a particular client. Dr. Shapiro and the research suggest that eye movements should move as fast as the client can tolerate in order to activate processing rather than just tracking. The therapist can tell the client that "I'm just guessing at the speed and number of passes, but you can tell me to stop or continue." By giving the client the power to continue or stop the saccades, the therapist becomes more attuned to the individual client's unique manner of processing.

Tactile Stimulation   Therapists can also provide bilateral stimulation through tactile stimulation such as tapping on the clients hands or using a device especially designed for therapist use during EMDR. The Neurotek® device is a small machine that can be purchased by therapists to create artificial bilateral stimulation with tactile stimulation (children often call these buzzies because the machine buzzes as you contact it) or auditory stimulation with tones or by connecting the device to a CD player or MP3 player to create auditory stimulation (discussed below). There are many different ways to use tactile forms of BLS with clients and some creative and fun ways to engage children with BLS including drumming, stomping, marching, or playing patty-cake, to list a few.

Auditory Stimulation   Therapists can provide auditory stimulation by using technological equipment like the Neurotek® that can either pulse in the client's ears or by attaching a CD player or iPod to the equipment in order for the client to use music as bilateral stimulation. When using the device that provides bilateral stimulation it is helpful to start by turning all controls including auditory and tactile volume and speed to the lowest level of the control. Proceed by slowly increasing the speed, intensity, or volume until the client chooses a setting that is most comfortable.

Some therapists use remote speakers that can be placed on either side of a play area or sand tray and then use a preprogrammed CD that provides alternating auditory stimulation. It is important to monitor whether actual BLS is occurring because children are active and may not stay between the two speakers.

Determining the Speed, Intensity, and Number of Saccades of BLS   In addition to determining the most appropriate type of BLS, the therapist needs to determine what speed and number of saccades work most effectively with the client. When the therapist is installing resources, safe/calm place, or mastery experiences, it is important to use short, slow sets. With children, two to four saccades are usually sufficient for installing something positive. The therapist needs to be ever aware of the goal of the BLS. If the therapist trying to install something positive, then the therapist should not attempt to evoke maladaptively stored information for reprocessing when longer, faster sets of BLS are indicated. This issue will be discussed further in the desensitization phase later in the chapter.

The process of instructing children about BLS can be diagnostic and give information about the child's preference for processing and suggest sensory integration issues. For example, if the child is not able to process with eye movements, the therapist may try tactile or auditory saccades and find that the child processes more effectively in an auditory or tactile mode.

Safe/Calm Place   As previously discussed, clients of all ages also need to have resources for titrating intense affect. The client needs to be able to metaphorically go to a safe/calm place during reprocessing with EMDR if the affect becomes overwhelming and the client cannot continue. No matter what the age, all clients need to have identified a safe/calm place and a stop signal with which to communicate with the therapist.

Finding a safe/calm place with child clients is important and can be elicited from even very young children with adjustments to the directions the therapist uses. For example, young children may need to draw a picture or several pictures of a safe/calm place that can be used in sessions. The protocol for teaching a safe/calm place is part of basic training in EMDR. In addition to teaching the child a resource for self-soothing and distancing from intense affect, this protocol is also diagnostic.

As the therapist elicits a safe/calm place from the child, the therapist can observe how the child processes and understands instructions. Installing a safe/calm place can be difficult with severely and chronically traumatized children; therefore, the therapist may need to install mastery experiences and resources before the child is able to identify a real or imaginary safe/calm place.

Assessing When the Child Is Sufficiently Prepared and Ready to Proceed   Case conceptualization in EMDR with children is a circular process in which the therapist is assessing, teaching, modeling, reinforcing, and monitoring the child's responses to treatment. The early phases are critical during specific episodes of care, and the therapist may need to return to those phases if the child needs additional skills for coping and stabilization. Depending on the child's symptoms and needs, the therapist may need to spend a great deal of time front loading children's resources in order to continue with the assessment phase of EMDR. This is a decision point in treatment where therapists may be reinforced by the child's progress and abatement of symptoms and by noticing that the child may enjoy new skills in dealing with symptoms. Therapists need to use their clinical judgment as to how much time to spend in the preparation phase. Therapists who do not spend sufficient time in preparation may find that the child will become overwhelmed during the trauma processing phases of EMDR, starting with the assessment phase. However, therapists who spend too much time in the preparation phase may never get to trauma reprocessing, and consequently maladaptively stored information will not get reprocessed. Thus, skipping later phases is not doing EMDR. Therapists need to resist the temptation to avoid children's pain and the consequent temptation to stick with the fun parts of treatment in which the child gets state changes but does not get the deeper trait change that is possible. If the maladaptively stored memory network is not reprocessed, the core of the symptomatology remains with the potential for significant developmental implications for child clients.

In order to approach this clinical issue, it is helpful to start with teaching safe/calm place and if the child has one resource with which to self-soothe, the therapist can proceed with the assessment phase. At any point in the treatment process, the therapist may assess that the child is in need of additional resources and return to the preparation phase to teach the child new skills. Case Example 6-5 describes how Julia was prepared for EMDR.

Case Example 6-5: Preparing Julia for EMDR

After developing a comprehensive treatment plan with Julia and her parents, at the next session the therapist taught Julia the mechanics of EMDR. The therapist first demonstrated the different types of bilateral stimulation (BLS), and Julia decided that she liked the "buzzies" in her pockets. (The buzzies are used for bilateral stimulation and described in detail later in the chapter.) Then the therapist told Julia they were going to do a safe/calm place exercise. Julia was asked if she could think of a calm relaxing place that made her feel safe. Julia immediately thought of her bedroom holding her stuffed bunny. The therapist had her draw a picture of the bunny and then had her think of the relaxed, calm place while the therapist turned on the "buzzies" for slow short sets of tactile saccades. The therapist did this several times until Julia continued to report feeling more and more relaxed. As part of preparing Julia for the reprocessing phases of EMDR, the therapist also conducted a resource development installation (RDI) with Julia.

JULIA'S RDI SESSION

The therapist asked Julia what was the good quality she needed to have to be able to go back to school. Julia said, "Be brave." The therapist asked Julia to recall a time she remembered feeling brave. She said, "When I stood up in class for the spelling bee last year." The therapist asked Julia what that looked like and how it felt. The therapist turned on the "buzzies" for a short amount of time and asked Julia how it felt. Julia said, "Good." The therapist continued on with that experience and the BLS until Julia felt her bravery become very strong.

ASSESSMENT PHASE

Description and Purpose   This is where the EMDR protocol is unique from other types of therapies. The assessment phase includes specific procedural steps therapists typically practice during the practicum of EMDR basic training. Identifying targets for reprocessing is one of the significant goals of the assessment phase. Even though targets have been noted during the client history and treatment planning phase as part of the targeting sequence plan, it is during the assessment phase that the therapist identifies a specific target for reprocessing through the remaining phases of the protocol. In phase 3 of EMDR, the therapist and client formally identify targets for reprocessing and complete the procedural steps of the protocol that include eliciting an image, negative and positive cognition, Validity of Cognition (VoC), emotions, SUD, and body sensations.

Selecting Targets   There are many ways to identify targets with clients. When working with children, there are imaginative ways to identify targets that tap into a child's way of processing. After the target is identified, the client is asked to pinpoint the worst part of the memory. Children may identify the worst part of the memory by drawing pictures, working in the sand tray, or using puppets and many other types of art and play therapy techniques.

Tools for Target Identification with Children   The targeting sequence plan organized during the client history and treatment planning phase of EMDR is revisited as the therapist and client select the first maladaptively stored event to reprocess. The therapist starts with exploring the validity of the touchstone event as the event the client wants to target with EMDR. Once the target is selected, the next procedural step of the EMDR assessment phase is to identify the image that represents the most distressing part of the target event.

Children can draw a picture of the target or create the target in the sand tray or with the toys in the therapist's office. Art therapy techniques such as painting the picture or creating the picture with clay are also some of the many creative techniques therapists can use with children.

The Image   Once the target is identified, the client is asked to select the image. The target and the image are not the same thing. A target is an issue or incident or experience or memory from the client's life that is believed to be the maladaptively stored incident that is contributing to the child's current symptom presentation. The image is a picture that represents the worst part of the target. Again with children, the image can be painted or drawn or created in the sand tray. Some therapists have children create collages of the image or take digital pictures that represent the image.

Negative and Positive Cognitions   Distilling the negative and positive cognitions is the next step of the procedural steps of the assessment phase. This process requires patience, creativity, and attunement to the client. The negative cognition is a presently held, negative belief about one's self that is believed to have its origins in the maladaptively stored events most likely originating in the touchstone event. Once a negative cognition has been identified that is a presently held belief that is also irrational, self-referencing, and generalizable, the therapist has essentially connected to the client's memory network. Along with a negative cognition, the therapist then identifies the positive cognition. The positive cognition is what the client would like to believe about themselves instead of the negative cognition. The positive cognition needs to be realistic, self-referencing, and generalizable.

The therapist needs to invest time in identifying a negative cognition that resonates for the client. If the therapist was able to develop a targeting sequence plan during the client history and treatment planning phase of EMDR, the therapist and client have already identified the client's negative cognition as part of the targeting sequence plan.

If the client was unable to develop a targeting sequence plan during client history and treatment planning because the client was not able to tolerate the exploration of past events because that process was too triggering and the therapist determined that the client needed to proceed with the preparation phase in order to improve self-soothing and calming skills and develop resources. At this point in treatment, the therapist may need to return to the process of distilling a negative cognition for the target identified by the client. If this is true, the therapist then asks the client, "When you bring up that image of the worst part of the event, what is your negative belief about yourself now?"

Having the client identify what he wants to believe is very important because it's an educational process of having the client consider possibilities. What is it that the client wants to be able to believe about himself instead?

It is very important that the negative cognition and positive cognition "match." Typically, they are polar opposites. If the negative cognition and positive cognition are different, the therapist needs to take the time to find negative and positive cognitions that match. For example, if the negative cognition is "I'm not good enough" and the positive cognition is "I'm safe now," the cognitions are significantly different, and the therapist needs to ask the client which resonates more for the specific image. If the positive cognition resonates more, it is appropriate to then change the negative cognition to match the positive cognition.

Also, it is important to ensure that the negative cognition makes sense with the specific target. For example, if the client's target is the memory of a rape and her negative cognition is "I'm not good enough," the therapist may want to explore whether that negative cognition truly fits for the client or if she is confused about the EMDR process.

Children may not be able to follow this explanation of the negative cognition, so therapists can simply ask the child, "When you think about that picture of that bad thing that happened, what is your bad thought about yourself now?" The words *bad thought* and *good thought* replace the terms *negative* and *positive cognition* if the child is unable to understand the concept. The negative and positive cognitions for children may be trauma specific and presented in fantasy or metaphor or even in third person. For example, young children may describe a bad thought as a monster rather than a specific traumatic event such as was described in Julia's case.

Again, the child can draw a picture of the bad thought and good thought or even create these thoughts in the sand tray. It is possible to divide the sand tray in half and have the child create the bad thought on the left side of the tray and the good thought on the right side of the tray with a bridge between the bad thought and the good thought implying that the goal is to move from the bad thought to the good thought.

Validity of Cognition   Continuing in the EMDR process, the therapist next assesses the validity of the positive cognition (VoC). The VoC is measured on a 7-point scale from 1 (completely false) to 7 (completely true). Measuring the VoC is often confusing for adult clients as well as children because the measurement needs to be more concrete. Although measuring the VoC is somewhat challenging, it is possible and important to attempt to obtain a VoC from even the youngest clients. As was described above when the therapist uses the sand tray to develop a good thought and a bad thought, it is possible to ask the child to identify which step of the bridge, with seven steps between the bad thought and good thought, the client is at now. Once the therapist has asked the client how true the positive cognition feels to him now, the process has moved from a cognitive level to an emotional level. Using a VoC bridge with children makes this measurement very simple and easy for children to understand and follow.

Expressing the Emotion   After the VoC, the therapist asks the client for the emotion associated with the target. Whatever emotion the client reports, the therapist notes the emotion the client identified and continues with the procedural steps. With children, the therapist may have taught emotional literacy, or the therapist may need to teach the child about identifying emotions at this point. The therapist may show the child her picture or the sand tray she designed and then ask the child how she feels about the bad thought. After identifying the emotion associated with the target and the bad thought, the therapist then needs to assess the level of disturbance.

Subjective Units of Disturbance (SUD)   The SUD is a standard measurement of disturbance on an 11-point-scale from 0 or no disturbance to 10, the most disturbing. Once the client has identified an emotion that is connected with the target, the therapist immediately asks the client to assess how disturbing the emotion feels to him now on the SUD scale.

Children may not understand this scale, so the therapist can simply demonstrate the amount of disturbance by asking the child, "Is it this big? This big? Or this big?" as the therapist moves his or her hands further and further apart. The therapist then notes the child's report of the level of disturbance and continues by assessing the location of the disturbance in the client's body.

Body Sensation   As soon as the client chooses an SUD level, the therapist asks the client for the body sensation, which is the client's noting the location of the emotion in his body. The therapist asks the child, "Where do you feel that disturbing feeling in your body?" The therapist may need to remind the child of what he taught him about body sensations, or he may need to teach the child about body sensations at this point in the protocol. EMDR is a comprehensive treatment approach because it has the client focus on cognitions, emotions, and body sensations.

The therapist then connects the image, negative cognition, emotion, and body sensation, and starts the bilateral stimulation, which signals the beginning of the desensitization phase of EMDR.

Children are often quite able to follow the steps of the assessment phase when the therapist can use age-appropriate language and explain the process to the child. More in-depth and creative explanations for eliciting each step of the protocol with even young children are described in *EMDR and the Art of Psychotherapy with Children* (Adler-Tapia and Settle, 2008).

DESENSITIZATION PHASE

Description and Purpose   The goal of the desensitization phase is to reprocess the maladaptively stored information that has been accessed and stimulated by the procedural steps of the previous phase. The desensitization phase begins when the therapist starts BLS after asking the client to hold together the previously identified image or picture and the negative cognition and to notice where the client feels the feelings in her body. The length of the desensitization phase can be only minutes within a single session or expand over several sessions that could take months, depending on the number of channels associated with the chosen target. If the negative cognition is connected to many experiences in the client's history, the links between memories can be extensive. For example, if the client's negative cognition is "I'm not good enough" and the client first remembered thinking "I'm not good enough" at age 2 when she was punished during potty training, and the client is now 40, the negative cognition or belief can have infiltrated 38 years of life experiences and memories for the client. The belief that "I'm not good enough" can be a foundational belief for the client. The connections may be clear or may appear to be tangential and irrelevant. This is when the therapist's patience and attunement is vital. The therapist's ability to hang in there and stay out of the client's way is crucial to the desensitization process.

For children, the memory networks will most likely be shorter due to the age of the child. This is one of the many reasons why EMDR is not only effective with children, but profound in changing cognitive beliefs about oneself.

Evidence of Reprocessing   Children evidence reprocessing in a variety of ways similar to adults, but also with nonverbal cues, including yawning, becoming more or less active, affective evidence like crying or sighing, and frequently avoidance or becoming sleepy. This is where the therapist needs to be closely attuned to the child because reprocessing with children can be more subtle. Yawning or becoming sleepy may be evidence of mild dissociation because children may feel like they are being flooded by emotion, and it is important for the therapist to have more training and skills in working with children.

While working with children, it is especially important for therapists to be actively involved and consider frequently changing the type of BLS and allowing the child to move. Children who can be active during reprocessing are more able to focus on reprocessing than children who are expected to sit still. A child may sit on a yoga ball and bounce during reprocessing in order to move, so the therapist may notice an increase or decrease in the child's bouncing. Or a child may need to take a break or get a drink or go to the restroom. Allowing children to be active as they reprocesses traumatic events allows them to discharge energy and to be able to engage in the process for longer periods of time.

Clinical Implications One of the challenges of the desensitization phase is for therapists to follow the client's process and stay out of the way. Therapists may feel the need to provide reflective statements or link with insights; however, the EMDR protocol is that the response from the therapist should be to say to the client "just notice" and follow the BLS during the desensitization phase. Therapists may feel the need to ask questions or repeat the client's responses; however, no interpretation is necessary with EMDR.

Another clinical implication of EMDR desensitization is that as the desensitization process occurs new memory networks are accessed, reprocessed, and moved to adaptive resolution. This process can involve the therapist's and client's moving through the previous phases in a circular rather than linear process. For example, after taking a thorough history and creating a treatment plan, the therapist may learn new and more detailed information about the client's history during the assessment phase of the protocol. It is also common to start desensitization and then realize the client needs additional preparation skills with which to process a particular memory network. The EMDR therapy process is often unpredictable and surprising as the therapist and client learn together how the client has experienced and stored the traumatic event. Often, a missing piece will arise that explains why the event has become encapsulated and not completed by the individual's natural healing process. At each phase of the EMDR protocol, the therapist needs to be aware that each client processes in unique ways, and it is the client's unique healing process that needs to be followed by the therapist using EMDR. This is where the previous tools you have learned as a therapist can be integrated into the phases of the EMDR protocol.

During the desensitization phase with children, clinical implications suggest that children may not have stored the traumatic events in ways that make sense. Instead, children may express fears of monsters, or sleeping in their own bed, or going to school; however, there is frequently no logic to the desensitization phase because it is the child's own perception of what occurred at the time that is encapsulated. Therefore, younger children may express traumas in fantasy or imagery or even in sensory–motor memories that are difficult to follow. It is important for the clinician to remember that what matters is not whether what the client reports makes sense to the therapist, but whether the child's symptoms improve. Case Example 6-6 describes the assessment and desensitization phases for Julia.

Case Example 6-6: Assessment and Desensitization of Julia's Memories of the Bus Accident

Again, Julia's case illustrates the efficacy of the EMDR protocol with young children. For the assessment phase, the therapist began by having Julia draw a picture of the last time she saw her brother. Julia's picture was her brother waving good-bye from the back window of the bus. Julia's negative belief about herself was "I'm never going to see him again." (This is a child's version of "I'm powerless" or "I can't let go." See the changes of languaging of the negative cognition later in the chapter.) The positive belief she wanted was "He's always in my heart." (This may be a child's version of acceptance.) Julia then drew a picture of her brother in a heart. The therapist had Julia measure how true the positive belief was on the VoC bridge. The VoC bridge was a drawing of a bridge with seven rungs. The seventh rung meant the good thought felt completely true, and the first rung meant it felt false. Julia picked the second rung, meaning the good thought felt only a little true. Next, the therapist asked how Julia felt when she looked at the picture of her brother waving good-bye and the bad thought, "I'm never going to see him again." Julia said really bad, really sad. The therapist asked her how bad that felt (SUD). The therapist held her hands wide apart and said, "This bad? This means the worst anybody can imagine." The therapist then held her hands in the middle and said, "This means pretty bad, but it's in the middle." Then the therapist put her hands together so they touched, and she said, "This means it's not bad at all. It's a zero." Julia held her hands out as wide as they would go and said, "This bad. The worst." The therapist said, "Where do you feel it in your body?" Julia said, "My heart." Julia looked like she was going to cry. The therapist had Julia put the "buzzies" in her pockets and turned them on for about 30 seconds. After the therapist turned them off, Julia was asked, "What are you getting?" Julia said, "My mom and I were in our car behind the bus that morning. My brother waved to us." The therapist said, "Go with that." The desensitization phase continued for about 20 minutes. Sometimes Julia remembered more details about that day. Sometimes she just felt things in her stomach. Toward the end, Julia said, "My brother is with God now. I see him on a cloud waving at us." The therapist said, "Go with that," and turned the "buzzies" on for 30 seconds. She then turned them off and asked, "What did you get?" Julia said, "God is in my heart, and he's putting my brother there."

The therapist asked Julia how she felt when she thought of the original incident. Julia said, "I feel better." The therapist asked her to rate it with her hands. Julia held her hands up with just a small space between her hands and said, "Just a little." The therapist asked, "Where do you feel that in your body?" Julia said, "In my tummy." The therapist said, "Go with that," and turned on the "buzzies" for approximately 30 seconds again. After the therapist asked, "What did you get?" Julia said, "I feel better. He is in my heart. I want to stop. Can I play with that puzzle?" The therapist said, "Yes, but can I ask you how bad it feels now?" Julia put her hands together, "It's zero." The therapist asked, "Can we do one more thing? Can you tell me on the VoC bridge how true the words 'he's in my heart' feel to you?" Julia looked at the bridge and put an "X" on the seventh rung, "It's true!" Then the therapist asked Julia to notice any feeling in her body when she thought of "he's in my heart." She said, "No, just the scratch on my knee hurts, that's all."

The therapist completed this session by inviting Julia's parents into the session, and as Julia played, the therapist explained what they had worked on. The therapist told Julia she did a good job and asked that she and her parents notice how she feels in between sessions. They were asked to notice any changes in behaviors, good or bad, and notice any dreams.

Procedural Considerations for Desensitizing Targets with EMDR   Many therapists will return to the original target, even though the client is continuing to process. It is necessary to return to the original target only if the therapist believes the client has completed a memory network and the therapist is reevaluating the original target. The therapist asks the client to return to the original target to assess where the client is in reprocessing the target during desensitization. The therapist simply asks the client to bring up the original incident and then report what he gets now. Whatever the client reports, the therapist instructs him to "Go with that" and continues with desensitization. If he identifies any disturbance at all, the therapist continues with desensitization.

If, in the clinical opinion of the therapist, the client's target appears to have been completed, the therapist then takes an SUD measurement. The therapist may suspect that the target has been reprocessed when the client's responses are neutral or positive. For example, the client may begin to make statements approximating the positive cognition. A client may say, "I was only a kid. I couldn't have stopped him." This would indicate client movement and the possibility that the target no longer has emotional valence. There is often a surprising amount of reprocessing to be completed between an SUD of one and zero.

Being aware of the client's nonverbal presentation is just as important as listening to what the client verbally reports. Some clients may overfocus on doing the desensitization process perfectly. They stare, hold their breath, or try to memorize everything they notice during BLS. This is when it is important to repeat the directions to just notice what is happening. For example, clients may stop blinking as they try to stare at the eye movements, and then their eyes may begin to tear. This can cause them to struggle with eye movements. Clients may need to be reminded that it is fine to blink while following the eye movements.

Client breathing is a significant factor in any type of therapy. As the therapist remains attuned to the client's nonverbal signals, breathing can mean many different things. Watching the client's breathing during reprocessing is critical. Anxious clients may take very shallow breaths. When a client is reprocessing a target, he many initially hold his breath and then may take a shallow breath and then a deep breath when he has reprocessed through the target. Clients may also stop breathing while reprocessing a memory, and the therapist may need to remind the client that it is very important to just notice his breathing. Other clients may think that they are supposed to hold their breath during BLS. These clients again need to be instructed to just notice their breathing.

Clients may also try to remember everything that comes up during BLS in order to report this to the therapist. It is helpful to tell the client that the therapist needs only a brief report of the last thing he noticed when the therapist paused the BLS. Although many clients like to report everything they became aware of during BLS, encouraging the client to report only the last thing he noticed facilitates the process. If the client appears distracted or confused, or reports that nothing is happening or that he is not noticing anything, the therapist can simply instruct him to just go with that. This may just be part of the client's progression.

Children may become very still as they are reprocessing or may become very agitated. What is important to notice is that either behavior reflects a significant change in behavior that was not evident prior to beginning the desensitization phase aimed at reprocessing an identified target. It is imperative to learn each client's unique presentation. Encouraging the client to just notice what is happening during reprocessing and go with whatever comes up is a hallmark of effective reprocessing in EMDR. It is important to know that it is during the desensitization phase that a substantial process occurs in EMDR. The transmutation of the target from a traumatic event with significant disturbance reprocesses through as associative chaining begins to link up with more adaptive responses in the present. Associative chaining occurs as the therapist follows the client's process as the client links up past events that are associated through some significance in the brain (shared images, cognitions, emotions, or sensations) as the client reports the links that arise during sets of BLS. How events are associated is not as important as the fact that the client's brain has made some type of association that now links maladaptively stored information that drives the client's current symptoms and that by reprocessing that data through to a healthy conclusion, the client's symptoms abate.

During EMDR, theoretically, the client links up maladaptively stored information with current adaptive resolutions; however, children may not possess the skills or information for adaptive resolution. This is when the introduction of emotional literacy, psychoeducational information, resource development, and mastery skills are helpful to provide children with new abilities to cope with previous traumatic events.

Implications of Developmental Milestones on Reprocessing Recognizing and integrating developmental milestones into psychotherapy with children is important with any type of therapy. Those developmental milestones related to cognitive processing, emotional literacy, mindfulness, physical and psychosocial development, and self-awareness impact how a child processes traumatic experiences and how those experiences are interpreted and reported by the child during desensitization. Since child development is often rapid but incongruent, therapists may note that a child has reprocessed a memory and later a different aspect of that memory arises, as is evidenced by the impact of the child's development from session to session. What is distressing or uncomfortable in one session may have resolved by the next session due to the child's development. A lack of resolution might indicate that the child may not have mastered a developmental task that is impacting the reprocessing of the maladaptively stored information.

Therapists working with children and adolescents will benefit greatly from understanding child development and the unique stages within which the individual child is experiencing the traumatic event *and* the therapeutic experiences. Case Example 6-7 illustrates how understanding child development can help when working with young children who try to explain something they cannot understand.

Case Example 6-7: Max's Narrative for Losing His Shoes

Children will often weave together evidence in their environment to try to create a coherent narrative in an effort to explain what they cannot understand. For example, 4-year-old Max kept getting in trouble for losing one of his shoes, and no matter how hard he or his mother tried, they could not figure out what was happening to Max's shoes. After losing the mate to at least six pairs of Max's shoes, Max's parents were so frustrated with Max that they gave him responsibility for doing extra chores to pay for a new pair of shoes.

Max was extremely frustrated because he did not feel responsible for losing his shoes. Max then told his parents how a shark had come through his bedroom window and eaten his shoes. To Max, this was a reasonable explanation for something he could not explain because he had watched a television show on sharks explaining how sharks eat many things, including shoes. Max's drive to find an explanation for what confused and challenged him was not a lie, but instead an effort to make sense of something that made no sense.

Later, Max's mother learned that Max's little sister had been using Max's shoes to make a loud noise in the trash can that made her giggle. Indeed, there was a logical explanation for a situation that originally did not make sense. Max did not lie, but the distress of repeatedly losing his shoes and having consequences from his parents caused Max to try to alleviate his discomfort by creating a coherent narrative based on information in his immediate environment. It is important to remember that children often will look for explanations for things that disturb them that make no sense. Max's associative chaining made sense to him in that when you cannot find your shoes and have no explanation, it is possible that sharks eat shoes even though you live in the desert. Max's distress was discharged when he was able to find a reasonable explanation for his distressing event.

Completing Desensitization Phase   Therapists need to use clinical judgment when deciding whether the client has completed the desensitization phase. When the therapist has had the client return to the original incident and the SUD is 0, the therapeutic process is moving from the desensitization phase to the installation phase. The therapist may decide to continue with the desensitization process if the VoC remains 5 or less. The therapist might consider a VoC of 5 or less as indicative of the need to continue with desensitization. By moving to the installation phase, the protocol calls for the VoC to be measured with each successive set of BLS, which can be very distracting, especially with children. During the desensitization phase, the therapist does not need to evaluate the VoC as frequently as during the installation phase.

The EMDR protocol suggests that once the therapeutic process has moved to the installation phase, the therapist evaluates the VoC with each successive set of BLS. However, therapists should keep in mind that repeated requests for VoC (as well as SUD ratings) can make clients feel pressured to say what they think the therapist wants to hear (i.e., a lower SUD rating or a higher VoC rating), rather than what they would say without feeling such pressure. To diminish or prevent that sense of pressure, therapists can emphasize that it is important for the child to tell them what they really feel or believe, even if the ratings are not changing or getting better.

If the therapist continues with desensitization until the client begins to report successive positive statements, it is then clinically indicated that the client is ready for installation of the positive cognition. Therapists need to determine the flow of the EMDR protocol by assessing when to continue with the desensitization phase versus when to move to the installation phase.

The process flows much more effectively and the therapist decreases the likelihood of demand characteristics with children when she is continuing with desensitization until the child repeats positive responses that are essentially the same for several saccadic sets. For example, the child may say, "I *am* a good kid." The therapist responds, "Just notice that," and continues with bilateral stimulation. The child then repeats, "I am a *good* kid," and the therapist responds, "Just notice that." If it is evident that the child is presenting with the positive cognition or a close approximation, the therapist then considers that the client is ready to move to the installation phase of EMDR.

Cognitive Interweaves   A cognitive interweave is a technique used to jump-start blocked processing when previous approaches have not worked. A cognitive interweave is a question or statement offered by the therapist to the client if the client appears to have encountered blocked processing. Blocked processing occurs when the reprocessing appears to be stuck because the client is repeatedly reporting that nothing is changing or the client is getting nothing.

If the client encounters blocked processing, the therapist should first attempt other, more subtle interventions, including changing speed and direction of BLS. It is important to read the chapter on blocked processing in Shapiro's book (2002) and attempt the procedures for blocked processing before using cognitive interweaves.

Because cognitive interweaves are taught at the second weekend of training, therapists tend to use them without attempting other techniques first to assist the client with blocked processing. This does not mean that they are the first choice of techniques that therapists use when the client encounters blocked processing, but rather that learning to use them is more challenging.

In addition to cognitive interweaves, children may also benefit from motor interweaves. Motor interweaves can be introduced when the therapist notes that the child may need to move to jump-start reprocessing. Since child memories are often stored in sensory–motor format, the actual action needed to be taken may assist in jump-starting the reprocessing. Motor interweaves are not typically part of the EMDR protocol, but were designed by child therapists to assist children during reprocessing with EMDR. Motor interweaves can be used when it appears that the child needs to move or express an untaken action from the traumatic event. The therapist may say to the child, "You couldn't get away then, but what do you need to do now?" Children may then yell, "Stop," or get up and move away or kick. These untaken actions elicited by motor interweaves appear to assist children in focusing and continuing to reprocess traumatic events to facilitate movement when there is blocked processing.

Procedural Considerations   Desensitization continues as long as the client identifies any disturbance associated with the original target event. If the client appears to have reprocessed the event and the disturbance is alleviated, the therapist asks her to return to the original event and report what is remaining from that original incident. So the protocol suggests that the therapist says to the client, "When you bring up that original incident, what do you get now?" Whatever she reports, the therapist adds a set of BLS. If the client's response is neutral or positive, the therapist then measures the SUD. If there is any remaining disturbance or the SUD is greater than 0, desensitization continues. If the SUD is 0, the therapist then continues with the installation phase. The installation phase is part of completing a target.

Children often process targets quickly, to the surprise of the therapist. Therapists may also suspect that the observant child has learned that by reporting no disturbance, she can avoid continuing reprocessing. The therapist can assess the accuracy of the child's response by observing changes in the child's behaviors and affect, and by monitoring improvement in symptoms between sessions as reported by the parent, teacher, and child. It is not unusual for a child to move from a high disturbance or SUD of 10 to a SUD of 0 with a few sets of BLS. Children are often just done and ready to go play. Therapists will need to assess the efficacy of the reprocessing and may need to encourage the child to stay with the process a bit longer by providing the opportunity to play at the end of each session.

Ending a psychotherapy session with play builds the therapeutic alliance and allows the child to transition from the disturbance of reprocessing to returning to the environment with reduced distress. The therapist may show the child a clock in the office and explain that reprocessing a target will continue for a specific amount of time, and then at a certain time the reprocessing will be contained and the child will be permitted to spend the remainder of the session in a positive activity with the parent and therapist. It is important to reinforce children's work in therapy by congratulating them for a job well done.

Completing a Target   With EMDR, the target is considered completed when the client reports an SUD of 0, a VoC of 7, and a clear body scan.

Closure of an Incomplete Target   Reprocessing may not be completed during a single session of therapy; therefore, the therapist will need to pace the flow and timing of therapy to allow appropriate time for shutting down disturbance and preparing the client for the period between sessions. As discussed above, with children, it is helpful to allow time to play and remind the child of his safe/calm place and resources to use if any disturbance arises outside the therapy session.

INSTALLATION PHASE

Description and Purpose   The goal of the installation phase is to check the validity of the positive cognition and to strengthen its validity until it reaches a VoC of 7. This begins once the client assesses the SUD to be at a 0, indicating that there is no more disturbance associated with the original target. The therapist begins the installation phase by combining the original incident and the positive cognition and checking with the client to make sure that the original positive cognition selected still applies. Once the client either stays with the original positive cognition or chooses a more fitting positive cognition, the therapist proceeds with BLS to strengthen the validity of the positive cognition selected by the client. With each successive set of saccades, the therapist evaluates the VoC. Installation continues as long as the VoC strengthens. When the VoC reaches a 7 or greater and holds, the process moves into the body scan phase of EMDR.

During installation, it is important to continue with the same number of passes of BLS as used with the individual client during desensitization because it is necessary to ascertain if any unprocessed material remains.

Therapists will note that children typically progress through the installation phase very quickly. When the therapist states to the child, ''When you bring up that incident we started with today (your drawing or what you made in the sand tray) and those words "I'm safe now, how true do those words feel on the VoC bridge?" Children will often move from the bad thought or negative thought to the good thought or positive cognition with only a few saccades of BLS.

BODY SCAN PHASE

Description and Purpose   After desensitizing the target to a SUD of 0 and installing the positive cognition to a VoC of 7, the EMDR protocol continues with the body scan. The goal of the body scan phase is to clear any remaining disturbance the client may be experiencing as physical sensations. During this phase, the client is asked to hold the original incident together with the positive cognition and to scan his body from head to toe for any remaining disturbance. If any disturbance is noted, he is asked to focus on the disturbance and instructed to "go with that" as the therapist continues with BLS at the same frequency and speed used throughout the desensitization phase.

Sometimes the client will quickly report feeling no disturbance in his body. The client may report that he is feeling fine or calm, and then the process proceeds to closure. If the client reports some type of physiological disturbance, this disturbance is again desensitized using bilateral stimulation. He is instructed to notice the disturbance and allow whatever comes up to come up, and the therapist provides additional BLS. This may be a link to another channel or memory, or sometimes clients may just notice things in their body. Once a clear body scan is achieved, the process continues with the closure phase of EMDR.

Completing the body scan phase with children can require additional education, instruction, and demonstration. Children may be distracted by an external cut or bruise and need to be redirected to internal sensations such as headaches or tummy aches. Teaching children how to scan their body can involve explaining that scanning their body is like an x-ray, where we are looking inside their body from the top of their head to the tip of their toes. Sometimes it is useful to use some type of toy to demonstrate how to scan your body. The therapist can use a magnifying glass and demonstrate to the child how she can use the handheld magnifying glass to scan from the top of his head to the bottom of his feet, exploring for any distress or discomfort.

Children may report unusual body sensations in their arms or legs and can then be instructed to "go with that." It is important to note that the body scan phase often moves quickly for children, and then they are ready to play.

Completing the Body Scan   The body scan is completed when the child reports no discomfort in his body. This is referred to as a clear body scan, which is the marker for proceeding to the next phase of the EMDR protocol.

When the therapist identifies a clear body scan, he then determines what steps to take for the remainder of the session. Is there time to begin with the next target, or is it important to reinforce the child's success in therapy and to end the session with play and reinforcing the child's newest success?

Closure Phase

Description and Purpose   The purpose of the closure phase is to end the session whether or not the client has completed a target. The goal is for the client to be grounded, stabilized, and prepared to cope with what happens between sessions. The progression of the closure phase of EMDR is dependent on the status of the EMDR session. If the client has completed all previous phases, closure continues with the future template (as described below). If the session is incomplete, closure continues with stabilization of the client with instructions for in between sessions.

Closure of a Completed Session of EMDR   With a completed session of EMDR the SUD is 0, the positive cognition has been strengthened and installed to a VoC of 7, and there is a clear body scan. This is where some confusion exists for therapists. If the past events and current issues have been reprocessed, it is then beneficial to continue with the future template if session time allows. Otherwise, the therapist can choose to continue with the future template in the next session. The decision to process all past events and all current triggers before moving to the future template must be driven by case conceptualization and clinical judgment. With children, it is beneficial to process one target through to the future template. The child then leaves the therapy session empowered with the belief that she can handle the presenting problem that initially brought her to treatment. The positive results that emerge from completing the EMDR protocol leave the client with a positive association with therapy and the motivation to continue with EMDR even when the process is distressing. This is especially true with children. When children experience the positive benefits of EMDR by experiencing mastery and successfully reprocessing a target through to the future template, many will return and initiate reprocessing of additional and sometimes even more difficult targets.

In case conceptualization with children, the therapist may consider reprocessing a more current target with a child as a mastery experience. With some children, going after the most disturbing target may be overwhelming and create a resistance to reprocessing in therapy. If the child seems to struggle and balk at desensitization, it is helpful to target an incident that is less disturbing in order to demonstrate for the child the benefits of reprocessing. Once the client experiences mastery of an incident, the child may be willing to tackle more difficult and complicated targets.

Closing an Incomplete Session   In addition to the variations for closure of a completed EMDR session, there are treatment interventions necessary following an incomplete session of EMDR. With an incomplete session of EMDR, it is essential for the therapist to stop the reprocessing in time to ground the client in the office and contain any disturbing materials, if necessary, before the end of the session. With adults, the therapist reminds the client that he has done work during therapy and then uses the analogy of a train by explaining to the client that in this trip from California to Miami, the therapist has estimated that she believes that in this session the client has made it to Dallas. The therapist then reminds the client that between sessions the client may continue on the train trip to Miami and even end up in the Bahamas, which often elicits a laugh because it is not possible to take a train from California to the Bahamas.

The goal of closure following an incomplete session is to stabilize the client in order that he may leave the therapist's office firmly grounded in the present with skills to manage any additional processing or distress that may arise.

With children it is important to teach children self-calming and self-soothing techniques to use between sessions. It is also important to explain to children and parents that reprocessing may continue between sessions and what children and parents can do in order to assist the child in coping with the continued reprocessing. It is necessary to teach techniques such as containers, relationship skills, and other tools for children to use to cope with intense emotions. If the therapist has taught the child these skills during the preparation phase, it is helpful to remind the child about previously acquired skills and ask the parent to cue the child to use these skills between sessions.

Future Template   The future template is the opportunity to rehearse future desired behaviors and outcomes. The entire EMDR protocol is symptom driven; thus, if you think of case conceptualization along the lines of symptom manifestation, this will help guide the choice of the future template. The symptoms with which the client presented at the initial intake guide the selection of the future template. Thus, as with Julia in Case Example 6-8, if the parents bring the child into therapy due to the child's refusal to go to school, the future template would focus on the child's imaging getting ready and going to school tomorrow. The future template protocol would continue until the child can imagine going to school with positive outcomes. This is a positive template for the future related to the symptoms that initially brought the child into treatment.

Case Example 6-8: Julia's Future Template

The therapist asked Julia to think about going back to school and identifying the worst part of that future event. Julia reported, "Just walking in the corridors—thinking about that." The therapist had Julia draw a picture of it.

"What's the bad thought?" the therapist asked.

"Something bad might happen," Julia said.

"What do you want to think?" the therapist asked.

"I'm okay. I can do it," said Julia.

The therapist then turned on the "buzzies," and Julia reprocessed successfully to "I can do it!" The therapist had Julia imagine each step of the future event of going back to school. Then the therapist had Julia's parents take her to school on the weekend to walk the corridors. The therapist explained that if Julia experienced any disturbance while visiting the school, he would process that with Julia in her next session. However, Julia's visit to her school was uneventful, and she was able to return to school that Monday.

Julia's case illustrates the three-pronged approach of EMDR that includes the past, present, and future issues that were impacting Julia's school phobia. When determining how many issues to address in one session, the decision is dependent on the length of time remaining in the session. Brief time remaining requires closure to end the session and help the client to return to her life without significant distress. Alternatively, with time available, the therapist continues with the future template to complete the EMDR protocol for the specific target. With children, it is possible to target the past, present, and future of one target in a session because children process so quickly. This is especially true when the therapist focuses on identifying clear, concrete future events when conducting a future template process with a child. As with Julia, the specific future event was returning to school on Monday. The therapist could process with Julia all her anticipatory anxiety so that Julia's distress was alleviated and she successfully returned to school.

REEVALUATION PHASE

Description and Purpose   The final phase of EMDR is the reevaluation phase. The goal of the reevaluation phase of EMDR is to evaluate progress in treatment. There are actually three different times that the therapy protocol may necessitate reevaluation: at the end of a completed target, at the beginning of the next session, and when evaluating the treatment process, in order to aid in discharge planning.

The first type of reevaluation is actually checking the target during a session. This occurs when the therapist has the client return to the original incident and asks the client, "When you bring up that original incident, what do you get now?" Whatever the client's answer, the therapist then instructs the client to "go with that." This occurs during the desensitization phase as the therapist works with the client to reprocess the event in order to clear any disturbance.

The second type of reevaluation occurs at the beginning of the next session following a session in which a target has been desensitized. The therapist asks the client to return to the original incident and asks the client, "When you bring up that original incident, what do you get now?" Clinical judgment guides how this process unfolds and was described earlier in this chapter.

The final type of reevaluation occurs when the therapist and client review all targets in order to make sure that no additional disturbance exists and all targets have been reprocessed. Once the therapist and client have agreed that all targets have been reprocessed successfully and the symptoms identified at the beginning of treatment have been addressed, the therapist and client together can plan for treatment discharge following their successful treatment process. This is the goal for all clients.

With children, using drawings or pictures or other tangible ways of organizing the work in therapy will help children remember what they have accomplished and the child's successes in therapy. The therapist monitors the child's progress in therapy based not only on the child's reports, but also on parent reports and symptom monitoring.

As mentioned earlier, the evidence of the adaptive resolution of trauma with EMDR is in symptom abatement. Discharge planning occurs when the symptoms that brought the child into treatment are no longer evident and the child is able to return to his individual course of normal development without the interference of trauma. This is the conclusion of the EMDR protocol that accompanies discharge planning; however, this comprehensive course of treatment may not be possible for all children. When comprehensive treatment with the full EMDR protocol is not possible, case conceptualization with EMDR allows for episodes of care.

EPISODES OF CARE

The ideal EMDR treatment intervention would entail all eight phases of the protocol, ending with discharge planning once all targets have been reprocessed and maladaptively stored information has been reprocessed to adaptive resolution and symptoms have abated. Unfortunately, the opportunity to complete this course of treatment is not always available due to time, client or therapist changes, or financial issues. This is especially true of children in the child welfare system. Even though a comprehensive course of treatment is not possible, therapists can still provide episodes of care by working through the stages of the EMDR protocol, as illustrated in Case Example 6-9. If case conceptualization suggests that the therapist will have abbreviated time with the client—as is true of clients in hospital or residential settings, children in foster care or shelters, or even with clients who are in transition and may be homeless—pieces of the EMDR protocol are still effective with limited treatment availability during an episode of care.

The therapist may need to think in episodes of care where a child in a 90-day residential treatment facility with a chronic history of abuse and neglect may require stabilization and resource development and mastery skills as are taught in the preparation phase. One of the extremely advantageous skills of the preparation phase is using a resource development and installation protocol (RDI) defined earlier in the chapter. With RDI, the therapist can focus on installing a positive future template, while containing past trauma. This can assist an adolescent who is experiencing a shortened sense of future to leave the residential placement with new hope for the future. The goal is that this positive future template will help the teen to realize the benefits of treatment and continue to seek treatment after leaving the RTC. In addition, children in a shelter are in such a state of transition that targeting the child's past history of abuse may not be clinically indicated. However, if the therapist can teach the child containment skills and focus on desensitizing current triggers, the child may stabilize during this episode of care sufficiently to be placed in a foster home versus being repeatedly hospitalized. The phases of the EMDR protocol offer a unique and efficacious treatment model in which therapists can conceptualize treatment planning in phases for episodes of care with realistic targets for each episode.

EMDR WITH CHILDREN IN FOSTER CARE AND WITH ADOPTIVE CHILDREN

Currently, there are no published studies on EMDR with children who have experienced abuse and neglect and are in foster care or with children who are adopted. These children most likely have experienced some degree of trauma (often chronic trauma) and present with a myriad of symptoms. Case conceptualizations for use with children in foster and adoptive care suggest that the development of resources and mastery skills in the preparation phase of EMDR are foundational for successful trauma processing with children with severe and chronic trauma. This is true of children with attachment trauma and dissociative symptoms.

Case Conceptualization with Children with Attachment Disorders

In case conceptualization with children with attachment trauma, it may be clinically indicated to start with the symptom and focus on a presenting problem while a targeting sequence plan is developed. Children with symptoms of reactive attachment disorder, especially those adopted internationally, may have no cognitive or verbal history, at least in English. So even if they do remember, they remember in another language that they may have forgotten, which makes tapping the memory network to reprocess it even more confusing! Again, this is part of learning about the unique issues of this population. At some point in treatment, it is helpful to have the child create a narrative of his own history and even make a life book that can be helpful to resolve the past history that is often unknown. Using Joan Lovett's narrative (from her previously mentioned book *Small Wonders*) is helpful to teach kids. Children can create a life book with a story that tells what is known about their birth parents and family, their former home(s), their childhood before adoption, what is known about the adoption process, and what has happened since adoption. Adoptive parents can help with some of the information, but this is the adoptive parents' story, not the child's story. Therefore, when the adoptive parents help provide information for the story, caution is needed to make sure that the story is about the child's experience and not the parents'. It is surprising what many children will report if asked to write their own story. This may seem like a subtle difference, but it is very important for therapists to focus on what the child experiences and reports rather than what the child may be mimicking from the parent. Once the story is written, it is possible to identify targets from the book that the child previously thought would have been uncomfortable to approach in psychotherapy.

Children Living in Residential Treatment Centers

It is helpful to teach children in residential treatment facilities RDI focused on installing mastery experiences to improve self-esteem and create a basis of positive current resources from which the child can draw to handle difficult situations. This is why, when working with children in residential treatment centers (RTCs), the therapist may need to focus on the preparation phase for a period of time. It is important to determine what the goal is for this episode of care for the child. Many children are in RTCs because they struggle with affect regulation and need to learn affect regulation and emotional literacy. Psychoeducational training, along with installing resources with RDI and mastery, can be extremely beneficial, but it may take some successes in therapy before the child is ready to proceed with trauma processing. With case conceptualization with EMDR, it is important to spend time in the preparation phase, teaching children the ability to experience, appropriately express, and tolerate both positive and negative emotions. We have previously discussed teaching children emotional literacy and emotional regulation skills; however, it may also be necessary to teach children positive affect tolerance. Positive affect tolerance is the ability to experience and appropriately express positive emotions.

Children in RTCs are often in high-stress situations and may need to focus on coping with issues in their RTC. So, in case conceptualization, ask the child about something that is happening at the RTC that is bothering them and then do a future template focused on the child's handling the situation in a different way. The therapist will need to determine if the child is experiencing anticipatory anxiety and/or missing information and then install the future template with the child's definition of being successful at the RTC.

This is not to suggest that targeting traumatic events and reprocessing with EMDR is not possible when working with children in RTCs, but when children balk at desensitization, it is often an indication that they need to develop more resources in order to continue with trauma processing, as illustrated in Case Example 6-9. It is the therapist's role to assist the child to be prepared for trauma processing. During the episode of care, when the child is placed in an RTC, the circumstances may or may not be conducive to trauma processing that will have to be included in a later episode of care.

Case Example 6-9: Treating James's Attachment Trauma and Abuse with EMDR

James was removed from his parents' custody at the age of 3 because his father sexually abused him. James was in three foster homes until he was adopted at 5 years of age. He was later removed from his adoptive family at the age of 8 because of his aggressive behaviors and sexualized behaviors with a younger sibling. After being placed in two more foster homes, James was placed in a therapeutic foster home. James had been in therapy since he was 3 years old, being diagnosed with attention deficit hyperactivity disorder (ADHD), PTSD, RAD, and bipolar disorder, and prescribed multiple medications. James was constantly in trouble at home and school for his rages, lying, and stealing. His therapeutic foster family feared that he would kill someone.

Even though he was on three different psychotropic medications and they were told he was unadoptable, James's therapeutic foster family searched for some resolution to James's distress and learned about EMDR. James began treatment and reported to his therapist that he wanted to learn to not hurt people. The therapist met with James weekly and worked on installing a safe/calm place and teaching him relaxation skills, guided visualization designed to improve bonding and attachment, and emotional literacy. James's symptoms greatly reduced.

Initially, James was avoidant of proceeding with the trauma reprocessing phases of the EMDR protocol. It appeared too painful to target his abuse directly. Because of James's early attachment traumas and ongoing abuse, James did not possess the resources and adaptive skills necessary to reprocess his traumas. It was not yet possible for James to link up his maladaptively stored experiences with new adaptive resources. The therapist needed to spend time in the preparation phase developing James's resources and providing the scaffolding for James to be able to reprocess his early life traumas.

After 8 months of preparation, James revealed his desire to help other children. The therapist had James metaphorically help another "child" with EMDR by using a teddy bear as the "child" that needed help. James held the "buzzies" in his hands on the teddy bear's paws. James's negative cognition was "It's my fault. I'm bad." His positive cognition was "I did the best I could." James was able to reprocess with the teddy bear until he progressed through the events of his traumatic early childhood.

During this time, James's school began to notice the positive changes in James in that he was calmer and more thoughtful. After learning of James's success in EMDR treatment and improvement in his symptoms, a family that had previously considered adopting James came forward to express their interest in making James a permanent member of their family. James is now in the process of becoming part of a forever family.

In conceptualizing James's case, his lack of a secure attachment followed by severe sexual and physical abuse created severe behavioral and mental health problems for a young boy. In order to reprocess his trauma, James needed internal resources as well as self-soothing and calming skills in order to move the maladaptively stored events of his early childhood to adaptive resolution. James's case is an all-too-familiar example of children in the child welfare system whose symptoms are medicated when they can't be managed in foster and adoptive homes. What James needed was to develop resources and mastery skills and then to reprocess the traumatic events in his life in order for his symptoms to abate.

ADDITIONAL SKILLS FOR GETTING STARTED WITH EMDR WITH CHILDREN

It is common for therapists to find that integrating EMDR into the practice of psychotherapy is difficult to grasp, especially upon returning to the office after the first weekend of training. Beginning to use EMDR psychotherapy with clients may seem awkward. It is also common to start desensitization and realize the client needs additional preparation skills with which to process a particular memory network. The EMDR therapy process is often unpredictable and surprising as the therapist and client learn together how the client has experienced and stored the traumatic event. It is not unusual for the therapist to realize that there is a missing piece that arises, which explains why the event has become encapsulated and not completed by the individual's natural healing process.

At each phase of the EMDR protocol, the therapist needs to be aware that clients process in unique ways, and it is the client's unique healing process that needs to be followed by the therapist using EMDR. This is where the previous tools one has learned as a therapist can be integrated into the phases of the EMDR protocol.

THERAPIST'S ROLE IN EMDR

The therapist's role in EMDR is that of guide, facilitator, educator, and coach. EMDR is a client-centered therapy in which the therapeutic relationship and alliance are significant to the healthy environment, as is true of most therapeutic interventions.

The therapist's ability to listen, be attuned, and use her or his own skills to listen and facilitate the process and provide translation from adult language to child language is essential to the treatment process throughout the eight phases of EMDR with children. One of the challenges for therapists first learning the EMDR protocol is to stay out of the way. Effective and appropriate clinical skills are often not necessary with EMDR, as it is the client's own healing process that leads the treatment. Therapists may be tempted to rephrase the client's statements, offer insights, or make suggestions to the client; however, this is not necessary with EMDR, especially once the process enters the desensitization phase. Such interventions can actually slow the client's reprocessing and change the direction of the client's process of adaptive resolution. Children often offer creative and unique resolutions to their own issues that are surprising and adaptive. Core to effective EMDR is the therapist's ability to trust that the client's own wisdom will prevail through the process of EMDR and the natural healing process of adaptive information processing.

CONCLUSION

As previously mentioned, this chapter is an overview to EMDR treatment of children and not sufficient to implement practice. Please refer to Shapiro's book, *Eye Movement Desensitization and Reprocessing*, 2nd edition (2001) to get in-depth direction for each piece of the protocol, and Adler-Tapia and Settle (2008) for additional guidance on the treatment of children. After completing basic training in EMDR, implementing EMDR in psychotherapy with children and adolescents requires experience and training in working with children. Adolescents may be more capable of following the adult protocol; however, it is important to use clinical skills especially designed for children in order to process the pieces of the EMDR protocol within a developmental framework appropriate to the individual child. Distilling the pieces of the protocol with play therapy or art therapy techniques is advisable with all clients, especially young children.

After therapists have gained competency with the basic EMDR protocol, it is possible to use the EMDR protocol to conceptualize treatment with children with a myriad of symptoms and diagnoses in an effort to provide efficacious treatment. Not only is this important to child clients, but it is part of best practice in working with children. Adaptive Information Processing theory and the EMDR treatment methodology offer clinicians advanced skills to treat trauma and other disorders that have traumatic etiology of both acute and developmental beginnings that frequently contribute to or underlie many other mental health and behavioral disorders in children. By treating the origins of trauma in children and adolescents, therapists can return children to healthy trajectories of development so that they continue toward adolescence and healthy adulthood.

REFERENCES

Adler-Tapia, R. L., & Settle, C. S. (Accepted for review). Establishing EMDR with children as evidence based practice: A review of the literature.

Adler-Tapia, R. L., & Settle, C. S. (2008). *EMDR and the art of psychotherapy with children*. New York: Springer.

Adler-Tapia, R. L. & Tapia, M. (2008). *My EMDR workbook*. Tempe, AZ: Author.

Adúriz, M., Bluthgen, C., Gorrini, Z., Maquieira, S., Nofal, S., & Knopfler, C. (in press). The flooding in Santa Fé, Argentina. *Journal of Psychotraumatology for Iberoamérica.*

Ahmad, A., Larsson, B., & Sundelin-Wahlsten, V. (2007). EMDR treatment for children with PTSD: Results of a randomized controlled trial. *Nordic Journal of Psychiatry, 61*(5), 349–354.

American Psychiatric Association. (2000). *Diagnostic and statistical manual of mental disorders* (4th ed., Text Revision). Washington, DC: American Psychiatric Press.

Armstrong, J., Carlson, E. B., & Putnam, F. (1997). Adolescent-Dissociative Experiences Scale-II (A-DES). Retrieved from www.energyhealing.net/pdf_files/a-des.pdf.

Chemtob, C., Nakashima, J., & Carlson, J. (2002). Brief treatment for elementary school children with disaster-related posttraumatic stress disorder: A field study. *Journal of Clinical Psychology, 58*(1), 99–112.

Cocco, N., & Sharpe, L. (1993). An auditory variant of eye movement desensitization in a case of childhood post-traumatic stress disorder. *Journal of Behavior Therapy and Experimental Psychiatry, 24*(4), 373–377.

de Roos, C., & de Jongh, A. (2008). EMDR treatment of children and adolescents with a choking phobia. *Journal of EMDR Practice and Research, 2*(3), 201–211.

de Roos, C., Greenwald, R., de Jongh, A., and Noorthorn, E. O. (In press). EMDR (Eye Movement Desensitization and Reprocessing) versus CBT (Cognitive Behavioral Therapy) for disaster-exposed children: A controlled study.

Felitti V. J., Anda R. F., Nordernberg, D., Williamson, D. F., Spitz, A. M., Edwards, V., et al. (1998). Relationship of childhood abuse to many of the leading causes of death in adults: The adverse childhood experiences (ACE) study. *American Journal of Preventive Medicine, 14*(4): 245–258.

Fernandez, I., Gallinari, E., & Lorenzetti, A. (2004). A school-based eye movement desensitization and reprocessing intervention for children who witnessed the Pirelli Building airplane crash in Milan, Italy. *Journal of Brief Therapy, 2*(2), 129–135.

Greenwald, R. (1994). Applying eye movement desensitization and reprocessing (EMDR) to the treatment of traumatized children: Five case studies. *Anxiety Disorders Practice Journal, 1*(2), 83–97.

Greenwald, R. (1999). *Eye movement desensitization and reprocessing (EMDR) in child and adolescent psychotherapy.* Northvale, NJ: Jason Aronson Press.

Gomez, A. (2007). Dark bad day go away. Phoenix, AZ: Author.

International Society for the Study of Dissociation (ISST-D) Task Force on Children and Adolescents. (2004). Guidelines for the evaluation and treatment of dissociative symptoms in children and adolescents. *Journal of Trauma and Dissociation, 5*(3), 119–150.

Jaberghaderi, N., Greenwald, R., Rubin, A., Dolatabadim, S., & Zand, S. O. (2002). A comparison of CBT and EMDR for sexually abused Iranian girls. *Clinical Psychology and Psychotherapy, 11*, 358–368.

Jarero, I. (2001). *The butterfly hug.* Retrieved July 29, 2008, from www.emotionalrelief.org/articles/article-butterflyhug-jarero.htm.

Jarero, I., Artigas, L., & Hartung, J. (2006). EMDR integrative group treatment protocol: A postdisaster trauma intervention for children and adults. *Traumatology, 12*(2), 121–129.

Jarero, I., Artigas, L., Mauer, M., Alcala, N., & Lupez, T. (1999, November). *EMDR integrative group treatment protocol and the butterfly hug*. Paper presented at the annual meeting of the International Society for Traumatic Stress Studies, Miami, FL.

Jones, R. T. (2002). The child's reaction to traumatic events scale (CRTES): A self-report traumatic stress measure. Blacksburg: Virginia Polytechnic University.

Korkmazlar-Oral, U., & Pamuk, S. (2002). Group EMDR with child survivors of the earthquake in Turkey (*ACPP Occasional Papers Series No. 19*). Academy of Child & Adolescent Psychiatry (1998). *Journal of the American Academy of Child & Adolescent Psychiatry, 37*(10 Suppl.), 4S–26S.

Leeds, A. (1998) Lifting the burden of shame: Using EMDR resource installation to resolve a therapeutic impasse. In P. Manfield (Ed.), *Extending EMDR: A case book of innovative application* (pp. 456–282). New York: Norton.

Lovett, J. (1999). *Small wonders: Healing childhood trauma with EMDR*. New York: Free Press.

Muris, P., Merckelbach, H., Holdrinet, I., & Sijsenaar, M. (1998). Treating phobic children: Effects of EMDR versus exposure. *Journal of Consulting and Clinical Psychology, 66*, 193–198.

Muris, P., Merckelbach, H., van Haaften, H., & Mayer, B. (1997). Eye movement desensitization and reprocessing versus exposure in vivo: A single-session crossover study of spider-phobic children. *British Journal of Psychiatry, 171*, 82–86.

Oras, R., Cancela De Ezpeleta, S., & Ahmad, A. (2004). Treatment of traumatized refugee children with eye movement desensitization and reprocessing in a psychodynamic context. *Nordic Journal of Psychiatry, 58*, 199–203.

Perry, B. (2006). Applying principles of neurodevelopment to clinical work with maltreated and traumatized children. In N. B. Webb (Ed.), *Working with traumatized youth in child welfare* (pp. 27–52). New York: Guilford Press.

Puffer, M., Greenwald, R., & Elrod, D. (1997). A single session EMDR study with twenty traumatized children and adolescents. International Electronic Journal of Innovations in the Study of the Traumatization Process and Methods for Reducing or Eliminating Related Human Suffering, 3(2), article 6. Retrieved February 3, 2008, from www.fsu.edu/~trauma/v3i2art6.html.

Putnam, F. (1997). *Child dissociative checklist, version 3*. Retrieved from www .energyhealing.net/pdf_files/cdc.pdf, July 28, 2008.

Rubin, A., Bischofshausen, S., Conroy-Moore, K., Dennis, B., Hastie, M., Melnick, L., et al. (2001). The effectiveness of EMDR in a child guidance center. *Research on Social Work Practice, 11*(4), 435–457.

Shapiro, F. (1989a). Efficacy of the eye movement desensitization procedure in the treatment of traumatic memories. *Journal of Traumatic Stress, 2*(2), 199–223.

Shapiro, F. (1989b). Eye movement desensitization: A new treatment for post-traumatic stress disorder. *Journal of Behavior Therapy and Experimental Psychiatry, 20*, 211–217.

Shapiro, F. (1995). *Eye movement desensitization and reprocessing: Basic principles, protocols, and procedures.* New York: Guilford Press.

Shapiro, F. (2001). *Eye movement desensitization and reprocessing: Basic principles, protocols, and procedures* (2nd ed.). New York: Guilford Press.

Shapiro, F. (2007). EMDR and case conceptualization from an adaptive information processing perspective. In F. Shapiro, F. W. Kaslow, & L. Maxfield (Eds.), *Handbook of EMDR and family therapy processes* (pp. 3–34). Hoboken, NJ: Wiley.

Siegel, D. (2007). *The mindful brain.* New York: Norton.

Siegel, D., & Hartzell, M. (2003). *Parenting from the inside out.* New York: Penguin.

Soberman, G., Greenwald, R., & Rule, D. (2002). A controlled study of eye movement desensitization and reprocessing (EMDR) for boys with conduct problems. *Journal of Aggression, Maltreatment and Trauma, 6*(1), 217–236.

Tinker, R. H., & Wilson, S. A. (1999). *Through the eyes of a child: EMDR with children.* New York: Norton.

Tufnell, G. (2005). Eye movement desensitization and reprocessing in the treatment of preadolescent children with post-traumatic symptoms. *Clinical Child Psychology and Psychiatry, 10*(4), 587–600.

van der Kolk, B. A. (2005). Developmental trauma disorder. *Psychiatric Annals,* 374–378.

Wilson, S., Tinker, R., Hofmann, A., Becker, L., & Marshall, S. (2000, November). *A field study of EMDR with Kosovar-Albanian refugee children using a group treatment protocol.* Paper presented at the annual meeting of the International Society for the Study of Traumatic Stress, San Antonio, TX.

Zaghrout-Hodali, M., Alissa, F., & Dodgson, P. W. (2008). Building resilience and dismantling fear: EMDR group protocol with children in an area of ongoing trauma. *Journal of EMDR Practice and Research, 2*(2), 106–113.

ADDITIONAL READINGS

Adler-Tapia, R. L., & Settle, C. S. (2008). *EMDR and the art of psychotherapy with children.* New York: Springer.

Based on the foundations of Shapiro's books, the authors have explained the unique challenges of each phase of the EMDR protocol, described the techniques and tools for using each procedural step of the EMDR protocol, and developed an approach for case conceptualization with AIP in psychotherapy with various populations of children by integrating case studies with children with regulatory, developmental, behavioral, and mental health issues. The book and accompanying treatment manual provide step-by-step protocols and forms for using EMDR with children.

Adler-Tapia, R. L., & Tapia, M. (2008). *My EMDR workbook.* Tempe, AZ: Author.

This workbook takes children through each step of the EMDR protocol and helps therapists organize the steps to provide opportunities for children to express their experiences through art and play interventions. This workbook, along with the storybook by Ana Gomez listed below, provides child friendly tools for using EMDR with even very young children.

Gomez, A. (2007). *Dark bad day go away*. Available for purchase online through the EMDR-Humanitarian Assistance Program store at www.emdrhap.org/os Commerce/index.php.

This storybook uses animal characters to explain EMDR and the mechanics of EMDR to children in a delightful presentation that engages children in developmentally appropriate language.

Greenwald, R. (1999). *Eye movement desensitization and reprocessing (EMDR) in child and adolescent psychotherapy*. Northvale, NJ: Jason Aronson Press.

Ricky Greenwald provides techniques for the treatment of children— techniques that are especially focused on working with adolescents. In addition to using EMDR with adolescents, Greenwald provides an emphasis on treating oppositional-defiant clients.

Lovett, J. (1999). *Small wonders: Healing childhood trauma with EMDR*. New York: Free Press.

Joan Lovett describes the parent narrative and how to use this process in EMDR with children. The parent narrative can be very useful for children who are nonresponsive. It is helpful to use the parent narrative for children with traumatic brain injuries who are unable to participate on their own.

Tinker, R. H., & Wilson, S. A. (1999). *Through the eyes of a child: EMDR with children*. New York: Norton.

Robert Tinker and Sandra Wilson provide a scholarly overview of psycho-therapy with children, detail the history of EMDR with children, discuss the theoretical underpinnings of EMDR with children and finally include many case examples of EMDR treatment with children.

ADDITIONAL RESOURCES

Study Groups

Ongoing support through consultation, study groups, and advanced train-ings can enhance therapists' confidence in their clinical ability to effectively use EMDR in psychotherapy with children. Study groups consist of col-leagues who have been trained in EMDR, who gather to study and share information on EMDR in order to advance clinical skills and enhance each participant's adherence to the protocol. Study groups can be formed to support therapists after basic training and to network with other clinicians for support, brainstorming, and sharing skills.

Listservs

Listservs are online communities formed by professionals who share information and offer the opportunity to post questions or request case consultation. There are many EMDR Listservs for individuals who have been trained in EMDR, including those accessed through the EMDR International Association (EMDRIA) and other EMDR organizations. There also are special interest groups (SIGS) for individuals who have an interest in a particular area including research, the military, children, eating disorders, and other topics. The EMDR HAP (Humanitarian Assistance Programs) is currently developing the HAPKIDS Project that focuses on providing training, research, consultation, and consumer information for anyone who works with or cares for children with mental health needs and especially for children experiencing traumatic events. The HAPKIDS project is developing a Listserv to provide support for clinicians who are using EMDR with children (EMDR Humanitarian Assistance Programs, 2007). Additional information is available at www.emdrhap.org.

EMDR Progress Notes

Many therapists have created their own progress notes that summarize the EMDR eight-phase protocol and the procedural steps. These progress notes assist therapists in adhering to the protocol and provide a quick way to monitor client progression through EMDR. It behooves therapists to use an EMDR specific progress note in order to prevent therapist drift and to document that the therapist has completed each step of the protocol. EMDR child progress notes and protocols are available in the books listed in the additional readings section.

Research on EMDR with Children

EMDR was originally designed by Francine Shapiro to treat symptoms of PTSD in adults; however, EMDR has been used to treat children with diagnoses other than PTSD when there is a suspicion that traumatic symptoms may also be contributing to the child's diagnoses (Adler-Tapia & Settle, accepted for review). Familiarity with the research on EMDR with children is important in order for therapists to explain to agencies and third-party payers the evidence that EMDR is a promising practice with children. Below, then, is a list of citations of research studies on EMDR with children. The full citations for these studies can be found in the References section of this chapter.

　　Ahmad, Larsson, & Sundelin-Wahlsten, 2007; Adúriz, Bluthgen, Gorrini, Maquieira, Nofal, & Knopfler, in press; Chemtob, Nakashima, & Carlson,

2002; Cocco & Sharpe, 1993; De Roos & de Jongh, 2008; De Roos, Greenwald, de Jongh, and Noorthorn, submitted; Fernandez, Gallinari, & Lorenzetti, 2004; Greenwald, 1994; Jaberghaderi, Greenwald, Rubin, Dolatabadim, & Zand, 2002; Jarero, Artigas, & Hartung, 2006; Jarero, Artigas, & Montero, 2008; Korkmazlar-Oral & Pamuk, 2002; Muris, Merckelbach, Holdrinet, & Sijsenaar, 1998; Oras, Cancela De Ezpeleta, & Ahmad, 2004; Puffer, Greenwald, & Elrod, 1997; Rubin, Bischofshausen, Conroy-Moore, Dennis, Hastie, Melnick, Reeves, & Smith, 2001; Soberman, Greenwald, & Rule, 2002; Tufnell, 2005; Wilson, Tinker, Hofmann, Becker, & Marshall, 2000; Zaghrout-Hodali, Alissa, Sahour, & Dodgson, 2008.

Afterword

ALLEN RUBIN

I F YOU HAVE just finished reading all the chapters in this book and have not had previous experience with or significant exposure to the interventions they describe, you may be feeling overwhelmed. There is quite a lot to learn if you are considering implementing a new, empirically supported intervention that you've never learned about or provided before. So much to learn, in fact, that even if you have only read one or two of the chapters on just one new intervention approach, you might still be feeling overwhelmed. If you are feeling that way, I urge you not to give up—particularly if the intervention approaches you have been providing to date have not been empirically supported and especially if they have been studied and found to be either ineffective or much less effective than the interventions described in this book.

No matter how overwhelmed you might feel, I hope you will persevere in trying to master one or more of the interventions described in this book. Perhaps the most important reasons for persevering are your professional ethics and compassion for your clients. A cornerstone of professional ethics is a devotion to serving clients in the most effective way possible. If you know that an intervention that you have read about in this book has significantly more scientific support for its efficacy with clients like yours than the one(s) you have been providing, and if you really believe that it is likely to be more effective with them, but you nevertheless are unwilling to do the hard work of trying to learn about that intervention or at least refer your client to another practitioner who can skillfully provide that intervention, then perhaps you are not being as professionally ethical as you should be.

I say "perhaps" because clinicians often express reasonable rationales for not switching to empirically supported interventions with which they are less familiar or comfortable. The evidence supporting such interventions may be based on studies with clients whose characteristics or problems are unlike those of their clients. The clinicians might perceive such interventions as requiring a manualized and mechanistic approach to practice that deemphasizes and devalues therapist flexibility, expertise, and relationship skills.

419

In that connection, they might cite studies that have supported the importance of the quality of the therapeutic alliance as having as much or more impact on client outcome than the specific intervention approach chosen. Perhaps the rationale is that their agency caseload and other requirements leave them no time to learn to become sufficiently skillful in a new intervention approach and there are no other clinicians in their area who are adept in the empirically supported intervention. Maybe there are such clinicians nearby, but their clients cannot afford the fees of those other clinicians.

If your rationale for sticking with interventions that are not evidence based is like one of the above reasons—or even if it is based on some other reason for thinking that switching would not be in your client's best interest—then even if your reasoning is debatable, you are being professionally ethical in that your reasoning is based on what you think is best for your clients. But your professional ethics could be questioned if your reason for refusing to learn more about a more empirically supported intervention or to refer to a clinician who can skillfully provide that intervention is based merely on what interests you or on your own unwillingness to invest the work required to try to learn more about something that you believe will be more helpful to your clients.

For example, occasionally I hear from clinical students near completion of their master's degree studies that they just want to provide the interventions that they find most interesting and with which they are most comfortable, regardless of the research evidence about the relative effectiveness of those interventions versus alternative ones. Admittedly, there is some merit to what they say. Clients will not benefit—and perhaps will fare worse—if clinicians provide an empirically supported intervention unenthusiastically and with skepticism about its efficacy or in an incompetent manner because they have not yet mastered the intervention or perhaps feel very awkward and unsure of themselves in providing it.

But there is no excuse for sticking with interventions that lack adequate empirical support merely because one finds those interventions to be more interesting or personally fulfilling than newer interventions that are known to have a greater likelihood of effectiveness. I often respond to students who express such a reason for disliking evidence-based practice with a medical analogy like the one in the box titled "Response to Students: Medical Analogy."

Response to Students: Medical Analogy

Imagine going to a physician for treatment for a medical condition that you recently developed and for which you learned that the most rigorous scientific research studies have agreed that Treatment A is by far the most effective remedy—much more effective than Treatment B. Your physician examines you and agrees that you have the condition you think you have and then tells you she or he will provide Treatment B. You then express your consternation about Treatment B in light of the scientific studies you learned about, and your physician tells you that despite knowing about those studies, he or she prefers to provide Treatment B anyway because of lack of skill or discomfort with Treatment A. How would you feel about that physician? My guess is that you'd view them as inadequately compassionate or ethical. You'd probably insist on being referred to a physician who could skillfully and comfortably provide Treatment A.

What if those studies favoring Treatment A existed, and your physician knew about them, but you didn't. What if he or she then merely provided Treatment B without informing you of the evidence supporting the superior effectiveness of Treatment A or offering to refer you to another physician who could skillfully provide it? What if you subsequently—after receiving Treatment B and not benefiting from it—learned about Treatment A's evidence and found out that your physician knew about that evidence but went ahead with Treatment B anyway for the reasons mentioned above? You might express more extreme terms to describe the physician than "inadequately compassionate or ethical."

Of course, psychotherapy with traumatized clients is not the same as treating a medical condition. Therapist relationship skills and the therapeutic alliance have a much greater impact on treatment outcome than in medical treatment. Even the most evidence-based psychotherapies will not be effective without a strong therapeutic alliance. Moreover, even though they may have the greatest likelihood of success, many clients do not benefit from them. Idiosyncratic client characteristics and preferences can have a profound impact on the choice of intervention, and therapist expertise is critical in determining whether an intervention with the best evidence is really the best fit for a particular client in light of that client's idiosyncrasies.

However, the issue is not an all or nothing matter. Being compassionate, professionally ethical, and evidence based does not require that you automatically choose empirically supported interventions in a mechanistic, cookbook fashion and without regard to client preferences. It just means that you will make such choices and intervene in light of the best evidence, and having integrated that evidence with your clinical expertise and knowledge of your client's characteristics and preferences. As is evident in every chapter in this book—and especially in Chapter 1 and Appendix B—clinical expertise and knowledge of client characteristics and preferences are important elements of evidence-based practice and can rightfully imply that an intervention without the best evidence might be the treatment of choice for some clients. Moreover, being evidence based does not mean providing an empirically supported intervention in a rigid manner without room for flexibility based on your clinical expertise. Again, the room for such flexibility is evident in every chapter of this book.

Likewise, your level of comfort and skill in providing a new, evidence-based intervention is not an all-or-nothing, black-and-white issue. Every clinician—no matter what interventions they are providing—has started out being less skillful, less confident, and less comfortable with those interventions than they are now. If you are not yet ready to begin providing an empirically supported intervention due to skill or comfort concerns, that's understandable. But those are not compelling reasons to avoid trying to become more skillful and comfortable with those interventions. And the chapters in this book have identified various additional resources and ways for trying to become more comfortable and skillful with them.

When psychotherapists consider their own medical treatment, it's easy for them to endorse the necessity of evidence-based practice. But when it comes to their own practice, some opt to keep providing interventions with which they are most comfortable and skillful regardless of the scientific evidence about their effects or without seeking to learn about that evidence. But many others embrace evidence-based practice. I hope that you, reader, are in the latter group or at least have been spurred by this book to learn more about evidence-based practice and about the interventions described herein. I also hope that this book may have given you enough expertise to begin gaining experience in providing one or more of these interventions.

APPENDIX A

Research Providing the Evidence Base for the Interventions in This Volume

ALLEN RUBIN

T HE INTERVENTION APPROACHES described in the chapters of this volume have had a substantial amount of research empirically supporting their effectiveness in the treatment of posttraumatic stress disorder (PTSD). However, several caveats bear noting. One is that distinguishing the evidentiary support for exposure therapy from that of trauma-focused cognitive behavioral therapy (TFCBT) is tricky because of the overlap between those two approaches. For example, exposure therapy includes CBT components, and TFCBT includes exposure components. Despite the overlap, some authors refer to their intervention approach as exposure therapy, while others refer to it as TFCBT. Although there are differences between the approaches using the different labels, the overlap is considerable. Adding to the terminological fuzziness, some authors refer to their interventions as *CBT*, omitting *trauma focused (TF)* from the label. To simplify things, in this volume we have kept the TF part of the label because all of the pertinent studies evaluated the effectiveness of CBT in treating *trauma*.

Another caveat concerns limitations in the PTSD diagnostic framework. In the first chapter of this volume, I discussed the disorders of extreme stress not otherwise specified (DESNOS) diagnosis. That diagnosis involves symptoms that go well beyond the classic PTSD symptoms and pertains to individuals whose traumas have been extremely severe and prolonged, such as early childhood sexual and physical abuse, repeated battering, being taken hostage, and being incarcerated and tortured. As noted by Foa, Keane, and Friedman (2000), little is known about how to treat effectively people with these trauma histories, and some evidence is beginning to suggest the need for multimodal interventions provided over a longer period of time than the interventions described in this volume. Likewise, many people suffering from PTSD have comorbid disorders such as substance abuse and major depression. The ample empirical support for the interventions described in this volume by and large is derived from studies of clients who do not have comorbidity. Volume 2 of this series, *Substance Abuse Treatment for Youth and Adults*, provides a chapter on seeking safety, which is an evidence-based approach for treating co-occurring PTSD and substance abuse. In addition, that volume's appendix reviews the outcome studies that provide the empirical support for the effectiveness of that approach.

EXPOSURE THERAPY

The evidence base supporting the effectiveness of exposure therapy in treating PTSD is both vast and rigorous. Many studies using randomized control trials (RCTs) have supported its effectiveness in treating PTSD resulting from a variety of traumas and with a variety of client characteristics. And, as noted above, because exposure therapy is part of TFCBT, its evidentiary support actually exceeds that depicted by the studies that evaluated it as a separate approach. In their review of the research supporting the effectiveness of exposure therapy, Riggs, Cahill, and Foa (2006) cite RCTs with female survivors of rape and physical assault, domestic violence, and childhood physical and sexual abuse. They also cite studies supporting its effectiveness with refugees and both male and female survivors of auto accidents. The effectiveness of exposure therapy also was supported in a meta-analysis conducted by Davidson and Parker (2001).

TRAUMA-FOCUSED COGNITIVE BEHAVIORAL THERAPY (TFCBT)

The evidence base supporting the effectiveness of TFCBT is also quite impressive. Two meta-analyses have supported the effectiveness of TFCBT with adults. One reviewed 25 RCTs that compared TFCBT with wait-list or other interventions and concluded that TFCBT has superior effects on PTSD symptoms (Bisson et al., 2007). The other meta-analysis of studies involving adults reviewed seven RCTs and concluded that TFCBT and EMDR are equally effective (Seidler & Wagner, 2006). In addition, five RCTs have supported the effectiveness of TFCBT with sexually abused children (Cohen & Mannarino, 1996, 1998; Cohen et al., 2004; Deblinger et al., 1996; Deblinger, Stauffer, & Steer, 2001). Moreover, Cohen, Mannarino, and Deblinger (2006) cite four reviews that concluded that TFCBT has the best evidence for its effectiveness in treating PTSD and related problems among sexually abused children.

COGNITIVE RESTRUCTURING

There have been far fewer RCTs supporting cognitive restructuring per se than have supported exposure therapy or TFCBT; however, cognitive restructuring has been a component of exposure therapy or TFCBT in many of the rigorous studies supporting each of those broader approaches. We decided to have a separate chapter on cognitive restructuring, rather than just let it be covered as part of exposure therapy or CBT, because of the amount of content readers would need to learn in order to employ it clinically. Resick and Schnicke (1992) found that it is effective (when compared to a wait-list control group) in treating sexual assault victims. However, the evidence is mixed on whether adding the adding a cognitive restructuring component significantly improves the effectiveness of exposure therapy. Two RCTs found that it did not (Foa et al., 2005; Foa & Rauch, 2004). Another found that it did (Bryant, et al., 2003). Marks, Lovell, Noshirvani, Livanou, and Thrasher (1998) found that cognitive restructuring alone is effective in treating PTSD among victims of mixed traumas. They also found that prolonged exposure therapy alone was effective and that the combination of the two interventions was not more effective than either alone. Resick, Nishith, Weaver, Astin, and Feuer (2002) found that cognitive restructuring is effective in reducing shame and guilt prior to starting exposure therapy with female rape victims.

EMDR

Although some deem eye movement desensitization and reprocessing (EMDR) to be controversial and less empirically supported than exposure therapy or TFCBT (Foa, Keane, & Friedman, 2000; Rubin, 2003), both the International Society for Traumatic Stress Studies and Division 12 (Clinical Psychology) of the American Psychological Association have—in light of its evidence base— designated EMDR as an effective treatment for PTSD (Chambless et al., 1998; Chemtob, Tolin, van der Kolk, & Pitman, 2000). A large number of well-controlled outcome studies and some meta-analyses have supported the effectiveness of EMDR in treating adults with noncombat, single-trauma PTSD (Bisson et al., 2007; Davidson & Parker, 2001; Seidler & Wagner, 2006; Van Etten & Taylor, 1998).

The evidence base for considering EMDR to be an effective treatment for PTSD is well summarized in two systematic review/meta-analysis studies. In one systematic review and meta-analysis, Bisson et al. (2007) appraised 38 RCTs and concluded that EMDR and trauma-focused cognitive-behavioral therapy (TFCBT) were more effective than stress management and other therapies in treating chronic PTSD among mainly adult participants (aged 17 and up). Twelve of the RCTs compared EMDR with wait-list controls or with other interventions and had, on average, clinically meaningful effect sizes.

In the other systematic review and meta-analysis, Seidler and Wagner (2006) concluded—based on several earlier systematic reviews and meta-analyses (Bradley et al., 2005; Davidson & Parker, 2001; National Collaborating Centre for Mental Health, 2005; Shepherd et al., 2000; van Etten & Taylor, 1998)—that the efficacy of EMDR is beyond doubt. However, those earlier reviews did not settle the question of whether EMDR or TFCBT was the superior treatment for PTSD. Seidler and Wagner appraised seven RCTs that compared the effectiveness of EMDR and TFCBT with adults and concluded both treatments are equally efficacious. Their study did not, however, resolve the debate as to whether the eye movement component is necessary for EMDR to be effective, and thus "whether the mechanisms underlying EMDR are just another form of exposure" (p. 1521). Despite these unresolved issues, evidence is emerging supporting the notion that EMDR treatment can achieve the same level of effects but with less time and homework as compared to other efficacious treatments for PTSD (Maxfield, 2007).

Uncertainty about the necessity of the eye movement component (more recently referred to as the *dual attention stimulation* component) is related to the need for a more persuasive theoretical explanation as to why and how that component makes a difference. Two brain imaging studies (van der Kolk, 1997; van der Kolk, Burbridge, & Suzuki, 1997) provided a possible explanation. Individuals with and without PTSD differ in brain activity, the size of the hippocampus, and the amount of right versus left brain hemisphere activity. Consequently, individuals with PTSD are more vulnerable to having their emotional system dominate over their cognitive system in processing information. In turn, they may be more susceptible to hyperarousal, dissociation and difficulties in stimulus discrimination. The dual attention stimulation component of EMDR conceivably activates neurological mechanisms in the brain that enable the brain's cognitive system to process and integrate information connected to the trauma that had been previously neurologically frozen.

The two studies by van der Kolk and associates observed brain changes after EMDR treatment in six traumatized individuals. The changes reflected improvements in (1) distinguishing past threats from present experiences and (2) learning from new information instead of staying focused on the past. Based on those findings, Barker and Hawes (1999) reasoned that perhaps the dual attention stimulation of EMDR activates neurological activity in the brain that helps the brain's cognitive system to process and integrate previously frozen information connected to the trauma. They also reasoned that perhaps the dual attention stimulation desensitizes the individual by producing a relaxation response that extinguishes the negative associations with the traumatic memory.

Despite the strong evidence base supporting EMDR with civilians, the evidence is mixed regarding its effectiveness in treating combat PTSD among military veterans (Rubin, 2003). More evidence also is needed as to its effectiveness in treating victims of multiple traumas experiencing complex PTSD (Rubin). In addition, there is insufficient evidence to support claims that EMDR is effective in treating a wider range of problems, including problems that may not be caused by trauma (Rubin; Shapiro, 1995).

Although only three experimental outcome studies were found that supported the effectiveness of EMDR with children, we decided to include that chapter in light of the strengths of those studies and the substantial support for the effectiveness of EMDR with adults. The three experimental outcome studies supporting the effectiveness of EMDR with children all pertained to treating PTSD symptoms among children whose symptoms are connected to specific traumas. Chemtob et al. (2002) found that EMDR alleviated PTSD symptoms of elementary school children (aged 6 to 12) who had experienced a hurricane. Jeffres (2004) found that EMDR alleviated PTSD symptoms among children (aged 8 to 12) who had suffered one or more traumas. Jaberghaderi, Greenwald, Rubin, Dolatabadim, and Zand (2004) found that it was effective in treating the trauma symptoms of a small sample of sexually abused Iranian girls.

REFERENCES

Bisson, J. I., Ehlers, A., Matthews, R., Pilling, S., Richards, D. A., Turner, S., et al. (2007). Psychological treatments for chronic post-traumatic stress disorder: Systematic review and meta-analysis. *British Journal of Psychiatry, 190*(2), 97–104.

Bradley, R., Greene, J., Russ, E., Dutra, L., & Westen, D. (2005). A multidimensional meta-analysis of psychotherapy for PTSD. *American Journal of Psychiatry, 162*, 214–144.

Bryant, R. A., Moulds, M. L., Guthrie, R. M., Dang, S. T., & Nixon, R. D. V. (2003). Imaginal exposure alone and imaginal exposure with cognitive restructuring in treatment of posttraumatic stress disorder. *Journal of Consulting and Clinical Psychology, 71*(4), 706–712.

Chambless, D. L., Baker, M. J., Baucom, D. H., Beutler, L. E., Calhoun, K. S., Crits-Christoph, P., et al. (1998). Update on empirically validated therapies, II. *Clinical Psychologist, 51*, 3–16.

Chemtob, C. M., Tolin, D., van der Kolk, B., & Pitman, R. (2000). Eye movement desensitization and reprocessing: Practice guidelines from the International Society for Traumatic Stress Studies. In E. B. Foa, T. M. Keane, & M. J. Friedman (Eds.), *Effective treatments for PTSD* (pp. 139–154). New York: Guilford Press.

Chemtob, C. M., Nakashima, J., & Carlson, J. G. (2002). Brief treatment for elementary school children with disaster-related posttraumatic stress disorder: A field study. *Journal of Clinical Psychology, 58*, 99–112.

Cohen, J. A., Berliner, L., & March, J. S. (2000). Treatment of children and adolescents. In E. B. Foa, T. M. Keane, & M. J. Friedman (Eds.), *Effective treatments for PTSD: Practice guidelines from the International Society for Traumatic Stress Studies* (pp. 330–332). New York: Guilford Press.

Cohen, J. A., Deblinger, E., Mannarino, A. P., & Steer, R. A. (2004). A multisite, randomized control trial for children with sexual abuse-related PTSD symptoms. *Journal of the American Academy of Child and Adolescent Psychiatry, 43,* 393–402.

Cohen, J. A., & Mannarino, A. P. (1996). A treatment outcome study for sexually abused preschooler children: Initial findings. *Journal of the American Academy of Child and Adolescent Psychiatry, 35*(1), 42–50.

Cohen, J. A., & Mannarino, A. P. (1998). Interventions for sexually abused children: Initial treatment findings. *Child Maltreatment, 3*(1), 17–26.

Cohen, J. A., Mannarino, A. P., & Deblinger, E. (2006). *Treating trauma and traumatic grief in children and adolescents.* New York: Guilford Press.

Davidson, P. R., & Parker, K. C. H. (2001). Eye movement desensitization and reprocessing (EMDR): A meta-analysis. *Journal of Consulting and Clinical Psychology, 69,* 305–316.

Deblinger, E., Lippmann, J., & Steer, R. (1996). Sexually abused children suffering posttraumatic stress symptoms: Initial treatment outcome findings. *Child Maltreatment, 1*(4), 310–321.

Deblinger, E., Stauffer, L. B., & Steer, R. (2001). Comparative efficacies of supportive and cognitive–behavioral group therapies for young children who have been sexually abused and their non-offending mothers. *Child Maltreatment, 6,* 332–343.

Foa, E. B., Keane, T. M, & Friedman, M. J. (2000) Introduction. In E. B. Foa, T. M. Keane, & M. J. Friedman (Eds.), *Effective treatments for PTSD* (pp. 1–17). New York: Guilford Press.

Foa, E. B., Hembree, E. A., Cahill, S. P., Rauch, S. A. M., Riggs, D. S., Feeny, N. C., et al. (2005). Randomized trial of prolonged exposure for posttraumatic stress disorder with and without cognitive restructuring: Outcome at academic and community clinics. *Journal of Consulting and Clinical Psychology, 73*(5), 953–964.

Foa, E. B., & Rauch, S. A. M. (2004). Cognitive changes during prolonged exposure versus prolonged exposure plus cognitive restructuring in female assault survivors with posttraumatic stress disorder. *Journal of Consulting and Clinical Psychology, 72*(5), 879–884.

Jaberghaderi, N., Greenwald, R., Rubin, A., Dolatabadim, S., & Sand, S. O. (2004). A comparison of CBT and EMDR for sexually abused Iranian girls. *Clinical Psychology and Psychotherapy, 11,* 358–368.

Jeffres, M. J. (2004). The efficacy of EMDR with traumatized children. *Dissertation Abstracts International: Section B: The Sciences and Engineering, 64*(8-B), 4042.

Marks, I., Lovell, K., Noshirvani, H., Livanou, M., & Thrasher, S. (1998). Treatment of posttraumatic stress disorder by exposure and/or cognitive restructuring. *Archives of General Psychiatry, 55,* 317–325.

Maxfield, L. (2007). Current status and future directions for EMDR research. [Electronic version]. *Journal of EMDR Practice and Research, 1*(1), 6–14.

National Collaborating Centre for Mental Health (2005). *Posttraumatic stress disorder: The management of PTSD in primary and secondary care.* London: National Institute for Health and Clinical Excellence (NICE).

Resick, P. A., Nishith, P., Weaver, T. L., Astin, M. C., & Feuer, C. A. (2002). A comparison of cognitive processing therapy with prolonged exposure and a waiting condition for the treatment of chronic posttraumatic stress disorder in female rape victims. *Journal of Consulting and Clinical Psychology, 70*(4), 867–879.

Resick, P. A., & Schnicke, M. K. (1992). Cognitive processing therapy for sexual assault victims. *Journal of Consulting and Clinical Psychology, 60*(5), 748–756.

Riggs, D. S., Cahill, S. P., & Foa, E. B. (2006) Prolonged exposure treatment of posttraumatic stress disorder. In V. M. Follette & J. I. Ruzek (Eds.), *Cognitive behavioral therapies for trauma* (pp. 65–95). New York: Guilford Press.

Rubin, A. (2003). Unanswered questions about the empirical support for EMDR in the treatment of PTSD. *Traumatology, 9,* 4–30.

Shapiro, F. (1995). *Eye movement desensitization and reprocessing: Basic principles, protocols, and procedures.* New York: Guilford Press.

van der Kolk, B. A. (1997). The psychobiology of posttraumatic stress disorder. *Journal of Clinical Psychiatry, 58*(Suppl. 9) 12–24.

van der Kolk, B. A., Burbridge, J. A., & Suzuki, J. (1997). The psychobiology of traumatic memory: Clinical implications of neuroimaging studies. In R. Yehuda & A. C. McFarlane (Eds.), *Annals of the New York Academy of Sciences, vol. 821): Psychobiology of posttraumatic stress disorder* (pp. 99–113). New York: New York Academy of Sciences.

Van Etten, M. L., & Taylor, S. (1998). Comparative efficacy of treatments for posttraumatic stress disorder: A meta-analysis. *Clinical Psychology and Psychotherapy, 5,* 126–144.

APPENDIX B

The Evidence-Based Practice Process

ALLEN RUBIN

A S MENTIONED IN this volume's introduction, in its original and most prominent definition, evidence-based practice is a five-step process for making practice decisions. The term *evidence-based practice* (EBP) sprang from the term *evidence-based medicine* (EBM), which was coined in the 1980s and was ultimately defined as "the integration of best research evidence with clinical expertise and patient values" (Sackett, Straus, Richardson, Rosenberg, & Haynes, 2000, p. 1). By including clinical expertise and patient values in the definition, EBM was distinguished from the notion of it being an unchanging list of approved interventions that physicians should implement even if they seemed to be contraindicated in light of the physician's knowledge about the patient. Nevertheless, as the concept of EBM spread to the nonmedical helping professions with the label EBP, some critics disregarded its integration component and misconstrued it as recommending that practitioners mechanistically implement scientifically approved interventions regardless of their clinical expertise and knowledge about client attributes, values, and preferences.

Pointing out the integration component of the EBP process is not meant to diminish the importance of the role of empirically supported interventions in EBP. As was displayed in Figure 1.1 of this volume's introduction, the best research evidence is a key component of the EBP process. Indeed, this entire volume has aimed to facilitate your ability to find and implement interventions that have the best research evidence regarding their effectiveness with traumatized clients. In fact, the ultimate priority of the EBP process is to maximize the chances that practice decisions will yield desired outcomes in light of the best scientific evidence. Thus, the integration component of EBP is not meant to give practitioners so much wiggle room that they can disregard or diminish the importance of the best scientific evidence in making practice decisions. It just recognizes the need to blend that evidence with clinical expertise and client attributes.

In this volume's introductory chapter, I discussed various practical obstacles to the feasibility of the EBP process often encountered by clinicians. Key among those obstacles are the time, expertise, and other resources required to find relevant research evidence, to critically appraise various studies and sort through their bewildering array of inconsistent findings to ascertain which interventions are supported by the *best* evidence, and ultimately to learn how to implement one or more of those interventions. This volume has been geared to practitioners for whom those daunting obstacles make implementing the entire EBP process infeasible. However, if you would like to try to implement that process, the remainder of this appendix can guide you in a step-by-step fashion.

STEP 1: FORMULATE A QUESTION

The first step in the EBP process involves formulating a question based on a practice decision that you need to make. As mentioned in this volume's introductory chapter, the question could pertain to any level of practice, including questions bearing on administrative or policy decisions. Here are four common types of EBP questions (Rubin, 2008):

1. What intervention, program, or policy is most effective?
2. What factors best predict desirable or undesirable outcomes?
3. What's it like to have had my client's experiences?
4. What assessment tool should be used?

At the clinical level, you are most likely to formulate the first type of question above—one geared to choosing the intervention that has the best chance to be effective for your client. This volume has been geared to that type of question.

In order to make the next step in the EBP process both expedient and productive, you'll need to add as much specificity to your question as possible—without making it so specific that you'll find no evidence bearing on it. To illustrate questions that are too broadly worded, while writing this appendix I went online to the PsycINFO literature database and requested that it show each published work that included all of the following three search terms somewhere in its text: *effective, treatment, trauma*. My implicit question was, "What intervention is most effective for treating trauma?" More than 1,000 published works came up. Too many!

My question was too broad. After all, there are many different types of trauma. So I redid my search, substituting *PTSD* for *trauma*. My implicit question was, "What intervention is most effective for treating PTSD?" That reduced the listed results to 677 publications. Still a lot. Assuming that my client was a victim of sexual abuse, I added the term *sexual abuse* to the search, with the implicit EBP question, "What intervention is most effective for treating PTSD among victims of sexual abuse?" That reduced the list to 51 published works—much more manageable and relevant to my hypothetical client.

To illustrate adding more specificity, I repeated my search by adding the term *African American* to the search, with the implicit EBP question, "What intervention is most effective for treating PTSD among African American victims of sexual abuse?" However, no works were found when I added that search term. The same happened when I substituted *Hispanic* for *African American*.

In formulating your EBP questions, it's usually best to go in the opposite direction, formulating a very specific question, and then broadening it in your search if necessary. That way, you can skip the search term tries that give you too many publications that are irrelevant or tangential to your specific practice decision or client, and add (broadening) terms only as needed.

Not all EBP questions about effectiveness are open-ended, without specifying one or more specific interventions in advance. For example, perhaps you know that both EMDR and exposure therapy are accepted as the most effective treatments for PTSD and are wondering which has the best evidence. Your EBP question therefore might be, "Is EMDR or exposure therapy more effective in treating PTSD?" When I asked PsycINFO to find all publications that contained all of the following search terms: EMDR, exposure therapy, and PTSD, it listed 23 results.

STEP 2: SEARCH FOR EVIDENCE

As a busy practitioner, the least time consuming way to search for evidence is to use Internet search engines and electronic literature databases. PsycINFO, as discussed above, is one useful option. Using it requires a subscription, but there are ways to get around that cost if your work setting does not have such a subscription. One way is to see if you can get free access through any university faculty members or internship students with whom you are affiliated (especially if you serve as an adjunct faculty member or a field internship instructor). Another way is through your local library. Many local libraries provide free access to databases like PsycINFO for residents with a library card. You probably will not have to go to the library to use their computers; you should be able to do it all online from your own computer. There are many alternative electronic literature databases, including Google Scholar and MedLine. The nice thing about MedLine is that the National Library of Medicine offers free access to it at www.nlm.nih.gov.

Although different professional literature databases typically require the entering of search terms to retrieve studies, they differ in their search rules and procedures. You'll need to scan their search guidelines before proceeding so that you can expedite your search. For some databases, you can connect the various parts of your search term with words like *and, or,* and *not.* Using *and* limits the number of studies that come up to only those that contain all of the keywords in your search term. For example, if you want to find studies that compare EMDR to exposure therapy, you could enter "EMDR and exposure therapy." Using *or* will expand the number of studies that come up. Thus, if you enter "EMDR or exposure therapy," studies that come up will include those that look only at EMDR, only at exposure therapy, and at both (whereas using *and* would include only those studies that look at both). If you enter "EMDR and exposure therapy not pilot study," the list of references that come up will include those that address *both* EMDR *and* exposure therapy, but will exclude pilot studies. For some databases, such as PsycINFO, you will not have to enter the connecting words like *and, or,* and *not.* Instead, you can enter the keywords in different boxes that are prefaced with the connecting words.

So far I've been discussing the search for evidence in terms of looking for individual studies. Implicit in this approach is the need to critically appraise (in the next step of the EBP process) the quality of the evidence in each of the relevant studies that you find. A more expedient alternative would be to look first for systematic reviews of the studies already completed by others. This would also include meta-analyses, which are systematic reviews that pool the statistical results of the reviewed studies. Systematic reviews are expedient in several ways. First, they save you the time of searching for and reading individual studies. Second, they spare you the difficulty of critically appraising the research methodology of each study, which can be a daunting task for clinicians with limited expertise in research design, methods, and statistics. Third, even those studies that are methodologically rigorous and that supply the best evidence often report findings that are inconsistent from one study to another, and for some EBP questions, that inconsistency can be bewildering. A good systematic review will synthesize the various findings and provide you with a bottom line as to which interventions have the best evidence, for what types of clients and problems, and under what conditions.

Of course, an even more expedient way for busy practitioners to engage in EBP is to rely on volumes like the one you are reading. If you read Appendix A, you saw a synopsis of the ample empirical support, including systematic reviews and meta-analyses, for the interventions selected for this volume. However, if your EBP question is one for which no systematic reviews or books like this have been published, you may have no alternative to searching for and appraising individual studies. When you start your search, you won't know in advance what you'll find. Assuming that time and other practical constraints make searching for individual studies an undesirable option from the standpoint of feasibility, I recommend that you begin looking for systematic reviews and volumes like this and then look for individual studies only as a last resort. That being said, however, you need to be careful that the authors of systematic reviews or books like this do not have a vested interested in the interventions that they depict as having the best evidence. If my coeditor and I, for example, had developed or ran workshops on the interventions described in this volume, then the credibility of our previous appendix on the supportive research would be highly suspect, and the value of this book's chapters therefore would suffer. In case you are wondering, we have no vested interests in any of the interventions described in this book.

You should also bear in mind that for some problem areas, different systematic reviews might produce different conclusions regarding which interventions have the best evidence supporting their effectiveness with that problem. For example, some authors with well-established reputations in EMDR have conducted reviews that concluded that EMDR is more effective than exposure therapy, while other authors have conducted reviews that reached the opposite conclusion, while still others conducted reviews that concluded that both interventions appear to be equally effective. Systematic reviews should be transparent about the presence or lack of vested interests by the authors of the review. Reviews that lack that transparency should be viewed with suspicion, as should reviews that admit to a vested interest, while reviews in which the authors have no vested interests probably should have the most credibility (all other criteria being equal, as will be discussed below).

Two highly regarded sources for unbiased and methodologically sophisticated systematic reviews are the Cochrane Collaboration and the Campbell Collaboration. Both are international nonprofit organizations that recruit into review teams researchers, practitioners, and consumers without vested interests in the subjects of their reviews. Each of their sites can be accessed online. If you can find a review bearing on your EBP question in the onsite library at either of those sites, you can probably rely on it to answer your question and thus save you the trouble of searching for and appraising other sources of evidence. Moreover, their libraries also contain comments and criticisms of their own reviews as well as abstracts of other reviews, bibliographies of studies, reviews regarding methodology, and links that can help you conduct your own review. The Cochrane Collaboration focuses on reviews in the areas of health and mental health and can be accessed at www.cochrane.org. Its sibling organization, the Campbell Collaboration, focuses on reviews in social welfare, education, and criminal justice. You can access its web site at www.campbellcollaboration.org.

STEP 3: CRITICALLY APPRAISE THE EVIDENCE

The next step of the EBP process involves critically appraising the evidence found in the previous step. Being published is no guarantee that study's evidence is sound. Some studies are better than others, and some have fatal flaws that severely undermine their utility for guiding practice decisions. All studies have at least one or two minor flaws. Your prime task is not looking for the holy grail of a perfectly flawless study, but rather looking for one or more studies (or systematic reviews) whose strengths and relevance to your practice decision far outweigh their minor flaws.

The criteria to use in critically appraising any study depend on the nature of your EBP question. For questions such as, "What's it like to have had my client's experiences?" studies that employ qualitative research methods are likely to provide better evidence than quantitative studies such as experiments or surveys. For questions like, "What factors best predict desirable or undesirable outcomes?" studies that employ multivariate correlation analyses along with survey designs, case-control designs, or longitudinal designs may be your best bet. For questions like, "What assessment tool should be used?" you'll need to examine studies that administer assessment tools to large samples of people and calculate the tools' reliability, validity, and sensitivity.

As mentioned earlier, however, the most commonly asked EBP question asks something like, "What intervention, program or policy is most effective?" For questions about effectiveness, the following evidentiary hierarchy table should guide your appraisal of the evidence.

It is beyond the scope of this appendix to explain everything in Table B.1. If you have had one or more good courses on research methods, perhaps you already have sufficient familiarity with the terminology and standards of research rigor to guide your appraisal. To brush up on that material, you might want to examine my book, *Practitioner's Guide to Using Research for Evidence-Based Practice* (Wiley, 2008). In the meantime, some key criteria to keep in mind when appraising individual studies are as follows:

1. Was a control group used?
2. Was random assignment used to avoid a selectivity bias that would make one group more likely to have a successful outcome than the other?

Table B.1
Evidentiary Hierarchy for Questions about Effectiveness (Best Evidence at the Top)[*]

Level 1	Systematic reviews and meta-analyses
Level 2	Multi-site replications of randomized experiments
Level 3	Randomized experiments
Level 4	Quasi-experiments
Level 5	Single-case experiments
Level 6	Correlational Studies
Level 7	Other: • Anecdotal case reports • Pretest-posttest studies without control groups • Qualitative descriptions of client experiences during or after treatment • Surveys of clients as to what they think helped them • Surveys of practitioners as to what they think is effective

[*]This hierarchy assumes that each type of study is well designed. If not well designed, then a particular study would merit a lower level on the hierarchy. For example, a randomized experiment with egregiously biased measurement would not deserve to be at Level 3 and perhaps would be so fatally flawed as to merit dropping to the lowest level. The same applies to a quasi-experiment with a severe vulnerability to a selectivity bias.

3. If random assignment was not used (i.e., in a quasi-experiment), do the authors provide solid evidence and a persuasive case for considering a selectivity bias to be unlikely?
4. Was outcome measured in an unbiased manner?
5. Were the attrition rates in both groups roughly equivalent?

Although the preceding list does not exhaust all the criteria to consider, if the answers to questions 1, 4, and 5 are all *yes*, coupled with an affirmative answer to *either* question 2 or 3, then chances are the study is supplying some relatively strong evidence regarding whether a policy, program, or intervention is effective.

When appraising systematic reviews (including meta-analyses), you should ask whether the reviewed studies were appraised in connection to the above types of evidentiary standards. Reviews can do so in two ways. One way is for the authors of the review to take the strengths and weaknesses of the reviewed studies into account when deriving their conclusions and guidelines for practice. The other way is to exclude from the review any studies that fail to meet certain evidentiary standards, such as the ones listed above.

As mentioned earlier, another important consideration when appraising a systematic review is whether the authors have vested interests in any of the policies, programs, or interventions addressed in the review and whether they are transparent about such vested interests. They also should identify the inclusion and exclusion criteria they used in selecting studies for their review and describe how comprehensively they searched for studies. For example, if they excluded studies of clients with substance abuse comorbidity from their review of treatment for PTSD, and your client has such comorbidity, then their review might have less value to you than one that included such studies. As to comprehensiveness, a key issue is whether the authors searched well for unpublished studies to include in their review, based on the notion that if only published studies are included, the deck might be stacked toward studies with findings supporting the effectiveness of interventions, since studies with null findings often are not submitted for publication.

STEP 4: INTEGRATION, SELECTION, AND IMPLEMENTATION

As mentioned earlier, the EBP process is not merely a mechanistic, cookbook approach in which practice decisions are made and implemented based solely on the best evidence regardless of clinician expertise and knowledge of client attributes and preferences. Consequently, after appraising the evidence, the next step of the EBP process involves selecting an intervention and implementing it only after integrating the critical appraisal of the evidence with your clinical expertise and knowledge of client circumstances and preferences. You might, for example, opt to implement an intervention that has the second or third best evidence because the studies done on that intervention involved clients like yours, whereas the studies done on the interventions with the best evidence involved only clients very unlike yours in ways that you deem to be very important. Likewise, your client might refuse to participate in an intervention supported by the best evidence, such as when some parents cannot be persuaded (through psychoeducation) to permit their child to undergo EMDR or exposure therapy because they fear such treatment would retraumatize their child.

Feasibility issues also must be considered. What if you lack training in the intervention supported by the best evidence? Is it possible to get the needed training? Can you afford the time and money that will be required? Can you get it soon enough? If you cannot get it, can you refer the client to another service provider who has the expertise to provide the desired intervention? If the answers to these questions are negative, the client might be better off if you provide an intervention that has the second or third best evidence, but is one that you have the expertise to provide competently. If the preferred intervention is one covered in this volume, perhaps reading the pertinent chapter will suffice to get you started.

STEP 5: MONITOR/EVALUATE OUTCOME

In the final step of the EBP process, you monitor or evaluate the outcome of the intervention (or other practice decision that is implemented in step 4). You might wonder why this final step is needed. After all, haven't you implemented the option that has already been evaluated and found to have the best evidence supporting its effectiveness? There are several answers to these questions. One reason is that even in studies providing the best evidence, some of the participants do not benefit from the empirically supported interventions. A related reason is that those studies might not have included participants with some of your client's key attributes. A third reason is that in step 4 you may have opted for an intervention that does not have the best evidence.

Moreover, you might complete all four preceding steps and find no empirically supported intervention that fits your client. You may therefore have to proceed according to theory or clinical judgment, alone, thus implementing an intervention that lacks empirical support. Keep in mind that doing so does not mean you have violated the EBP process. The fact that you completed the preceding steps means you have implemented the EBP process even if your search is fruitless. But if that is so, then it is all the more important to complete the final step of the process; that is, to evaluate whether the intervention you have chosen attains the desired outcome.

A final reason for the final step of the EBP process is the possibility that you might not implement the selected intervention in a sufficiently competent manner. Remember, even the best evidence is only probabilistic. Rather than assure treatment success, it merely means that the chosen intervention has the best *likelihood* of success.

Now that you see the rationale for this final step, you might wonder how to do it. Your options are many, and some might be a lot more feasible for you than you think. The most feasible options pertain to situations where you have implemented an intervention that has already been supported by strong studies. In such situations, you should not feel the need to employ a sophisticated evaluation design aimed at producing causal inferences about whether the chosen intervention is really the cause of any client outcomes. Instead, all you need to do is monitor client outcomes. That is, you just need to see if the client achieves his or her desired outcome, regardless of the cause. That's because previous studies have already produced probabilistic causal evidence about the intervention, and your task as a practitioner (and not as a

Instructions: At the end of each day, enter the day's date and then circle a number to approximate how depressed you felt on average for that day.

Average Level of Depression† for the Day

DATE	NOT AT ALL ──────→			MODERATE ──────→			SEVERE	
_____	0	1	2	3	4	5	6	7
_____	0	1	2	3	4	5	6	7
_____	0	1	2	3	4	5	6	7
_____	0	1	2	3	4	5	6	7
_____	0	1	2	3	4	5	6	7
_____	0	1	2	3	4	5	6	7
_____	0	1	2	3	4	5	6	7

* The development of this scale was inspired by ideas in Bloom, Fischer, and Orme (2006).
† This scale can be adapted for other target problems or goals by substituting those problems (anxiety, anger, etc.) or goals (self-confidence, assertiveness, etc.) for depressed or depression.

Figure B.1. An Individualized Daily Rating Scale for Depressed Mood*

researcher) therefore is merely to see if your client gets where he or she wants to go after receiving that intervention and whether (assuming a desired outcome is not attained) a different intervention may need to be introduced.

For a comprehensive guide to monitoring client progress, you can examine Chapter 12 of the book I mentioned earlier (Rubin, 2008). For example, if you are monitoring a client's PTSD symptoms, the client could self-monitor one or more symptoms (including perhaps just one overall rating of the day's symptoms) by completing an individualized self-rating scale each day, such as the one shown in Figure B.1 from Rubin (2008, p. 259)

You could graph the daily ratings chronologically, as appears below to see if the desired level of progress is being achieved. The graph in Figure B.2 (from Rubin, 2008, p. 257) would indicate a successful outcome was being achieved in reducing an undesirable symptom (or overall rating of PTSD symptoms in general).

In contrast, the graph in Figure B.3 (from Rubin, 2008, p. 257) illustrates an outcome in which progress was not being made with the selected intervention (Intervention A), but then after an alternative intervention (Intervention B) was introduced the desired progress was being achieved in reducing an undesirable symptom (or overall rating of PTSD symptoms in general).

If you have implemented an intervention that lacks adequate prior empirical support, you might want to employ a more sophisticated evaluation

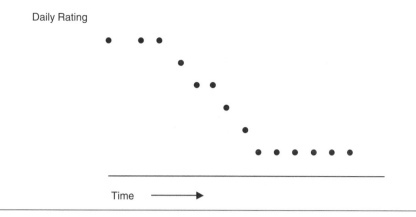

Daily Rating

Time

Figure B.2. Illustration of a Successful Outcome in Reducing an Undesirable Symptom

design that aims to produce causal inferences (assuming, of course, that such a design is feasible for you). Such designs include experiments, quasi-experiments, time-series designs, and single-case experiments.

The preceding examples were discussed in the context of clinical practice with a specific client. However, they can be adapted to a macro level of practice in which you want to monitor or evaluate outcome with a large number of clients or with an entire community. For example, if you want to see whether a new crisis intervention modality is more effective than previous efforts to prevent PTSD among victims of natural disasters, you could compare the incidence of PTSD among its recipients to the incidence among victims who received alternative or no crisis intervention modalities. To learn more about such macro evaluations, you can read Rubin and Babbie (2008).

The main thing to keep in mind about this phase of the EBP process, however, is to implement it in whatever way that is feasible for you. As a

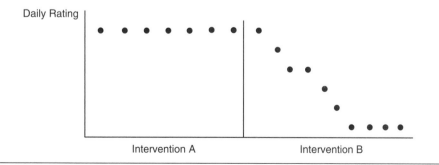

Daily Rating

Intervention A　　　Intervention B

Figure B.3. Illustration of an Unsuccessful Outcome for Intervention A Followed by a Successful Outcome for Intervention B

practitioner, you should not feel immobilized just because a rigorous research evaluation research design is beyond your reach. Remember, all practitioners routinely have to make judgments as to whether what they are doing is working or not and whether they need to try something different. The same applies regardless of what you find and implement in the previous steps of the EBP process. The ideas presented here and in the suggested reference volumes can help you make your monitoring or evaluation efforts more systematic and doable. Just do the best you can, and good luck!

REFERENCES

Bloom, M., Fischer, J., & Orme, J. G. (2006). *Evaluating practice: Guidelines for the accountable professional* (5th ed.). Boston: Allyn & Bacon.

Rubin, A. (2008). *Practitioner's guide to using research for evidence-based practice.* Hoboken, NJ: Wiley.

Rubin, A., & Babbie, E. (2008). *Research methods for social work* (6th ed.). Belmont, CA: Thomson Brooks/Cole.

Sackett, D. L., Straus, S. E., Richardson, W. S., Rosenberg, W. M. C., & Haynes, R. B. (2000). *Evidence-based medicine: How to practice and teach EBM* (2nd ed.). New York: Churchill Livingstone.

Glossary of EMDR Terms[1]

ADAPTIVE INFORMATION PROCESSING: A model of the accommodation and assimilation of experiences into state and trait memories that includes a natural process of moving toward an adaptive integration of information (memories) into a verbally accessible memory system.

AFFECT SCAN: A process in which the client brings to mind an incident or experience, notices the emotions and bodily sensations that he or she is feeling, and goes back in his or her mind to see if this resonates with an earlier experience.

ASSESSMENT PHASE: Third phase of EMDR, which precedes the reprocessing phases of desensitization, installation, and body scan. The assessment relates to a specific target and includes drawing together the memory and associated image, negative and positive cognitions, Validity of Cognition, emotions, Subjective Units of Disturbance, and bodily sensations prior to desensitization.

ASSOCIATIVE CHAINING: Occurs as the therapist follows the client's process as the client links up past events that are associated through some significance in the brain (shared images, cognitions, emotions, or sensations) as the client reports the links that arise during sets of bilateral stimulation.

AUDITORY STIMULATION: One form of bilateral stimulation used during reprocessing or resource installation that utilizes sounds that alternate back and forth from ear to ear either by the therapist snapping his or her fingers on each side of the client's head or using a mechanical device with a headset set that produces alternating tones.

BILATERAL STIMULATION: Visual, auditory, or tactile stimulation (such as eye movements, tones, or taps) delivered from side to side by the clinician using manual or electronic means.

BLOCKED PROCESSING: Occurs when a client is unable to access new information and is not spontaneously reprocessing during the desensitization phase.

---

1. The EMDR-related terms in the glossary were provided by the authors of the EMDR chapters in this volume.

BODY SCAN: The sixth phase of EMDR in which the body is mentally scanned for any sensation that may indicate residual material to be reprocessed or adaptive resolution of material or information and a sense of well-being.

CALM PLACE: An EMDR protocol that uses a place or situation in imagination or reality to bring to mind a sense of safety and is installed with short, slow sets of bilateral stimulation. (Also called *safe place*.)

CHANNEL: Part of a memory network relating to an incident or experience in which associated information (images, cognitions, emotions, and bodily sensations) is stored and accessed in EMDR, especially in the reprocessing phases.

CLOSURE: The seventh phase of EMDR, which includes closure of a session after completion of reprocessing (in which the SUD score is 0 or 1 and the VoC score is 7 or 6), or of an incomplete session in which material has not been fully reprocessed (in which the SUD score is greater than 1 and the VOC score is less than 6).

COGNITIVE INTERWEAVE: A brief comment or question made by the clinician during the desensitization phase of EMDR to start or restart processing when this has become stuck or repetitive and has not responded to other strategies to facilitate blocked processing.

COMPLEX TRAUMA: A term to describe the impact of traumatic experiences repeated over a period of time and often of an interpersonal nature and involving a restriction of physical or emotional liberty.

DESENSITIZATION PHASE: The fourth phase of EMDR in which the use of bilateral stimulation facilitates the desensitization, or reduction in disturbance, associated with a specific memory or experience.

DESNOS: Disorder of extreme stress not otherwise specified, synonymous with complex trauma.

DEVELOPMENTAL TRAUMA: Prolonged and repeated trauma, usually interpersonal in nature and often occurring within the child's caregiving system. The trauma is proposed to have an adverse and chronic effect on the child's developing brain.

DUAL ATTENTION STIMULUS: Usually bilateral stimulation from a source external to the client that shifts the client's attention between internal and external stimuli.

EGO STRENGTH: In psychoanalysis, the degree to which the ego is capable of handling the demands of the id and the superego without disruption, a person with high ego strength being self-confident, strong-willed, and robust in response to frustration. More generally, a person's capacity to handle emotional material and maintain emotional stability and a sense of self.

EMDR: Eye movement desensitization and reprocessing: a complex, integrative psychotherapy approach for the treatment of the psychological sequelae of trauma and other difficulties. The aim of EMDR is to enable the adaptive processing of stored memories that seem locked in the nervous system with the original images, thoughts, emotions, and bodily sensations.

FEEDER MEMORY: A memory of an incident or experience that was experienced as significant and feeds into a more recent experience or incident and may inhibit reprocessing. May be part of a cluster or chain of memories or stored information, the earliest of which will be a touchstone event.

FLOATBACK: An approach similar to the affect scan but differs in its focus on cognitions. In the floatback technique, a person brings to mind a present experience, noticing what he feels and experience in his body, and the negative belief associated with it, and lets himself float back to an earlier time when he experienced the same or similar thoughts and feelings.

FUTURE TEMPLATE: A representation of the planned outcome of therapy in relation to a previously traumatizing situation or a situation that triggered responses linked with earlier traumatic experiences.

HISTORY PHASE: The first phase of EMDR in which a client describes her background and is able to identify significant experiences that will become the focus of the reprocessing phases of EMDR.

INITIAL TARGET: An incident stored in the memory system that is used as the initial focus of the reprocessing phase and has associated memory networks or channels of association.

INFORMATION: An experience or experiences, including images, thoughts, emotions, and bodily sensations stored in a memory (neural) network.

INSTALLATION PHASE: The fifth phase of EMDR in which a target incident or experience is coupled with the positive cognition and a dual-attention stimulus to facilitate the adaptive resolution of a memory.

"LARGE T" TRAUMA: An extremely distressing incident or experience that meets Criterion A of the DSM-IV.

MEMORY: Storage of information in the brain and nervous system.

MEMORY NETWORK: Network of associated information (memory) stored in the brain and nervous system. Memory networks connect through common links such as the same smell, sound, body sensation, or other sensory relationship where the individual's brain made the association between experiences.

MOTOR INTERWEAVES: A form of a cognitive interweave that involves the client making a movement or taking action to assist in blocked processing and return to spontaneous reprocessing.

NEGATIVE COGNITION: A presently held negative belief about the self that is evoked by a current memory or experience of a negative, unprocessed event and is generalizable to other situations.

NODE: An incident or experience, stored in the memory system as a pivotal memory or experience, that may be a target of EMDR reprocessing.

PAST–PRESENT–FUTURE: The three-pronged approach of EMDR that addresses past experiences; present triggers of cognitive, emotional, and physiological responses that are linked to past trauma or unprocessed experiences (information); and future possibilities that are rehearsed, together with positive beliefs about the self, in the third stage of the EMDR approach to psychotherapy.

PHASE: One of the eight elements that comprise EMDR: history; preparation; assessment; desensitization; installation; body scan; closure; reevaluation.

POSITIVE AFFECT TOLERANCE: A client's ability to experience and accept positive emotions and body sensations.

POSITIVE COGNITION: A presently held positive belief about the self that is associated with the outcome of reprocessing future situations or likely experiences and represents a desired belief. It is in the same domain as the negative cognition but 180° opposite. It is not simply a negation of the negative cognition—it is a generalizable positive self-statement.

PREPARATION PHASE: The second phase of EMDR in which the clinician and client work together to prepare the client for the reprocessing phases of EMDR. This includes developing resources for the client to regulate affect, introducing the client to the seating arrangements, the logistics of bilateral stimulation, or the dual attention stimulus, and to the possibility of continued reprocessing between sessions.

PRESENT TRIGGERS: Events in the present that trigger experiences from the past and the associated images, beliefs, emotions, or sensations.

PROTOCOL: Framework for the practice of EMDR by reprocessing past memories or experiences, present triggers, and processing future templates.

REEVALUATION PHASE: The first part of any session after the first. Draws on reflection by the clinician after the close of the preceding session and focuses on the experience of the client between sessions and the client's evaluation of the targets addressed in the previous session, using the SUD and VoC scales.

REPROCESSING: The process in which a dysfunctionally stored memory reaches an adaptive resolution.

RDI: Resource development and installation. The development of personal (imaginal and actual) resources, including relaxation, visual imagery, and safe place techniques to enable a person to manage or regulate affect and give a sense of safety.

SACCADE: One saccade is counted as one bilateral stimulation movement where the therapist moves the sensory stimulation (eye movement, sounds, or tactile) from the far right to the far left.

SAFE PLACE: A place or situation in imagination or reality in which a person can bring to mind a sense of safety or well-being. Sometimes called "special place" or "calm place."

SET: A series of bilateral stimulation (visual, auditory, or tactile) in which one "track" comprises a complete movement from one side to the other and back again. Typically, in the desensitization phase, a set will be 24 to 30 rapid return movements but may be considerably longer. Slower, shorter sets of about six are typical in the preparation phase and during resource development and installation.

"SMALL T" TRAUMA: A term used to describe any incident or experience that is experienced as traumatic or disturbing.

SOCRATIC QUESTIONING: Based on Socrates's approach of asking students a series of questions that would draw out their responses. Ostensibly to seek clarification or challenge assumptions, to help a person change perspectives or challenge a rationale, and sometimes to draw attention to possible consequences of a point of view, the Socratic method aims to help the student come to their own understanding of the issues and their own conclusions. The method has been adapted for use in classical Adlerian psychotherapy and cognitive therapy, as well as being used in EMDR.

STATE: In the present moment, the emotional, cognitive, or physiological state of a person.

SUD: Subjective Units of Distress Scale: an 11-point scale in which 0 represents no disturbance or neutral and 10 represents the worst disturbance a person can imagine.

TACTILE STIMULATION: One form of bilateral stimulation that uses the sense of touch such as tapping or mechanical device that can be held and vibrates in each of the client's hands, back and forth.

TARGET: A recent or distant memory of an incident or experience that is a focus of the reprocessing phase.

TARGETING SEQUENCE PLAN: The therapist determines which incident to target first, second, third, and so on, using the three-pronged approach of past, present, and future.

THREE-PRONGED APPROACH: Case conceptualization with the AIP model that includes targeting traumatic events from past and current triggers and addresses future templates.

TOUCHSTONE EVENT: The earliest incident or experience that is stored in memory and acts as a feeder memory carrying an emotional, cognitive, and/or physiological charge to a more recent incident or experience.

TRAIT: The enduring emotional, cognitive, or physiological characteristics of a person that are likely to evolve or change during reprocessing.

VoC: Validity of Cognition Scale: a 7-point scale that is used to evaluate the validity of a positive cognition, in which 1 represents "feels completely false" and 7 represents "feels completely true," used to evaluate the degree to which a positive cognition in relation to a target incident or experience feels true or false in the present moment.

Author Index

Subject Index

abuse
  avoidance symptoms and, 6
  control and empowerment concerns about, 13
  emotional/psychological, 179, 180, 259
  impact on children of, 179–82, 356, 361
  perpetration of, 41
  physical, 179, 180, 185, 259
  safety issues and, 10
  validation of, 14
  See also domestic violence; sexual abuse
active ignoring, 201
acute stress disorder, 7, 354
acute trauma, 354–55
Adaptive Information Processing, 22, 261–63, 278, 299, 350–51
  case formulation and, 272, 363
  children and, 353, 358, 359, 360, 361, 411
addiction, 12, 278. *See also* substance use/abuse
adjustment disorders, 354
Adolescent-Dissociative Experiences Scale, 369
adolescents
  domestic violence education and, 239
  EMDR and, 23, 349–411
  emotion modulation and, 213, 214
  episodes of care and, 406
  pregnancy/paternity and, 181, 182
  sex education and, 239
  TFCBT and, 188, 204–5
  trauma's impact on, 179, 181
  trauma symptoms and, 356–57, 360
adopted children, 406–7
Adverse Effects of Childhood Scale, 360
affect expression/regulation, 210, 212–14, 407–8
affect management, 275, 298, 314–15
  children and, 374, 379, 381–82, 385
  closure and, 320, 321
  dissociation and, 287–88
  techniques for, 267, 270, 299, 302–5
affect scan, 274–75, 298, 319
agitation, 158
AIP. *See* Adaptive Information Processing
alcohol use/abuse, 8, 12, 286
Allegheny General Hospital (Pittsburgh, Pa.), 182
alternative thoughts, 146–54
anger, 12, 108–9, 140
anger management, 12, 212–13
anxiety
  anticipatory, 362, 408
  avoidance behavior and, 34, 37, 104
  cognitive restructuring and, 108–9
  EMDR and, 278, 362

prolonged exposure and, 38, 58, 62
in vivo gradual exposure and, 232–33
anxiety disorders, 36, 157
anxiety management training, 31, 36
arousal, 213, 245, 257, 259, 359
  window of tolerance and, 304, 307, 314
  See also hyperarousal symptoms
art therapy, 352, 361, 365, 378, 381, 388, 411
assertive communication, 240, 242
assertiveness training, 374
assessment, 5–9, 13
  of children, 8–9, 356–57, 368–69, 386, 387–91
  cognitive restructuring and, 110–12
  EMDR and, 267–68, 272, 305–10, 356–57, 368–69, 386, 387–91
  exposure therapy and, 31, 45, 46–47, 68–70, 73–88
  TFCBT and, 31, 192–94
assessment instruments, 7, 70, 111–12, 193
  for children, 8–9, 356, 368, 369
  See also specific measures
associative chaining, 396
attachment, 259, 330, 359, 369
  trauma and, 180–81, 352, 356, 371
attachment disorders, 407
attachment therapy, 352, 362
attention deficit hyperactivity disorder, 363
Attributional Style Questionnaire, 111
auditory stimulation, 267, 285, 300–301, 384, 385
automatic thoughts, 126, 133, 152
avoidance/avoidance symptoms, 37, 245, 313
  exposure therapy and, 35, 38, 39, 41, 42, 231–32
  homework completion and, 128
  information processing and, 40
  mindfulness and, 214
  operant conditioning and, 34, 104, 105
  trauma and, 6, 7, 257, 259
awareness skills, 240

Beck Depression Inventory, 2nd edition, 193
Behavior Assessment Scale, 193
behavior management skills, 199, 200–202
behavior problems, 8, 382
  TFCBT and, 183, 185, 190, 193, 200–202, 244, 245–46
beliefs, 32, 106, 114
  cognitive restructuring and, 133–34, 146–47
  See also negative cognitions; positive cognitions
benzodiazepines, 286